A History of

INTEREST RATES

Photo of Sidney Homer by George E. Joseph

A History of
INTEREST RATES

SIDNEY HOMER and RICHARD SYLLA

THIRD EDITION

RUTGERS UNIVERSITY PRESS

New Brunswick and London

Library of Congress Cataloging-in-Publication Data

Homer, Sidney, 1902–
A history of interest rates / Sidney Homer and
Richard Sylla. —3rd ed.
p.   cm.

Includes bibliographical references and index.
ISBN 0-8135-1628-5
1. Interest rates—History.   2. Credit—
History.   I. Sylla, Richard Eugene.   II. Title.
HG1621.H6   1991
332.8′09—dc20   90-37645
                                                                  CIP

British Cataloging-in-Publication information available

Foreword

Sidney Homer's watershed HISTORY traced interest rates from their earliest beginnings. Richard Sylla's extensive revisions and updating to 1990 have continued that unbroken line through the burgeoning volume, instruments, and data bases of recent decades.

This was a remarkable book written by a remarkable man. Sidney Homer called himself a bond man, but he was far more than that. It is true that he ran his own bond firm early in his career and later on became a senior bond portfolio manager for Scudder, Stevens and Clark, but this only scratches the surface of his accomplishments and talents. Sidney Homer did pioneering work in fixed-income analysis. He labored for a good part of his career when bonds were not as popular as they are today and when interest rates were not in the forefront of the financial press.

Sidney Homer spearheaded the use of such analytical tools as the analysis of relative values, the yield curve, and the linkages of the financial world to the economy. He was among the first to utilize the analysis of flow of funds in the financial markets, well before the Federal Reserve formalized this approach.

When he came to Salomon Brothers in 1961, he organized and managed the first in-depth research department devoted strictly to fixed-income markets. This was an extraordinary undertaking for Sidney and for Salomon Brothers. Bill Salomon and Charles Simon were responsible for hiring Sidney. While they were completely unlike this very classical man, they realized that Sidney had a mine of untapped knowledge that could benefit Salomon Brothers. They were right. By the time he retired as a general partner in October 1971, he had built the leading fixed-income research department. It had no match and included a quantitative group, which only became popular elsewhere much later on.

His frequent writings clearly showed that he was more than just a bond man. They had a current relevance with great historical perspective and insights and ranged from technical aspects in the money and bond markets to the broad underlying economic and financial issues of the day. To him, interest rates were more than just statistics. As he states so well in this book, "it seems fair to say that free market long-term rates of interest for any industrial nation, properly charted, provide a sort of fever chart of the economic and political health of that nation."

My first examination of A HISTORY OF INTEREST RATES was of the first edition, and it was a most detailed one. During my early weeks at Salomon Brothers, Sidney Homer asked me to read the galleys of the book, but, as was typical of him, he wanted it done in a meticulous way. I read the entire book, then encompassing 594 pages and 81 statistical tables, out loud to my secretary. It apparently left an imprint on my career.

Much has transpired in the financial world since the first two editions were published. New credit instruments have been introduced. The volume of outstanding fixed-income obligations has mushroomed, both here and abroad. Capital now moves quickly across the globe. Thus, the third edition is highly timely. The revisions and updating have been accomplished by a prominent scholar, Professor Richard Sylla. His grasp of markets and historical background fits well into the Sidney Homer mold. The subject matter remains as relevant today as it was in 1963 when the first edition went into print. The book has no peer. It will continue to be a classic.

Henry Kaufman

Preface to the Third Edition

After presenting the revised edition, Sidney Homer lived long enough to see interest rates in the leading markets climb to their highest levels since the Middle Ages. What Mr. Homer said in his 1977 preface could well be said of the period since that time:

> When a historian attempts to record and discuss a span of many centuries, indeed millennia, it would seem unlikely that the events of a single decade or so would require a wholly new perspective and hence a significant revision. And yet, during the fourteen years that have elapsed [since the previous edition] interest rates, both here and abroad, have made more history than they did in the several preceding centuries. The extraordinary recent fluctuations not only add dramatic new facts to this historical record but require new perspectives on the recent centuries.

Interest rate fluctuations from 1975, when the revised edition left off, to 1990 were more than extraordinary. They were unprecedented. Thus, a new edition of his HISTORY should be of more than usual interest. As Mr. Homer passed away in 1983, another would have to undertake the revision.

When Rutgers University Press asked me to prepare this edition, I accepted for both professional and personal reasons. As a financial historian and economist, I have often used Mr. Homer's HISTORY in my own work and have recommended it to others. There is no study even remotely like it in the comprehensiveness of its coverage across time and space, and in the insights it extracts from the long record of interest-rate levels, trends, and fluctuations extending back to antiquity. To bring such a work up to date is both an obligation and an honor for a financial historian. But I also redeem a personal debt. When I was a graduate student working at Harvard in the 1960's on my doctoral dissertation, I faced the knotty problem of determining the effective yields of U.S. government bonds during and after the Civil War, when there was considerable uncertainty about whether interest and principal would be paid in gold dollars or in greenback dollars. Knowing Mr. Homer's HISTORY I corresponded with him about my problem. He gave me help and encouragement at a crucial time in my career. More than two decades later, I am attempting to pay my debt—with interest—to the memory of Sidney Homer.

Most of the revisions in this edition are in Parts Four and Five, which deal with the twentieth century. The United States, for which detailed information is provided, is now treated in two chapters rather than one. Some rearrangement is made of other chapters and of countries within chapters to reflect changes in recent decades. For example, the European Community now deserves more focus, and the old sterling area less. Moreover, Japan clearly requires more prominence in modern discussions of interest rates. New interest-rate series are introduced in the tables and charts; an example is the U.S. federal funds rate, which did not appear in the previous editions but has now become one of the most important of all short rates. Real interest rates—rates adjusted for the effects of inflation—were not treated explicitly by Mr. Homer, but no up-to-date discussion of interest-rate trends can leave out this important concept. Inflation also led to financial innovations; some, such as the inflation-indexed bonds introduced in the 1980's by the British government, are discussed here. The pre–twentieth century chapters have been little revised, but it is my hope that in a subsequent edition they will include additions to the historical record that have been made since these chapters took shape thirty years ago. Finally, it should be noted that the 1989 data in the summary tables and charts are full-year data for the United States, but generally part-year data for other countries because of lags in the publication of sources as this volume went to press.

It is a pleasure to acknowledge the assistance of a number of people and institutions that made this edition possible. Above all, I thank Katty Ooms, who, as a graduate research assistant at North Carolina State University, performed what I can best describe as miracles. She located and retrieved data, both in this country and in her native Belgium, from obscure and not-so-obscure sources written in a number of languages. She computerized the text and tables, repeatedly revising the latter. And she utilized her substantial skills in modern computer technology to produce near-perfect replicas—with extensions, of course—of Sidney Homer's numerous charts, which have been and are, I think, a distinctive feature of this HISTORY. Dr. Henry Kaufman, whose association with this work extends all the way back to the first edition, helped with data not easily accessible, as did Jerry Pegden, his associate at Henry Kaufman and Company. This included data compiled by the firm of Saloman Brothers, with which both Sidney Homer and Henry Kaufman were long associated.

Others who helped with data gathering include Orlando da Silva, another graduate research assistant at North Carolina State; Ralph Monaco of the Economic Research Service of the U.S. Department of Agriculture; members of the staff of the Office of Thrift Supervision; Jack Wilson, Daniel Sumner, and James Seagraves of the North Carolina State faculty; and countless staff members of the libraries of North Carolina State and other universities who gladly helped without ever asking my name or telling me theirs. Word processing was ably provided by Ann Phillips especially, and also by Karen Carlton, Joan Grimes, Judy Johnson, and Gwen Joyner, all at North Carolina State. Marlie Wasserman, associate director and editor-in-chief of Rutgers University Press, swapped advice and encouragement with me at all stages of the project, and offered the gentle prods that an author expects and usually deserves to receive from a fine editor. Lyn Grossman superbly copyedited a complex manuscript, and Marilyn Campbell of the Press carefully guided it through the publication process.

More than the usual acknowledgment of support must be made to my family. Edith Sylla, herself a scholar, knows well the efforts involved in a project such as this and always made them easier. Our daughters also assisted. Anne, fresh out of Harvard, proved to be an excellent editor of my drafts. Peggy, in the best teenager tradition, helped by offering me as much of her advice as she normally accepts of mine. A scholar is fortunate to have such support at home.

Richard Sylla

Contents

Contents

Summary Tables

Charts

A History of

INTEREST RATES

INTRODUCTION

The spectacular rise in interest rates during the 1970's and early 1980's pushed many long-term market rates on prime credits up to levels never before approached, much less reached, in modern history. A long view, provided by this history, shows that recent peak yields were far above the highest prime long-term rates reported in the United States since 1800, in England since 1700, or in Holland since 1600. In other words, since modern capital markets came into existence, there have never been such high long-term rates as we recently have had all over the world.

The recent fluctuations of interest rates and the succession of market crises that accompanied them imply that a history of interest rates cannot fail to be dramatic. Most readers will be startled merely by the extremities of many ancient and modern interest rates. As the story of interest rates unfolds here, some readers may find profound significance in the sustained trends of interest rates upward or downward over many decades and centuries.

In the charts and tables of interest rates over long periods, students of history may see mirrored the rise and fall of nations and civilizations, the exertions and tragedies of war, and the enjoyments and the abuses of peace. They may be able to trace in the fluctuations the progress of knowledge and technology, the successes and failures of political forms, and the long, hard, and never-ending struggle of democracy with the rule of tyrants and elites.

Students of economics may read in the ebb and flow of interest rates the success of some communities and the failure of others to develop effective commercial ethics and laws and suitable monetary and fiscal techniques and policies. They may recognize the effects of economic growth and of economic decline as these two forces alternate over the dimensions of time and space.

Around the turn of the last century, a famous Austrian economist, Eugen von Böhm Bawerk, declared that the cultural level of a nation is mirrored by its rate of interest: the higher a people's intelligence and moral strength, the lower the rate of interest. He was speaking of free market rates of interest, not of controlled rates of interest. In his time, market rates of interest throughout the principal trading nations of the world were historically low: 2½ to 3½% for long-term prime credits. And inflation was not then the problem that it would become in this century.

If Böhm Bawerk had said "financial strength" instead of "moral strength" and "technological level" instead of "cultural level," more people today would agree with him, but we think he meant exactly what he said. Indeed, if these substitutions had been suggested to him, he might well have responded that moral strength in a nation as a whole is a necessary precondition for financial strength and that a high cultural level is a necessary precondition for a high technological level.

In any case, thirty years ago few students of the money market would have accepted Böhm Bawerk's sweeping generality. Interest rates were higher than in his era, but so, some thought, were intelligence, moral strength, and cultural levels. In light of the extraordinary events of the 1960's, 1970's, and 1980's, however, he might win some recruits. In the last analysis, it will depend on how one measures cultural level and moral strength, and here there is room for wide differences of opinion.

The primary purpose of this history is not to explore sociological or economic causes or effects of interest-rate fluctuations but rather simply to seek out, record, and analyze the prevailing rates of interest themselves over a centuries-long period in many countries. Nevertheless, a reader of these pages will not be able to avoid noticing sustained trends and repetitious patterns over the centuries. The reader may correlate them in his or her mind with the rise and fall of nations and, indeed, of whole civilizations.

The chapters on interest rates in ancient Babylonia, Greece, and Rome show, in each case, a progressive decline in interest rates as the nation or culture developed and throve, and then a sharp rise in rates as each "declined and fell." In our culture (Western Europe and North America), interest rates declined most of the time from the Middle Ages to the middle of the twentieth century. But now? Recent high rates have not lasted long enough, perhaps, to show a significant trend in the charts. But will they?

It is not necessary to assume that history repeats itself in any neat pattern. It is not necessary, after a glance at the charts, to cry doom. There is plenty of opportunity to reverse unfavorable trends. It seems fair to say, however, that the free market long-term rates of interest for any industrial nation, properly charted, provide a sort of fever chart of the economic and political health of that nation. Wars and political and economic calamities are recognizable at sight on the charts.

CREDIT IN ANCIENT TIMES

Credit is sometimes considered a modern device, or even a modern vice. It is true that new credit forms have been developed in our country, and the statistics reflecting the growth of the volume of credit during recent decades are impressive. But a glance through the pages of financial history will dispel any notion of great recent novelty. Credit was in general use in ancient and in medieval times. Credit long antedated industry, banking, and even coinage; it probably antedated primitive forms of money. Loans at interest may be said to have begun when the Neolithic farmer made a loan of seed to a cousin and expected more back at harvesttime. Be this as it may, we know that the recorded legal history of several great civilizations started with elaborate regulation of credit.

For example, about 1800 B.C., Hammurabi, a king of the first dynasty of ancient Babylonia, gave his people their earliest known formal code of laws. A number of the chief provisions of this code regulated the relation of debtor to creditor. The maximum rate of interest was set at 33⅓% per annum for loans of grain, repayable in kind, and at 20% per annum for loans of silver by weight. All loans had to be accompanied by written contracts witnessed before officials. If a higher than legal interest rate was collected by subterfuge, the principal of the debt was canceled. Land and movables could be pledged for debt, as could the person of the creditor, his wife, concubine, children, or slaves. Personal slavery for debt, however, was limited to three years.

Twelve hundred years later, around 600 B.C., the legal history of classical Greece began with the laws of Solon. At that time, drastic reforms were necessitated by an economic crisis in Athens, stemming in part from excessive debt and widespread personal slavery for debt. In contrast to the Code of Hammurabi, the laws of Solon did away with all limits on the rate of interest. They reduced or canceled many debts. They permitted hypothecation, but they forbade personal slavery for debt. These laws endured for centuries.

The Romans also began their legal history with a body of laws regulating credit. This, too, was forced by a crisis characterized by excessive debt. The famous semitraditional Twelve Tables, dating from around 450 B.C., insofar as they deal with credit, resembled the Code of Hammurabi more than they did the laws of Solon. Interest on loans was limited to no more than 8⅓% per annum. Higher than legal interest was penalized by fourfold damages. Personal slavery for debt was permitted, but the physical well-being of the slave was protected.

These three examples from the earliest days of historical Babylonia, Greece, and Rome are enough to support the conclusion that credit at interest was widespread enough to create major political problems before the emergence of written history. The entire 5,000-year span of written history, however, is equal to only about one-half of one percent of the duration of human life on this planet. People had plenty of time to learn a lot about credit and interest before they began to write it down.

Moving forward in time, we note that the Capitularies of Charlemagne, circa 800 A.D., also dealt with credit. They flatly forbade all increments on loans. The sin of usury, and the desire for legal exceptions, provoked major theological and legal controversies for more than a thousand years of the Middle Ages. After the Reformation had justified the charging of interest in northern Europe, the interest rate controversy was taken up by economists, financiers, and politicians, usually in terms of laissez faire versus state control. England eventually followed Solon and abandoned all fixed legal limits on the rate of interest. The states of the United States in their usury laws set fixed maximum rates of interest and in this respect continued the legal traditions of Hammurabi and Rome.

Interest rates in the twentieth century are as much a subject of political and economic controversy as they were in antiquity. American political parties and European political parties are as divided on interest rates as were the patricians and plebeians of republican Rome. Some like them high, and some like them low. Modern economists, if anything, have an even wider and more complex range of opinion. The issues are not new.

A comprehensive view of the history of interest rates will unsettle most preconceived ideas of what is a high rate or a low rate or an average rate. Each generation tends to consider as normal the range of interest rates with which it grew up; rates much higher suggest a crisis or seem extortionate, while rates much lower seem artificial or inadequate. Almost every generation is eventually shocked by the behavior of interest rates because, in fact, market rates of interest in modern times rarely have been stable for long. Usually they are rising or falling to unexpected extremes. Students of the history of interest rates will not be surprised by volatility. Their backward-looking knowledge will not tell them where interest rates will be in the future, but it will permit them to distinguish a truly unusual level of rates from a mere change.

It is easy enough to cite seemingly fanciful interest rates. In fact, we do not have to look beyond our own century to find the highest and lowest rates in the entire span of this history: a 10,000% high in Berlin; an 0.01% low in New York. Both rates were quoted on standard money-market credits under very unusual circumstances. This is a range of 1 million to 1. On January 2, 1990, *The Wall Street Journal* reported that banks in Argentina were offering large depositors 600% interest per month!

Hammurabi's legal limit of 20% per annum on loans in silver cannot be usefully compared with today's money-market interest rates. It was well above most twentieth-century rates on prime business loans, savings bonds, savings deposits, and the like, but was below the 30–45% per annum legal limits and actual charges in many states of the United States for small personal loans. It will be very difficult throughout this history to compare rates with like rates. There are more types and varieties of credit contracts in ancient and modern history than are dreamed of in the philosophy of the modern bond salesperson.

When, in the second millennium B.C., the god Shamash of Sippar in Babylon loaned silver through his priests at 6¼%, the rate was so low for the times as to be considered an act of pious charity. The Temple of Arbela (732–625 B.C.) in Assyria loaned silver at 25%. When Demosthenes in the fourth century B.C. permitted a client to defer paying his legal fee, he added 12% per annum interest to his bill; this was precisely the top of the range of "normal rates" in Athens at his time. When Caesar's sometime friend, the noble Brutus, attempted to charge the City of Salamis 48% for a loan, he shocked his contemporary, Cicero, who reminded Brutus that the legal limit for interest was then 12%. Money in Rome was in fact, then offered at rates as low as 4% per annum.

While we are thus gossiping about the financial behavior of earlier generations, we should not forget the loan sharks. In classical Athens certain usurers used to lend money at 48% a month; this adds up to 576% a year, uncompounded. Even this rate was below the 25% a week ($4 loaned on Monday for $5 to be repaid on Friday) that frequently is reported in New York law courts in trials of unlicensed loan sharks, a rate theoretically equal to 1300% a year. Finally, we should mention Theophrastus's (*d.* 287 B.C.) usurer, who charged 25% a day; this was 9125% a year and may have been a literary exaggeration. Only during twentieth-century inflations will we again find such a high rate specifically reported, as in Germany in the 1920's and Argentina in the last days of the 1980's.

The Middle Ages left its share of interest rate oddities and contrasts. In the twelfth century, personal loans in England were made at 52–120% a year, depending on the collateral, while at the same time in the Netherlands long-term loans secured by real property were made at 8–10%. There were also reports of odd collateral for loans. Baldwin II, king of Jerusalem, under pecuniary pressure on one occasion, hypothecated his beard. In the next century, another Baldwin, Emperor of Constantinople, borrowed in Venice on the security of the Crown of Thorns; when he defaulted, the collateral was redeemed by King Louis IX of France. In the fourteenth century, the 5% bonds of the Republic of Venice sold for a few years over par, while in the same period Frederick the Fair of Austria was borrowing at 80% interest. In the fifteenth century, Charles VIII of France paid up to 100% interest in Italy for a war loan, while merchants in Italy could borrow at 5 to 10%. In the seventeenth century, Holland refunded her 8⅓% state debt at 3¾%, and Dutch merchants borrowed at rates as low as 1¾%, while at about the same time the Crown of Spain was paying 40% interest for short-term loans.

These scraps and oddities were rarely part of the mainstream of interest rate history with which this book is primarily concerned. They are cited at the outset to limber up the imagination and widen the perspective. They illustrate the great actual range of historical interest rates when all countries, eras, and types of loans are considered, and the sharp contrasts to be found from time to time or from place to place, and even at the same time and place, between loans of one type and loans of other types.

Most of this history will be devoted to interest rates on standard, repetitive types of loans, usually on recognized good credits, reflecting as nearly as possible the conventional types of interest rates in antiquity and the various prime market rates of interest in modern times. The going rates on these standard types of loans, however, are supplemented in several chapters by examples of eccentric, specialized, risk, or usurious rates. A history of interest rates, even for twentieth-century America, would be incomplete and misleading if it confined itself to money-market quotations.

THE PLAN OF THIS BOOK

Interest rates can be viewed as changing through many dimensions. The principal dimensions are time, space, quality of the loan, and maturity of the loan. Other distinguishing characteristics are marketability, size of loan, redemption terms, legality, tax status, class of debtor, and class of creditor. Rates on one specific type of loan at one place will change from day to day or from year to year; this is the dimension of time. Or at any one time, the rates on otherwise similar types of loans will change from city to city or from country to country, the dimension of space. Again, at one specific time and place, there usually is a great range of interest rates, according to quality, maturity, size, marketability, and other surrounding circumstances. This history attempts to cover the range of all of these dimensions, with the following limitations and degrees of emphasis:

Time.   The dimension of time is covered from 3000 B.C. without any limit except that enforced by the data that have become available. Since there are more good interest-rate data for the nineteenth and twentieth centuries than for all the rest of human history combined, this history reports much more fully on these centuries than on earlier centuries.

Place.   It is natural and fortunate that those nations that have been most advanced for their times in the development of personal or commercial credit have left us the fullest records of their interest rates. For ancient and medieval times, therefore, this history has not had to formulate any plan of geographic selectivity; it has attempted to be inclusive. The mainstream of interest rate history as it has been reported to us followed a course similar to that of Western political history, coming down from prehistoric times through Mesopotamia, Greece, and Rome to Eastern Europe in medieval times and to Europe and America in modern times. Only occasional early rates are available from other areas. For modern times, some degree of geographical selectivity has been necessary. By far the greatest space has been allotted to interest rates in the principal commercial and financial countries of the

West. Nevertheless, for purposes of background and comparison, some history of interest rates is included for many other countries.

Quality. Some examples of rates of interest on loans entailing a wide range of risk are included when they are available. Rates on high-grade credits are rendered more understandable by such comparisons and also are more easily identified. Nevertheless, this history is concerned chiefly with the course of rates on loans considered high grade by contemporary standards. Such a general and inclusive definition is essential because only such a definition will hold good through the shifting standards of many eras of history. In modern advanced countries, government loans usually set a standard for high quality, followed by loans of the best corporations. In medieval and ancient times, there were no great corporations, and government credit was usually inferior to the credit of propertied individuals. From period to period, therefore, the character of best credits shifted and with it the type of loan that receives the most attention here.

Maturity. This history attempts to report the rates on loans of all maturities, from very short-term personal or trade loans and government bills to perpetual annuities with no maturity date at all. For modern times, maturity is accurately defined, and no reporting problem arises except for the ambiguities inherent in bond averages or optional redemption features. Later chapters present tables showing gradual and unbroken series of interest rates, from the shortest to the longest maturity.

The attempt to cover all maturities, however, succeeds only for a few countries in this century because of lack of earlier data. For the earlier centuries of modern times, the data will consist largely of rates on very long-term bonds or mortgages and rates on many forms of very short-term credit. Rates on medium-maturity loans will usually be lacking. Nevertheless, the definition of maturity will usually be precise.

For the Middle Ages, we will often have to be satisfied with two broad maturity categories, "long" and "short," because the bulk of the data is not more precise. "Long-term" loans will include the perpetual debt of Italian cities, the French *rentes*, the perpetual annuities issued by many European towns, and other loans that were clearly intended to run for many years. "Short-term" loans will include bills of exchange, bank deposits, pawnshop and other collateral loans, and the floating debt of princes. Much of this short-term debt, in fact, probably ran for years, but the form of contract was short term. There is uncertainty, however, as to the term of many medieval credits; when there is doubt, they have been classified as short term, but a description of the term is given to the reader whenever it has come down to us.

For ancient times, distinctions between interest rates arising from maturity are almost nonexistent. The legal limits of Babylonia and Rome applied equally to long- and short-term loans. Historians report "normal" interest rates on best credits, usually without mention of maturity. There is, however, a great deal of evidence that most ancient loans were intended to run only a few months or at most from one to three years. Rates were usually quoted at so much a month. Even loans secured on real property usually specified repayment in one year; occasionally a longer period was specified, but there was no distinction of rate according to term. Long-term capital projects were not generally financed on credit, and states rarely borrowed. There were no large corporations. Some credits were in fact outstanding for years, but this was apparently due to regular renewal or to default. For these reasons, no attempt has been made to classify ancient rates by term of maturity, although in all cases where it is available the specific maturity has been given. Otherwise it is usually assumed they were short-term loans.

Marketability. The rates of interest here reported are sometimes derived from marketable securities, such as bonds, notes, and treasury bills, and sometimes from nonmarketable loans, such as personal loans, bank loans, mortgages, and deposits. Each type is classified separately. No bourse type of market is reported for any form of credit instruments before medieval times. It is probable that an active exchange of obligations did take place in ancient Athens and Rome, but no quotations have come down to us. The history of the modern money market began in twelfth-century Italy.

Rates. The rates quoted here for nonmarketable debt are the nominal rates set forth in the loan contracts. For marketable debt, both nominal rates (the interest expressed as a percentage of the nominal, face, or par value of the loan) and market yields (the rate of return to the buyer at the market price) are reported whenever they have come down to us. If both are available, the market yield is always preferred as an indication of the going rate of interest on loans of the particular sort described. In the absence of market prices, nominal rate alone is considered an adequate indication of prevailing rates only if the securities were newly and successfully sold at approximately face value. Nominal rates that do not reflect voluntary contracts, such as the rates on forced loans and forced conversions are so labeled and are not carried down to the summaries of prevailing rates.

This history does not attempt to go more deeply into the many mathematical concepts of interest and yield than do its sources. Simple interest at annual rates is the form that is attempted throughout, but it is not always precisely achieved. Rates of discount, for example, are quoted from time to time as interest rates, and these provide a higher simple interest than the rate of discount. The sources do not always distinguish. Where a discount is known as such, it is pointed out. Most ancient rates, like modern small-loan rates, were quoted by the month, and these are simply multiplied by twelve without compounding, and without allowing for variations in the calendar, to give an annual rate.

Other attributes, such as *size, redemption* features, *legality,* and *tax status,* are reported, when available, to the extent that they may affect the record of the trend and level of interest rates.

CONTINUITY AND ACCURACY

The economist eager to discover or to support a theory of the causes or effects of interest rates may object to the inclusion in one volume of such unlike rates of interest as the legal interest limits of Babylon and Rome and the modern treasury bill rates of New York and London. For purposes of interest rate theory, the economist will rightly seek to compare only like with like, and might ask that the data, both modern and ancient, be winnowed so that only those rates are presented for all ages that were charged for loans of uniform quality, form, and maturity. No such comparable data exist or could exist over the ages. This fact may explain why economists have shied away from compiling universal histories of interest rates.

Valid interest-rate trends can at times be discerned over periods of as much as several centuries where reasonable (but never perfect) comparability has prevailed. We shall find comparable rates tending to decline in many areas at specific periods of history and tending to increase at others. Economic historians have called attention to these long-term trends in interest rates and their findings are summarized here.

Great caution, however, should be used in comparing the modern interest rates quoted here with their early ancestors, which are also quoted here. The social and economic environments were very different. Customs, taxes, currencies, and laws all differed. These changes might seem to disqualify all comparisons over the centuries. And yet our present money market did not spring fully grown from the brow of Senator Carter Glass, the legislative father of the Federal Reserve System. It grew to its modern form over the centuries. Its birth is lost in antiquity.

Those who are reluctant to make any comparison at all of rates centuries ago with rates today should, to be consistent, refuse to compare the rates of the 1980s with rates twenty or forty years earlier. The economic environment surrounding the U.S. Treasury bill rate in 1989 was very different from that surrounding the U.S. Treasury bill rate in 1945, and this again was very different from that of the 1960's. Basic changes have taken place in a few year's time in the structure of the money market that sets the interest rate. In some respects, there was more difference between 1945 and 1989 in the environment influencing New York interest rates than there was between London in 1755 and New York in 1965. We should not refuse to compare effects because causes have changed.

There is more continuity over the centuries in interest rates than there is in most prices. This is because the interest rate is a ratio of like to like. Like rates produce the same mathematical result in any era, in any currency, and at any given price structure. Compound interest at $x\%$ net will double principal in exactly the same number of years today as in the days of Socrates, and the net purchasing power of $x\%$ interest will be increased or reduced by changes in the value of money or burden of taxes in the same proportion. Because it is such a mathematical ratio, the rate of interest is one of our closest statistical links with our economic past. This book will therefore provide a comparison of rates of interest over the ages in spite of the very unlike credit forms and economic environments. It will, however, summarize the changes in credit forms and in economic environment.

It is not the purpose of this book to analyze the causes of interest-rate levels and trends. There is a vast literature on this subject but little area of agreement. Some interest-rate theories will be mentioned, but none will be sponsored. Patterns of change coinciding with external political or economic events, such as wars and inflations, will be noted, and from these the reader is free to infer cause and effect. It is not the purpose of this history, however, to support or enforce such inferences.

For ancient and medieval times, this book is as inclusive as the scanty data permit. No one who has not diligently sought out ancient and medieval interest rates can appreciate how scarce they are. Contemporaries did not proclaim and rarely recorded the rates of interest they charged. Often interest was illegal or considered sinful, and at other times legal limits encouraged secrecy. In the literature of ancient and medieval economic history, few actual interest rates are mentioned. Most historians ignore the subject or treat it in very general terms.

Furthermore, economic historians inevitably differ on the reliability of the sources. Old data are constantly being amended or refuted by new. There is a splendid opportunity for more original research on ancient, medieval, and even modern interest rates. The authors hope this history will encourage such research. No doubt the scarcity of reliable data is a reason why historians have not compiled universal histories of interest rates. Nevertheless, it should be useful to proceed now by collating and reviewing the material that is available to us even though some of it will be changed. There is no doubt that the record here presented can, and will, be improved by further research.

The earlier rates quoted are almost all derived from books on history or economics, and the modern rates are mostly derived from official sources. Original sources—loan contracts, surviving securities, and the like—usually have not been reexamined. Thus, the economic historian will not find new material in this book. He or she will find familiar material summarized and reorganized to isolate the history of just one type of variable—the rate of interest on loans.

POLITICAL AND ECONOMIC BACKGROUND

Most of the chapters in this history are introduced by subsections that summarize the political and economic events and financial customs at the time and place for which the interest rates are quoted. It is hoped thereby to place the rates and the credit forms to which they were attached in context and to make them understandable.

Much of the ancient and medieval backgound material is controversial. While financial and economic history is constantly being debated, revised, and improved by modern historians, the authors have nowhere attempted to burden the reader with these controversies or to improve upon the texts that provide the background. The reader should be warned, however, that little is certain about early interest rates or early financial usages.

Great gaps will be evident in the background history, as in the history of interest rates themselves. Why are several centuries of Hellenistic Greece described in one paragraph, whereas several pages are devoted to one earlier century of Athenian supremacy? The answer is twofold: First, developmental periods require and deserve detailed description, whereas ensuing periods are likely to be repetitious. Second, the sources themselves apportion far more space to periods of financial development than they do to subsequent, longer periods of repetitious activity. Nevertheless, there are many periods that seem to deserve fuller treatment than this history has been able to provide. The gaps, such as the later Greek, the later Roman, the Byzantine, and the early Dutch periods will some day be filled in.

The authors' choice of background material is not intended to espouse any one of the many theories that undertake to explain interest-rate trends. However, they have not avoided the selection of background facts that might seem to support one or another of these theories. Major wars, price-level trends and currency conditions, for example, are mentioned because they are often considered relevant. The coincidence of events is occasionally pointed out.

PREPARATION OF THIS BOOK

"Our earth is degenerate in these latter days; bribery and corruption are common; children no longer obey their parents; every man wants to write a book, and the end of the world is evidently approaching."—From an ancient Assyrian tablet.

This book was originally written because the late Sidney Homer's long search for a history of interest rates was unsuccessful. It seemed incredible to him that comprehensive histories of this universal and basic economic and commercial price did not exist.

Sidney Homer's search for a history of modern interest rates arose from the practical requirements of business in Wall Street. This was, and still is, vitally concerned day by day with prevailing rates of interest on many sorts of obligations and their fluctuations. Present rates and trends become more comprehensible when compared with past rates and past trends. All markets have historical characteristics that deserve study even though the findings of an individual scholar may eventually be modified.

In the 1930's, when Mr. Homer started this collection of interest rates, short-term American market rates of interest were well reported. But many bond-yield averages were faulty: They combined too wide a variety of qualities and terms. Therefore, he began original research on the history of American bond yields. Subsequently, the science of averaging improved, and several excellent new yield averages became available. The old averages, however, were still widely used and served to distort the history of the markets. Even today, the task of correctly picturing levels and trends of past and present American bond yields is far from completed.

Also evident was the fact that American interest rates did not move in isolation from interest rates in the rest of the world in spite of the breakdown in the international gold standard. In the 1930's, while gold was pouring into the United States and apparently depressing our interest rates to low levels, interest rates were also declining in most of those countries that were being drained of their gold reserves. The great money market of London deserved attention. A glance revealed a rich history of a market not too different in structure from our own that antedated ours by at least a hundred years. Therefore, working always backward, Mr. Homer carried this collection of rates of interest across the Atlantic and moved it back to 1752, the date when the presently outstanding issue of British consols was floated.

All this was carried out while Mr. Homer was seeking without success some inclusive record of the history of all sorts of interest rates and bond yields. Without such a record, he had to gather material laboriously from an enormous variety of sources. From time to time, some serious gaps were filled in by excellent studies published by the National Bureau of Economic Research and other persons and organizations, but all were limited in scope. After twenty years of collecting and analyzing the data and seeking in vain for an organized study of interest rates, the idea presented itself to Mr. Homer of collating all the interest-rate data collected for business purposes into some sort of publication that might be useful to others.

How far back should the study be carried? What came before the London market of 1752? What about the history of the famous French *rentes*? What of the possibility that the English money market was itself merely a copy of earlier continental markets? What was "Dutch finance"? Were there useful precedents to be found by looking far back into antiquity?

Business considerations continued to motivate Mr. Homer's search. At some point, however, he admitted that purely historical curiosity was added. Few business or professional persons have no curiosity about the history of their calling. Doctors defer to Hippocrates and lawyers quote Demosthenes. Why should not those who finance their communities' economic life be as fully aware as history permits of the antiquity of their economic function?

For these reasons, this history has evolved over the years from very practical beginnings. The first edition traced the history of interest rates from 1960 back to antiquity. The second edition carried the story forward to 1975, a period that saw interest rates in leading financial centers advance to what were then record highs. After that edition appeared, interest rates and market yields continued their rise to dramatic new highs in 1981 and 1982. These new record highs made the previous highs of the 1970's appear moderate indeed. As the 1990's began, rates and yields were much lower than they were less than a decade ago. In context, they appeared moderate. The student of interest-rate history will note, however, that the "moderate" rates prevailing as the 1990's opened were about the same as the then-record rates of 1974, shortly before the previous edition of this history went to press. The 1970's and 1980's added much more than one might have expected, or possibly desired, to the recorded history of interest rates covering several millennia. The result is a story worth continuing. No reader will be more surprised than were the authors at the exciting economic drama uncovered by a history of interest rates.

PART ONE

Ancient Times

Chapter 1

Prehistoric and Primitive Credit and Interest

In historical times credit preceded the coining of money by over two thousand years. Coinage is dated from the first millennium B.C., but old Sumerian documents, circa 3000 B.C., reveal a systematic use of credit based on loans of grain by volume and loans of metal by weight. Often these loans carried interest.

In prehistoric times, even before the development of common measures of value or of mediums of exchange, credit probably existed. There are many ethnological instances of credit in kind in communities where no trace of any medium of exchange or even standard of value can be discovered. Credit existed from the very earliest phases of economic activity, even before the evolution of barter proper. (1)

When we consider credit in its broadest meaning we can infer something of its earliest forms. Primitive credit need only have consisted of a loan of seed to a son or brother or neighbor until harvest time or a loan of an animal or of a tool or of food. Such transfers are called gifts if no repayment is expected, loans if repayment is expected, and loans at interest if the repayment of a certain amount more than was loaned is .expected. These transactions in kind required no money, no exchange, and no barter.

Today a transfer without immediate quid pro quo is usually classified in one of three ways: a gift, a loan, or a theft. Those of us who remember our dormitory years know that the distinction between gift, loan, and theft is not always clear. The conventional euphemism is "loan," and it is understood that the aggrieved party, whose necktie is missing, may reciprocate at a convenient opportunity by "borrowing" something belonging to his roommate. Thus loans occur even when not formally negotiated; credit can exist without being clearly defined.

This ambiguity is not new. Thefts, of course, were common in primitive times as they are now. However, before the evolution of governments, the logical response to a theft was a countertheft; a cattle raid for a cattle raid. "Gifts" between chieftains were at times the principal form of peaceable international trade; gifts from one chieftain were expected to be met with a return of gifts, preferably of greater value, from the other. If time elapsed, this could be called credit.

Loans without interest undoubtedly were always common as they are today: friendly or charitable or interested help to a relative or neighbor. They may take the form of the loan of a lawn mower or a cup of sugar or a large or small sum of money or the use of an empty residence. We are here concerned with loans at interest and with the amount of interest expected. The earliest historical records show that interest was already a usual and accepted concomitant of credit. What can we say about its origin?

The loan of a tool to a neighbor suggests no payment of interest, even today: merely the return of the tool in equivalent condition, and the implied privilege of borrowing one of his when needed. Nor does the loan of food or shelter to needy friends or relatives suggest repayment with interest. In fact, such loans are customarily gifts with sometimes a vague hint of reciprocity. But other sorts of loans exist and existed at very early times, which do suggest repayment with interest: loans of seeds and of animals. These were loans for productive purposes. The seeds yielded an increase. At harvest time the seeds could conveniently be returned with interest. Some part or all of the animal's progeny could be returned with the animal. We shall never know but we can surmise that the concept of interest in its modern sense arose from just such productive loans.

By earliest historical times productive loans of this sort, repayable in kind with an agreed rate of interest, had become common. Also common was the friendly charitable loan of nonproductive goods without interest. A confusion of these two types of credit, leading to nonproductive loans at interest, is also evident at an early date. Such loans were subject to amelioration and regulation in the earliest legal codes as they are in our modern legal codes.

Another early distinction that has endured was that between the loan of an identifiable object, say an animal, a tool, or a farm, which must itself be returned, and the loan of a commodity (seed, money, or food), which need not itself be returned but must be returned in kind; the original no longer existed or was indistinguishable from its like. The type of loan repayable in kind required standards of quality and measurement. Indeed such loans could have led to the development of primitive measurements and monetary standards. The use of grain as a medium of exchange was common in the ancient Orient, and it was so used until recent historical times. A later and sophisticated development was the establishment of a common denominator for all repayments; namely, money. Loans of grain or land or animals or money itself could all be repaid in money with or without interest.

Loans of land or loans secured by land are forms of credit which were developed before historical times. Here the source of interest is obvious —the first fruits. Those were payable first, no doubt, in kind and much later in money. The repayment of principal could be in a different form than the payment of interest. The land itself could be returned—a hardship to most farmers of all ages; or principal could be amortized out of the fruits; or, in fact, the principal might never be returnable but might remain the basis of a perpetual annual payment.

This is by no means a complete catalogue of the forms of primitive credit. Among others should be mentioned loans to provide ransom, to finance marriages (bride money, dowry), to finance the shipment of goods, to finance religious donations, and to finance wars. There are fundamental differences that distinguish four types of credit, which persist throughout this history: (a) long-term productive loans, (b) short-term working capital loans, (c) nonproductive consumption loans, and (d) loans to governments.

As early as the Paleolithic Age, probably before 10,000 B.C., a primitive exchange of goods had begun between European and Asiatic tribes which involved amber, shell jewelry, flint, and other commodities suitable for exchange. (2) In a wide area from the Red Sea to Switzerland, Paleolithic shell hoards of sufficient uniformity to suggest their use as a form of money have come down to us. This hypothesis is reinforced by the modern use of just such shells as money by certain South Sea tribes. It is very doubtful, however, that these exchanges and this shell money formed a suitable basis for credit. At the beginning, loans were more likely to have been within tribes or families and in kind.

It was only later, after 8000 B.C., during the Mesolithic Age, and especially after 5000 B.C., during the Neolithic Age (the dates, of course, are conjectural and differ widely for different locations), that capital and credit became important and provided a main impetus toward human progress. Paleolithic man went out to find his food. Neolithic man produced his own food through agriculture and animal culture. His capital took the form of seeds, improved tools, and especially herds of animals. Capital accumulation led to a great increase in population and the opening up of vast new areas in Asia and Europe. Such capital permitted the further accumulation of possessions, the support of chieftains, and the building of cities.

Cattle breeding has supplied us with many financial terms used in later money economies. For example, there is our own word *capital* and our term *pecuniary*, from *pecus*, meaning a "flock" in Latin. Sumerians used the word *mas* for calves and for interest. The Egyptian term *ms*, meaning interest, is derived from the verb *msj*, which means "to give birth." Early Greeks, in fact, valued their precious metals in terms of cattle. In the Odyssey one of the suitors promised to bring Ulysses a contribution "of bronze and gold to the value of twenty oxen."

Cattle probably comprised the first true productive assets or capital of tribes or individuals. Ownership of cattle determined the social position of individuals and families and still does in parts of Africa and, indeed, in parts of the United States. Surplus labor could be stored and retained in the form of cattle. Furthermore, servants and slaves could be profitably employed to speed the accumulation.

As cattle and grain became available and in demand in quantities above consumption requirements, they provided a form of primitive money; that is to say, they became commodities of sufficient value and uniformity that they could conveniently be used as a standard medium of exchange for other commodities. They could also be loaned out at interest. In addition, they provided a standard of valuation.

As early as 5000 B.C., in the Middle East dates, olives, figs, nuts, or seeds of grain were probably lent to serfs, poor farmers, or dependents, and an increased portion of the harvest was expected to be returned in kind. (3) We shall find later abundant evidence of this type of transaction surviving in modern primitive tribes. Animal money could be, and was, loaned out and provided its own increment. Foods and animals were the most important forms of money used by the original Sumerian, Indo-Germanic, and Semito-Hamitic peoples and were so used in Egypt, Mesopotamia, America, India, and China before town civilizations developed. (4)

With the development of town culture in the ancient Orient, credit became very important. Mining had developed, and now inanimate objects, especially metals, such as gold, silver, lead, bronze, and copper, were loaned out at interest. This is as much as to say that they were treated as though they were living organisms with the means of reproduction. (5) Before coined money, metals were exchanged by weight. Capital thus became a powerful economic force. Loan transactions in metals are recorded in numerous early Sumerian and some Egyptian texts. Early Hindu law provided for the right to negotiate such loans.

Coined money is sometimes considered to have originated as pieces of metal stamped by the state as a guaranty of weight or fineness. Alternatively it may have originated as religious tokens. It probably first appeared very late, perhaps in the seventh century B.C. in Asia Minor. But uncoined metal was used for money for thousands of years before that time. Such pieces of metal have been excavated in Troy, Asia Minor, Minoan and Mycenean settlements, Babylonia, Assyria, Syria, Egypt, and Iran. We shall see in the next chapter how at the start of recorded history this uncoined metal money was adapted to trade and banking operations of a remarkably sophisticated nature.

Along with the early development of money and credit there also grew up abuses and prejudices. Some have continued to this day. Most of the earliest legal codes sought to prevent the abuse of credit or to prohibit the use of it. The Israelites did not permit lending at interest. As late as 450 B.C. the Iranians considered that the taking of interest on a loan dishonored a man. (6) Ancient Indian literature reviled usurers and set interest maxima. Nevertheless, loans based on real estate or pawns are mentioned in the Bible, the Zend Avesta, and the Veda. The Babylonians and Romans permitted credit but limited the rate of interest. The Greeks encouraged credit without limit as to rate of interest but forbade personal bondage for debt.

In attempting to judge rates of interest on loans in prehistoric times, we must be content with indirect evidence. Earliest historic rates were reported in the range of 20–50% per annum for loans of grain and metal. The necessity of setting legal maxima and the elaborate machinery of enforcement suggest that higher rates than these would otherwise often have been charged. We can guess that loan sharks existed then as now, willing to accommodate a friend in need at rates 10 or 20 times the legal limit. We can also guess that lower rates were common for credit transactions between solvent capitalists. Beyond such inferences and conjectures we have guidance only from the customs of modern primitive tribes. These rates, while highly suggestive and perhaps acceptable as a rough measure of the natural terms of similar transactions, are presented separately here lest they be mistaken for true ancient history.

A study of primitive money (7) catalogues some 173 objects and materials which in ancient and modern times have had monetary attributes in one or more places and at one or more times. Those most frequently mentioned include beads, cattle, cloth, copper, gold, grain, iron, rice, salt, shells, silver, skins, slaves and tobacco. It has been suggested that currencies in some areas became standardized because of the difficulty that debtors often met in making exact repayments in kind. Law or custom eventually provided an alternative means of debt repayment in some commonly acceptable commodity of value. This "legal tender" then became even more valuable. Be that as it may, the ethnological records reveal abundant instances of loans, repayments, and interest in primitive economies using uncoined money. A few may be cited:

1. In backward parts of India, grain in modern times has been an important medium of exchange and a standard for deferred payments. Sowing seed and food were borrowed for repayment at the next harvest. The usual repayment was double the quantity borrowed. This in modern banking terms would be interest of $100\% \times 12/x$ per annum if x equals the number of months until harvest time. Since interest charged for rupee loans in the same backward districts was reported as 24–36% per annum, the grain rate seems high. However, it is necessary to allow for the fact that grain was no doubt cheaper at harvest time than at seed time, and also that many borrowers of seed were not eligible for rupee loans. In rice districts of India, paddy seed loans were reported at 60% interest (term unstated). Among the Naga tribes cows and buffaloes have been loaned out; after one year the amount repayable was double, which equals 100%. (8) Loans of coin among the Naga brought less interest; for these 50% was quoted.

2. In Indo-China, in the early twentieth century loans were granted in rice at an interest rate of 50% repayable at the end of the next season. (9)

3. In the Philippines in this century credit among the remote Ifugao tribes took the form of loans in kind on which interest was regularly exacted. Rice loaned at any time had to be doubly repaid at the next harvest; this equals $100\% \times 12/x$. The loan of a pig required the return of two pigs of the same size. Loans of legal metallic money also commanded a 100% rate of return and compounding was rapid. A man who borrowed 3 pesos to meet a funeral expense owed 24 pesos three years later. The Ifugaos even had a form of discount called "patang," in terms of which interest on the loan of an animal was paid in advance. (10)

4. On the Banks Islands in the Southwest Pacific a very highly developed credit and currency system in terms of strings of shells was closely connected with a system of men's clubs or secret societies. This was more ceremonial than economic. Admission to the clubs cost a large quantity of shell money, and promotion in rank cost even more. Shell money was little needed and little used for everyday life, but a poor man required shells to make a start in life by joining a society. The standard rate of interest for borrowing shells was 100% for any period. If a man had insufficient shells to join a society, he could loan what he had to others and in time the interest would provide him with his initiation fee. The unusual feature of this system was that a man was entitled to impose a loan on an unwilling borrower who had to repay with interest under threat of severe penalties. Nor is this the only case we find of coerced debtors. The situation was not unlike the gift economies

of Homeric and medieval times, when a gift had to be requited by a larger gift. Kings gave abundantly to other kings and to their own nobles, but such gifts were often costly to the recipients. Even today social customs at times have encouraged retributive giving: for example, at Christmas time, birthdays, and weddings. The giver sometimes may contemplate a return with an agio. (11)

5. On Vancouver Island, in Canada, not long ago, blankets had taken the place of furs and wampum as the monetary unit of the Kwakiutl. These cheap white blankets, then valued at about 50 cents, formed the medium of exchange and valuation and were above all the standard of deferred payments. An elaborate credit system was developed which was also more ceremonial than economic. Five blankets borrowed for six months became seven; for a year they became ten. In modern banking terminology these returns equate to annual interest rates of 80% for a six-month loan and 100% for a one-year loan. A young man got his start in life by borrowing blankets to be repaid double in a year, and then he distributed them to his relatives as forced loans repayable within a few months at 300%. (12) This system of forced loans, called "potlatch" (gifts with a string attached), became so widespread that it had to be prohibited by the Canadian government. Wealthy Indians vied with each other to see who could give away the most blankets, all with the understanding that even more would be given back—usually double. This became a reductio ad absurdum of the old gift custom more generally described as "Indian giving." (13)

6. In Namaland, in Southwest Africa, cattle and beads were the original currencies. Debts were incurred in cattle (no rates quoted), and the difficulty of repayment often led to cattle raids into neighboring states. (14) In the Belgian Congo, brass rods were used extensively as a standard of deferred payment. Credit was frequently granted by native traders, and tribal law gave creditors extensive power to collect. In the French Sudan cattle were used until recently as currency for large transactions. Cattle loans were granted *free of interest*, but if a cow which was lent had a calf, the calf and the cow was claimed by the creditor. (15) Similarly, in Uganda and French Equatorial Africa cattle and sheep were the bases of credit. In the former the creditor expected every third new birth as interest.

7. In Northern Siberia, at least until recently, domesticated reindeer served as money. Loans were granted in reindeer. Among the Kirghiz of Siberia, horses and sheep served as money and were loaned out. The usual interest for such loans was 100%. (16)

These scraps of primitive interest rates are in fact all a part of modern history, not of ancient history or of the prehistory of credit. Inferences from them should be made with caution. They do, however, serve to illustrate the actual operation of primitive credit in kind and in very general terms show the type and magnitude of return the creditor often expected. In most cases per annum rates were not conventional and our translation into modern credit terms is forced. The term was the natural term of the transaction: from seed time to harvest, for example. But since such a seed loan can often be made only once a year, it might have been a matter of indifference to both debtor and creditor whether the term was six months or twelve months.

The earliest historical customs relating to credit and interest, which will now be examined, should not be considered the direct successors of the primitive customs and rates which have just been cited. Most, and probably all, civilizations that were able to record their own histories were already highly advanced, complex, and mature when their recorded history began. Long ages of development must have intervened between the first primitive cattle economies and the first historical societies of Mesopotamia, Egypt, Greece, and Rome. In fact, some of the characteristics and customs of the cattle economies of modern times were never known by the prehistoric ancestors of these peoples. Productive loans in kind, however, were certainly a survival. We shall now find history beginning with an elaborate effort to regulate the complex relationship between debtor and creditor.

Chapter II

Mesopotamia: Sumer, Babylonia, and Assyria

BACKGROUND

This historical era may be divided into four parts: (a) the earliest recorded Sumerian history, circa 3000 B.C. down to the first Babylonian dynasty, circa 1900 B.C.; * (b) the Babylonian Empire, 1900 B.C. down to the period of Assyrian domination, 732 B.C.; (c) the period of Assyrian domination of Babylonia, 732–625 B.C.; and (d) the Neo-Babylonian Empire, 625–539 B.C. Thereafter followed Persian rule, 539–333 B.C., and later the Hellenistic period.

In ancient Sumer in earliest times barley was the medium of exchange for most transactions. In this rich agricultural region grain continued throughout these centuries to be a standard of payment and repayment. (17) However, even before 3000 B.C., ingots of copper and silver were also exchanged. There were two standards of value: grain and silver. Silver was used mainly in the town economies that developed in Mesopotamia, while grain was used in the country. Their relative values varied and this led to frequent state intervention to provide rules for exchange and repayment. There was no coined money until the first millennium B.C.; payments in metal were by weight.

Many documents dealing with property and credit have come down to us from the Sumerian period. There was no sharp break with the past at the beginning of the Babylonian Empire. Many of the financial cus-

* Most of the dates in this era are highly controversial.

toms of the early Sumerians were codified and perpetuated in the Baby., lonian Code of Hammurabi (circa 1800 B.C.).

In Sumer, property in land was vested in individuals and in social groups, such as temples. (18) Transfers and loans were carefully recorded in legal documents which were witnessed before officials and deposited in temples. This practice was already far ahead of the primitive customs of modern tribes. Deeds of sale of land have been discovered which date from before 2800 B.C. The law then restricted the sale of private property in favor of the family; in principle real property could only be alienated from the family by debt. Uncultivated land was at the disposal of the first occupant; he, however, had to clear it, irrigate it, and farm it.

The Code of Hammurabi regulated the terms of ownership of land, the employment of agricultural labor, civil obligations, land rental, credit, and much besides. Creditors must wait until after the harvest before pressing a farmer for repayment. Crop failure caused by storm or drought served to cancel interest due on a land loan for that year. Land could not only be hypothecated at interest, but could also be leased, usually for three years. Rent was payable sometimes in produce and sometimes in metallic money.

Town houses as well as farms might be hypothecated. Owing to the scarcity of wood, doors were rare and were not considered part of a house but a separate commodity separately salable and sometimes separately hypothecated for loans. The Code even fixed the fees of the architect and made him responsible for replacing bad construction and liable even to pay with his life if the owner were crushed in the ruins. Sometimes the holder of a loan on a house came to live in the house in lieu of interest.

From early times trade played an important part in Mesopotamian life. This was partly due to the strategic location of the country on navigable rivers midway between east and west; it was also due to the necessity of importing a great number of primary materials, such as wood. (19) When a merchant traded with distant countries, he formed a sort of share-partnership with a commercial traveler.

Commercial transactions were carefully regulated by the Code. Exact accounts had to be kept; negligence was penalized; the division of profits and provision of capital had to be spelled out in writing in advance. Partners did not necessarily contribute capital; they might contribute only their credit and jointly borrow the whole sum needed. Partnerships were known in ancient Sumer long before the Code.

From early times down to the time of the Persian Empire, a span of thousands of years, this legislation on credit was remarkably stable. (20) Loans without interest of consumable commodities were recognized and they could, but need not, provide a penalty for nonpayment. Such penalty rates are common throughout history and must be sharply distinguished from contract rates of interest. The Code also recognized loans at interest, both loans of silver and loans of grain, secured and unsecured. A maximum interest rate was fixed on all loans. These maxima were altered only once in two thousand years.

Like early Sumerian custom, the Code set a higher maximum interest rate on loans of grain than on loans of silver. Twelve hundred years later, circa 600 B.C., the interest rate maximum on grain loans was reduced to equal the rate on silver loans. Higher than maximum rates were occasionally permitted. Very often, however, loans were negotiated below the maximum rates of interest.

To prevent violations, the Code required that all loan contracts be drawn up in the presence of an official and witnessed. Otherwise the lender would lose all rights to repayment. A higher than legal rate collected by subterfuge also canceled the debt. Provision was made for compromise settlements when the debtor could not pay in full.

To protect the creditor, pledges and sureties were permitted. Pledging of farmland was regulated in detail; the creditor could not take more at harvest time than the principal, if due, plus legal interest. Any property, real or personal, could be pledged—wife, concubine, children, slaves, land, houses, utensils, credits, the door. But servitude for debt could not last more than three years. Later this time limit was extended. Many contracts show that interest (and sometimes principal) on a debt was earned by the labor of a pledged slave or child. The debtor, unable to pay, might himself be reduced to slavery for three years. More often an indemnity was provided. Provision was made for court settlement if there were several unsatisfied creditors. The wife's signature was often required in a loan contract. Women's property rights were protected by the Code; the husband alone could not pledge or dispose of joint property.

The temples not only owned great wealth but were active in finance. They granted loans of silver and loans of grain. Sometimes they made loans to the poor without interest (21) and at other times they made loans at interest. Often they charged rates below the legal maximum; sometimes one half or one third of this maximum. The Temple of Marduk at Babylon would lend money to slaves to enable them to purchase freedom. At Sippon, the Sun God, acting through priests and priestesses, was the chief banker. The temples were also seats of justice and depositories of documents and valuables.

Such banking operations, including deposits, transfers, and loans, date back to the third millennium B.C., but did not lead to the creation of specialized professional banking firms until the Assyrian and Neo-Babylonian period. (22) Early royal and temple households and private individuals conducted banking business as part of their other economic activities and generally in small volume.

From the time of Hammurabi, and probably earlier, loans in the form of exchange bills were known and were negotiable. Some bills were payable to the original creditor, others to any bearer; some on demand, some at a fixed date. Remittances were made by a documentary order on a debtor. Deposits were common: valuables were placed with another for his administration subject to withdrawal at a given time or on demand. The business of changing money for a profit was combined with transferring sums from one account to another without the use of cash. Also there was payment and receipt on behalf of another without a previous money deposit. Money was loaned on pawns, credit instruments, or real estate or on general credit without security.

Some of these financial transactions were international as well as local. There are clear records in cuneiform of such transactions between Babylonians and Assyrians, Syrians, Hittites, Elamites, but not with Egyptians. The highly authoritarian economy of ancient Egypt, which largely dispensed with the domestic use of money, left few records of credit and interest.

The stability of credit customs in Mesopotamia over thousands of years has been mentioned. Evolution, development, and great change there must have been, especially considering the long history of wars, destruction, invasion, and conquest. And yet in broad outline the financial usages of the year 1800 B.C. and earlier still seemed to be current in the sixth century B.C.

After 600 B.C. there grew up a more advanced form of banking practice in private hands. For example, the Egibi Sons and the Murassu, merchant bankers of Babylon, carried on large and complicated businesses, lending large sums to governments and to individuals, transferring deposits on order from one merchant to another, paying interest on deposits, buying loans on land, and entering business ventures as partners. The use of modern terminology, however, must not suggest a picture of modern finance in Babylonia. An absolute Oriental monarch ruled as a god. It is sufficient to note that by 600 B.C. Neo-Babylonian finance was at least as far ahead of the primitive as twentieth-century finance is ahead of the Neo-Babylonian.

The history of Assyria long antedates the period when Assyria ruled over Babylonia. Assyrian dynasties are known as early as 2000 B.C., but the nation's rise to empire came much later. Financial usage in Assyria did not differ greatly from financial usage in Babylonia. However, credit transactions appeared less frequently and were more primitive. Assyrian loans were scarcely ever granted without real security in the form of a substantial pawn. Collateral changed hands at the granting of a loan rather than at default, as in Babylonia. Loans free of interest for a short term were frequent in Assyria, but with heavy penalties for default. Interest rates were probably higher in Assyria than in Babylonia.

We do not know of formal legal limits for interest in Assyria, but customary rates were recognized. There, too, the temples loaned money. As in Babylonia, wives, slaves, and children could be given as pledge for a loan. The law protected such human pledges from mistreatment and they could not be sold. By the first millennium B.C., at least, banking operations similar to those of Babylonia were widespread in Assyria. We begin to hear of specialized banking firms. By law anyone starting a legal action arising from a business contract was required to deposit a large sum of money for the duration of the action.

The following are translations (sometimes abbreviated) of a few business documents of Babylonia and Assyria which may serve to illustrate specific types of transactions:

1. Circa 2040 B.C.: "The house property, next the house of X. . . . one end abutting on the street, . . . from the hands of I., son of S., X., son of K. has bought. The full price, two thirds mina and nine shekels of silver has he paid. The transaction is completed; his heart is satisfied. Never shall the one make any claim against the other. In the names of [gods] and King Samsu-Iluna have they sworn . . . [Names of twelve witnesses and the date]." (23)

2. Circa 2000 B.C.: "Two shekels of silver have been borrowed by Mas-Schamach, the son of A., from the sun-priestess Amat-Schamach, daughter of W. He will pay the Sun-God's interest. At the time of the harvest he will pay back the sum and the interest upon it."

3. Circa 1800 B.C.: "Ka-enlilla, the son of N., borrowed one mina of silver from Bur-Sin on the interest of the temple of Shamash. He will repay the capital and its interest in [the month of] Napri. [Names of 5 witnesses]"

4. Assyria, probably 1000–700 B.C.: "Five imer of barley belonging to the heir apparent, in the hand of Taquni II, placed at the disposal of Hamathutha of. . . . The barley increases by 50 qua the imer." (24)

5. Babylon 595 B.C.: "One-half mina of silver, the possession of Nabu-Usabsi, the son of N., the son of N., is owed by Nabu-sar-ahesu, the son of. . . . Yearly upon one mina, ten shekels of silver shall accumulate (16⅔%). All his property . . . , all that there is, shall be a pledge. . . . Another creditor has no right of disposal over it until Nabu-Usabsi gets his money, full repaid. The men he caused to appear [4 witnesses, the priest] City of Uruk, month of Ululu, 11th day of the 9th year of Nebuchadnessar, King of Babylon." (25)

MESOPOTAMIAN INTEREST RATES, 3000–400 B.C.

In the Sumerian period, 3000–1900 B.C., the customary rate of interest for a loan of barley was 33⅓% per annum and for a loan of silver was 20% per annum. (26) There are examples, however, of silver loans at

25% and a likelihood of rates below these customary rates, including interest-free loans. (In the twenty-fourth century B.C., the Laws of Manu in India set 24% as an established rate of interest.) (27)

In the Babylonian period, 1900–732 B.C., the Code of Hammurabi recognized the old customary interest rates and established them as legal maxima which lasted more than 1200 years: 33⅓% per annum for loans of grain and 20% per annum for loans of silver. (26) Again there are examples of silver loans as high as 25%, but much more often capitalists accepted a smaller return. The state sometimes granted loans of silver at 12%, and the temple administrators sometimes demanded even less. The God Shamash, of Sippar, used to lend barley at 20% and silver at 6¼%. The normal rate on silver loans seems to have ranged between 10% and 25% in Babylonia and on grain loans between 20% and 33⅓%. (22) In neighboring countries rates were often higher.

During the period of Assyrian domination, 732–625 B.C., the legal interest maximum in Babylonia was still 33⅓% on grain and 20% on silver; no change in the range of normal rates is reported. In Assyria, however, interest-free loans with penalties were more common; penalty rates were often high: 40%, 100%, 141%. Examples of silver loans at interest in Assyria at this time are:

The Temple of Arbela charged.......................... 25%
Unstated creditor charged............................. 30%
In 667 B.C. Nergal-shar-utsin lent 5 shekels of silver at..... 20%
In 668 B.C. Suka borrowed 3 mina of silver at............. 40%(28)

There must have been a customary rate of interest in Assyria, but since documents rarely mention the interest rate, it has not been determined. For advances in grain the interest was often 50%; in one document, it was as low as 30%. The evidence suggests that interest rates were higher in Assyria than in Babylonia.

In the Neo-Babylonian Empire, 625–539 B.C., the legal maximum on silver loans remained at 20%, but the maximum on barley loans was reduced to 20%. (29) Specific examples of actual loan transactions are:

618–581 B.C. Professional moneylenders lend at 11⅔%. (27)

595 B.C.   One-half mina of silver borrowed by N-S from N-U on security of all his possessions, on which interest of 16⅔% shall accrue each year. (25)

555 B.C.   N. borrowed ½ mina of silver from G. against his house at 20%. (30)

544 B.C.   Loan through an agent at 20%. (30)

542 B.C.   Banking house of Egibi loaned ½ mina which bore interest at 20% per annum if not paid in a month. (31)

540 B.C.   Loan at 20%. (31)

539 B.C.   Loan at 20%. (27)
536 B.C.   Loan at 16⅔%. (27)
518 B.C.   Nabu-mukin-zer, a scribe, lent at 20%. (27)

After the Persian Conquest, 539 B.C., there is some evidence that 40% became a common rate of interest in Babylonia. This was after Mesopotamia had lost her independence. Babylonia was no longer a great capital city. Her old civilization had all but vanished. The center of economic progress and activity had shifted to the Mediterranean and especially to Greece, which will be reviewed in the next chapter.

This survey of Mesopotamian interest rates is not able to distinguish different characteristic rates of interest for different types of credit, with the exception of grain loans and silver loans. Long-term and short-term credits are not characterized by different interest rates or legal limits; nor are production loans distinguished from consumption loans, nor real estate credit from trade credit. All these types of loans existed and differences in rates no doubt existed when the prevailing rate was below the legal maximum. But the raw data, which are abundant, have not yet been organized to reveal these distinctions. Nor do they trace rate fluctuations over the dimension of time, except over vast eras. Judging from the known commercial activity, the importance of private capital, and the prevalence of borrowing below legal limits, such interest rate fluctuations must have existed. The data only give us a picture of the generally accepted range of interest rates on "standard credits" during this long span of history.

TABLE 1

SUMMARY OF MESOPOTAMIAN INTEREST RATES: 3000–400 B.C.

Dates B.C.	Normal Rates, %		Legal Maxima, %	
	On grain	On silver	On grain	On silver
Sumer				
3000–1900	$33\frac{1}{3}$	20–25		
Babylonia				
1900–732	20–$33\frac{1}{3}$	10–25	$33\frac{1}{3}$	20
732–625	20–$33\frac{1}{3}$	10–20	$33\frac{1}{3}$	20
625–539	?–20	10–20	20	20
Fifth–fourth centuries		40 (?)		
Assyria				
Ninth–seventh centuries	30–50	20–40		
Persia				
Sixth century	40	40		

Chapter III

Greece

BACKGROUND

The Bronze Age civilization of the Aegean Sea, which rose and fell between 2400 and 1200 B.C., reached a high level of culture and economic activity, but left no specific information on its credit forms and rates of interest. Cattle were the first standard of value, and metals later became mediums of exchange. (33) The metal ingot represented great wealth in small bulk. Ingots were often flat sheets of copper of fixed weight in the shape of an ox hide, which bore a weight stamp: mina, shekel, and so on. Gold and silver were also exchanged by weight. As this was essentially an island civilization, centered at first in Crete, maritime trade was active. Trademarks and commercial documents were in regular use and so probably was credit.

With the fall of Crete in 1400 B.C., and especially following the Dorian invasion of 1200 B.C., this Minoan-Mycenaean civilization was destroyed. The Iron Age was ushered in by a decline to barbarism. The poems of Homer purported to describe events of the early heroic golden age of Mycenaean Greece, but many of the economic customs Homer described were more characteristic of the late barbaric period, just before 800 B.C.(?), when the epics were supposed to have been written. The forms of government and the economy they describe were feudal, and in some respects resembled Europe's Dark Ages. (34) "Gifts" often took the place of royal revenues, taxes, and payments. Kings gave "gifts" and furnished elaborate dinners to the nobles who had a right to come uninvited. Kings also received "gifts" regularly and on special occasions. Foreign traders on arrival in port brought "gifts" to the king and received "gifts" in return. Even craftsmen were often paid for their services in "gifts." Royal revenues also were derived from the king's personal estate, the duty of personal service, tribute, the spoils of war, piracy, and cattle raids. Armies lived off plunder; conquerors were free from taxation.

There are many references in the Iliad and the Odyssey to the use of the ox as a unit of account. (35) The Homeric Greeks had been nomads from the grassy steppes. A big tripod was "at the worth of twelve oxen." A skillful woman was "worth four oxen." Each of the gold tassels on the shield of Pallas was "a hundred oxen's price."

These are references to a standard of value, not necessarily to a medium of exchange. Payment was probably more often made in metals: "We will pay in bronze and gold to the value of twenty oxen." Homeric trade was often by barter. Fines were sometimes in cauldrons and tripods, by capacity, not by weight, because there were no facilities for weighing base metals. This was a steep descent from the elaborate civilization of Minoan Crete where metallic currency had all but reached the stage of official coinage and where gold was abundant. One of the later reforms of Solon, 594 B.C., was the recomputation of fines and bounties in coined money instead of cattle.

Iron also assumed importance as a monetary material during the barbaric period following the Dorian invasions. Iron spits, or obols, were exchanged in bundles. Sparta early adopted iron bars for currency and retained them through most of her history.

There are no records of interest-bearing loans for productive purposes during this archaic Greek period, but Hesiod speaks of interest-free seed loans repayable in kind. (36) The Iliad has an account of loans to strangers, probably loans of cattle, which if not repaid could be reclaimed by legal robbery. Cattle raids on land and piracy at sea were normal forms of economic activity and, if successful, became the subject of royal self-congratulation.

The official coinage of money is supposed to have originated in Lydia in the seventh century B.C., although some credit the Ionians or earlier peoples. This coinage consisted of pieces of stamped metal that may have originated as religious tokens and came to be officially stamped by the state. They provided a sort of legal tender for the payment of debts and taxes. The first Lydian coins were attributed to the nebulous King Gyges (686?–656 B.C.). They were of electrum, a mixture of gold and silver. King Croesus of Lydia (560–546 B.C.) is credited with providing the first ingots of pure gold; Lydia was then a leading gold producer. (37) During the seventh century B.C. the Lydian innovation of striking coins was adopted by the greater part of the Greek world. (38) Since the Greeks had little gold, they coined silver. In classical Attica 1 talent of silver equaled 60 minas; 1 mina equaled 100 drachmas; 1 drachma equaled 6 oboli.

In the course of the "Dark Ages" the Dorian Greek invaders were absorbed and civilized by the old culture. Personal ownership replaced collective tribal ownership. (39) The agricultural insufficiency of Greek land led to active maritime trade. Meat, so abundant in Homeric times, became very scarce; even grain was insufficient. There were in Greece, however, exportable surpluses of wine and olive oil and of such manufactured articles as pottery and metal implements. The necessities of trade led to standardized weights and measures.

The Greeks of the seventh century B.C. developed an economic system that was commercial, urban, and monetary. Credit facilitated trade. There was extensive borrowing at interest, especially on ship loans. "In next to no time the commercial genius of the Greek rises to the notion of speculation . . . capital accumulated is only an investment with a view to accumulating more." (40) The poets of the day bitterly compared the new standards with the old ideals. The power of the old kings, once based on soil, cattle, and descent from the gods, was gone. Oligarchy had supplanted hereditary monarchy. Even the landed nobility, except in Sparta, sought after movable wealth; some used their surplus wealth to become merchants and shipowners and compete with the lower class tradesmen. "Virtue and glory follow riches." "Money makes the man." The stage was set for a social struggle between economic classes.

In Attica, at the beginning of the sixth century B.C. the tenant farmers were under severe economic pressure and threatened rebellion. They were sometimes able to keep only the sixth part of their produce. Personal slavery of whole families for debt was permitted and became common. Freemen had to compete with slaves. In spite of the relief provided by extensive colonization, discontent grew. Pawn credit was widespread. Debt had become an insupportable burden. At this crucial point (594 B.C.) the poet and wiseman Solon was called upon by Athens to assume supreme legislative power for a limited period and revise her laws. (32)

Solon's reforms were radical and for the most part they endured. He probably canceled many debts secured by land and scaled down others. All those enslaved for debt were freed; those sold abroad for debt were redeemed at state expense. All restrictions were removed from rates of interest and from loan transactions, except that personal slavery for debts was forbidden. Political power was reapportioned according to property. The drachma was devalued by about one quarter. Weights and measures were increased in size. Citizenship was granted to immigrants who were skilled artisans. Judging from these reforms and their acceptance, the economic crisis of 594 B.C. must have been severe indeed.

In 508 B.C. democracy was established in Athens. From this time on Athens so rapidly outdistanced other Greek cities in trade and finance that the history of Greek credit and interest rates is largely, but not entirely, a history of Athenian credit and Athenian interest rates.

Before the beginning of the fifth century B.C., the minting of money in Greece was hampered by a scarcity of metals. (41) After 483 B.C. a series of marvelous finds occurred, and precious metals spread throughout Greece. Each city struck its own coinage. Every foreign transaction thus required a money-changing transaction. Many cities engaged in unscrupulous alloying, but such frauds could only work internally. A few cities by their integrity gained universal acceptance for their coinage. Athens had the advantage of the silver mines of Laureion. The Athenians took every precaution to maintain the integrity of their famous "owls." Even in times of tragic national disaster, when the treasury was empty and Attica occupied by an enemy, Athens refused to debase this silver coinage. As a consequence, the Athenian "owl" became current in all markets and an article for export. It remained a most acceptable currency throughout the Mediterranean for 600 years, long after the disastrous defeat of Athens in the Peloponnesian War, 431–404 B.C. (42) This tragic event, immortalized by Thucydides and mourned to this day by lovers of human excellence, was not a turning point in the financial history of Greece.

Before the Persian wars, 499–479 B.C., the hoarding of coin was general in Greece. Cities and temples, especially the temple at Delphi, accumulated treasure. Temples made loans to states and to individuals. But after 450 B.C., and especially after 400 B.C., investment in productive capital became common. (43) Recorded estates of wealthy Athenians then showed little ready cash and large holdings not only of land but of rental housing, slaves let out for hire, business investments, and loans bearing interest. Even Socrates, the philosopher, had a friend to whom he entrusted his investment problems. At going rates of profit and interest the fortunes of minors often doubled or trebled in a few years. Traders and manufacturers borrowed to carry their stock, and farmers borrowed on land. Interest was generally reckoned at so much per mina per month. Loan sharks abounded and small debtors in difficulty dreaded "the end of the moon."

Sea loans, sometimes called "bottomry loans," were very popular. These were contracts wherein a lender advanced his money secured by hull or cargo. In case of shipwreck the borrower usually owed nothing; if he completed his voyage, he repaid the capital with a specific "interest." As this reward was either a form of insurance premium or the profit from a partnership at full risk, these rates should not be considered interest rates. They were very high. For a return voyage from Athens to the Bosphorus a rate of 30% was quoted in wartime and 22½% in peacetime. This rate could be earned twice a year and thus profits of 40–60% per season were common. Sometimes 100% was asked for longer and more hazardous trips. (44) The creditor frequently went with the ship to look after his investment.

Personal loans secured by real estate were common in Greece as they were elsewhere at most periods of history. The medieval term "mortgage" is often used by economic historians to describe such loans, but it obscures some differences in legal thinking and economic context from those of the present day. (45) The Athenians used three terms: "hypotheke," signifying that the property remained with the debtor until default, as distinguished from a pawn; "prasis epi lysei," meaning a conditional sale which could be released from the buyer's claim; and "apotimena," meaning an evaluation of security put up to guarantee performance of a contract.

In the period 500–200 B.C. it was the custom in Attica to designate the ownership of real estate by marking stones, called "horoi," which meant limit or boundary. The visible half of these horoi was sometimes blank and sometimes engraved. There were severe penalties for tampering with the horoi. Several hundred have come down to us. Certain of them give notice that the property is encumbered, and a few say how, for how much due to whom, and on what terms. The debtor remained in physical possession and, therefore, his name did not appear. At about 450 B.C. the deme Myrrhinus instructed its temple officials to obtain real security for all its loans and to place horoi on the encumbered property. An example of an unusually explicit Attic horoi inscription from about 300 B.C. is: "In [date] N. and H. . . . put up as security to K. . . . their lands, house and roof . . . in full—for 5000 drachmas in silver. N. will pay K. for each year 500 drachmas in silver." (46)

Such loans were not usually for productive purposes, such as improvements to the property or to finance business ventures, but were often loans to wealthy or average farmers to meet personal emergencies. (47) There are indications that these real estate loans were usually for moderate periods, perhaps one year. However, certain transactions like the one quoted above appear to be for indefinite periods. The state itself was never mentioned in the horoi; public lending or borrowing was unusual. Groups of individuals, comprising lending clubs, often made such secured loans to friends, sometimes without interest. The horoi often refer to loan contracts on deposit with bankers or in temples. A number of specific horoi transactions are listed below under "Interest Rates, Real Estate Loans."

Public finance in Greece tended to be conservative and traditional. In contrast to the present day, states rarely borrowed. (48) Instead they accumulated treasure in their treasuries. Most famous is the vast treasure of the Athens of Pericles, removed in 454 B.C. to Athens from Delos, where it had been the war chest of the Delian League. Direct taxes were considered servile and were unknown in the fifth and fourth centuries B.C. (49) However, voluntary direct taxes, that is, "liturgies," or gifts to the state, were common, and much later they were merged into capital levies on wealthy men. The mines provided most of the ordinary revenue of Athens. Her armies were supposed to be self-supporting; a good general could find money.

Loans to states were thus exceptional until the third and second centuries B.C. There were occasional early loans to states, but these were compulsory or of a political character. The famous loans of the Temple of Athena to the city of Athens during the fifth century B.C. were a religious fiction: the money was the war reserve of the people of Athens. Interest on these loans was nominal and was rarely paid, but an effort was made to return the principal to the Temple, that is to say, to restore the war reserve. (50)

The credit of most Greek states was in fact very poor. It generally rated far below the credit of wealthy citizens. This situation existed also in the Middle Ages in Western Europe. Greek cities were often arbitrary with their creditors; money was usually scarce, and sound principles of public finance were unknown. Public loans were usually due within five years and hence repayment of principal was a burden. They were not amortized. They were usually secured by valuable pledges, and sometimes the security took strange forms. For example, state fortifications were sometimes hypothecated. Cyme pledged her public colonnades, and when the city defaulted her citizens could not use them to get out of the sun or the rain. Creditors were sometimes offered tax exemption. Public revenues were sometimes pledged. For example, Demosthenes, 385?-322 B.C., once lent one talent (a large sum) to the city of Oreos at 12% secured by all the public revenues of the city.

Often Greek states wishing to borrow had to offer the guarantee of individual citizens in good standing, who were called "foreloaners" or "underwriters." In 377-373 B.C., thirteen states borrowed from the temple at Delos, and only two proved completely faithful; in all, four fifths of the money was never repaid. Thereafter the temple preferred loans to individuals, secured by land.

The financial difficulties of Greek states reached their height after the Macedonian conquest. Athens then resorted to the "eisphora," or capital levy, instead of loans. Athens was never a debtor. In 205 B.C., the city of Miletus experimented with a new credit form: the city borrowed from its citizens on life annuities. It paid back 360 drachmas a year for life for every 3,600 drachmas it borrowed; this innovation proved very popular.

Although there is general agreement that in Greece the banking functions of deposit and loan originated in the temples, as they did in Babylonia, there is a difference of opinion as to the scope of temple lending in the classical period. The shrine at Delphi, the greatest of them all, is sometimes described as the great banker of the Greek world. There is certainly a long history of lending by the temple at Delos, largely to private persons, but sometimes to states and to money changers.

Industry in classical Greece was generally on a small scale, consisting of workshops with a handful of slaves and limited capital. Local trade was left to shopkeepers and peddlers and was despised, (51) but foreign trade was held in high esteem in Athens. Since the state was not self-sufficient, commerce was encouraged and was largely free of tariffs and restrictions. Athens became the trading metropolis of the Mediterranean world. By 450 B.C. it had monopolized the trade of the Black and Aegean seas and traded with Egypt, Cyprus, and Italy.

In the fourth century B.C., private banking began to play an important role. Bankers, the "trapezitai," changed money, received deposits, made loans to individuals and states, made foreign remittances, collected revenues, issued letters of credit and money orders, honored checks, and kept complete books. (52) Some of their loans were on cargoes, others on pawns, and others on real estate. Unsecured loans also became common. "Of all kinds of capital," said Demosthenes, "the most productive in business is confidence, and if you do not know that you do not know anything." Phormio, an ex-slave turned banker, became the richest man in Athens. (53) By the third century B.C. Greek finance was highly developed and the use of credit was general. By 200 B.C. the real estate loan, once dreaded, came to be regarded as a convenient means of procuring money at a moderate rate, especially by the small farmer. (54)

During the Hellenistic and Roman periods there were many records of endowment funds set up in Greek cities by wealthy men. These endowments were usually to perpetuate some festival or religious observance and often stipulated a rate of return on a principal sum, sometimes loaned out on landed security.

Finally, there were the loan sharks, those small-scale purveyors of unsecured loans to the distressed poor. They are frequently mentioned in Greek literature. As we shall see, some of the highest of the rates attributed to them come close to setting a record for this history.

The end of the classical period of Greek history and the beginning of the Hellenistic period is usually dated from the conquests of Alexander, circa 325 B.C. These wars had revolutionary economic effects, two of which should be mentioned here. Alexander seized and distributed a vast hoard of Persian gold and silver. Much of it was subsequently coined, and it is said that the money stock of the Mediterranean world was multiplied several-fold in a few years. Prices rose and interest rates declined. Also, the opening of the East and of Africa and the unifying of the known world created a much wider trading area. This vastly increased the demand for, and supply of, goods and expanded trade. (56)

After the conquests of Alexander, Athens was no longer in a position to dominate Mediterranean commerce. She had lost her Empire. Athenian prosperity declined after 300 B.C. (55) In 229 B.C., Athens was released from Macedonian domination, and money came out of hiding. Trade at the Piraeus, the Port of Athens, revived and mining was resumed. In 197 B.C. Roman domination began and with it peace and another trade revival. (57) During the ensuing centuries, however, Rome, not Greece, dominated the history of the Mediterranean world. Rome for a while strove to help Athens, and Athenian trade was prosperous in the early years of the first century B.C. Many Italian "negotiators" were busy in Athens. Nevertheless, Athens never regained her position as the great commercial and financial center. As a consequence of Roman policy, trade shifted to Rhodes, Antioch, Seleucia, and especially to Alexandria.

GREEK INTEREST RATES

Although there were many forms of credit in classical Greece, a precise classification of interest rates according to the term or form of loan or according to the type of debtor or creditor is often impossible. More often than not historians quote an Athenian interest rate as "the prevailing rate on normal safe loans" or as "the customary interest rate." Ranges of rates are often quoted by centuries. These vagaries are probably not due to errors of omission but rather are a consequence of the financial customs of the times.

Information on Greek interest rates is more abundant than information on interest rates in earlier times or in the Roman period. The data are sufficient to suggest a general range of rates that was considered normal at each period of time. Suprasecular trends of interest rates may be discerned and some relationships between rates for different types of loans.

Greek interest rates quoted here are all for loans of silver. Although the rates were often designated as so much a month, they are stated here as annual rates for a twelve-month year. Six types of Greek loans are distinguished:

1. *Normal loans.* This unfortunately general title is most frequently used by historians. It must include some loans of the other types listed below. The term appears for the most part to represent loans to men of

substance, usually for personal use, sometimes for productive purposes, often unsecured. Many of these loans were probably not too different from modern personal bank loans to the average small business man. Most were probably short term.

2. *Loans secured on real estate.* These loans are sometimes subdivided according to city and country real estate; most probably ran for one year; some for five years or longer.

3. *Loans to cities.*

4. *Endowments invested at, and paying, a specified rate of return.* These may be based on real estate loans and other types of investments.

5. *Loans to industry and commerce.* Since there was no large industry and little safe trading, these were probably speculative short-term loans. Rates on sea loans are excluded.

6. *Personal, usurious, and miscellaneous loans.* These range all the way from rates on "hard bargains" and pawnshop rates to the very much more extreme loan-shark rates. They were certainly short-term rates by contract, but probably they were also often compounded over long periods.

All of these rates are for Athens unless otherwise specified.

NORMAL LOANS

Sixth century B.C.	"In Solon's time the customary rate was probably"	18%	(58–59)
	"In Solon's time the customary rate was probably"	16	(60)
Fifth century B.C.	"Perfectly safe loans"	10–12	(59)
Fourth century B.C.	"Perfectly safe loans"	10–12	(59)
	"Common rate of interest"	12	(61)
	"Normal rate"	12	(62)
	"A favor"	10	(62)
350 B.C.	"Common rate"	12	(63)
	"Average rate"	12	(64)
Third century B.C.	"Normal rate declined"	12 to 10	(65)
	"Normal rate had fallen to"	10	(61)
	"Rate fell to (or lower)"	10	(66)
Circa 297 B.C.	"Maximum and middle interest rate in Ephesus"	$7\frac{1}{7}$–$8\frac{1}{3}$	(67)
	"Perfectly safe loans"	10	(59)
Late	"Safe investment"	6–10	(64)
Second century B.C.	"Normal rate outside Athens"	6–9	(68)
200–150 B.C.	"Normal rate declined"	10 to 7	(65)
	"Perfectly safe loans"	6–8	(59)
200–150 B.C.	"Rates generally below 10%"	6?–9?	(66)
	"As low as"	$6\frac{2}{3}$	(61)
First century B.C.	"Perfectly safe loans"	6–8	(59)
	"Probably"	9–11	(69)
	"Loans at Tenos"	8–12	(70)
First century A.D.	"On safe investments"	8–9	(71)

Real Estate Loans

Fifth century B.C.	City property, at least	8%	(59)
	Country property	8–12	(59)
Fourth century B.C.	City property, at least	8	(59)
	Country property	8–12	(59)
	Town mortgages	8	(64)
400 B.C.	Mortgage loans at	16–18	(62)
369 B.C.	A man borrowed on multiple dwelling at	16	(74)
346 B.C.	Horoi pledge, mill and slaves at	12	(72)
305 B.C.	5000 drachmas, on horoi at	10	(73)
Third century B.C.			
300 B.C.	Horoi pledge on extensive land at	10	(75)
	Horoi pledge on home, roof, and land at	10	(72)
210–195 B.C.	Land in Thera pledged at	7	(76)
Second century B.C.	Gift to Aegiale to be loaned on land at	10	(76)
160 B.C.	Gift to Delphi to be loaned on land worth at least twice the loan, 5-yr. term	$6\frac{2}{3}$	(76)

Loans to Cities

Fourth century B.C.	To Amorgos (an island of the Cyclades) at	$8\frac{1}{2}$–10–12%	(67)
	To Oreos; Demosthenes loan secured by revenues at	12	(77)
Third century B.C.	To Amorgos	$8\frac{1}{2}$–10–12	(67)
213 B.C. *ff.*	To Melita	10	(67)
213 B.C. *ff.*	To Peria	10	(67)
	Safest public loans, at least	10	(77)
205 B.C.	Miletus borrowed on life annuity at 10		(79)
Second century B.C.			
200 B.C. *ff.*	To Oropus	10	(67)
	Rate fell to	7	(79)
First century B.C.	Loans by Romans:		
70 B.C.	To Tenos	8–12	(67)
71 B.C.	To Gythium (poor credit)	24–48	(78)
56–50 B.C.	To Salamis (poor credit); loan by Marcus Junius Brutus	48	(67)
	Legal limit for Roman loans to provincial cities	12	(67)

Endowment Funds (Rate Earned)

Third century B.C.			
221–205 B.C.	At Thespia	6–8%	(67)
210–195 B.C.	At Thera	7	(67)
210–195 B.C.	At Aegilia to be loaned on real estate	10	(76)
Second century B.C.			
200–199 B.C.	At Lietus	10	(67)
162 B.C.	Donation of Attalids to Delphi	$6\frac{2}{3}$	(76)
	At Corcyra (Corfu)	16	(67)
	At Ilium	10	(67)
First century B.C.			
100 B.C.	At Amorgos	10	(67)

Loans to Industry and Commerce

Fifth and fourth centuries B.C.	On movable capital	12–18%	(59)
	Commerce, usually	$16\frac{2}{3}$	(59)
	Loans secured by slaves	30–38	(59)
Fourth century B.C.	Highest rates were for industry at	18–36	(62)
	For commerce the usual rate	16–18	(62)

Personal, Usurious, and Miscellaneous Loans

The variety of types is so wide that no trends or typical rates should be read into these figures.

Fifth century B.C.	Usurious rates	36%	(59)
Fourth century B.C.	48% a month by usurers	576	(80)
	Common usurers loaned money from—	62	(81)
	up to $1\frac{1}{2}$ ob a day on a loan of 6 ob	9000	(81)
	Pasion loaned on pawns at	36	(81)
	Aeschines the philosopher (390–330 B.C.) borrowed at	36	(82)
	and later refunded his obligations at	18	(82)
	Phormio the banker borrowed at	$16\frac{2}{3}$	(82)
	Stratocles loaned his money out at	18	(83)
	Demosthenes mentions rates as high as	16	(81)
	and as low as	10	(81)
	Usurious rates	36	(59)
	A public fund loaned to the people at	20	(84)
	Professional moneylenders	$12–33\frac{1}{3}$	(27)
	Penalty for delinquency over 1 year	200	(27)
Third century B.C.	Safe investments in Greek Asia	24	(64)

The temple at Delos charged 10% on all loans made during the fifth, fourth, third, and second centuries B.C. Most of these loans were made to individuals and were secured by land. These loans were usually made for five years, some were for one year only, and others ran for long terms, possibly due to delinquency. In one case in the fourth century a loan ran for thirty-three years; in another in the third century, for fifty-five years. Interest was payable annually. The temple also loaned to the city of Delos, which probably paid interest if the loan ran more than a few months. At first this 10% temple rate at Delos was below the "normal" rate at Athens; later, by the third century, it was about "normal"; whereas by the second century it was above "normal." The temple then reported that it had difficulty in loaning out its funds. (85)

TABLE 2

SUMMARY OF GREEK INTEREST RATES

Century	Normal Loans, %	Real Estate Loans, %	Loans to Cities, %	Earnings of Endowments, %	Loans for Commerce and Industry, %
B.C.					
Sixth century	16–18	—	—	—	—
Fifth century	10–12	8–12	—	—	12–18
Fourth century	10–12	8–12	$8\frac{1}{2}$–12	—	12–18
Third century					
(early)	$7\frac{1}{7}$–12	10	$8\frac{1}{2}$–12	—	—
(late)	6–10	7	10	6–10	—
Second century					
(early)	6–9	$6\frac{2}{3}$–10	10	$6\frac{2}{3}$–10	—
(late)	6–9	—	7	10	—
First century	6–12	—	8–12	10	—
A.D.					
First century	8–9	—	—	—	—

Chapter IV

Rome

BACKGROUND: THE REPUBLIC

The Romans were a nation of farmers and soldiers. They left manufacture, commerce, and banking largely to foreigners. Cato said: "In preference to farming one might seek gain by commerce on the seas, were it not so perilous, and in money lending, if it were honorable. . . . How much worse the money lender was considered by our forefathers than the thief. . . ." Nevertheless, Plutarch says that Cato himself invested in mercantile loans, probably secretly.

This attitude probably explains why so few Roman rates of interest were recorded for posterity. Most of Roman interest-rate history consists of legal maxima. Nevertheless, a summary of Roman financial history should serve to explain the significance of those few rates of interest which are quoted.

In prehistoric Italy cattle and perhaps other domestic animals constituted the earliest known form of money. The word "pecus," cattle, sheep, goats, singly or in herds, led to "pecunia," money. As late as 452 B.C., Roman law, like early Greek law, fixed fines in cattle and sheep as well as in metal. (86) But the Twelve Tables, circa 443 B.C., make no mention of cattle money. Raw copper and bronze became the principal mediums of exchange; bronze remained a monetary standard to the end of the Republic. Gold and silver also changed hands by weight. By the second century B.C., Rome coined silver; seven silver denarii to the ounce of silver, and twelve ounces, or eighty-four denarii, to the pound. Republican Rome coined no gold.

At the time of the ancient Etruscan monarchy, before the beginning of systematic, written history, Rome is believed to have been a strong, wealthy city with a large population surrounded by rich farmland. The land was so intensively drained and cultivated as to suggest overpopulation. Rome was then in touch, through trade, with the Greek Mediterranean world. The revolution of 509 B.C., which created the Republic, was followed by a loss of power and population and by isolation from commerce. (87)

The republican government was at first oligarchic. For 200 years after the revolution there occurred a bitter, but largely bloodless, struggle between Roman patricians and Roman plebeians. Out of this give and take evolved an elaborate body of legal checks and balances. Much of this early struggle was economic. Famines and food commissions were frequent in the fifth century B.C. Extremely severe property laws permitted debtors to be reduced to slavery and to be sold in foreign lands. Several political and economic crises were resolved by new legislation regulating credit.

The most famous of these early reforms resulted in the promulgation of the Twelve Tables, a codification of Roman law that remained basic for many centuries. Their traditional date is 443 B.C. On judgments of debt or admitted debt, thirty days were allowed for payment; on default, the debtor could be brought before a magistrate. Unless the debt was discharged, the creditor could seize and fetter the debtor, but he had to feed him; several creditors could seize and divide one debtor's property. A creditor exacting higher interest than the legal maximum of one ounce per pound per annum ($8\frac{1}{3}\%$) was liable to fourfold damages.

The Gallic invasion of 387 B.C. was accompanied by great destruction of property and by popular distress. (88) A heavy ransom was paid and debt was incurred for rebuilding ruined farms. In 367 B.C. relief legislation provided that interest paid should be deducted from the principal of a debt and the remainder discharged in three equal annual installments. In 357 B.C. the maximum rate of interest was again fixed at $8\frac{1}{3}\%$, suggesting that the old law had lapsed and that this rate had been exceeded. In 352 B.C. a commission was appointed to lend state funds, to adjust real estate loans by just valuations, to permit bankruptcies, and to obtain relief in the matter of interest rates. In 347 B.C. the legal rate of interest was reduced to one-half ounce per pound per annum ($4\frac{1}{6}\%$), and a moratorium on loans was arranged. At some time circa 342, interest was altogether forbidden, but this law soon became a dead letter, and the legal rate returned to $8\frac{1}{3}\%$. In 326, for the first time it was forbidden to imprison Romans for debt.

By 240 B.C. the plebians had gained at least equal rights with the patricians. There was no sign of class struggle during the desperate Second Punic War, 218–201 B.C. In 192 B.C. several moneylenders were fined for exceeding the legal interest rate, and the usury law was extended to cover loans by foreigners. Maritime loans, however, were not restricted as to rates.

The Roman state first paid its soldiers in 406 B.C. This was a heavy financial burden. (89) Generally speaking, the state, like most ancient states, did not borrow. During the Second Punic War, however, it borrowed supplies from merchants, presumably without interest; it also financed public building contracts on credit and seized trust funds at a stipulated but unreported rate of interest. The state's income came ordinarily from war indemnity, booty, mines, port dues, rental of public lands, provincial tithes, and, until 167 B.C., taxes on citizens. In 187 B.C. the treasury refunded the super taxes of the Punic wars. Women were then tax-exempt. By 169 B.C. so much property had passed into the hands of women that the law forbade a man to will as much as half his property to women. (90)

The Roman citizens, largely soldier-farmers, pursued a policy of indifference toward commerce. Rome was always an open port. By 348 B.C. there was still little industry or foreign trade, but by 312 B.C. there had grown up a large free industrial class in Rome engaged in the manufacture of arms and household wares; as yet there were few slaves. The heavy colonizations of the third century B.C. stopped this industrial development and reduced class disturbances. (91) Political power then developed suddenly, and Romans had vast opportunities to invest in land throughout Italy. Although Italian commerce increased, it was largely in the hands of south Italians from Greek cities and of Greeks. After 200 B.C., vine and olive culture and a rapid increase in the number of slaves led to a great increase in property values. However, with small use of machinery there was no feverish production. Economic crises arose principally from political disturbances and wars. (92)

These early centuries of Roman history have left us very little evidence of organized financial activity or credit other than personal debt secured by real estate. Large banking firms were unknown. The state, however, encouraged foreign traders to come to the city, and for their convenience it rented out money booths in the forum. The bankers were called by the Greek name "trapezita" and probably were mainly Greeks, as they were later in Cicero's day. They were trusted with large sums, lent money at interest, paid interest on deposits, changed money, bought and sold as agents, and later kept agents in the provinces and issued foreign drafts. Cicero kept an account with the bank of Egnatius and paid by drafts on his bankers. (93) By the first century B.C., Rome was the financial center of the world. Nevertheless, banking firms were still not large and well-known. This may have been because Roman law discouraged limited liability companies for commercial and financial purposes.

Joint stock companies with limited liability, however, were permitted to finance public projects. Such companies of "knights" after 179 B.C. contracted to collect taxes and to construct public works. They became prominent after the late second century B.C., when Asiatic tax collecting was farmed to Roman publicans. Extensive opportunities then developed for lucrative business in the conquered provinces, especially placing loans on land and lending to cities or to individuals delinquent in taxes. A period of wide expansion into such provincial investments followed in the first century B.C. Italian "negotiators" were everywhere, probably very few of them Romans. By this time wealthy Romans frequently borrowed and frequently invested in Asiatic loans, but this was usually done quietly through agents. Cicero said any serious disaster in Asia caused a panic in the forum.

For the first century B.C. and the first century A.D., we have a better record of Roman interest rates than for any earlier or later periods. The rates were very volatile. The volume of gold and silver in Italy had increased rapidly during the late second century B.C., and was largely absorbed by commercial expansion and investment in Gaul and Asia. A period of plentiful money and large profits came to an end with the Social War of 90 B.C. This led to complete state bankruptcy. In 88 B.C., Sulla set the maximum rate of interest at 12%, which suggests that the old $8\frac{1}{3}$% limit had fallen into disuse. In 86 B.C. the Valerian law remitted three fourths of all debts. State debts were repaid only 25%. The Catalinian conspiracy was partly an uprising on behalf of hard-pressed debtors.

In the provinces Sulla plundered the temples at Delphi and Olympia of vast fortunes in gold. He imposed unbearable fines on Asiatic cities that had opposed him, and they were often forced to borrow from Romans at high rates of interest. Lucullus, during 74–69 B.C., took drastic measures to reduce these Asiatic debts: he limited Asiatic interest to 12%; he provided that accumulated interest could not exceed principal and that creditors should receive one fourth, but no more, of a debtor's income. Somewhat later, in 44 B.C., the loans reported in Chapter III were made by Senator Marcus Junius Brutus through agents to the King of Cappedocia and to the city of Salamis at an interest rate of 48% per annum. Cicero, then governor of Cilicia, was shocked at the rate and pointed out to Brutus that 12% was the legal rate. Unfortunately for Brutus' financial reputation, Cicero or one of his literary slave ghost writers immortalized this probably not uncommon transaction. Few financial histories of Rome omit the episode. (94)

For a while after 67 B.C. the seas were safe and commerce prospered, largely in foreign ships. Imports of luxuries were common. All ports were kept open, and there were no monopolies or forbidden goods. There was also heavy investment in the provinces and a large balance of trade against Rome. Money became tight. To remedy the shortage of money, provincials were forbidden to borrow money in Rome. In 63 B.C. the state forbade the export of gold and silver from Italy. When Caesar and Pompey brought in new supplies, the scarcity of money was turned into an abundance. By 54 B.C. safe loans in Rome were available at far below the legal limit, but the rate would rise during political campaigns. (95) Only risky loans brought the legal limit.

Soon after this interval of monetary ease, the civil wars of 49–31 B.C. again bankrupted Rome and led to ruinous confiscations and a return of high interest rates. Caesar removed the "knights" from tax collecting and from moneylending in Asia and ended their abuses. He attempted to restore credit by permitting bankruptcies at prewar prices. He introduced an issue of gold coin. Caesar personally was a daring borrower and financed an important part of his political rise on credit. Financial stability, however, was not restored until the battle of Actium, 31 B.C., and the beginning of the reign of Augustus.

BACKGROUND: THE EMPIRE

The civil wars destroyed faith in property rights and brought on financial stagnation. Money was hoarded and was scarce and expensive. Confiscation made real estate dangerous to own. Augustus changed all this. He respected property and restored peace and good faith. Hoarded money returned to circulation. The treasures of Egypt were coined and put in circulation. Public building activity was resumed and real estate prices rose. (96) As debts were liquidated interest rates again fell to very low levels. (97) Augustus followed Caesar's policy of expanding the volume of coin.

After Augustus' death in 14 A.D., Tiberius reduced coinage to a trickle, cut expenses, and hoarded metal in his treasury. At the same time money was moving east to pay for imports. Interest rates rose to the legal limit and beyond. A crisis occurred in 33 A.D., due largely to credit disturbances. It began with the prosecution of bankers for overcharging. As a result more loans were called, and the crisis was intensified. The crisis was resolved when finally large sums were withdrawn from the treasury and loaned out for a three-year term without interest. (98) Succeeding emperors coined much more freely than Tiberius, and Nero even lightened the coins moderately.

After Nero's death in 68 A.D., renewed civil wars brought devastation, but the Emperor Vespasian, 69–79 A.D., restored order and economy.

Rome never again saw the wasteful luxury of the Claudians. High living made men marked characters; it went out of style, and cultural pursuits became popular. (99)

During the first century A.D. the metal content of Roman coins was reduced about 25%, and during the second century A.D. it was reduced substantially more. Silver coins were reduced to the status of token coins. In the third century A.D. monetary inflation on a grand scale accompanied a succession of revolutions and civil wars. These later centuries have left us little information on credit and finance. The chaotic fifty years before Diocletian, 284–305 A.D., were, in the opinion of Tenney Frank, the period when Rome fell. There was anarchy and looting. Provincials lost faith in Rome. Industry and trade disintegrated, and even the Latin speech decayed. (100)

Under the Roman Empire banking, manufacture, and shipping were more than ever tabooed to wealthy Romans. The aristocracy was still largely agrarian. Articles were made and sold in small shops. Large factories were few and were worked generally by slaves and financed by individuals. There was a rich mercantile class, but it consisted largely of foreigners. Imports were far larger than exports. Italian industry and agriculture could not stand the competition of the provinces.

Large fortunes under the Empire, as under the Republic, came not from commerce or industry or banking, but from military rewards and land investment. History tells of no bankers of importance. Industrial loans are not mentioned, but there are reports of sea loans. On these there were no legal interest rate limits; rates of 20% per voyage were reported. Personal loans were common. There was no organized investment in production and few private joint-stock companies. However, individual "negotiators" were common—moneylenders, investors in the provinces, importers, traveling salesmen and merchants, agents of wealthy Romans. Auction rooms enjoyed a great vogue. Finance, with the exception of real estate loans, was still probably surreptitious.

During the reign of Augustus the rate of interest on best credits fell far below the legal limit. It later rose again under Tiberius. Thereafter it fell. Nerva 96–98 and Trajan 98–117 advanced public money in loans secured by land and used the annual interest to support the children of the poor, the "alimenta." These land loans were at 5%, which was considered a moderate rate. There was no revision of the 12% legal maximum rate of interest over the centuries of the Western Empire: it was still in force or was renewed in the fourth century under Constantine. (101 and 102) Later in the fourth century the legal limit was increased to 12½%. (103) Lower legal limits were established in sixth-century Byzantium. (134, 135)

THE ROMAN PROVINCES

Egypt. Ancient Egypt has provided almost no record of interest rates. The state controlled the principal resources of the country most of the time. Nevertheless, the existence of loans at interest during at least the first millennium B.C. is proved by a few documents. Interest on loans of corn is mentioned in certain papyri. (105) A ninth century B.C. papyrus records a deposition in which a man declares that he has received 5 deben of silver and promises to pay back 10 deben of silver in exactly one year; this is a rate of 100%. (106) A document of 568–567 B.C. mentions 40% interest, terms unstated. (107) A tablet at the Metropolitan Museum of Art in New York, dated before 664 B.C., records a grain loan for eight months at 50% interest; this equals a 75% annual rate. A papyrus in the British Museum, dated around 568 B.C., records a silver loan for six months apparently without interest but with a penalty for nonpayment of 40% per year. A Louvre papyrus records a grain loan in 499 B.C. repayable in one year 1½-fold with a penalty of 10% a month for nonrepayment; this should probably equate to a rate of 50%. A silver loan of 488 B.C. was repayable in seven months, 1½-fold plus a penalty of 10% a month for nonrepayment, a rate of about 85% per annum. (108)

After 300 B.C. the Ptolomies enforced state control of Egypt's growing industry and commerce. Loans were made in kind (largely in wheat) and in metallic money. In the metropolis of each section of the country a government bank acted as receiver and distributor of state funds. These were in large part grain banks, receiving surplus production both as tax payments and for deposit or transfer. They could transfer grain or metal on order to all parts of the kingdom. At times they loaned seed and perhaps metal. There were also private bankers but money lending was done largely by temples and lending clubs. (109) Legal maxima are not mentioned, and they were not in the Greek tradition. A "normal" interest rate of 12% is repeatedly mentioned over the centuries and must have been a tradition or in fact a limit. (110) Higher penalty rates for nonpayment were common. Land was often pledged. Debt was chronic with the Egyptian peasant. Personal loans were usually private and were a favorite form of investment.

Under Roman rule, Egypt became a private possession of the imperial household. The country was deliberately isolated from the rest of the world by a fiat currency that circulated only in Egypt. The tremendous tribute exacted by Rome forced industrial development. State monopolies were surrendered to private enterprise, and Alexandria became one of the world's most important centers of trade and industry. Wheat was still the most important export.

During the first and second centuries A.D., Egypt was rich and prosperous. The early emperors regulated credit. They established the old 12% traditional interest rate as a legal maximum: 1 drachma per mina per month. Compound interest was not permitted, and interest accumulations could not exceed the principal. Specific penalties for default were provided up to 50%. Pawnbroker rates were recorded both below and far above the legal limit. There were also private loans of grain at higher rates and at times government seed loans at lower rates. There are no records of endowments or trust funds in Egypt.

In the third century A.D. the disorders of the Roman Empire broke through the barriers of Egypt's economic isolation. Famine, plague, and inflation devastated the land, and banditry became widespread. (111)

Roman Africa. The history of Roman Africa began with the destruction of Carthage in 146 B.C. The motive for destruction was entirely political and the Romans permitted the extensive trade of Carthage to fall to Greeks and Greek-Italians. Africa became an agricultural province. (112) Its material prosperity was at its height in A.D. 150–200. Towns then advanced in status and wealthy Romans developed large estates. The only records of credit and interest that have come down to us are derived from the many endowment funds set up by wealthy men for public purposes, which were generally lent at 5–6%. (113)

Asia Minor. Asia Minor became a Roman province in 133 B.C. under the will of its King Attalus. In 89–84 B.C. the First Mithradatic War was followed by heavy penalties and fines levied by the Roman General Sulla against cities. Many cities were forced to mortgage their property and to borrow from Italian Greeks and Roman "knights" at high rates of interest. Roman publicans in Asia Minor worked in large companies called "societates," which had shareholders; they collected taxes in kind, traded, and made loans. Pompey seized and brought to Rome most of the cash resources of the province and this sent interest rates up in Asia Minor. In 67 B.C. a new Roman law forbade provincials to borrow in Rome and limited the rate of interest in Asia Minor to 12%. (115) The catastrophe of the civil wars left the province bankrupt for a generation. Augustus had to cancel debts. Finally, in the first and second centuries A.D. the Asiatic cities recovered and were prosperous.

Sacred, private, and public banks existed in Asia Minor from the Hellenistic period. The temples were places of safe deposit; they made some loans, mostly of high quality and secured by real estate. They also made seed loans but made no reported commercial or bottomry loans. (116) Private bankers exchanged money, made secured loans, and engaged in business ventures.

The legal interest limit of 12% in Asia Minor continued during the Empire. It apparently was above normal rates at times in the first century A.D. In one case Trajan was advised by Pliny that "the money [of an Asiatic city] must lie unemployed because no persons will borrow from the municipality at 12%." Trajan replied in favor of offering the money at lower rates. (117) "Under the Empire available capital increased and the rate of interest in Asia was somewhat diminished." (118)

ROMAN INTEREST RATES

The Roman rates of interest are here listed in four groups:
1. Roman legal maxima.
2. Normal loans in Rome. These have the same general definition used under Greece. A large part of these normal loans were probably secured by real estate. Most were probably for short periods; there is little evidence of long-term loans.
3. Provincial interest rates.
4. Byzantine legal maxima.

ROMAN LEGAL MAXIMA

Fifth century B.C.			
443 B.C.	The Twelve Tables established a limit of	$8\frac{1}{3}\%$	(87)
Fourth century B.C.			
357 B.C.	The old limit reinstated	$8\frac{1}{3}$	(119)
347 B.C.	Limit reduced to	$4\frac{1}{6}$	(119)
342 B.C.	Interest forbidden briefly	0	(119)
340 B.C.?	Old limit reinstated	$8\frac{1}{3}$	(119)
First century B.C.			
88 B.C.	A new limit valid for centuries set at	12	(120)
Fourth century A.D.			
325	Constantine reaffirmed the limit of	12	(101)
	Limit later raised to	$12\frac{1}{2}$	(103)

Normal Interest Rates. For the first three centuries of the Roman Republic there are no interest rate quotations except legal limits. We may infer, however, from the frequent political and economic crises in the fifth and fourth centuries B.C., which involved credit and the enforcement of the legal rate of interest, that the normal rate was often above the highest legal limit of $8\frac{1}{3}\%$. At this time normal rates in Athens were reported at 10–12%. Furthermore, the attempts in the fourth century B.C. to reduce the legal limit below $8\frac{1}{3}\%$ did not meet with lasting success.

Since no credit controversies are reported during the third century B.C. and interest rates were declining elsewhere in the Mediterranean, it may be that normal rates were then at, or below, the $8\frac{1}{3}\%$ limit. For the second century B.C. there are scraps of evidence of rates as low as 6% and also evidence that the $8\frac{1}{3}\%$ limit was at times exceeded.

For the first century B.C. much better data suggest volatility in a wide range, possibly reflecting the social turmoil. Early in the century rates must have frequently exceeded $8\frac{1}{3}\%$ because the legal limit was raised to 12% in 88 B.C. But in 54 B.C. a "customary" rate of 6% (121) was reported, and at times money in Rome was freely available at 4%. It would then rise to 8% during political campaigns. (95) Only risky loans were made at 12%. Rates soon rose during the Civil Wars, 49–31 B.C., probably to, or above, the legal limit of 12%. The peace of Augustus brought back rates as low as 4% (97) by about 25 B.C.

The first century A.D. began with rates at 4–6%, but during the credit

Normal Interest Rates

Fifth century B.C.	Probably above legal limit of $8\frac{1}{3}\%$	$8\frac{1}{3}\%+$	
Fourth century B.C.	Probably above legal limit of $8\frac{1}{3}\%$	$8\frac{1}{3}+$	
Third century B.C.	Probably at limit in peacetime around	$8\frac{1}{3}$	
Second century B.C.			
192 B.C.	Probably above legal limit of $8\frac{1}{3}\%$	$8\frac{1}{3}+$	
150 B.C.	Cato reports that farm capital costs	6	(122)
First century B.C.			
100 B.C.	Probably close to limit of $8\frac{1}{3}\%$	$6-8\frac{1}{3}$	(123)
90–88 B.C.	Social war. Probably above new limit of 12%	12+	
60 B.C.	Probably well below limit of 12%	6–10	
54 B.C.	With peace, money lends freely at	4–6	(121)
	Rose during political campaigns to	8	(95)
	Risk loans at 12%		(95)
	In the provinces loans at 12–48%		(95)
49–31 B.C.	In civil wars, probably at times above limit of 12%	12+	(124)
Circa 25 B.C.	Rates fell to	4–6	(124)
First century A.D.			
Circa 10 A.D.	Probably still	4–6	
33 A.D.	Crisis. Rates probably rose above limit of 12%	12+	(98)
34 A.D.	End of crisis; rates much lower	6–10?	
50 A.D.	Columella reports that farm capital costs	6	(125)
Circa 97 A.D.	Government agricultural loans at 5% termed "low"		
	Normal range for first century	4–6	(126)
Second century A.D.			
	Probably rose from	6	
	to legal limit of 12%	12	
Third century A.D.			
	No actual quotations. Probably at times exceeded limit of 12%	12+	
Fourth century A.D.			
	No actual quotations. Probably at times exceeded limit of 12%	12+	
	and later exceeded new higher limit of $12\frac{1}{2}\%$	$12\frac{1}{2}+$	

Provincial Interest Rates

Ninth century B.C.	*Egypt**—Silver loan (one example)	100%	(106)
Seventh century B.C.	*Egypt*—Grain loan (one example)	75	
Sixth century B.C.	*Egypt*—Silver loan (one example)	40	(107)
Fifth century B.C.	*Egypt*—Grain loan (one example)	160	(108)
	Silver loan (one example)	85	(108)
	Penalty rate (one example)	120	(108)
Third century B.C.	*Egypt*—Government banks lend on pawns	24	(101)
	A professional moneylender, Zenon	100	(101)
Second century B.C.	*Asia*—Cash loans on land	8–12	(127)
	Egypt—"Safe investment brought"	5–10	(127)
First century B.C.	*Asia*—Cash loans on land	8–12	(127)
	Asia—Loans to cities in distress	24–48	
	Asia—(84 B.C.) In one case normal rate was	14	
	Asia—(70 B.C.) Legal limit set at conventional		
	rate	12	(128)
	Egypt—Normal rate for cash loans	12	(130)
	Penalty rates 24–50%		
First century A.D.	*Asia*—Legal limit remains at	12	
	Asia—Normal rate	below 12	(129)
	Egypt—Normal rate for cash loans	12	(131)
	Egypt—Loans of grain payable at harvest	50	(131)
	Egypt—Government seed loans	6	(131)
	Egypt—Bank of Didymus charged	18–22	(101)
	Egypt—Heraclius, a moneylender, charged 18%		(101)
Second century A.D.	*Asia*—Legal limit remained at	12	
	Asia—Normal rate	below 12	(129)
	Foundation in Ephesus based on	9	(129)
	Foundation in Aphrodisias based on	6	
	Egypt—Legal limit established at	12	(131)
	Egypt—Pawnbroker in one case charged	48	(131)
	Egypt—Pawnbroker in another case charged	12	(131)
	Egypt—Loans of grain payable at harvest	50	(131)
	Egypt—Government seed loans at	6	(131)
	Africa—Largest foundation based on	5	(132)
	Another foundation based on	6	
	Another foundation based on	6	
	Another foundation based on	12	

* Egypt was not a Roman province during these early centuries.

crisis of A.D. 33 it was hard to borrow at the legal limit of 12%. (98) Thereafter, rates probably came down at least to 6%. By the early second century, 6% was considered normal. For the next three centuries we again have only legal limits as a guide. The turmoil and inflation of the third century suggest that the 12% limit was probably exceeded. This supposition is supported by the increase in the legal limit to 12½%, which occurred during the fourth century, although this revision was probably due largely to convenience because currency units had been changed.

Byzantine Interest Rates. For the thousand-year history of the Eastern Roman Empire, virtually no interest rates except legal limits have come down to us. Therefore, no discussion is attempted on credit forms and financial history. As Constantinople was a center of trade for centuries, this is a serious gap which probably can be filled out. Although most of Byzantine history chronologically belongs to the Middle Ages, its financial history is so much an outgrowth of Greek and Roman financial history that the few Byzantine rates available have been included in this chapter.

Byzantine interest rate policy for centuries vacillated between the Christian hostility to all interest and the traditional Roman policy of regulated rates. (136) Justinian's Code (sixth century) expressed the Roman tradition and favored bankers who were important to the state. He declared that "the ancient rate of interest is exorbitant" and reduced the 12–12½% legal limit of Constantine to a range of 4–8%, depending on the status of the creditor. Bankers could charge the highest rate, 8% per annum; ordinary citizens could charge 6%; while an "illustrious creditor," a senator, for example, could not charge above 4% a year. Maritime loans, which had been unlimited, were limited to 12% a voyage. Loans of commodities payable in kind could be made up to 12%. For the province of Thrace, loans to farms were limited to 12½% if in commodities and to 4½% if in money. Loans to churches and foundations were limited to 3%. Accumulated interest could not exceed principal.

Byzantine Interest Rates

Fourth century A.D.	Legal limit raised from	12 to $12\frac{1}{2}\%$	
Fifth century A.D.	Legal limit still	$12\frac{1}{2}$	
Sixth century A.D.	Legal limit on bottomry 12% a voyage		(134)
	Legal limit on property loans by bankers	8	(134)
	Legal limit on property loans by other lenders	6	(134)
	Legal limit on property loans by senators	4	
	An annuity (date?)	9.72	(137)
Seventh and eighth centuries A.D.	Same legal limits as in sixth century	4–8	
Ninth and tenth centuries A.D.	Legal limit, bankers	$11\frac{1}{8}$	(135)
	Legal limit, private moneylenders	$8\frac{1}{3}$	(135)
	Legal limit, bottomry $16\frac{2}{3}\%$ the voyage		(135)
Fourteenth century	An actual bottomry loan $16\frac{2}{3}\%$ the voyage		(134)

The Code of Justinian dominated the subsequent span of Byzantine history. From time to time all interest was prohibited, but subsequently the laws of Justinian were reinstated. There were slight modifications in the rates based on changes in currency denominations. In the ninth century, however, the limits were raised from 8 to $11\frac{1}{8}\%$. (135)

TABLE 3

SUMMARY OF ROMAN AND PROVINCIAL INTEREST RATES

Century	Rome		Egypt		Asia		Africa
	Legal Maxima, %	Normal, %	Normal, %	Grain, %	Normal, %	Trusts, %	Trusts, %
B.C.							
Fifth	$8\frac{1}{3}$	$?8\frac{1}{3}+$					
Fourth	From $8\frac{1}{3}$ to $4\frac{1}{6}$ to $8\frac{1}{3}$	$?8\frac{1}{3}+$					
Third	$8\frac{1}{3}?$	$?8\frac{1}{3}$	24				
Second	$8\frac{1}{3}?$	$6-8\frac{1}{3}+$	5-10		8-12		
First	From $8\frac{1}{3}$ to 12	From $6-8\frac{1}{3}+$ to $?12+$ to 4 to $12+$ to 4	12		8-12		
A.D.							
First	12	From 4 to 6-12? to 6	12	50	Below 12		
Second	12	6-12?	12	50	Below 12	6-9	5-12
Third	12	Over 12?					
Fourth	From 12 to $12\frac{1}{2}$	Over $12\frac{1}{2}?$					
Fifth	$12\frac{1}{2}$	$12\frac{1}{2}+?$					

BYZANTINE LEGAL MAXIMA

Century	Loans by Bankers, %	Loans by Others, %	Loans by Senators, %
Sixth	8	6	4
Seventh	8	6	4
Eighth	8	6	4
Ninth	$11\frac{1}{8}$	$8\frac{1}{3}$	?
Tenth	$11\frac{1}{8}$	$8\frac{1}{3}$	

Chapter V

A Summary and Analysis of Ancient Interest Rates

All of the caveats that were elaborated in the introduction to this book apply with special force to the whole body of data on ancient interest rates. Perhaps each caveat should be repeated with each ancient quotation, but the reader would soon be bored. Furthermore, the danger of overworking such data becomes even greater when mere historical narrative is supplemented by an attempt to analyze trends. It would be safer to omit analysis altogether, but much would be lost.

Nothing resembling a modern time series of exactly comparable interest rates is available from antiquity. There are no rates on comparable credit forms quoted day after day or month after month or year after year.

The preceding chapters have presented data which may be categorized as follows:

1. Spot rates on specific loan transactions. These by themselves do not establish the rate quoted as typical of that year, much less of that century, but they do serve to support other data.

2. Estimates by historians of prevailing interest rates at a given time and place for certain types of loans (sometimes vaguely defined). These were derived presumably from an examination of a number of spot rates or from contemporary comment that a certain rate was "high" and another rate was "low."

3. Legal limits. These are factual enough and usually provide a good indication of what was considered reasonable at the time of the legis-

tion. But often there are enormous time gaps between legislation and little information on the no doubt variable degree of enforcement.

Such data obviously do not permit short-term trend analysis. The question is whether they permit long-term trend analysis or international comparisons or even general judgments on levels of interest rates.

When we consider the great range of interest rates on prime marketable securities in our own century, we may wonder what significance should be attached to the assertion, for example, that "in Athens in the fourth century B.C. the normal rate for best credits was 10–12%." It is especially when such estimates are placed as they are here in columns, one century under another and sometimes even charted, that there appears to be an implication of uniformity and universality which may be unwarranted by our knowledge. Finally, gaps in the data tempt the analytical mind to interpolations which may be erroneous.

These doubts, however, may be based too much on false analogy with the volatility of the modern market rate structure. A consideration of the differences, as well as similarities, over the ages may lead to a meaningful use of these ancient data.

The ancient interest rates quoted here were not volatile money market rates of interest. It seems probable that at times, such as in ancient Athens at the height of her commercial activity, something like a fluctuating money market existed, with daily bargaining among merchants and traders for credit at a price. Laissez faire was the policy, and sharp wits were competing for every small advantage. Bargaining was not beneath the dignity of the Greek, and survival amidst intense and active competition was the stake. And yet there was no daily press to record such activity. No doubt, over long periods "market rates of interest" influenced the type of rates which have come down to us, but our data are not market rates. They are mainly rates of a traditional and stable sort.

Up to recently in the United States many types of interest rates fluctuated very sluggishly. A 6% tradition lasted for at least two centuries. Usury limits generally lasted unchanged until the 1960's. The rates on bank loans charged by banks far removed from money market centers and from "Big Business" were relatively stable for long periods. Personal small loan rates rarely changed except with legislation.

The "normal" rates, which are frequently quoted for Mesopotamia, Greece, and Rome, appear for the most part to be rates paid for conventional short-term personal loans, usually but not always secured, and often secured on real estate. A difference in rate for differences in term is rarely apparent from the data. As business organizations of size and complexity did not exist, these were loans to persons or to partnerships, probably most often to meet personal needs but sometimes to finance trade or industry.

The quotations are generally for "best credits." This assertion by historians is supported by the risk rates which, when the law allowed, ran up far higher. There also are pawnshop rates and "loan shark" rates which are far higher than the "normal" rates. These latter, therefore, were probably well secured, either by land or movable valuables or by the established credit of a wealthy citizen. If he desired, the Greek or Roman investor could get three to ten times these normal rates by taking the bottomry risk.

Finally, we have excellent evidence of great stability in these "normal" interest rates over known long periods of time. This stability was due no doubt in part to tradition. Even today tradition plays an important role in determining interest rates on loans far removed from a money market.

These ancient "normal" loans, if they are to be compared at all with modern loans, were probably most like modern personal loans made by small banks or by individuals. The rate ten years ago in New England might have been 6%, as it was one hundred years earlier. Western rates would have been higher but would rarely have been influenced by fluctuations in the Eastern money market. If indeed this analogy is even partly correct, the sluggishness of ancient rates is understandable, and the data from century to century, especially during the Greek and a portion of the Roman period, are meaningful.

A few of the differences between the credit structure of antiquity and that of the present day should be noted here before ancient rates are analyzed in detail. There were few loans floated in volume by states. States were not in high credit standing. They were not often able to pledge the private resources of their people. They had not learned the principles of deficit financing. There were no large private corporate debtors. There was no bourse market to permit creditors to liquidate loans in advance of maturity; this device had to await the Italian financiers of the Middle Ages. There were no large banking organizations able to supplement the metallic currency with a large volume of credit instruments, able to create deposit money in volume, and able to act as convenient intermediaries between debtor and creditors. As a consequence there could be no large organized money market capable of reflecting quickly the supply and demand for credit and of mobilizing large credit resources.

The risk factor in ancient loans is probably overstressed in explaining high "normal" interest rates. The implication is that there were no safe loans in antiquity. But the margin of security was often very large, the term was short, and the sanctions for default were very severe: personal slavery in Babylonia and Rome. Risk loans certainly were common, and their rates were many times the concurrent "normal" rates. In Greece, at least, anyone could speculate if he desired. Furthermore, in modern times there is an enormous range of certain prime rates, and when such rates are high, this cannot be explained in terms of an increase in risk. American Telephone 8.80s seemed just as safe when they were issued in 1974 as American Telephone 2⅝s were twenty-eight years earlier. No doubt the legal status of Greek and Roman creditors improved as time passed and this facilitated credit. But the sanctions of creditors seemed in some respects better under the Code of Hammurabi than they do today.

Instead of overemphasizing risk, another basic difference from today should be emphasized—the relative inconvenience of lending or investing money in ancient times. A lack of institutional intermediaries would today bring our credit structure to a standstill. The mechanics of lending as individuals to other individuals on pawns or real estate or general credit is complex, burdensome, and potentially unpleasant, however gilt-edged the collateral. This difference of convenience alone may outweigh the factor of risk in explaining the tendency of ancients to hoard metal and invest in land.

Keeping always in mind these differences of ancient credit from modern credit, as well as the fact that nevertheless in ancient times the use of credit was widespread, the data on ancient interest rates can now be reviewed to see to what extent it may yield generalities and comparisons. Table 4 summarizes those rates from Tables 1, 2, and 3 which purport to represent either rates on good credits or legal limits. They are stated in terms of centuries (except for the earliest period) and as ranges wherever available. Spot rates, usurious rates, risk rates, and eccentric rates are omitted. The data are subdivided geographically and by types of loan wherever that is definable. No attempt is made to distinguish the term of the loans because the data rarely specify term, and the legal limits never do. With a few exceptions most "normal" loans were for a year or a fraction thereof; occasionally, 2–5 years. Long-term loans existed at these rates, but were often "renewals" of shorter loans. Loans in kind are omitted from the table.

Table 4 gives the impression that most Babylonian rates were higher than most Greek rates, and most Greek rates were higher than most Roman rates. Roman rates were usually also lower than the rates in Roman provinces.

Almost nothing can be inferred concerning the stability of Babylonian rates or concerning their century-by-century trends. The very wide range quoted for most of this vast Babylonian epoch—10–25%—could imply

TABLE 4

REVIEW OF INTEREST RATES IN ANCIENT TIMES

Century	Sumer and Babylonia		Greece				Egypt	Rome		Roman Asia		Roman Africa
	Normal, %	Legal, %	Normal, %	Real Estate, %	To Cities, %	Trusts, %	Normal, %	Normal, %	Legal, %	Normal, %	Trusts, %	Trusts, %
B.C.												
3000–1900	20–25											
1900–700	10–25	20										
Seventh	10–20	20										
Sixth	10–20	20	16–18									
Fifth	40		10–12	8–12	$8\frac{1}{2}$–12			$8\frac{1}{3}$+	$8\frac{1}{3}$			
Fourth	40		10–12	8–12	$8\frac{1}{2}$–12			$8\frac{1}{3}$+	$4\frac{1}{6}$–$8\frac{1}{3}$			
Third			6–12	7–10	7–10	6–10	24	$8\frac{1}{3}$	$8\frac{1}{3}$			
Second			6–9	$6\frac{2}{3}$–10	8–12	$6\frac{2}{3}$–10	5–10	6–$8\frac{1}{3}$	$8\frac{1}{3}$	8–12		
First			6–12			10	12	4–12+	$8\frac{1}{3}$–12	8–12		
A.D.												
First			8–9				12	4–12	12	Below 12		
Second							12	6–12	12	Below 12	6–9	5–12
Third								12+?	12			
Fourth								$12\frac{1}{2}$+?	12–$12\frac{1}{2}$			
Fifth									$12\frac{1}{2}$			
									Byzantine Empire			
Sixth									6–8			
Seventh									6–8			
Ninth									$8\frac{1}{3}$–$11\frac{1}{8}$			
Tenth									$8\frac{1}{3}$–$11\frac{1}{8}$			

Rates are derived from Tables 1, 2, and 3. Minimum rates used in Chart 1 are underlined.

great volatility over a period of time, but could also imply a variety of types of loans. Greek rates seem the most stable over a long time, while Roman rates became very volatile from 100 B.C. to A.D. 200. Perhaps something like a true money market had developed in Rome by that time, but if so it was largely under the counter.

There was a good measure of continuity in the development of credit forms over this entire ancient era, even though the center of civilization shifted at least twice and the customs and traditions of the peoples were very different. The Greeks adopted certain Babylonian weights and measures. It is likely that the elaborate but small-scale banking methods of Babylonia were also imitated by the Greeks; in any event the Greeks used similar forms. These credit forms were exploited by the Greeks in an atmosphere of freedom and laissez faire very different from that of Babylonia. Finally, Roman bankers were largely Greeks who must have brought with them to Rome all of their techniques and there re-adapted them to an authoritarian society.

Together with this continuity of credit forms, other trends and events influenced the entire Mediterranean world with some uniformity. These included the supply of precious metals, the activity of trade, the safety of the seas, and the prevalence of war or peace.

The trends of "normal" interest rates, insofar as the tables reflect them even roughly, were downward in both Greece and Rome (and Egypt) during the centuries before the beginning of the Christian Era. Many historians have reported this decline in interest rates. Contemporaries commented upon it.

The decline occurred earlier in Greece. Some economists attribute the lower rates to the vast increase in the volume of coined money which flooded the Mediterranean world after the conquests of Alexander. There are a number of alternative explanations. The decline in Mediterranean interest rates seemed to spread to Rome and Egypt during the second century B.C. Rates declined little further in Greece, which had by then become a Roman dependency and had lost her economic ascendancy.

During the first century B.C. and the first century A.D., there is some evidence that Greek rates increased; in any event they declined no further. In Rome, however, it was for these centuries that the lowest rates in antiquity are quoted. This is the only period when a rate as low as 4% is to be found in ancient times. Four percent is within the range of modern prime rates.

Roman interest rates rose during the second century A.D., but were at times still moderate by ancient standards. Roman endowments in Asia and Africa were at that time often based on a conservative earnings expectancy. There is not much difference between second century A.D. Roman and provincial rates and third-century B.C. Greek rates.

During the late second and the third centuries A.D., Roman interest rates probably rose sharply. The period of relatively low interest rates was ended for Western Europe for a thousand years or more.

Finally, the decline in Byzantine legal limits from the fifth to the sixth century A.D. should be noted. They rose again in the ninth century A.D. At their lowest, Byzantine limits were not as low as the lowest free rates of the early Roman Empire.

One step further in simplification and analysis is possible. Chart 1 is based on the interest rates in Table 4. The chart traces only the minimum rates reported for each period. If eccentric and charitable rates are omitted, lows may be a consistent guide to trends. As Babylonian rates are not reported by centuries until the seventh century B.C., and because of the vast span of time covered by meager data, Babylonian rates before the seventh century are only roughly sketched in the chart with dotted lines. The descent from the 20% minimum reported for 3000–1900 B.C. to the 10% minimum reported for the era 1900–700 B.C. is arbitrarily treated as an even slope.

For each of these three great peoples the suprasecular patterns of minimum interest rates provided by this method of analysis had a good deal of similarity. In all three cases interest rates seemed to decline from earliest history until a period of late commercial development, and later to advance during the final centuries of political breakdown.

Only Greek interest rate history ended with lower rates than it began, and this is probably an accident of economic reporting. No doubt during the disastrous third century A.D. "normal" loans in Greece were at rates at least as high as Roman rates. The possibility also remains that in late Roman periods, when it is assumed that "normal" loans were at legal limits or above, they might have been available at much lower rates, since the rates have not been reported. This, of course, would alter the hypothetical curves. However, the political turbulence of the times, the extreme inflation, and the renewed political concern with legal limits leave the impression that "normal" rates were then more likely to be above than below the limits.

For each nation the pattern resembled a vast saucer or trough. The Roman amplitude exceeded the Greek. The poorest data are derived from the earliest and latest periods for all three peoples, that is to say from the times when charted rates were highest. The best data are derived from periods when rates were lowest.

The dates when each curve begins and ends are arbitrary. The beginning coincides with the accidental emergence into history of crude

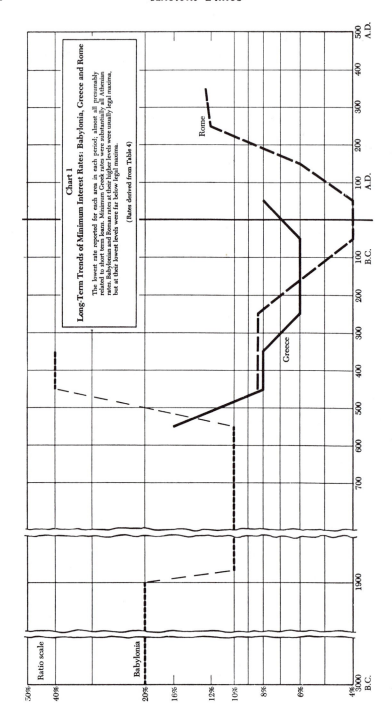

Chart 1

Long-Term Trends of Minimum Interest Rates: Babylonia, Greece and Rome

The lowest rate reported for each area in each period; almost all presumably related to short term loans. Minimum Greek rates were substantially all Athenian rates. Babylonian and Roman rates at their higher levels were usually legal maxima, but at their lowest levels were far below legal maxima.

(Rates derived from Table 4)

data and the end coincides with the break-up of the organized economic life of each of these peoples.

Western European interest rates, when in medieval times they finally again emerge from centuries of darkness, were higher than the highest of the late Greek and Roman rates and very much higher than simultaneous Byzantine interest rate limits.

PART TWO

Medieval and Renaissance Europe

Chapter VI

Usury Doctrines and Their Effect on European Credit Forms and Interest

"If thou lend money to any of my people that is poor by thee, thou shalt not be to him as an usurer."—Exodus 22:25

"Thou shalt not lend upon usury to thy brother; usury of money; usury of victuals; usury of anything. . . . Unto a stranger thou mayest lend upon usury; but unto thy brother thou shalt not lend upon usury. . . ."—Deuteronomy 23:19-20

"He that hath not given forth upon usury, neither hath taken any increase . . . he is just, he shall surely live, saith the Lord God."—Ezekiel 18:8

". . . lend freely, hoping nothing thereby."—Luke 6:35

"Accordingly all the saints and all the angels of paradise cry then against [the usurer], saying, 'To hell, to hell, to hell.' Also the heavens with their stars cry out, saying, 'To the fire, to the fire, to the fire.' The planets also clamor, 'To the depths, to the depths, to the depths.' "—ST. BERNARDINE, *De Contractibus*, Sermon 45, art. 3: c. 3

> "Upon the outermost
> Head of that seventh circle . . .
> Where sat the melancholy folk (the usurers)
> Out of their eyes was gushing forth their woe."
> —DANTE, *Divine Comedy*,
> Inferno: Canto VII

We shall better understand interest rates and credit forms in Europe during the medieval and renaissance periods if we first review the restrictions then placed on usury by Church doctrine. These restrictions at times seemed to approach absolute prohibition, and for many centuries they enjoyed widespread and official support. They therefore not only curtailed the use of credit but vitally influenced financial usage and those credit forms which gradually developed and gained acceptance.

As early as 325 the first general council of the Christian Church, the Council of Nicea, passed a canon prohibiting usury by clerics and citing the Psalm 15. (138) Saint Jerome, 340–420, argued that the prohibition of usury among brothers in Deuteronomy (above) had been universalized by the Prophets and the New Testament; the troublesome permission to take usury from strangers was no longer warranted. Saint Ambrose, 340–397, argued that usury was only licit against the notorious foes of God's people, the enemy whom it would not be a crime to kill. (139) Pope Leo the Great, 440–461, forbade clerics to take usury and declared laymen who take it to be guilty of "shameful gain." During the reign of Charlemagne, circa 800, not only did the Hadriana, a collection of canons, repeat and quote these earlier prohibitions, but for the first time the state, in the Capitularies of Charlemagne, forbade usury to everyone. Usury was defined; it was "where more is asked than is given."

From this time for 300 years the attack against usury was pressed intermittently by both Church and State. In 850 lay usurers were excommunicated by the Synod of Pavia. However, it was not until the eleventh century, when European learning and trade revived, that the Church's doctrine on usury was examined in detail by scholars and the prohibitions were spelled out by Church authorities. Usury was then declared to be even a form of robbery: a sin against the Seventh Commandment. (140) It became subjective: mental usury, according to St. Augustine, occurs when you "expect to receive something more than you have given." In 1139 the Second Lateran Council prohibited usury and declared that usurers shall be held infamous. Pope Eugene III decreed that "mortgages, in which the lender enjoyed the fruits of a pledge without counting them towards the principal, were usurious." (141) Restitution was required as in theft. Pope Alexander III, 1159–1181, declared that credit sales at a price above the cash price were usurious. *Manifest* usurers were excommunicated. Usurers were now guilty not only of lack of charity and of avarice, but of a sin against justice. Usury had become an invasion of a property right.

The condemnation was not against gain as such. "All usury is profit, but not all profit is usury," said St. Bernardine. Gain from work leading to the purchase and sale of goods was not questioned if at "fair prices." Gain from work in industry and agriculture was a matter of course.

Loans were regarded, not through mercantile eyes, but as forms of help that a neighbor owes to his neighbor in distress. To profit from his distress as you profit from industry seemed at first evil and then unjust. This point of view, arising no doubt from personal consumption loans, had evidently been generalized to include other forms of credit. Mental usury was a sin: in 1210 William of Auxerre declared that "a usurious will makes the usurer"; he compared the sin of usury to the sin of unlawful desire. (142) The prohibition is even more rigorous than the commandment against murder; there is no exception to the law against usury, whereas it is on occasion even meritorious to kill. The troublesome permission in Deuteronomy (above) to take usury from strangers had been superseded by the concept of universal brotherhood: there were no strangers. (143) The essence of the approach to usury was expressed in the opinion of St. Raymond: "One ought to lend to one's needy neighbor only for God and principally from charity." (142) The criterion was intention.

St. Thomas Aquinas, 1225?–1274, cited Aristotle who considered that money was sterile and hence that the breeding of money from money is unnatural and justly hated. Aristotle in fact objected to gain from all commercial transactions. St. Thomas summarized his own doctrine thus: "To take usury from any man is simply evil. . . ." The Jews were permitted to take usury from foreigners only in order to avoid a greater evil, that is, that they should take usury from fellow Jews. (144) The permission in Deuteronomy to lend to strangers proved troublesome throughout the Scholastic period. It sharpened the distinction between tribal law and universal law. It seemed to some to permit Jews to lend to Christians and to permit both Christians and Jews to lend to Saracens, which they did. This latter conclusion was not generally accepted by the Scholastics, many of whom condemned all usury.

The sweeping clerical condemnation of usury was accompanied during the eighth to twelfth centuries by civil prohibitions which varied widely from country to country (or county to county) in form but even more in enforcement. Usury was not completely stamped out in Europe and probably not in any large area of Europe for any important period of time. However, it would be a mistake to regard the Church's sweeping prohibition as a sort of Volstead Act respected only by partisans, casually enforced, and lightly regarded by social and political leaders and the common man. The fear of the sin of usury weighed heavily on the consciences of political and Church leaders and of merchants and bankers. As trade revived in the eleventh and twelfth centuries, governments and enterprises made great efforts at large expense in inconvenience and outlay to finance their activities without the aid of usury. Those credit forms which developed were sometimes designed to avoid the sin. The consciences of financial leaders were constantly tortured by the apprehension that they might be guilty, directly or indirectly, of usury.

Now that we have reviewed the prohibition in all its full and almost universal force, we shall examine the limits of the prohibition, the exceptions that were common in practice, the evasions, and, especially, those forms of credit which were not considered usurious. We shall also examine the gradual evolution and modification of the usury doctrine during the thirteenth to fifteenth centuries and the new credit forms that eventually obtained general and ecclesiastic acceptance. These developments will not be arranged in historical sequence, but rather according to the nature of the credit forms that existed from the start or that evolved as trade and industry revived after the eleventh century.

PAWNSHOPS

The phrase "manifest usurers" suggests that an early distinction was made between those whose daily bread came from consumption loans to individuals and those who incidentally and occasionally profited from lending. It appears as though the attack was primarily against pawnbrokers and those whom we today would call "loan sharks" and send to jail. But the prohibition became generalized. This was due in part to the difficulty of making exceptions and in part to the early absence of legitimate commercial credit machinery or the demand for it.

The "manifest usurers" were usually regular pawnbrokers who made secured consumption loans. Pawnshop rates of 32½% to 300% are quoted below, and these were mostly legal maxima. It can be surmised that in the Middle Ages "loan sharks" also existed as they do today and as they apparently existed in classical Greece. These might have charged, and often today do charge, 25% a week for unsecured credit. The rate multiplied by 52 can be called the equivalent of 1300% a year. A distinction therefore should be kept in mind between legally established pawnshops and such illegal dealers in small unsecured loans.

In spite of the usury prohibition, professional pawnbrokers probably always existed in medieval Europe. They were often tolerated and even officially licensed. They might be tolerated by the state, according to certain Church authorities, as necessary evils, but not approved or encouraged. (145) In fact, in the Low Countries and elsewhere in the twelfth century public usurers were under the special protection of the prince, who participated through heavy license fees. The State often devoted most of its efforts to eliminating unlicensed competition, but occasionally, in waves of reform, it suppressed licensed usurers.

Often "manifest usurers" were Jews. They were, of course, unaffected by excommunication. They were not excused, and their traffic was deplored and morally condemned. However, the Jews held no monopoly on medieval usury. They were early in the field, but their operations were usually small and marginal. In the tenth or eleventh century they were partly supplanted by the Lombards. These were men from Northern Italy who spread through Europe. (146) Later on, the State in the Low Countries and Italy set up public pawnshops which charged lower interest in an effort to supplant Lombards and Jews.

Although social opinion was probably directed largely against these "manifest usurers," the moral code was also opposed to commercial credit if it involved profit from loans. It was this wider prohibition which directly affected the development of trade and banking and the structure of commercial loans and interest rates.

INTEREST AS DISTINCT FROM USURY

In the doctrinal discussion up to this point, the term "interest" has not been emphasized. The prohibition was against usury, "where more is asked than is given." The Latin noun *usura* means the "use" of anything, in this case the use of borrowed capital; hence, usury was the price paid for the use of money. The Latin verb *intereo* means "to be lost"; a substantive form *interisse* developed into the modern term "interest." Interest was not profit but loss.

It was from exceptions to the canon law against usury that the medieval theory of interest slowly developed. Compensation for loans was not licit if it was a gain to the lender, but became licit if the compensation was not a net gain, but rather a reimbursement for loss or expense. The doctrine of intention was overriding. The scholastic analysis of usury came to center on the distinction between usury and interest. (147)

Interest was considered the compensation due to a creditor because of a loss which he had incurred through lending. (148) The concept derived from Roman law, where it was considered the difference between the lender's or other injured party's present position and that in which he would have stood if he had not loaned. It was "damages" in the broad sense of sometimes including the profit that the lender might have made with the money loaned. The term "interesse" in this sense became standard about 1220. It was often a compensation or penalty for delayed repayment of a loan. Such damages might arise (a) when guarantors of a loan were forced to borrow to make good and thus to pay usury; they could recapture the usury as damages; (b) when a loan was not repaid at the agreed time, and a penalty for delay might be charged, provided that the lender would prefer repayment to the delay plus interest. In the latter case penalties sometimes ran to double the sum lent. (149) Much of the profits of the Belgian Lombards were from these penalties. But there was an ecclesiastical tendency to limit the penalties to actual damages suffered. St. Thomas Aquinas declared that a debtor in delay may be held to repay probable lost profits on the money borrowed. (150)

In early cases loans were supposed to be interest-free from the beginning, acts of charity which, however, incurred a penalty, that is, interest, if not repaid promptly. But soon interest as a penalty was by some, and in certain circumstances, permitted from the beginning of a loan. One such case was as compensation for time and effort in making loans, a sort of wage. Another was when the money could clearly have been used profitably if not loaned, and still another was when loss was incurred by the lender, say in selling property, in order to raise the money to lend. Again, in the case of the census (annuity secured by property) discussed below, interest from the start was allowed if it was no greater than the gain from investing the money in the outright purchase of the property. Finally, interest on a forced loan by a state was by some considered licit as damages as long as the loanholder would rather have his principal back than receive the interest. (151) Risk was generally not considered a legal ground for accepting interest or profit on a loan. Perhaps this was because loans were usually secured by property worth many times the principal of the loan.

STATE LOANS

Forced loans were levied on wealthy citizens by Venice, Florence, and Genoa from a very early date. The controversy on the legality of their interest payments was keen. In a sense these loans were a form of tax. The taxpayer, however, got a claim to interest as a return on his payment. These loans were assessed by the rich against the rich in proportion to their known wealth. In Venice such forced loans, usually for defense, were organized in the form of a government fund called a *mons*. Every lender received a share in the *mons* and these shares became the object of trade. (152) Daily Bourse prices were eventually quoted. There was no obligatory redemption date, but the State generally retained the right of redemption. Annual payments were made "as gift and interest." These were defended against usury laws on the ground that the interest was so low that no one would voluntarily make the loan.

By 1400 most Scholastics had agreed that increments on public loans were interest, that is, compensation for damages, not usury.

PARTNERSHIPS AND ASSOCIATIONS

The *societas,* or partnership, was a normal and recognized form of commercial organization from Roman times. (153) Its profit objective was recognized and approved as an earned reward for effort and risk. Only where partnership agreements tended to limit or eliminate the work and risk of one partner were payments to him challenged as usury. The usury prohibition was not intended to curb the high profits of risk enterprise.

Later, in Renaissance times, special partnerships were permitted under the so-called "triple contract." Here the partnership agreement was supplemented by two other agreements: the active partner insured the special partner against loss, and the active partner promised the special partner a fixed rate of return. These "triple contracts" were sometimes called "five-percent contracts," from the customary rate promised. They were a subject of active Scholastic contention in the fourteenth and fifteenth centuries because they came close to simple riskless loans at usury. However, as trade and banking increased, there came to be a different attitude toward finance. Banking was no longer concerned largely with consumer loans to unfortunate neighbors in an agricultural community; it had become dealings between wealthy merchants. It had social utility.

Insurance developed in the fourteenth century in Mediterranean ports. The owner of property transferred risks to an insurer for a fee. This was defended as the rendering of a service for a price. (154) By the end of the fourteenth century the principle of insurance of a fixed rate of return was extended to *societas* partnerships.

In fifteenth-century Germany such partnership contracts, known as "five-percent contracts," were, after a controversy, upheld. In 1567 Pope Pius V unofficially approved of the five-percent contract. (155) Wards, widows, and the Church were supported by interest from such investments in special partnerships. Although they continued to be controversial, they gained general acceptance.

ANNUITIES: THE CENSUS

In the Middle Ages the "census" was a normal form of investment in land and a regular instrument of state credit. (156) Farmers, nobles, and states sold a "census" secured by their lands, monopolies, and tax receipts; this was usually licit, rarely considered usury, and very extensive.

A "census" was "an obligation to pay an annual return from fruitful property." (157) These contracts somewhat resembled the modern annuity, by which term the "census" is usually rendered, and also resembled the modern mortgage. The buyer of a "census" often paid cash; the seller was a debtor and must make annual payments.

This form of contract developed in early feudal times. At first, the returns were paid in real fruits, and hence they were considered as sales of future goods. They became the sale of a right to future money, sometimes in variable, and more often in fixed, amounts. A life "census" ran for the life of buyer or seller and resembled a life annuity. A perpetual "census" ran forever. A temporary "census" ran for a fixed number of years and resembled a mortgage. A "census" might be nonredeemable or redeemable at the option of the buyer, or of the seller, or of both. Some of these forms were the equivalent of personal loans and were challenged as such. Most, however, were accepted if the rate was not exorbitant. In 1425 and 1455, respectively, Popes Martin V and Calixtus III authorized redeemable real and personal "census" contracts.

This form of long-term investment, usually based on real estate, became a favorite credit form. Monasteries invested large bequests in this way. In the twelfth and thirteenth centuries a *rentier* class developed in Italy and the Netherlands. States and cities frequently financed improvements and contingencies by the sale of a "census." These could be resold at times by the investor at a premium or discount just as the forced loans of Italian cities were salable.

DEPOSIT BANKING

The safekeeping of goods or money by a deposit contract goes back to Greek and Roman times and earlier. It was an early medieval practice. (158) By the thirteenth century in Italy the deposit had become a means of investment. Deposits of money were left with merchants, often at a variable rate of profit, depending upon the success of the merchant's ventures. In Genoa deposit banking was well established, and in Florence the merchant banks paid well for deposits from nobles, businessmen, and clergy. In the fifteenth century the Medici Bank was organized on the basis of deposits made partly by the owners, which drew interest only when earned. Wards and widows were often dependent on interest from deposits.

Merchant bankers also created additional deposits by making loans or investments. In fourteenth-century Barcelona, the rate of credit expansion by the banks was estimated at $3\frac{1}{2}$ times the specie reserve; in Bruges, the specie reserve was typically 29% of deposits. (159) The assets of the banks, however, were probably devoted largely to investments rather than to loans; their loans were often forced levies by the government. (160)

Such deposits at interest were criticized as usury, especially when there was no risk and a fixed rate. However, as time passed, the prohibition of usury was applied in its full severity only against manifest usurers, exploiters of the personal needs of individuals, and not against commercial lenders. Deposit banking was permitted, and other forms of commercial credit were tolerated. In spite of the usury controversy, "a banker's social standing in thirteenth-century Florence was probably at least as good as in twentieth-century New York." (161)

THE BILL OF EXCHANGE

As early as the twelfth century, and probably much earlier, the remittance of foreign exchange was combined with credit. In Genoa, for example, foreign exchange was bought or sold, payable at the next Champagne Fair. These great fairs, held several times a year, which brought together importers and exporters from all over Europe, were at times largely financed by Italian bankers. A standard bill of exchange for foreign remittance was developed and became a common instrument of credit in the fourteenth and fifteenth centuries. (162)

These bills, however, were not discountable; they were not explicitly in the form of loans. Often the profit was variable and speculative, depending on the exchange rate at a future date at which the banker could reacquire his own currency. Such a profit could not be called either usury or true interest.

A medieval bill of exchange, unlike a modern draft, always originated in an exchange contract. A merchant gave a sum in local currency to another merchant and received a bill payable at a future date in another place and in another currency. (164) A typical contract involved four parties: (a) the "delivered," who bought the bill at the city of origin; (b) the "taker," who received the money and made out the bill to a foreign agent of the "delivered"; (c) the "payor," in a foreign city on whom the bill was drawn, usually a correspondent of the "taker"; and (d) the "payee" in the foreign city, usually a correspondent of the "delivered."

There existed in the later Middle Ages organized money markets at which the cash price of bills was set by supply and demand. (165) Most such bills were payable "at usance," that is, at the conventional time for transit of goods between the city of origin and the city of destination —one month, two months, three months, etc. The bills were usually paid, not in specie, but rather by the transfer of a deposit at a bank.

While the purchase of bills involved the extension of credit, interest could not be charged openly and was, therefore, concealed in an exchange rate higher than would have prevailed in a cash transaction. (166) Not all these bills were commercial; medieval bills were not usually drawn by an exporter on his foreign customer. On the contrary, goods were more often sent on consignment. A large proportion of bills were issued by one merchant-banker on a correspondent to adjust balances or to make a profit on arbitrage. Conditions of the money markets often encouraged a flow of funds; in one city there might be tight money (*strettezza*), and in another easy money (*larghezza*).

Such bills were allowed by the Church and by custom, but not without controversy and not without pangs of conscience on the part of pious bankers. However, the rate was often uncertain; in modern terms it was usually a profit, not an interest rate. One variation, called "dry exchange," eliminated much of the uncertainty and sometimes became a pure loan. In "dry exchange" the outward and the inward bills were negotiated simultaneously. This negotiation could provide the banker with an assured gain—a true rate of interest. No goods or shipments were involved and no actual foreign currency. The borrower simply had the use of the money during x months (x usances) while the bills traveled abroad to the correspondents and other bills returned.

Exchange banks were widely used by the Holy See to effect remittances throughout Europe without the dangerous shipment of specie. Their fees in the fourteenth century for this business were very moderate: (167) sometimes nothing; sometimes 5%. On actual loans to the Holy See they charged nothing, but, over all, the business was highly lucrative. For example, the favored bankers could lend to newly appointed bishops the sums required to secure such appointments. The bankers would purchase bills of exchange in Rome, payable in the diocese later out of revenues. Such loans were noted as early as 1200. (168) Also, the banks had the use of idle papal funds on deposit with them.

In the thirteenth, fourteenth, and fifteenth centuries, Bruges was an important center of exchange banking, as were also the Italian cities. In the sixteenth century, Lyons and Antwerp developed as financial centers. Princes and cities borrowed large sums there for wars and public works, and much of this credit took the form of exchange sales. There was a vast expansion of financial transactions on the Antwerp Exchange. In the seventeenth century, Amsterdam assumed much of the leadership formerly held by Antwerp and Lyons. It was not until the eighteenth century that London became a dominant financial center. And with London's dominance, exchange banking as a method of credit and finance receded. New credit forms were introduced by the English, which were not affected by clerical doctrine on usury. The English in the seventeenth century developed circulating notes and discounted domestic commercial paper at undisguised rates of interest.

PUBLIC PAWNSHOPS: MONS PIETATIS

In the fifteenth century there was a strong effort to correct the abuses of the "manifest usurers," although they had been recognized as a necessary evil. Shortly after 1461, Barbarus, Governor of Perugia, instituted the first *mons pietatis:* a public pawnshop financed by charitable donations and run for the benefit of the poor. It was to charge a small fee for the care of the pawns and the expense of administration. This was at first 6%, in contrast to 32½%–43½% previously permitted to private pawnshops. (169) In spite of theological opposition, Pope Paul II approved. It was agreed that sums repaid above the principal were not usury but were interest contributions to defray the cost of operation. The *montes* needed capital over and above charitable contributions. Therefore, they were permitted to accept deposits and to pay interest to depositors as compensation for the loss of the use of this money. Gradually they came to lend to business as well as to the poor. They were something like modern savings banks.

In 1618 the southern Netherlands suppressed private usurers and also organized a system of public *montes*. Funds were obtained through census sales at 6¼%, secured by the business. These *montes* were permitted to charge 15%. The Belgian bishops approved. (171) However, the Infanta Isabella, in 1625, forced the *montes* to lend to her; furthermore, their rates on all loans were reduced by law to 10%. Misfortunes and mismanagement forced a suspension of payment on the census. By 1652 census payments were resumed at a reduced rate. The interest charged went back to 15%. These *montes* continued down to the French Revolution. They were government pawnshops, but they never developed the savings bank character of the Italian *montes*. Nevertheless, the idea of institutional loans at interest had been established and overwhelmingly accepted.

MODIFICATION OF CHURCH DOCTRINE

By the sixteenth century credit on a vast scale was financing wars and trade in Europe. Interest was generally accepted. Nevertheless, the theological controversy continued. Condemnation, however, came to be more overtly confined to those whom we today call usurers.

During the Reformation many Protestant leaders defended interest and credit. As a result, the usury doctrine, which had held a firm grip on Jews and Christians for 2000 years, was weakened and finally deserted. (172)

Martin Luther, 1483–1536, declared that a Christian was under no obligation to observe dead Mosaic ordinances. At first, however, he opposed the census and the wealthy *rentier* class as even worse than manifest usurers. He condemned interest. However, as the radical reformers were calling for a return to communal life, a defiance of authority, and a repudiation of debts, Luther's position seemed to change. It was not, he said, complicity in sin to pay usury. The common man must obey the temporal authorities. Private property must be respected. Reform must come from the princes and not from the people. The Christian man was free to lend his money. Considerations of public utility should regulate loans at interest. Those who take only 5–6% are not to be treated as extortioners. Even 8% was permissible as long as it was from a redeemable security on land. But some creditors, he reports, were demanding as high as 60%, and these were responsible for the fearful inflation and woes of Germany. The widely used 5% contract must not be questioned.

Zwingli, 1484–1531, the Swiss reformer, did not concede that a strict prohibition of usury might be inferred from Scriptures. (174) The obligation to pay interest flows directly from the commandment to "render to all their dues." Nevertheless, he condemned professional usurers. According to another Protestant reformer, Bucer, 1491–1551, the sole test of the legality of loans is the Golden Rule. The objections of the Old Testament were directed, not against all increment on loans, but against biting usury.

John Calvin, 1509–1564, attacked the Aristotelian and Scholastic doctrine that money is sterile and of itself yields no natural fruits. He interpreted biblical rules of conduct in the light of equity, the Golden Rule, and public utility. (175) Scripture, he taught, forbids only biting usury. If all usury is evil, God would not have allowed the Hebrews to lend at usury to Gentiles (see Deuteronomy 23:19–20 above). There remains of ancient law only the rules of charity, equity, and justice. There is a grave difference between taking usury in the course of business and setting up as a usurer. Usury is permissible only if it is not injurious to one's brother. (176) In 1547 at Geneva, Calvin fixed the maximum legal rate of interest at 5%.

Now that certain outstanding religious leaders had expressed doubts about, or opposition to, the biblical doctrine against usury, commercial interests moved rapidly to assure its demise. (177) The controversy lost its religious overtones, but was by no means ended. By 1650, in Protestant countries, the economic effects of different rates of interest were being discussed by the mercantilists. John Locke insisted that the "price of the hire of money" cannot be regulated. (180)

In Catholic countries a decisive break with tradition did not come until the eighteenth century. We have seen that the 5% contract had been defended within the Church as early as the fifteenth or sixteenth century. Later it was argued that the civil law had the power to make usury legal and again that it was no sin to take usury from a rich man at customary rates. State loans were defended. However, the old law retained stout defenders and gave way only gradually.

More forms of credit were accepted during the eighteenth century by the Catholic Church. Finally, between 1822 and 1836, the Holy Office decreed that all interest allowed by law may be taken by everyone. (178) Laws, of course, remained which variously limited rates of interest, licensed usurers, and controlled banking and credit. Finally, as far as the Roman Catholic position is concerned, Pope Pius XII, in 1950, declared that bankers "earn their livelihood honestly." He approved of the banking system. (179)

It will be gathered from this survey that the medieval attack on usury was by no means only an ecclesiastical debate. It was not wholly effective, exceptions gradually developed, certain evasions were probably always easy. Nevertheless, for long centuries the ordinary consumer loan, and, for that matter, the ordinary commercial loan, was opposed by effective popular and clerical censure and often by civil law. Respectable citizens were forced to develop expedients to finance the growing trade of Europe following the eleventh century. Out of these expedients have developed banking methods and credit forms which endure. Nevertheless, it is probable that in essence the early attack on usury was aimed not very differently than it is today: against exorbitant rates.

The controversy did not end with the Reformation and the modification of Church doctrine. It continued and continues. It is now couched largely in terms of justice and expediency, laissez faire or economic controls, controlled rates (supposed to be low) versus free rates (supposed to be higher). Bentham, 1748–1832, declared that "no man of ripe years and sound mind, acting freely and with his eyes open, ought to be hindered . . . from making such bargain, in the way of obtaining money, as he thinks fit: nor anybody hindered from supplying him upon any terms he thinks proper to accede to." (170) The rate of interest in twentieth-century America is often limited by law. It is still a subject of controversy, not only among economists, but equally among politicians and economic groups. Some like it high; some like it low.

Chapter VII

The Dark Ages

The Dark Ages which followed the fall of the Western Roman Empire provide no contributions to this history of interest rates. Nevertheless, it may be useful to summarize briefly the state of the Western European economy during these centuries, so that the earliest recorded medieval rates of interest can be placed in an historic setting and the kind of economic activity to which they were related can be understood.

We can be sure that credit existed throughout these centuries. This is suggested by the ecclesiastical campaign against usury and by frequent civil ordinances forbidding or regulating usury. The fact of loans at interest is also recorded, but the rates charged are not a part of this record.

During much of the Middle Ages the Western European economy can be discussed in terms of geography rather than of nations. Great organized states usually did not exist, the powers of kings were limited, and the powers of local nobles were often absolute. People did not think and act in terms of nationality. Trade and currencies often crossed national boundaries as easily, or with as great difficulty, as they crossed county boundaries.

FIFTH AND SIXTH CENTURIES

Following the sack of Rome by the Goths, in 410, and by the Vandals, in 455, barbaric kingdoms prevailed throughout Western Europe: Franks in Gaul, Visigoths in Spain, Ostrogoths and later Lombards in Italy, Angles, Saxons, and Jutes in Britain. These kingdoms, however, generally retained what they could of the Roman civilization. (180) The barbarians had been taught to admire Rome and Roman culture. Their kings often accepted honorary titles from the Roman emperor at Constantinople with appreciation. They sometimes requited him with services. "No violent break had intervened between the centuries officially Roman and those officially barbaric." (181)

Much of the old Roman economic system was retained. Roman towns remained centers of commerce and of clerical and civil administration. While the trade of northern Europe became more localized and tended to withdraw from its Roman orbit, much trade continued along the old Roman routes. These trade routes throughout southern Europe essentially fanned out from Mediterranean ports. The Mediterranean Sea was the main artery of commerce, and through it communication was still maintained with Constantinople, Africa, and the East. (182) Although trade, the circulation of money, and probably population were declining, there was less change in the economic system of important parts of western Europe than occurred later, after the Mohammedan attack. For example, although the Franks invaded Flanders circa 400, they continued the manufacture of Flemish cloth and exported it to Italy. (182) Professional merchants carried on an export and import trade throughout the former empire. The trade fair of St. Denis, near Paris, dates back to this time. Roman gold coins continued to circulate. Manorial self-sufficiency was spreading rapidly, and the trade of merchants and the industry of cities were declining, but important trade with the Orient remained and, in fact, never entirely ceased. Trade between northern European countries probably was increasing.

SEVENTH AND EIGHTH CENTURIES

In 622 occurred the fateful Hegira of Mohammed, which led to economic consequences as important as its political and religious consequences. In 632 the Arabs conquered Syria, Egypt, and Persia; in 669 they seized Asia Minor; and in 698, Carthage. In 711 they crossed over to Spain, defeated the Visigoths, and held this European western flank for centuries thereafter. Although their further attempt to complete the conquest of Europe was defeated by Charles Martel at the Battle of Tours in 732, the Arabs almost held southwest Europe in siege. An essential economic fact was that the Mediterranean was all but closed to commerce. Only the ports of southern Italy, the Adriatic, and the Aegean remained open. Syrian navigation between the ports of the west and Asia and Egypt ceased.

From the beginning of the eighth century, western European commerce was profoundly depressed. (183) Although the Arabs had been stopped at the Pyrenees, no counterattack to reopen the seas could even be attempted. The empire of Charlemagne was essentially land-locked. (185) The Danes were plundering England. The Vikings dominated the northern waters. This interruption of commerce accelerated the ruin of merchants and the decline of cities. Western Europe at the time of Charlemagne, 742–814, stopped using imported luxuries. It was sinking back into a largely agricultural economy. The Latin tongue was forgotten, culture vanished, and superstition throve. Roman serfdom became the basis of feudalism. Absolute self-sufficiency, however, was never achieved even by the great estates. (184) Trade in salt, metals, food, wines, and cloth continued. (186) The nadir of economic activity probably was reached for different commodities and in different parts of Europe in different centuries.

Money was used regularly throughout the darkest of the dark ages, but the lack of commerce reduced its circulation. Yet, just at this point, Charlemagne devised a new silver coinage to supplant the Roman gold coinage. His new small-denomination silver coins were well suited to an agricultural economy that did not know trade on a great scale. His currency subdivisions survived to this century. The only tangible coin was the silver penny (denier), but for accounting purposes twelve pence equaled one shilling (sou), and twenty shillings equaled one pound. (187)

Charlemagne was the first prince to forbid all usury. From this we can surmise that credit not only existed but probably was widespread. Unfortunately this review is able to cite no specific loans at known rates of interest for this crucial period which linked the declining ancient world with the emergent modern world.

NINTH CENTURY

The ninth century perhaps marked the low ebb of European economic life in many places, in spite of the formation of the Holy Roman Empire in 800. Arab pirates now infested the Mediterranean shore. They advanced to Rome and even beseiged the castle of St. Angelo. They were masters of Africa, and after 878 they dominated Sicily. They controlled the islands of the Mediterranean and the coastal waters, and Europeans all but abandoned the sea.

To the North, the Vikings similarly destroyed or dominated the ports of the North Sea and the Channel. They came first as pirates; later as invaders, and still later as merchants. They established camps on the Scheldt, the Meuse, and the Seine. They beseiged Paris. At the same time they established camps in Russia along the Dnieper; they penetrated through Russia to the Black Sea; they traded through Russia with

Constantinople. They became the Russ—the early princes of Russia. In England Alfred the Great was struggling to hold back the Danes.

Thus beleaguered, Europe had become a largely rural civilization. Feudalism marked the disintegration of public authority. Exchange and the movement of goods sank to a low ebb. (188) The merchant class almost disappeared, and serfdom was general. The Church was the great financial power and ran the whole business of government. The Church all but monopolized literacy. Some markets developed, but they were small local affairs permitting a local exchange of goods. The famous Roman roads had deteriorated and in places almost vanished. (189) Municipal trade and commerce were almost extinct, and the towns remained largely as administrative centers for the Church. Nobles ruled from country estates and disregarded higher authority. They usurped the royal rights of coinage.

There were exceptions, however, to the utter collapse of trade. Venice, a community of refugees on the sand islands of the Adriatic, had been able to repel the barbarians and also the Carolingians and to develop a secure independence. Venice continued to acknowledge a relationship with Constantinople, and the Eastern Empire had maintained its civilization and its trade in luxuries. Venice traded not only with Constantinople but with the Arabs of Africa and with Syria as well. (190) The Doges themselves engaged in commerce. At this time Venice began her remarkable expansion. Venetian merchants even this early probably carried their imported goods to northern Europe. Perhaps they frequented the plain of Champagne where the famous trade fairs were soon to develop.

TENTH CENTURY

The tenth century has been called the century of transition. (191) In superficial respects the plight of much of western Europe grew worse. Many economic activities deteriorated further. Simultaneously history records the quiet beginnings of trends and forces that can be recognized as the forces behind a new economic revival. They can be seen with the benefit of hindsight, but it is safe to say that contemporary seers can hardly have made favorable forecasts.

Petty warfare continued throughout much of western Europe. There was still very little communication between it and the Saracen ports of Spain, Africa, and the East. Arab pirates pillaged Pisa in 935 and again in 1004; they destroyed Barcelona in 985. The Arabs even established an outpost in the Alps. Coastal bishoprics in the south had to be transferred inland. (192) To compound evils, terrible cavalry raids from Hungary began and were combined with Arab threats from the south and

Viking threats from the north and west. Europeans built castles: "burgs" garrisoned by knights, living off the land but making no economic contribution.

Royal power in France was at its low ebb. The Norse, under Rollo, were granted Normandy by Charles the Simple, King of France, in 911. However, in 936, Otto I, the Great, King of Germany, finally defeated the Magyars, created a kingdom for himself, became Emperor, reformed the Papacy, and helped revive Europe.

The signs of revival this early were tenuous. No new Arab successes had occurred for a long time, and the Arab World was weakening in its faraway center. At the end of the century Arab countries began to import slaves, metal goods, timber, and other commodities from Europe and to pay for them in gold. (193) In the meantime the Vikings were not followed by a host of invaders. Instead, these pillagers, who had been traders earlier, became traders again. Their boats reappeared on the Meuse and Scheldt in quest of merchandise. (194) They frequented Hamburg, Kiel, and London. They became middlemen between the East and the northwest and dominated the maritime trade to the Baltic. They also traded from Kiev to Constantinople and with the Arabs and Jews of the Caspian Sea. With their aid Flemish woolen cloth found a great northern market. Native Flemish wool became insufficient for the demand, and a superior quality of wool was imported from England to Flanders. The counts of Flanders now organized a peaceful and progressive state favorable to the arts, to trade, to manufacture, and to towns. (195)

The population of Europe, which had been declining for centuries, probably began to increase after the middle of the tenth century. (196) Europe had been delivered from the pillages of the Arabs, the Norse, and the Hungarians. (197) Surplus serfs ran away and tried their luck in the world. The younger sons of knights sought adventure and gain.

Traveling merchants were the only group independent of the land. They formed a class apart. They traveled over the wretched roads or waterways in armed bands, which became *fraires, compagnies,* gilds, or hanses. These wanderers sought the protection of the new "burgs"; outside them they built *faubourgs,* portuses, places of transit. They frequented London and Champagne. Their economic significance was as yet slight, for trade was small, but their future development revolutionized the European economy.

It was in this century that Venice obtained decisive concessions from the Emperor at Constantinople: freedom from customs and the establishment of a Venetian factory and colony on the Bosphorus. In Venice serfdom was unknown. Almost the entire population engaged in maritime trade. There was continuous trouble with the pirates of the Adriatic, but relations were extended to Pavia, Ravenna, and many coastal ports. In spite of opposition from the Papacy, Venice also developed its trade with the Moslem world. Venetians began investing money in maritime ventures on a scale requiring some financial organization. Coiners and money changers rose steadily in power and prestige, and commercial contracts were developed in rudimentary form. Italian merchants replaced Greeks, Syrians, and Jews as middlemen with the East. (198)

ELEVENTH CENTURY

During the eleventh century, political and economic revival in western Europe became general. Pisans and Genoese took the offensive against the weakening Arab power. They conquered Sardinia and attacked Arab Sicily and the coast of Africa. They freed the Tyrrhenian Sea. They recaptured Corsica in 1091. The Normans destroyed Arab power in Sicily. Finally, the first Crusade, 1096, established the control of the Mediterranean by the Italian cities. (199) European trade with the East was thereby greatly enlarged.

At the same time trade on the North Sea revived. The Vikings had turned merchant traders. They traded from the Thames and the Rhine to Iceland and Greenland, to the Dvina and Constantinople. (200) Canute, 1017–1035, for a while united England, Denmark, and Norway. Later, the Norman Conquest strengthened England's commercial ties with the continent. Tiel became a commercial center. Ships began to put into Bruges, and industry expanded in Flanders. The most famous of the old international trade fairs began in Champagne. In such places a feudal peace replaced feudal anarchy. Italian traders came northward through the Alps and began to meet northern traders at these fairs. More continental merchants frequented London. There was a growing trade in wine, cloth, and timber.

In this century something like a commercial code was developed among merchants, a collection of usages. (201) Arbitrators were agreed upon. Already there were merchants wealthy enough to lend large sums to princes, and they thereby obtained political and economic concessions. Italian merchants specialized in small luxury items, such as spices and fine cloth, which could easily be transported overland and sold at great profit. Byzantine and Arab gold coins began to circulate in Europe, and the mobility of money increased. Currencies continued in frightful confusion and were progressively debased and "called down," but silver mining in Hungary and Saxony was rapidly developing.

This was the period when the towns of northern Europe obtained power and autonomy. (202) They built walls. Municipalities were organized, financed, and dominated by the new merchant class, the burghers. Many Italian cities achieved their freedom. Rising population led to land reclamation along the estuaries of the North Sea and the founding of new towns which were often populated by escaped serfs. Urban artisans began forming craft fraternities to control the quality and price of their wares. (203) Education spread, partly because the new merchant class, although often ex-pirates and adventurers, found education advantageous in their business.

Venice now had many wealthy merchants with extensive shipping interests. She dominated the Adriatic and had developed a monopoly of transport to all the dependencies of Constantinople. (204) "Commenda" contracts, which involved sleeping partnerships and insurance, became widespread. Genoa, however, was just beginning its recovery.

In spite of this evidence of progress, the new economic activity was still small scale. Detailed records of credit and credit forms are lacking for another century or so. The Church had been the indispensable moneylender for centuries. (205) It had liquid capital which it advanced to nobles, usually secured by a form of census called a "land gage," a "live gage" when the revenue contributed to repayment of principal, or a "dead gage" (mortgage) when the debt was not reduced by the payments. (206) In this century commercial credit developed in forms more fully reported at later dates.

Chapter VIII

Late Medieval Times

TWELFTH CENTURY

Background

During the twelfth century the economic development of western Europe accelerated. It mattered little that the Turks drove the Europeans from Jerusalem in 1187; the Turks had no fleet. The Italians continued to control the Mediterranean. They traded with the Turks and with the Arabs. The Crusades were very good for shipping and commerce. (207) Genoa came forward to compete with Venice for Eastern trade; by this time both cities rivaled in wealth the great commercial centers of antiquity. Marseilles and Barcelona joined the competition. Westerners monopolized Byzantine trade.

European culture borrowed from Byzantine and Arabic sources. Learning revived and Gothic cathedrals were built in the north. The power of the victorious Papacy reached its height under Innocent III, 1198–1216. Kings allied themselves with the growing towns in their struggles with the nobles and with the Church. In France and elsewhere the power of the kings began to increase.

The new Mediterranean commerce penetrated inland. As a result of enlarged consumer demands, agriculture and industry revived. The wine trade became extensive. Silk was manufactured in Lombardy and exported. Flanders became a land of weavers and fullers who moved from the country to the towns: Ghent, Bruges, Ypres, Lille, Donai, and Arras. (208) Flemish cloth traveled by land to Italy and by sea to Novgorod. Flemish, Italian, and northern traders met at the fairs of Champagne.

Active trade was assisted by a growing supply of money from mines. Prices rose. The supply of, and demand for, luxuries increased. Since feudal rents were often fixed in terms of a depreciating currency, many great landowners became poor; manorial industry disappeared in favor of urban industry. Serfs readily purchased their freedom; they could pay higher free rents than their traditional tribute. Agriculture became specialized. As the population increased rapidly new free cities sprung up with charters and strong walls, ruled by merchants. There was a general migration from country to town. (209)

In the North the German Hansards took the place of the Scandinavians as maritime traders. They controlled the North Sea; they established trading centers in London, Bruges, Novgorod, and, of course, in the German cities. (210) Cologne became rich. The Germans started to conquer, colonize, and populate the Slavic country to the East; they founded Lübeck in 1143 and traded thence into the Baltic.

Commercial capitalism now developed rapidly. Private fortunes were accumulated by urban merchants. Canal transportation was improved and extended and merchants negotiated the lifting of some private transit tariffs.

The Champagne fairs attracted merchants and bankers from all parts of Europe. Here the prince granted a special peace, guards, immunities from tariffs and seizures, and immunity from the prohibition of usury, provided that fixed maximum rates of interest were observed. There were six Champagne fairs a year, and each continued for six weeks. (211) At each fair settlements of accounts took place among merchants, partly by book entry and offset. In this way debts from preceding fairs were cleared. Rudimentary letters of credit were used. Commercial debts were generally made payable at a certain fair. (212)

By this time in Italy trading societies and maritime insurance were well developed. Merchants there received deposits and arranged foreign remittances. Italian towns, such as Genoa, assigned specific taxes to creditors who formed themselves into organized groups to collect and distribute the proceeds. Rich merchants made loans on land and on houses at interest, and thus a *rentier* class developed. Flemish and Italian financiers made loans to English wool growers. (213) Italian merchant-bankers spread their branch offices all over Europe and came to dominate international finance.

TWELFTH CENTURY

Interest Rates

At this point the history of specific interest rates can be resumed after a lapse of almost a thousand years. As might be expected, the data at first are scarce and general. Creditors probably rarely recorded their usury for the enlightenment of posterity. Definitions are uncertain. We must be satisfied with scraps of evidence: this or nothing.

Money lending in England was then largely in the hands of Jews. (214) If security was excellent, their usual rate, according to one report, was 2 pence on the pound per week; this was the equivalent of 43⅓% a year or over 52% if compounded. If the security was poor, the annual rate might be 80–120%. Because the majority of medieval loans were repayable in less than a year, interest was often stated at weekly rates. Continental pawnbrokers also often charged 43⅓% a year, (215) but rates were frequently higher. An Englishman, Richard of Anestey, borrowed from moneylenders to sustain his claim on his uncle's estate; he paid an average of just under 60% a year. (216)

At about the end of this century commercial and official loans in the Netherlands were reported at rates between 10 and 16% per annum. In 1200 in Genoa, an interest rate of 20% was stipulated for commercial loans by banks. (217) Rates of 43–50% on bottomry (sea) loans are reported. Bottomry rates, however, are not classified here as interest rates, because the lender generally assumed the loss in case of maritime catastrophe. (218)

It is probable that in the Netherlands, as early as 1200, rich merchants

TABLE 5

SUMMARY OF TWELFTH-CENTURY INTEREST RATES *

Personal Loans (Short Term)

England	Best credits	$43\frac{1}{3}$–52%
England	Poorer credits	80–120
England	An individual	60
Europe	Pawnshops	$43\frac{1}{3}$ and higher

Commercial Loans (Short Term)

Netherlands, end of century	10–16%
Genoa	20

Annuities and Mortgages (Long Term)

Netherlands, end of century	8–10%

* As explained more fully elsewhere, the subtitles "short term" and "long term" in these summaries are in part arbitrary. Thus, princely and state loans not specifically designated as annuities were usually floating debt and so are tabulated as short term, even though in fact they may have been outstanding for a long period. Similarly, mortgages and annuities are assumed to be long term, although some may have had near-term maturity dates.

bought land *rentes* and house *rentes*, that is, loaned money at long term against real security, at 8–10% per annum. Such long-term annuities or mortgages, the census described in an earlier chapter, were generally at rates lower than the rates on short-term loans either princely, personal or commercial. (219)

Few twelfth-century rates are available from Italian towns although credit there was well advanced. Information becomes far more plentiful in the next century. In 1164 Genoa farmed some of her revenues to a group of capitalists for eleven years in return for a loan, rate unstated. Such loans were later consolidated into the debt administered by the famous *Casa di San Giorgio* (Bank of St. George), which played a leading role in financing the rise of Genoa.

In Venice in 1171 the government exacted a forced loan from its citizens. (220) It gave them bonds in return, but did not make regular interest payments on these bonds until the next century. Interest on forced loans does not, of course, represent a going or acceptable rate of interest. This, however, was the beginning of Venice's famous funded debt.

THIRTEENTH CENTURY

Background

This was a century of continued economic expansion. It was the century of the Mongol conquest of Asia, from which the Arab World never recovered. This conquest led to a great Asiatic peace which opened Asia as far as China to European trade. It was the century of Marco Polo, 1254?–1324, and of St. Thomas Aquinas, 1225?–1274. It saw the end of the great Crusades, with the defeat of St. Louis (IX), 1214–1270. Western Europeans, backed by the Venetian fleet, for a while ruled Constantinople. The Teutonic knights completed their conquest of Eastern Germany, Prussia, and Lithuania. Cordova and Seville were recaptured from the Moors. Trade and prosperity rose to their highest medieval level. Roads, however, were still wretched and, local tolls were still multiplying. (221)

The population of Europe continued to increase (222), and free labor grew very fast and became urbanized. Prices continued to rise. (223) Nobility often incurred debt and ruin. Emancipated peasants often owned their soil in return for a census (mortgage), which sometimes was an hereditary obligation. (224) Rural peace was reestablished in many places and trade security grew. Therefore, merchant adventurers began to stay at home and send agents abroad. This trend later led to the decline of the fairs. Foreign hosts, called brokers, who had entertained traveling merchants, began to act for them and later developed brokerage monopolies. Many merchants became purely investors; others joined forces in great companies which supplanted the individual adventurer.

Venice now was forced to see Genoa dispute her supremacy in the Levant. The Genoese pioneered winter navigation. Cloth came from Flanders to Genoa for export. Aristocrats, merchants, workers, and even servants in Genoa now practically all had an interest in, or investments in, business, deposits with bankers, or a holding of government bonds. (225) Italians, especially Florentines, brought international banking to its highest development thus far. They had representatives throughout Europe. They made long-term loans to English wool growers. Credit sales and installment sales were common. Bank accounts were used for business and in everyday life. Speculation in foreign money and in shares of public loans was active.

Men of Cahors and Lombards of northern Italy supplanted the Jews as pawnbrokers throughout Europe. While ecclesiastical establishments now rarely lent money, the Order of Knights Templar, retiring from the Levant, became a great banking organization.

The French and Flemish civilizations revived brilliantly. French wines began to enjoy a dominant position in trade. Flemish cloth, now made of superior English wool (226), became another dominant item of trade. Italian, Spanish, German, and English merchants installed factories at Bruges, which was called the "Venice of the North." It was the point of entry for English wool. Bruges later supplanted the Champagne fairs (227) as the meeting place of north and south; it was not periodic like the fairs. Philip the Fair of France later helped Bruges by closing the great trade routes through Champagne and ruining the cloth industry of Artois. (228)

By the close of the thirteenth century the Germans in Bruges had become the chief exporters of Flemish cloth and the principal buyers of Italian imports. The German Hanseatic League dominated the trade of northern Europe. Cologne was then the leading trading and cultural town of Germany. The German trade route led through Hamburg and Lübeck to the Baltic and Scandinavia and the East. At the same time great English merchant families grew up in the city of London, financed the king, and held large investments in land and mortgages. The wool trade continued to be dominant in England.

The currencies of Europe were still in debased confusion. In order to provide reliable currency, some superior gold coins were struck by trading cities: the florin in Florence, 1252; the ducat in Venice, 1284.

The *rentier* class continued to expand. Towns resorted increasingly to borrowing by the sale of *rentes* (census annuities) for one or two lives or longer. Bruges borrowed in this manner ten times between 1283 and

1305. Genoa and Venice consolidated their debts and recognized the right of creditors to sell their holdings in the open market. Nobles and monasteries were often in debt to the new bourgeoisie.

THIRTEENTH CENTURY

Interest Rates

Loans to Princes and Personal Loans. The credit of the best merchants and the credit of free towns was generally much better than the credit of princes. Towns could pledge the wealth of their burghers to perpetuity. Towns generally had to make good on commitments in order to preserve their prized sovereignty, and their credit enjoyed continuity from generation to generation. Their sources of revenue were systematic and reliable and, therefore, could be pledged. Merchants' credit was in effect secured by their physical assets, which were generally realizable in case of a shortage of cash; furthermore, merchants were under necessity to maintain good credit or else lose their power to trade. (229)

Princes, on the other hand, could not bind their subjects to pay their debts. Usually they could not even pledge the credit of their successors. Their credit was thus ephemeral, depending often on youth, good health, and military success. With the death, disaster, or bad faith of the prince, his creditors often lost everything. Furthermore, deliberate default often could be punished only by the sanction of a future denial of credit. Thus it was that princely loans, when not amply secured by enforceable pledges of assets or revenues, usually were made at much higher interest rates than prime commercial loans or loans to sound free cities. Lenders might have been even better advised to heed the words of Ecclesiastes: "Lend not to him who is mightier than thou." (VIII:13)

The Emperor Frederick II, 1211–1250, for example, usually paid 30–40% interest to his creditors. (230) Similar high princely rates were common when the collateral was not liquid. The Latin Byzantine Emperor Baldwin II, in 1237 borrowed from Morosini, a Venetian merchant, 13,000 perperi on short term, secured by the Crown of Thorns, rate unstated. When the loan went into default, the collateral was redeemed by Louis IX of France (St. Louis). (231) In 1221 the Countess Jeanne, in order to ransom her husband, Ferdinand of Portugal, borrowed at 18% (232) for one year; the relatively low rate suggests that she pledged good collateral.

High interest rates were a subject of widespread complaint at this time by Church, State, the common man, and especially by the entrepreneur. States tried to fix legal limits above which would be incurred the sin of usury. In Milan, 15% was the legal maximum; in Sicily, 10%. In Verona, in 1228, it was 12½%. In Modena, in 1270, it was 20%, and in Genoa throughout the thirteenth century it was 15%. (230) In England pawnshop limits were set at 43⅓% in the thirteenth century; in some places pawnshop limits were much higher: for example, 300% in Provence and 173% in Germany. (233)

Commerical Loans. It has been reported that rates of 20% per year, and even 25%, were customary in Italy on good commercial credits in the thirteenth century. (234) These were similar to twelfth-century rates. Apparently, however, these rates fell in the late thirteenth and early fourteenth centuries. A Sienese trading company in 1260 advised its agent at the Champagne fair that rates for merchants in Siena were "high" at 12½–15%. It also reported that borrowers, other than merchants, had to pay 25–30%. (235) In Venice, while 5% nominal and 6⅝–8⅜% market rates were being paid on long-term government securities and 8–12% for voluntary short loans to the government, private commercial loans, which bore maritime risk, were made at 20%.

Commercial rates in northern Europe at the Champagne fairs, circa 1270, are quoted at 15–20%. A range of 10–16% is quoted as the going rate for good commercial loans in the Netherlands from 1200 to 1350, with extremes of 5% and 24%, respectively, depending in part on risk.

Deposits. In Florence, the Peruzzi, the great thirteenth-century merchant-bankers, were willing to pay as much as a 20% annual rate for a deposit for four months. All the bankers would pay 10% per year for demand deposits. (236) A century later most Florentine bankers paid 5–10%, and the Peruzzi were down to 8%.

Annuities and Mortgages. In the Netherlands long-term real estate loans (the census) were reported at 8–10% in the thirteenth and early fourteenth centuries. At the end of the thirteenth century, however, the *rentiers* of Arras, who had accumulated fortunes in the cloth trade with Genoa and at the Champagne fairs, invested in land and loans at rates as high as 14%. (237)

Loans to States. In Florence, interest on the public debt was reduced from 15% in the thirteenth century to 10% and finally, by 1390, to 5%. (238) Whether this reflected a decline in the rate of interest or was an arbitrary economy is not stated.

The long-term loans floated by the Republic of Venice, called the *prestiti*, were all forced loans such as were reported during the twelfth century. Subscriptions were obligatory on wealthy citizens in proportion to their wealth. In 1262, when international affairs had become ominous with the loss of Constantinople, these loans, which earlier had been considered temporary, were consolidated into one permanent fund called the *"monte vecchio."* These *prestiti* payed a nominal interest rate of 5% per year on the unpaid face value. (239) Repayments of principal, while subordinated to interest, were made from time to time, but were often less than new levies. New levies were very heavy between 1287 and 1314, when competition from Genoa became severe and the Genoese began winning occasional naval victories. However, the 5% nominal interest was paid regularly in two annual installments of $2\frac{1}{2}$% each for more than 100 years.

No certificates were given to the owners of these *prestiti*, which could be called Venetian government bonds, but their claims were recorded in the Loan Office. These claims could be sold and transferred to others. Thus, although the nominal rate of 5% did not represent a going or acceptable rate of interest, this rate, divided by the price paid freely in the open market and modified by other advantages or disadvantages of ownership, should reflect the value of money on a long-term annuity basis. The purchase of *prestiti* in the open market became a popular form of voluntary investment by Venetian nobles. They were used for the endowment of charities and the payment of dowries. Their market price was a matter of public record. The purchaser had all the rights of the original creditor.

These forced loans were originally occasioned largely by war. It was provided that all state revenues after expenses must be applied to repayment of this debt and only thereafter could it be accumulated as a war chest. Although no promise to repay principal at a fixed date was made, earlier loans were repaid first. This sometimes occurred while new loans were being assessed. The market price of the *prestiti* was no doubt heavily influenced by the balance between repayment and new emissions. Their market was also supported by the fact that *prestiti* were ·exempt until 1378 from assessment of new forced loans if held by the original owner. Assessments were levied largely on real estate valued at ten times its yearly yield.

In 1285 the Venetian *prestiti* were quoted in the open market at 75% of face value. Because 5% per year interest was being regularly paid on face value, this price equaled a perpetual annuity rate of $6\frac{5}{8}$% plus any expectation there might have been of repayment at face value. This was in fact a period when new assessments were small and were exceeded by repayments.

By 1288, during a local war, new assessments rose sharply. A price of 70 was quoted on outstandings, equal to $7\frac{1}{8}$% plus. By 1299, during a disastrous war with Genoa, a price of 60 was quoted, equal to $8\frac{3}{8}$% plus. Shortly thereafter, with peace, the price rose importantly, large repayments were resumed, and in fact by the mid-fourteenth century a price of over 100 was occasionally quoted.

Confidence in the *prestiti* grew with their long record of regular payment of interest in spite of war and disaster. It was helped by the growth in the prosperity of Venice and, hence, by her ability to service her debts. Later the appropriation of a fund to buy in the *prestiti* when they sank in value contributed to their popularity and price.

The government of Venice also borrowed in other ways. At times it floated voluntary loans at rates unstated. It also borrowed in anticipation of tax collections. The salt office, which supervised the salt monopoly, one of the original sources of Venetian wealth, borrowed in anticipation of collections. The supervisor of butcheries also borrowed. This kind of short-term government loan was concentrated in the *Camera del*

TABLE 6

SUMMARY OF THIRTEENTH-CENTURY INTEREST RATES

	Loans to Princes (Short Term)	
Germany	Example	30–40%
Portugal (?)	Example	18
	Personal Loans (Short Term)	
Italy		25–30%
Italy	Legal limits for pawnshops	10–20
England	Legal limits for pawnshops	$43\frac{1}{3}$
Provence	Legal limits for pawnshops	300
Germany	Legal limits for pawnshops	173
	Commercial Loans (Short Term)	
Italy	Early in century	20–25%
Italy	Late in century	8–15
France (Champagne fairs)	Ca. 1270	15–20
Netherlands	Usual	10–16
	Deposits (Short Term)	
Florence	Demand or time	10–20%
	Loans to States (Short Term)	
Venice	Voluntary	8–12%
	Annuities and Mortgages (Long Term)	
Netherlands	Census loans on real estate	8–10%
Arras	Census loans on real estate: example	Up to 14
	Loans to States (Long Term)	
Florence	Forced	10–15
Venice	No maturity date—nominal rate	5
Venice	No maturity date—market rate, 1285	$6\frac{5}{8}+$%
Venice	No maturity date—market rate, 1288	$7\frac{1}{8}+$
Venice	No maturity date—market rate, 1299	$8\frac{3}{8}+$

Frumento, the grain warehouse, which had become accustomed to borrowing to buy grain and to pay off with the proceeds of sales. This office finally became the agent for all government revenue collecting bureaus. It even loaned out its surplus funds to assist business and thus became a kind of bank. It paid 8% in 1285, 10% in 1287, and 12% in 1288 for loans. In 1289 a regulation set 10% a year as the maximum. The terms of these *Camera* loans are uncertain, and there is evidence that funds intended for repayment were frequently diverted to other uses. When creditors of the *Camera* clamored for repayment, special levies or other funds were assigned to restore its solvency.

FOURTEENTH CENTURY

Background

During the fourteenth century, the medieval commercial expansion culminated. As a result of severe calamities and economic maladjustments, the economy of Europe during the second half of this century either grew more slowly or contracted. (240) This was a century of humanism and also of economic and political progress in many areas and fields of enterprise. But it was also the century of the Hundred Years' War and of the Black Death. This plague carried off one third to two thirds of the population in parts of Europe.

The decline in population was especially pronounced in towns. (241) It was accompanied by a rise in wages and a sharp and sustained fall in important agricultural prices. Civil discontent and social struggles occurred in France, England, Flanders, Germany, and Italy. Discontent among apprentices and journeymen led to strikes. Local protectionism and urban attempts to exclude competition hampered trade. Land values and rents fell in France and elsewhere. The German expansion into the Baltic area had reached its limits. An authority on the period says that "in the larger part of Europe the prosperous level of 1300 was not reached again before the 16th or 17th century." (242)

In the course of the Hundred Years' War both the king of England and the king of France defaulted on their debts. (243) Most of the big banks in Italy broke (244), and this led to reforms: in 1374 Venetian banks were forbidden to trade in speculative commodities; in 1403 they were required to hold two fifths of their assets in public debt; bank examiners were appointed.

The Hundred Years' War also dealt the Champagne fairs a decisive blow. Toward the middle of the century the cloth industry of Flanders declined rapidly because of a rise in wages, local hostilities, obsolete technical processes, and the curtailment of English wool exports. Workers migrated to Florence and to England. English wool was now more often than before manufactured into cloth in England. (245) With the growth in royal power and nationalism, economic protectionism spread.

Bruges, nevertheless, continued to be a trade center. The Italians now organized fleets to go by sea from the Mediterranean to Bruges and to London. Ships of the German Hanseatic League carried French wines to the Baltic. Backward areas, such as Bohemia and Poland, became substantial importers and exporters.

Trade, if not expanding as heretofore, was evolving its modern forms. Great commercial companies now grew rapidly. Princes cooperated with merchants to their mutual advantage. The coinage of gold spread. Modern bookkeeping methods began to develop. In spite of frequent wars between Venice and Genoa, the closing of the trade routes to the East, and bank failures, Italy retained its trade supremacy. Greater and greater concentrations of Italian capital were accumulated.

FOURTEENTH CENTURY

Interest Rates

Loans to Princes. Princes still did not enjoy the good credit of the best merchants or of the wealthy towns. (246) Princely loans, as recorded by historians, tended to very high interest rates, perhaps in part because high rates are selected for mention.

For example, Frederick the Fair of Austria, 1286?–1330, borrowed at 80% interest. (247) In 1319 the Angevin King of Naples, Robert of Anjou, 1275–1343, borrowed at 30% from Florentine bankers. With good security the rate of interest was much less. In 1328, for example, the Duke of Cambrai borrowed in Florence with precious jewels as collateral at 15%. In 1364 the Countess of Bar pawned her gold coronet for a loan at 50%. (248)

Philip the Fair (IV) of France, 1285–1314, borrowed heavily at unstated rates, but instead of repaying his bankers he banished them, canceled his own debts and decreed that the principal of all other debts must be paid to the Crown. His principal creditor, the Order of Knights Templar, which had become largely a banking organization, was utterly destroyed. Edward III of England, 1312–1377, likewise repudiated his debts, rate unstated, and ruined his Florentine bankers. These episodes did not improve the credit of princes.

Personal Loans. The Lombards often charged necessitous debtors in the Netherlands as much as 50%, and on occasion more than 100%, although the usual legal pawnshop rate was still 43⅓%. In 1306 the Lombards in Bruges were again licensed to lend at no more than 43⅓% (249), which was 2 pence per pound per week. However, Lombard loans in 1364 in Flanders were quoted at 20, 22, 24, 30, and 50% annual rates. In Burgundy at the end of the century the legal maximum for usury was 87%, but records exist of charges from 25% up. (250)

In Italy consumption loan rates ranged up to 50%, but were usually less: in a range of 15–50%. (251) In Florence a rate of 30% is mentioned. In France, in 1311, the legal pawnshop maximum was fixed at 21⅔%, and in Lombardy, in 1390, at 10%. But in France the legal maximum later ranged up to 173⅓%, and in 1361 it was 86%. These wide variations were probably not caused by economic change but by a conflict between popular opinion and the needs of the national budget which shared in the profits of usury. Jews in Nuremberg borrowed money from the Holzschuher firm at an average of 94%, and presumably charged more, although the legal limit was also 43⅓%. (252)

Commercial Loans. A very general statement on commercial interest rates in the Netherlands quotes the same range of rates for the first part of the fourteenth century as for the thirteenth century: usually 10–16%, but at extremes 5–24%. The usual rate for good commercial credits was elsewhere quoted at 10–25%. Rates at the Champagne fairs were reported at 15–20%, with the dates not precisely stated.

In Florence and Pisa, merchants and entrepreneurs in the fourteenth century could finance private business ventures at 7–15%. (253) It is stated that a decline in interest rates occurred at this time. In Venice loans were made to traders for activity within the city at 5–8% in the middle of the century. Later in the century 5% became the rule.

Philip the Fair (IV) of France, attempted to distinguish between usury and trade loans made at fairs. In 1311 he allowed 2½% to be charged for commercial loans from one fair to the next. This probably averaged 15% per annum, although the time span was highly variable. (254)

Deposits. In 1369 pawnbrokers in Brussels paid 10% a year for deposits. (255)

In Italy the rate paid on bank deposits declined from the 10–20% of the thirteenth century to the more modest figures of 5–10%. In 1300–1325 the Peruzzi paid a fixed 8%. Such payments on deposits were not always fixed; sometimes they depended upon profits. (256)

Historians cite a decline in interest rates in the fourteenth century. Rates on deposits, government loans, and real estate investments in Italy are quoted at 8–12%. (257)

Annuities and Mortgages. Rates of 8–10% on real estate loans are cited in this century for the Netherlands; this range was unchanged from the thirteenth century. At this time the city of Bruges did most of its financing by selling life annuities and *rentes* to private individuals; the rates it paid are not stated, but are said to have been far below commercial rates.

Loans to States. The rates of interest on long-term forced loans to the commune of Florence are reported to have declined from 15% in the thirteenth century to 10% and then to 5% in 1370. (258) We are given no terms.

In this century Venice provided a well-reported market-price history for its *prestiti*. These were the long-term government assessments which paid interest and could be sold. For more than 100 years, through many wars and crises, the republic persisted in paying interest regularly on these forced loans. It was at 5% of face value, until the defeat of Venice by Genoa in 1379. There was no promised maturity, although some part was often redeemed. The *prestiti* became popular for investment throughout Europe. Foreign princes and capitalists bought them as a secure investment. The right to own them was a privilege that a foreigner could obtain only by an act of the Council of Venice. This right was much sought after. *Prestiti* were used to endow charities and to secure dowers. They were voluntarily held in the estates of many Venetian nobles even though their original issue was still by assessment.

From 1200 to 1400 these forced loans took the place of all other forms of direct Venetian taxes. Ordinary revenues, such as a tax on the important salt monopoly, paid the peacetime expenses of the republic and at times yielded a surplus which was applied to redeeming the *prestiti*. Wars were frequent, however, and the most costly were the wars with Genoa. In wartime new *prestiti* were issued in volume, and the voluntary principal repayments were suspended. In one difficult period, 1311–1313, such internal loans, although large, did not cover the deficit, and the assets of the republic had to be pledged for a loan from Florence.

For 1299, it was reported that the market price of the *prestiti* had declined to 60, which equaled 8⅜% plus whatever hope there was of recovering the discount by eventual retirement. In the war with Genoa, 1294–1299, new assessments had been very large. From this date quotations become more frequent. Reported prices, with the minimum rates of current yield at these prices, were as shown on page 102. (259)

Because of the many changes in administration of the *prestiti* after 1377 and the interruption of regular interest payments at a fixed rate, it does not seem advisable to attempt interest calculation after that date. Substantial interest payments were made, however. Venetian prosperity was not yet approaching its decline.

Prices and Yields of Venetian Prestiti

Time	Events	Price of 5%* Prestiti	Current Yield, %
1299	War with Genoa	60	$8\frac{3}{8}$
1303	Large repayments on *prestiti*	$77\frac{1}{2}$	$6\frac{1}{2}$
1304	War with Padua; new assessments	$76\frac{1}{4}$	$6\frac{5}{8}$
1311–14	Large new assessments	60–76	$8\frac{3}{8}$–$6\frac{5}{8}$
1315–16	Repayments exceed assessments	73–70	$6\frac{3}{4}$–$7\frac{1}{8}$
1319–20	Large repayments	75–80	$6\frac{2}{3}$–$6\frac{1}{4}$
1323–24	Repayments exceed assessments	90–86	$5\frac{1}{2}$–$5\frac{7}{8}$
1325–26	Small assessment	81–80	$6\frac{1}{4}$
1332–34	Large repayments	86–100	$5\frac{7}{8}$–5
1335	War; small new assessment	97–99	$5\frac{1}{8}$–5
1336–37	War; large assessment	85–$95\frac{1}{2}$	$5\frac{7}{8}$–$5\frac{1}{4}$
1339–43	Large repayments	$94\frac{1}{2}$–100	$5\frac{1}{4}$–5
1344	Large repayments	102	$4\frac{7}{8}$
1347	War; large assessments	94	$5\frac{1}{4}$
1348	War; small assessments	93	$5\frac{3}{8}$
1349		95–$97\frac{1}{2}$	$5\frac{1}{4}$–$5\frac{1}{8}$
1350	War with Genoa; large assessments	$98\frac{1}{2}$–99	$5\frac{1}{8}$–5
1353	All charities were required to sell their real estate and accept *prestiti* in payment at 100, and were forbidden to invest in commercial loans		
1355	Very large assessments	76–$77\frac{1}{2}$	$6\frac{5}{8}$–$6\frac{1}{2}$
1356–57	War; very large assessments	77–65	$6\frac{1}{2}$–$7\frac{3}{4}$
1359		$77\frac{1}{2}$–83	$6\frac{5}{8}$–6
1360		82–86	$6\frac{1}{8}$–$5\frac{7}{8}$
1361–62		$87\frac{1}{2}$–90	$5\frac{3}{4}$–$5\frac{1}{2}$
1363	Rebellion	$92\frac{1}{2}$–95	$5\frac{3}{8}$–$5\frac{1}{4}$
1364	Large assessments	89–91	$5\frac{5}{8}$–$5\frac{1}{2}$
1365–67		89–91	$5\frac{5}{8}$–$5\frac{1}{2}$
1368		$92\frac{1}{2}$–96	$5\frac{3}{8}$–$5\frac{1}{4}$
1369–70	War of Trieste; large assessments	87–93	$5\frac{7}{8}$–$5\frac{3}{8}$
1371		89	$5\frac{5}{8}$
1372	War; assessments	90	$5\frac{1}{2}$
1373	War; very large assessments	78–83	$6\frac{5}{8}$–6
1374		77	$6\frac{1}{4}$
1375		$92\frac{1}{2}$	$5\frac{3}{8}$
1377	War of Chioggea with Genoa; very large assessments; suspension of interest payments; *prestiti* no longer immune from tax levies. The debt expanded to 6–9 times the debt of 1344.	19–43	
1380	Large assessments	30–43	
1381	Large assessments	18–30	
1382	Assessments	40–45	
1385–86		34–38	
1389	Small assessments	43–46	
1390	No assessments	40–43	
1391		$42\frac{3}{4}$	
1392–93		$45\frac{1}{2}$–53	
1394		56–$58\frac{1}{2}$	
1396–97		58–61	
1399		63	
1403	Small assessments	65–66	

* Percent of face value.

TABLE 7

SUMMARY OF FOURTEENTH-CENTURY INTEREST RATES

Loans to Princes (Short Term)

Austria	Example	80%
Italy	Example	30
Italy	Example	15
Italy	Example	50

Personal Loans (Short Term)

Netherlands		$43\frac{1}{3}$–50–100%
Netherlands	Usual rate; legal maximum	$43\frac{1}{3}$
Flanders		20–30–50
Burgundy	Legal maximum	87
Burgundy	Examples	25 and up
Italy		15–50
Italy		30
Lombardy	Legal maximum	10
France		$21\frac{2}{3}$–86–$173\frac{1}{3}$
Germany	Example	94+
Germany	Legal maximum	$43\frac{1}{3}$

Commercial Loans (Short Term)

Netherlands	Usual	10–16%
Netherlands	Usual	10–25
Italy		7–15
Italy		5–8
Italy	Late in the century	5
France		15–20
France		15

Deposits (Short Term)

Netherlands	Pawnbrokers pay	10%
Italy	Bankers pay	5–10
Italy	Bankers pay	8
Italy	Bankers pay	8–12

Annuities and Mortgages (Long Term)

Netherlands	Census loans on real estate	8–10%

Loans to States (Long Term)

Florence	Forced		10–5
Venice	*Prestiti*	Nominal	5
Venice	*Prestiti* 1299	Market rate	$8\frac{3}{8}$%
Venice	*Prestiti* 1303–1304	Market rate	$6\frac{1}{2}$–$6\frac{5}{8}$
Venice	*Prestiti* 1311	Market rate	$8\frac{3}{8}$
Venice	*Prestiti* 1314–1320	Market rate	$6\frac{1}{4}$–$7\frac{1}{8}$
Venice	*Prestiti* 1323–1332	Market rate	$5\frac{1}{2}$–$6\frac{1}{4}$
Venice	*Prestiti* 1333–1350	Market rate	$4\frac{7}{8}$–$5\frac{7}{8}$
Venice	*Prestiti* 1355–1359	Market rate	$6\frac{1}{2}$–$7\frac{3}{4}$
Venice	*Prestiti* 1359–1375	Market rate	$5\frac{1}{4}$–$6\frac{3}{4}$
Venice	*Prestiti* 1377–1400	Market rate	10–?

Chapter IX

The Renaissance

FIFTEENTH CENTURY

Background

The fifteenth century was a century of economic transition. Its opening decades saw a continuation of the past century's wars and disorders, agricultural depression (260) and local restrictions on free and prosperous trade. Yet, this century later saw the rapid rise of humanism, science, the arts, and worldwide discovery. Printing was invented. Royal power began to reassert itself and point the way toward modern nationalism. This was the century of Louis XI of France, 1461–1483; Henry VII of England, 1485–1509; and Ferdinand and Isabella of Spain, 1474–1504. In 1480 Ivan III freed Moscow from the Mongols. In 1453 the Turks finally captured Constantinople, but in 1486 Diaz of Portugal rounded Africa and opened the way for new trade routes to the Orient. In 1492 Columbus discovered the New World.

The population of Europe still did not grow. (261) Epidemics recurred early in the century. Towns struggled for advantage by monopolistic and restrictive measures. There were sixty-four tolls on the Rhine and seventy-seven on the Danube in Austria alone. (262) The mining of metals was depressed (263) until near the end of the century, when technological improvements brought an impressive revival. Agricultural prices continued to decline sharply in a number of places and for certain commodities on which records were kept.

In this century, in spite of the disastrous Hundred Years' War, 1337–1453, and the Wars of the Roses, 1455–1485, economically backward

England took a few tentative steps to challenge the trade and industry of the Continent. The wool trade had long financed the English Crown. Disorders in Flanders now brought skilled textile labor to England. Local cloth manufacture was fostered by royal policy, and English cloth exports rose while English wool exports declined. (264) English ships began to challenge the Hanseatic League in the Baltic and elsewhere.

At the same time the rise of the Dutch as a trading people began. (265) Leiden became one of the foremost cloth centers of the world. Dutch beer brewing and Dutch fishing were developed for export. After a struggle with the German Hanseatic League, the Dutch won freedom to trade in the Baltic.

The manufacture of cloth in Flanders now declined rapidly as a result of English competition, internal disorders, and restrictive policies. (266) Bruges continued to be the leading market of the north during the first half of the century, but then began to lose its advantageous position. (267) Its harbor silted up. Flemish industry migrated. Soon Antwerp assumed the role of the leading port and the financial and trading center of northern Europe.

Commerce and manufacture also grew in South Germany and Switzerland, in Nuremberg, Augsburg, and Geneva. (268) Great merchants from these areas began to compete for northern and southern trade; they were in contact with the Germans, Dutch, and English in the north and with the Italians in the south. They provided Europe with nonprecious and precious metals.

The victories of the Turks and the interruption of the Oriental trade route through the Mediterranean led to the discovery of alternative trade routes. This ultimately deprived the Italians of their central trading position. Nevertheless, in this century Italian prosperity continued at a high level. Between 1430 and 1480, the Medici Bank at Florence was by far the greatest financial organization in Europe (269), with branches throughout Europe, the Levant and North Africa. It was the chief bank for the Curia. Many other Italian banks had large capital and a worldwide business. Venice kept ahead of Genoa and was the first seaport of the Mediterranean.

The structure of trade and industry changed. Europe now had great capitalists possessed of large and diversified interests. These men were not local merchants; they were no longer dependent on the restrictive regulations of the town burghers. They could move their operations from place to place: to the country or to other towns. (270) They began to operate on credit on a large scale and to speculate. They supported royalty and financed wars.

The manorial economy of the early Middle Ages had thus been transformed by degrees into a pecuniary economy in which money and credit played a central role. While land had once been synonymous with wealth and power, now all men wished to possess money. Gold, not trade, became the object of exploration. The doctrine *Pecunia nervus belli* gave new power and dignity to the banking profession. (271) War had become an industry requiring financial management. The mercenary soldier could be hired by any town or prince who possessed the necessary cash or credit. Foreign policy often turned on financial considerations.

Forced loans to the Crown were still the rule in France and England. These often paid no interest. They sometimes took the form of tax anticipations. (272) Princes mortgaged specific revenues, sometimes in perpetuity. Often the need for cash was so urgent that they borrowed on short term from bankers at ruinous rates. When their floating debt became unwieldy, they sometimes enforced a funding into permanent annuities, sometimes called *rentes*, secured by branches of their revenue. These annuities became salable and sometimes were dealt in at premiums or discounts. (273) The Castilian Crown, however, discriminated against holders of annuities who had bought their claims to income at a discount. Spanish financial customs, in fact, remained backward throughout most of her long history and in spite of her wealth and power.

FIFTEENTH CENTURY

Interest Rates

Loans to Princes. When Charles VIII of France invaded Italy in 1494, he found himself possessed of one of the first national armies in Europe. Such armies are expensive, as we know today. Charles had to borrow at the last minute, and the Medici refused to lend. He borrowed from the Lyons office of the Genoese banking firm of Sauli. He is variously reported to have paid interest at rates of 42% (275), 56% (274), and 100% (276) per annum.

Personal Loans. It was at this time that many towns established *montes pietatis* in an effort to reduce pawnshop rates. (277) The Italian *montes pietatis* began in 1462; they charged 6% as compared with 32½–43½% sometimes charged by private usurers. (278) However, private pawnshops in Florence continued to make loans at the legal rate of 20% a year.

Commercial Loans. Historians offer evidence that the rate of interest was still declining in Italy. One states that 5–8% "was now regarded as a fair interest rate on commercial loans." (279) As a result of lower profits and lower interest rates, commerce lost men and capital to other forms of activity. Bankers used a larger part of their capital for loans to aristocrats and to belligerent states and less for commercial loans and ventures.

Another historian also says that during this century rates on commercial loans in Italy fell: they declined from 12 to 10% and then to 5%. (280) A third historian considers that the normal range of rates for merchants in Italian trading towns was still 7–15%. (281) A fourth considers 5% to be indicative of the usual level of prime commercial rates (282) in Venice. This type of market rate is very variable over short periods today. By sixteenth-century evidence it covered a large range in a few weeks. Therefore, a typical level is probably not so informative as a range or a minimum level.

Deposits. The 5% rate, which was relatively low when it first formed the basis of the "five per cent contracts" or "triple contracts" discussed in an earlier chapter, now became common in Western Europe on safe deposits or special partnerships. At the end of this century the Hochstetter Bank in Germany paid 5% on small deposits. (283)

In England the return expected by special partners may have been much higher. It may have averaged in excess of 10%, (284) insofar as can be judged from imperfect evidence.

In Florence the State now held guardians of wards and widows responsible for a flat 5% minimum rate of return. (285) The Medici Bank in Florence paid 10%, then 7¼%, and then 5% on deposits; these payments, however, were often contingent on earnings. Some of these deposits were short term, and some stipulated one year's notice of withdrawal; the latter usually paid the higher rates. Nobles, ecclesiastics, and statesmen were attracted by the higher return paid by the Medici. But late in this century the Medici Bank was crushed between the steady fall of prices and its mounting burden of commitments. In 1494, the year when Charles VIII invaded Italy, the bank was liquidated, and its assets were not enough to satisfy all creditors. (286) At this time the *Banchi a Minuto* shops in Florence, which sold jewelry on installment and dealt in money, paid 9–10% on time deposits. (287)

Annuities and Mortgages. Census loans, sometimes called *rentes,* on land in Lombardy were now usually at 6%, although it was not unusual to find lower and higher rates. In Southern France the prevailing rate for such loans was 10%. (288) By 1500 a census loan on land in Italy and Germany was usually at 5%. (289)

In 1452 Pope Nicholas V determined that in Aragon and Sicily a redeemable "census" was licit, provided that it paid not over 10%. (290)

Loans to States. Louis XI of France, 1461–1483, raised forced loans, rates unstated, which, if not repaid, would be funded into *rentes* at 5–10% interest.

In 1489, when King Ferdinand and Queen Isabella of Spain were in pressing need to finance their war against the Moors, they invited cities and individuals to make loans to them and granted 10% annuities for the sums so obtained. (291) Castile had long financed itself by such perpetual annuities. These annuities became such a burden that in her last will Isabella advised her successors never to sell perpetual annuities; she ordered that all free revenues of Granada should be applied to repayment of these loans. Her injunctions were not obeyed, and in subsequent centuries the record of the Spanish Crown became a dreary succession of defaults in spite of the wealth of Spanish possessions in the new world.

In the Netherlands the government, the provinces, and the towns contracted loans from time to time which often took the form of life annuities or perpetual annuities with sinking funds. At the end of this century the rates they paid were 8 to 12% (292), but these rates later declined. As these were not all perpetual annuities, some part of these higher payments was a return of principal.

The rate of interest on long-term loans to the city of Genoa in the fifteenth century ranged between 4 and 10%, while rates on perpetual annuities issued by the city of Barcelona ranged between 4 and 5½%.

For Venice in the thirteenth and fourteenth centuries a series of quotations have been reported on the 5% *prestiti*, covering a period of more than 100 years. These forced loans, redeemable only at the option of the republic, had commanded universal respect and had at one time even commanded a price above face value. In the war of Chiogga with Genoa, 1378–1381, even though Venice won a crushing victory, the republic suspended regular interest payments on the *prestiti* and revoked their exemption from new capital levies. They evidently lost status because they declined in the market from 92½ in 1375 to a range of 19–43 by 1381. (293)

By 1400 the *prestiti* had recovered to a range of 60–66% of par. Quotations during the fifteenth century were between 13 and 67, usually in the higher part of this range. The nominal rate of interest was then 4%, which gives a yield of 6% on a price of 67. (282) Unfortunately, however, there is not sufficient evidence of regular interest payments to translate most of these prices into market rates of interest. This nevertheless was a century of progress and prosperity for Venice. She won most of her wars. There was a long period of peace and prosperity after 1423, (294) during which the debt was reduced and interest was paid. Nevertheless, expenses were heavy. There were extraordinary taxes and abuse of credit, a stoppage of amortization, and at times a stoppage or reduction of interest payments. Price quotations of the *prestiti* (orginally paying 5%; later 4% or variable rates) are reported as follows (293):

PRICES OF VENETIAN PRESTITI

Time	Events	Price *
1399		63
1403	Small assessments	65–66
1405	Very large assessments	40–50
1407–10		$43–58\frac{3}{4}$
1411	Very large assessments	$54\frac{3}{4}$
1412	Very large assessments; victorious war with Hungary	$41\frac{1}{2}–44\frac{1}{4}$
1413–15		$47\frac{1}{2}–50$
1416	War with Turks, easily won	56
1417		$59\frac{1}{4}$
1419	Large assessments	41–56
1420	War with Milan	60
1421–22		64–66
1423	Long peace and prosperity	67
1424	Debt reduced	64–67
1425	Unfavorable war with Turks	65–67
1426	Successful war with Milan; heavy assessments	58
1427	Heavy assessments	$55\frac{1}{2}–58$
1429		57
1431–33	Heavy assessments	42–43
1434–35	Heavy assessments	36
1436–38	Heavy assessments	34–36
1439	Heavy assessments	20–24
1440–41	Very heavy assessments	20
1443	Very heavy assessments	23–28
1444	Assessments	24–25
1445		30
1446–49	Heavy assessments	24–28
1450	War against Florence and Milan	28
1451	Fall of Constantinople, 1453	24–25
1458		24
1465	Disastrous war with Turks, 1464–1479	22
1465–67		23–20
1482	New series of *prestiti* begin at 5%	Near 100
1495	Heavy assessments	80
1500		52
1502		74

* Percent of face value.

In 1482 a new series of *prestiti* was started, the *Monte Nuovo*, based on a new kind of tax in order to restore the rate of 5%. They sold near 100 until heavy issues in 1495 sent them down to 80 to yield 6.25%; then to 52, or 9.60%, in 1500. In 1502 they sold at 74 to yield 6.76%. In 1509, during the war with the League of Cambrai, a still newer series was

TABLE 8

SUMMARY OF FIFTEENTH-CENTURY INTEREST RATES

Loans to Princes (Short Term)		
Italy, 1494	Example	42–56–100%
Personal Loans (Short Term)		
Florence	Legal rate for pawnshops	20%
Italy	Pawnshops	$32\frac{1}{2}$–$43\frac{1}{2}$
Italy	*Montes pietatis*	6
Commercial Loans (Short Term)		
Italy	"Fell to"	5–8%
Italy	Early fifteenth century	10
Italy	Late fifteenth century	5
Italy	"Normal range"	7–15
Venice	"Usual rate"	5
Deposits (Short Term)		
Western Europe, Germany, Netherlands	Special partnership	5%
England	Special partnerships	10+
Florence	Trustees minimum payment	5
Florence	Medici Bank, demand and time	10
Florence	Medici Bank, demand later	$7\frac{1}{4}$
Florence	Medici Bank, demand later	5
Florence	*Banchi a Minuto*, time	9–10
Annuities and Mortgages (Long Term)		
Lombardy	Land census loans	6%
Southern France	Land census loans	10
Germany and Italy	Land census loans by 1500	5
Aragon and Sicily	Redeemable census loans	Not over 10
Loans to States (Long Term)		
Spain	Crown, patriotic annuity loans	10%
Netherlands	Towns and state, life and perpetual annuities	8–12
Genoa	Voluntary?	4–10
Barcelona	Perpetual annuities	4–$5\frac{1}{2}$
Venice	*Prestiti*	5–10+

started, the *Monte Novissimo*. (295) They were paid off in the late sixteenth century, but on what terms and in what currency we are not told. With the evidence at hand it is thought best not to attempt regular interest-rate calculation from their prices.

SIXTEENTH CENTURY

Background

This dynamic century was dominated by the power of the newly great monarchies. England, France, and Spain struggled for economic or military supremacy in Europe, and for control of the Atlantic. This was the century of the Reformation, the century when the New World was first exploited and new routes to the Orient were developed. It was the century of Francis I of France, 1515–1547, and his wars with the Holy Roman Emperor, Charles V, 1516–1556; the century of Henry VIII, 1509–1547, and Elizabeth I, 1558–1603, of England; and of Philip II of Spain, 1556–1598, and his Armada, 1588.

The population of Europe resumed its rise, (296) and the economy of Europe began again to expand rapidly. (297) Capital wielded increasing power. Commodity prices rose sharply. Between 1550 and 1620, in fact, prices in northern Italy rose about 2½ times; (298) this is called the price revolution and is attributed by some to the influx of American gold and silver.

Because of a change in trading conditions in the north, the structure of the English wool trade was again altered. Exports of unfinished cloth were increased, and exports of finished cloth were reduced. More English cloth was now dyed and finished in Flanders and Holland. This rearrangement revived the ties of England to the Low Countries. Antwerp became the greatest commercial center in Europe. Gradually English and Dutch traders supplanted the Germans in the commercial leadership of northern Europe. (299)

The Italians, in spite of the loss of their trade route and of their trade monopoly, found ways of doing business with the Turks and of financing trade between Spain and her new American possessions. They retained for the time being a large share of western European finance. (300) Nevertheless, Italy's days as a leader were numbered. The "price revolution" devalued the capital of Italian financiers, and their royal debtors defaulted.

Finance supported the great wars of the sixteenth century, and war gave Italian and German bankers great power and led to their ruin. Unpaid mercenaries sacked Antwerp and Rome. (301) The wars of Francis I and Charles V more than once came to a full stop when money ran out. In this century there were only twenty-five years when there was no large-scale warlike operation in Europe. Finance on a vast scale was required; military payments were often necessary far from home and in hard cash. Bankers mobilized liquid resources at the demand of princes. The medieval financial machinery was first over-stimulated by royal patronage and then destroyed by royal defaults.

Currency depreciation was still indulged in by princes. Merchants, however, had learned to protect themselves and accepted depreciated currencies only at discounts. (302) Princes, as an alternative source of funds, strove to exploit the superior credit of their own towns. As the power of princes now increased, such exploitation became possible, to the ultimate ruin of many towns, notably Antwerp. Princes also availed themselves of the doctrine against usury to default on loans, especially if creditors were foreigners. In France and England forced loans to the Crown were still common, usually without interest.

All these expedients were insufficient for the costs of the wars. Princes had to supplement them by "anticipations" of future revenues. These were short-term loans—in other words "floating debt"—usually at high rates of interest.

This floating debt, when it became overburdensome, was often "re-funded" (sometimes forcibly, as in Spain) into perpetual annuities at lower interest rates. These annuities promised a fixed income until re-paid at the convenience of the creditor; the income was secured on specific revenues. From early times recurrent expenses and income grants by princes had been secured by such pledges of specific revenues. Parliaments and towns had raised loans in this way, sometimes on behalf of princes. Now even the Popes began to raise money by the sale of perpetual annuities on the model of those of Venice and Florence. (303) In 1522 the city of Paris raised such a loan on behalf of the Crown, secured by royal revenues. Thus began the famous *rentes*. In England no funded national debt was issued until the last years of the seventeenth century. But in the Netherlands perpetual and life annuities, which had long been sold by towns, were now increasingly floated by towns on behalf of princes.

Bankers now performed "miracles of finance" in support of their royal patrons. The German bankers, especially those of Augsburg, and more especially the firm of the Fuggers, came to the fore. They controlled the mining of metals in the Tyrol. Fugger bills at Antwerp were considered "as safe as gold." (304) "Anton Fugger and Nephews" of Augsburg in 1546 had a capital of 5 million guilder, the largest, until then, ever held by one firm. In the seventeenth century much of this wealth was lost because of defaults by the Spanish Crown.

In the early sixteenth century the Exchange at Antwerp had come to dominate European transactions in bills of exchange. It also dealt in other credit instruments, such as demand notes, deposit certificates, and the bonds of states and towns; these were all usually short-term debts. This Exchange at one time had 5000 members. (305) Sometimes 500 ships a day would enter the port of Antwerp. Commodities were exchanged in another part of town; the Exchange dealt largely in credit instruments.

In 1570 Antwerp defaulted on its debts. It could no longer stand aloof from the financial vicissitudes of the Spanish Crown. In 1576 an unpaid Spanish army sacked Antwerp and ruined its commercial prosperity. Amsterdam, which was soon to gain its independence from Spain after a war of exhaustion, maintained a solid credit standing, which it retained. In the seventeenth century Amsterdam assumed the position of financial center enjoyed by Antwerp in the sixteenth century.

SIXTEENTH CENTURY

Interest Rates

Loans to Princes. In 1547 Edward VI of England, 1547–1553, paid 14% in London for a loan, although the legal rate had recently been set at 10%. In 1558 Queen Mary, 1553–1558, borrowed in London at 12%. (306) In 1561 Queen Elizabeth I, 1558–1603, who was the first to enforce the legal maximum, borrowed 30,000 pounds in London at 10%. These rates are more moderate than some of the very high rates quoted in earlier centuries for loans to princes. Perhaps this decline was due to the active credit markets that had grown up at Antwerp and elsewhere. Bankers found it tempting to borrow on the Exchange on their own bills, which commanded relatively low rates, and relend to their royal patrons at a worthwhile differential without tying up their own capital. The English Crown now kept financial agents at Antwerp, the most famous of whom was Sir Thomas Gresham, 1519?–1579. English Crown loans at Antwerp were reported (308) at the following rates: 1546, 13%; 1548, 12–13%; 1552, 12–14%; 1554, 14%; 1558, 14%.

As a consequence of the wars of Charles V, the Spanish Crown became Europe's largest debtor. It was no longer feasible to make a sharp distinction between the credit of the Spanish Crown and the credit of the government of the Spanish Netherlands, or even of the city of Antwerp, because the Crown forced both to borrow for it. In practice much of this borrowing was done on the Antwerp Exchange. In addition, the great banking houses, especially the Fuggers, made direct loans to Charles and his family. Most of these Fugger loans were well secured by concessions, such as the lease of mining property. Others, however, were unsecured. Some were obtained by great pressure and were made largely to ensure collection of earlier debts. The following are examples of loans by the Fuggers to the Hapsburgs: (307)

1508 8000 florins to the Emperor Maximilian I, 1493–1519, secured by the right to farm salt in the Tyrol, and 128,750 florins secured by copper and silver production (no rate).

1518 A three-month loan to Charles V at an annual rate of 10%, endorsed by several receivers general (of taxes) in the Netherlands and by several towns.

1530 275,000 florins to Ferdinand I, 1531–1564, brother of Charles V, to secure his election as king of Rome, repayable in five yearly installments, secured by an annuity on revenues at 10% per year plus a 15% bonus.

1536 100,000 ducats to Charles V. payable in one year, secured on the revenues of the kingdom of Castile and on the first gold or silver to arrive from "India," at 14%.

1548 150,000 ducats to Charles V, secured on the revenues of Naples, at 12%.

1556 Philip II of Spain, 1556–1598, consolidated his debts to the Fuggers at 12% secured on Netherlands tax receipts and guaranteed by the receivers general of the Netherlands.

1560 Philip II, who now was paying the Fuggers 12–14% on a vast debt, sought to settle at 5% interest, but was refused. An arrangement was made in 1562.

1572 Philip II borrowed from the Fuggers at 12%.

Loans by various bankers to the Spanish Netherlands government are reported in some detail for a few years as follows: (309)

Date of Loan	Term	Description	Annual Rate, %
March, 1509	Approx. 6 mos.	Borrowed at Antwerp	$11\frac{1}{2}$
March, 1509	Approx. 12 mos.	Borrowed at Antwerp	$11\frac{1}{2}$
June, 1510	Approx. 18 mos.	Borrowed at Antwerp	$7\frac{1}{2}$
June, 1510	Approx. 4 mos.	Borrowed at Antwerp	24
Oct., 1510	Approx. 6 mos.	Borrowed at Bruges	$13\frac{1}{4}$
May, 1511	Approx. 10 mos.	Borrowed at Antwerp	$6\frac{1}{4}$
May, 1511	Approx. 7 mos.	Borrowed at Antwerp	10
July, 1511	Approx. 17–23 mos.	Borrowed at Antwerp and Bruges	15
Jan., 1512	Approx. 8 mos.	Borrowed at Bruges	$8\frac{1}{2}$
Jan., 1512	Approx. 7 mos.	Borrowed at Bruges	$12\frac{1}{4}$
March, 1516	Approx. 6 mos.	Borrowed at Antwerp	20
May, 1516	Approx. 6 mos.	Borrowed at Antwerp	$15\frac{1}{2}$–$31\frac{1}{2}$
? 1516	Approx. 12 mos.	Borrowed from Fugger, gtd. by Antwerp	11
Sept. 1516	Approx. 12 mos.	From Genoese merchants, gtd. by Antwerp	$13\frac{1}{2}$
Dec., 1516	Approx. 6? mos.	Borrowed at, and gtd. by, Antwerp	$14\frac{3}{4}$
? 1518	Approx. 3 mos.	Fugger loan gtd. by cities	10
Aug., 1519	Approx. 5 mos.		16
May, 1519	Approx. 10 mos.		7
June, 1520	Approx. 7 mos.		10–13
Sept., 1520	Approx. 7 mos.		$15\frac{1}{2}$
Dec., 1520	Approx. 5 mos.		$16\frac{1}{4}$
May, 1521	Approx. 6 mos.		17
July, 1521	Approx 6 mos.		$21\frac{1}{2}$
Oct., 1521	Approx. 3 mos.		$27\frac{1}{2}$
Oct., 1521	Approx. 6 mos.		16–18

Over a longer period of time the following ranges of interest rates are reported (310) on many loans to Charles V, the Netherlands government, and the city of Antwerp.

Year	%	Year	%
1508	$11\frac{1}{2}$	1540	12–16
		1542	10–12
1510	$7\frac{1}{2}$–24	1544	9–16
1512	$6\frac{1}{4}$–27	1546	11–$13\frac{1}{2}$
1516	11–20	1548	9–12
1518	7–20		
		1550	11–12
1520	10–$27\frac{1}{2}$	1552	12–16
1522	13–27	1554	11–14
1526	14	1556	12–13
1528	14–22	1558	14
1530	12–24	1560	12–14
1536	13–15		
1538	10–13	1570	12
		1572	12

In addition the Fuggers made emergency loans to Charles V at rates as high as 24–52%.

The great range of these rates in many years was no doubt due in part to differences in terms, although these were probably all negotiated as relatively short-term loans. In the early years of the century the Spanish Crown was considered a good credit, and the rates were not far above the prime commercial bill rates at Antwerp, listed below. Most of the range may be ascribed to daily fluctuations in the money markets of Europe. Stress alternated with ease as funds were shifted from market to market and as the supply of liquid capital was exhausted by wars and restored by imports of metal and the expansion of bank credit. As a sequel we have the history of six bankruptcies of the Spanish Crown in one century: 1557, 1575, 1596, 1607, 1627, 1647.

The king of Portugal also often borrowed at Antwerp. His loans were usually in anticipation of the arrival of spices from India. These loans were reported at rates of 12 to 18%.

The king of France bid high for short-term funds at Lyons, where he fostered a competitive credit market. He paid above commerical rates. In 1551 his 12% bills sold briefly at a discount to yield 28%, but were soon back to par. He then set a legal limit of 15% for all private loans at Lyons. In the financial crisis of 1557 both the king of Spain and the king of France suspended payments. French Crown short-term loans at Lyons were reported at 12% in 1536, but from 1542 to 1558 they often paid 16% on face value. By 1575 the French Crown's credit was gone. Interest was long unpaid and royal bills sold far below face value. In 1586 the king settled at 25–40% of principal in long-term *rentes*, rate unstated.

Personal Loans. In the Netherlands the public pawnshop at the end of this century loaned on pawns at 15%, later at 12%. Private pawnshop rates are not specifically reported for this century, but probably continued within the very wide range of the fifteenth century.

Commercial Loans. By 1550 the *montes pietatis* of Italy, which accepted deposits at 5%, loaned to business at 8–10%. (311)

The market rate of interest on best short-term credits at Antwerp is reported as follows:

Year	%	Year	%
1530	7–12 *	1552	10–12
1536	4–6	1554	12
		1556	8–12
1540	12	1557	10–12
1546	$8\frac{1}{2}$–13	1558	8–10
1548	10		
		1560	7–8
		1562	8–10

* Usual range for many years.

In 1563, when the Fuggers were in trouble, they borrowed at 22% (312) in Spain and at 30% in Antwerp. Soon they were again borrowing in Antwerp at 8–10%.

In France the important credit market at Lyons was dominated by Florentine bankers. At this market King Francis I and his successors bid against Charles of Spain and Germany and his successors for funds. Ranges at Lyons for short commercial bills were reported as follows:

Year	%	Year	%
1530	8–9	1550	11
1534	7–8	1551	8–10
1542	5–8	1554	10–12
1546	12	1556	8
1548	10–12	1558	12

Deposits. In Germany by 1515 the "triple contracts," by which inactive partners and others kept money with a bank or merchant without sharing in the risk of the business, usually paid 5%. In Spain in 1550 such contracts are reported at 4%, but by 1575 the rate in Spain had gone up to 5%. (313) In the Netherlands by 1600 this rate was 6¼%.

Montes pietatis in Italy and the Netherlands, circa 1540, accepted deposits from wealthy men and paid 4–6% interest. (311)

In 1505 the House of Hochstetter, of Amsterdam and Augsburg, received deposits up to a total of 1 million guilders and paid 5% on them. (315)

In 1527 the House of Fugger paid only 2–3% on large deposits by the family and more on other deposits. (316) By 1536 the Fuggers had expanded and paid 4½–5% for much larger deposits. In 1553 the banking house of Haug, in Augsburg, paid 7% on deposits of special partners. In 1570 the Imhof Bank, also of Augsburg, paid 5% to special partners. (317)

Annuities and Mortgages. In the sixteenth century, in Germany and Italy the going rate on a census contract secured by land was usually 5%. (318) The public pawnshops of the Netherlands financed themselves by the sale of a census at 6¼%; other census rates reported there were at 4–10%.

Loans on London real estate are reported to have run as high as 12% in 1553 and to have risen to 14% in 1560. (306) In 1546 interest in England was legalized at a 10% maximum rate, which is said to have represented the fair value of money on best security. However, it was not until 1571 that Elizabeth I enforced this maximum.

Long-Term Loans to States and Cities. In 1546 Ferdinand I, 1531–1564, sold to the Fuggers a perpetual annuity of 11,000 ducats secured by his revenues from Calabria in return for a payment of 110,000 ducats; this was a 10% annuity. In 1557 the Fuggers bought a similar 10% annuity secured by the revenues of Brabant and Flanders. (320)

One of the best German credits was the city of Nuremberg. Nuremberg in 1540–1550 often borrowed on perpetual annuities at 5%. When in 1553 there was an emergency caused by the need to build new walls quickly, the city floated an annuity loan at a rate as high as 12%. By 1555 the rate was down to 10%; by 1558, 8%; 1561, 6%; and by 1565 it was back to 5%. (321)

In France, in 1522 perpetual annuities, called *rentes,* were floated free of coercion at 8⅓%. These were secured by the tax on wine. They proved popular and more were sold at the same rate in 1536, 1537, and 1543. The rate was forcibly reduced to 4% in 1597.

At about this time a long and very significant history of annuity rates developed in the province of Holland. Holland was the most important province in that part of the Netherlands which became Protestant and at first resisted, and later effectively threw off, the dominion of the

Spanish Crown. It secured and held its independence in spite of a small population and limited resources. The province and the cities of Holland and their instrumentalities and neighboring Dutch provinces had often borrowed from private persons on life annuities and perpetual annuities sometimes amortized by sinking funds. About 1500 annuity rates were considered "high" at 8–12%. In 1552 the perpetual sinking fund annuities of the province of Holland that were outstanding paid 8⅓%. (322) However, as the opinion was then held that life annuities were more profitable to the province, these were sold at 12½% and the proceeds used for redemption of perpetual sinking fund annuities. In 1544 the average interest rate paid by the province on all debt was 12%. In 1550–1560 perpetual sinking fund annuities were again sold at 8⅓%. By 1570 their rate had declined to 6⅙%. In 1572 during the War of Independence the rate increased again to 8⅓%. After 1590 political and economic conditions improved, and interest rates started to decline again. By 1606 the rate on sinking fund perpetuals was down to 7¹⁄₇%. (322)

For Venice the available data in this century do not permit the derivation of many interest rates from the *prestiti*. In 1470 a new series of *prestiti* was floated, the *Monte Nuovo,* and in 1509 another new series was floated, the *Monte Novissimo.* Yields were probably 9.60% in 1500 and 6.76% in 1502. They were paid off late in this century, but we do not know on what terms. Following the war with the League of Cambrai, 1508–1510, Venice lost her mainland power, and in a series of wars with the Turks, she lost much of her Eastern empire. Genoa in contrast lived under Spanish protection and prospered.

Genoese financial records now provide an extraordinary and detailed series of interest rates. (323) The Bank of St. George issued, on behalf of the Republic of Genoa, placements or perpetual bonds, called *luoghi,* at a nominal value of 100 lira each. Their income was secured by specific taxes farmed out to the bank. The *luoghi* did not pay a fixed rate of interest, as the Venetian *prestiti* originally did, but paid dividends which depended on the amount of taxes collected after payment of the expenses of the bank. These *luoghi* changed hands freely and were negotiated by citizens and foreigners. Prices fluctuated above or below par, following the course of supply and demand, and these prices were recorded. The *luoghi* were not forced loans, but were voluntarily subscribed. Retirement, although discussed from time to time, was never attempted on a large scale. In addition to issuing the *luoghi,* the bank received deposits and carried on a regular banking business, but the income from these other activities went directly to the officers of the bank and was not distributed to security holders.

Demand for *luoghi* was stimulated by bequests to charities, and this led to the practice of *moltiplechi*. Under *moltiplechi* the legatee was required not to sell, but to hold, the *luoghi* and to reinvest the dividends in more *luoghi* until the principal reached a specified higher figure. Demand was also stimulated by the fact that the bank was required to keep a certain reserve in *luoghi*.

During the sixteenth and seventeenth centuries the dividends on the *luoghi*, which were declared annually, were paid one half in the fourth year after declaration and one half in the fifth year. Holders registered their divided claims on declaration and could discount their dividend claims in the market at the current rate of discount. It is this market rate of discount for dividends payable in 4–5 years that is reported below as a rate of interest. The yield on the *luoghi* themselves is not reported because it resembled a dividend yield on a stock.

In the table we see that the rate of discount between 1522 and 1534

ANNUAL RATE OF DISCOUNT FOR 4–5 YEARS OF DEFERRED DIVIDENDS OF BANK OF SAINT GEORGE (323)

(Annual Average)

Year	%	Year	%	Year	%	Year	%
		1540	$4\frac{1}{4}$	1560	$6\frac{1}{4}$	1580	$4\frac{3}{8}$
		1541	4	1561	$6\frac{1}{2}$	1581	$2\frac{7}{8}$
1522	$4\frac{1}{4}$	1542	$3\frac{7}{8}$	1562	$5\frac{5}{8}$	1602	$2\frac{7}{8}$
1523	3	1543	$4\frac{1}{8}$	1563	$4\frac{1}{4}$	1583	$2\frac{3}{8}$
1524	4	1544	$4\frac{5}{8}$	1564	$4\frac{5}{8}$	1584	$2\frac{1}{2}$
1525	$2\frac{7}{8}$	1545	$5\frac{1}{4}$	1565	$7\frac{1}{4}$	1585	$1\frac{7}{8}$
1526	$5\frac{1}{2}$	1546	$3\frac{1}{2}$	1566	9	1586	$2\frac{3}{4}$
1527	$6\frac{1}{2}$	1547	$3\frac{3}{4}$	1567	$6\frac{1}{4}$	1587	3
1528	$5\frac{1}{4}$	1548	$4\frac{1}{4}$	1568	$5\frac{7}{8}$	1588	$3\frac{1}{4}$
1529	$4\frac{1}{4}$	1549	$4\frac{5}{8}$	1569	$4\frac{7}{8}$	1589	$3\frac{3}{8}$
1530	4	1550	$4\frac{3}{8}$	1570	5	1590	$3\frac{1}{4}$
1531	4	1551	$4\frac{1}{2}$	1571	$4\frac{3}{8}$	1591	$3\frac{1}{4}$
1532	$5\frac{1}{8}$	1552	$4\frac{1}{4}$	1572	$3\frac{5}{8}$	1592	$3\frac{3}{8}$
1533	4	1553	$4\frac{5}{8}$	1573	$2\frac{1}{2}$	1593	$3\frac{1}{4}$
1534	$5\frac{1}{4}$	1554	$7\frac{1}{4}$	1574	3	1594	$3\frac{3}{4}$
1535	$4\frac{1}{4}$	1555	9	1575	$4\frac{1}{4}$	1595	$3\frac{3}{4}$
1536	$4\frac{5}{8}$	1556	$6\frac{1}{4}$	1576	$3\frac{3}{4}$	1596	$3\frac{1}{2}$
1537	$4\frac{1}{4}$	1557	$5\frac{7}{8}$	1577	$3\frac{3}{4}$	1597	$3\frac{1}{8}$
1538	$4\frac{3}{8}$	1558	$5\frac{1}{2}$	1578	$2\frac{3}{4}$	1598	$2\frac{1}{2}$
1539	$4\frac{7}{8}$	1559	$6\frac{1}{4}$	1579	$3\frac{1}{4}$	1599	$2\frac{7}{8}$
						1600	$2\frac{7}{8}$

generally ranged between 4 and 6%. This was a period of war and unrest, the dividend rate was reduced, and the volume of *luoghi* outstanding was increased. Commodity prices were rising. From 1534 to 1546 the discount rate tended to decline from 5 to 4% and then to 3½%. Commodity prices were declining, and the outstanding issue again increased. From 1546 to 1570 the discount rate increased sharply from 3½% to a 4–6% range, with occasional peaks at 7–9% in times of war. This was a period of large-scale building and commercial activity.

From 1570 to 1600 the discount rate declined from 5% to a 3–4% range and then to a 2½–2⅞% range. In 1570 Genoa became the banker for the Spanish Crown, a role previously held by German and Netherlands bankers. Probably as a result of recent Spanish defaults to northern creditors, the Genoese obtained good security: the gold and silver which was coming from America. The metal on which advances had been made came to Genoa rather than to Spain and eventually flooded the market. This was the time when commodity prices in Italy rose 2½ times from 1550 to 1620.

The astonishing feature of this series is the lowness of the discount rates in the late sixteenth century and early seventeenth century. It suggests that money was advanced freely for a term of years at between 1½% and 3% at a time when other European interest rates were much higher. *Moltiplechi*, tax advantages and reserve requirements may have depressed these rates below all other prime interest rates which have been reported. Pending further research, these Genoese rates are not carried forward in the summary tables as indicative of prevailing prime interest rates in sixteenth- and seventeenth-century Europe.

TABLE 9

SUMMARY OF SIXTEENTH-CENTURY INTEREST RATES

Loans to Princes (Short Term)

England	Crown in England	10–14%
England	Crown in Antwerp, 1546–1558	12–14
Hapsburgs	From Fugger, 1518–1572	10–16
Hapsburgs	From Fugger (under stress), 24–52%	
Hapsburgs	On Antwerp Exchange, 1508–1572	$6\frac{1}{4}$–$31\frac{1}{2}$
Portuguese	Crown on Antwerp Exchange	12–18
France	Crown at Lyons	12–16
France	Crown (under stress), 28+%	

Personal Loans (Short Term)

Netherlands	*Montes pietatis*	12–15%

TABLE 9 *(Continued)*

Commercial Loans (Short Term)

Italy	*Montes pietatis*, loan to business at	8–10%
Antwerp	Market rate on best bills, 1530–1550	4–13
Antwerp	Market rate on best bills, 1550–1562	7–12
Antwerp	Fuggers when in trouble paid (1563), 22–30	
Antwerp	Fuggers when strong paid	4–10
Lyons	Market rate on best bills, 1530–1550	5–12
Lyons	Market rate on best bills, 1551–1558	8–12+

Deposits (Short Term)

Germany	Special partnerships	5%
Spain	Special partnerships	4–5
Netherlands	Special partnerships	$6\frac{1}{4}$
Italy and Netherlands	Deposits with *montes pietatis*	4–6
Amsterdam and Augsburg	Hochstetter deposits	5
Augsburg	Fugger deposits 1527, family (2–3+)	
Augsburg	Fugger deposits 1536	$4\frac{1}{2}$–5
Augsburg	Haug deposits 1553	7
Augsburg	Imhof deposits 1570	5

Annuities and Mortgages (Long Term)

Germany, Italy, and Netherlands	Census contracts on land, usually	5%
Germany, Italy, and Netherlands	Census contracts on land, range	4–10
Netherlands	Census on *montes pietatis*	$6\frac{1}{4}$
England	Real estate mortgages	10–14

Loans to Cities and States (Long Term)

Germany	Hapsburg annuity (example)	10%
Germany	Nuremberg annuity, normal times	5
Germany	Nuremberg annuity, emergency	6–8–10–12
Holland	Sinking fund perpetual annuities	$6\frac{1}{6}$–$7\frac{1}{7}$–$8\frac{1}{3}$
Holland	Life annuities	$12\frac{1}{2}$
Genoa	Rate of discount on declared dividends of Bank of St. George, payable in 4–5 years: 1522–1534, $2\frac{7}{8}$–$6\frac{1}{2}$% 1535–1546, $3\frac{1}{2}$–$5\frac{1}{4}$ 1547–1570, $3\frac{3}{4}$–9 1571–1600, $1\frac{7}{8}$–$4\frac{3}{8}$	
Venice	*Prestiti* (payments irregular), 1502, 1522	$6\frac{3}{4}$–$9\frac{5}{8}$?
France	*Rentes* (perpetual annuities), 1522–1543	$8\frac{1}{3}$
France	*Rentes* arbitrarily reduced in 1597 to	4

SEVENTEENTH CENTURY

Background

Seventeenth-century European finance was a study in contrasts. The wars, the excessive loans, the inflations, and the defaults of the late sixteenth century brought the Crowns of Spain and France, and with them their great Italian and German bankers, to financial ruin. At the same time in a remote northern corner of Europe, the new Dutch Republic won its independence from Spain, achieved a trading empire, and developed the high modern standards of state credit. England, a century later, successfully adopted the Dutch principles of national debt and learned how to use a sound credit structure for national purposes.

The seventeenth century is often classified by historians as "modern." From the point of view of credit markets, however, it is convenient to review it as the last of the Renaissance centuries. Only a little before 1700, when Dutch financial principles were brought to England by William III and his Whig supporters and were there greatly improved upon, did the history of modern banking and credit really start.

The presentation of interest-rate history must now be modified in one essentially modern respect: financial events and interest rates must now be arranged according to national boundaries. No longer was Europe financially international. No longer did Italian bankers dominate an international money market and shift their balances at will to or from Italy, Spain, France, Germany, England, and the Netherlands. Credit conditions had never been uniform throughout all the geographical regions of Europe, but the earlier distinctions were based less on nationality than on local economic and financial circumstances. In the seventeenth century, financial history became nationalized.

Spain, recently the most powerful of European states, sank into financial decrepitude in spite of her empire in the New World and in spite of inpouring gold and silver. Spanish state bankruptcies occurred about every twenty years: 1607–1627–1649. (324) Spain's imported gold and silver were pledged in advance to Genoese bankers. While the pledged Spanish gold and silver flowed to Genoa, Spain sank to a copper standard of currency. Often money was lacking to supply the king's table. Revenues were pledged five to ten years in advance. At times it turned out that Crown property had been pledged several times. These bankruptcies meant that payment was stopped on the floating debt of the Crown; the floating debt was later forcibly consolidated into low-interest annuities. Even these annuities were reduced in amount and not always honored. By 1627 nearly everybody in Genoa had an interest in Spanish claims, and the ruin there became general. The big Genoese banks reached the end of their resources. The Fuggers who had clung to old Spanish claims dating back to the sixteenth century were now completely ruined. Spain never recovered her international political and financial power.

In France the Italian bankers to the Crown were ruined in a more orderly and fastidious way. The power of France grew under Louis XIII, 1610–1643, and Louis XIV, 1643–1715, and these absolute monarchs were strong enough to exploit their creditors. There were, however, a number of enlightened efforts by French finance ministers to reform the state credit, and in the course of these France made some valuable contributions to techniques of government finance. Under Henry IV, 1589–1610, Sully, the French finance minister, consolidated the debts during a state bankruptcy into low-rate *rentes*. He avoided floating debt, introduced economy, improved the national finances, and brought on a period of prosperity. (325) In 1610 a new period of mismanagement began. The aggressive foreign policy of Richelieu, 1624–1642, and the extravagance of the court led again to a new and huge floating debt. At this time the term "partisans" was coined: people who had *partis*, money transactions with the government, and thus became its unconditional adherents. Another French state bankruptcy in 1648 eliminated the Italian bankers, mostly Florentines. State revenues by that time had been anticipated three years ahead by borrowing from the partisans who charged the Crown ruinous rates. Even the *rentes* (perpetual loans) were not always serviced in full. From 1639 French *rentes* enjoyed a market on the new Paris Exchange.

In 1665, Colbert, the new finance minister to Louis XIV, again reformed French finances. He greatly increased revenues and reduced the *rentes* arbitrarily or paid them off at low rates. He set a maximum interest rate of 5%, saying that high interest rates created unemployment and retarded trade. He also said that "a banker should behave toward a finance minister like a soldier toward a general." (326) The war of 1672 again required enormous loans. Colbert, in 1674, founded a State Savings Bank, which paid 5% interest, secured by taxes. In 1679 he successfully issued new *rentes* at public subscription. He then devised the art of oversubscription. In 1683 Colbert died, and thereafter French finances again went the way of Spain's.

Germany in this century was still a collection of independent states. The Thirty Years' War, 1618–1648, in part a struggle between Protestant Europe and Catholic Europe, resulted in irreparable losses of men and wealth in Germany. Nothing more was heard of great German financiers like the Fuggers.

England, under the Stuarts, clung to old financial methods. In the sixteenth century Gresham had reformed English government finance, instilling principles of commercial honor, order, and economy. Foreign bankers had gradually been excluded. Elizabeth never broke her word, but her loans were usually forced loans in the old style. She left a small debt. James I, 1603–1625, and Charles I, 1625–1649, incurred large floating debts. There was still no funded debt. The lack of popular enthusiasm for the Stuarts finally brought an end to forced loans. Goldsmiths became bankers. They gave short-term credit to the Crown (327) at high rates and obtained the money from their depositors. Goldsmiths also helped finance Cromwell, 1649–1660, and Charles II, 1660–1685. In 1672 Charles II "stopped the Exchequer": he stopped payment on his large floating debt during a war with Holland. Charles settled with 6% perpetual annuities. This was the last English forced loan.

Only after the Revolution of 1689, when King William III and the Parliament could borrow in the name of the united country and could offer some promise of joint fiscal responsibility, was English national credit established. Until the 1690's England, although making great commercial progress at home and abroad, had no central bank and no organized money market.

The seventeenth-century financial history of Holland contrasted strikingly with the dismal succession of defaults by the rulers of great powers. The new Dutch Republic was a union of the northern provinces of the Spanish Netherlands. Her successful war of liberation from Spain lasted from 1568 to 1648—eighty years. In spite of the war, the period 1600–1650 was the golden age of Dutch arts and literature. Because Spain closed Lisbon to Dutch commerce, the Dutch found their own way to the Far East and to the New World and displaced the Portuguese. The Dutch East India Company was founded in 1602, and the Dutch West India Company was founded in 1621. (328) With such extensive trade Holland became the commercial center of Europe. Amsterdam replaced Antwerp, which was still under Spanish rule, as a financial center.

In 1652 and 1665 the Dutch Republic fought wars with England. The Dutch fleet even sailed up the Thames and destroyed one of the suburbs of London. In 1672–1678 France invaded Holland. The Dutch saved themselves only by opening the dikes. Nevertheless, under William of Orange (later William III of England, 1689–1702) the France of Louis XIV was held to a draw.

A good part of the military success of this small new nation may be attributed to the excellence of Dutch state credit. Provincial and town annuities at moderate rates had been popular in Holland for centuries. There was no expensive court. The frugal people saved and invested. There were no expensive foreign wars—all wars were right at home. The navy, which was also a merchant marine, brought in more than it cost. (329) With good credit, German mercenaries could be hired for land defense. Since the country was united and the people trusted their government, it could pledge the nation's credit effectively: the whole future surplus of all the people.

Dutch credit was freely used for defense; it was not abjured. The national debt increased during these wars and became large. But it was almost all funded debt; floating debt was only used for emergencies and was promptly funded. The provinces and towns kept faith with their creditors who were their own people. With prosperous trade there was usually more capital seeking investment than there were safe borrowers. Creditor groups several times effectively objected to plans to raise taxes and pay off the national debt. Sixty-five thousand people in one province alone had money in Dutch state annuities. These annuities were advertised and sold by voluntary subscription. There were many kinds of annuities: life, 30–32 year, perpetual bonds, and lotteries. These loans were not, as in France and Spain, secured by specific revenues, but only on the general credit of the issuing provinces or towns. Confidence in the honesty of administration was unshaken. However, there was no published budget, and the people could only guess at the amount of the public debt. It remained for the English to develop the principle of complete disclosure.

Interest rates in Holland declined further during the seventeenth century. Modern "easy money" was discovered. In a series of important refundings the provinces reduced the annuity rates. However, there were great fluctuations in the market for Dutch annuities, the price often depending on the fortunes of war.

The Amsterdam Exchange, brought indoors in 1613, at first dealt largely in shares, such as those of the Dutch East India Company. On this exchange was developed most of the peculiar techniques of modern stock speculation. (330) The seventeenth-century Dutch even speculated in tulip bulbs. In the course of the famous "tulipomania" one speculator in 1636 bought a single bulb for 4600 florins. Government bonds were first dealt in on the Exchange in 1672 when the invasion by France created a precipitous price decline to 30% of par and thus attracted the attention of speculators.

SEVENTEENTH-CENTURY INTEREST RATES

England

"To them that lend money my caveat is, that neither directly nor indirectly, by art, or cunning invention, they take above ten in the hundred; for they that seeke by sleight to creepe out of these statutes, will deceive themselves and repent in the end."—Sɪʀ Eᴅᴡᴀʀᴅ Cᴏᴋᴇ, *Institutes of the Laws of England,* Book I, Sec. 1.

The *legal rate* of interest in England was as follows: (331) 1571–1624, 10%; 1624–1651, 8%; 1651–1714, 6%. It did not apply to Crown loans.

Short-term loans to the Crown were made at widely varying rates, probably depending on the quality of security offered. As the Antwerp bill market no longer existed, and as London goldsmiths had developed banking operations based on deposits, Crown loans were now largely in the form of floating debt borrowed from London goldsmiths. In addition there were forced loans at rates unstated. Some rates on goldsmith loans to the Crown have come down as follows:

1640	To Charles I	"Usual rate"	8%	(333)
1660–70	To Charles II		8	(332)
1665	To Charles II	Secured by taxes	8–10	(333)
1660–85	To Charles II		10–20	(331)
1660–85	To Charles II	Maximum rate	30	(331)
1680	To Charles II	Secured by revenue	6	(334)
1690	To William III	Secured by revenue	10–12	(335)
1690	To William III	Unsecured	25–30	(335)

The first English *national debt* of long maturity was floated in 1692 to finance the war with France. At that time 1 million pounds was borrowed, secured by duties on beer and liquor, as life annuities at 10% to 1700, and 7% thereafter on a semitontine basis (survivors take all); one subscriber survived seventy-seven years. In 1693, 1 million pounds more was borrowed, secured by the duty on salt, at 10% interest for sixteen years plus lottery prizes, raising the total cost of the money to 14%. (336)

These high rates for Crown borrowing appeared intolerable. Other rates of interest in England were far lower, and in the Dutch Republic the government was borrowing at 3%. England envied the Dutch banking arrangements. In 1694 the war with France continued to be costly and the English government offered a new loan of £1,200,000 secured by the duty on tonnage and paying 8%; as an extra inducement, subscribers received the right to incorporate themselves as the Governor and Company of the Bank of England. (336)

For *short-term commercial credits* there is very little English data until the end of this century. As rates of 4–6% were paid by goldsmiths for deposits, we can surmise that commercial credits early in the century commanded something over 6%. That good loans did not regularly bring much over 6% can be surmised by the frequent 8% rate cited above for well-secured Crown loans. However, the legal limit of 8%, later 6%, probably distorted the record as it comes down to us. There was as yet no evidence of a "money market" or "bill market" in seventeenth-century London.

In the 1630's the Chamber of London loaned to merchants at 7% and to the East India Company at 6%. In 1640 the market rate for good London loans was reported to be 8%, the legal limit, and in 1688 to be 4–6%, or below the legal limit. After the financial innovations of William III, the Bank of England, founded in 1694, discounted trade bills at the following rates: (337) 1694, 4½–6%; 1695, 3–6%; 1698, 4½%; 1699, 4½%.

For rates on *short-term deposits* in the city of London, the data may be summarized as follows:

1660	Goldsmiths paid	6%	(332)
1665	Goldsmiths paid for money to lend to Charles II	4–6	(338)
1690	Goldsmiths paid for money to lend to William III	6	(338)

For *mortgages, annuities and other longer-term loans,* the legal maximum of 10% in 1600–1625 was said to represent a full market rate for loans with normal security. (339) By 1675–1700 the effective market rate was said to be below the legal maximum, then 6%. In 1666 there was much more money lent out at 4–4½% on landed security than at 5% or 6%. In the 1670's John Locke wrote that "a great part of the moneyed men will now let their money upon good security at 4%." It was stated in a lawsuit that "5% was the highest rate in 1687 that was generally paid on mortgages." Macaulay, however, says that in 1696 the market rate of interest on the best mortgages was 6%. (340) However, in 1694 the Bank of England anticipated making mortgage loans at 5% although it did not develop this business. In 1677 the Africa Company converted the whole of its bonded debt, contracted at 6% in 1675, to a rate of 5%. (339)

The Dutch Republic

Dutch interest rates for this century are quoted on the *long-term loans* of the individual provinces, the United Provinces, and the towns. These loans were mostly in the form of annuities of many kinds: some with sinking funds, some limited in time, some perpetual. Quoted rates do not always distinguish the precise terms of each loan quoted. A remarkable series of conversions of the securities of the provinces of the Republic may be summarized as follows: (341)

1600	Sinking fund perpetual annuities were still sold at	$8\frac{1}{3}$%
1606	Sinking fund annuity rates were reduced to	$7\frac{1}{7}$
1620?	Sinking fund annuity rates were reduced to	$6\frac{1}{6}$
1640–49	All sinking fund annuities and bonds were converted to a rate of	5
1654–55	Outstanding securities were converted to a rate of	4
1665	The Deputies of Amsterdam tried to induce the states to reduce the rate to 3%, but investors objected	
1672	Another conversion brought the rate down to	$3\frac{3}{4}$
1672	After the French invasion, government securities sold down to 30 on the Amsterdam Exchange (342) to yield	$12\frac{1}{2}$?
1672	After formation of a defensive alliance, government securities recovered to prices of 60–75–95 to yield	4–$6\frac{1}{4}$?
1673	They sold down to 50, then up to 75, to yield	5–$7\frac{1}{2}$?
1678	They recovered to 100 on or before this year to yield	$3\frac{3}{4}$
1679–1700	In times of peace new loans could sometimes be floated as low as	3
1679–1700	In war new loans could be floated at	4–$6\frac{1}{4}$

One specific example of a perpetual Dutch annuity of the seventeenth century may be cited. In 1624 one Elsken Jorisdochter (Elsie, the daughter of George) invested 1200 florins in a bond issued for repairs to a dike. (343) She received a bond of the Lekdyk Bovendams Company (chartered 1323), which was a semipublic enterprise with taxing power. The company and this bond survived at least to 1957. This perpetual bond originally paid $6\frac{1}{4}$% interest per annum, about the same rate then paid by the provinces. It promised no repayment of principal. At some time in the eighteenth century the then owner agreed to a reduction of interest to $2\frac{1}{2}$%. In 1957 this bond was still paying $2\frac{1}{2}$% per annum. The bond must be presented at Utrecht for interest payments at least once every five years, and payments are recorded on the back. The bond states that it is "free of all taxes, impositions or charges whichsoever, however called or disguised, with no single exception." In 1938 this bond was presented to the New York Stock Exchange, which collected interest as it became payable.

This scrap of financial history illustrates the long history of perpetual Dutch annuities. It suggests that small local issues then did not differ greatly in rate from national annuities. Tax privileges were probably a factor in securing low rates, as they were in Venice in the fourteenth century. However, too much weight should not be given to tax exemption, because all forms of interest rates appeared to decline sharply to low levels in Holland.

For other Dutch loans the sources do not always distinguish between deposits and advances and between long- and short-term loans. The following scraps of information are, however, informative:

1603	The rate paid by the city of Amsterdam on deposits withdrawable one month after request was reduced from	$8\frac{1}{3}\%$
	to	$6\frac{1}{6}$
1659–1660	The city of Amsterdam borrowed money on deposit at	$3\frac{3}{4}$
	later at	$3\frac{1}{4}$
1670	The Guardians Supervisory Council of Amsterdam, finding it impossible to lend money at $3\frac{1}{4}\%$, asked permission to loan at	3
1679	The treasurer of the city of Amsterdam urged a reduction of interest paid from	4
	to	$3\frac{1}{2}$
	He pointed out that Alkmaar and other towns paid	3

For rates on *short-term commercial credit* in seventeenth-century Holland there is as yet no chronological record. There is, however, good evidence of low rates at least during the second half of the century. "In Holland" declared Josiah Child, in 1668, "any man that is a competent good husband, prudent and careful in his business, may take up 500 pounds or 1,000 pounds at 3% upon his own note only." Another contemporary said "it is a great advantage for the Traffick of Holland that money may be taken up by merchants at 3½% for a year without pawn or pledge." Amsterdam merchants are cited as borrowing at 3–4½% and lending in England and France at 6% or better. Interest rates in Holland are elsewhere cited at 3–4% on medium- and long-term credits. Finally, at the turn of the eighteenth century the rate of interest on the Amsterdam Exchange was reported as falling to 2% or even to 1¾%. (344) This is the first record of such low rates that we have for northern Europe, although a century earlier even lower rates may have prevailed in Genoa.

France

The State bankruptcy of 1557 marked the end of the prosperity of the Lyons bill market. In 1586 the king settled in *rentes* for 25–40% of principal due. In 1597, in a great financial reform (bankruptcy), the annuity rate on Crown *rentes* was forcibly reduced to 4%. This, however, was presumably not a market rate of interest. In fact, there is little evidence of an organized money market in France in the seventeenth century.

Toward the end of Cardinal Mazarin's power, 1643–1661, the *partisans* charged the Crown for *short-term floating debt*, at least 15%, but at times as high as 50–60%. (345)

The French Crown had two sources of credit, the bankers (*partisans*), who made short loans at high rates, and the *rentiers*, who purchased long-term annuity claims. Some of these annuities had been created by State bankruptcies when floating debt was forcibly refunded. There are few data on the rates paid on French *rentes* in this century except the imposed rates. In the sixteenth century several issues of *rentes* were voluntarily purchased at 8⅓%. Finance Minister Colbert, in 1660, in a "reform" kept back one third of the *rentes* due on the Hôtel de Ville in Paris. He tried to pay off other *rentes* forcibly at a heavy discount. There were riots, and in 1665 Colbert reduced the legal rate on *rentes* to 5% and resumed payment. In 1674 he founded a State Savings Bank which paid 5% and promised to repay capital on demand. He so far improved public credit that in 1679 he could offer *rentes* for public subscription at 5–5⅞% and have them oversubscribed, using some part of the proceeds to pay off old *rentes* that carried higher rates. After his death in 1683 the French budget was again disorganized. Some rentes were created between 1688 and 1697 which again paid 8⅓%. (401)

Spain

The record of interest rates in seventeenth-century Spain is, as usual, very brief. Crisis followed crisis, and compulsory consolidations of debt were customary. The resulting annuities (rate unstated) were serviced in copper, if at all. Theologians helped by accusing the creditors of usury. In the bankruptcy of 1647, when the debt to all creditors except four Genoese banks (which presumably held, as usual, precious metal as collateral) was annulled, the royal revenues were found to be mortgaged seven years ahead. In 1673 an interest rate of 40% was paid by the Spanish Crown for short-term floating debt. (346) State bankruptcies occurred again in 1686 and in 1700, throughout the eighteenth century, and in 1820, 1837, 1851 and 1873. Thus, in this century of contrasts, the trends and levels of interest rates were very different in the various countries reviewed and often foreshadowed much of the future economic and political power of each country.

Italy

In the seventeenth century the history of Italian international banking faded away. It had long outlasted the prosperity of Italian commerce.

For Venice we have no reliably reported rates. In a war, 1645–1658, Venice lost most of what remained of her overseas empire. This war was financed by a consolidation of government debt and the sale of treasury bonds under their value. (347)

For the first quarter of this century there is a continuation of the series of *rates of discount* for the 4–5 year deferred dividends of the Bank

TABLE 10

SUMMARY OF SEVENTEENTH-CENTURY INTEREST RATES

Loans to Princes (Short Term)

England	Crown loans by goldsmiths, usual	1640–1690	6–12%
England	Crown loans by goldsmiths, emergency	1640–1690	20–30
France	From *partisans*	1643–1661	15–60
Spain	Example	1673	40

Commercial Loans (Short Term)

England	Legal limit (all private loans)	1571–1624	10%
England	Legal limit (all private loans)	1624–1651	8
England	Legal limit (all private loans)	1651–1714	6
England	Chamber loans to merchants	1630	6–7
England	Good credit loans	1640	8
England	Good credit loans	1688	4–6
England	Bank of England discounts	1694–1699	3–6
Holland	Private loans	1650–1675	$3–4\frac{1}{2}$
Holland	Private loans as low as	1700	$1\frac{3}{4}$–2

Deposits (Short Term)

England	Goldsmiths pay	1660–1690	4–6%
Holland	City of Amsterdam	1603	$6\frac{1}{6}$–$8\frac{1}{3}$
Holland	City of Amsterdam	1659–1700	3–4
France	State Savings Bank pays	1674	5

Annuities and Mortgages (Long Term)

England	Mortgage loans	1600–1625	10%
England	Mortgage loans	1666	4–6
England	Mortgage loans	1670	4
England	Mortgage loans	1687	?–5
England	Mortgage loans	1696	5–6
England	Private bonded debt (example)	1675–1677	5–6

Loans to States (Long Term)

England	A government life annuity	1692	10%
England	A government 16-year lottery loan	1693	14
England	A government perpetual annuity; advanced by Bank of England	1694	8+
Holland	Sinking fund annuities of government	1600–1640	$6\frac{1}{6}$–$8\frac{1}{3}$
Holland	Sinking fund annuities of government	1640–1672	$3\frac{3}{4}$–5
Holland	Sinking fund of government (war)	1672–1700	4–$12\frac{1}{2}$
Holland	Sinking fund of government (peace)	1672–1700	3–$3\frac{3}{4}$
France	*Rentes*	1679	5–$5\frac{7}{8}$
France	*Rentes*	1688–1697	$8\frac{1}{3}$
Genoa	Rate of discount on declared dividends of Bank of St. George payable in 4–5 years: 1600–1606?, $2\frac{1}{8}$–$4\frac{3}{8}$? 1607–1621?, $1\frac{1}{8}$–$2\frac{5}{8}$? 1622–1625?, $3\frac{3}{4}$–$5\frac{1}{2}$?		

of St. George (see sixteenth-century "Loans to States," page 119). These were as follows: (323)

Year	%	Year	%	Year	%	Year	%
1600	$2\frac{7}{8}$	1606	$4\frac{3}{8}$	1613	$1\frac{5}{8}$	1619	$1\frac{1}{8}$
1601	3	1607	$2\frac{3}{8}$	1614	$1\frac{3}{4}$	1620	$1\frac{1}{4}$
1602	$2\frac{7}{8}$	1608	$2\frac{5}{8}$	1615	$1\frac{5}{8}$	1621	$1\frac{5}{8}$
1603	$3\frac{5}{8}$	1609	$2\frac{5}{8}$	1616	$1\frac{5}{8}$	1622	$4\frac{1}{4}$
1604	$2\frac{3}{8}$	1610	$2\frac{3}{8}$	1617	$1\frac{3}{8}$	1623	$3\frac{3}{4}$
1605	$2\frac{1}{8}$	1611	$1\frac{7}{8}$	1618	$1\frac{3}{8}$	1624	$5\frac{1}{2}$
		1612	2			1625	$5\frac{1}{4}$

Although the *luoghi* of Genoa were outstanding long after 1625, a disturbance after that date in the value relationship between money of account and effective money as used by the bank makes further interest calculations unreliable. The speculative character of the boom between 1615 and 1619 was marked by a rise in the price of the *luoghi* from 3920 per 1000 to 5100 per 1000, without any increase in the dividend; thus their dividend yield declined to around 1.1% per annum. Thereafter the price dropped sharply to 3965. While the dividend yield on the *luoghi* rose only to 1.3%, the discount rate of interest rose sharply from 1.1 to 5.5%, the highest annual average since 1568. This decline in price and rise in rates was probably associated with the financial difficulties of Genoa's great protector and creditor, Spain.

Chapter X

A Summary and Analysis of Medieval and Renaissance Interest Rates in Western Europe

When the history of Western European interest rates was resumed in the twelfth century, after nine centuries of darkness, the types of credit were stated very generally, and the rates were sparsely reported. Nevertheless, the credit forms were much more recognizable than were many ancient credit forms. In fact, although some were different from modern credit forms, the evolution of modern credit forms can be traced directly from those of the Middle Ages.

As early as the twelfth century short-term commercial credit was represented by an early form of the bill of exchange. Medieval census annuities somewhat resembled the modern bond or mortgage or perpetual annuity. For the thirteenth century some quotations were preserved on interest from deposits with bankers and on rates on the marketable perpetual debt of the Republic of Venice. From this century on the data improve, thanks to the excellent research of a few modern economic historians who are also medievalists. There are serious gaps in the data and a great deal of room for additional research, but rates are much more often specifically defined and differentiated than are ancient interest rates.

VOLATILITY

A new problem for this history arises with the development of the medieval money market and the volatility of the rates on such instruments as the commercial bill. No longer do the data represent principally interest rates on conventional, sluggish "normal" loans, such as the consumer loans which dominated ancient credit. Consumer credit existed in the Middle Ages in volume, but it was largely illicit and probably was often under cover, in part obtained from the pawnshops, in part from the loan sharks, and in part disguised as commercial transactions. The high rates sometimes paid by monarchs have been cited. It can be conjectured that the lesser nobility sometimes paid similar high rates when in need. This history, however, from now on is primarily concerned with volatile commercial rates, deposit rates, annuity rates, and rates paid by free cities.

The new factor which complicates rate reporting is the volatility of some of the rates, especially the volatility of commercial loan rates. In this respect medieval rates resembled modern money market rates much more than they did ancient "normal" rates. In the sixteenth century, for example, prime bill rates in Antwerp were quoted as low as 4% and as high as 13%, and it might be wrong to read a trend into the range; the year 1546 alone saw a range of at least 7 to 13%. This degree of short-term volatility is not unlike that seen in the modern bill market in New York or in London. It is, however, far greater than the range of the stable rates usually reported from antiquity. When such a wide range was reported for commercial loans, it did not necessarily mean differences in credit risk, although there were big differences, but could be accounted for by day-to-day differences in the condition of the money market. From this distance it is impossible to distinguish.

Today, the statistical problem of volatility is met by averaging rates on uniform loans, and thus computing monthly average rates or yearly average rates, and also by reporting highs and lows. No such complete data exist for the Middle Ages. Therefore, the tables often are based only on wide ranges. However, the data are sufficient to provide a good general impression of the sort of interest rates prevailing for good credits most of the time from the twelfth century onward. Interest rate trends can also be distinguished.

Table 11 below attempts to summarize medieval and Renaissance interest rates on best credits. All princely and usurious rates have been omitted. The nominal rates on forced loans and usually the rates on annuities sold by princes have also been omitted, because these latter often represented involuntary compositions. The table consists only of the reported high and low rates of interest for each half century on commercial bills, deposits, and long-term annuities, mortgages or bonds of citizens, towns, and governments.

CREDIT STRUCTURE

Before attempting to analyze these rates, a few of the differences in the medieval credit structure from ancient and also from modern times should be reviewed together with the similarities and the evolution toward modern forms.

In medieval times there was far more evidence of state loans, city loans and princely loans than in ancient times. Credit gradually became a political device and has remained so ever since: an essential weapon of politics and of national defense or offense. The princes, however, rarely managed to develop efficient state credit. Something like modern methods of state finance were developed only by the northern free towns and by the Italian republics; these methods were later adopted by Holland and England. The consent of the propertied public was the essential ingredient. The ultimate triumph of more democratic governments throughout much of northern Europe was probably due in part to the ability of these governments to mobilize their enormous public resources. Spain failed absolutely. The French monarchy at times seemed to succeed but quickly relapsed into arbitrary state finance.

The principal credit form of the free towns and provinces was the traditional census annuity, the long-term pledge of annual income payments, often running to perpetuity, with no obligatory repayment of principal. No such instruments were in general use in ancient times, although there were one or two experiments with annuities. Out of these perpetual annuities have evolved the modern funded debts of the nations. A more or less distant maturity is now added to funded debts, but if maturity is twenty, thirty, or fifty years off, the practical difference from the perpetual annuity is slight.

These annuities in northern Europe apparently had no secondary market in early centuries. However, the perpetual obligations of Venice developed an active secondary or bourse market in the thirteenth century; their form was almost identical with the northern town annuities, but they were originally issued as forced assessments and they were uniform. There was also an active bourse market for Genoese obligations in the sixteenth century. In the seventeenth century, Dutch annuities became marketable, and some sort of market developed at times for French *rentes* (another term for perpetual annuities). In each case marketability seemed to coincide with lower interest rates, but this may or may not have been a result of cause and effect. The lower rates may have been due to the simple fact that all interest rates were declining throughout most of the period under review. By the end of the Renaissance, something close to modern governmental long-term bonds had thus developed. The modern short-term government "bill market," however, had not yet appeared.

Deposit banking existed throughout the Middle Ages, but in a form at first more resembling ancient banking than modern. Bankers were private merchants. In Italy they were subject to official rules and regulations. They carried on all of the banking activities of antiquity and these included most of the modern banking functions in rudimentary form. There were even a few official or quasi-official banks organized very early. Dates of origin and the functions of these banks were as follows:

1157	The Bank of Venice	Deposit and transfer
1401	The Bank of Barcelona	Transfer
1407	The Bank of St. George (Genoa)	Transfer
1587	The Bank of the Rialto (Venice)	Deposit and transfer
1609	The Amsterdam Wisselbank	Deposit and transfer
1656	The Bank of Sweden	Deposit and issue (first)
1694	The Bank of England	Deposit, transfer, loan, and issue

A basic difference from the present was the lack of large private corporations. Toward the end of the Renaissance trading companies that had commercial monopolies along nationalistic lines were organized, and their securities soon enjoyed an active market. But industry, and hence modern capitalism, had to await the industrial revolution. Long-term private loans, therefore, were not yet in modern form. They comprised principally the census annuities issued by farmers on their land, or issued by quasi-public authorities on their revenues; they were sometimes perpetual and at other times redeemable or for one or more lives.

Investment of the surplus funds of the private man of wealth in credit instruments was not yet convenient and well organized. Merchants, with their expert knowledge, capital, and connections abroad, could manage to invest well enough, but the amateur capitalist still usually hoarded metal, deposited with bankers or bought land. There is good evidence, however, that investable surpluses were accumulating rapidly in the sixteenth and seventeenth centuries. When convenient and suitable credit forms were developed, such as the Dutch and British funded debt, they quickly attracted very large funds.

THE TREND OF INTEREST RATES

Table 11 supports the opinion often expressed by economic historians that interest rates declined during much of the later Middle Ages and

TABLE 11

Review of Medieval and Renaissance Interest Rates in Western Europe

Century	Commercial Loans—Short				
	Spanish Netherlands	Dutch Republic	Italy	France	England
Twelfth					
1st Half					
2nd Half	10 *–16		20		
Thirteenth					
1st Half	10–16		20–25		
2nd Half	10–16		8–15	15–20	
Fourteenth					
1st Half	10–25		7–15	15–20	
2nd Half	10–25		5–15	15–20	
Fifteenth					
1st Half	(8)–(17) †		5–15		
2nd Half	(8)–(17)		5–15		
Sixteenth					
1st Half	4–13		(4)–(13) +	5–12	
2nd Half	7–12 +		(7)–(12)	8–12 +	
Seventeenth					
1st Half		6–12			6–10
2nd Half		1¾–4½			3–6

Century	Deposits—Short					
	Spanish Netherlands	Dutch Republic	Italy	England	Germany	Spain
Twelfth						
1st Half						
2nd Half						
Thirteenth						
1st Half			10–20			
2nd Half			10–20			
Fourteenth						
1st Half			5–12			
2nd Half	10		5–12			
Fifteenth						
1st Half	5		5–10	10	5	
2nd Half	5		5–10	10	5	
Sixteenth						
1st Half	4–6¼		4–6		4½–5	4–5
2nd Half	6¼		5–6		5–7	5
Seventeenth						
1st Half		6⅙–8⅓		6		
2nd Half		3–4		4–6		

TABLE 11 (*Continued*)

Century	Census Annuities, Mortgages, Other Long-Term Debts						
	Spanish Nether-lands	Dutch Re-public	Italy	France	Germany	England	Spain
Twelfth							
1st Half							
2nd Half	8–10						
Thirteenth							
1st Half	8–10						
2nd Half	8–10		$6\frac{5}{8}$–$8\frac{3}{4}$	14?			
Fourteenth							
1st Half	8–10		$4\frac{7}{8}$–$8\frac{3}{4}$				
2nd Half	8–10		$5\frac{1}{4}$–10+				
Fifteenth							
1st Half	8–12		6–10+	10			4–10
2nd Half	8–12		5–10	10	5		4–10
Sixteenth							
1st Half	4–10	$8\frac{1}{3}$	4–10	$8\frac{1}{3}$	4–10	10–14	
2nd Half	4–10	$6\frac{1}{6}$–$8\frac{1}{3}$	4–10	$8\frac{1}{3}$+	4–12	10–14	
Seventeenth							
1st Half		5–$8\frac{1}{3}$		$8\frac{1}{3}$		8–10	
2nd Half		3–$12\frac{1}{2}$		5–$8\frac{1}{3}$		4–6	

NOTES

* The lowest reported rate for each half century is underlined.

† Because of the importance of Italian bankers in the Netherlands, the lack of Netherlands rates in the fifteenth century is supplied by interpolation influenced by Italian rates, while the lack of Italian rates in the sixteenth century is supplied by assuming the same range as in the Netherlands.

Rates are derived from Tables 5, 6, 7, 8, 9, and 10.

Renaissance. The earliest short-term rates quoted were somewhat higher than the last and highest of the western Roman legal limits. They were not too different from early Greek rates and were within the range of Babylonian rates, although the credit forms were very different from ancient credit forms. The later Renaissance rates were well within the range of modern rates and the lowest were far below modern rates in periods of credit stringency.

As most of Western Europe throughout most of this period was in effect one money market dominated by Italians, very little weight should be put on variations of bill rates from place to place. The Italians dominated the Netherlands bill market, and, therefore, differences in quotations between Italy and the Netherlands may be accidents of reporting.

Only in the seventeenth century did the money markets divide by national boundaries. In the seventeenth century, low rates developed in England and Holland, while the markets formerly dominated by Italians, including that of Antwerp, were disorganized following the disasters to their chief debtor, the Spanish Crown.

One more step in simplification for trend analysis is possible, and this is presented in Charts 2 and 3. The charts picture the principal rates for the period under review in terms of minimum rates reported for each half century. Chart 2 is arranged by type of credit, and Chart 3 is arranged geographically.

The method of using minimum rates to determine interest rate trends is informative. Today the use of "prime rates" and AAA averages is customary to indicate interest rate trends. There is a very large range of rates higher than minimum rates at all times, and there is no top limit except legal maxima. Averages of rates, if they did exist, might be merely averages of good credits with bad credits. The lowest regularly reported rates, excluding eccentric rates, comprise a practical limit comparable over time. Minimum rates will not show us where most funds were lending, but they should provide a fair index number for measuring long-term interest rate trends.

Chart 2 pictures the lowest reported rates of Western Europe, regardless of country, subdivided according to three types of credit: commercial loans, assumed to be short term; deposits with bankers, short term; census loans, mortgages, and annuities, assumed to be long term. For each type the country from which the low quotation is derived at each period is designated by a letter. Thus the geographical shift of minimum reported rates can be traced, although national boundaries only become significant toward the end of this period.

Chart 2A suggests that a substantial decline in minimum commercial loan rates occurred in the late thirteenth and fourteenth centuries; that there was stability in the fifteenth century; that a further decline occurred in the early sixteenth century, followed by a sharp rise in the late sixteenth century, the period of Spanish and French defaults. The decline was resumed in the seventeenth century, but now the lowest rates were to be found in England and Holland, whereas earlier the lowest rates were reported largely from the Spanish Netherlands and Italy. The lowest commercial rates at the end of the seventeenth century—around 2%—were within the modern range.

Such tables and charts as these are useful to summarize our data. Unfortunately, our data are not adequate to assure us that they adequately portray the level of the market at many periods of time. The general levels, however, and the trends are probably valid.

Chart 2B pictures in the same way the more sluggish deposit rates.

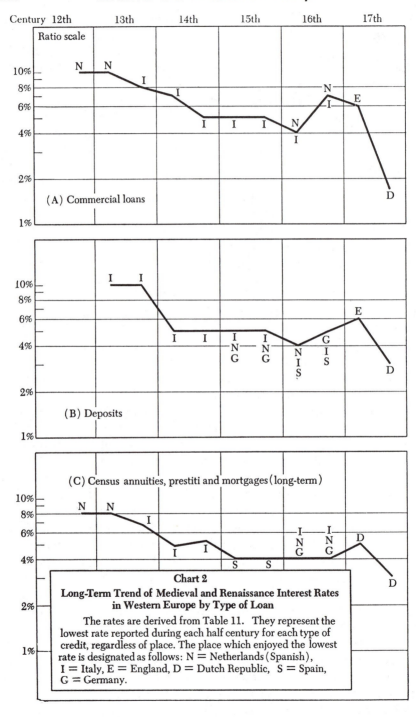

Century 12th   13th   14th   15th   16th   17th

(A) Commercial loans

(B) Deposits

(C) Census annuities, prestiti and mortgages (long-term)

Chart 2

Long-Term Trend of Medieval and Renaissance Interest Rates in Western Europe by Type of Loan

The rates are derived from Table 11. They represent the lowest rate reported during each half century for each type of credit, regardless of place. The place which enjoyed the lowest rate is designated as follows: N = Netherlands (Spanish), I = Italy, E = England, D = Dutch Republic, S = Spain, G = Germany.

They show a very sharp decline between the thirteenth and fourteenth centuries, then a rise in the late sixteenth century, and a sharp decline in the seventeenth century. They confirm the trends shown by commercial rates.

Chart 2C, which deals with long-term credits, suggests that in the twelfth and thirteenth centuries these annuities commanded rates below minimum rates on short-term credits. However, during the lower interest rate periods of the fifteenth and sixteenth centuries there was not much difference between the long and the short rates, whereas late in the seventeenth century, when minimum rates were lowest, the lowest rates were commanded by short-term credits. A suprasecular decline in interest rates is evident for long-term loans in these centuries. The decline of long rates was especially noticeable in the thirteenth, fourteenth, and fifteenth centuries, the rise was moderate in the late sixteenth century, and the decline was sharp in the seventeenth century.

Chart 3 gives the same picture of declining interest rates geographically. Chart 3A suggests very little variation of minimum rates in the Netherlands, either short or long, in the twelfth, thirteenth, and fourteenth centuries; a decline in the fifteenth and especially the early sixteenth centuries, when Antwerp became the money market for Europe and was dominated by Italian and German merchant-bankers; and a final fillip in the late sixteenth century when Antwerp was destroyed. Dutch rates started the sixteenth century higher than Antwerp (Spanish Netherlands) rates, soon declined sharply, and plunged in the late seventeenth century.

Chart 3B suggests that the decline in interest rates may have begun in Italy a century or more before it began elsewhere. We have no early census quotations for Italy, but by the time the Venetian *prestiti* were quoted in the late thirteenth century their range was not very different from minimum commercial and deposit rates. Minimum commercial rates rose sharply in the late sixteenth century.

Chart 3C shows that French minimum commercial rates, also dominated by Italian bankers, remained high—in fact, above Netherlands and Italian rates—in the thirteenth and fourteenth centuries, were low in the early sixteenth century, and then rose sharply with the late sixteenth-century defaults. The rates on French *rentes* declined over the centuries. English rates are included on this chart for convenience only; they were very little influenced by French or other continental rates before the seventeenth century. The earliest reported English long-term rates in the early sixteenth century were far higher than most continental minima, but in the seventeenth century they declined sharply.

These charts do not reflect the great rise and fall of whole civilizations such as were embraced within Chart 1, which summarized ancient in-

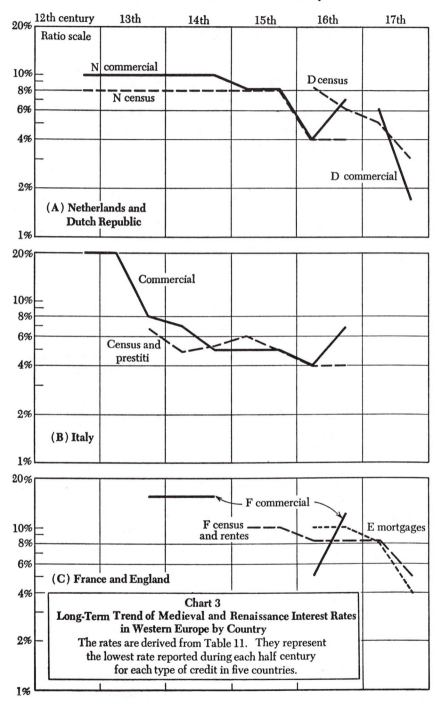

Chart 3
Long-Term Trend of Medieval and Renaissance Interest Rates
in Western Europe by Country
The rates are derived from Table 11. They represent
the lowest rate reported during each half century
for each type of credit in five countries.

terest rates. The time span was shorter. The political entities, instead of great empires, were at first local; most of the time they were not even organized as great nations. These charts cover a period which contained the gradual evolution of modern banking techniques, but it breaks off just as these were becoming fully formed and effective. The terminal date of 1700 is artificial. The history of interest rates in Western Europe is continued in succeeding chapters.

PART THREE

Modern Europe and North America to 1900

Chapter XI

England in the Eighteenth Century

THE ORIGIN OF THE FUNDED DEBT AND OF THE BANK OF ENGLAND

England was transformed financially as well as politically by the Revolution of 1688. Under the reigns of the Tudors and the Stuarts, no money or investment markets comparable to those of Antwerp, Lyons, and Amsterdam had appeared in London. On the Continent during the fifteenth and sixteenth centuries the Italians had played a leading role in developing a complicated system of private international banking. During the seventeenth century the Dutch had developed effective state finance based on confidence in a popular government's ability to pledge the resources of a town, province, or nation. It was now England's turn to achieve financial leadership. Within the first few decades of the eighteenth century, England improved upon the Italian banking techniques and upon the Dutch principles of funded debt. The city of London learned how to mobilize the savings of the people for commercial and for national objectives.

Because this transformation has an important bearing on the history of interest rates, it is presented here in some detail and with retrospective background. Furthermore, the history of English credit and interest rates in the eighteenth and nineteenth centuries is discussed in greater detail than that of other European countries because of the leading role that England then played in the development of all modern money markets.

Up to the last decade of the seventeenth century England had no money market, no substantial bank, and no organized national debt. Stuart kings borrowed haphazardly from goldsmiths on short term; sometimes they paid very high rates of interest. They occasionally defaulted in the Spanish manner. These were personal princely loans in the style of the Middle Ages.

Nevertheless, during the seventeenth century great wealth was accumulating in England. New credit forms also were being developed which when combined with continental banking methods were to prove highly effective. As a result of the growth of domestic and foreign commerical ventures, land was no longer the only important form of income-yielding wealth in England. Capital could be held in trade ventures.

Owners of cash could deposit it with London goldsmiths. The goldsmiths issued receipts for the cash. Presently these receipts became payable to bearer: this was the birth of the modern bank note.

The check also was developed to permit distant remittances when bills of exchange or bank notes were not appropriate, but it was not widely used. An early check, dated July 11, 1676, was worded as follows:

> Mr. Hoare:
> Pray pay to the bearer hereof Mr. Witt Morgan fifty-four pounds ten shillings and ten pence and take his receipt for the same.
>
> >   Your loving friend
> >   Will Hale.
>
> For Mr. Richard Hoare at the Golden Bottle in Cheapside. (348)

An influx of American gold and silver augmented liquid capital. Also London goldsmiths discovered what Italian bankers had long since discovered, namely, that they needed to keep on hand only a fraction of the cash deposited with them and could lend or invest the larger part. Therefore, instead of charging a fee for accepting deposits, they began to pay interest on deposits. Since there were in England no laws forbidding interest, but only laws limiting the rate of interest, the merchants and the goldsmiths developed the "inland bill of exchange." This was an undisguised loan instrument at explicit rates of interest created by trade between domestic merchants. It was uncomplicated by a foreign exchange contract, such as was used to obscure the interest in many Italian bills of exchange. London merchants borrowed openly from each other and from the goldsmiths at interest.

There was in England, as yet, no officially recognized and generally respected public bank. The need for such a bank was felt keenly when in 1672 Charles II stopped payments on the deposits of the goldsmiths at the Exchequer and ruined several of the most prominent of them. The Italian republics had enjoyed the protection of officially chartered banks for several centuries. The Dutch, with the help of the Bank of Amsterdam, had attracted foreign funds, had stabilized dealings in currencies, and had provided their merchants with a reliable depository.

Proposals for organizing a Bank of London to provide security of deposit and credit on reasonable terms were in the air throughout the closing decades of the seventeenth century. Sir William Temple told his countrymen that the province of Holland had borrowed the equivalent of £5 million at 4%, that interest in Holland was always paid on the day due, and that when any of the principal of the province's debt was paid off, the public creditor "received his money with tears, well knowing he could find no other investment equally secure." (349) Some Dutch interest rates were down to 3%, while at the same time the English Crown was paying 6–30% for short-term loans.

A political environment favorable to the creation of an English national debt and a state-sponsored bank was provided by the revolution of 1688. This was not just because a Dutch prince became King William III of England, but primarily because this king was a strictly constitutional monarch with no pretensions to absolute personal power. Thus the government might now aspire to borrow in the name of the English people. It would be more accurate to say that William borrowed in the name of himself and of the great Whig mercantile interests which backed him and dominated the Parliament. Nevertheless, a union of king and country was developing. By the 1720's the English national credit could be effectively pledged behind the loans of the government in the manner of the medieval Italian republics, the provinces of seventeenth-century Holland, and modern democracies.

William III immediately engaged England in a costly war with Louis XIV of France. At first William borrowed from city goldsmiths and merchants in the old way and paid high rates, sometimes up to 30%. But the time was ripe for financial reform. The need of the government for long-term loans on reasonable terms was matched by the need of Englishmen to find suitable safe investments for their rapidly accumulating investable funds. In the absence of convenient credit instruments, metal was still hoarded, the price of land pushed up, and there was a rash of speculation in new commercial ventures. The word "stock-jobber" was coined for what is now called a promoter. "The spirit of the cogging dices of Whitefriars took possession of the grave Senators of the City." (350)

The first attempts of William's Whig government to create a funded debt were experimental and costly. They were born of the government's desperate need for cash to carry on the war with France. In 1692 the Parliament provided new duties on beer and other liquors to be set aside as security for a long-term loan of £1 million in the form of life annuities which would pay 10% until 1700 and thereafter 7% plus tontine benefits to long survivors. (351) The creditors' risk seemed considerable because William's regime was contested; if the Stuart Kings returned, they would repudiate the debts of William's government. In 1693 another long-term loan of £1 million was floated, secured by a duty on salt, at 10% interest for 16 years plus lottery benefits, which brought the cost of the loan up to 14%. (352) This type of finance was costly and unsatisfactory. The provinces of Holland were borrowing at 3–4%, and did not have to pledge specific revenues.

In 1694 another large war loan was required by the government. This time a momentous expedient was devised. As is usual with such innovations, doubts, fears, and prejudices were resolved by the acute national need and the uninviting character of the alternatives. The Parliament passed an ambiguously worded bill to impose a new duty on tonnage for the benefit of such persons as should advance money toward carrying on the war. The plan was to borrow £1,200,000 at what was then considered the moderate rate of 8%, secured by these duties; as an added inducement, the subscribers to the loan were to be given the privilege of pooling their funds and of incorporating themselves under the name of the "Governor and Company of the Bank of England." (353) In return for lending its entire capital of £1.2 million to the government, this bank would receive from the government a perpetual annuity of £100,000, or 8% interest plus £4000 a year for management, all tax-exempt. It would have the right (but not as a monopoly) to trade in bullion and bills of exchange and implicitly the right to carry on a banking business and, therefore, to issue bank notes up to an amount equal to its capital funds. (354)

The bank was at first forbidden to loan otherwise to the Crown or to trade in commodities. Its privileges would cease when the principal of the loan was repaid, but not before 1706. The loan, however, never was repaid, and the bank survives. No one was permitted to subscribe to more than £20,000 of the bank's stock. A quarter of the subscriptions was to be paid in prompt cash. The bank's liabilities were not to exceed its capital. (355) Dividends were to be paid only out of profits. The books were opened for stock subscription on June 21, 1694, and the promoters were allowed six months to find the funds. The entire amount was subscribed in twelve days. The bank commenced its operations on January 1, 1695, in the house of the Company of Grocers, with a staff of fifty-four people.

These were boom days for stock subscriptions of all sorts. The government had found a way to enlist in its support the general desire for capital gains. It repeatedly appealed to speculative hopes in its subsequent financing by selling long-term debt with lottery privileges.

The "tonnage bank," as the Bank of England was called from the nature of the tax that secured its revenue, was a political institution from the start. The Whig ministry, which supported the "Protestant succession" against the French-sponsored Stuarts, had devised a valuable ally. As it was supposed that the Stuarts would not recognize the debt to the bank, the bank could be relied upon to support the Whig government in its wars with France. This it did, but not without protracted bargaining between the cabinet and the bank. "Dutch finance," as the political enemies of the ministry called this new bank and its emissions, was distrusted by the Tories because it facilitated a large government debt, stimulated investment activity, furthered the ascendancy of the city over the country gentlemen, and financed a Whig government and a Whig war. (356)

The Bank of England accepted deposits from the government and the public. It issued bank notes payable to bearer. It issued deposit receipts, anticipating the modern passbook, and it honored drafts against deposits, anticipating the modern check. For a few years it also issued its own time paper, called "sealed bills," some of which paid no interest, and some of which bore interest at annual rates of 3% and 4½% and occasionally more. The Exchequer accepted the bank's notes as cash and paid them out to its creditors. The public used the notes to make substantial remittances. The bank discounted inland and foreign trade bills and also dealt in bullion and foreign exchange.

During its early years the bank had great difficulty in meeting the growing demands of the government and at the same time warding off competing banking schemes. The government continued to require heavy loans, and war news was often unfavorable. In 1695 the bank had to borrow £300,000 from the Estates of Holland. In 1697 some of the bank's bills were protested for nonpayment in Amsterdam; (357) the bank then offered to pay 6% in London for loans of specie and to give in return "specie notes" payable on demand in specie. In spite of these early troubles, the bank was able to advance further sums to the government when the need was desperate. In 1697 the bank almost doubled its original loan to the government. This time it received as security temporary exchequer obligations at 8%, which it was agreed would be paid off as soon as the government was in a position to do so. As an added inducement the bank was for the first time given a monopoly of joint-stock banking. So favorable were these terms that the bank could make the new loan without increasing its own capital. Peace in 1697, although brief, restored the bank to a strong position. During the next decade victory and prosperity gave the bank permanent strength.

In 1696 the government developed a new form of short-term obligation called "exchequer bills." The old exchequer tallies had been informal tax-anticipation obligations that were paid off irregularly as tax receipts permitted. Exchequer bills bore fixed interest, could not be cashed on demand, circulated by endorsement, and were to be met by the exchequer receipts of the following year. (358) They were later accepted in payment of taxes.

In 1709 the bank's charter was renewed until 1732. The government received an additional loan, and the rate of interest on its debt to the bank was reduced from 8% to 6%. The bank received the right to double its capital and hence its note issue. It also retained its monopoly of joint-stock issue banking in England.

The Bank of England was not yet a bankers' bank in the modern sense. "Bank rate" did not have its modern significance of a penalty rate charged by the lender of last resort. The bank did a retail banking business directly with merchants. It also financed the government and provided a stable circulation. Throughout the eighteenth century all banking in England that was not done by the Bank of England was done by private individuals and small partnerships. Other joint-stock banks were not yet permitted.

EIGHTEENTH-CENTURY BACKGROUND

For England the eighteenth century was a century of growing economic and political strength at home and abroad. Constitutional parliamentary government and a limited monarchy were gradually accepted by both political parties. The challenge of the Pretenders of the House of Stuart and the associated challenge of the French Monarchy were laboriously but decisively defeated. When Queen Anne, 1702–1714, was succeeded by George I, 1714–1727, this accession of the House of Hanover marked the final acceptance of the Revolution of 1688. By the time of the French Revolution in 1789, England had achieved what was essentially the modern parliamentary system. The nation was governed by a cabinet responsive to the wishes of the enfranchised voters.

The Treaty of Utrecht, 1713, ended the war with Louis XIV, who renounced the Stuarts. Nevertheless, there were attempted Stuart invasions of England in 1715–1716 and in 1745–1746. There was a war with Spain in 1717–1720, another war with Spain, the War of Jenkins's Ear, in 1739–1748, the War of the Austrian Succession in 1740–1748, and the Seven Years' War in 1755–1763. By 1763 England was for the time being at the summit of her power. She had acquired Canada, Florida, Gibraltar, and many other foreign possessions; she had established her position in India. There followed fifty years of crisis and disaster: the loss of the American colonies in the War for Independence, 1775–1783, the shock of the French Revolution, 1789, and the wars with France, which continued intermittently from 1793 until 1815.

During the eighteenth century, Englishmen turned away from religious controversy to assert themselves effectively in finance and in the world beyond their shores. They became busy with warships and cargoes and ledgers. Instead of *Pilgrim's Progress,* they read *Robinson Crusoe.* (359) The population increased by two thirds. (360) Food prices were stable in the first half of the century. Roads were still primitive, and the chief highway was the sea, but canals and turnpikes were being built by privately promoted companies. Manufacture gradually became big business. All manner of men took to inventing machines, generally aimed at the application of power to work. Marine and other forms of insurance developed. There was no deliberate debasement of the coinage throughout this century, and the currency was almost always convertible. In 1717 gold was given the status of legal tender along with the traditional silver. In 1774 a gold standard was implicitly created when payments in silver were restricted to £25. (361)

During this century of finance, the government was the chief borrower, always for wars. Government loans, which were usually in the form of perpetual annuities, set the going rate for all long-term loans. Other borrowers had to compete with government bonds, called "the funds," and were restricted by the 5% usury limit, which applied to all but government loans. The widely variable market rate of interest on government bonds was an important stimulant or break on private economic activity. (362) When the funds were high in price, that is, yielding around 3%, new private enterprises could be financed with ease at 4 or 5%; canals and turnpikes were projected, mortgages were floated to finance agricultural enclosure, and company promotions were stimulated. When the funds were low, that is, yielding 5% or so, only the government could borrow heavily, and private credit expansion was sharply curtailed. Thus, in wartime the government could pre-empt the savings of the people.

The eighteenth century was also a century of speculation. A large number of companies were promoted, and trading was active in their shares. Insurance became a popular means of gambling on ships and on lives. State loans with lotteries attached were the rule; from 1694 to 1784 there were forty-two state lotteries. They facilitated the flotation of a large national debt. Life annuities introduced another element of chance.

The South Sea Bubble of 1720 grew out of a scheme, backed by the government, to persuade the holders of almost all the new government debt to exchange their government obligations for shares in a semi-official trading company, the South Sea Company, which would hold the government debt. These shares stood at very high premiums, so that debt holders who seemed to be gaining a big premium by accepting the exchange were in reality parting with half or more of their investment. South Sea stock appreciated that year from £128 to £1000 a share. At such prices half of the government debt was exchanged for South Sea stock. By November of 1720 the bubble had burst, and South Sea stock was back to £135. As a result the Chancellor of the Exchequer was imprisoned, and the "Bubble Act" was passed, which restricted the formation of new companies.

Nevertheless, expansion, promotion, and speculation continued throughout most of this century. Stockjobbers frequented the Royal Exchange, the coffee houses, and the streets. They dealt at first largely in shares, but later also in government tallies and bills and in "government stock," which was, and is, a term used for government bonds. When, in 1719, speculation was widely denounced, a speculator replied that "there is only one way to get rid of us; pay off the national debt." In 1773 the words "the Stock Exchange" were written over the door of New Jonathan's Coffee House, and admittance was permitted only by fee. In 1802 the Stock Exchange built its own home.

Mortgages at this time did not provide, as they do today, a fixed rate of return over long periods of time. Interest was variable because usually either party could withdraw from the contract on six months' notice. Furthermore, real estate mortgages, which were a principal form of borrowing and lending between individuals, could change hands by assignment or sale. (363) Thus, mortgage rates tended to follow the rates on the funds with a lag, and mortgages became very hard to negotiate when the funds were at high rates of interest.

Although the Bank of England enjoyed a monopoly of joint-stock banking, private banking by individuals and small partnerships grew rapidly, especially during the latter half of the eighteenth century. There were between twenty and thirty private banks in London in 1750, and seventy in 1800. They accepted deposits, handled remittances, dealt in bills, and made loans. Country banks also multiplied at this time; they kept deposits with London banks, though rarely with the Bank of England. Some country banks sent the savings of agricultural communities to London to be invested, and others drew on London to finance growing manufacturing communities. The bill brokers acted as intermediaries. In 1775 the London Clearing House was established, and by its means these private London bankers were permitted to settle their daily balances by draft on the Bank of England.

At the time of the accession of William III, in 1689, the English national debt totaled under £1 million, and all of it was of a temporary character. There was no funded debt. But 128 years later, at the end of the Napoleonic Wars, the national debt totaled £900 million. During the first half of the eighteenth century the Dutch methods of funding a public debt were well learned, and two improvements were added: Complete disclosure was made of the size and terms of every issue; and uniformity and interchangeability were achieved through large issues carrying identical claims. England became a world power by the use of her national credit.

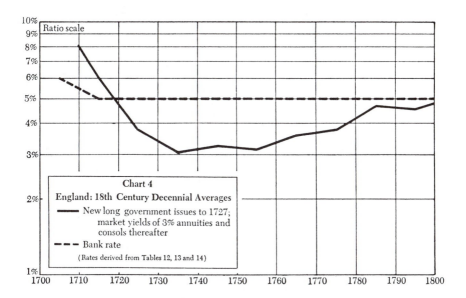

Chart 4
England: 18th Century Decennial Averages
—— New long government issues to 1727; market yields of 3% annuities and consols thereafter
--- Bank rate
(Rates derived from Tables 12, 13 and 14)

LONG-TERM INTEREST RATES

The history of the trends of long-term government bond yields in eighteenth-century England may be divided into two parts: (a) From 1700 to mid-century, the yields declined most of the time; starting at 6–8% they finally broke through 3% (Chart 5). This first, easy money period culminated in the flotation of the famous British 3% consols in 1751. (b) From 1754 on, consols fell in price, and yields rose in a highly erratic pattern. During the Napoleonic Wars at the end of the century, consols sold briefly below 50, and the government on one occasion paid over 6½% for a new loan.

When a new war with France began in 1702, it met with early success at Blenheim and Gibraltar. It was financed relatively smoothly by loans at the Bank of England for short-term requirements and by the sale to the public of annuities for long-term requirements. These annuities were negotiated at a wide variety of terms and at rates between 6 and 8.7% or higher (see Table 12). They were sometimes for one, two, or three lives, or ran to 96–99 years, or were perpetual. They were often accompanied by prizes and lotteries. Therefore, their nominal rates cannot always be translated accurately into a rate of interest.

TABLE 12

YIELDS ON NEW BRITISH GOVERNMENT LONG-TERM ISSUES:
EIGHTEENTH CENTURY

Year	Conditions of Issue	Estimated Effective Yield, %
1702	Nominal rate; yield undetermined	(6.0?)
1706	Nominal rate; yield undetermined	(6.0?)
1710	With lottery privileges	8.3
1711	With lottery privileges	8.7
1712	With lottery privileges	8.7
1713	With lottery privileges	5.9
1714	With lottery privileges	6.5
1715	New money and conversion	5.0
1717	Funding	4.0–5.0
1718	Funding	4.0–5.0
1719	New money and conversion	4.0
1721		5.0
1722	Funding; nominal rate; yield undetermined	(3.0?)
1726	With lottery privileges	3.0
1727	Conversion	4.0
1731	3s, lottery; $3\frac{1}{2}$s, new money	3.0–3.5
1736		3.0
1739		3.0
1743	Some with lottery privileges	3.0
1744	Some with lottery privileges	3.0
1745	Also lottery at 5.6% cost	3.0
1746	Also lottery at 10.2% cost	3.0
1747	With lottery privileges	4.0
1748	With lottery privileges	4.4
1749	Funding	4.0–3.0
1750	Conversion	3.0
1751	Conversion with lottery privileges	3.0
1755	With lottery privileges	2.7
1756	With lottery privileges	3.4
1757		3.7
1758	With lottery privileges	3.4
1759	With lottery privileges	3.4
1760	With lottery privileges	4.1
1761	With lottery privileges	4 0
1762		4.9
1763	Some with lottery privileges; funding	4.0
1766	With lottery privileges	3.0
1767	With lottery privileges; conversion	3.0
1768	With lottery privileges	3.0
1770	With lottery privileges; conversion	3.0
1776	With lottery privileges	3.2
1777	With lottery privileges	4.2

TABLE 12 (*Continued*)

Year	Conditions of Issue	Estimated Effective Yield, %
1778	With lottery privileges	4.5
1779	With lottery privileges	5.2
1780	With lottery privileges	5.7
1781	With lottery privileges	5.5
1782	With lottery privileges	6.8
1783	With lottery privileges	4.6
1784	Conversion and cash; some with lottery privileges	5.2–5.4
1785	Conversion	5.6
1793		4.15
1794		4.5–5.05
1795		4.70–5.40
1796		4.62–5.62
1797		6.35–6.57
1798		6.25–5.25
1800		4.41

SOURCES

Principally Jacob Cohen, "The Element of Lottery in British Government Bonds 1694–1919," *Economica* (London; The London School of Economics and Political Science), XX (1953), 242–243.

Yields at issue price are not always a simple calculation, because in many instances loans were raised by the issuance of a term annuity along with a perpetual annuity, as discussed under the Nineteenth Century. The above yield calculations are based on capitalizing the present value of the term annuities according to the nominal rate of interest on the perpetual annuities

During Queen Anne's reign, 1702–1714, the legal limit of 6% became the usual rate for public loans, although the government was not subject to the limit. (365) At this time the Bank of England first managed the subscriptions to a government loan, and after 1715 the bank generally managed the funded debt of the government as well as its floating debt. Government loans became enormously popular. In 1710, during a lottery loan at 8.3%, £500,000 was reserved for "such as brought their silver plate into the mint."

Interest rates fell in the second decade. England was on the verge of its first easy-money period. In 1714 the usury laws were amended, reducing the maximum rate from 6 to 5%. In 1715 the government sold a 5% perpetual annuity, and in 1717 it sold a 4% funding loan. This was a period of moderate debt reduction and close cooperation between the Bank, and the Exchequer. "Dealings with the state were eased and

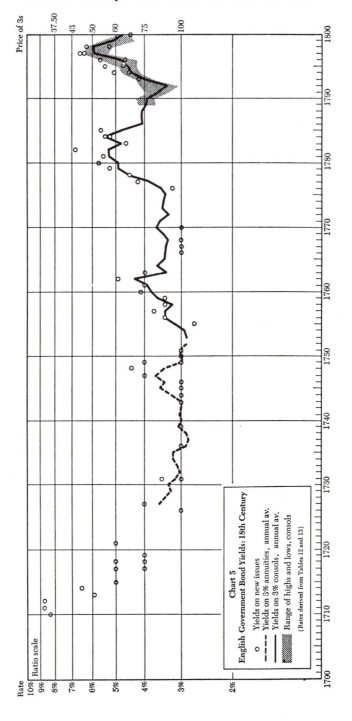

Chart 5
English Government Bond Yields: 18th Century

o   Yields on new issues
– – –   Yields on 3% annuities, annual av.
———   Yields on 3% consols, annual av.
▓   Range of highs and lows, consols

(Rates derived from Tables 12 and 13)

sweetened . . . by a pretty habit the Bank had of making a New Year's gift to the officers of the Exchequer . . . three hundred and forty guineas." (366)

As early as 1722 the government created some perpetual annuities with a nominal rate as low as 3% in a funding operation. In 1726 a loan was floated at 3% with lottery privileges attached. (365) The market value of these issues was probably well below par. Secondary market prices on an issue of 3% perpetual annuities are reported from 1727 in Table 13 (page 161). (367) Market yields of 3¼–3½% in the 1720's show that rates had indeed fallen far from the 6–8% level of two decades earlier. This was the century's only extended period of peace. There were funding and debt redemption, but there was little new financing.

In the late 1730's, with interest rates low and 3% perpetual annuities selling at times at a premium, a movement developed to reduce all public interest rates to 3%. It was pointed out that "in Holland 3% was a maximum rate; often money there yielded only 2%." (368) Low rates of interest were considered to be to the advantage of commerce and the government. But in the 1740's war began again, and the 3s declined far below par; new government debt was floated at 4%. In 1745, during the last Jacobite rebellion, the first "black Friday" occurred, and the 3s were quoted below 75 to yield over 4%. (369)

With peace in 1749, the 3s rose again to par. Henry Pelham, the Chancellor of the Exchequer, then sought to take advantage of this period of peace and low interest rates to reduce the burden of debt. He began to convert a number of funds, comprising the greater part of the national debt, into an issue of "3% consolidated annuities," the original consols. These funds are still outstanding, although they now bear a rate of 2½%. He offered holders of £57 million of 4% stock that was then selling above par and was redeemable at the option of the government, the new stock to bear 4% until 1750, 3½% until 1757, and thereafter 3%. Holders of £54 million accepted, and the balance of the 4s was paid off. Holders of other government securities received and accepted similar offers.

The new 3% consols sold above par until 1755. But by 1756, when the Seven Years' War began, consols had slipped below 90, or 3.33%; by 1858, below 80, or 3.75%; and during the final years of this highly successful war, 1761–1762, they fell below 75, or 4%. In 1762 the government paid 4.90% for a new war loan; it offered perpetual 4s at 100, and subscribers also received without extra charge a 100-year annuity worth almost 1% per annum additional income.

Pelham's famous conversion provided the historian of interest rates with a valuable tool: an issue of prime long-term debt, the consols, outstanding in large volume and actively traded for over two hundred years. The consols were and are perpetual, and in this they resembled the

Venetian *prestiti:* holders could never claim their principal, but the stock could, after a specified date, be retired at the option of the government at 100. Their yield, figured by a simple ratio of price to nominal rate, gave a rough picture of the level and also of the fluctuations of long-term prime interest rates in eighteenth- and nineteenth-century England. Two qualifications, however, must be mentioned. First, when the price of consols was high, that is, not far below 100 or at a premium, their yield was apt to be higher than other long-term rates because of the possibility of redemption, which might not apply to funds selling at a lower price. Second, when the price was very low their yield was apt to fall below other long-term rates partly because of their almost total immunity to early redemption and partly because of expectation of large price recovery.

Table 13 gives annual prices and yields of the old 3% annuities from 1727 to 1752 and of the 3% consols from 1753 to 1800. Table 12 gave estimates of the rates paid by the government on its principal new long-term issues. Chart 4 summarizes the data by means of decennial averages, and Chart 5 pictures it in annual averages. For a chart of British consol yields continuously to 1989, see Chart 52 in Chapter XIX.

By 1762 the national debt totaled £110 million, and annual interest payments totaled £3.79 million, a ratio of 3.42%. Of this debt 70% was managed at the Bank of England, and of this the larger part was the consolidated 3% funds and the later 3½ and 4% funds. (370) The bank itself owned some £11.7 million of government debt. During the peace that began in 1763, following the victorious Seven Years' War, some debt was repaid. The 3% consols recovered to prices above 90.

In 1775 the long and costly War for American Independence broke out, in the course of which France, Spain, and Holland came in against England. Consols declined disastrously. At one time they sold as low as 54, or 5.56%. The national debt more than doubled, reaching £244 million, and stood at an average interest cost of 3.8%. Many new loans were floated at rates rising from 3.22 to 4.50 to 6.80%, allowing for bonuses paid to subscribers and discount prices. During the respite following the Treaty of Paris, 1783, consols rallied to 97. They almost doubled in price from their low.

In 1793 the wars with France broke out. These turned out to be the most costly and terrible of all wars up to that time. Consols declined to new lows. They sold at 47¼ in 1798, a high yield of 6.35%, the highest yield in their long history until 1961. In 1796 the government floated its famous Loyalty Loan in the form of 5% annuities at 89% of par to yield 5.62%. In 1797 it paid 6.57% for new long-term funds. The eighteenth century ended as it had begun, in a period of war and of very high interest rates. It was not until well after the end of the Napoleonic Wars

TABLE 13

Prices and Yields of Long-Term British Government Securities: Eighteenth Century

Left section — **Old 3% Annuities** (and, for 1753–1755, **3% Consols**):

Year	Price *	Yield, %
1727	84	3.57
1728		
1729	93	3.24
1730	91	3.30
1731	96	3.12
1732	99	3.03
1733	97	3.09
1734	94	3.19
1735	94	3.19
1736	105	2.86
1737	106	2.83
1738	105	2.86
1739	98	3.06
10-yr. av.		3.05
1740	100	3.00
1741	99	3.03
1742	100	3.00
1743	101	2.97
1744	93	3.24
1745	85	3.53
1746	88	3.41
1747	82	3.66
1748	88	3.41
1749	101	2.97
10-yr. av.		3.22
1750	100	3.00
1751	99	3.03
1752	105	2.86
3% Consols		
1753	$104\frac{7}{8}$	2.86
1754	$103\frac{1}{16}$	2.91
1755	$95\frac{1}{2}$	3.14

Right section — **3% Consols**:

Year	Annual Average Price *	Yield, %	Other Quotations Price	Yield, %
1756	89	3.37		
1757	$88\frac{1}{2}$	3.39		
1758	$93\frac{7}{16}$	3.21	89	3.37
1759	$83\frac{9}{16}$	3.59	81	3.71
10-yr. av.		3.13		
1760	$79\frac{9}{16}$	3.77	82	3.66
1761	$76\frac{15}{16}$	3.90	74	4.06
1762	$69\frac{15}{16}$	4.29	80	3.75
1763	89	3.37	84	3.58
1764	$83\frac{1}{8}$	3.61	83	3.62
1765	88	3.41	89	3.38
1766	$88\frac{1}{2}$	3.39	87	3.45
1767	89	3.37	88	3.41
1768	$90\frac{5}{8}$	3.31	89	3.38
1769	$86\frac{7}{16}$	3.47	88	3.41
10-yr. av.		3.59		
1770	$82\frac{3}{8}$	3.64	78	3.86
1771	$84\frac{1}{2}$	3.55	87	3.45
1772	$90\frac{15}{16}$	3.30	89	3.38
1773	$86\frac{7}{16}$	3.47	87	3.45
1774	$87\frac{7}{16}$	3.43	88	3.41
1775	$88\frac{1}{2}$	3.39	89	3.38
1776	$85\frac{1}{2}$	3.51	83	3.62
1777	$77\frac{15}{16}$	3.85	78	3.86
1778	$66\frac{1}{2}$	4.51	64	4.70
1779	$61\frac{1}{2}$	4.88	61	4.91
10-yr. av.		3.75		
1780	$61\frac{1}{2}$	4.88	63	4.76
1781	$57\frac{1}{2}$	5.22	56	5.36
1782	57	5.26	57	5.26
1783	63	4.76	66	4.55
1784	$55\frac{7}{16}$	5.41	54	5.56
1785	63	4.76	65	4.61
1786	74	4.06	74	4.06
1787	$73\frac{1}{2}$	4.08	69	4.35
1788	74	4 06		

* Price is always quoted as a percent of par.

TABLE 13 (*Continued*)

Year	3% Consols					
	Annual Average		Annual High Prices		Annual Low Prices	
	Price	Yield, %	High Price	Yield, %	Low Price	Yield, %
1789	76½	3.92	81¼	3.69	71⅝	4.19
10-yr. av.		4.64				
1790	76⅞	3.90	80⅞	3.71	70½	4.25
1791	83¾	3.58	89¾	3.34	75¾	3.96
1792	90	3.33	97⅛	3.08	72½	4.14
1793	75¾	3.96	81	3.70	70½	4.25
1794	68 3/16	4.40	72⅜	4.14	62¾	4.78
1795	66⅜	4.52	70½	4.25	61	4.91
1796	62½	4.80	70⅝	4.24	53¼	5.63
1797	50 13/16	5.90	56½	5.30	47½	6.31
1798	50½	5.94	58	5.16	47¼	6.35
1799	59 3/16	5.07	69	4.34	52⅝	5.69
10-yr. av.		4.54				
1800	63 11/16	4.71	67¼	4.46	60	5.00

SOURCES

T. S. Ashton, *The Economic History of England: 18th Century*. London: Methuen & Co., Ltd., 1955. P. 251.

G. F. Warren and F. A. Pearson, *Prices*. New York: John Wiley & Sons, Inc., 1933. P. 273.

Charles Fenn, *Fenn's Compendium of the English and Foreign Funds*. London: Effingham Wilson, 14th ed., 1889. P. 29.

that England again experienced a period of sustained low interest rates.

The market yield on the funds usually set the minimum market rate of interest for long-term loans of all sorts. Although there is no systematic record of other long-term rates, investment opportunities at much higher rates were common. In 1735, when government annuities yielded 3.19%, a loan floated in London on the security of the German emperor's silver mines carried interest at 7%. (371) In 1744 a loan to the King of Sardinia was floated at 6% when the consols were at 3.24%. In 1753 a loan to the city of Danzig was floated at 5% when consols were at 2.86%.

Interest rates on real estate mortgages were subject to usury laws and, therefore, were not always free to reflect supply and demand. Furthermore, as the terms were subject to renegotiation from year to year, the rates were not true long-term contractual rates of interest. Neither were they rates on short-term self-liquidating loans. A series of mortgage rates charged by the Sun Fire office of London may be summarized as follows:

Period	Average Mortgage Rate, %	Average Yields on the 3% Funds, %
1736–1739	4	2.93
1740–1749	$4\frac{1}{2}$	3.22
1750–1759	$4\frac{1}{4}$	3.13
1760–1769	$4\frac{5}{8}$	3.59
1770–1779	$4\frac{1}{4}$	3.75
1780–1789	$4\frac{7}{8}$	4.64
1790–1799	$4\frac{3}{4}$	4.54

The fluctuations of these mortgage rates were largely independent of bank rate, which was fixed at 5% throughout this period. They tended to change in the same direction as the yield on the funds, but at highly variable differentials. Other real estate mortgage rates are quoted at 4 to 5% from 1725 to 1800. Cases of public utility loans for turnpikes and improvements are cited at 3½ to 5% (372), usually fluctuating with, but above, consol yields.

SHORT-TERM INTEREST RATES

From the time of its organization the Bank of England dominated the British bill market. The bank's discount rates were not, as now, penalty rates, at which other bankers would borrow only in case of need. The bank was a commercial bank in almost the modern sense, and its discount rates were the rates at which it would discount prime short bills for its depositors and, at its discretion, for others. The bank had the privilege of issuing its own bank notes in exchange for bills or of creating deposits for the same purpose. Discounting rapidly became an important source of its revenue.

In the eighteenth century English trade both large and small was carried on by bills. Every manufacturer and merchant wrote bills freely. At times manufacturers even paid wages in their own small bills, which were redeemed by retailers at various discounts. The usury laws put a ceiling on the rate of discount of bills. The legal limit was 6% to 1714 and 5% thereafter. Of course, there were violations; for example, one usurious rate of 250% a year is quoted as the charge of an individual moneylender. (373) We have, however, no annual data reporting the history of English bill rates at this period except for bank rate.

The history of bank rate in the eighteenth century showed no such volatility as the history of yields on the funds or the history of discount rates in the nineteenth century. The bank's discount rate was usually at or near the legal maximum, except for a few sharp dips early in the century. There is no recorded evidence of anything like the volatile international bill market of sixteenth-century Antwerp. From 1746 to 1822 the Bank of England's discount rate for domestic bills stood unchanged at the legal maximum of 5%. This was true when the funds yielded 3% and also when the funds yielded 5–6%. Lower bill rates were negotiated by private banks from time to time, but nothing like the low commercial rates of Holland were reported for eighteenth-century England.

In its early years the bank's discount window clearly depressed bill rates below the very high levels at times charged by seventeenth-century goldsmiths. In 1694 the bank set its discount rate at 6% for all domestic bills. At first it also set a 6% rate for foreign bills, but a month later it lowered the discount on foreign bills to 4½% and a few months later restored it to 6%. In 1695 it kept the 6% rate for the generality of domestic and foreign bills, but for those who kept their accounts with the bank it made preferential discount rates of 4½% and then 3%. This was a revolutionary decline in rates in a few years. It looked indeed like "Dutch finance." But by 1719, 5% was more usual. The low rates achieved by the funds after 1720 were not duplicated by low discount rates in this century.

Table 14 is based largely on the established rates of discount of the Bank of England. The table is not complete. There are indications that market rates were at times below bank rate. Chart 4 (page 155) compares bank rate with the effective yields of new long-term government securities until 1728, and thereafter with decennial averages of the market yield of 3% annuities and consols, derived from Table 13. It is evident that bank rate averaged above long-term rates after 1720. Scraps of information on short market rates, which are not regularly reported, show they were at times below bank rate, especially when consol yields were low; but it is doubtful that they were often sufficiently below bank rate to bring them down to the lower consol rates.

In the eighteenth century Britain did not achieve the very low level of Dutch interest rates. However, the gap was importantly narrowed. The funding of the national debt had been achieved, but the banking system, the money market, and the organization of the floating debt were still far from modern.

TABLE 14

Short-Term English Interest Rates: Eighteenth Century

Year	Bank of England Discount Rates (374)				Other Rates; Conditions	Sources
	Inland Bills		Foreign Bills			
	For Depositors	Un-specified	For Depositors	Un-specified		
1690					Usury limit 6% since 1651; government borrows at 10–12%	
1694	6	6		6–4.5	Bank prepares to discount bills up to 3 months	
1695	3–4.5	6	3	6	Bank favors depositors; exchequer bills first issued; pay $7\frac{1}{2}\%$	
1696					Economic crisis; bank pays 6% on its own specie bills	(378) (376)
1698			4.5			
1699	4.5					
1701					Economic crisis	(378)
1705		4	5			
1707					Run on bank; bank pays 6% on its own specie bills	(377)
1710				5		
1711	6		6		Discount rules formulated; discounts only for depositors	(382)
1713					Bank loans to East India Co. at 6%	(379)
1714					Usury limit reduced to 5%; market rate well below 6%	(380)
1716	4		4			
1717					Bank loans to East India Co. at 4%	(381)
1719	5		5			
1720			5		Discounting suspended during South Sea Crisis	
1722				4		
1727					Bank loans to Royal Bank of Scotland at 4%	(383)
1728					Rates on exchequer bills reduced from 4 to $3\frac{1}{2}\%$ and to 3%	(384)
1730					Bank loans to East India Co. at 4%	(379)
1742		5		4		
1745				5		
1746		5		5–4	5% rate on inland bills unchanged until 1822	
1753					Economic crisis	(378)
1763					Economic crisis	(378)
1772					Economic crisis	
1773				5	The 5% rate on foreign bills was unchanged until 1822	
1774					De facto gold standard introduced	(385)
1775					Clearing house established	(386)
1783					Economic crisis	(378)
1791					Bank considered, but did not approve, dropping discount rate from 5 to 4%	(387)
1793					Economic crisis; failure of 26 country banks	(378) (388)
1797					Specie payments suspended	(389)

Chapter XII

Europe in the Eighteenth Century

FRENCH BACKGROUND

A study of interest rates on the continent of Europe in the eighteenth century must center on developments in France and Holland. Italy had long since lost its financial importance and financial markets had never developed in Spain. Germany was still an aggregation of separate nations, each with its own tariff barriers and its own currency. Although Prussia and Austria had become powers of great strength, many of their financial customs were still medieval.

During this last century of the French monarchy, the Crown struggled unsuccessfully to improve its financial methods and thus to retain its power at home and its empire abroad. The century began with the defeat of Louis XIV by an effective coalition of foreign states; it ended with the French Revolution and the victories of Napoleon. France was involved in the War of the Spanish Succession, 1701–1714; the war with Spain, 1718–1720; the War of the Polish Succession, 1733–1738; the War of the Austrian Succession, 1740–1748; the Seven Years' War, 1756–1763; the War for American Independence, 1778–1783; and the wars of the revolution, from 1792, which merged into the Napoleonic Wars. By the end of the century France had lost most of her colonial empire, but had temporarily gained a dominating military position on the continent.

Industrialization did not progress far in France in this century. The guilds of France controlled industry; they guarded their monopolies, restricted membership and output, and opposed new methods. One of the forces behind the revolution was the demand of the excluded workers for the abolition of the guilds. Some sort of industrial freedom was achieved in 1791. (390) The factory system, however, did not develop rapidly until the third or fourth decade of the nineteenth century. French commerce in the eighteenth century was hampered by internal tolls and tariffs, which survived from the Middle Ages until they were also swept away by the revolution.

France was unfortunate almost in the proportion that England was fortunate in eigtheenth-century experiments with banking and with money. In 1702 the government of France founded a *Caisse des Emprunts* (loan office) to finance a general recoinage; the *caisse* issued interest-bearing billets against deposit of coin. The Crown used the billets to pay the purveyors of the state. Owing to the requirements of the war with England, the billets were not promptly redeemed and fell to discounts of 25–50%. (391) An active market in these billets developed on the Rue Quincampoix; speculation in them, called *agiotage*, spread to other government securities. This led, in 1724, to the establishment of the Bourse. (392)

In 1716 the Scotsman John Law persuaded the government of France to permit him to establish a bank called the *Banque Generale*. The bank began business with the power to issue notes, accept and transfer deposits, and deal in bills of exchange and in promissory notes. Its capital was paid in, one quarter in coin and three quarters in government billets. Success was immediate. The bank note issue proved very convenient, for the notes were made acceptable for taxes. In 1718 the government guaranteed the bank's obligations and set up branch banks in several cities. (393) Huge issues of notes were used to retire outstanding government indebtedness. Interest rates fell to $4\frac{1}{2}\%$ and, temporarily, even to 2–3%. Prices of commodities rose 88% at Paris as the supply of circulating medium was trebled in four years.

In the meantime the Crown, impressed by Law's initial success, had permitted him to charter several trading monopolies, including the Mississippi Company. A fever of wild speculation in these shares swept Paris. Law merged his various companies into each other and finally into the bank. In 1720 he was given the management of the mint and of the national revenues. In return, he undertook to repay the entire national debt. Many *rentiers* turned in their *rentes* for company stock. In 1720 a huge speculation carried the price of stock up tenfold. Opposition to Law appeared and created alarm. The market crashed, and the bank and its notes fell with it. The result of the Mississippi Bubble, as it is now known, was a profound popular distrust of paper money and of big banks, which had an enduring effect on French finance. The country returned to coin, and for the rest of the century French banking was carried on largely by private banks. In the same year of 1720 the Bank of England survived the similar South Sea Bubble and dominated English finance throughout the century.

In 1776 the French government organized the *Caisse d'Escompte* (discount office). It was modeled somewhat after the Bank of England, but it was not called a bank. It loaned its capital to the government at a rate not to exceed 4% and had the power to issue notes payable to bearer. (394) It proved a quietly successful and useful institution. In 1800, it was succeeded by the Bank of France.

We have seen that the recorded history of French *rentes* began in the fifteenth century. As early as the reign of Louis XI, 1461–1483, there were forced loans to the Crown, which provided that at maturity lenders, if not paid off, would be reimbursed with *rentes* at rates varying from 5 to 10% a year. The concept of *rentes* followed naturally from the feudal practice of granting incomes to subjects as a reward for services or in return for material considerations. In the reign of Francis I, 1515–1547, perpetual *rentes* in almost modern form were created (395): in 1522 an edict created a *rente* at 8⅓% secured by the wine tax. This was a reciprocal contract by virtue of which the state assumed the payment of an annuity for an indefinite period, but not the repayment of the principal, reserving the right to redeem at its own discretion. The mayor and aldermen of the city of Paris became arbiters to settle differences between the two contracting parties. The *rentiers* understood the benefit of having taxes imposed on their behalf and offered additional loans at 8⅓% in 1536, 1537, and 1543.

The disorganization of French finance during the latter half of the sixteenth century led to bankruptcy and reforms under Henry IV, 1589–1610. *Rentes*, nevertheless, continued popular with French investors in spite of another composition in 1615, a suspension of payments in 1648, and another suspension in 1659. Many finance ministers audited the *rentes* created by their predecessors, disallowed or reduced many, and created many more of their own. Variations were introduced, such as life annuities and tontines. There was no uniformity and often the amount of the government obligations outstanding was not known.

At the very end of the seventeenth century, the war with England forced the flotation of a large body of new *rentes*, some at high rates. In 1710 and in 1713 the high rates payable on certain *rentes* were arbitrarily reduced. This meant a cancellation of up to three fifths of their capital value. During the Mississippi Bubble, 1718–1720, some *rentes* were reduced temporarily to very low rates. After the bubble burst, the government tended to be more scrupulous with its creditors.

In spite of these vicissitudes, a substantial demand evidently continued for this form of investment. Each war saw further increases in *rentes* outstanding. In 1756 a large volume was created at 5%. Between

1774 and 1789 the total government debt tripled; half of it was in *rentes,* half was unfunded; interest amounted to half of the budget. By 1789 half of the *rentes* were perpetual, the rest for a life or for two, three, or four lives. In spite of disordered finance, the government had retained its ability to borrow throughout much of this century. When it could no longer borrow, the revolution followed fast. A crop failure in 1785 and an industrial crisis in 1787 were followed by the revolution in 1789.

The credit of the revolutionary government was poor. It financed itself by issuing assignats, which were obligations supposedly backed by the lands of the Church and nobility that had been seized. At first the assignats bore interest and were to be redeemed within five years by sale of Church land. (396) They were used in large part to pay off the floating debt. In 1790 their interest was reduced. Later, the interest payments were abolished, and assignats were issued in small denominations. They rapidly became paper money. As they were not redeemed, they lost value. After an enormous overissue, they were declared valueless in 1797. Also in 1797 the "two-thirds bankruptcy" law was passed, under which only one third of the interest on the national debt and one third of pensions was to be paid in cash and the balance in land warrants, which turned out to have little value.

As a result of inflation and repudiation, France ended the eighteenth century with a small national debt. This was in sharp contrast to England's vast funded debt. Napoleon reformed the national finances. He established a budget and increased taxes; he refunded the national debt into an issue of consolidated *rentes;* he rarely borrowed. Instead, he followed a pay-as-you-go policy by exploiting the conquered countries. (397) He adopted the English custom of statutory interest rate limits, setting the maximum at 6% for commercial loans and 5% for loans on real property. (398)

FRENCH INTEREST RATES IN THE EIGHTEENTH CENTURY

No systematic records of the market prices of French *rentes* are available until the last years of the eighteenth century. This is probably, in part, because the old *rentes* were not uniform in the manner of British consols. The lack is regrettable because wide and informative fluctuations in *rentes* must have recurred during this eventful century, reflecting the Mississippi Bubble, the many disastrous wars, the growing financial problems of the government, the revolution, and the assignat inflation. Only after 1796 do we have regular market quotations for *rentes,* and they are dramatic indeed. Something, however, is known of earlier market yields on *rentes.*

In the 1670's the French finance minister had sold *rentes* freely at 5–5⅞%, and had even managed to induce oversubscriptions. (399) Also, a State Savings Bank was established in 1674, paying 5%, which enabled small depositors to accumulate funds and then convert their deposits into *rentes* paying a similar rate. A highly generalized statement is made that during the later years of the seventeenth century "many loans with good security were made at from 4 to 5%." (400) This, however, was during peacetime. To finance the war of 1688–1697, some *rentes* were created that paid as high as 8⅓%. (401)

During the first decade of the eighteenth century, these higher wartime interest rates continued. A rate of 7% is mentioned on private credits, and more *rentes* were created at 8⅓%. (400) Thereafter rates declined, and for much of the century a range in quiet times of 4–5% prevailed on good private credits and 5–6% on loans to the State. (400) In 1766 a law sought to lower the legal rate for private credits from 5 to 4%, but it was not obeyed.

In addition to these general statements about interest rates in eighteenth-century France, there are some more precise data on interest rates at specified dates. In 1710 all the *rentes* were converted to a 5% basis. (402) This was a wartime forced conversion; the 8⅓% rate previously quoted is probably a better guide to the market. During 1713–1715 the payments on some *rentes* were arbitrarily cut to 4%. (402) In 1718 the funded debt was unified at 4%. (400) In 1720, at the height of the Mississippi boom, when many *rentes* were being turned in for stock, their rate was again cut briefly to 2–2½%. (402) This was peacetime. It was also the period when the English were bringing the rates on their funds down from 6 to 3%. Evidently the ideas behind "Dutch finance" were spreading through Europe.

The French experiment, however, did not enjoy the firmer political and economic foundations that existed in Holland and England. While Law's bank was exchanging its stock and its bank notes freely for government securities, an initial decline in interest rates occurred, but this episode lasted only a very few years. Quotations for *rentes* during the collapse of the boom in 1720–1721 would be interesting, but have not come down to us. Around 1735, however, the Church and the Chamber of Commerce of Marseilles both borrowed at 5%, and the government created new 5% *rentes* without compulsion. (400) In 1749 the first bearer *rentes* were created; these were at 5%. In spite of the many vicissitudes of the century, very high yields on *rentes* were not quoted until after the revolution. There is evidence of persistent saving by the *rentiers* and a demand for safe investment. Five percent seemed to be the magic rate throughout most of the seventeenth and eighteenth centuries. Lower and higher rates proved to be temporary.

In 1756, when the Seven Years' War began, the government created a huge volume of new 5% *rentes* and apparently sold them without co-ercion. In 1776 the *Caisse d'Escompte* was established and provided credit as low as 4% at short term. By the end of the old regime, in 1789, the volume of *rentes* outstanding had increased enormously, but there was no record of nominal rates in excess of 5%.

This same rate of 5% was initially paid on the assignats of 1789. Their rate was reduced to 3% in 1790, but owing to their forced issue and heavy discounts, no market rate of interest can be read into their nom-inal rate. In 1795 the government established a 6% legal maximum for commercial credit and a 5% legal maximum for credit secured by real estate. (398) Following the two-thirds bankruptcy of 1797 and as a part of Napoleon's financial reforms, the entire national debt was forcibly refunded into 5% *rentes.*

These rates were nominal interest rates of the revolutionary decade. What were the market rates? As might be expected following the po-litical turbulence of this period, its destruction, its wars, its inflation, and its bankruptcies, the market prices of *rentes* were not very high. A series of consecutive market quotations on *rentes* was begun in the year 1797. This was the year when two thirds of the income of the *rentes* was made payable in almost valueless land warrants. It was the year of Napoleon's initial victories, a year when France had no firmly established government and was at war with most of Europe. It was the year when Napoleon was expected momentarily to invade England. (He invaded Egypt instead.) In 1797 the 5% *rentes* were quoted as fluc-tuating in price between $6\frac{1}{8}$ and $36\frac{1}{8}$ as a percent of 100. If their nominal rate of 5% is applied to these prices, the computed yields were 82–14%. The mean price in 1798 was $16\frac{5}{8}$, and at this price the yield was 30% (403) if the government paid the interest, and 10% if it paid only one third of the interest.

In 1799, when Napoleon was established as First Consul for a ten-year term and began his reform of the government finances, the price of 5% *rentes* ranged from $22\frac{1}{2}$ high to 7 low; $14\frac{3}{4}$ was the mean. Obvi-ously payment in full was not expected, or the medium of payment was not wanted.

In 1800 there was a sharp improvement in the price of *rentes*. This coincided with several of Napoleon's greatest victories and also with progress in his financial reforms. This was the year when the Bank of France was organized. The 5% *rentes* sold up to 44, or over six times their recent lows. Their range for 1800 was 44 high and $17\frac{3}{8}$ low; $30\frac{3}{8}$ was the mean. These prices equaled yields of $28\frac{5}{8}\%$, $11\frac{3}{8}\%$, and $16\frac{1}{4}\%$, respectively, if 5% interest had been paid. (403) A later chapter tells that the 5% *rentes* continued to recover rapidly. They reached 68, or 7.35% yield, in 1801 and 93⅜, or 5.38%, in 1807.

In France, then, the trends of interest rates in the eighteenth century seemed to follow a pattern not too different from that of eighteenth-century England, but at very different levels. Rates at first were high in both countries, declined importantly during the first two or three decades, remained relatively low for a while, and then rose in both countries to high levels. During the Napoleonic Wars the 3% British consols sold below 50, and the 5% French *rentes* sold below 10.

In spite of wars and revolutions, a taste for bond investment evidently developed in England and France and throughout much of Europe during the eighteenth century. Investors were ready to buy safe

TABLE 15

FRENCH INTEREST RATES: EIGHTEENTH CENTURY

Period	Conditions	Miscella-neous, %	*Rentes*, %	Sources
Late 17th century	Rates generally range	4–5		(400)
Late 17th century	*Rentes* sold by subscription at		5–8⅓	
1700–10	During war rates rose to	7	8⅓	(400)
1710	All *rentes* arbitrarily cut to		5	(402)
1713–15	Some *rentes* arbitrarily cut to		4	(402)
1720	Some *rentes* arbitrarily cut to, briefly		2–2½	(402)
1720	Interest rates depressed in Law period to	2–3		(400)
After 1720	Private rates generally	4–10		(400)
After 1720	Government rates generally		5–6	(400)
1735	Church and Chamber of Marseilles pay	5		(400)
1735	Government borrows without coercion at		5	(400)
1756	Large volume of *rentes* floated at		5	(402)
1766	Unsuccessful attempt to reduce rates below	5	5	(400)
1766	*Caisse d'Escompte* discounts at	4		(394)
1766–1800	Discount rate did not exceed	6		(400)
1789–1790	Assignats issued at	3–5		(396)
1797	Charity loans at 36%			(373)
1797–1799	Bankruptcy; government debt refunded at 5%			(398)
1798	Mean market rate for 5% *rentes*		30⅛	(403)
1799	Mean market rate for 5% *rentes*		34	(403)
1800	Mean market rate for 5% *rentes*		16¼	(403)
1801	Mean market rate for 5% *rentes* (low of 7⅜%)		9¼	(403)
1807	Mean market rate for 5% *rentes*		5⅜	(403)

long-term government obligations in volume. Their appetite persisted in spite of severe vicissitudes and discouragements and heavy market declines. Long-term funds, or *rentes*, provided a suitable medium to mobilize the savings of the peoples. In the nineteenth century a quieter Europe brought its industrial capitalism to a high state of productivity by the use of these same methods of channeling savings into investment by means of long-term marketable debt securities. While the eighteenth century concentrated a large part of its negotiable savings in national debt, the nineteenth century spread its funds among much more varied types of securities.

DUTCH BACKGROUND

During the seventeenth century the new Dutch Republic had developed a worldwide trading empire. It had achieved a near monopoly of European shipping and commerce. Defoe, in 1728, described the Dutch as "the carriers of the world, the middle persons in trade, the factors and brokers of Europe." (404) The Dutch had fought successfully against Spain, France, and England. Amsterdam had become the financial center of Europe. Usury laws were unknown in Holland, but interest rates there were the lowest in Europe. A frugal, prosperous population saved enough to finance, not only its own wars and its own commerce, but also enough to finance foreign governments and foreign enterprise. As the seventeenth century ended, the Dutch stadtholder became King of England. "Dutch finance" was soon to be practiced by the English government.

In the eighteenth century it was impossible for the Dutch Republic to maintain the commercial leadership of Europe. Larger countries developed their own shipping and ports. In their military partnerships with England, the Dutch inevitably became the junior partners; England was also a nation of seamen and of foreign traders. Therefore in the eighteenth century the Dutch turned gradually from trade to finance. Amsterdam remained active and usually prosperous, interest rates remained low, and Dutch banks and investors continued to be very important in international finance. However, there were recurrent crises of overspeculation, which eventually sapped confidence in Amsterdam. A larger, more stable money market was developing in London, which at the end of the century displaced the Amsterdam market.

After the generally successful, but costly, War of the Spanish Succession, 1702–1713, when England was an ally against France, there was an economic decline in Holland. (405) After the War of the Austrian Succession, 1740–1748, when Holland was again an ally of England, another deterioration of the Dutch position became evident. In 1780–1784 during the War for American Independence, the Dutch went to war against England over the question of the right to search ships at sea and as a result lost a good part of their empire. Finally, the French Revolution foreshadowed the end of the Dutch Republic. In 1793 Holland was again an ally of England against France. In 1794–1795 the French captured the Dutch fleet while it was frozen in the ice and overran the country. The Batavian Republic, 1795–1806, modeled on the French revolutionary pattern, was an ally of France, and in consequence England seized the remaining Dutch colonies. Finally, a Kingdom of Holland was incorporated into Napoleon's empire. In spite of these political and economic vicissitudes, there is evidence that interest rates at Amsterdam remained relatively stable and apparently rose only moderately until very late in the eighteenth century.

The Bank of Amsterdam, founded in 1609, had achieved a dominating position in the international bullion trade. At times its deposits even commanded a small premium over coined money. It made large loans to the Dutch East India Company at moderate rates and financed the municipality of Amsterdam; otherwise, it rarely loaned money. In the eighteenth century the bank maintained its position as a chief bullion market, although London was obtaining a large volume of Brazilian gold and was providing strong competition. (406) An active foreign exchange market was maintained at Amsterdam. Drafts on Amsterdam were used to finance the trade of many countries. The use of bank acceptances increased. Dutch private bankers financed not only foreign trade but foreign governments, such as those of Austria and Russia. They financed foreign producers and foreign consumers a century before English bankers became international bankers.

Dutch capital was very important in the eighteenth-century London money market. (407) When the yield on safe investments in London rose well above the level in Amsterdam, Dutch capital flowed to London, and the rate of exchange moved in favor of London. Dutch capital in this way supported the exchange value of sterling in several crises.

The peace of 1763 was followed by a crisis and panic in Amsterdam. There were many bankruptcies. Another crisis in 1773 brought rescue from the Bank of England. The Dutch speculated increasingly in English securities as well as in their own and the results were costly. In 1781 the Bank of Amsterdam could not meet its obligations. (408)

The perpetual government annuities, which the Dutch had so successfully developed in the sixteenth and seventeenth centuries, were used throughout the eighteenth century without important improvements. State credit was based on the established Dutch habit of making provision for their old age and for their families by buying these perpetual annuities. (409) Large groups lived on investment income. Although temporary floating debt was occasionally created by the government, it was soon funded and usually commanded the same low rates paid on the funded debt. But this funded debt was heterogeneous: nothing like a uniform interchangeable stock, such as the British consols, was created. There were obligations of the Dutch Republic, obligations of the individual provinces, obligations of the separate towns, of the special colleges, of the admiralties, and of the Dutch East India Company. These instruments were not even uniformly worded and hence were often difficult to sell. They included many kinds of annuities. Most were perpetual annuities, but there were also annuities on lives and for thirty or thirty-two years, and lottery loans. Few, however, were secured by specific revenues in the French and English manner. They were backed solely by confidence in the general credit of the issuing body. Confidence in the honesty of the financial administration remained unshaken until late in the eighteenth century, when the secrecy which surrounded public finance led to suspicion of corruption. (410) No one knew the extent of the debts of the country or of the provinces. It was the English who introduced uniformity and full disclosure into public finance.

The Amsterdam Exchange in the early seventeenth century dealt principally in shares of the Dutch East India Company, in commodities, and in bills. Speculation was active. By the eighteenth century it had developed into a world market dealing in goods and bills and securities. (411) There were well-organized syndicates. Those sponsoring rising prices were called "lovers"; those sponsoring or seeking falling prices were called "counterminers." (412) Future contracts, margins, short sales, and many of the techniques of modern stock exchange trading were developed.

As time went by, foreign securities were also traded on the Amsterdam Exchange. Some of these were guaranteed by the authorities of the Dutch Republic; this was a form of foreign aid. By 1747 the Amsterdam Stock Exchange dealt in twenty-five different kinds of home, state, and provincial bonds, three home shares, three English shares, four English government securities, and six German loans. By the end of the eighteenth century, the list had increased from 41 to 110 issues. (413)

DUTCH INTEREST RATES IN THE EIGHTEENTH CENTURY

The record of Dutch interest rates in the eighteenth century remains imprecise. The basic data are probably available, but have not yet been published as a satisfactory continuous series of rates of interest. There is little doubt about the general level. Interest rates on best credits were often very low. There were high rates available to Dutch investors, but they were not usually provided by prime domestic loans. It is small wonder that Dutch capital sought foreign investment.

At the beginning of the eighteenth century, commercial loans were negotiated on the Amsterdam Exchange at as low as 1¾–2%. (413) The range for a long period was 2–3%. (414) The rate was estimated to average 2½–3% for the entire century up to the French Revolution. (415) During the years 1735–1738 the English Parliament was informed that Dutch traders could borrow at 2–3%. (416) After 1750 the Dutch government could still borrow at 2% and individuals at 3%. (417)

There is some evidence that short-term commercial rates crept up during the century. Perhaps they were influenced by opportunities to loan abroad at higher rates or by recurrent financial difficulties. By 1775 Dutch commercial rates, earlier at 1¾–2%, were quoted at 3–4%. The period of French domination and disruption of Dutch trade brought a further and sharp increase in commercial rates: 4–8% was quoted in 1795; 4–12% in 1797; but in 1799 discounts were quoted at 3–5%.

The long-term obligations of the various provinces and of the government of the Dutch Republic in 1717 required annual interest payments averaging 3½–4% of principal. The perpetual bonds of the seven provinces that shared in the debt of the Republic then paid an average nominal rate of 3.9%, while the Republic's own perpetual bonds paid 3% nominal. In 1712, 1744, and 1747 the province of Holland floated 2½s, and in 1735 and 1746 it floated 2s. In 1786 the East India Company floated 3s. These, however, were nominal rates and not market quotations. By 1786 the average paid on the combined debt was down from 3½% to 3%. (418) Loans of the Republic ranged from 1¼ to 5% nominal rates; the most usual nominal rate was 2½%. Loans of various admiralties were at 2½–4% nominal, and loans of the East India Company were at 2–4½% nominal. (418)

In 1762 market quotations for perpetual bonds of the provinces of Holland and Utrecht indicate yields of 2.51 and 2.84%, respectively. There were 2¾s selling at 97, 2½s selling at 96 and 99½, and 2s selling at 73.

The calamities of the 1790's are vividly reflected in the market quotations of May, 1798. (418) The 2½s of the province of Holland were then quoted at 36–39 to yield 6.95–6.42%; the 2s were quoted at 28–30 to yield 7.15–6.66%. East India Company 2% debentures were quoted at 20–25 to yield 10–8%, and some East India Company 3s, guaranteed by the Republic, were quoted at 30–31 to yield 10–9.7%.

England during the eighteenth century succeeded in bringing the rate of interest paid on her funded debt down from 8% or higher to an

TABLE 16

DUTCH INTEREST RATES: EIGHTEENTH CENTURY

Description	Short, %	Long, %	Sources
General			
Market rate	2–3		(414)
Public debts of the Republic ranged, nominal		$1\frac{1}{4}$–5	(418)
Many debentures of Holland were at, nominal		$2\frac{1}{2}$	(418)
Debentures of the various admiralties were at, nominal		$2\frac{1}{2}$–4	(418)
Debentures of East India Co. were at, nominal		2–$4\frac{1}{2}$	(418)
Commercial interest rates averaged	$2\frac{1}{2}$–3		(415)
Dated			
1700–1725 Market rate on Amsterdam Exchange as low as	$1\frac{3}{4}$–2		(413)
1717 Debts of the provinces paid a nominal average of		3.90	(418)
Debts of the Republic paid a nominal average of		3	(418)
1735–1738 English Parliament informed Dutch rates were	2–3		(416)
1750–1795 Loans to government	2		(417)
Loans to individuals	3		(417)
1762 Bonds of provinces sold at market prices to yield		$2\frac{1}{2}$–$2\frac{7}{8}$	
1775–1795 Rates gradually rose during century; now market rate	3–4		(413)
1786 Debt of the provinces paid an average of nominal		3	(418)
1795 Rate of discount at Amsterdam	4–6		(398)
1796 Rate of discount at Amsterdam	4–6		(398)
1797 Rate of discount at Amsterdam	4–12		(398)
1798 Rate of discount at Amsterdam	4–5		(398)
1799 Rate of discount at Amsterdam	3–5		(398)
1800 Rate of discount at Amsterdam	4–6		(398)
1798 Bonds of provinces sold at market price to yield		6.42–7.15	
1798 Bonds of East India Company sold at market prices to yield		8–10	

almost uniform 3% by mid-century, but thereafter England was unable to keep the rate down. Dutch long-term rates, when quoted, remained usually below English rates, but by no such margin as prevailed in the seventeenth century. The Dutch rates were usually far below the standard 5% that prevailed for French *rentes*.

The contrast was even more striking in short-term commercial rates. The English bank rate never stayed below the legal limit of 5% for long. Discounts in Holland were often in the lower part of a 2–4% range until the French Revolution.

In the eighteenth century Holland finally lost most of her trading advantages, much of her empire, and eventually her freedom and her republican form of government. Nevertheless, the country seemed to retain its financial poise and stability until it became a part of the French Empire. Low interest rates were still associated with the name of Dutch finance.

INTEREST RATES IN OTHER EUROPEAN COUNTRIES IN THE EIGHTEENTH CENTURY

Earlier chapters suggest that a rate of 5% became generally accepted in Europe during the sixteenth and seventeenth centuries as a fair and just rate. It was a common rate on long-term census annuities secured by landed property or by state revenues. It also was common for business loans in the form of silent partnerships or deposits.

In the eighteenth century in Germany and Italy, 5% was still considered normal for census annuities; this rate was sometimes as low as 4%. (419) The rate on guaranteed capital was also at times as low as 4%. Even in eighteenth-century Russia, 5% was recognized by law and became the legal maximum, although loans in Russia were often at higher rates, in the range of 8–10%. (420)

In Basel in the latter half of the eighteenth century, the rate of interest on long-term loans fell from 5 to 4%. This decline in rate created hardship for religious and benevolent associations because debtors threatened to repay old loans. Therefore, local governments sought to keep the rate up. However, the decline could not be resisted. (421)

Higher rates, of course, persisted, as in all ages, for loans of a more hazardous or administratively more expensive kind. The Belgian *montes* (public pawnshops) continued to charge 15% on pawns up to the French Revolution. (422) While no specific rates are quoted here, it is certain that far higher rates were charged and collected on usurious personal loans and risk loans of a commercial and political character.

Sweden during the seventeenth and eighteenth centuries made an interesting contribution to the history of European interest rates, even though the data are confined to rates established by law. The Bank of Sweden was founded in 1656. This was shortly after the abdication of Queen Christina and on the eve of the absolute rule and military adventures of her successors, Charles X, XI, and XII. The bank in 1661 started the first official issue of bank notes in Europe thirty-three years before the founding of the Bank of England. However, the experiment was not pressed, and note issue was discontinued in 1664.

In the laws governing the Bank of Sweden the interest rate paid on deposits was fixed at 6% in 1668, while the rates charged for bank loans were fixed at 8% for large loans, $8\frac{1}{4}$% for smaller loans, and $10\frac{5}{32}$% for small loans. (423) These were roughly comparable to English commercial loan rates at the time, but were far above the very low 3–4% Dutch rates. The Dutch example impressed the Estates of Sweden, which expressed the desire that their bank would eventually lower its loaning rates at least to 6%. The bank in fact lowered the rate that it paid on deposits to $4\frac{1}{2}$% in 1669 in compliance with a royal decree, and in 1687 it lowered its maximum loan rate to 6%. In 1700 the bank raised its deposit rate from $4\frac{1}{2}$ to 5%, but in 1701 it was again lowered by decree to $4\frac{1}{2}$%.

Apparently the decline in interest rates which during the first half of the eighteenth century spread from Holland to England and even to France eventually found reflection in Sweden. This was after the spectacular military success of Charles XII of Sweden in his war against Peter the Great of Russia, after his final defeat in 1709–1714, and after constitutional government was re-established in Sweden, 1718–1720. In 1741 the rate for bank loans on precious metals was reduced from 6 to $4\frac{1}{2}$%, while other loans were made at 5–6%. In 1748 the minimum loan rate was reduced to 4%. In 1756 the rate on loans secured by metals was set at 3% and on other loans at 4%; deposit rates were also cut by decree to 2% for private depositors, 3% for public institutions, and 4% for welfare organizations. This was about the same period in the eighteenth century when English long-term interest rates were at their lows and Dutch rates continued very low. English and Dutch rates, however, were market rates while the Swedish rates were by decree.

During the second part of the eighteenth century Swedish official rates at first rose, as did English and Dutch market rates. Later in the century they fell. In 1766 the Swedish discount rate on loans against deposit receipts was raised from 3 to 4%. In 1768 the minimum rate charged for loans on gold and silver was raised to 6%, but in 1770 it was reduced again to 4%. In 1792 the rate on loans secured by metals was again reduced to 3%, while the rate of interest paid on private deposits was raised to 3%. In 1800 deposits of gold and silver were paid 4% interest. These rates of interest for seventeenth- and eighteenth-century Sweden, all set by official decree, are summarized in Table 17.

TABLE 17

OFFICIAL INTEREST RATES OF THE SWEDISH RIKSBANK (423)

Year	Interest Paid on Deposits, %	Interest Charged on Loans, %	Year	Interest Paid on Deposits, %	Interest Charged on Loans, %
1668	6	8–$10\frac{5}{32}$	1750	2–4	3–4
1669	$4\frac{1}{2}$		1766		4
1687		6	1768		6
1700	5		1770		4
1701	$4\frac{1}{2}$		1792	3–4	3
1741		$4\frac{1}{2}$–6	1800	4	
1748		4			

Chapter XIII

England in the Nineteenth Century

GENERAL BACKGROUND

In England the nineteenth century was one of rapid economic growth, of hard money, and of declining interest rates. The Industrial Revolution ran its full course. Railroads and factories transformed the economy, and the population quadrupled. Commerce increased fourteenfold. (424) Specie payments were resumed soon after the end of the Napoleonic Wars, and the gold value of the pound was maintained throughout the century. Commodity prices ended the century far below their high wartime levels at the beginning of the century and also below the peacetime levels prevailing directly before and after the Napoleonic Wars. (425) Market yields on British consols started the century at 4½–6%; they were never above 4% after 1830, never above 3½% after 1850, and were below 2½% throughout the final decade of the century. This decline in yield exceeded 60%, and the appreciation in the price of the funds far exceeded 100%.

After Waterloo, 1815, this was a century of relative peace. British wars were small, brief, and victorious. There was war with China in 1839–1842, the Crimean War with Russia in 1854–1855, the Indian mutiny in 1857, another war with China in 1857–1858, the Afghan War in 1878, the Zulu War in 1878–1879, the intervention in Egypt in 1882, and, finally, the longer Boer War in 1899–1902. The British navy, however, saw no fleet action for almost one hundred years.

British supremacy was generally acknowledged. The Dutch had been eliminated as major commercial and financial rivals. British trading policies and willingness and power to grant long-term foreign credits made economic cooperation with Britain attractive to most foreign commercial interests. Many countries imitated British monetary and financial techniques and British interest rate policies. In one way or another, they tried to fit themselves into her worldwide trading community. The rules of the game were set in London. They were built around the gold standard, free access to markets, and respect for investment.

A chronological review of the century starts with the war with Napoleon, which was resumed in 1803. It brought great financial stress, inflation, and high interest rates. From time to time, such as 1808–1810,

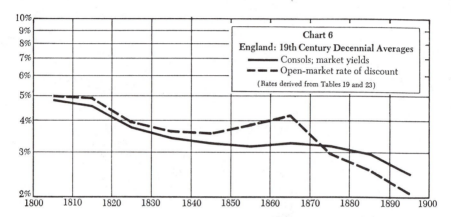

Chart 6
England: 19th Century Decennial Averages
—— Consols; market yields
– – – Open-market rate of discount
(Rates derived from Tables 19 and 23)

there were industrial booms and feverish activity. The fortunes of war swung from extreme to extreme and were often reflected in the market for the funds. After Waterloo, 1815, came the great peace, which lasted through the reigns of George IV, 1811–1830, William IV, 1830–1837, and Victoria, 1837–1901.

The early years of this peace were eventful for English money and capital markets. A severe economic depression began in 1815 and brought falling commodity prices, falling interest rates, and unemployment. Its trough was in 1816. The note issue was thereafter reduced, interest rates rose briefly, and specie payments were resumed in 1821.

A trend toward the construction of large factories then set in, based in part on the recent successful application of steam power to machinery. Imports of cotton increased fivefold by 1830. (426) The first railway was built in 1825, and in that year the repeal of the "Bubble Act of 1720," which had restricted joint stock promotions, led to widespread "projecting" of new companies. In one month the shares of one company advanced 4000% in price. There were crises in 1825 and 1826 and a crash in 1827, which took with it 400 of the 600 new companies. (427) Severe depression lasted until 1832. However, capital promotions continued. At this time, the concept of preferred stock (preference shares) was developed and proved useful in financing the forthcoming railway boom. However, limited liability for stockholders did not become general until 1855–1862.

In the 1830's there was continued industrial expansion accompanied by speculation in United States land and United States companies, a brief start at a railway construction boom, and a further fall in interest rates. Prosperity was interrupted by the effects of the American crisis of 1837. After a period of stagnation, the great railway construction boom of the 1840's got under way. Even the Bank of England bought railway debentures. Interest rates declined further; 3% consols briefly crossed par, up over 100% since the lows of the Napoleonic Wars. Another financial crisis in 1847 brought a sharp rise in interest rates and very severe bankruptcies. It was followed by the revolutions of 1848–1849 on the continent of Europe, which had adverse effects on European markets.

In 1849 a period of heavy gold imports to London began, which arose from new discoveries in California and Australia. Commodity prices rose. Interest rates at first declined and then advanced. Large sums were loaned abroad. Britain financed railways in Europe and North America, and stock speculation became widespread. British supremacy was now unquestioned.

The crisis of 1857 has been called the first worldwide crisis (428) and the first that was purely economic, without political or natural cause. Many United States banks failed or suspended, and there was a run on the Bank of England. A depression in 1858–1859 was followed by the stimulation and disturbances associated with the American Civil War. There was prosperity in 1862–1863, a cotton famine in 1864, rising interest rates, speculation and boom until 1866. In that year Overend, Gurney & Company, the leading London discount firm, failed. This unexpected event led to panic and another "Black Friday."

The next few years, 1867–1873, marked a turning point in nineteenth-century political and economic history. The United States was united and on its way to becoming a world power. Germany emerged from the Franco-Prussian War of 1870–1871 as a great power. The opening of the Suez Canal in 1869 signalized the vital concern of England in the affairs of the entire globe. There was furious industrial activity and the building of new railroads. In the United States, 24,000 miles of railroads were built in four years. Germany expanded rapidly. Gossip had it that colliers were drinking champagne. In 1873 there was an American crisis, a German crisis, and twenty-four changes in Britain's bank rate. In London and New York company shares crashed, and bankruptcies in America involved $225 million.

A period of stagnation followed. Commodity prices declined for 20 years, until 1893. (430) Interest rates declined almost steadily from 1866 to 1897. At times there was deep depression, such as 1879 and after 1882. However, there were no more major financial crises and no more crisis bank rates. In 1888 Chancellor Goschen undertook his famous conversion of most of the national debt from 3% consols to $2\frac{1}{2}$% consols and met with spectacular success.

Business improved after 1889. There were booms in shipbuilding, new flotations, African gold, foreign loans, and the organization of investment trusts. The Baring trouble of 1890, based on overextension of credit to Argentina, was not allowed to have wide effect. The years 1894–1896 were remarkable for the fact that interest rates reached their lowest point in this century. The yields of consols reached their historic low, never approached before or since.

THE INVESTMENT MARKETS

London finance before 1750 was primarily devoted to serving commerce and the State. After 1750 finance began also to serve industry. However, it was not until 1850 that industry began to depend heavily on finance. Thereafter, large aggregations of capital began to seek liquidity and diversification through the market place. (431) Industrial capital heretofore had been largely accumulated internally, but now the markets were called upon and were able to mobilize large resources from many segments of the population at home and abroad. The capitalist spirit was triumphant.

A glance at the investment markets of mid-nineteenth-century London suggests that this history has indeed reached modern times. Almost all the principal services provided by today's City and today's Wall Street were then available in London. A twentieth-century Yankee investor would probably not have felt at home in Victoria's Court, but he would have felt very much at home in the City of the 1850's, provided, of course, that he learned a few differences of terminology.

Bonds were and are called stocks. Stocks were called ordinary shares or preference shares, as they are today. Government bonds were called the "funds" or the "gilt-edged." Information on domestic and foreign government bonds was sought, not in Moody's *Manuals,* but in *Fenn on the Funds.* Balance sheets presented liabilities to the left and assets to the right. Credit ratings, as established in the discount department of the Bank of England, were not based on alphabetical symbols, but started with "persons in extensive business"; continued with "dealers in greatest respectability and opulence"; and ran downward through "persons in a more confined scale of business" to "persons in low estimation." Among the assets of the Bank of England, the item "desperate debts" meant just what it seems to mean; the amount of the item was negligible. Individual issues of government securities had their nicknames, just as they do today. The "Goschens" were the consols issued a few years later by Chancellor Goschen in the greatest of all refundings, that of 1888; the "Deadweight" was a debt issue put out to fund the burdensome military pensions of the Napoleonic Wars. The personalized and almost familiar term "bank rate" (not *the* bank rate) was, and still is, given to the minimum rate of discount charged by the Bank of England. Funded-debt obligations usually did not mature in the modern sense; they were redeemable after a future date, but this was usually at the option of the government or other issuing body. In essence, they were perpetual annuities and were often called just that—true descendants of the medieval census. The investor bought income, and he was free to sell his claim to income to another investor. In the nineteenth century, however, maturity was, in fact, provided in issues of exchequer bonds, and some other public and private securities.

These are but slight and superficial differences from modern American terminology and usage. The similarities were much more basic. The man of property in the London of 1850 could buy shares in railroads, manufacturers, commercial companies, or public utilities; domestic or foreign; blue chip or speculative; outright or on credit. Daily or hourly quotations were available to him. Tips and promotions abounded. Alternatively, he could buy trusteed securities, principally the funds, both for sure income and for capital gain. Substantial capital gains were, in fact, always eventually realized on the funds if care were taken to avoid issues selling close to redemption value. Again, the investor could deposit with his bankers at interest or buy short-term securities. If he distrusted his own investment acumen, he could always ask his bankers to manage his investments for him.

Periods of prosperity alternated with financial crises and depression, and capital values fluctuated. After a few years of feverish "projecting" and "stockjobbing," there would suddenly be announced an unseasonal sharp rise in bank rate. Perhaps the bank knew something. The funds would falter. Then, another rise in bank rate and another, all the way up from 2 or 3% to a crisis rate of 8 or 10%. Rumors of commercial insolvencies would lead to a drain on the Bank of England's reserves. The government would "suspend the Bank Act," which meant that the bank was relieved of the necessity of maintaining its statutory reserves. Commercial failures usually followed as expected, sometimes of large and important houses. Then came a period of trade stagnation and falling prices. The government was blamed and the City was blamed. "The country was going to pot." Then came trade revival and stirring new projects.

THE BANKING SYSTEM

In the early nineteenth century the Bank of England was not yet a conscious regulator of the rate of interest. It was as it had always been—first of all, the banker for the government. It also competed with private bankers for commercial business; it accepted private deposits; it made private loans. It jealously guarded its monopoly of joint-stock banking and of the power to issue notes in the London area.

All other English bankers were private bankers. The law forbade them to be joint-stock companies. Nevertheless, during the decade following the suspension of specie payments in 1797, when notes of small denomination were permitted, private country banks increased in number from 230 to 800. This was a period of note issues and wartime inflation. (432)

A commodity price index rose during the war from 100 in 1790 to 166 in 1801 and to a high of 200 in 1814. Thereafter, it declined to 130 in 1816, 103 in 1826, and 93 in 1830. Prices were even lower by the end of the nineteenth century. (429)

During the paper money period of the Napoleonic Wars, the Bank of England did a large business in discounting bills for the market. Its unchanged 5% rate, limited by the usury laws, was below the market. Money brokers could charge more than the legal limit in the form of commissions and thus use its facilities. (434) While the bank rarely took the initiative in seeking discounts, it considered it to be its duty to discount all short bills of good traders offered to it. The bank was directed by the leading merchants of London, and the liquidity of the bill market was a primary concern of all of them. Good bills must always be salable. The bank took this responsibility very seriously, but its credit policy was as yet passive. Some of its directors even denied that its huge wartime advances to the Exchequer, its huge private discounts, and its consequently swollen note issue had "any effect whatever" on the 43% wartime premium commanded by gold over notes.

After the Napoleonic Wars, all was reversed. (435) The market rate of discount sank below the bank's unchanged 5% rate, and its bill business was taken elsewhere. In 1820 Parliament set a mint price for gold. Before the war the gold standard had been unofficial, but now it became explicit. Specie payments were easily resumed in 1821. With lower interest rates and a fixed high 5% bank rate, discounting was so poor, except during crises, that the bank sought business. For a few years it loaned on real estate mortgages. One was at 4% to the Duke of Rutland, and there were a few others, all large. It loaned freely to Rothschild at $3\frac{1}{2}\%$.

At times of crisis, the bank's specie reserves, rarely large, declined sharply. In 1825 there was a crisis and a run on the bank. The minutes of the bank's "Court" say, "It was mentioned to His Majesty's Government that we thought we were likely to run dry." (436) They did not run quite dry. By 1827 the bank was again seeking business and opening branches. It feared competition from the new joint-stock banks that were now authorized by law.

In 1833 the first effective step was taken toward a conscious monetary policy as we know it today. The usury law was suspended for bills under three months' maturity. This permitted the use of bank rate to protect the reserves. Thereafter, money would still always be available at the lender of last resort, but at a price.

In 1844 dissatisfaction with the state of the note issue led to the Bank Charter Act which divided the bank into an issue department and a banking department, provided the bank with what became a monopoly of English note issue, and limited the size of the bank's fiduciary note issue. The unintended consequence was that in future crises the government was led to "suspend the Bank Charter Act," that is, to permit the note issue to rise without limit; this was only done when the bank agreed to charge a penalty bank rate of 10%. "Suspension of the Bank Act" always succeeded in restoring confidence and the reserves. (437) In 1854 the usury laws were finally repealed for all forms of credit.

In the 1860's joint-stock banking began to grow rapidly and to replace private banking. The London joint-stock banks, unlike the Bank of England, paid interest on deposits. They were finally accorded limited liability. Toward the end of the century, when they developed branch banking, the Bank of England's competitive position in commercial banking declined.

Balances between clearing banks were settled on the books of the Bank of England. The London discount market for prime merchants' bills was also used to settle bankers' balances. In 1890 the Bank of England definitely accepted the discount houses as the principal channel for rediscounting bills, that is, for providing cash to the market. (438) Alternatively, the bank would buy or sell government securities from or to the market. In fact, at times it borrowed from the market by selling consols for cash and buying them back for future delivery. (439)

A flexible bank rate became the chief weapon used to maintain an appropriate currency reserve and, indeed, to regulate the flow of gold reserves all over the world. (440) Bank rate was changed only nine times in the first four decades of the nineteenth century; twenty times in the fifth decade; forty-seven times in the sixth decade; ninety-six times in the seventh decade; one hundred and nine times in the eighth decade; and thereafter at a declining frequency. The range of bank rate became extremely wide—usually up 1% at a time, and soaring from 3 to 8% in a few months, and back again in ½% stages, with several changes in a single month and frequent reversals of direction. It is small wonder that the market for the funds became at times almost indifferent to bank rate and moved as little as ½ point in price for a 2% change in bank rate. During 1868–1869 the funds, in fact, sold at exactly the same yield with a 4½% bank rate as with a 2% bank rate. Stability of long-term rates was combined with extreme volatility of short-term rates.

THE NATIONAL DEBT

The British national debt remained essentially a war debt. The history of its size during two centuries is summarized in political terms in the accompanying table.

SIZE OF THE BRITISH NATIONAL DEBT (441)

Period	Events	Change, Million £	Principal at End, Million £
1688			0.6
1688–1727	Wars	+52.2	52.8
1727–1739	Peace	−6.3	46.6
1739–1748	Spanish War	+29.2	75.8
1748–1756	Peace	−1.2	74.6
1756–1763	Seven Years' War	+52.2	126.8
1762–1775	Peace	+0.4	127.2
1775–1783	American Revolution	+104.7	231.8
1783–1793	Peace; French Revolution	+16.0	247.9
1793–1815	French Wars	+652.5	900.4
1815–1855	Peace	−91.9	808.5
1855–1857	Russian War	+30.4	838.9
1857–1900	Peace	−199.9	639.0

During this entire period most of the national debt was funded. The composition of the debt in 1882, tabulated on page 189, illustrates the principles of debt management used.

Englishmen in the eighteenth and nineteenth centuries were as alarmed by the size of their national debt as are many Englishmen and Americans today. Other countries had been relieved by inflation and bankruptcy of much of the burden of debt, but the victorious English, proud of their credit and dependent on confidence and on imports, probably considered no such alternatives. Thomas Babington Macaulay in 1885 commented eloquently on the fears inspired by the national debt: (442)

At every stage in the growth of that debt the nation has set up the same cry of anguish and despair. [After the Peace of Utrecht] the nation owed about fifty millions; and that debt was considered, not merely by . . . fox-hunting squires . . . but by profound thinkers, as an incumbrance which would permanently cripple the body politic. Nevertheless . . . the nation [became] richer and richer.

Then came the war of the Austrian Succession; and the debt rose to eighty millions. Pamphleteers, historians and orators pronounced that now, at all events, the case was desperate.

Under the prodigal administration of the first William Pitt, the debt rapidly swelled to £140 million. . . . Men of theory and men of business almost unanimously pronounced that the fatal day had now really arrived. . . . It was possible to prove by figures that the road to national ruin was through the national debt. It was idle, however, now to talk about the road; we had reached the goal; all was over; all the revenues of the island . . . were mortgaged. Better for us to have been conquered by Prussia. . . . And yet [one] had only to open his eyes to see improvement all around him, cities increasing, marts too small for the crowd of buyers, harbors insufficient to contain the shipping . . . houses better furnished . . . smoother roads.

[After the Napoleonic War] the funded debt of England amounted to £800 million. It was in truth a . . . fabulous debt; and we can hardly wonder that the cry of despair should have been louder than ever. . . . Yet like Addison's valetudinarian, who contrived to whimper that he was dying of consumption till he became so fat that he was shamed into silence, she went on complaining that she was sunk in poverty till her wealth . . . made her complaints ridiculous. The . . . bankrupt society . . . while meeting these obligations, grew

STRUCTURE OF THE BRITISH NATIONAL DEBT, MARCH 31, 1882 (441)

Elements of the Debt	Million £	Percent of Total
Funded at $2\frac{1}{2}\%$	5.6	0.7
Funded at 3%	671.6	88.0
Funded at $3\frac{1}{2}\%$	0.2	N
Irish debt funded at 3%	32.1	4.0
Total funded debt	709.5	92.7
Actuarial value of terminable annuities	35.5	4.6
Long-term debt	745.0	97.3
Exchequer bills	5.2	0.7
Treasury three-month and six-month bills	5.4	0.7
Exchequer bonds at $3\frac{1}{2}\%$ (limited term)	7.4	1.0
Total debt	763.0	100.0

richer and richer so fast that the growth could almost be discerned by the eye.

A sum exceeding [£240 million, about one third of the national debt] was in a few years voluntarily expended by this ruined people on [the construction of railroads]. Meanwhile taxation was . . . becoming lighter; yet still the Exchequer was full. . . . The prophets of evil were under a double delusion. . . . They saw that the debt grew; and they forgot that other things grew as well as the debt.

A long experience justifies us in believing that England may, in the twentieth century, be better able to pay a debt of £1,600 million than she is at the present time to bear her present load. [In 1990 the British national debt was over £200 billion.]

During the war years up to 1815, the government financed its huge deficits principally through the sale of 3% consols at large discounts. They were sold as low as 55–57% of par to yield 5.45–5.25%, but more often at higher prices. These offerings were not worded, however, in terms of a percentage of par, but rather in terms of the value if redeemed. Thus, in 1800, as Table 18 indicates, the investor was offered by the government for each £100 of cash a face value of £147 of 3s. This equaled an annuity of 4.41% on his investment. In 1801 he was offered £175¾ of 3s for £100, which equaled 5.26%. Income would be supplemented by a large profit if the 3s were ever redeemed. There was no promise of redemption, but eighty-seven years later the 3s were all redeemed at par. At times, high rate securities were also offered. These were usually 5s. For example, £105 of 5s were offered for £100 in 1808, to yield 5.25%. This equaled a price of about 95% of par. Packages were often offered. In 1802 the investor was offered for £100 the following package: (443) £50 of 3s, plus £50 of 4s plus £25 of 5s, plus an annuity of 0.54% per year to 1860. This package yielded 5.24%.

Discount 3s were more popular than high-priced 5s. It was argued that with peace and easy money the government could refund the 5s while the 3s would simply appreciate. Just this happened. Because of the large volume of financing at discounts, the face value of the war debt increased much more than the sums raised.

In the last years of the Napoleonic Wars the floating debt rose very rapidly—a most unusual circumstance in nineteenth-century English fiscal history. Between 1811 and 1815 bank advances to the government replaced a good part of the bank's private discounts. (444) As soon as the war ended, demobilization, economy, fiscal and monetary reform, and debt conversion were pushed forward vigorously. In 1816 the rate on exchequer bills was reduced from 5 to 4%, and in 1818 they were refunded. High-rate securities were redeemed at par whenever their terms permitted, and the holders were offered lower rate securities with protec-

TABLE 18

PRINCIPAL NEW ISSUES OF LONG-TERM BRITISH GOVERNMENT
SECURITIES IN THE NINETEENTH CENTURY (443)

Year	Security Issues	Estimated Effective Yield, %
1800	3s £147 face amount for £100 cash	4.41
1801	3s £175¾ for £100	5.26
1802	3s £50 4s £50 5s £25 } all for £100 plus annuity of .54% to 1860 *	5.24
1804	3s £182 for £100	5.45
1805	3s £172 for £100	5.15
1806	3s £166 for £100	4.97
1807	3s £140 5s £12⅖ } all for £100	4.83
1808	4s £118⅜ for £100	4.75
	5s £105 for £100	5.25
1809	5s £103¼ for £100	5.16
1810	5s £103¼ for £100	5.16
	3s £140⅜ for £100	4.22
1811	5s £103.7 for £100	5.18
	3s £120 4s £20 } all for £100 plus annuity of .35% to 1860 *	4.71
1812	3s £176 for £100	5.29
	5s £115½ for £100	5.75
1813	3s £177 to £100	5.33
1814	3s £103½ 5s £30 } all for £100	4.61
1815	5s £117 for £100	5.85
	3s £174 4s £10 } all for £100	5.64
1822	Conversion of 5s to 4s	4.00 †
1824	Conversion of 4s to 3½s	3.50 †
1825	Conversion of 5s to 3s (at a discount)	3.50 †
1826	Conversion of 5s to 4s	4.00 †
1830	Conversion of 4s to 3½s	3.50 †
1834	Conversion of 4s to 3½s	3.50 †
1844	Conversion of 3½s to 3¼s	3.25 †
1847	Consol 3s (Irish famine) at 89	3.36
1854	Conversion of 3¼s to 3s	3.00 †
1856	Consol 3s (Crimean War) at 90	3.33
	Consol 3s (Crimean War) at 93	3.23
1876–79	Funding into 3½s	3.50 †
1884	Conversion of 3s to 2½s (at a discount)	2.80? †
1888	Conversion of 3s to consols paying 2¾% for fourteen years and 2½% thereafter	2.70 †

* The additional yield provided by the terminable annuities is calculated by capitalizing their present value at the nominal rates of the perpetual annuities.
† Conversion yields are estimated, based on approximate market value of the new securities.

tion against early redemption. Conversions occurred in 1822, 1824, 1825, 1826, and 1830, some in very large volume.

In 1853 there was an important experiment: a refunding issue of exchequer bonds was offered. This was a new type of security, paying 2¾% for ten years, and 2½% for thirty more years, and then maturing. The bonds were not popular. Maturity was a novelty, and the rate was low.

In 1877 the systematic issue of treasury bills was begun. The bills were sold at a discount and normally had a three months' maturity, although they occasionally ran for twelve months. Treasury bills became an important money-market instrument, tending to replace trade bills. Other innovations included an issue of exchequer Suez Canal bonds of 1876, repayable in full by sinking fund in thirty-six years, and regular issues of exchequer bonds in 1877–1879, with a fixed maturity of three years. Such repayable debt was not considered a part of the funded debt. The funded debt was a charge on the income of the nation, but not a principal charge on its liquid resources.

A few 2½% annuities were created at a discount in 1855, and these were substantially augmented in 1884. By this time, the 3% consols were selling around 100. At such prices, the consols were no longer a good guide to the market rate of long-term interest, because they were redeemable by the government at 100. The new 2½s now began to provide a better guide. By 1880, the 2½s were up to 83 and at that price yielded 3%—the same as consols. During the next eight years consols remained around their redemption price of 100, but the 2½s advanced almost steadily and in 1888 reached 97, to yield 2.56%.

At this point, Chancellor of the Exchequer Goschen, a former director of the Bank of England, moved rapidly to convert the greater part of the entire national debt into new consols. The new consols promised to pay 3% for one year, 2¾% for 14 years (that is, until 1903), and 2½% thereafter. The conversion was a great success. In 1889 the new 2¾–2½% consols declined several points in price, but by 1897 they stood at a price of 114, to yield 2.21%.

LONG-TERM INTEREST RATES: THE "FUNDS"

The market rate of interest on long-term English government securities declined most of the time from 1816 to 1896. In these eighty years the market moved from high rates to much the lowest rates for modern times. Chart 7 (p. 193) suggests that this gigantic fluctuation can be broken down into three parts: first, the postwar conversion period of 1816–1845, when, starting from 5½%, a large part of the decline in yields occurred and the 3% level of 1750 was regained; second, an interim pe-

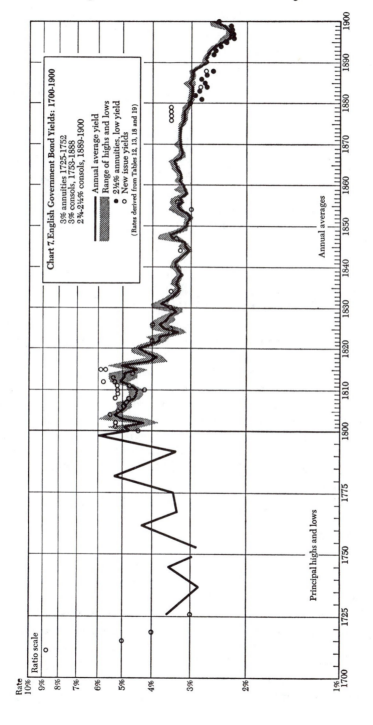

Chart 7. English Government Bond Yields: 1700-1900

3% annuities 1725-1752
3% consols, 1753-1888
2¾-2½% consols, 1889-1900

—— Annual average yield
▨ Range of highs and lows
● 2½% annuities, low yield
○ New issue yields

(Rates derived from Tables 12, 13, 18 and 19)

Rate
Ratio scale

Annual averages

Principal highs and lows

riod from 1846 to 1866, when consol yields increased moderately, moving narrowly in a 3–3½% band, usually in the higher part of this range; and, finally, the golden age of low interest rates from 1866 to 1897, when yields on consols plunged to new low levels of 2.21%, never duplicated before or since.

Table 19 and Chart 7 summarize the market yields of British consols from 1800 to 1900. The chart also indicates the yields from Table 18 on the principal new long-term government offerings for cash and the yield on some of the frequent exchange offerings, called conversions. The chart also contains a condensed version of the yield history of the British funds during the eighteenth century, so that the record of the nineteenth century can be seen in perspective. The complete history of this one rate throughout a span of 240 years of modern history is summarized in Chart 52, Chapter XIX. Table 19 and Chart 7 are based on annual averages of the yields, together with yields at annual high and low prices.

Consol yields in the twentieth century are not always representative of long-term British gilt-edged yields, but they were representative throughout most of the nineteenth century. However, during the ninth decade of the nineteenth century, the yields on the 3% consols were not representative of the going rate on long-term funds. The chance of redemption prevented a large price rise above 100, and consols were, in fact, redeemed after the conversion of 1888. Therefore, during this decade, the table and chart include market prices and yields on an issue of 2½% perpetual annuities, which were in less danger of redemption. The 2½s sold to yield slightly more than 3% consols from 1865 to 1881 and thereafter rose in price to yield substantially less than 3% consols, as shown by the table on page 214. As the yield on 3s was distorted by redemption price and the yield on 2½s was not, the history of yields during the ninth decade must be stated in terms of the 2½% annuities.

After the giant refunding of 1888, a new statistical complication was created by the terms of the refunding. The new consols promised 2¾% until 1903 and thereafter 2½%. Their yield during the interim period 1889–1903 is sometimes calculated by dividing their price into 2¾%. However, they did not carry a long-term promise of 2¾%, and, therefore, this is an overstatement of their yield; the overstatement is proved by comparison with simultaneous lower yields on the old 2½s. The new consols sold at substantial premiums after 1893. As they were redeemable at the option of Parliament after 1923, some have calculated their yield by amortizing a 2½% bond downward to par in 1923, and adding the current value of the extra ¼%. This calculation, resulting in yields below 2% at the market highs of 1896–1898, is probably an understatement. The possibility of redemption of 2½s twenty-seven years hence may have had

TABLE 19

Prices and Yields of Long-Term British Government Securities: Nineteenth Century

Year	3% Consols						2½% Annuities			
	Annual Average		Annual High Price	Yield, %	Annual Low Price	Yield, %	Annual High Price	Yield, %	Annual Low Price	Yield, %
	Price	Yield, %								
1800	63$\frac{11}{16}$	4.71	67$\frac{1}{4}$	4.46	60	5.00				
1801	61	4.92	70	4.30	54$\frac{1}{4}$	5.51				
1802	70$\frac{15}{16}$	4.23	79	3.80	66	4.54				
1803	60$\frac{1}{2}$	4.99	73	4.12	50$\frac{1}{4}$	5.99				
1804	56$\frac{5}{8}$	5.30	59$\frac{7}{8}$	5.01	53$\frac{3}{4}$	5.56				
1805	59$\frac{1}{2}$	5.04	62	4.83	57	5.26				
1806	61$\frac{5}{8}$	4.87	64$\frac{5}{8}$	4.62	58$\frac{1}{2}$	5.12				
1807	61	4.92	64$\frac{3}{8}$	4.63	57$\frac{5}{8}$	5.20				
1808	65$\frac{15}{16}$	4.55	69$\frac{1}{8}$	4.32	62$\frac{5}{8}$	4.79				
1809	66$\frac{13}{16}$	4.49	70$\frac{3}{8}$	4.26	63$\frac{3}{8}$	4.71				
10-yr. av.		4.80								
1810	67$\frac{1}{8}$	4.47	71	4.25	63$\frac{1}{4}$	4.75				
1811	64$\frac{1}{4}$	4.67	66$\frac{3}{4}$	4.50	61$\frac{1}{4}$	4.85				
1812	59	5.08	63	4.76	55$\frac{1}{8}$	5.42				
1813	61	4.92	67$\frac{1}{2}$	4.44	54$\frac{1}{2}$	5.49				
1814	61	4.92	67$\frac{1}{2}$	4.44	54$\frac{1}{2}$	5.49				
1815	67	4.48	72$\frac{1}{2}$	4.12	61$\frac{1}{4}$	4.86				
1816	59$\frac{3}{4}$	5.02	65$\frac{3}{4}$	4.56	53$\frac{7}{8}$	5.56				
1817	73$\frac{3}{16}$	4.10	84$\frac{1}{4}$	3.56	62	4.83				
1818	77$\frac{1}{2}$	3.87	82	3.66	73	4.12				
1819	71$\frac{15}{16}$	4.17	79	3.80	64$\frac{7}{8}$	4.61				
10-yr. av.		4.57								
1820	67$\frac{7}{8}$	4.42	70$\frac{1}{4}$	4.29	65$\frac{5}{8}$	4.56				
1821	73$\frac{3}{4}$	4.07	78$\frac{3}{4}$	3.81	68$\frac{3}{4}$	4.36				
1822	79$\frac{1}{8}$	3.79	83	3.60	75$\frac{3}{8}$	3.99				
1823	78$\frac{15}{16}$	3.80	85$\frac{3}{4}$	3.50	72	4.17				
1824	90$\frac{15}{16}$	3.30	96$\frac{5}{8}$	3.10	84$\frac{3}{4}$	3.54				
1825	84$\frac{3}{4}$	3.54	94$\frac{1}{4}$	3.19	75	4.00				
1826	79$\frac{3}{8}$	3.79	84$\frac{1}{2}$	3.55	73$\frac{7}{8}$	4.08				
1827	83$\frac{1}{8}$	3.61	89$\frac{1}{2}$	3.35	76$\frac{3}{4}$	3.92				
1828	84$\frac{3}{4}$	3.54	88$\frac{3}{8}$	3.40	80$\frac{7}{8}$	3.72				
1829	89$\frac{13}{16}$	3.34	94$\frac{1}{4}$	3.19	85$\frac{5}{8}$	3.50				
10-yr. av.		3.72								
1830	86	3.49	94$\frac{1}{4}$	3.19	77$\frac{1}{2}$	3.98				
1831	79$\frac{3}{4}$	3.76	84$\frac{3}{4}$	3.54	74$\frac{7}{8}$	4.01				
1832	83$\frac{3}{4}$	3.58	85$\frac{3}{4}$	3.50	81$\frac{5}{8}$	3.68				
1833	87$\frac{3}{4}$	3.42	91$\frac{1}{4}$	3.28	84$\frac{1}{4}$	3.56				
1834	90$\frac{3}{8}$	3.32	93	3.22	87$\frac{1}{2}$	3.44				
1835	91$\frac{3}{16}$	3.29	92$\frac{7}{8}$	3.22	89$\frac{1}{4}$	3.36				
1836	89$\frac{1}{2}$	3.35	92$\frac{1}{4}$	3.25	86$\frac{5}{8}$	3.47				
1837	90$\frac{15}{16}$	3.30	93$\frac{7}{8}$	3.20	87$\frac{7}{8}$	3.42				
1838	92$\frac{7}{8}$	3.23	95$\frac{1}{4}$	3.15	90$\frac{5}{8}$	3.31				
1839	91$\frac{1}{2}$	3.28	93$\frac{7}{8}$	3.20	89$\frac{1}{4}$	3.36				
10-yr. av.		3.40								

TABLE 19 (*Continued*)

Year	3% Consols						2½% Annuities			
	Annual Average		Annual High Price	Yield, %	Annual Low Price	Yield, %	Annual High Price	Yield, %	Annual Low Price	Yield, %
	Price	Yield, %								
1840	89½	3.35	93⅛	3.22	85¾	3.50				
1841	88¾	3.38	90½	3.30	87¼	3.45				
1842	91¾	3.27	94⅞	3.17	88½	3.39				
1843	94⅝	3.17	97⅝	3.07	92⅛	3.25				
1844	99	3.03	101⅜	2.96	96½	3.11				
1845	96⅛	3.12	100⅝	2.98	91⅞	3.27				
1846	95 13/16	3.13	97¾	3.07	94	3.20				
1847	87¼	3.44	93⅞	3.20	78¾	3.82				
1848	85½	3.51	90	3.34	80	3.76				
1849	92⅝	3.24	97⅞	3.07	88⅝	3.39				
10-yr. av.		3.26								
1850	96½	3.11	98⅜	3.05	94⅜	3.18				
1851	97	3.09	99⅛	3.02	95⅝	3.14				
1852	99⅜	3.02	102	2.94	95⅞	3.13				
1853	97¾	3.07	101	2.97	90¾	3.30				
1854	91¾	3.27	95⅞	3.14	85⅛	3.52				
1855	90⅝	3.31	93¾	3.20	86¼	3.47				
1856	93 3/16	3.22	95⅞	3.14	85¾	3.50				
1857	91¾	3.27	94¼	3.19	86½	3.46				
1858	96¾	3.10	98¾	3.04	93⅞	3.20				
1859	95¼	3.15	97⅜	3.08	88¼	3.40				
10-yr. av.		3.16								
1860	94	3.19	95⅞	3.14	92½	3.24				
1861	91½	3.28	94¼	3.19	89	3.37				
1862	92⅞	3.23	94¾	3.18	90⅜	3.31				
1863	92 9/16	3.24	94	3.20	90	3.34				
1864	90	3.33	92	3.26	87⅛	3.45				
1865	89½	3.35	91½	3.28	86¾	3.46	74	3.39	69	3.64
1866	88	3.41	90⅜	3.33	84⅝	3.54	72	3.49	67½	3.71
1867	92⅞	3.23	96⅜	3.11	89¾	3.35	77½	3.23	71	3.52
1868	93¾	3.20	96⅛	3.12	91⅞	3.27	77½	3.23	74½	3.38
1869	92⅞	3.23	94¼	3.19	91¾	3.27	76½	3.27	73½	3.40
10-yr. av.		3.27								
1870	92⅝	3.24	94½	3.19	88¼	3.40	76½	3.27	71	3.52
1871	92⅞	3.23	94	3.20	91⅜	3.28	76	3.29	73	3.41
1872	92⅝	3.24	93⅜	3.21	91¼	3.28	75½	3.32	73½	3.40
1873	92⅝	3.24	94	3.20	91⅝	3.27	75½	3.32	73½	3.40
1874	92⅝	3.24	93¾	3.20	91¼	3.28	76	3.29	73½	3.40
1875	93¾	3.20	95¾	3.14	91⅝	3.27	77½	3.23	73½	3.40
1876	94 15/16	3.16	97½	3.08	93⅜	3.21	79	3.16	75	3.34
1877	95¼	3.15	97⅜	3.08	93	3.22	79	3.16	76	3.29
1878	95¼	3.15	98	3.06	93⅝	3.20	79	3.16	75½	3.32
1879	97⅜	3.08	99⅝	3.01	94¼	3.19	82	3.06	75½	3.32
10-yr. av.		3.19								

TABLE 19 (*Continued*)

Year	3% and 3–2¾–2½% Consols						2½% Annuities			
	Annual Average		Annual High Price	Yield, %	Annual Low Price	Yield, %	Annual High Price	Yield, %	Annual Low Price	Yield, %
	Price	Yield, %								
1880	98⅜	3.05	100¾	2.98	97⅜	3.08	83	3.02	78½	3.19
1881	100	3.00	103	2.91	98¼	3.05	90½	2.78	81	3.09
1882	100⅜	2.99	102½	2.92	99	3.03	86	2.91	83½	2.99
1883	101	2.97	102¾	2.92	99⅜	3.02	88¼	2.84	86½	2.90
1884	101	2.97	102⅝	2.92	99⅛	3.03	92⅞	2.69	90⅜	2.75
1885	99⅜	3.02	103⅝	2.89	94⅝	3.16	91⅜	2.72	87	2.87
1886	100⅝	2.98	102¼	2.93	99¼	3.02	89¾	2.79	88½	2.83
1887	101 11/16	2.95	103⅝	2.89	100⅛	2.99	93¼	2.68	88¼	2.84
1888	101	2.97	103⅜	2.90	99⅛	3.02	97¼	2.56	94¼	2.64
1889	97⅞	2.81	99¼	2.77	96	2.86				
10-yr. av.		2.97								
1890	96½	2.67	98¾	2.62	93⅜	2.76				
1891	95 13/16	2.70	97½	2.65	94¼	2.74				
1892	96 13/16	2.65	98¼	2.62	95	2.71	97½	2.56	96	2.61
1893	98 5/16	2.61	99⅝	2.57	97	2.65	99½	2.52	98⅛	2.55
1894	101⅛	2.52	103½	2.46	98⅜	2.59	103¼	2.42	99	2.53
1895	106 3/16	2.39	108⅜	2.35	103⅜	2.46	107¾	2.32	104	2.40
1896	110⅞	2.28	113⅞	2.22	105⅛	2.42	113⅝	2.20	107	2.34
1897	112¼	2.25	113⅞	2.21	110	2.31	113	2.21	111⅝	2.24
1898	110⅞	2.28	112⅞	2.22	108⅞	2.32	112⅝	2.22	109	2.29
1899	107	2.36	111½	2.26	97¾	2.59	111	2.25	99½	2.51
10-yr. av.		2.47								
1900	99⅝	2.54	103¼	2.44	96¾	2.62	101¼	2.47	97¼	2.57

Consol yields calculated at the 3% nominal rate, 1800 through 1888; thereafter, calculated as described in text as a perpetual 2½ paying an extra ¼% until 1903.

SOURCES

Great Britain Central Statistical Office, *Statistical Abstract.*

G. F. Warren and F. A. Pearson, *Prices*, New York, 1933, John Wiley & Sons, Inc., p. 273.

Charles Fenn, *Fenn's Compendium of English and Foreign Funds*, London, Robert Lucas Nash, 1883, pp. 29ff.

Bankers Almanac, London, Thomas Skinner & Co.

R. G. Hawtrey, *A Century of Bank Rate*, London, Longmans Green & Co., 1938, pp. 155ff. and pp. 289–290.

little weight with investors interested in current income. The objection is also borne out by the simultaneous 2.20 minimum yield on the old 2½% annuities. Table 19 shows yields on the 2¾–2½% consols during this interim period of fourteen years calculated by reducing the market price of the 2¾s by an amount approximately equal to the discounted value of the extra ¼%. From this lower price the yield of a perpetual 2½ is derived. The resulting yields were very close to the market yields on the 2½% annuities.

At this point it is possible and desirable to deal more systematically with those capital values which are the inverse of long-term interest rates—in other words, with the market prices of long-term debt instruments. Heretofore, only a few prices have been quoted, such as the market prices of Venetian *prestiti,* the prices of British funds during most of the eighteenth century, and the prices of French *rentes* in the final years of that century. The long history of the British 3% consols from 1751 through 1888 provides an ideal medium for reviewing those changes in capital values which accompany changes in long-term interest rates. Modern interest rate history will give many other opportunities for reporting actual price histories of long-term bonds and also the history of bond price indices.

Bond market analysts frequently chart bond yields along inverted yield scales so that their curves rise when bond prices rise and yields decline, and fall when bond prices fall and yields rise. Such charts give a good picture of market price trends, while the reader is invited to look in the margin and see that yields are lowest at the top of the chart and highest at the bottom. Since this history is also concerned with short-term interest rates, which involve little inverse movement of capital values, and is primarily a history of interest rates rather than of capital values; and since it is the rate of interest that is to be compared from period to period rather than the market value of any one security, inversion of yield scales does not suit. Instead, yields are charted right side up and a few yield charts are supplemented by charts showing price histories, also right side up. The price of British consols and annuities from 1727 to 1900 is charted on Chart 8.

One more technicality of charting should be noted. Most of these interest rate and bond yield charts are in semilogarithm scale. This form of presentation recognizes the fact that a yield increase from 1 to 2% is a far more significant change than an increase from 4 to 5%. The doubling of rate from any level occupies equal height on these charts; and thus fluctuations in a higher yield range are not exaggerated to the eye, and fluctuations in a lower yield range are not minimized. Similarly, the long-range price charts are set in semilogarithm scale so that a price rise from 50 to 60 will seem to the eye as large as a rise from 100 to 120, and so on.

Chart 8 immediately reveals the vast changes in the price of consols in the eighteenth and nineteenth centuries. These followed from the changes in the going rate of long-term interest which have already been discussed. From a market price of 105 (in round numbers) in 1753, consols declined to 70 in 1762, rose to over 90 in 1768 (an appreciation of 30%), declined to 54 in 1784 after the American War, recovered to 97 in 1792 (an appreciation of 80%), and then declined to their all-time low (as 3s) of 47¼ in 1798 when Napoleon threatened invasion.

Investors at 100 had lost more than half their principal. No period in the nineteenth century saw a price so low or a yield so high. No nineteenth-century crisis saw the Treasury paying a rate as high as the 6.57% it paid in 1797 for new long-term funds.

After the brief peace of 1802, consols recovered to 79, an appreciation of 67% from their low. The next year, with renewed war, they dipped to 50—the low of the nineteenth century. They recovered to 71 in 1810 and fell again to about 54 in 1813; in the year of the Battle of Waterloo they ranged between 61½ and 72½. In one year, 1816–1817, they rose 55%

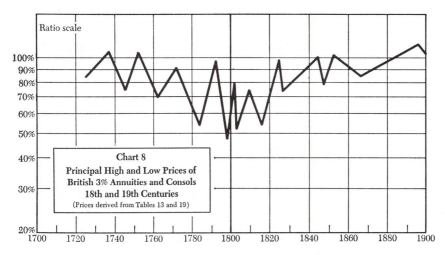

Chart 8
Principal High and Low Prices of British 3% Annuities and Consols 18th and 19th Centuries
(Prices derived from Tables 13 and 19)

from 54 to 84, and after some fluctuations were back to 96⅞ by 1824—an eight-year appreciation in principal value of 79%. They never again rose so rapidly in a comparable period of years, even in the 1930's. They did not lose the reputation they then gained of being "a good thing" until the wars of the twentieth century. The conventional yield calculations, made when the consols were at heavy discounts, do not and cannot include the added return which was correctly expected from capital gains.

From 1824 until 1880 a price range of 80–95 was maintained most of the time, with occasional dips to 74 or so during crises and occasional brief excursions upward to a slight premium. In the first part of this fifty-six-year period, from 1824 to 1852, prices advanced more often than they declined. From 1852 to 1866 moderate price declines predominated, which aggregated 17% when consols "came back" to 85. A renewed trend toward higher prices began in 1866 and lasted until 1897. The profit on consols, however, was then restricted by the redemption option. Consols rose to a 103⅝ high in 1887 and then were redeemed. Their 22% appreciation from 1866 low prices compared with a simultaneous appreciation of 45% for the 2½% annuities. The new consols after the conversion went on up to a price of 114 in 1896. The total gain from 1866 was 34% for holders of consols who accepted the refunding, as compared with 68% for holders of the old 2½% annuities. The funds were still a good thing.

The last decades of the nineteenth century could be called the golden age of easy money. Low yields did not seem transitory, as they were in the 1750's. This was not a period of deep depression or of war, such as characterized the easy money periods in the twentieth century. Short rates were volatile and occasionally high, but the yields on the gilt-edged were low by modern and by ancient standards. Yields had declined and prices had advanced most of the time for one hundred years. This somewhat resembled the easy-money periods in Holland in the seventeenth and early eighteenth centuries.

Almost all important trading nations enjoyed low long-term interest rates in the latter decades of the nineteenth century. Low interest rates were not then primarily a doctrine of reformers. Conservative business leaders were proud of their low market rates. They enjoyed the easy terms of credit available to finance the vast industrial installations then under construction. Conservative governments were delighted to ease their burden of debt by converting at low rates. The business community liked to see the funds rise in the market. A prominent editor of *The Economist* wrote some years later: "For British Consols to yield more than 3% in time of peace and prosperous trade is certainly abnormal." (445) It was then that Eugen Böhm von Bawerk declared that the higher are a people's intelligence and moral strength, the lower will be the rate of interest. (446) Central banks referred to their low discount rates as a measure of achievement. (447)

OTHER LONG-TERM INTEREST RATES

The spectrum of yields available to British investors was always very wide. The low yields from the funds were by no means representative of the entire market. Many kinds of long-term debt instruments were traded in volume on the London Stock Exchange of the nineteenth century. Many new issues of securities were offered by prospectuses to the public. There were loans to United Kingdom municipalities and governmental boards, loans to colonial governments, loans to foreign governments, and loans to domestic and foreign companies. No continuous and uniform series of interest rates on these various types of securities is available to us, and lack of standard ratings and uniformity would make such a series of questionable value. Some examples of debt issues other than the funds will illustrate the level and range of available long-term yields and the differences between other yields and yields on the funds.

The lowest yields, next to those from the funds, were understandably provided by issues of domestic governing bodies. These yields, however, sometimes covered a sizable range, as illustrated by Table 20, which lists representative issues from 1869 through 1886.

During the limited period of time covered by the above table, yields on consols were declining gradually, and thus the market was favorable. The yields on the only repetitive offerings, those of the Metropolitan Board of Works of London declined even faster than consol yields. Thus, their yield premium narrowed from almost 50 basis points in 1869 to 15 basis points twelve years later. Obviously, these securities achieved

TABLE 20

NEW ISSUES BY BRITISH LOCAL GOVERNMENTS (448)

Year	Local Government Issue	Price	Current Yield at Offering, %	Yield Difference from Annual Average Yield of Consols, in Basis Points *
1869	Metropolitan Board of Works $3\frac{1}{2}$s, due 1929	$94\frac{1}{2}$	3.70	+47
1873	Metropolitan Board of Works $3\frac{1}{2}$s, due 1929	$95\frac{1}{2}$	3.66	+42
1874	Metropolitan Board of Works $3\frac{1}{2}$s, due 1929	$94\frac{1}{2}$	3.70	+46
1876	Metropolitan Board of Works $3\frac{1}{2}$s, due 1929	$100\frac{1}{8}$	3.49	+33
1877	Metropolitan Board of Works $3\frac{1}{2}$s, due 1929	100	3.50	+35
1878	Metropolitan Board of Works $3\frac{1}{2}$s, due 1929	$100\frac{3}{4}$	3.47	+32
1878	Stockton $4\frac{1}{4}$s, due 1908	$102\frac{1}{2}$	4.15	+100
1879	Metropolitan Board of Works $3\frac{1}{2}$s, due 1929	$101\frac{3}{8}$	3.44	+36
1880	Metropolitan Board of Works $3\frac{1}{2}$s, due 1929	$102\frac{1}{8}$	3.41	+36
1880	Liverpool, $3\frac{1}{2}$s	100	3.50	+45
1880	Liverpool, $3\frac{1}{2}$s	105	3.33	+27
1881	Metropolitan Board of Works 3s, due 1941	95	3.15	+15
1881	Birmingham $3\frac{1}{2}$s, redeemable 1946	98	3.57	+57
1882	Metropolitan Board of Works 3s, due 1941	$97\frac{1}{8}$	3.08	+17 †
1882	Isle of Man $3\frac{1}{2}$s (1% sinking fund)	$98\frac{1}{2}$	3.56	+65 †
1882	Reading $3\frac{1}{2}$s redeemable (70-year sinking fund)	92	3.80	+89 †
1886	Corporation of London $3\frac{1}{2}$s	100	3.50	+66 †

* The difference is expressed in "basis points."

A "basis point" is one hundredth of 1% in yield. The difference between a yield of 2% and a yield of 3% is called 100 basis points. When Liverpool $3\frac{1}{2}$s were offered to yield 3.50 and consols were simultaneously selling to yield 3.05%, the difference, or spread, is said to be +45 basis points in favor of the Liverpool $3\frac{1}{2}$s.

† Yield difference from $2\frac{1}{2}$% annuities.

a prime credit rating with investors. Most other issues sold at larger differentials from the funds. The table shows that it was possible to obtain domestic obligations of a non-speculative character at yields in the range of 3.50–4% when the funds were yielding close to 3%.

Much higher yields were available from the obligations of colonial governments reported for 1860–1882 in Table 21. The colonial loans and the other foreign loans discussed later were all borrowings in sterling in the London market. Therefore, they are presented as a part of the history of rates prevailing in London on foreign securities rather than as part of the interest-rate histories of the debtor countries.

The sample of colonial sterling issues in Table 21 reflects the gradual decline in consol yields over most of this period, the improving popularity of colonial obligations, which resulted in declining yield spreads from consols, and the diversity of rates and ratings within this department of the investment market. It illustrates the use of the concept of bond maturity as a claim of investors rather than a privilege of borrowers.

British investors, however, were not limited to domestic and colonial securities. London was the banker for the world. Most foreign countries could borrow in London at a price. The British investor's appetite was good for high-yielding foreign bonds. It survived a long succession of defaults. History tends to emphasize newsworthy defaults and leaves in obscurity a great volume of routine periodic debt repayments between nations. When a credit was dubious or off the beaten path, British nineteenth-century investors insisted on high rates of interest.

Foreign loans were made in volume soon after the Napoleonic Wars. Demand for foreign bonds in the 1820's was no doubt stimulated by the rapid conversions of the British government debt from 5s to 4s and later to 3s. Recognition of the new South American republics after their secession from Spain probably also encouraged investors. Between 1818 and 1832, twenty-six foreign governments floated issues in London. By 1837 only ten of these still paid. Nevertheless as the century progressed and the yield on the funds continued to decline, British investors continued to absorb foreign securities. Some of these new issues and their yields are recorded in Table 22.

British investors were by no means restricted to investment in domestic and foreign bonds. Domestic and foreign equities were increasingly available. Also prime short bills could be bought in times of credit stringency at 4–7%. Good mortgages could be bought at rates up to 1% above consols. In 1866, Australian banks offered to pay 8% to Londoners for deposits.

Securities listed on the London Stock Exchange had a total value of £1.2 billion in 1843, of which 63% were obligations of the British government, 17% of British colonial and foreign governments, while 20% were

TABLE 21

NEW STERLING ISSUES BY COLONIAL GOVERNMENTS (449)

Year	Colonial Government Issue	Price	Current Yield at Offering, %	Yield Difference from Annual Average Yield of Consols, Basis Points *
1860	Canada Consolidated 5s ($\frac{1}{2}$% sinking fund)	$97\frac{1}{2}$	5.12	+193
1863	British Columbia 6s (9% sinking fund)	100	6.00	+276
1863	Ceylon 6s (redeemed in 1878)	100	6.00	+276
1865	Vancouver Island 6s due 1880	100	6.00	+265
1865	New South Wales 5s, redeemable 1888	96 high	5.20 †	+185
1865	New South Wales 5s, redeemable 1888	89 low	5.62 †	+227
1866	New South Wales 5s, redeemable 1895	$85\frac{1}{2}$	5.85	+244
1866	New Zealand 6s, due 1891 (2% sinking fund)	90	6.66	+325
1867	New Zealand 6s, due 1891 (2% sinking fund)	$104\frac{1}{4}$	5.77	+254
1867	Ceylon 6s (redeemed 1878)	108	5.55	+228
1868	New Zealand 5s (36-year sinking fund)	97	5.16	+196
1868	New South Wales 5s, redeemable 1896	$94\frac{1}{8}$	5.31	+211
1870	New South Wales 5s, redeemable 1888	$103\frac{1}{2}$ high	4.85 †	+161
1870	New South Wales 5s, redeemable 1888	96 low	5.27 †	+203
1871	New South Wales 5s, redeemable 1900	98.80	5.06	+183
1872	New South Wales 5s, redeemable 1902	100	5.00	+176
1872	New South Wales 4s, redeemable 1902	86	4.65	+141
1874	New South Wales 4s, due 1903	90	4.44	+120
1874	Canada 4s, due 1904	90	4.44	+120
1874	India 4s, redeemable 1888	$101\frac{3}{8}$	3.94	+70
1874	Quebec 5s, due 1904	$97\frac{1}{2}$	5.17	+176
1874	New Zealand $4\frac{1}{2}$s, due 1904	98	4.59	+135
1875	New South Wales 5s, redeemable 1888	111 high	4.50 †	+130
1875	New South Wales 5s, redeemable 1888	105 low	4.80 †	+150
1876	Ceylon $4\frac{1}{2}$s (39-year sinking fund)	102	4.43	+123
1876	Canada 4s, due 1906	91	4.40	+120
1877	British Columbia 6s, due 1907	100	6.00	+285
1879	New South Wales 4s, due 1909	$98\frac{1}{4}$	4.09	+101
1880	New South Wales 5s, redeemable 1888	112 high	4.45 †	+140
1880	New South Wales 5s, redeemable 1888	103 low	4.86 †	+181
1880	Ceylon 4s (41-year sinking fund)	98	4.11	+106
1880	India $3\frac{1}{2}$s redeemable 1931	$103\frac{5}{8}$	3.38	+33
1881	Ceylon 4s (41-year sinking fund)	102	3.92	+92
1882	New South Wales 4s, due 1910	102	3.92	+93

* See note below Table 20.
† Market prices of seasoned issues.

TABLE 22

NEW STERLING ISSUES BY FOREIGN GOVERNMENTS (449, 450)

Year	Foreign Government Issue	Price	Current Yield at Offering, %	Yield Difference from Annual Average Yield of Consols, Basis Points *
1818	Prussia 5s	72	6.95	+308
1821	Naples 5s	92	5.52	+145
1821	Spain 5s	56	8.90	+483
1822	Chile 6s	84	7.12	+333
1822	Denmark 5s, redeemable	77½	6.45	+266
1822	Russia 5s	82	6.10	+231
1823	Spain 5s	30¼	16.50	+1270
1824	Brazil 5s (redeemed in 1863)	75	6.66	+336
1824	Buenos Aires 6s	85	7.05	+375
1824	Colombia 6s	84	7.14	+384
1825	Greece 5s	56½	8.85	+531
1825	Brazil 5s (redeemed in 1863)	85	5.89	+235
1829	Brazil 5s (redeemed in 1863)	54	9.25	+546
1839	Brazil 5s (redeemed in 1863)	78	6.41	+313
1849	Denmark 5s (redeemed in 1860)	86	5.82	+258
1850	Russia 4½s (2% sinking fund)	93	4.84	+173
1851	Italy 5s (sinking fund)	85	5.89	+280
1852	Brazil 4½s	95	4.74	+172
1859	Russia 3s	66½	4.51	+136
1862	Portugal 3s	44	6.71	+348
1862	Egypt 7s (to be redeemed by 1892)	82½	8.50	+527
1862	Italy 5s (sinking fund)	74	6.75	+352
1862	Denmark 4s (redeemable)	91	4.40	+117
1864	Egypt 7s (to be redeemed by 1879)	93	7.55	+423
1865	Brazil 5s (due 1902, sinking fund)	74	6.75	+340
1866	Argentina 6s (1% sinking fund, lottery)	75	8.00	+459
1867	Egypt 9s (to be redeemed by 1882)	90	10.00	+677
1867	Russia 4s	60	6.66	+343
1870	Egypt 7s (to be redeemed by 1870)	78½	8.93	+569
1870	Argentina 6s	88	6.82	+358
1870	Japan 9s (10% sinking fund)	98	9.19	+595
1873	Russia 5s	93	5.48	+224
1874	Belgium 3s	75½	3.98	+74
1875	Brazil 5s (1% sinking fund)	96½	5.17	+197
1875	China 8s	95	8.42	+522
1876	China 8s (5–15% sinking fund)	100	8.00	+484
1879	Brazil 4½s (3⅓% sinking fund)	96⅜	4.69	+161
1880	Portugal 3s	50	6.00	+295
1881	Italy 5s (sinking fund)	90	5.55	+255
1882	Argentina 6s	91	6.60	+360
1882	Russia 3s	55	5.45	+245

* See note below Table 20.

securities of private companies. By 1875, the total listing had quadrupled to £4.5 billion. Obligations of the British government now comprised only 13% of the total; obligations of British municipalities and colonial and foreign governments comprised 55% of the total (up £2.2 billion in twenty-two years); and securities of private companies, domestic and foreign, comprised 32% of the total (up £1.2 billion in twenty-two years). (451) The funds were no longer the dominant outlet for British investors.

Finally, for those in search of a really worthwhile return, there was, as always, the opportunity to lend to a friend in need. After the repeal of the usury law, the courts came to consider 48% a ceiling above which they would not enforce collection. About 1840, Benjamin Disraeli was forced to pay 40% to meet a "pressing liability." (452) Farmers were reported borrowing at rates as high as 50%. (453)

SHORT-TERM INTEREST RATES

Short-term market rates of interest of the sort quoted on prime commercial bills also declined during the nineteenth century, but their decline followed a different pattern from that of long-term prime interest rates. By mid-century, these short rates were at times much higher, and at other times much lower than they were during the early wartime decades. Toward the end of the century, these short rates averaged much lower than they did at the start of the century or at mid-century, but every few years, at least, they would rise for a while to levels far above the uniform 5% legal limit of the Napoleonic Wars. The trend of quotations on short rates was influenced not only by supply and demand in the money market, but also by two other factors—the repeal of the usury law and the evolution of monetary policy.

The 5% limit of the usury law applied to bank rate and to the entire bill market until 1833. This law prevented quoted short rates from rising to the high levels that probably would otherwise have prevailed much of the time during the Napoleonic Wars. The 5% limit did not apply to government loans or to the market rate on consols, which was often above 5% before 1817. Discount houses were allowed to add commissions to the standard 5% rate, and thus effective rates of 5½ or 6% often were charged during the war period. (454) However, no official market quotations were recorded above 5% during the entire period 1714–1833 when the 5% legal limit was in force. Thus, the record does not reveal a true market rate of short-term interest until 1817, when quotations fell below the legal limit.

A deliberate monetary policy through manipulation of bank rate was unknown in the eighteenth century. It was impossible until the exemption of short bills from the usury laws in 1833. It was first attempted in 1839. Thereafter, the reserves were defended or trade was promoted more and more deliberately by changes in bank rate. By the 1850's bank rate was put up as high as 7–10% in emergencies and then quickly depressed to 2–3%.

The legal restrictions early in the century, their subsequent removal, and later the vigorous use of very high and very low bank rates help to explain the pattern of short-term market rate of interest in Britain during the nineteenth century. Chart 9 below reveals stability followed by increasing volatility and a great bulge at mid-century. After 1866, however, a declining trend is evident, even allowing for occasional high rates. In the final decade, the open market discount rate was usually below 2% and fell below 1%. With the funds yielding less than 2½%, the British had indeed achieved "Dutch finance."

Table 23 shows the fluctuations of bank rate throughout this century, including the annual average rate and the annual extremes of fluctuation. The table provides the same data for the open-market rate of discount for first-class commercial bills. These were bills of nonuniform maturity of a few months before 1855; thereafter, they were uniformly three-month bills. Decennial averages are also provided for convenience in discerning longer-term trends, and these are pictured in Chart 6 above.

Toward the end of the century, call loans became increasingly important. Loans at call were made by banks overnight to dealers in commercial bills and were secured by a part of the dealer's bill portfolio. Both lender and borrower could at their convenience terminate the loan on the following day. Thus, a very economical and flexible medium was provided for all participants in the money market, permitting a rapid investment and recovery of temporary balances. As would be expected, the call loan rates were very volatile and often fell far below the open market rate of discount. The open-market rate of discount in its turn was usually below bank rate. Bank rate had become a penalty rate set by the lender of last resort.

CALL LOAN RATES: MONTHLY AVERAGES

Year	Low, %	High, %	Year	Low, %	High, %
1889	1.06	3.27	1895	0.25	0.92
1890	1.30	5.40	1896	0.37	3.47
1891	0.47	3.20	1897	0.42	2.60
1892	0.44	2.20	1898	0.41	3.10
1893	0.50	2.95	1899	1.31	4.60
1894	0.28	1.80	1900	1.69	3.53

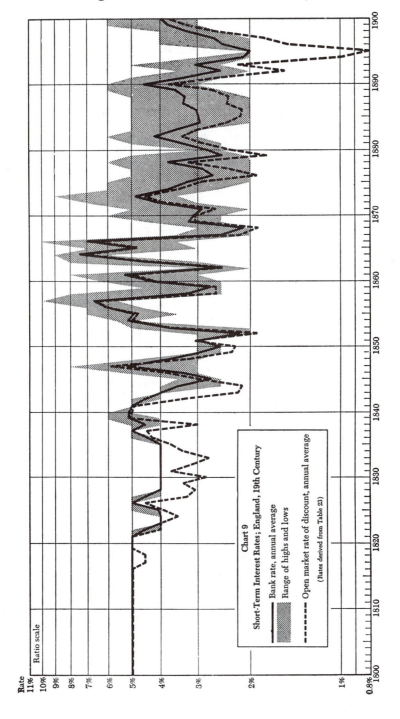

Chart 9

Short-Term Interest Rates; England, 19th Century

——— Bank rate, annual average

▨ Range of highs and lows

- - - - Open market rate of discount, annual average

(Rates derived from Table 23)

TABLE 23
SHORT-TERM BRITISH INTEREST RATES: NINETEENTH CENTURY

Year	Bank Rate, %			Open-Market Rate of Discount, %			Year	Bank Rate, %			Open-Market Rate of Discount, %		
	Annual Average	Low	High	Annual Average	Low	High		Annual Average	Low	High	Annual Average	Low	High
1800	5.00	5.00	5.00	5.00	5.00	5.00	1830	4.00	4.00	4.00	2.81	2.50	4.00
1801	5.00	5.00	5.00	5.00	5.00	5.00	1831	4.00	4.00	4.00	3.69	3.00	4.00
1802	5.00	5.00	5.00	5.00	5.00	5.00	1832	4.00	4.00	4.00	3.12	2.75	4.00
1803	5.00	5.00	5.00	5.00	5.00	5.00	1833	4.00	4.00	4.00	2.75	2.25	3.50
1804	5.00	5.00	5.00	5.00	5.00	5.00	1834	4.00	4.00	4.00	3.37	2.75	4.00
1805	5.00	5.00	5.00	5.00	5.00	5.00	1835	4.00	4.00	4.00	3.70	3.25	4.00
1806	5.00	5.00	5.00	5.00	5.00	5.00	1836	4.42	4.00	5.00	4.25	3.25	5.50
1807	5.00	5.00	5.00	5.00	5.00	5.00	1837	5.00	5.00	5.00	4.45	3.25	5.50
1808	5.00	5.00	5.00	5.00	5.00	5.00	1838	4.12	4.00	5.00	3.00	2.50	3.50
1809	5.00	5.00	5.00	5.00	5.00	5.00	1839	5.10	4.00	6.00	5.10	3.75	6.50
10-yr. av.	5.00			5.00			10-yr. av.	4.30			3.62		
1810	5.00	5.00	5.00	5.00	5.00	5.00	1840	5.10	5.00	6.00	5.00	4.25	6.00
1811	5.00	5.00	5.00	5.00	5.00	5.00	1841	5.00	5.00	5.00	4.90	4.50	5.50
1812	5.00	5.00	5.00	5.00	5.00	5.00	1842	4.26	4.00	5.00	3.33	2.50	4.75
1813	5.00	5.00	5.00	5.00	5.00	5.00	1843	4.00	4.00	4.00	2.18	2.00	2.50
1814	5.00	5.00	5.00	5.00	5.00	5.00	1844	3.50	2.50	4.00	2.12	1.75	2.75
1815	5.00	5.00	5.00	5.00	5.00	5.00	1845	2.70	2.50	3.50	2.96	2.50	4.50
1816	5.00	5.00	5.00	5.00	5.00	5.00	1846	3.33	3.00	3.50	3.80	3.00	5.00
1817	5.00	5.00	5.00	4.50	4.00	5.00	1847	5.17	3.00	8.00	5.88	3.25	10.00
1818	5.00	5.00	5.00	4.50	4.00	5.00	1848	3.71	3.00	5.00	3.20	2.50	4.25
1819	5.00	5.00	5.00	5.00	5.00	5.00	1849	2.95	2.50	3.00	2.31	2.00	2.50
10-yr. av.	5.00			4.90			10-yr. av.	4.00			3.57		
1820	5.00	5.00	5.00	5.00	5.00	5.00	1850	2.51	2.50	3.00	2.25	2.00	2.50
1821	5.00	5.00	5.00	5.00	5.00	5.00	1851	3.00	3.00	3.00	3.06	2.75	3.25
1822	4.50	4.00	5.00	4.00	4.00	4.00	1852	2.17	2.00	3.00	1.89	1.75	2.50
1823	4.00	4.00	4.00	4.00	4.00	4.00	1853	3.71	2.00	5.00	3.68	2.25	5.25
1824	4.00	4.00	4.00	3.50	3.50	3.50	1854	5.12	5.00	5.50	4.95	4.50	5.75
1825	4.06	4.00	5.00	3.88	3.50	4.50	1855	4.89	3.50	7.00	4.73	3.15	6.93
1826	5.00	5.00	5.00	4.50	4.00	5.00	1856	6.06	4.50	7.00	6.01	4.67	6.93
1827	4.50	4.00	5.00	3.25	3.00	4.00	1857	6.67	5.50	10.00	6.60	5.86	8.71
1828	4.00	4.00	4.00	3.05	3.00	3.50	1858	3.23	2.50	8.00	2.60	2.09	4.38
1829	4.00	4.00	4.00	3.35	3.00	4.00	1859	2.71	2.50	4.50	2.61	2.12	3.86
10-yr. av.	4.40			3.95			10-yr. av.	4.01			3.84		

TABLE 23 (*Continued*)

Year	Bank Rate, %			Open-Market Rate of Discount, %			Year	Bank Rate, %			Open-Market Rate of Discount, %		
	Annual Average	Low	High	Annual Average	Low	High		Annual Average	Low	High	Annual Average	Low	High
1860	4.17	2.50	6.00	4.10	2.57	4.81	1880	2.79	2.50	3.00	2.30	1.48	3.44
1861	5.27	3.00	8.00	5.00	2.46	7.35	1881	3.48	2.50	5.00	2.90	2.14	3.71
1862	2.52	2.00	3.00	2.49	2.18	2.87	1882	4.18	3.00	6.00	3.38	2.76	4.53
1863	4.45	3.00	8.00	4.40	3.15	7.20	1883	3.58	3.00	5.00	3.03	1.61	5.82
1864	7.38	6.00	9.00	7.29	5.77	10.29	1884	2.93	2.00	5.00	2.40	1.44	3.13
1865	4.81	3.00	7.00	4.79	3.21	6.65	1885	2.99	2.00	5.00	2.14	1.16	3.39
1866	6.95	3.50	10.00	6.60	3.41	10.02	1886	3.02	2.00	5.00	2.12	1.28	2.78
1867	2.51	2.00	3.50	2.16	1.30	2.99	1887	3.33	2.00	5.00	2.39	1.14	3.65
1868	2.11	2.00	3.00	1.88	1.50	2.67	1888	3.30	2.00	5.00	2.36	1.38	3.48
1869	3.21	2.50	4.50	3.06	2.38	4.13	1889	3.58	2.50	6.00	2.69	1.77	3.78
10-yr. av.	4.34			4.18			10-yr. av.	3.32			2.57		
1870	3.10	2.50	6.00	3.06	2.14	5.49	1890	4.52	3.00	6.00	3.74	2.07	6.26
1871	2.88	2.00	5.00	2.62	1.97	4.29	1891	3.28	2.50	5.00	2.51	1.66	4.60
1872	4.10	3.00	7.00	3.90	2.64	5.68	1892	2.51	2.00	3.50	1.53	1.01	2.04
1873	4.81	3.50	9.00	4.49	3.40	6.53	1893	3.05	2.50	5.00	2.19	1.21	4.49
1874	3.72	2.50	6.00	3.41	2.62	4.94	1894	2.10	2.00	3.00	0.99	0.48	1.69
1875	3.21	2.00	6.00	2.89	1.99	3.76	1895	2.00	2.00	2.00	0.81	0.53	1.15
1876	2.60	2.00	5.00	1.89	0.78	3.46	1896	2.48	2.00	4.00	1.50	0.73	2.72
1877	2.89	2.00	5.00	2.35	1.10	3.45	1897	2.63	2.00	4.00	1.80	1.08	2.42
1878	3.77	2.00	6.00	3.23	1.47	4.83	1898	3.25	2.50	4.00	2.62	1.64	4.29
1879	2.49	2.00	5.00	1.76	1.03	2.99	1899	3.74	3.00	6.00	3.26	2.02	4.87
10-yr. av.	3.36			2.96			10-yr. av.	2.96			2.09		
							1900	3.94	3.00	6.00	3.70	3.13	4.51

SOURCES

John Clapham, *The Bank of England*, New York, 1945, The Macmillan Company, Vol. II, pp. 429–431.

R. G. Hawtrey, *A Century of Bank Rate*, London, Longmans Green & Co., 1938, pp. 14, 281ff.

Open-market rates are based in part upon data compiled by the National Bureau of Economic Research from British Parliamentary papers, 1857, and from *The Economist*, 1858–1900.

The Bank of England's Statistical Office.

The history of bank rate and the history of the market rate of discount on bills provide a sufficient picture of the trends of short-term money rates of interest in nineteenth-century Britain. There were, however, many other forms of short-term credit and many diverse rates of interest charged and paid. The table below includes a number of rates associated with the banking system and with good credits. Its data are for three selected years: 1890, the year of highest market rates for this easy money decade; 1895, the year of lowest market rates for this decade and for this century; and 1900, a year when market rates had risen substantially from their lows.

Table 24 reveals a wide range of fluctuation for almost all these rates. An exception was the rate paid on deposits in English towns. All rates in country towns were more stable than city rates and were generally higher. Rates in Scotland and Ireland were usually higher than London rates, especially in 1895, when the extreme ease in the London money market had not found full reflection elsewhere.

TABLE 24

ANNUAL AVERAGE RATES ON SHORT-TERM LONDON,
PROVINCIAL, SCOTCH, AND IRISH LOANS (455)

Type of Loan	1890	1895	1900
Bank rate	4.52	2.00	3.94
First-class bills, two months, London	3.50	0.79	3.62
First-class bills, three months, London	3.68	0.82	3.42
First-class bills, six months, London	3.51	0.94	3.89
Call money	3.49	0.54	2.66
Overdrafts, London	Bank rate and upward		
Paid on bank deposits, London	3.02	0.50	2.44
Loans on stocks, a/c to a/c, London	Bank rate +0.25	Bank rate +0.50	4.26
Good bills, English country towns	4.60	3.50	4.00
Overdrafts, English country towns	5.10	4.00	4.50
Paid on deposits, English country towns	2.50	2.50	2.50
Good bills, three months, Scotland	4.75	2.79	4.92
Overdrafts, Scotland	6.13	5.04	5.96
Paid on deposits, Scotland	2.32	1.04	2.45
Good bills, three months, Ireland	4.84	3.00	4.47
Overdrafts (secured), Ireland	5.20	2.30	4.60
Paid on deposits, Ireland	1.76	1.00	1.50

This table is included, not because it is desirable here to analyze the differences in rates between Scotland, Ireland, and England or the differences between rates on deposits, overdrafts, and marketable bills, but largely as another illustration that in a modern industrial nation there is a vast complex of interest rates, of which this survey is following in detail only a few. Every city, town, and hamlet has, in fact, its own interest-rate history, usually unrecorded and unstudied.

THREE EPISODES

The following sections examine in greater detail certain important periods in the money market of nineteenth-century England.

The 1860's. The decade of the 1860's was one of stability in the market for British consols. Its interest rate history, and especially the history of the crisis of 1866, is presented in detail in Charts 10 and 11 in order to illustrate the behavior of these markets in a period when monetary management by bank rate had become fully developed.

The range of consol yields in this decade was 3.11% low and 3.54% high, which equals a range of about 12 points in price. In contrast, the range of bank rate was 2–10%, and the range of the monthly averages of open-market discounts was 1.30–10.29%. This was more than twenty times the range of consol yields.

Almost every nineteenth-century decade had its financial crisis. In this decade the crisis of 1866 was marked by the failure of Overend Gurney & Co., "The Corner House," London's largest discount house. Half of the business of the bill market was in its hands. (456) The failure came at the crest of a great boom which followed the end of the American Civil War. The year of the crisis, 1866, is shown in even greater detail on Chart 11.

Consols had been declining in price irregularly since 1863 and were down from 93 to 87½ by January of 1866. They declined a point more before the panic started. On May third the bank, which knew of the trouble to come, raised its rate 1% to 7% and 1% more on May eighth, up to 8%. On May tenth the failure of Overend Gurney & Co. for £5 million was announced.

Friday, May 11, 1866, was another "Black Friday." (457) True panic came. *The Times* wrote that the shock would be felt "in the remotest corners of the Kingdom" and that "panic . . . swayed the City to and fro." The banking reserve dropped from £5.7 million to £3 million in one day. Bank rate was raised to 9%. The government "suspended the Bank Charter Act" and, as usual in such emergencies, required that bank rate be put up to 10%. Many other failures followed. There were rumors

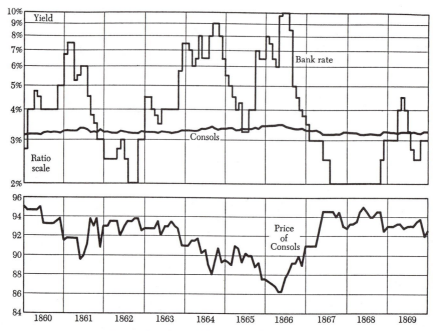

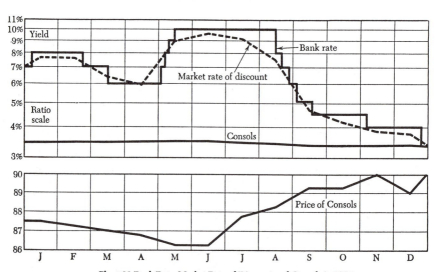

Chart 10. Bank Rate and Consols in the Decade of the 1860's
(Based on monthly data not included in the Tables)

Chart 11. Bank Rate, Market Rate of Discount and Consols in 1866
(Based on monthly and daily data not included in the Tables)

that the bank had even refused to lend on government securities. Bank rate remained at 10% for an unprecedented three months.

These details of crisis and panic are provided primarily to relate them to the structure of the market for the funds. In April, 1866, directly before the panic, the market yield on consols averaged 3.46% and the price averaged 86¾. During the panic month of May, when bank rate rose to 10%, consol yields averaged 3.48%, a price of 86¼. By June, consols were rising; and by August, with bank rate still at 10%, they reached 88½—a new high price for the year. After bank rate came down sharply, they advanced further. This episode illustrates dramatically the remarkable stability which the funds displayed throughout most of the nineteenth century in the face of frequent violent changes in short-term interest rates.

The Conversion of 1888. The decade of the 1880's is described in some detail here to present the events that made possible the great conversion of 1888. Business activity was quiet to depressed in the early part of this decade. However, there were no crises. The nation was at peace and was generally prosperous.

Bank rate and the market rate of discount on prime short bills fluctuated widely every year during this decade, partly in response to seasonal pressures. Bank rate often was lifted to 5%, but more often was held down to 3 or 2½%, or even to 2%. The market rate for bills ranged occasionally up to 4%, but more often fell to 2%, and even occasionally below 1%. Short-term market rates in this decade averaged lower than ever before.

Against this background, the yield of consols was stable at around 3%. Consol prices were close to 100 throughout, occasionally rising to 102 and only once falling to a low of 97. This stability, however, was deceptive. Consols were held down by the privilege of the government to redeem at par.

The true level of long-term rates should be derived for this decade from the price of a relatively obscure issue of 2½% annuities created earlier at a discount. A sharp rise in the market for the 2½s during this decade provided the clue to future events (see Table 19 and Chart 7). From a 78½ low in 1880, they rose to a 90½ high in 1881, to 92¾ in 1884, and then up to 97¼ in the conversion year of 1888. This represented a decline in yield from 3.19% in 1880 to 2.56% in 1888. Clearly, a 2½% rate was in sight. It might prove acceptable if some special inducements were offered. A decade or two earlier, when the consols had been selling at a discount of 5–10 points, the market had preferred the 3s to the 2½s, which probably reflected a general opinion that the 3s would not be redeemed. The gradual swing in preference toward the 2½s is shown by the following summary of yield differentials between these two issues:

YIELD ON $2\frac{1}{2}$s VS. YIELD ON 3s AT ANNUAL HIGH PRICES

Year	Basis Points	Year	Basis Points
1865–69, average	+11	1883	−8
1870–74, average	+10	1884	−23
1875–79, average	+10	1885	−17
1880	+4	1886	−14
1881	−13	1887	−21
1882	−1	1888	−34

Chancellor of the Exchequer Goschen picked a strategic moment to effect his giant conversion. In March of 1888 the country was optimistic, money was cheap, and the 2½s were above 95. The chancellor offered holders of most of the entire national debt new consols, which would pay 3% for one year, 2¾% for 14 years until 1903, and 2½% thereafter. He offered a bonus to holders of stock not then redeemable as an inducement to convert. He assumed that all holders of redeemable debt, such as the 3% consols, were willing to accept the conversion unless they protested in form. Those not accepting would be paid off. He offered a commission to brokers and others who brought in stock. The Bank of England was very cooperative: bank rate was held down to 2–3% until fall. After the conversion, Mr. Collet, the Governor of the Bank of England, was given a baronetcy. Holders of 96% of the £591 million of debt involved in the conversion accepted the new consols. The national debt was now funded at what would soon become a 2½% rate of interest.

The Crest of the Market, 1892–1900. By 1892, the great bull market in British funds was at least seventy-five years old. There had been brief reversals in times of financial crises. There had also been one longer period, 1852–1866, when moderate price declines predominated. However, the experience of several generations of British investors proved that market declines in the funds were always temporary, that new high prices always eventually rewarded the patient holder, and that every sharp decline in price was just one more opportunity to buy which probably would never recur. Three percent was now considered a high return for Her Majesty's funds. It was worthwhile to buy funds in spite of the low yields because the buyer was virtually sure of a handsome capital gain.

Against this background of precedent, the market for the funds a few years after the great conversion staged one more sweeping advance. This occurred during the final decade of the nineteenth century. The funds established their all-time highs in 1896–1897. The new 2¾–2½% consols advanced from 95 in 1892 to 113⅞ in 1896, a final capital gain of 20% —not large by earlier standards. This represented a decline in yield from 2.71 to 2.21%. The funds never again sold so high, even during the easy-money era of the 1930's and during the Labor administration of the 1940's. By 1920, consols were down to a price of 44¼, to yield 5.65%.

The year 1896 marked the true crest of a great market fluctuation that filled a full century of time. A tendency to go to extremes is often observed at the highs or the lows of a protracted market trend. At such times, precedent and overwhelming psychological expectations reinforce prevailing economic factors.

The renewed advance in the consols in 1894–1895 was accompanied by very low short rates. Bank rate was down to 2% for more than two years, which was without precedent. The open market rate of discount ranged below 1%.

Late in 1896 short rates advanced sharply to about 4%. They declined again in mid-1897 and advanced again in late 1897. Throughout these months of higher short rates, consols generally maintained their low yields. It was not until 1899, when bank rate remained between 3 and 6% throughout the year, that consols turned definitely downward in price (see Table 19 and Chart 7). They crossed 100 in late 1899. At the close of the century consols yielded 2½%, and simultaneously the open-market rate of discount was above 6%. These 2½% consols are still outstanding. In the mid-1970's, they sold down below a price of 14 to yield 18%. By the late 1980's, they had recovered to yield less than 10%.

Chapter XIV

France in the Nineteenth Century

GENERAL BACKGROUND

The year 1815 divided the nineteenth-century financial history of France and of most European countries into two parts. The years before 1815 were marked by wars, intense pressures on financial resources, and high interest rates. The years following 1815 were marked by comparative peace, a hard currency, industrial development, and declining interest rates. Toward the end of the century interest rates became very low in almost all of the principal trading nations of the Western world, including France.

The political history of France during the nineteenth century revealed little of the political stability enjoyed by England. France's interest rate history was also far more erratic than England's. Napoleon's empire, 1804–1815, was followed by the rule of the Bourbons, 1815–1830, the revolution of 1830, the rule of Louis Philippe, 1830–1848, the revolution of 1848, the Second Republic, 1848–1852, the Second Empire of Napoleon III, 1852–1870, the disastrous Franco-Prussian War of 1870, and then the Third Republic. Each large rise in long-term interest rates coincided precisely with each of the revolutionary changes in regime, that is, 1830–1831, 1848–1849, 1870–1871. After each political crisis, stability, peace, and low interest rates quickly returned.

In spite of political instability and two major military disasters, the nineteenth was a century of orderly finance and great economic growth for France. The nation ended the century with a world-wide empire, a powerful military establishment, an efficient banking system, great finan-

cial resources, and a modern industrial plant and system of railroads—
almost all financed by the savings of the prosperous and frugal French
people. French savings were even sufficient to help finance the industrialization of her gigantic ally Russia. The contrast with the disorganized French finances of earlier and later centuries is striking. Modern
methods for the effective mobilization of the savings of the people had
been pioneered in seventeenth-century Holland, developed as an effective means of world-wide power in eighteenth-century England, and in
the nineteenth century were adopted throughout the Western world.

The Bank of France was organized by Napoleon in 1800. It was at

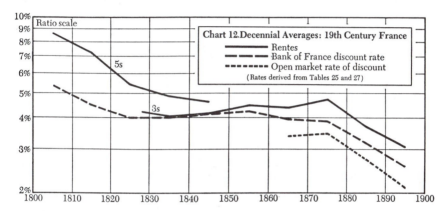

Chart 12. Decennial Averages: 19th Century France
——————— Rentes
— — — Bank of France discount rate
■■■■■■■ Open market rate of discount
(Rates derived from Tables 25 and 27)

first a semiprivate company. It was the banker for the government, but
it did not enjoy a monopoly of banking. (458) It managed the *rentes,*
issued notes, and engaged in private banking. It was not a banker's bank.
Eventually it established branches and was given a monopoly of note
issue. It discounted small bills and made possible the conduct of all
sorts of business with small capital. It kept much larger metallic reserves
than the Bank of England and did not rely so much on the discount rate
to control credit and protect its resources. Other French banks were
then largely private partnerships. Investment banking and commercial
banking grew up side by side and were not differentiated as they were
in England. In the latter half of the century great joint-stock banking
companies spread their branches over France, squeezed out many small
country bankers, and diminished the importance of the old private
houses. (459)

Other important financial reforms had been accomplished by Napoleon. He reformed the budget and the currency, refrained from large
borrowing, and made debt service a first charge on revenues. The 5%
rentes rose from a price below 10% of their nominal value in 1797 to a
high of 93% by 1807; they rarely sold below 60% of par during the Em-

pire. In 1815 the national debt, partly liquidated by the assignat inflation, was moderate.

The government of the Restoration which assumed power in 1815 pursued careful and conservative financial policies. It paid off the war indemnity rapidly, funded the floating debt and maintained public credit
on a firm foundation. (460) By 1824 the 5% *rentes* sold at a premium
and debt refunding at lower interest rates was begun.

The 1820's were a period of prosperity and growth. The value of a
seat on the Paris Bourse rose from 30,000 francs to 850,000 francs between 1816, when it was reorganized, and 1830. Except for canal-com-
pany stocks, however, there were few company shares listed. Trading
was largely in government securities. The people still preferred to invest in land or in government *rentes*. They distrusted industrial securities, banks, and bank notes.

From 1827 to 1832 there was a period of business depression, in the
midst of which occurred the Revolution of 1830. (461) From 1833 to
1837 there was rising prosperity, railroad construction, the formation of
many companies, and a great increase in securities listed on the Bourse.
In 1837 there occurred a collapse; the price of railroad securities dropped
sharply, but the price of *rentes* continued to rise.

Prosperity returned in 1842. Railroad construction reached boom proportions in 1845 with huge speculation on the Bourse. In 1846 a series
of crises began with crop failures and led to unemployment, the first
increase in the discount rate at the Bank of France since 1820, financial stringency, a sharp fall in the price of *rentes,* and finally the Eu-
rope-wide revolutions of 1848.

Under the Second Empire, 1852–1870, prosperity returned. *Rentes* recovered and the discount rate was for the first time dropped below 4%.
Many measures were taken to improve the availability of credit to smaller
entrepreneurs, such as the establishment of a land bank, the *Crédit Fon-
cier,* in 1852. French trade doubled between 1851 and 1870. (462) There
was another crisis in 1857 which again embarrassed the railroads and
which was accompanied by a brief excursion of the discount rate up to
8%, but it had a very small effect on the market for *rentes*. Financial
stringency recurred in 1864. However, the *rentes* were not importantly
depressed until the disastrous defeat of 1870–1871; this was followed
by a few years of very high interest rates.

After 1872 the last three decades of the century saw stability, peace
and the same remarkable decline in interest rates which occurred in
England and in most other industrial countries. There were periods of
hard times, such as 1883 and 1896, but no financial crisis, no very high
discount rates, and no depressed markets for *rentes*. This was for all
Europe a period of growth and of nationalism; it was an age of steel

and mass production. Industrially, France ended the century far behind England, but France was catching up rapidly. Germany and the United States, however, were catching up even more rapidly.

Commodity prices in France followed a pattern similar to those in England. They declined from 1820 to 1850, rose to 1856, and then declined almost steadily to a new low in 1896. They ended the century far below their wartime levels of the first decades.

LONG-TERM INTEREST RATES

Long-term French interest rates opened the nineteenth century at very high levels and closed it at very low levels. In between, however, their course was extremely erratic: the declining trend was frequently interrupted by brief returns to very high rates. While in England and in Holland the development of low mid-nineteenth-century interest rates was a reversion to rates that had prevailed at times in earlier centuries, for France these low rates were a novelty. French *rentiers* who remembered a long tradition of 5% *rentes* gradually, however, became accustomed to 4% and finally to 3%.

The French *rentes* were similar in structure to the British consols and to the earlier Dutch annuities. All three were direct descendants of the medieval census annuities. These contracts all undertook to provide an income to the creditor at a fixed rate. The debtor retained the right to redeem eventually but made no promise ever to do so. Probably over those long centuries, when interest rates were often declining from very high levels, continuity of income was exactly what creditors wanted.

The modern uniform French *rente* probably can be dated from 1793 when the *Great Book of the Public Debt* was created, in which were inscribed all the valid loans and in which were recorded the many confusing titles to *rentes*. (463) Uniformity and legality of claim were thus assured. However, the unhappy *rentiers* were, in 1793, still being paid in depreciated assignats. *Rentiers* lost all confidence. In 1797 the 5% *rentes* were quoted between 6⅛ and 36⅛ francs per 100 francs face value.

In 1799 the debt was consolidated into 5% *rentes*. These were then quoted at 14¾ to provide a current yield of about 34%—if paid. The budget was put in order and the *Caisse d'Amortissement* was re-established to service the debt. In 1800 the Bank of France was organized, and a metallic currency was restored. By 1801 the *rentes* were up to a high of 68 to yield 7.35%.

For the years from 1797 to the present time there exists at least one, and sometimes several, series of market quotations on various French *rentes*. By the means of these quotations the fluctuations from year to

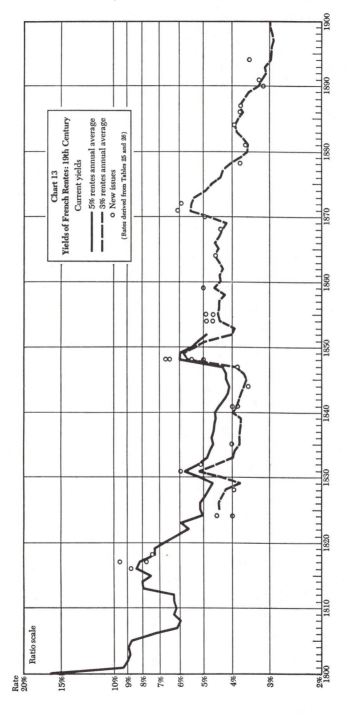

Chart 13
Yields of French Rentes: 19th Century
Current yields

——— 5% rentes annual average
- - - 3% rentes annual average
○ New issues

(Rates derived from Tables 25 and 26)

year in these market rates of long-term interest on government credit can be approximated. There were and are, however, many issues of *rentes* outstanding, and their terms varied greatly. No one series always provided a representative picture of the level of long-term French interest rates in the manner usually provided for Britain by the British consols.

Table 25 contains prices and current yields of the two most important series of nineteenth-century *rentes* stated in terms of annual averages and annual high and low prices. These yields are pictured on Chart 13, together with the yields on new issues of *rentes* from Table 26. Chart 12 above pictures decennial average yields.

At the beginning of the century the quoted debt consisted entirely of 5% *rentes*. In 1824 some 4½% *rentes* were created at a price of 100 and some 3% *rentes* at a price of 75, which equaled 4% current yield. In 1828 some 4% *rentes* were created at a small premium. *Rentes* at these four nominal rates—3, 4, 4½, and 5%—comprised the market during most of this century, although the 5s were redeemed and disappeared temporarily in 1852. A comparison of the simultaneous current yields of *rentes* with various nominal rates shows great differences. A lower current yield usually prevailed for the *rentes* with lower nominal rates selling at larger discounts. The difference was pronounced during periods of declining interest rates. In 1840, a period of low yields, and in 1873, a period of high yields, the prices and current yields are compared as follows:

Issue	1840		1873	
	High Price	Low Yield, % *	High Price	Low Yield, % *
5s	119⅜	4.18	93¾	5.36
4½s	113½	3.96	84½	5.31
4s	109	3.68	73	5.49
3s	86⅝	3.40	59⅛	5.05

* All yields quoted for *rentes* are current yields, nominal interest rate divided by price, and thus make no allowance for possible capital gains or losses.

These yield differences were due in large part to differences in terms and in prospects of redemption. Investors preferred discount issues with longer probable life and a greater chance of price appreciation. Premiums would probably be lost.

TABLE 25

Prices and Yields of Long-Term French Government Securities: Nineteenth Century

Year	5% Rentes						3% Rentes					
	Annual Average		An-nual High Price	Yield, %	An-nual Low Price	Yield, %	Annual Average		An-nual High Price	Yield, %	An-nual Low Price	Yield, %
	Price	Yield, %					Price	Yield, %				
1797			36⅛	13.80	6⅛	82.00						
1798	16⅝	30.10	24¼	20.60	9	55.50						
1799	14¾	34.00	22½	22.22	7	71.40						
1800	30⅝	16.28	44	11.36	17⅜	28.60						
1801	53¾	9.30	68	7.35	39½	12.60						
1802	54½	9.00	59	8.40	50⅛	9.90						
1803	56¾	8.80	66⅝	7.50	47	10.65						
1804	56	8.90	59¾	8.30	52¼	9.50						
1805	57⅝	8.70	63¼	7.85	51⅞	9.60						
1806	68¾	7.30	77	6.48	60⅜	8.30						
1807	82⅜	6.10	93½	5.38	71¼	7.00						
1808	83⅛	5.98	88⅛	5.66	78⅛	6.40						
1809	80⅛	6.25	84	5.95	76¼	6.55						
10-yr. av.		8.66										
1810	81½	6.15	84½	5.98	78⅜	6.40						
1811	80½	6.22	83⅜	6.00	77¾	6.40						
1812	80	6.25	83⅝	6.00	76½	6.50						
1813	63⅞	7.90	80¼	6.20	47½	9.60						
1814	62½	8.00	80	6.25	45	11.11						
1815	67	7.45	81⅝	6.10	52¼	9.60						
1816	59⅜	8.35	64⅜	7.75	54¼	9.30						
1817	62	8.15	69	7.25	55	9.00						
1818	70	7.20	80	6.25	60	8.15						
1819	69	7.25	73⅛	6.80	64⅞	7.70						
10-yr. av.		7.29										
1820	74⅞	6.70	79⅝	6.30	70⅛	7.10						
1821	82¼	6.15	90⅝	5.50	73¾	6.80						
1822	89⅜	5.60	95	5.25	83¾	5.95						
1823	84½	5.95	93⅝	5.35	75½	6.65						
1824	98⅞	5.04	104¾	4.80	93	5.60						
1825	98⅜	5.09	106¼	4.69	90½	5.52	68⅛	4.40	76⅜	3.94	59¾	5.10
1826	98⅜	5.09	101	4.94	95¾	5.21	67⅝	4.42	72⅜	4.16	63	4.80
1827	101⅝	4.95	104¾	4.80	98½	5.06	70	4.30	73¾	4.10	66⅛	4.55
1828	105⅛	4.76	109	4.58	101¼	4.93	71½	4.20	76⅛	3.96	66¾	4.50
1829	108½	4.62	110⅝	4.51	106½	4.68	80	3.75	86⅛	3.46	74	4.10
10-yr. av.		5.40					5-yr. av.	4.21				
1830	97½	5.12	109⅞	4.54	84½	5.95	70¼	4.28	85⅜	3.52	55	5.45
1831	86⅞	5.76	98⅞	5.06	74⅞	6.66	58¼	5.15	70½	4.22	46	6.55
1832	96	5.20	99¾	5.01	92	5.42	66½	4.51	71	4.20	62	4.85
1833	102¾	4.86	105½	4.73	100¼	4.99	75¼	3.98	80½	3.73	70	4.30
1834	105⅜	4.73	106⅝	4.67	104	4.80	76¾	3.91	80	3.75	73⅝	4.10
1835	108¼	4.61	110¼	4.53	106⅜	4.68	79½	3.77	82⅜	3.65	76¾	3.91
1836	106¾	4.67	110¼	4.53	103¼	4.84	79½	3.77	82¼	3.66	76⅞	3.90
1837	108¾	4.59	111	4.50	106¼	4.68	79⅝	3.76	81½	3.68	77¾	3.85
1838	109½	4.56	111⅞	4.46	107	4.66	80⅛	3.74	82¼	3.66	78⅛	3.80
1839	110½	4.52	112⅞	4.43	108¼	4.61	80⅛	3.74	82½	3.64	77¾	3.85
10-yr. av.		4.86						4.06				
1840	110	4.54	119⅜	4.18	100½	4.98	76¼	3.98	86⅝	3.40	65⅞	4.55
1841	113¾	4.40	117	4.26	110½	4.52	78⅛	3.84	80⅝	3.72	75⅝	3.96
1842	118½	4.21	120⅞	4.14	116	4.30	79½	3.78	82¼	3.65	76⅝	3.94
1843	121⅝	4.11	123¾	4.04	119½	4.18	81	3.71	83¼	3.62	78¾	3.81
1844	122⅛	4.08	126¼	3.96	118⅛	4.21	82¾	3.63	85⅝	3.52	79¾	3.76
1845	119⅝	4.17	122⅞	4.05	116½	4.28	83⅝	3.58	86⅜	3.45	80⅞	3.70
1846	119¾	4.17	123⅝	4.04	116	4.30	82¾	3.63	85	3.53	80⅜	3.74
1847	116¼	4.29	119⅛	4.19	113⅜	4.41	77½	3.88	80¼	3.74	74⅝	4.05
1848	83¾	5.97	117½	4.27	50	10.00	53⅞	5.58	75¼	3.98	32½	9.25
1849	83½	5.98	92¾	5.40	74	6.72	51⅝	5.80	58½	5.14	44¾	6.70
10-yr. av.		4.59						4.14				

TABLE 25 (*Continued*)

Year	*5% Rentes*						*3% Rentes*					
	Annual Average		Annual High Price	Yield, %	Annual Low Price	Yield, %	Annual Average		Annual High Price	Yield, %	Annual Low Price	Yield, %
	Price	Yield, %					Price	Yield, %				
1850	92	5.43	97⅜	5.14	86¾	5.75	56⅜	5.33	58⅞	5.12	53⅞	5.55
1851	96⅛	5.19	103	4.85	89⅛	5.59	60¾	4.94	67	4.48	54½	5.50
1852	102⅞	4.85	106½	4.67	99⅛	5.04	75	4.00	86	3.48	63⅞	4.70
1853							77	3.90	82⅛	3.66	71¾	4.15
1854							69	4.34	76⅜	3.94	61½	4.88
1855							67¾	4.42	71¾	4.20	63⅞	4.70
1856							68½	4.39	75½	3.98	61½	4.88
1857							68½	4.39	71⅛	4.18	65⅞	4.55
1858							71¼	4.21	75	4.02	67½	4.40
1859							66½	4.55	72½	4.14	60½	4.95
10-yr. av.								4.45				
1860							69¼	4.34	71⅜	4.20	67⅛	4.40
1861							68½	4.38	70⅛	4.30	66⅞	4.48
1862							70⅛	4.28	72⅞	4.12	67⅜	4.38
1863							68⅜	4.39	70⅝	4.25	66⅛	4.44
1864							66⅛	4.54	67¾	4.45	64½	4.65
1865							67½	4.42	69½	4.33	66¼	4.45
1866							66	4.55	70⅝	4.29	62½	4.80
1867							68	4.41	70¾	4.28	65¼	4.70
1868							70⅛	4.27	72	4.22	68¼	4.55
1869							71⅜	4.17	73⅞	4.08	69¾	4.49
10-yr. av.								4.37				
1870							63	4.76	75⅛	4.00	50¾	5.95
1871							54⅜	5.51	58½	5.12	50⅜	5.97
1872							54¾	5.47	57¼	5.24	52⅜	5.70
1873							56⅛	5.34	59⅛	5.05	53¼	5.60
1874							61¼	4.90	64¾	4.60	57¾	5.22
1875							64¼	4.66	67	4.48	61⅝	4.90
1876							69	4.35	73	4.03	65	4.80
1877							70¼	4.27	74⅜	4.02	66⅛	4.55
1878							73⅜	4.06	77¾	3.80	70	4.30
1879							80⅜	3.73	84½	3.55	76¼	3.98
10-yr. av.								4.71				
1880							84¼	3.56	87¼	3.45	81⅛	3.74
1881							84⅝	3.54	87¼	3.45	82	3.66
1882							81¾	3.67	84¾	3.52	78⅝	3.83
1883							78⅜	3.83	82⅝	3.62	74⅛	4.04
1884							77¼	3.88	79½	3.78	75⅛	4.00
1885							79¼	3.79	82⅜	3.64	76¼	3.95
1886							82	3.66	83⅞	3.60	80⅛	3.74
1887							79½	3.78	82⅞	3.63	76	3.97
1888							82¾	3.63	84⅝	3.51	80⅞	3.70
1889							85½	3.51	88⅜	3.40	82½	3.60
10-yr. av.								3.68				
1890							91⅞	3.26	96⅜	3.11	87⅜	3.41
1891							94½	3.18	96¾	3.08	92¼	3.25
1892							97⅞	3.07	100¾	2.97	95	3.18
1893							96⅝	3.10	99⅝	3.01	93⅝	3.20
1894							100⅝	2.98	104½	2.88	96⅞	3.10
1895							101⅜	2.96	103¾	2.90	99⅝	3.02
1896							101⅞	2.94	103¼	2.91	100⅝	2.99
1897							103½	2.90	105¼	2.86	101⅝	2.96
1898							102⅞	2.92	104¼	2.88	101⅜	2.97
1899							100⅞	2.98	103	2.92	98¾	3.08
10-yr. av.								3.03				
1900							100¾	2.98	102⅜	2.94	99⅛	3.04

SOURCES

Leonidas J. Loutchitch, *Des Variations du Taux de l'Intérêt en France de 1800 à Nos Jours*, Paris, 1930, Libraire Félix Alcan, pp. 42–45.

Georges Robert, *Des Variations du Taux de l'Intérêt*, Lyons, 1902, A. Storck et Cie., p. 78.

J. M. Fachan, *Historique de la Rente Française*, Paris, 1904, Berger-Levrault et Cie., pp. 263–264.

TABLE 26

PRINCIPAL NEW ISSUES AND CONVERSIONS OF FRENCH
RENTES: NINETEENTH CENTURY

Year	New Issues and Conversions	Nominal Rate, %	Price	Current Yield, %
1799–1807	Various consolidations of debt into *rentes* @	5		
1816	Debt consolidated into *rentes* @	5		
1816	Cash offering of *rentes* @	5	$57\frac{1}{4}$	8.73
1817	Cash offering of *rentes* @	5	$\begin{cases}52\frac{1}{2}\\64\frac{1}{2}\end{cases}$	9.52 / 7.75
1818	Cash offering of *rentes* @	5	$67\frac{5}{8}$	7.39
1824	Conversion of 5% *rentes* into *rentes* @	$4\frac{1}{2}$	100	4.50
	Conversion of 5% *rentes* into *rentes* @	3	75	4.00
1828	Cash offering of *rentes* @	4	102	3.92
1831	Cash offering of *rentes* @	5	84	5.96
1832	Cash offering of *rentes* @	5	$98\frac{1}{2}$	5.08
1835	Cash offering of *rentes* @	4	100	4.00
1841	Cash offering of *rentes* @	4	100	4.00
	Cash offering of *rentes* @	3	$78\frac{1}{2}$	3.83
1844	Cash offering of *rentes* @	3	$84\frac{3}{4}$	3.54
1847	Cash offering of *rentes* @	3	$78\frac{1}{4}$	3.84
1848	Cash offering of *rentes* @	5	100	5.00
	Cash offering of *rentes* @	3	55	5.46
	Cash offering of *rentes* @	3	46.4	6.48
	Cash offering of *rentes* @	5	$75\frac{1}{4}$	6.65
1852	Conversion of 5% *rentes* into *rentes* @	$4\frac{1}{2}$	—	—
1854	Cash offering of *rentes*	$4\frac{1}{2}$	$92\frac{1}{2}$	4.86
	Cash offering of *rentes*	3	$65\frac{1}{4}$	4.61
1855	Cash offering of *rentes*	$4\frac{1}{2}$	92	4.89
	Cash offering of *rentes*	3	$65\frac{1}{4}$	4.61
1859	Cash offering of *rentes*	$4\frac{1}{2}$	90	5.00
	Cash offering of *rentes*	3	60	5.00
1862	Conversion of $4\frac{1}{2}$s and 4s into *rentes* @	3	—	—
1864	Cash offering of *rentes*	3	66.3	4.53
1868	Cash offering of *rentes*	3	$69\frac{1}{4}$	4.34
1870	Cash offering of *rentes*	3	60.6	4.95
1871	Cash offering of *rentes*	5	$82\frac{1}{2}$	6.06
1872	Cash offering of *rentes*	5	$84\frac{1}{2}$	5.91
1878	Cash offering of *rentes* (amortized)	3	$80\frac{1}{2}$	3.74
1881	Cash offering of *rentes* (amortized)	3	$83\frac{1}{4}$	3.60
1883	Conversion of 5% *rentes* into *rentes* @	$4\frac{1}{2}$		
1884	Cash offering of *rentes* (amortized)	3	76.6	3.92
1886	Floating debt converted to perpetual *rentes*	3	79.8	3.76
1887	Conversion of $4\frac{1}{2}$% and 4% *rentes* into *rentes* @	3	80.1	3.74
1890	Cash offering of *rentes* (amortized)	3	95.27	3.14
1891	Cash offering of *rentes* (perpetual)	3	92.55	3.24
1894	Conversion of $4\frac{1}{2}$% *rentes* into *rentes* @	$3\frac{1}{2}$	100	3.50
1901	Cash offering of *rentes* (perpetual)	3	100	3.00
1902	Conversion of $3\frac{1}{2}$% *rentes* into *rentes* @	3	100	3.00

SOURCES

Principally J. M. Fachan, *Historique de la Rente Française*, Paris, 1904, Berger-Levrault et Cie.; and Charles Fenn, *Compendium of English and Foreign Funds*, London, 1889, Robert Lucas Nash.

The detailed chart is supplemented by Chart 14 which compares nineteenth-century yields on French *rentes* with nineteenth-century yields on British consols. This chart helps to identify the peculiarities of the market trends in France. Consols may be treated as a sort of norm in the nineteenth century because of Britain's dominant position in finance. A norm, however imperfect, facilitates multiple comparisons. Such comparisons, however, must be considered relative, not absolute; rough and not precise. Differences in terms, in currencies, in taxation, in laws complicate any measurement of international interest rate differentials. French *rentes* were not the equivalent of British consols with a higher

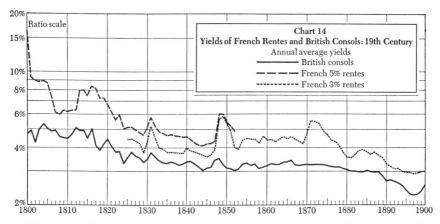

yield. But differences in trend and big changes in the differentials do carry a significance for this history.

Under Napoleon I the 5% *rentes,* after their initial tenfold recovery from bankruptcy prices of 6⅛–24¼ to 60–90, fluctuated in a range where their yield was still comparatively high, usually from 6 to 8%. British consols at the time averaged 4.25–5.25%. The British, nevertheless, were borrowing heavily during these years and Napoleon was not.

Under the Bourbons, 1815–1830, the trends of debt creation were reversed: the French funded debt trebled while the British funded debt was being reduced. Nevertheless, after 1815, market yields declined sharply in France as well as in Britain. The 5% *rentes* rose in price year by year without an important reversal from 52¼, or 9.6% in 1815, to par in 1824, and then to a price of 104¾. In 1816 the French government sold new 5s at 57¼, to yield 8.73%. (464) In 1824 it created new *rentes* by conversion as 4½s at 100 and as 3s at a discount. By 1829, the 5s had risen to 110⅝; and the 3s, to an average of 80, to yield 3.75%. The yields of 3% *rentes* were then only moderately above British yields. This close relationship, however, was very temporary. It was not to occur again during most of the century.

The revolution of 1830 sent the *rentes* down sharply in price. The 5s sold down to a low of 74⅞, to yield 6.66%; and the 3s, to a low of 46, to yield 6.55%; these were price declines of 34% and 41%, respectively.

Again, as after every crisis throughout this century, the French *rentes* recovered sharply and swiftly. Yields again became low. By 1833 the 5s were up to 105½ in the market and the 3s were up to 80½, to yield 3.73%. This decline in French interest rates was not seriously interrupted by the boom and crisis of 1834–1837. The early 1840's were years of great prosperity when yields of *rentes* reached their low point for the first half of the century, not to be duplicated for thirty-five years. This was also a temporary low point for British consol yields. However, the sharp rise in French yields which occurred in 1847–1849, was again not accompanied by a large increase in British yields. Fluctuations in both countries continued to be similar in direction, but in France they were much wider in scope than in Britain.

The crisis of 1847 and the revolution of 1848 carried the 3% *rentes* down from 86⅜ to a temporary low of 32½, at which they yielded 9.25%. In 1848 new 5s were created at 75¼, to yield 6.65%; and new 3s, at 46.40, to yield 6.48%. By 1851–1853, however, another swift recovery had set in which carried the 3s back to a high of 86, to yield 3.48%, and the 5s up again to 106½.

The period from 1853 through 1866 was the only period of sustained rise in long-term French yields in this century. A modest rise in British consol yields also was sustained between 1852 and 1866. This was the period of military expansion of the Second Empire; the perpetual debt increased by two thirds.

In 1866 the yields on British consols began a decline that continued almost steadily until 1897. In 1866 the yields on French *rentes* also started to decline, but this trend was interrupted by the war of 1870. The 3% *rentes* dropped from a high of 75⅛, or 4% in 1870, their highest price in thirteen years, to a low of 50⅜, or 5.97% in 1871, a price decline of one third. Even this was smaller than the 47% price decline during the Revolution of 1830–1831 and the 63% price decline during the revolutionary period of 1846–1848. In fact the War of 1870 only briefly interrupted a period of peace, prosperity, and declining interest rates. It had no noticeable effect on British consols.

The treaty of peace in 1871 imposed a gigantic 5-billion-franc indemnity on France, which was enforced by German occupation. French investors, however, placed unexpected resources at the disposal of their government when it offered very high rates. (465) In 1871 a large domestic loan was floated as 5% *rentes* priced at 82½, to yield 6.06%, and was heavily oversubscribed. In 1872 an even larger domestic loan was floated as 5% *rentes* priced at 84½, to yield 5.91% and was oversubscribed nearly tenfold. Thus ended occupation, war, and high interest rates in nineteenth-century France.

Economic recovery was rapid. The prices of *rentes* rose most of the time from 1873 until the end of the century. From 50⅜ low in 1871 the 3% *rentes* rose to 87¼, or 3.45% in 1880, an appreciation of almost 75%.

In 1878 the government created a novelty, a 3% *rente* that was amortized rather than perpetual. A sinking fund was provided sufficient to retire the issue over a period of seventy-five years; otherwise, these new *rentes* were not redeemable or convertible. They were sold at 80½, to yield 3.74% currently plus amortization.

By 1890 the perpetual 3s were up to a 91⅞ average, or 3.26%. This yield was still well above the average yield of 2.67% which prevailed in 1890 for British consols. The further drop in yields to 1897 was far less pronounced in France than in Britain. The French 3% perpetuals reached their low yields of the century in 1897, when they sold at 105¼, to yield 2.86%. In view of the premium it is possible that even lower yields might have been bid for issues with a lower nominal rate, but none was created to test the market.

In the period 1883–1902 the government undertook an important series of debt conversions by which it exchanged 5s for 4½s, 4½s for 3½s, and finally, in 1902, 3½s for 3s. The French debt was largely funded at 3%, whereas the British debt was largely funded at 2½%. The decline in yields from 1815 was very similar in both countries, although the size of the British debt was heavily reduced and the size of the French debt was greatly enlarged.

Nineteenth-century Ministers of Finance or Chancellors of the Exchequer thought of the burden of their national debts in terms of the annual interest charge against the revenues rather than in terms of a principal amount which must be repaid. Principal repayment only occurred when it was considered a benefit to the state. Refundings were almost always conversions at lower rates. Floating debts were looked upon very differently: here the liability was to pay principal. They were usually temporary affairs refunded as soon as possible into perpetual debt.

In France, as in England, the investor was by no means restricted to government securities. In France, however, distrust of promotions and of industrial securities continued throughout this century. The corporate form came late. Much French capital remained in land mortgages on which an effective interest rate of 10% was common at least until mid-century. (466) If usury laws interfered, this rate could be achieved by a loan at 5% on twice the principal actually advanced. There was also investment in canal shares and, later, railroad shares. Much railroad financing was undertaken by the government, but railroad bonds were also publicly floated. In 1860 a yield of 5.61% is quoted for a highly regarded railroad bond issue; this was 127 basis points over the average of the yield of the 3% *rentes*. (467) In the crisis of 1871–1873 the differential became very small when yields of both railroad bonds and *rentes* were around 5.50%, while in 1880 the government-sponsored railroad obligations were quoted at 4.23% and *rentes* at 3.56%, a differential of 67 basis points. Foreign government bonds at high yields were also favorites with French investors as they were with English investors. Large sums were loaned in this way to Russia and lost.

SHORT-TERM INTEREST RATES

The Bank of France, when it was organized in 1800, established its minimum rate of discount at 6%. In a few years the rate was reduced to 4%, where it was held most of the time until 1852. Only then was a flexible discount rate policy adopted, somewhat on the model established in Britain thirteen years earlier. The stability of the discount rate during the first half century contrasted strikingly with its volatility during the second half century.

Other bankers were free to charge less than the Bank of France and at times did so. However, it would have been difficult to charge a higher rate on the discounts of recognized prime borrowers because the Bank of France competed directly for this business. Therefore, the discount rate of the Bank of France during the first half of this century probably provides a good picture of the highest prime rate at any one time, but not the lowest. This conclusion is reinforced by the fact that the open-market discount rate, when it was regularly reported after 1862 always averaged below the Bank of France's discount rate. It is reported that in the 1830's, with the bank's rate at 4%, good commercial paper was at times discounted privately as low as 2–3%. (468)

Table 27 and Chart 15 are based on only two series: (a) the discount rate of the Bank of France, all the fluctuations of which from 1800 are fully reported as annual averages and as annual ranges; and (b) a series of open-market discount rates for prime short-term bills reported as annual averages and as the annual range of monthly averages from 1863. There were, of course, many other short-term rates of interest in nineteenth-century France, most of which are not regularly reported, but these two must suffice.

The rigidity of the first half century was, of course, a matter of central bank policy and not of market stability. For example, the revolution of 1830 brought no fluctuation at all in the bank's discount rate and the revolution of 1847–1848 brought only a brief excursion from 4 to 5% and quickly back to 4%. Chart 13 showed the sharp fluctuations in the *rentes*

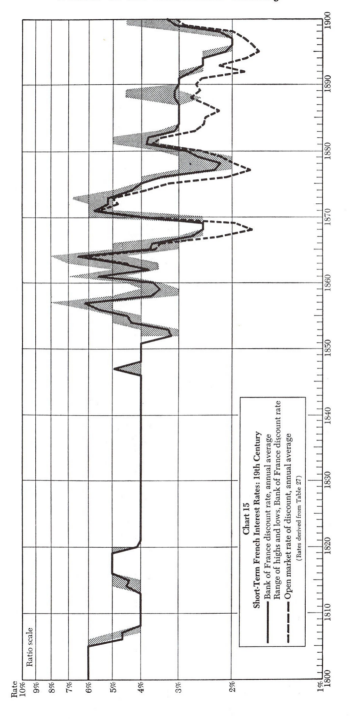

Chart 15

Short-Term French Interest Rates: 19th Century

—— Bank of France discount rate, annual average

Range of highs and lows, Bank of France discount rate

- - - - Open market rate of discount, annual average

(Rates derived from Table 27)

TABLE 27

SHORT-TERM FRENCH INTEREST RATES: NINETEENTH CENTURY

Year	Discount Rate of the Bank of France			Open-Market Discount Rate			Year	Discount Rate of the Bank of France			Open-Market Discount Rate		
	Annual Average, %	High	Low	Annual Average, %	High	Low		Annual Average, %	High	Low	Annual Average, %	High	Low
1800	6.00	6.00					1828	4.00	4.00				
1801	6.00	6.00					1829	4.00	4.00				
1802	6.00	6.00					10-yr. av.	4.01					
1803	6.00	6.00											
1804	6.00	6.00											
1805	6.00	6.00					1830	4.00	4.00				
1806	4.60	6.00	5.00				1831	4.00	4.00				
1807	4.59	5.00	4.00				1832	4.00	4.00				
1808	4.00	4.00					1833	4.00	4.00				
1809	4.00	4.00					1834	4.00	4.00				
10-yr. av.	5.32						1835	4.00	4.00				
							1836	4.00	4.00				
							1837	4.00	4.00				
1810	4.00	4.00					1838	4.00	4.00				
1811	4.00	4.00					1839	4.00	4.00				
1812	4.00	4.00					10-yr. av.	4.00					
1813	4.00	4.00											
1814	4.48	5.00	4.00										
1815	4.37	5.00	4.00				1840	4.00	4.00				
1816	5.00	5.00					1841	4.00	4.00				
1817	5.00	5.00					1842	4.00	4.00				
1818	5.00	5.00					1843	4.00	4.00				
1819	5.00	5.00					1844	4.00	4.00				
10-yr. av.	4.49						1845	4.00	4.00				
							1846	4.00	4.00				
							1847	4.95	5.00	4.00			
1820	4.10	5.00	4.00				1848	4.00	4.00				
1821	4.00	4.00					1849	4.00	4.00				
1822	4.00	4.00					10-yr. av.	4.10					
1823	4.00	4.00											
1824	4.00	4.00											
1825	4.00	4.00					1850	4.00					
1826	4.00	4.00					1851	4.00					
1827	4.00	4.00					1852	3.17	4.00	3.00			

TABLE 27 (*Continued*)

Year	Discount Rate of the Bank of France			Open-Market Discount Rate			Year	Discount Rate of the Bank of France			Open-Market Discount Rate		
	Annual Average, %	High	Low	Annual Average, %	High	Low		Annual Average, %	High	Low	Annual Average, %	High	Low
1853	3.23	4.00	3.00				1878	2.18	3.00	2.00	1.97	2.81	1.53
1854	4.30	5.00	4.00				1879	2.58	3.00	2.00	2.16	2.78	1.62
1855	4.44	5.00	4.00				10-yr.						
1856	5.51	6.00	5.00				av.	3.87			3.43		
1857	6.15	8.00	5.00										
1858	3.70	5.00	3.00				1880	2.81	3.50	2.50	2.52	3.28	2.16
1859	3.45	4.00	3.00				1881	3.84	5.00	3.50	3.68	4.91	3.16
							1882	3.80	5.00	3.50	3.41	4.97	3.02
10-yr.							1883	3.08	3.50	3.00	2.67	3.25	2.50
av.	4.20						1884	3.00	3.00		2.48	2.69	2.03
1860	3.63	4.50	3.50				1885	3.00	3.00		2.45	2.78	1.84
1861	5.52	7.00	4.50				1886	3.00	3.00		2.20	2.60	1.09
1862	3.77	5.00	3.50				1887	3.00	3.00		2.42	2.78	2.08
1863	4.64	7.00	3.50	4.42	6.62	3.56	1888	3.10	4.50	2.50	2.73	4.03	2.02
1864	6.50	8.00	4.50	6.25	7.38	4.95	1889	3.09	4.50	3.00	2.54	3.42	2.20
1865	3.72	5.00	3.00	3.60	4.56	2.85	10-yr.						
1866	3.67	5.00	3.00	3.44	4.97	2.44	av.	3.17			2.71		
1867	2.71	3.00	2.50	2.22	2.62	1.91							
1868	2.50	2.50		1.72	2.25	1.38	1890	3.00	3.00		2.62	2.97	2.31
1869	2.50	2.50		1.95	2.25	1.50	1891	3.00	3.00		2.51	2.88	2.18
				3.37			1892	2.70	3.00	2.50	1.81	2.70	1.12
10-yr.				7-yr.			1893	2.50	2.50		2.22	2.44	1.97
av.	3.92			av.			1894	2.50	2.50		1.79	2.34	1.30
							1895	2.10	2.50	2.00	1.63	2.12	0.98
1870	3.99	6.00	2.50	3.86	6.17	2.00	1896	2.00	2.00		1.71	1.88	1.50
1871	5.71	6.00	5.00	5.63	5.50	4.70	1897	2.00	2.00		1.82	2.00	1.66
1872	5.15	6.00	5.00	4.78	5.42	4.38	1898	2.20	3.00	2.00	1.99	2.88	1.68
1873	5.15	7.00	5.00	5.00	5.94	4.69	1899	3.06	4.50	3.00	2.84	3.38	2.69
1874	4.30	5.00	4.00	3.86	4.60	3.09	10-yr.						
1875	4.00	4.00		3.22	3.72	3.00	av.	2.51			2.09		
1876	3.40	4.00	3.00	2.08	3.06	1.25							
1877	2.28	3.00	2.00	1.74	2.06	1.28	1900	3.25	4.50	3.00	3.04	4.19	2.62

SOURCES

Leonidas J. Loutchitch, *Des Variations du Taux de l'Intérêt en France de 1800 à Nos Jours*, Paris, 1930, Libraire Félix Alcan, pp. 42–45.

R. G. Hawtrey, *A Century of Bank Rate*, London, 1938, Longmans, Green & Co., p. 302.

Open-market rates based on data compiled by the National Bureau of Economic Research from various published sources.

during both these episodes. We can conjecture that discounts were very hard indeed to negotiate during these crises at the rigid discount rate and that lower rates were available during periods of ease. We have no real market history of short rates until 1863, while after 1863 the market rate of discount was evidently importantly controlled by the Bank of France's discount policy. As in Britain, the short-term market rate of discount was limited by central bank policy. Much freer market rates are provided in most countries, even today, by the yields on long-term obligations than by the rates on short-term prime paper.

Broadly speaking, the pattern of French prime short-term interest rates during the nineteenth century was similar to the British pattern. In both countries there was rigidity during the first four of five decades of the century, usually at rates neither very high nor very low, that is to say, between 4 and 5%. After mid-century the ranges in both countries became very wide, for example, $1\frac{1}{2}$–8% in France and $1\frac{1}{2}$–10% in Britain during the 1860's. In both countries a high degree of volatility at sharply declining average levels characterized the last three decades of the century.

While the yields on French *rentes* were higher than the yields on British consols throughout this century, French short rates here quoted were often lower than the British short rates quoted. For example, the Bank of France lowered its discount rate from 6 to 4% in 1807, fifteen years before the Bank of England reduced its traditional 5% rate to 4%. Again in the 1860's the French open-market rate of discount often was below the British. For the years 1863 through 1869 the French average was 3.37% and the British was 4.31%. This was the only period in the century when British rates maintained a rising trend. In the 1870's and 1880's the French open-market rate was again above the British. During the 1890's, the decade of extreme ease in both countries, the decennial averages of French and British open-market discount rates were identical at 2.09%. At this time French *rentes* continued to yield much more than British consols.

The decennial averages in Chart 12 indicated that the short-term French interest rates reported almost always averaged lower than the long-term French interest rates as measured by the *rentes*. This contrasted with the relationship in Britain where the short rates averaged higher than the long rates until the easy-money period at the end of the century. The spread of long-term rates in France above short-term rates was very large in the early decades, but seemed to vanish briefly in the 1820's when the yield of 3% *rentes* fell to 3.75% while the discount rate remained at 4%. However, a true market short rate at that time may well have been below 4%. Similarly in the 1830's the rigid 4% discount rate did not reflect lower market rates which at times at least prevailed.

However, following the development of a flexible discount rate policy in the 1850's, the discount rate and the open-market rate always averaged well below the average yield on *rentes*.

Occasions when short market rates rose above long were rare in nineteenth-century France and frequent in nineteenth-century Britain. In Britain bank-rate policy was much more vigorously used to regulate the international flow of funds and to protect the small reserves, whereas the Bank of France relied more on its large metallic reserves and less on its rate to protect the currency.

These short-term money market rates of interest were, of course, far below short-term rates charged in France for less marketable and less well known credits. There were very few large banks in France. Frenchmen generally complained of high interest rates and looked with envy on the low rates in Britain. French private bankers often paid 4–5% for their funds and loaned them to small business concerns at 7–10%. (469) In some purely agricultural districts at mid-century a rate of discount of 15–20% was charged landowners. At Bordeaux around 1820, 15% is quoted for money at the season of the wine harvest and 5% during other seasons. In the 1830's rates of 6–12% are quoted at Chateauroux. Quotations of this sort are ill-defined and haphazard. They merely serve to re-emphasize that the main stream of money-market rates is at the low limit of a very wide band of rates of interest. During the second half of the nineteenth century the benefits of lower interest rates were gradually extended to the French provinces by the spread of branch banking and by the establishment of specialized popular lending institutions under government auspices. Small consumer-credit loans, however, continued to be obtainable chiefly from pawnshops and individual moneylenders; the lowest rates quoted were 20–30%.

Chapter XV

Other European Countries in the Nineteenth Century

THE NETHERLANDS

Background. The history of the Dutch as an independent nation was resumed in 1815. The treaty of peace which liquidated Napoleon's Empire reunited Belgium (the Austrian Netherlands) with the provinces of the former Dutch Republic to form the Kingdom of the Netherlands under the Dutch House of Orange. This reunion was unpopular with the Belgians because of religious, cultural, and economic differences and because of the Dutch political supremacy. The burden of the public debt was equally divided, even though in 1814 the debt of Holland was many times greater than that of more populous Belgium. In 1830, shortly after the July Revolution in Paris, the Belgians revolted. With the help of France and with the agreement of Britain and other powers, they again separated from the Dutch provinces and established the Kingdom of Belgium in 1831.

The political history of the Kingdom of the Netherlands for the rest of the nineteenth century was peaceful. After the European disturbances of 1848 a new Dutch constitution created a limited monarchy, somewhat on the British model. During the latter part of the century there was great commercial expansion and much internal development. Only then did modern commercial banking and large-scale industry appear. The Dutch overseas empire in the East Indies and the West Indies, which had been restored after 1815, was actively developed as a source of great wealth.

234

The financial history of the Kingdom of the Netherlands in the nineteenth century was not a history of innovation and international leadership, such as was the history of the Dutch Republic in the seventeenth century and the early part of the eighteenth century. Following the financial disasters of the late eighteenth century and the period of French domination, the Dutch quickly reverted to stable and orthodox financial policies. Their funded debt had been consolidated in the French and English manner. A new central bank was organized. Dutch finance was

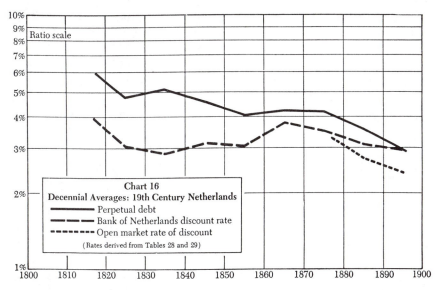

Chart 16
Decennial Averages: 19th Century Netherlands
———— Perpetual debt
— — — Bank of Netherlands discount rate
▪▪▪▪▪▪▪ Open market rate of discount
(Rates derived from Tables 28 and 29)

fitted nicely into the accepted European system under the leadership of London. The financial methods then employed in Holland could be called an imitation of the eminently successful British methods, but their sources were not quite so simple. The British system of national debt had in fact been copied from earlier Dutch innovations; it had been adopted and modified by the French, who in turn influenced the terms of the new Dutch financial reorganization. For the purposes of interest rate history, however, the essential components of the system were three: (a) a public which saved regularly and sought safe income from its savings through the obligations of a trusted and respected government, (b) a funded national debt largely in the form of uniform and marketable perpetual annuities, and (c) a money market designed to promote trade and dominated by a central bank which provided funds at varying rates of interest.

Interest Rates. Dutch interest rates declined sharply during the nineteenth century after 1815, as did interest rates in other European countries. The decline in Netherlands rates was especially pronounced in the market yields on the long-term perpetual debt. However, unlike the yields in Britain, France and other countries, the nineteenth-century lows of long-term Dutch rates were not new historic lows. They did not quite reach the 2½% level attained at least once in eighteenth-century Holland, although in the last decade of the nineteenth century they got close to it. In contrast, the nineteenth-century low rates on British funds and French *rentes* were far below their respective eighteenth-century lows.

At the very end of the eighteenth century the financial disasters of the Dutch Republic and conquest by France had brought the price of the 2½% perpetual annuities of the Province of Holland down from 99½ in 1762 to 36 in 1798, a rise in yield from 2.51% to 6.95%. These are random quotations and are not necessarily highs or lows. During the French rule the debt of the Dutch central government had been consolidated. Our earliest consecutive quotations begin in 1814. Then the range of the Dutch 2½% perpetuals was 38 high and 30½ low, which represented yields of 6.56% and 8.20%, respectively. These were strangely high rates for Holland; they were above the peak rates on British consols, but they were below the rates on French *rentes* prevailing at the same time. The nineteenth-century history of the 2½% Dutch perpetuals is given in Table 28 and Chart 17.

After 1814 the market for Dutch perpetuals at first recovered only slowly. However, it moved up sharply in 1824 to 62¼ high and in 1830 to 66⅝, to yield 3.75%. This price was not exceeded until 1881.

The war with the Belgians in 1830–1831 was accompanied by a sharp decline in the 2½s to a price of 34, to yield 7.35%. However, the price recovered rapidly and reached 58½ in 1835 and 65¼ in 1845, to yield 3.83%.

During the disturbance of 1848 the Dutch perpetuals again declined sharply from a high of 60 in 1847 to a low of 34 in 1848, to yield 7.35%; they were again back to their low price range of 1814. This disturbance, however, was brief in the Netherlands. By 1849 the perpetuals were back to 55½, and by 1852 at 66½ they about duplicated their high price level of early 1830.

After 1852 the price declined irregularly for nineteen years, with sharp temporary drops in 1854, 1859, 1866–1867, and 1870. It reached a low during the Franco-Prussian War of 48½, to yield 5.15%. Up to 1870, therefore, the nineteenth was not a century of low long-term interest rates for the Dutch, such as the seventeenth and eighteenth centuries had been.

From 1872 until 1895, however, the price of Dutch perpetuals rose almost steadily. In this period interest rates declined in most European countries. The perpetuals reached a high of 96 in 1895, to yield 2.60%.

TABLE 28

PRICES AND YIELDS OF LONG-TERM DUTCH GOVERNMENT
SECURITIES: NINETEENTH CENTURY

Year	$2\frac{1}{2}\%$ Perpetual Debt of the Central Government					
	December 31		Annual High Price	Yield, %	Annual Low Price	Yield, %
	Price	Yield, %				
1814	$37\frac{1}{4}$	6.66	38	6.56	$30\frac{1}{2}$	8.20
1815	41	6.09	$46\frac{3}{4}$	5.35	33	7.56
1816	44	5.69	$44\frac{3}{4}$	5.59	$40\frac{3}{4}$	6.14
1817	$43\frac{1}{4}$	5.76	$44\frac{1}{2}$	5.61	$42\frac{7}{8}$	5.84
1818	43	5.80	$45\frac{1}{4}$	5.53	$41\frac{5}{8}$	6.00
1819	$43\frac{3}{4}$	5.70	45	5.55	$42\frac{5}{8}$	5.86
		5.95 6-yr. av.				
1820	$45\frac{1}{4}$	5.52	$46\frac{1}{2}$	5.37	$43\frac{5}{8}$	5.73
1821	$47\frac{1}{2}$	5.25	$48\frac{3}{8}$	5.17	$44\frac{1}{4}$	5.65
1822	$47\frac{1}{2}$	5.25	$49\frac{1}{8}$	5.09	$46\frac{1}{8}$	5.43
1823	48	5.20	$48\frac{1}{2}$	5.15	$46\frac{1}{4}$	5.40
1824	$58\frac{1}{4}$	4.29	$62\frac{1}{4}$	4.02	$47\frac{7}{8}$	5.23
1825	56	4.45	$60\frac{1}{4}$	4.15	$51\frac{1}{4}$	4.87
1826	51	4.90	$57\frac{1}{2}$	4.35	49	5.10
1827	$52\frac{1}{2}$	4.76	$55\frac{7}{8}$	4.48	$50\frac{5}{8}$	4.94
1828	57	4.37	$57\frac{5}{8}$	4.34	52	4.80
1829	$63\frac{1}{2}$	3.94	64	3.90	$56\frac{1}{2}$	4.43
10-yr. av.		4.79				
1830	40	6.22	$66\frac{5}{8}$	3.75	$34\frac{5}{8}$	7.23
1831	$41\frac{1}{2}$	6.02	$43\frac{7}{8}$	5.70	34	7.35
1832	$41\frac{3}{4}$	5.97	$44\frac{3}{4}$	5.59	$38\frac{3}{8}$	6.51
1833	50	5.00	$51\frac{5}{8}$	4.84	$40\frac{7}{8}$	6.12
1834	54	4.62	55	4.55	$49\frac{1}{2}$	5.05
1835	55	4.54	$58\frac{1}{2}$	4.28	$53\frac{3}{4}$	4.65
1836	$53\frac{3}{4}$	4.62	$57\frac{5}{8}$	4.34	$49\frac{1}{2}$	5.05
1837	$52\frac{1}{2}$	4.75	$54\frac{1}{2}$	4.59	$51\frac{1}{2}$	4.86
1838	$54\frac{1}{4}$	4.60	56	4.47	$52\frac{3}{4}$	4.74
1839	52	4.79	$55\frac{1}{2}$	4.50	$50\frac{1}{2}$	4.95
10-yr. av.		5.11				

TABLE 28 (*Continued*)

Year	December 31 Price	December 31 Yield, %	Annual High Price	Yield, %	Annual Low Price	Yield, %
	\multicolumn{6}{c}{$2\frac{1}{2}\%$ Perpetual Debt of the Central Government}
1840	$49\frac{3}{4}$	5.01	$54\frac{3}{8}$	4.60	$46\frac{1}{4}$	5.40
1841	$51\frac{1}{2}$	4.85	$52\frac{3}{4}$	4.74	$49\frac{3}{4}$	5.03
1842	$52\frac{1}{2}$	4.78	53	4.72	$51\frac{1}{8}$	4.89
1843	$54\frac{3}{4}$	4.56	58	4.31	$52\frac{1}{2}$	4.76
1844	65	3.84	65	3.85	$54\frac{3}{8}$	4.60
1845	$61\frac{3}{4}$	4.04	$65\frac{1}{4}$	3.83	$58\frac{3}{8}$	4.28
1846	$59\frac{3}{4}$	4.18	$61\frac{3}{4}$	4.05	$58\frac{1}{4}$	4.30
1847	55	4.52	60	4.16	$53\frac{1}{2}$	4.67
1848	$49\frac{1}{2}$	5.02	$55\frac{1}{2}$	4.50	34	7.35
1849	$55\frac{1}{4}$	4.51	$55\frac{1}{2}$	4.50	$45\frac{1}{2}$	5.50
10-yr. av.		4.53				
1850	$57\frac{1}{2}$	4.36	$58\frac{1}{4}$	4.30	$51\frac{1}{2}$	4.86
1851	$58\frac{1}{2}$	4.28	59	4.24	55	4.55
1852	$66\frac{1}{2}$	3.76	$66\frac{1}{2}$	3.76	$57\frac{1}{2}$	4.35
1853	$62\frac{3}{4}$	3.99	$66\frac{3}{8}$	3.77	60	4.16
1854	60	4.16	$63\frac{1}{4}$	3.95	$50\frac{1}{4}$	4.97
1855	63	3.98	$63\frac{7}{8}$	3.92	$59\frac{1}{2}$	4.20
1856	$63\frac{1}{2}$	3.94	$64\frac{3}{4}$	3.86	$61\frac{1}{4}$	4.08
1857	$63\frac{1}{2}$	3.94	$64\frac{1}{4}$	3.89	$60\frac{7}{8}$	4.11
1858	$64\frac{3}{4}$	3.88	$65\frac{1}{2}$	3.82	63	3.97
1859	64	3.90	65	3.84	$53\frac{1}{2}$	4.67
10-yr. av.		4.02				
1860	$62\frac{1}{2}$	4.00	65	3.84	$61\frac{3}{4}$	4.05
1861	63	3.97	$64\frac{1}{4}$	3.89	$61\frac{1}{2}$	4.06
1862	$64\frac{1}{2}$	3.89	$64\frac{1}{2}$	3.87	$62\frac{3}{8}$	4.01
1863	$63\frac{3}{4}$	3.92	$64\frac{3}{4}$	3.86	61	4.10
1864	62	4.01	64	3.90	59	4.24
1865	$61\frac{1}{2}$	4.05	$63\frac{1}{4}$	3.95	60	4.16
1866	$55\frac{1}{2}$	4.50	$61\frac{1}{4}$	4.08	$53\frac{1}{2}$	4.67
1867	$52\frac{1}{4}$	4.76	$57\frac{1}{2}$	4.35	$50\frac{3}{4}$	4.93
1868	57	4.39	58	4.31	$52\frac{1}{2}$	4.76
1869	$53\frac{3}{4}$	4.65	$57\frac{1}{4}$	4.36	$52\frac{3}{8}$	4.77
10-yr. av.		4.21				

TABLE 28 (*Continued*)

Year	$2\frac{1}{2}\%$ Perpetual Debt of the Central Government					
	December 31		Annual High Price	Yield, %	Annual Low Price	Yield, %
	Price	Yield, %				
1870	$52\frac{1}{2}$	4.75	$57\frac{1}{4}$	4.36	$48\frac{1}{2}$	5.15
1871	$57\frac{3}{4}$	4.33	$58\frac{1}{4}$	4.30	$51\frac{3}{4}$	4.73
1872	$54\frac{3}{4}$	4.66	58	4.31	$54\frac{1}{4}$	4.61
1873	$57\frac{3}{4}$	4.33	$58\frac{1}{2}$	4.28	$54\frac{3}{4}$	4.56
1874	$62\frac{1}{4}$	4.01	$62\frac{1}{4}$	4.02	$57\frac{3}{4}$	4.33
1875	$63\frac{1}{4}$	3.96	$64\frac{1}{4}$	3.89	$61\frac{3}{4}$	4.05
1876	$63\frac{1}{4}$	3.96	$64\frac{1}{4}$	3.89	61	4.10
1877	64	3.91	$65\frac{1}{4}$	3.83	$60\frac{3}{8}$	4.14
1878	$62\frac{3}{4}$	3.98	$64\frac{3}{4}$	3.86	$61\frac{1}{4}$	4.08
1879	$64\frac{3}{4}$	3.86	66	3.79	$62\frac{3}{4}$	3.98
10-yr. av.		4.17				
1880	65	3.84	$66\frac{1}{2}$	3.76	$63\frac{3}{4}$	3.92
1881	$67\frac{1}{4}$	3.72	$68\frac{7}{8}$	3.63	$64\frac{3}{4}$	3.86
1882	$66\frac{3}{4}$	3.75	$68\frac{5}{8}$	3.64	$65\frac{3}{8}$	3.83
1883	$65\frac{1}{4}$	3.84	$67\frac{1}{4}$	3.71	$63\frac{7}{8}$	3.91
1884	$66\frac{3}{4}$	3.75	$68\frac{3}{4}$	3.63	$65\frac{3}{8}$	3.83
1885	$69\frac{1}{2}$	3.60	$69\frac{3}{4}$	3.58	$64\frac{3}{4}$	3.86
1886	$74\frac{1}{2}$	3.36	$76\frac{3}{8}$	3.27	$69\frac{1}{4}$	3.61
1887	74	3.38	$75\frac{1}{2}$	3.31	72	3.47
1888	$77\frac{1}{4}$	3.25	$84\frac{1}{2}$	2.96	$72\frac{5}{8}$	3.44
1889	$83\frac{3}{4}$	2.99	84	2.98	$77\frac{5}{8}$	3.22
10-yr. av.		3.55				
1890	$78\frac{1}{4}$	3.19	$79\frac{1}{2}$	3.15	$75\frac{1}{4}$	3.33
1891	$79\frac{1}{4}$	3.15	80	3.12	$76\frac{1}{4}$	3.28
1892	83	3.01	$83\frac{1}{2}$	3.00	$78\frac{1}{4}$	3.20
1893	$84\frac{1}{2}$	2.96	$84\frac{1}{2}$	2.96	$82\frac{3}{4}$	3.02
1894	94	2.66	$95\frac{1}{4}$	2.63	$84\frac{1}{2}$	2.96
1895	93	2.69	96	2.60	92	2.72
1896	$89\frac{1}{4}$	2.80	$93\frac{1}{2}$	2.68	$88\frac{1}{2}$	2.83
1897	$87\frac{3}{4}$	2.84	90	2.78	$86\frac{1}{2}$	2.89
1898	$86\frac{3}{4}$	2.88	88	2.84	$84\frac{1}{2}$	2.96
1899	$79\frac{3}{4}$	3.14	$87\frac{1}{2}$	2.86	$79\frac{1}{2}$	3.15
10-yr. av.		2.93				
1900	$76\frac{1}{2}$	3.26	$82\frac{1}{2}$	3.03	75	3.34

SOURCE

The Netherlands Central Bureau of Statistics.

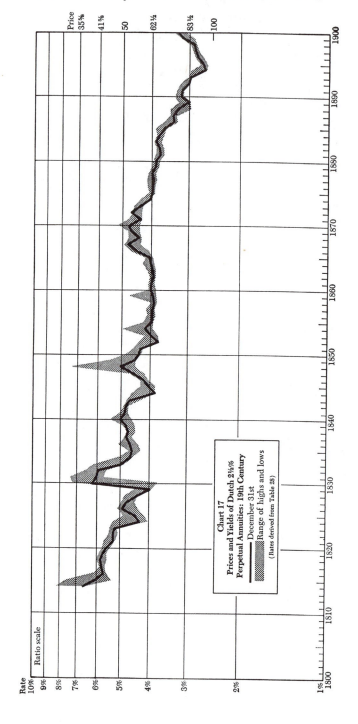

Chart 17
Prices and Yields of Dutch 2½%
Perpetual Annuities: 19th Century
—— December 31st
▨ Range of highs and lows
(Rates derived from Table 28)

By the end of the century, however, they were down to a price of 79½, to yield 3.15%.

Chart 18 compares the annual yields of the Dutch perpetual 2½s with those of British consols during the nineteenth century. The Dutch long rates were usually far higher than the British long rates. This was in striking contrast to the opposite relationship which prevailed in the seventeenth and eighteenth centuries. The closest approach to the British yields came in 1888–1892, when the great British refunding into 2½% consols was under way. It was then that the British for the first time achieved the low 2½% nominal rate on a large part of their debt that

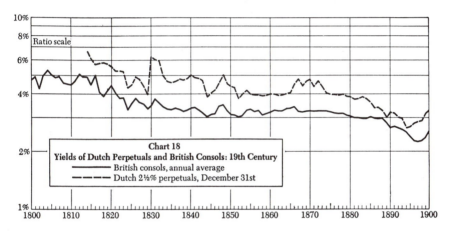

Chart 18
Yields of Dutch Perpetuals and British Consols: 19th Century
——— British consols, annual average
- - - - Dutch 2½% perpetuals, December 31st

had become common in the Dutch Republic more than a century earlier. But in the 1890's the British 2½s sold at good premiums while the Dutch 2½s did not quite reach 100. A great change had occurred in a period of two centuries in the relative economic stature of these two countries.

The chart shows that the nineteenth-century pattern of long-term yield trends in the Netherlands was similar to that in Britain. The two patterns differed, however, in important respects. At times the course of Dutch perpetuals more closely resembled the course of French *rentes* (see Chart 14, page 225), especially when yields rose sharply during the crises of 1830, 1848, and 1870. Each of these crises was reflected in far smaller increases in British yields. On the whole, Dutch perpetuals were far more volatile than British consols during this century.

Short-term Dutch interest rates during the nineteenth century are tabulated in Table 29 and pictured in Chart 19. The rates given are the discount rate of the Bank of the Netherlands after 1814 and the market rate of discount in Amsterdam after 1872.

The broad pattern of these short Dutch rates was not unlike the pattern of short British rates in the nineteenth century. Both showed

TABLE 29

SHORT-TERM DUTCH INTEREST RATES: NINETEENTH CENTURY

Year	Discount Rate of the Bank of the Netherlands			Market Rate of Discount in Amsterdam	Year	Discount Rate of the Bank of the Netherlands			Market Rate of Discount in Amsterdam
	Annual Average, %	High, %	Low, %	Annual Average, %		Annual Average, %	High, %	Low, %	Annual Average, %
1814	4.25	4.50	4.00		1840	2.95	5.00	2.50	
1815	3.72	4.00	3.00		1841	3.00	3.00	3.00	
1816	3.00	3.00	3.00		1842	2.61	3.00	2.50	
1817	4.31	5.00	3.00		1843	2.50	2.50	2.50	
1818	4.12	5.00	3.50		1844	2.50	2.50	2.50	
1819	4.08	5.00	3.00		1845	3.16	5.50	2.50	
					1846	4.28	5.50	4.00	
6-yr. av.	3.91				1847	4.09	5.00	4.00	
					1848	3.68	5.00	3.00	
1820	3.00	3.00	3.00		1849	2.55	3.00	2.50	
1821	3.00	3.00	3.00						
1822	3.00	3.00	3.00		10-yr. av.	3.13			
1823	3.33	5.00	3.00						
1824	3.16	5.00	3.00		1850	2.08	2.50	2.00	
1825	3.16	5.00	3.00		1851	2.00	2.00	2.00	
1826	4.41	5.00	3.50		1852	2.00	2.00	2.00	
1827	3.50	3.50	3.50		1853	2.21	3.00	2.00	
1828	1.75	3.50	1.50		1854	3.00	3.00	3.00	
1829	2.20	2.50	1.50		1855	3.20	4.00	3.00	
					1856	4.32	5.50	4.00	
10-yr. av.	3.05				1857	5.00	7.00	4.00	
					1858	3.74	7.00	3.00	
1830	2.91	5.00	2.00		1859	3.00	3.00	3.00	
1831	3.02	4.00	3.00						
1832	2.58	3.00	2.00		10-yr. av.	3.06			
1833	2.00	2.00	2.00						
1834	2.00	2.00	2.00		1860	3.00	3.00	3.00	
1835	2.00	2.00	2.00		1861	3.07	4.00	3.00	
1836	3.42	5.00	2.00		1862	3.74	4.00	3.50	
1837	4.25	5.00	3.50		1863	3.57	5.00	3.00	
1838	2.53	3.50	2.50		1864	5.35	7.00	4.50	
1839	4.00	5.00	2.50		1865	4.05	6.00	3.00	
					1866	5.95	7.00	4.50	
10-yr. av.	2.87				1867	3.00	4.50	2.50	

TABLE 29 (*Continued*)

Year	Discount Rate of the Bank of the Netherlands			Market Rate of Discount in Amsterdam	Year	Discount Rate of the Bank of the Netherlands			Market Rate of Discount in Amsterdam
	Annual Average, %	High, %	Low, %	Annual Average, %		Annual Average, %	High, %	Low, %	Annual Average, %
1868	2.66	3.50	2.50		1884	3.18	3.50	3.00	2.80
1869	3.48	5.00	2.50		1885	2.70	3.00	2.50	2.37
					1886	2.50	2.50	2.50	1.92
10-yr. av.	3.79				1887	2.50	2.50	2.50	2.13
					1888	2.50	2.50	2.50	2.13
1870	4.27	6.00	3.00		1889	2.50	2.50	2.50	2.18
1871	3.24	4.00	3.00						
1872	3.24	5.00	2.50		10-yr. av.	3.10			2.72
1873	4.84	6.50	4.00	4.69					
1874	3.63	5.00	3.50	3.50	1890	2.79	4.50	2.50	2.59
1875	3.32	3.50	3.00	3.19	1891	3.12	4.50	3.00	2.75
1876	3.00	3.00	3.00	2.75	1892	2.70	3.00	2.50	2.00
1877	3.00	3.00	3.00	2.75	1893	3.40	5.00	2.50	2.88
1878	3.45	4.00	3.00	3.31	1894	2.58	3.50	2.50	1.75
1879	3.17	4.00	3.00	3.00	1895	2.50	2.50	2.50	1.54
					1896	3.03	3.50	2.50	2.44
10-yr. av.	3.52			3.31	1897	3.13	3.50	3.00	2.32
				7-yr. av.	1898	2.83	3.00	2.50	2.49
					1899	3.58	5.00	2.50	3.24
1880	3.00	3.00	3.00	2.50					
1881	3.27	4.50	3.00	3.07	10-yr. av.	2.97			2.40
1882	4.49	5.50	3.50	4.26					
1883	4.12	5.50	3.50	3.81	1900	3.61	5.00	3.50	3.44

SOURCES

The Netherlands Central Bureau of Statistics.

Kurt Eisfeld, *Das Niederlandishe Bankwesen*, 1916, Vol. II, pp. 39–40.

volatility. High rates at 5–7% alternated each few months or few years with low rates in the range of 2–3%. In both countries volatility increased after 1850; in both the decennial average of short rates declined until the 1830's or 1840's, rose until the 1860's and thereafter declined again.

There were, however, these differences: the Dutch discount rate was highly variable after 1815, while the British bank rate was relatively stable at a fairly high level until 1839. Dutch short rates after 1815 were

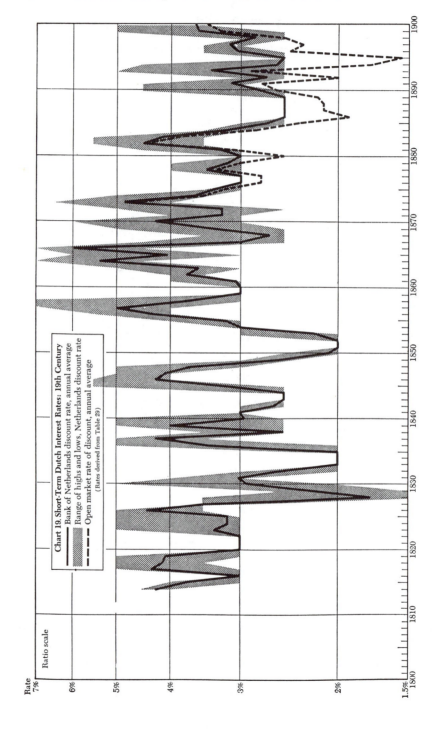

Chart 19. Short-Term Dutch Interest Rates: 19th Century

——— Bank of Netherlands discount rate, annual average

▨ Range of highs and lows, Netherlands discount rate

- - - Open market rate of discount, annual average

(Rates derived from Table 29)

below British short rates. Perhaps the newly liberated Dutch were making an immediate effort to return to their very low commercial rates of the seventeenth and eighteenth centuries. They put the discount rate down to 3% as early as 1815, when the British bank rate was at 5%. In the 1820's the Dutch discount rate was usually at 3–3½%, although it occasionally rose to 5%. In 1828 the Dutch discount rate was lowered to 1½% for a brief period when the British bank rate was at 4% and Dutch perpetuals were at 4–5%. This suggests an effort of policy.

Such low short rates, however, did not last. Never again in this century did the Dutch discount rate go below 2% and rarely below 2½%. In the 1830's it ranged from 2 to 5%, and in the 1850's and 1860's it ranged usually from 3% up to an occasional crisis high of 7%. It never reached the British crisis high of 10%, and after 1853 it never reached the British customary low of 2%. In other words, as the century progressed, the British bank rate became more volatile than the Dutch discount rate, whereas early in the century bank rate had been less volatile.

When market rates in Amsterdam were reported after 1872, they were below the discount rate of the Bank of the Netherlands. They were highly volatile, like British market rates, but they never went as high or as low as the British rates. Toward the end of the century, Dutch short-term market rates were low on the average, usually ranging between 1½ and 2¾%.

The generally successful efforts of the Dutch to maintain low short-term commercial rates is clearly reflected by the decennial averages in Chart 16 above. These Dutch short rates averaged far below the Dutch long-term bond yields at all times, although the differential narrowed during the easy-money period of the last two decades. In contrast similar British short-term rates averaged above the British long-term bond yields throughout the century until the last two decades. In the final three decades the relatively high Dutch long rates fell more rapidly than the relatively low Dutch short rates. At the period of lowest interest rates in this century the long and short rates in both countries were as shown in the accompanying table.

LOW RATES OF 1894–1897

	British, %	Dutch, %
Long-term government bond yields, extreme lows	2.22	2.60
Central bank rate, extreme lows	2.00	2.50
Short-term market rate of discount, low annual averages	0.81	1.54

BELGIUM

Background. The Kingdom of Belgium was established in 1831 as an "independent and perpetually neutral state." Belgium fought in no wars in this century and almost entirely escaped the revolutionary disturbances which swept Europe in 1848. It pursued a liberal trade policy on the British model and adopted the prevailing methods of banking and finance. It acquired an empire in the African Congo. Its mineral resources were so rich and its economic growth was so rapid that by the end of the century Belgium was the fourth-ranking manufacturing power in Europe.

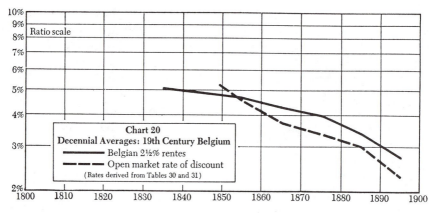

Chart 20
Decennial Averages: 19th Century Belgium
————— Belgian 2½% rentes
— — — Open market rate of discount
(Rates derived from Tables 30 and 31)

Antwerp, however, never regained the central position in trade and in finance that it had occupied in the fifteenth and sixteenth centuries. Leadership had passed first to Amsterdam and then to London. But an important international money market nevertheless developed in nineteenth-century Belgium. The Belgian currency and Belgian securities acquired an enviable reputation. State finance was largely modeled on the new European methods: (a) A moderate debt was funded in long-term *rentes*, which were uniform and hence marketable; (b) a national bank established an official discount rate which importantly influenced free-market rates of discount.

Interest Rates. Belgian interest rates were relatively high in 1830–1831 when the new nation was established. They remained high until 1849, and then declined almost steadily until 1895. Thus they followed a trend broadly similar to the declining trend of rates in most northern European countries, but different in detail.

Throughout the middle decades of this century Belgium had simulta·neously outstanding a number of series of *rentes* with widely different nominal rates of interest ranging from 2½ to 5%. Prices and yields on several series are presented in Table 30 and Chart 21.

TABLE 30

Prices and Yields of Long-Term Belgian Government Securities: Nineteenth Century

Year	Annual Averages									
	5% Rentes		*4½% Rentes*		*4% Rentes*		*3% Rentes*		*2½% Rentes*	
	Price	Yield, %	Price	Yield, %	Price	Yield, %	Price	Yield, %	Price	Yield, %
1831									$38\frac{1}{2}$	6.49
1832									$42\frac{5}{8}$	5.86
1833	95	5.26							$46\frac{1}{2}$	5.37
1834	$96\frac{7}{8}$	5.16							$51\frac{1}{2}$	4.85
1835	$101\frac{3}{8}$	4.93							$53\frac{7}{8}$	4.64
1836	$100\frac{3}{8}$	4.98							$53\frac{3}{8}$	4.68
1837	$101\frac{3}{8}$	4.93							$53\frac{1}{4}$	4.70
1838	$97\frac{5}{8}$	5.12					$73\frac{3}{4}$	4.07	$54\frac{1}{2}$	4.59
1839	101	4.95					70	4.29	$53\frac{7}{8}$	4.64
		5.05 7-yr. av.								5.09 9-yr. av.
1840	100	5.00					$71\frac{1}{8}$	4.22	56	4.46
1841	$100\frac{3}{4}$	4.96					70	4.29	$52\frac{1}{2}$	4.76
1842	$102\frac{1}{2}$	4.88					$71\frac{3}{4}$	4.18	$52\frac{5}{8}$	4.75
1843	$103\frac{1}{4}$	4.84					$73\frac{1}{2}$	4.08	$55\frac{1}{2}$	4.51
1844	$103\frac{1}{4}$	4.84	$105\frac{5}{8}$	4.26			$77\frac{1}{8}$	3.89	$59\frac{1}{2}$	4.20
1845	102	4.90	$101\frac{3}{8}$	4.44			77	3.90	60	4.17
1846	$100\frac{3}{4}$	4.96	$99\frac{3}{8}$	4.53			$74\frac{1}{8}$	4.05	$56\frac{1}{8}$	4.45
1847	$99\frac{3}{8}$	5.03	$93\frac{3}{4}$	4.80			$69\frac{1}{8}$	4.34	$52\frac{1}{2}$	4.76
1848	$76\frac{3}{8}$	6.55	$70\frac{1}{2}$	6.39			47	6.38 *	35	7.15 †
1849	$91\frac{3}{4}$	5.45	84	5.36			60	5.00	$45\frac{3}{4}$	5.47
10-yr. av.		5.14						4.43		4.87
1850	$98\frac{1}{4}$	5.09	$90\frac{3}{4}$	4.96			$64\frac{1}{8}$	4.68	$49\frac{1}{2}$	5.05
1851	$99\frac{3}{4}$	5.01	$90\frac{7}{8}$	4.95			$63\frac{3}{4}$	4.70	$50\frac{1}{4}$	4.97
1852	$100\frac{3}{8}$	4.98	96	4.69			$69\frac{1}{8}$	4.34	$53\frac{7}{8}$	4.64
1853	$99\frac{3}{4}$	5.01	$97\frac{1}{2}$	4.62			$74\frac{1}{8}$	4.05	$55\frac{1}{4}$	4.52
1854	$96\frac{7}{8}$	5.16	89	5.06			69	4.35	$50\frac{1}{4}$	4.98
1855	$99\frac{3}{4}$	5.01	93	4.84			$72\frac{1}{2}$	4.14	$53\frac{1}{4}$	4.70
1856	100	5.00	$96\frac{3}{4}$	4.65			$73\frac{3}{4}$	4.07	$54\frac{3}{8}$	4.60
1857	$98\frac{3}{4}$	5.06	$97\frac{5}{8}$	4.61			$73\frac{1}{2}$	4.08	$55\frac{3}{4}$	4.48
1858	$98\frac{3}{4}$	5.06	$98\frac{5}{8}$	4.56			$73\frac{3}{4}$	4.07	$55\frac{3}{4}$	4.48
1859	$98\frac{3}{4}$	5.06	$97\frac{3}{8}$	4.62			$74\frac{1}{8}$	4.05	$55\frac{1}{2}$	4.51
10-yr. av.		5.04		4.76				4.25		4.69
1860			$97\frac{3}{8}$	4.62			$76\frac{1}{2}$	3.92	$55\frac{5}{8}$	4.49
1861			$99\frac{1}{8}$	4.54			$79\frac{1}{8}$	3.79	$56\frac{5}{8}$	4.42
1862			$99\frac{3}{4}$	4.51			$82\frac{5}{8}$	3.63	$57\frac{1}{4}$	4.37
1863			100	4.50			$82\frac{5}{8}$	3.63	61	4.10
1864			$99\frac{3}{4}$	4.51			$82\frac{3}{8}$	3.64	$58\frac{5}{8}$	4.26

* High 8.57%. † High 9.80% ($25\frac{1}{2}$).

TABLE 30 (*Continued*)

Year	5% Rentes Price	Yield, %	4½% Rentes Price	Yield, %	4% Rentes Price	Yield, %	3% Rentes Price	Yield, %	2½% Rentes Price	Yield, %
						Annual Averages				
1865			$99\frac{1}{2}$	4.52			$82\frac{1}{8}$	3.65	$58\frac{3}{4}$	4.25
1866			$98\frac{1}{4}$	4.58			$85\frac{1}{4}$	3.52	$57\frac{3}{8}$	4.36
1867			$99\frac{3}{8}$	4.53			85	3.53	$56\frac{1}{2}$	4.43
1868			$101\frac{1}{8}$	4.45			$85\frac{1}{2}$	3.51	$59\frac{1}{8}$	4.23
1869			$102\frac{3}{4}$	4.38			89	3.37	$62\frac{1}{8}$	4.02
10-yr. av.				4.51				3.62		4.29
1870			$101\frac{3}{4}$	4.42			$90\frac{5}{8}$	3.31	$62\frac{1}{8}$	4.02
1871			$102\frac{1}{4}$	4.40			$93\frac{1}{2}$	3.21	$61\frac{7}{8}$	4.04
1872			$102\frac{1}{4}$	4.40	$100\frac{1}{2}$	3.98	$97\frac{1}{8}$	3.09	64	3.91
1873			$101\frac{1}{2}$	4.43	100	4.00	$77\frac{3}{8}$	3.86	$64\frac{1}{2}$	3.87
1874			$102\frac{3}{8}$	4.38	$98\frac{1}{2}$	4.06	$73\frac{7}{8}$	4.06	$61\frac{1}{4}$	4.08
1875			$103\frac{5}{8}$	4.34	$98\frac{3}{4}$	4.05	$73\frac{3}{4}$	4.07	$61\frac{1}{4}$	4.08
1876			$104\frac{1}{8}$	4.32	99	4.04	$74\frac{1}{8}$	4.05	$61\frac{1}{4}$	4.08
1877			103	4.37	$99\frac{3}{4}$	4.01	$76\frac{3}{5}$	3.94	$62\frac{1}{4}$	3.98
1878			104	4.33	$99\frac{3}{4}$	4.01	$76\frac{1}{2}$	3.92	63	3.97
1879			$104\frac{3}{8}$	4.31	$102\frac{7}{8}$	3.89	$80\frac{3}{8}$	3.73	$65\frac{5}{8}$	3.81
10-yr. av.				4.37				3.72		3.98
1880					$104\frac{3}{4}$	3.82	$84\frac{1}{2}$	3.55	$68\frac{1}{2}$	3.65
1881					$105\frac{1}{4}$	3.80	$85\frac{1}{2}$	3.51	$70\frac{1}{4}$	3.56
1882					$103\frac{7}{8}$	3.85	$84\frac{1}{2}$	3.55	$70\frac{1}{4}$	3.56
1883					$103\frac{5}{8}$	3.86	$82\frac{7}{8}$	3.62	$69\frac{7}{8}$	3.58
1884					$104\frac{1}{8}$	3.84	84	3.57	$70\frac{1}{4}$	3.56
1885					$103\frac{1}{8}$	3.88	89	3.37	$73\frac{1}{2}$	3.40
1886					$103\frac{5}{8}$	3.86	$94\frac{3}{8}$	3.18	$79\frac{7}{8}$	3.13
1887					$101\frac{1}{4}$	3.95	$92\frac{1}{2}$	3.24	$80\frac{1}{8}$	3.12 ‡
1888					$3\frac{1}{2}$% Rentes		$92\frac{7}{8}$	3.23	$80\frac{5}{8}$	3.10
1889					102	3.43	$93\frac{3}{4}$	3.20	$80\frac{3}{8}$	3.11
10-yr. av.								3.40		3.38
1890					$102\frac{3}{8}$	3.42	$97\frac{3}{8}$	3.08	$84\frac{1}{8}$	2.97
1891					$101\frac{1}{8}$	3.46	$98\frac{5}{8}$	3.04	$88\frac{3}{4}$	2.83
1892					$102\frac{3}{8}$	3.42	99	3.03	$88\frac{5}{8}$	2.82
1893					$102\frac{5}{8}$	3.41	$101\frac{3}{8}$	2.96	93	2.69
1894					$102\frac{5}{8}$	3.41	102	2.94	$97\frac{5}{8}$	2.56 §
1895					102	3.43	$100\frac{5}{8}$	2.98	$97\frac{1}{4}$	2.57
1896							101	2.97	$94\frac{3}{8}$	2.65
1897							$101\frac{3}{8}$	2.96	95	2.63
1898							$100\frac{5}{8}$	2.98	$95\frac{3}{8}$	2.62
1899							$98\frac{3}{8}$	3.05	90	2.78
10-yr. av.								3.00		2.71
1900							$95\frac{1}{4}$	3.15	$85\frac{5}{8}$	2.92

‡ Low 3.02%. § Low 2.52%.
All yields are current yields.

SOURCE
Bulletin de l'Institute des Sciences Economiques, Université Catholique de Louvain. Article by Von Der Rest, November, 1933, pp. 103–4; and article by J. M. Drappier, August, 1937, pp. 428–435, 437–440.

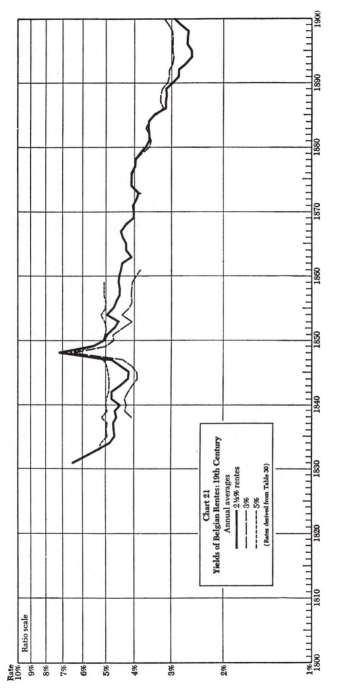

Chart 21
Yields of Belgian Rentes: 19th Century
Annual averages
2½% rentes
3%
5%
(Rates derived from Table 30)

The variety of simultaneous yields is noteworthy. It illustrates the caution with which the yield calculations on any one security should be treated as representing a whole market. A part of the yield differences can be explained in terms of discounts and premiums below or above par value: the 5s never sold to yield much less than 5%; the 4½s never sold to yield much less than 4½%; and so on. This was due no doubt to fear of redemption. Therefore, as interest rates declined, a large yield differential developed in favor of the *rentes* with high nominal rates, and they became less representative of long-term rates of interest; investors were willing to accept a lower yield on a discount security protected against redemption. The same differentials have been found in other markets. However, the chart shows that discount was not the only cause of lower yields. In the period of relatively high rates in the 1830's the 3s at 4.10–4.25% commanded a lower current yield than the 2½s at 4.50–4.75%. In fact the 2½s provided the highest current yields at the earliest reported dates and the lowest at the close of the century. Despite differences in terms between various issues which prevent the yield of any one issue from representing the whole market, an informative picture on trends is provided by the long-continued history of the 2½% *rentes*.

The earliest quotations on the Belgian 2½s are for 1831, when they sold at 38–39 to yield 6.58–6.41% currently. This was directly after the War of Belgian Independence and at a time of general unsettlement in Europe. Dutch perpetuals were then yielding over 6% and French *rentes* over 5%. Even British consols had recently declined in price, but their yield at about 3.75% was far below other European yields.

During the new nation's first few years the Belgian *rentes* improved rapidly in price. By 1845 the 2½s were up to an average of 60, to yield 4.17%. These were the high prices and low yields for 15–20 years to come.

The revolutions of 1848, although none occurred in Belgium itself, had a demoralizing effect on Belgian as well as other European markets. The Belgian 2½s actually declined to a low price of 25½ in 1848, to yield 9.8%, their lowest price in the period covered by this history. French 5% *rentes* simultaneously had declined from 119⅛ to 50, to yield 10%, and the Dutch 2½s from 65 to a low of 34, to yield 7.35%. British consols dropped from 97¾ to a low of 80, to yield 3.76%. Up to mid-century Britain alone among these countries had consistently low long-term rates; she enjoyed a large measure of immunity from the social disturbances on the continent. Belgian long-term rates by mid-century had not yet become low by nineteenth-century standards.

From 1848 on throughout the whole second half of the century until 1894, these Belgian long-term interest rates declined almost steadily.

The yield decline and the price advance were far better sustained than those in Holland or France or Britain. In a two-year period from 1848 to 1850 the Belgian 2½s doubled in price, moving up from 25½ to 50¾. By 1863 they exceeded their previous 1846 high of 61⅝. After a brief setback in 1863–1867 they advanced again to a new high price of 64½ in 1872, thus breaking through the 4% yield level. During the years 1872–1894 the 2½s moved up rapidly from 64½ to an all-time high of 99, to yield 2.52%. By 1898 they had come back to 85¾, to yield 2.91%.

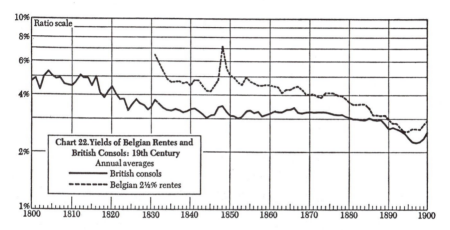

Chart 22. Yields of Belgian Rentes and British Consols: 19th Century
Annual averages
——— British consols
------- Belgian 2½% rentes

The distinctive feature of the history of these Belgian long-term rates in this century was the continuity and sharpness of their decline following 1848. The comparison with British consols in Chart 22 brings this out forcefully: both series declined most of the time but British rates were already at comparably low levels at mid-century and thereafter Belgian rates declined much faster, much further, and much more persistently. At 1848 low prices Belgian 2½s yielded 504 basis points more than consols; at 1894 high prices they yielded only 6 basis points more than consols.

Comparison of Chart 22 with Charts 14 and 18, which summarize the histories of French *rentes* and Dutch perpetuals, reveals that after 1870 all three yields tended to decline faster than the yields of British consols. The unusual feature of the Belgian series was its steady yield decline in the period 1852–1871 when rates on French *rentes* and Dutch perpetuals advanced sharply. In summary, Belgian *rentes* tended to behave more like French and Dutch obligations up to 1850, reaching very high yields in the crises of 1830 and 1848; after 1850, Belgian *rentes* ignored continental crises, and their yields declined swiftly and steadily until they came very close to consol yields, closer than did the French and Dutch yields.

TABLE 31

SHORT-TERM BELGIAN INTEREST RATES: NINETEENTH CENTURY

Year	Official Discount Rate, %		Free-Market Rate of Discount				
	High	Low	Annual Aver-age,* %	Quarterly Averages, %			
				1st	2nd	3rd	4th
1823	3.50	3.00					
1824	3.00	3.00					
1825	4.00	3.00					
1826	4.50	4.00					
1827	4.00	4.00					
1828	4.00	4.00					
1829	4.00	4.00					
1830	4.50	4.50					
1831	5.00	5.00					
1832	5.00	5.00					
1833	5.00	5.00					
1834	5.00	5.00					
1835	5.00	3.00					
1836	5.00	4.00					
1837	5.00	4.00					
1838	5.00	4.00					
1839	5.00	4.50					
1840	5.00	3.50					
1841	4.00	3.00					
1842	4.00	3.00					
1843	4.00	3.00					
1844	4.00	3.00					
1845	5.00	4.50					
1846	5.00	4.50					
1847	5.00	4.50					
1848	5.00	5.00	5.50		6.00	5.00	
1849	5.00	5.00	5.00	5.00	5.00		5.00
1850	5.00	5.00	5.00			5.00	5.00
1851	4.00	4.00	4.50			4.50	4.50
1852	4.00	3.00	4.33	4.50	4.50		4.00
1853	3.00	3.00	4.00	4.00		4.00	4.00
1854	3.00	3.00	4.33	4.00		4.50	4.50
1855	3.00	3.00	4.50	4.50		4.50	4.50
1856	4.00	3.00	4.75		4.50		5.00
1857	5.50	3.50	5.00	5.00	5.00	5.00	5.00
1858	5.00	3.00	4.75		5.00	4.50	
1859	4.00	3.00	4.75			5.00	4.50
10-yr. av.			4.59				
1860	4.00	3.00	4.33	5.00	4.00		4.00
1861	5.00	3.00	4.50	4.00			5.00
1862	4.00	3.00	3.25	4.00	3.00	3.00	3.00
1863	5.50	3.00	3.25	3.00	3.00	3.00	4.00
1864	6.00	4.00	5.31	5.75	4.00	5.75	5.75

TABLE 31 (*Continued*)

Year	Official Discount Rate, %		Free-Market Rate of Discount				
	High	Low	Annual Average,* %	Quarterly Averages, %			
				1st	2nd	3rd	4th
1865	6.00	3.00	3.87	4.00	3.50	3.00	5.00
1866	6.00	3.00	4.69	5.25	4.50	6.00	3.00
1867	3.00	2.50	3.00	3.00	3.00	3.00	3.00
1868	2.50	2.50	2.50	2.50	2.50	2.50	2.50
1869	2.50	2.50	2.50	2.50	2.50	2.50	2.50
10-yr. av.			3.72				
1870	6.00	2.50	3.00	2.50	2.50	2.50	4.50
1871	5.50	2.50	4.12	3.50	4.00	4.00	5.00
1872	5.50	2.50	3.25	2.50	2.50	4.00	4.00
1873	7.00	3.50	5.00	5.00	4.00	6.00	5.00
1874	6.00	3.50	4.50	6.00	5.50	3.50	3.00
1875	4.50	3.00	3.75	4.00	3.75	3.00	4.25
1876	3.50	2.50	2.62	3.50	3.00	2.00	2.00
1877	3.50	2.50	2.12	2.25	2.00	2.17	2.06
1878	4.50	2.50	2.68	2.50	2.12	3.12	3.00
1879	4.00	2.50	2.52	3.50	2.50	2.07 †	2.00
10-yr. av.			3.36				
1880	3.50	3.00	2.72	3.12	2.94	2.25	2.50
1881	5.50	3.50	3.45	3.12	3.06	3.50	4.12
1882	6.00	3.50	3.78	4.75	3.25	3.00	4.12
1883	4.50	3.50	3.61	4.12	4.12	3.00	3.20
1884	4.00	3.00	2.96	3.50	2.75	2.75	2.75
1885	4.00	3.00	2.90	3.75	2.60	2.50	2.75
1886	4.00	2.50	2.47	3.25	2.25	2.12	2.25
1887	3.50	2.50	2.62	2.40	2.25	2.60	3.25
1888	5.00	2.50	2.42	2.20	2.00	2.50	3.00
1889	5.00	3.00	3.21	4.25	3.20	2.40	3.00
10-yr. av.			3.01				
1890	4.00	3.00	2.90	3.54	2.56	2.75	2.75
1891	3.00	3.00	2.57	2.75	2.50	2.44	2.62
1892	3.00	2.50	1.99	2.62	1.87	1.87	1.62
1893	3.00	2.50	2.03	1.69	1.50	2.19	2.75
1894	3.00	3.00	2.22	2.69	2.62	1.81	1.81
1895	3.00	2.50	1.65	1.62	1.50	2.00	1.50
1896	3.00	2.50	2.10	1.75	1.75	2.25	2.62
1897	3.00	3.00	1.94	2.12	1.75		
1898	4.00	3.00	2.16	2.12	1.75	2.50	2.25
1899	5.00	3.50	3.28	3.75	2.75	3.06	3.75
10-yr. av.			2.29				
1900	5.00	4.00	3.92	4.75	3.75	3.62	3.62

* Average of recorded quotations, which are not always complete.
† 1.75% at low.

SOURCE

J. M. Drappier, *Bulletin de l'Institute des Sciences Economiques,* Université Catholique de Louvain, August, 1937, pp. 438–443, 449.

Short-term interest rates in Belgium, as represented by the official discount rate and the free-market rate of discount, fluctuated very similarly to other European short-term rates. They became highly volatile in the 1860's and 1870's. Their annual averages tended to decline sharply throughout the second half of the century. They are reported in Table 31 and Chart 23.

Although no open-market series of short rates is presented until 1848, official rates suggest that short-term rates may have remained relatively high in Belgium until 1850. In fact the Belgian free-market rate averaged 4.59% during the decade of the 1850's, when the British open-market rate averaged 3.84%, the French official rate averaged 4.20%, and the Dutch official rate averaged 3.06%. Belgian short rates, however, declined rapidly after 1850. They reached a decennial average of 2.29% in the 1890's, which was close to the British and French open-market average of 2.09% and below the Dutch average of 2.40%.

The decline of Belgian short-term rates and Belgian long-term rates during the second half of the nineteenth century was almost parallel as shown in Chart 20 above. Although at their highs around 1850, the average of these short rates was briefly above the average of these long rates; during all the rest of the century these short Belgian rates averaged below these long Belgian rates by a roughly constant differential. By the end of the century both were among the lowest in Europe.

GERMANY

Background. The financial history of Germany in the nineteenth century turned upon two dates—1815 and 1870. After the defeat of Napoleon I in 1815, Germany was reorganized in its ancient form as a group of independent nations, each a separate political and financial entity. After the defeat of Napoleon III in 1870, these states were for the first time united as a great nation, the German Empire, and thereafter had a common political and financial history.

The social disturbances which led in 1830 to the July Revolution in Paris had repercussions throughout Germany, but they were strongly suppressed and no important political changes occurred. However, the generally accepted desire to attain greater economic and political unity led to the organization of the *Zollverein,* 1834–1844, under the leadership of Prussia. This was a customs union of many German states which aimed to overcome the irksome and hampering restrictions of multiple tariffs.

The revolutions of 1848 disturbed the various German states profoundly. Ineffective uprisings occurred demanding liberal constitutions and a unification or federation of German states. In 1862 Otto Von Bismarck became Minister-President (later Chancellor) of Prussia. Im-

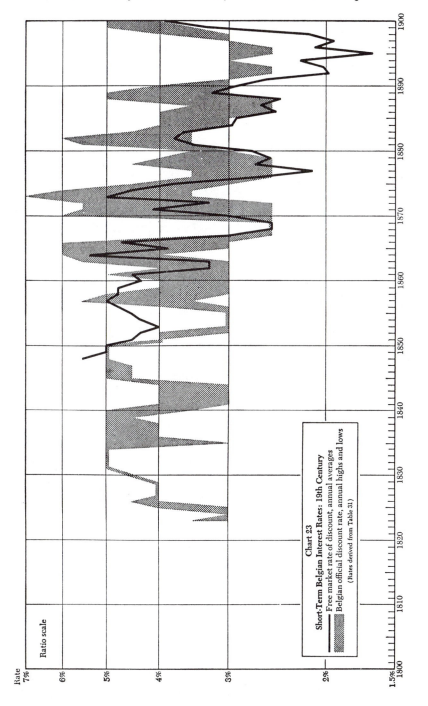

Chart 23
Short-Term Belgian Interest Rates: 19th Century
—— Free market rate of discount, annual averages
▒ Belgian official discount rate, annual highs and lows
(Rates derived from Table 31)

mediately an effort was begun to achieve German unification without concessions to the movement for liberal and constitutional reform. War with Denmark in 1864 secured the duchies of Schleswig-Holstein and Lauenberg for Prussia. War with the Austria-Hungarian Empire in 1866 resulted in a complete Prussian victory and the organization of the North German Confederation under Prussian leadership. War with France in 1870 was quickly victorious and led in 1871 to the formation of the German Empire.

Immediately an ambitious program of political expansion and empire building was matched by rapid economic development at home. A gold standard was adopted in 1871. After a financial crisis in 1873 and an ensuing depression, the Reichsbank was organized in 1876. It substituted one currency for nine and helped to stabilize the economy and to make Berlin a leading financial center. A system of gigantic branch banks grew up and forced the old private banks out of business, although savings banks, mortgage banks, and cooperative credit societies survived.

German industry underwent a phenomenal development. Germany soon passed France and England as a producer of iron and steel. Railway mileage trebled between 1870 and 1914, while the German merchant marine grew fivefold. German foreign trade grew to be almost as large as England's. Urbanization, industrialization, and growth probably without precedent were crowded into the last three decades of the century. Nevertheless, German commodity prices remained stable and, in fact, declined until 1896, the national debt remained relatively moderate, and interest rates declined. (470)

German finance after 1815 followed the general European model, with a few differences. The debts of the various states were largely in the form of long-term bonds essentially similar to British funds and French *rentes*. German states and cities had financed themselves by the issuance of perpetual annuities since the days of the medieval census annuities. There were bonds of the various provinces of Prussia and bonds of the states of Prussia, Bavaria, Würtemberg, Baden, Hanover, Saxony, Nassau, Hesse, Brunswick, the Palatinate, Hamburg, and so on. Many of these are quoted regularly, beginning in 1815. There was no unified German debt until loans of the Imperial Reich were floated in the late 1870's.

Mortgage banks were a characteristic German institution. The first mortgage bank, the Land Mortgage Credit Association, was founded in Prussia in 1770 under government auspices. Such institutions helped finance redemption payments by tenants to their former lords and assisted landowners to purchase and develop more land. Their capital was provided by the sale of bonds. Land mortgage bonds were dealt in extensively and were quoted frequently in nineteenth- and twentieth-century Germany. The efforts of the land banks were supplemented by agricultural cooperative banks, of which there were some 17,000 by 1910.

In Germany there were many rival centers of banking and finance, but Berlin was predominant. These money markets were organized after 1815 in the usual European manner, with a central bank, an official discount rate, and an open market for prime short-term commercial bills. The principal central banks were the Royal Bank of Berlin until 1846, the Prussian Bank until 1875, and thereafter the Reichsbank. There were different market rates of discount in Berlin, Frankfort on the Main, Hamburg, and elsewhere. For the purposes of this history it is sufficient to follow

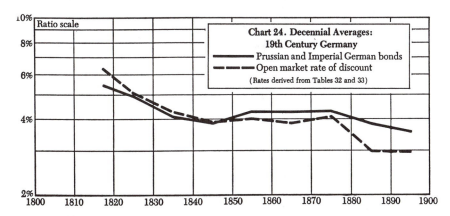

interest rates in Prussia from 1815 until the 1870's and thereafter to follow Imperial German interest rates; this is merely to follow the Berlin market throughout the century.

Interest Rates. German interest rates, both long-term and short-term, declined during the nineteenth century in the sense that their averages were lower in the fifth and sixth decades than in the second and lowest in the last decade. The decline, however, was more moderate than the decline in most other countries. It was far from continuous, and during the latter part of the century it did not carry rates down to the low levels prevailing elsewhere. Germany was a relatively high interest rate country in the nineteenth century.

When such generalizations on the course and level of German interest rates are offered for the nineteenth century, they must be qualified by the consideration that the quotations are for rates on Prussian government securities until the 1870's and on Imperial German government securities thereafter. Bavarian bond yields, for example, were often lower than Prussian bond yields. There were other complications, such as a variety of Prussian issues with different nominal rates.

Table 32 and Chart 25 below contain only a few of the available series

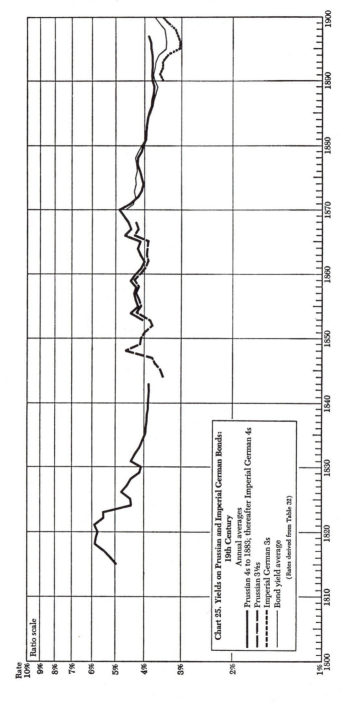

Chart 25. Yields on Prussian and Imperial German Bonds:
19th Century
Annual averages
———— Prussian 4s to 1883; thereafter Imperial German 4s
– – – – Prussian 3½s
▪▪▪▪▪▪ Imperial German 3s
———— Bond yield average
(Rates derived from Table 32)

TABLE 32

PRICES AND YIELDS OF LONG-TERM GERMAN BONDS: NINETEENTH CENTURY

Year	Annual Averages								
	Prussian State 3½s		Prussian State 4s		Bavarian 4s		Imperial German 4s		Computed Average of Bond Yields, %
	Price	Yield, %	Price	Yield, %	Price	Yield, %	Price	Yield, %	
1815			81⅛	4.94					
1816			77	5.19					
1817			73¼	5.46					
1818			68¼	5.86					
1819			69¼	5.79					
				5.45 5-yr. av.					
1820			70	5.72	73¾	5.42			
1821			68⅛	5.87	74⅜	5.38			
1822			73	5.47	85½	4.68			
1823			73	5.47	88½	4.55			
1824			91	4.40	94	4.26			
1825			90¾	4.41	93⅜	4.28			
1826			84⅛	4.74	90½	4.42			
1827			88⅛	4.54	93⅞	4.26			
1828			90¾	4.41	97¼	4.12			
1829			97¼	4.12	100¼	3.99			
10-yr. av.				4.91		4.54			
1830			97⅞	4.09	100¾	3.98			
1831			90¾	4.41	95	4.21			
1832			93¾	4.27	96⅝	4.15			
1833			97⅛	4.13	99¾	4.01			
1834			99¼	4.03	102	3.93			
1835			101⅛	3.96	102½	3.90			
1836			101⅞	3.94	101⅞	3.94			
1837			102⅜	3.91	102⅛	3.92			
1838			102⅞	3.90	102⅛	3.92			
1839			103½	3.86	100⅜	3.98			
10-yr. av.				4.05		3.99			
1840			103¾	3.86	100⅞	3.97			
1841			104⅛	3.84	3½s				
1842			104½	3.83	101⅝	3.44			
1843			104	3.84	101⅜	3.45			
1844	101¼	3.45			101¾	3.44			
1845	99½	3.52			101⅛	3.46			
1846	95¾	3.66			98	3.56			
1847	93	3.76			93¼	3.75			
1848	76⅛	4.60			73⅞	4.73			
1849	84¾	4.13			80	4.37			
		3.85 6-yr. av.		3.84 4-yr. av.		3.78 8-yr. av.			

TABLE 32 (*Continued*)

Year	Prussian State 3½s		Prussian State 4s		Bavarian 3½s		Imperial German 4s		Computed Average of Bond Yields, %
	Price	Yield, %	Price	Yield, %	Price	Yield, %	Price	Yield, %	
1850	$85\frac{1}{2}$	4.10			$82\frac{7}{8}$	4.22			
1851	$87\frac{3}{4}$	3.99			$90\frac{1}{4}$	3.88			
1852	93	3.76			$93\frac{1}{2}$	3.74			
1853	$91\frac{3}{4}$	3.82	$99\frac{1}{2}$	4.02	$94\frac{1}{4}$	3.71			
1854	$83\frac{1}{4}$	4.21	$90\frac{1}{2}$	4.44	$87\frac{1}{4}$	4.01			
1855	$85\frac{1}{2}$	4.10	$95\frac{3}{4}$	4.17	85	4.09			
1856	$84\frac{1}{8}$	4.15	$94\frac{1}{8}$	4.24	87	4.02			
1857	$82\frac{3}{4}$	4.23	$93\frac{1}{2}$	4.30	$92\frac{3}{4}$	3.77			
1858	$84\frac{1}{8}$	4.15	$94\frac{1}{2}$	4.23	$96\frac{3}{4}$	3.61			
1859	$81\frac{3}{4}$	4.29	$90\frac{1}{4}$	4.42	$94\frac{7}{8}$	3.69			
10-yr. av.		4.08		4.26		3.87			
				7-yr. av.	4s				
1860	$85\frac{1}{8}$	4.11	$94\frac{1}{2}$	4.24	99	4.04			
1861	$88\frac{3}{4}$	3.94	$98\frac{1}{4}$	4.07	101	3.95			
1862	$90\frac{3}{4}$	3.86	100	4.00	$101\frac{1}{8}$	3.96			
1863	$89\frac{1}{2}$	3.91	$97\frac{1}{2}$	4.10	$101\frac{1}{8}$	3.96			
1864	$90\frac{1}{4}$	3.88	$95\frac{7}{8}$	4.19	$98\frac{1}{2}$	4.06			
1865	$90\frac{1}{4}$	3.87	$97\frac{1}{2}$	4.10	$98\frac{7}{8}$	4.05			
1866	$81\frac{1}{8}$	4.31	$86\frac{1}{2}$	4.62	89	4.49			
1867	$83\frac{3}{4}$	4.18	$90\frac{3}{8}$	4.42	$90\frac{1}{8}$	4.44			
1868	$82\frac{1}{4}$	4.25	$88\frac{1}{4}$	4.52	$90\frac{1}{8}$	4.44			
1869					$88\frac{3}{8}$	4.54			
10-yr. av.		4.03		4.25		4.19			
		9-yr. av.		9-yr. av.					
1870			$82\frac{1}{4}$	4.87	$85\frac{5}{8}$	4.66			4.60
1871			90	4.45	$92\frac{1}{4}$	4.33			4.44
1872			96	4.18	94	4.25			4.26
1873			98	4.08	$94\frac{5}{8}$	4.22			4.30
1874			$99\frac{5}{8}$	4.02	98	4.07			4.24
1875			$98\frac{3}{8}$	4.09	94	4.26			4.25
1876			97	4.12	93	4.30			4.21
1877			$95\frac{1}{8}$	4.20	$94\frac{3}{8}$	4.24			4.22
1878			$95\frac{7}{8}$	4.19	$94\frac{5}{8}$	4.22	$95\frac{3}{4}$	4.18	4.26
1879			$98\frac{1}{8}$	4.07	$97\frac{7}{8}$	4.08	$97\frac{7}{8}$	4.09	4.17
10-yr. av.				4.23		4.26		4.13	4.29
								2-yr. av.	
1880			$99\frac{3}{8}$	4.03	$99\frac{3}{8}$	4.03	$99\frac{7}{8}$	4.00	4.05
1881			$101\frac{1}{2}$	3.94	$101\frac{1}{8}$	3.96	$101\frac{1}{2}$	3.94	3.96
1882			101	3.96	$101\frac{3}{8}$	3.95	$101\frac{1}{2}$	3.94	3.94
1883			$101\frac{7}{8}$	3.93	$101\frac{3}{4}$	3.94	$102\frac{1}{8}$	3.92	3.92
1884							$103\frac{1}{8}$	3.88	3.88
1885							$104\frac{1}{4}$	3.84	3.81
1886							106	3.77	3.74
1887							$106\frac{1}{4}$	3.76	3.70
1888							108	3.71	3.64
1889							$108\frac{1}{8}$	3.70	3.60
10-yr. av.				3.97		3.97		3.85	3.82
				4-yr. av.		4-yr. av.			

TABLE 32 (*Continued*)

Year	Annual Averages								
	Prussian State 3½s		Prussian State 4s		Imperial German 3s		Imperial German 4s		Computed Average of Bond Yields, %
	Price	Yield, %	Price	Yield, %	Price	Yield, %	Price	Yield, %	
1890					87	3.45	106¾	3.75	3.68
1891					85⅛	3.52	106	3.77	3.71
1892					86¼	3.48	106⅞	3.74	3.68
1893					86¼	3.48	107¼	3.73	3.65
1894					90¾	3.31	106½	3.75	3.56
1895					98⅞	3.03	105⅝	3.79	3.36
1896					99¼	3.02	105½	3.79	3.35
1897					97⅝	3.07	103⅝	3.85	3.36
1898					95½	3.14			3.40
1899					90¾	3.31			3.55
10-yr. av.						3.28		3.77 8-yr. av.	3.53
1900					86¾	3.46			3.68

SOURCES

Dr. Julius Kahn, *Geschichte des Zinsfusses in Deutschland seit 1815*, Stuttgart, 1884, J. G. Cottaschen Buchhandlung, pp. 209–217. Prices are averages of periodic prices supplied by source. Yields are a simple division of nominal rate by average price.

National Monetary Commission, *Statistics for Great Britain, Germany, and France*, Washington, D.C., Vol. XXI, Tables 7 and 9, pp. 279, 281.

Averages 1870–1900 compiled by the National Bureau of Economic Research from various sources.

of German long-term interest rates in the nineteenth century. Prices and yields in the table are provided on Prussian 4s until 1883 and 3½s until 1868; on Bavarian bonds until 1883; on Imperial German 4s from 1878 and 3s from 1890; and on a computed average of German bond yields from 1870.

For 1815 the earliest quotations on Prussian state 4% bonds ranged from 85 down to 78 and averaged 81⅛. (No true average is available; these "averages" are merely halfway between high and low quotations.) From these prices current yields can be computed, ignoring the possibility of capital gains and ultimate redemption; these were 4.72%; 5.14%; 4.94% average. After 1815 for five years Prussian yields tended to rise while most other European yields were declining. They reached an average of 5.87% in 1821. This was the highest average yield for the century after 1815.

After 1821 prices rose and yields declined sharply in common with general European experience. By 1830 the average price of Prussian 4s was 97⅞, to yield 4.09%, an appreciation of 43%. The disturbances of 1830 brought only a small interruption of the trend toward lower yields. By

1840 the yield of the 4s was no longer representative because of a market premium. In fact the newly floated Prussian 3½s in 1844 also commanded a small premium, averaging 101¼, to yield 3.45%. This was the period of lowest German bond yields for the nineteenth century until the last decade.

The revolutions of 1848 were accompanied by a sharp increase in the yields of Prussian 3½s. From a premium in 1844 they declined to an average price of 76⅛, to yield 4.60% in 1848. The yield decline in 1849–1852 did not restore the low yields of 1844. After 1852 yields rose gradually until 1859 and declined again in 1862. The wars of 1864, 1866, and 1870 were all accompanied by a rise in yields, so that by 1870 yields were back to the levels of 1824, but by no means as high as they were in 1820. A new series of Prussian state 4s sold in 1870 at an average of 82¼, to yield 4.87%. The year 1870 ended three and a half decades of rising interest rates.

From 1870 to 1895–1897 German interest rates declined sharply and almost steadily in keeping with a general European trend. In 1878 a

LONG-TERM GERMAN YIELDS AT THREE DATES

	1820		1850		1875	
Prussia	4s	5.72%	3s	4.10%	4s	4.09%
Bavaria	4s	5.44	4s	4.22	4s	4.26
Wurtemberg			4½s	4.73	4s	4.18
Baden			3½s	4.39	4s	4.16
Saxony			4s	4.18	4s	4.14
Nassau			3½s	4.16		
Hesse			4s	4.56		
Province of E. Prussia	4s	4.50	3½s	3.92	3½s	4.11
Province of Pomerania	4s	3.90	3½s	3.76	3½s	4.09
Province of Silesia	4s	3.83	3½s	3.80	3½s	4.10
Bavarian Mortgage Bank Bonds					4s	4.22
Real estate mortgages in Berlin		5.00		5.00		5.00–6.00
Real estate mortgages in Danzig		4.00–5.00		6.00		5.00
Real estate mortgages in *junker* estates in Mecklenberg		3.50–5.00		3.50–4.00		4.00
Real estate mortgages in Dresden		5.00		4.00–4.50		5.00

SOURCE

Kahn, *op. cit.*, pp. 209–245.

computed average of German high-grade bond yields stood at 4.26%. By 1890 the computed average stood at 3.68% and by 1896, the year of lowest interest rates, the computed average stood at 3.35%: these yields were only moderately below the low yields of 1843–1844 and were above most European yields on comparable securities. As in other countries, the last few years of the century saw a rise in yields which in fact was the beginning of a long-term upward trend.

Space does not permit an attempt to trace the great variety of rates on the many types of German state and mortgage securities which were

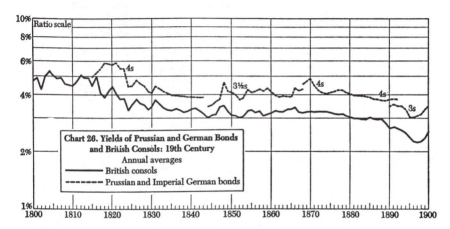

Chart 26. Yields of Prussian and German Bonds
and British Consols: 19th Century
Annual averages
——— British consols
- - - - - Prussian and Imperial German bonds

outstanding in the nineteenth century. However, the table on page 262 will serve to illustrate the variety of yields at long term that were simultaneously available, reflecting differences in credit, differences in terms and customs, and transient factors of supply and demand.

Chart 26 compares the yields on British consols with the yields on Prussian and Imperial German bonds. It brings out important similarities and differences in trend. In both countries yields declined sharply from 1820 to 1844 and from 1870 to 1895–1897. In both countries the period from 1844 to 1870 was one of irregularity during which yields tended to rise—substantially in Germany and moderately in Britian. In both countries many minor fluctuations coincided, such as the rises in 1826, 1830–1831, 1845, and 1866. German bond yields, however, were almost always substantially higher than yields on British consols; after 1845 there was a tendency for the differential to widen. The most striking differences in trend were the rise in German yields from 1815 to 1818 while British yields were declining and the much sharper rise in German yields in 1848 and 1870.

German short-term interest rates were usually volatile early in the century. Table 33 and Chart 27 give the discount rate of the Reichsbank

TABLE 33

SHORT-TERM GERMAN INTEREST RATES: NINETEENTH CENTURY

Year	Minimum Rate of Discount of Reichsbank and Its Predecessors			Open-Market Discount Rate at Berlin		
	Annual Average, %	High, %	Low, %	Annual Average, %	High, %	Low, %
1814				7	$9\frac{1}{2}$	$4\frac{1}{2}$
1815				8	12	4
1816				$5\frac{7}{8}$	$8\frac{3}{4}$	3
1817	$7\frac{1}{4}$	10	$4\frac{1}{2}$	$6\frac{3}{8}$	$9\frac{1}{2}$	$3\frac{1}{4}$
1818	$6\frac{1}{4}$	8	$4\frac{1}{2}$	$6\frac{3}{8}$	$8\frac{3}{4}$	4
1819	$4\frac{1}{2}$	6	3	$4\frac{1}{4}$	$6\frac{1}{2}$	2
	6 3-yr. av.			6.33 6-yr. av.		
1820	$5\frac{1}{4}$	7	$3\frac{1}{2}$	$5\frac{1}{2}$	8	3
1821	$5\frac{1}{2}$	8	3	$5\frac{1}{4}$	8	$2\frac{1}{2}$
1822	$4\frac{1}{2}$	6	3	5	7	3
1823	$4\frac{3}{4}$	6	$3\frac{1}{2}$	5	$7\frac{1}{2}$	$2\frac{1}{2}$
1824	$6\frac{3}{4}$	10	$3\frac{1}{2}$	$7\frac{1}{2}$	12	3
1825	$5\frac{1}{2}$	8	3	$5\frac{1}{4}$	$8\frac{1}{4}$	3
1826	$4\frac{1}{2}$	6	3	5	$6\frac{1}{2}$	$3\frac{1}{2}$
1827	4	5	3	4	4	4
1828	4	5	3	4	4	4
1829	4	$4\frac{1}{2}$	$3\frac{1}{2}$	$4\frac{1}{4}$	$4\frac{1}{2}$	4
10-yr. av.	4.87			5.07		
1830	$5\frac{1}{2}$	6	5	$5\frac{1}{4}$	$6\frac{1}{2}$	4
1831	4	4	4	$4\frac{1}{4}$	5	$3\frac{1}{2}$
1832	$5\frac{1}{4}$	$5\frac{1}{2}$	5	$4\frac{1}{2}$	$5\frac{1}{2}$	$3\frac{1}{2}$
1833	$4\frac{1}{2}$	5	4	$4\frac{1}{2}$	5	4
1834	$3\frac{3}{4}$	4	$3\frac{1}{2}$	$4\frac{1}{4}$	$4\frac{1}{2}$	4
1835	4	5	3	$4\frac{1}{4}$	$4\frac{1}{2}$	4
1836	$4\frac{1}{2}$	5	4	$4\frac{1}{2}$	5	4
1837	$4\frac{1}{2}$	5	4	4	5	3
1838	4	4	4	$3\frac{1}{2}$	4	3
1839	4	4	4	$3\frac{3}{4}$	4	$3\frac{1}{2}$
10-yr. av.	4.40			4.28		
1840	4.00	4	4	$3\frac{3}{4}$	4	$3\frac{1}{2}$
1841	4.00	4	4	$3\frac{5}{8}$	$3\frac{3}{4}$	$3\frac{1}{2}$
1842	4.00	4	4	$3\frac{1}{2}$	$3\frac{3}{4}$	$3\frac{1}{4}$
1843	4.00	4	4	$3\frac{3}{8}$	$3\frac{1}{2}$	$3\frac{1}{4}$
1844	4.11	$4\frac{1}{2}$	4	$3\frac{3}{4}$	4	$3\frac{1}{2}$

TABLE 33 (*Continued*)

Year	Minimum Rate of Discount of Reichsbank and Its Predecessors			Open-Market Discount Rate at Berlin		
	Annual Average, %	High, %	Low, %	Annual Average, %	High, %	Low, %
1845	4.35	5	4	$4\frac{1}{2}$	5	4
1846	4.68	5	4	$4\frac{1}{2}$	5	4
1847	4.85	5	$4\frac{1}{2}$	$4\frac{1}{4}$	$4\frac{1}{2}$	4
1848	4.67	5	$4\frac{1}{2}$	$4\frac{1}{2}$	5	4
1849	4.04	$4\frac{1}{2}$	4	$3\frac{1}{4}$	$4\frac{1}{2}$	2
10-yr. av.	4.27			3.90		
1850	4.00	4	4	$3\frac{1}{2}$	5	2
1851	4.00	4	4	$3\frac{1}{4}$	4	$2\frac{1}{2}$
1852	4.00	4	4	$3\frac{1}{4}$	4	$2\frac{1}{2}$
1853	4.25	5	4	4	5	3
1854	4.36	5	4	4	5	3
1855	4.06	$4\frac{1}{2}$	4	$3\frac{7}{8}$	$4\frac{1}{2}$	$3\frac{1}{4}$
1856	4.91	6	4	$4\frac{7}{8}$	6	$3\frac{3}{4}$
1857	5.76	$7\frac{1}{2}$	5	$6\frac{1}{8}$	$7\frac{1}{2}$	$4\frac{3}{4}$
1858	4.13	$6\frac{1}{2}$	4	4	5	3
1859	4.21	5	4	$3\frac{3}{8}$	$4\frac{1}{2}$	$2\frac{3}{4}$
10-yr. av.	4.37			4.03		
1860	4.00	4	4	$3\frac{3}{8}$	4	$2\frac{3}{4}$
1861	4.00	4	4	3	$3\frac{1}{2}$	$2\frac{1}{2}$
1862	4.00	4	4	$3\frac{1}{8}$	$3\frac{3}{4}$	$2\frac{1}{2}$
1863	4.07	$4\frac{1}{2}$	4	$3\frac{3}{4}$	$4\frac{1}{2}$	3
1864	5.32	7	$4\frac{1}{2}$	$4\frac{1}{2}$	6	3
1865	4.94	7	4	$4\frac{7}{8}$	7	$2\frac{3}{4}$
1866	6.22	9	4	$6\frac{1}{4}$	9	$3\frac{1}{2}$
1867	4.00	4	4	$3\frac{1}{4}$	$3\frac{3}{4}$	$2\frac{3}{4}$
1868	4.00	4	4	$2\frac{3}{4}$	3	$2\frac{1}{2}$
1869	4.24	5	4	$3\frac{1}{2}$	$4\frac{1}{2}$	$2\frac{1}{2}$
10-yr. av.	4.48			3.84		
1870	4.87	8	4	$6\frac{3}{4}$	10	$3\frac{1}{2}$
1871	4.16	5	4	$4\frac{1}{8}$	5	$3\frac{3}{8}$
1872	4.29	5	4	$4\frac{4}{5}$	5	$3\frac{1}{4}$
1873	4.95	6	4	$4\frac{5}{8}$	$5\frac{3}{4}$	$3\frac{1}{2}$
1874	4.38	6	4	$3\frac{1}{2}$	$4\frac{3}{8}$	$2\frac{1}{2}$
1875	4.71	6	4	$4\frac{1}{4}$	$5\frac{5}{8}$	$2\frac{7}{8}$
1876	4.16	6	$3\frac{1}{2}$	$3\frac{7}{8}$	$5\frac{1}{2}$	$2\frac{3}{8}$
1877	4.42	$5\frac{1}{2}$	4	$3\frac{3}{8}$	$4\frac{3}{4}$	$1\frac{7}{8}$
1878	4.34	5	4	$3\frac{3}{8}$	$4\frac{1}{2}$	$2\frac{1}{8}$
1879	3.70	$4\frac{1}{2}$	3	$2\frac{7}{8}$	$4\frac{1}{4}$	$1\frac{3}{8}$
10-yr. av.	4.40			4.09		

TABLE 33 (*Continued*)

Year	Minimum Rate of Discount of Reichsbank and Its Predecessors			Open-Market Discount Rate at Berlin		
	Annual Average, %	High, %	Low, %	Annual Average, %	High, %	Low, %
1880	4.24	$5\frac{1}{2}$	4	$3\frac{3}{8}$	5	$1\frac{7}{8}$
1881	4.42	$5\frac{1}{2}$	4	$4\frac{1}{8}$	$5\frac{3}{8}$	$2\frac{7}{8}$
1882	4.54	6	4	$3\frac{7}{8}$	$4\frac{7}{8}$	$2\frac{7}{8}$
1883	4.00	5	4	$3\frac{1}{2}$	$4\frac{5}{8}$	$2\frac{1}{2}$
1884	4.00	4	4	2.89	$3\frac{7}{8}$	$2\frac{1}{8}$
1885	4.12	5	4	2.85	$4\frac{1}{4}$	$2\frac{1}{8}$
1886	3.28	5	3	2.16	$4\frac{1}{2}$	$1\frac{1}{8}$
1887	3.41	5	3	2.30	$3\frac{3}{8}$	$1\frac{1}{2}$
1888	3.32	$4\frac{1}{2}$	3	2.11	4	$1\frac{1}{4}$
1889	3.68	5	3	2.63	5	$1\frac{1}{4}$
10-yr. av.	3.90			2.98		
1890	4.52	$5\frac{1}{2}$	4	3.78	$5\frac{1}{2}$	$2\frac{5}{8}$
1891	3.78	4	3	3.02	$4\frac{1}{4}$	$2\frac{1}{4}$
1892	3.20	4	3	1.80	$3\frac{1}{4}$	$1\frac{1}{4}$
1893	4.07	5	3	3.17	$4\frac{7}{8}$	$1\frac{1}{4}$
1894	3.12	4	3	1.74	$3\frac{3}{8}$	$1\frac{3}{8}$
1895	3.14	4	3	2.01	$3\frac{7}{8}$	$1\frac{1}{2}$
1896	3.66	5	3	3.04	$4\frac{7}{8}$	2
1897	3.81	5	3	3.09	$4\frac{3}{4}$	$2\frac{1}{4}$
1898	4.27	6	3	3.55	$5\frac{5}{8}$	$2\frac{3}{8}$
1899	5.04	7	4	4.45	$6\frac{3}{8}$	$3\frac{1}{2}$
10-yr. av.	3.86			2.97		
1900	5.33	7	5	4.41	$5\frac{5}{8}$	$3\frac{5}{8}$

Averages of official discount rates are unweighted arithmetic means of high and low from 1817 to 1843 and are weighted averages thereafter. Averages of open-market rates are unweighted until 1883 and are weighted averages thereafter.

SOURCES

Arthur Spiethoff, *Die Wirtschaftlichen Wechsellagen*, Zurich, 1955, Table 12.

National Monetary Commission, *Statistics for Great Britain, Germany and France*, Washington, D.C., Vol. XXI, Table 18, p. 140.

Vergleichende Notenbankstatistik, 1876–1913, Berlin, 1925, Table 113, pp. 186–187.

Average open-market rate from 1884 compiled by the National Bureau of Economic Research from various published sources.

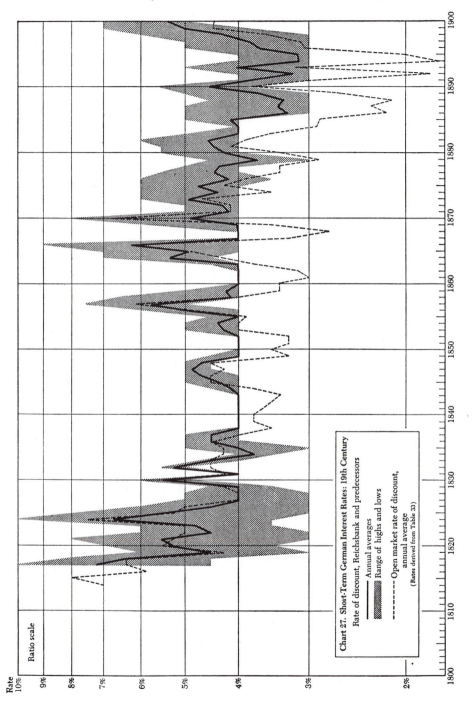

Chart 27. Short-Term German Interest Rates: 19th Century
Rate of discount, Reichsbank and predecessors
——— Annual averages
▨▨▨ Range of highs and lows
– – – Open market rate of discount,
annual average
(**Rates** derived from Table 33)

and its predecessors as a range and as annual averages and also give the open-market rate of discount in Berlin. They suggest that a widely ranging discount rate and a volatile open-market rate existed in Berlin several decades before English and French discount rates became very volatile.

In the 1820's the German discount rate ranged between 3 and 10%, while the French discount rate was fixed at 4% and the British bank rate was held in a range of 4–5%. Berlin open-market rates moved from an average of 8% in 1815 (halfway between 12% high and 4% low) to an average of 4¼% in 1819 (6½–2%) during a period when Prussian bond yields were advancing. By 1824 the average was back to 7½%, and by 1827 it was down to 4%. The Berlin discount rate was as low as 3% frequently from 1819 on to 1828, but rarely thereafter until 1879. It was as high as 10% twice before 1825, but never thereafter. Open-market Berlin rates were as low as 2½% and as high as 12% in the 1820's in a period when few data are presented for open-market British and French rates.

Whatever may have been the local cause of this early volatility, short Berlin rates tended to stabilize around 4% in the 1830's and 1840's just when British short rates began to fluctuate widely. It was not until the late 1850's that Berlin rates again became highly volatile. Thereafter they fluctuated widely and tended to decline.

The decennial averages on Chart 24 indicate that the short rates selected were moderately above the long rates selected early in the century. From 1845 when long German rates tended to rise more sharply, short rates in Germany began to average moderately below long rates. In the two easy-money decades at the end of the century the German short rates fell far below the German long rates.

SWISS INTEREST RATES

In 1815 the Congress of Vienna restored the old frontiers of Switzerland. However, it provided for a very loose federation of cantons which could not act effectively as a nation in political or financial affairs. Twelve different currencies existed, together with local customs barriers.

A severe Swiss economic crisis around 1820 was followed by a protracted struggle between the conservative and the liberal cantons, which organized themselves into rival confederations. Finally, in 1845–1846, a civil war resulted in a victory for the liberal anticlerical cantons. They moved swiftly to organize a stronger central government under a new constitution modeled after that of the United States. In 1850 the currency was unified. However, a central bank with a monopoly of note issue was not established until 1905. (471) Throughout this century Swiss finance was local in character rather than national. There were many banks of issue which charged different rates of interest. Geneva, Basel, Zurich, and St. Gallen were all independent financial centers.

Table 34 and Chart 28 are based on the rates of interest charged by the banks of issue in these four financial centers. These rates are grouped together so that for each year the highest and lowest rate charged at any of these centers provides the limit of a range. This range is supplemented by a computed annual average of rates in all four cities. No prices or yields on long-term securities are provided.

The pattern of Swiss discount rates from 1837 to the end of the century was somewhat different from the pattern in most European financial centers. The range of the annual averages was more moderate in Switzerland, almost always between 3 and 6%, while the British bank rate averaged between 2 and 7% and the French discount rate between 2 and 6½%. The Swiss rates only occasionally declined to 2% and very occasionally rose above 7%.

Swiss rates were usually higher than those in other European centers. Although they rose in the seventh decade and fell in the eighth and ninth decades, a pattern similar to that of other countries, they did not decline sharply toward the end of the century in the manner of short-term rates in other countries. In fact, the last decade saw an increase in Swiss rates.

In 1837–1839, when Swiss discounts were first quoted, they averaged 4.14% and ranged from 4 to 5%. Comparison with short rates in other countries is obscured by the fact that these Swiss rates were not official central bank rates, and that they also were not open-market rates of discount. During the 1840's these Swiss rates usually remained close to 4–4¼%. In the years 1847–1850 they declined to around 3½%. The Swiss civil war of 1845 and the European revolutions of 1848 had no noticeable effect. These Swiss rates averaged 4.11% in the decade of the 1840's when the British bank rate averaged 3.97% and the British open market rate averaged 3.57%. Swiss short rates were then not far from most other European short rates.

During the 1850's the Swiss rates continued to average 4.11%, fluctuating in a wider range at 2–7%. This was close to the British, French and German average. In the 1860's the Swiss average rose to 4.57%, and individual rates reached a peak of 8.50% in 1864. This was the decade of highest Swiss rates. British short rates also rose to a thirty-year peak, as did Dutch short rates.

During the decades of the 1870's and 1880's Swiss rates suffered their only important sustained decline during this century. They moved down from a 4.57% average in the 1860's to a 3.35% average in the 1880's or

TABLE 34

SHORT-TERM SWISS INTEREST RATES: NINETEENTH CENTURY

Year	Discount Rates at Various Banks of Issue			Year	Discount Rates at Various Banks of Issue		
	Annual Average, %	Annual Low, %	Annual High, %		Annual Average, %	Annual Low, %	Annual High, %
1837	4.00	4.00	4.00	1870	4.38	3.00	6.00
1838	4.04	4.00	4.50	1871	3.79	3.00	5.50
1839	4.39	4.00	5.00	1872	4.53	3.00	7.00
				1873	5.34	4.00	7.00
3-yr. av.	4.14			1874	4.55	3.00	6.50
				1875	4.13	3.00	6.00
1840	4.36	4.00	5.00	1876	3.50	2.50	5.50
1841	3.92	3.50	4.50	1877	3.52	2.00	5.00
1842	4.43	4.00	5.00	1878	3.71	2.50	5.00
1843	4.21	4.00	5.00	1879	3.31	2.00	4.50
1844	4.21	4.00	5.00				
1845	3.98	3.29	5.00	10-yr. av.	4.08		
1846	3.95	3.00	5.00				
1847	4.57	3.00	5.00	1880	3.02	2.00	5.00
1848	3.99	2.50	5.00	1881	4.11	2.50	6.00
1849	3.46	2.50	5.00	1882	4.45	3.50	7.00
				1883	3.04	2.50	4.00
10-yr. av.	4.11			1884	2.88	2.50	4.50
				1885	3.09	2.50	4.00
1850	3.31	2.25	4.00	1886	3.01	2.50	4.00
1851	3.27	2.00	4.00	1887	2.93	2.50	4.50
1852	3.51	2.50	4.00	1888	3.14	2.50	4.50
1853	3.89	3.00	5.00	1889	3.72	3.00	5.00
1854	4.43	3.75	5.00				
1855	4.51	3.50	6.00	10-yr. av.	3.35		
1856	4.73	4.00	6 00				
1857	5.43	4.50	7.00	1890	3.90	3.00	5.00
1858	4.12	3.50	6.00	1891	3.93	3.50	5.00
1859	3.95	3.00	5.00	1892	3.06	2.50	4.50
				1893	3.37	2.50	4.50
10-yr. av.	4.11			1894	3.17	3.00	4.25
				1895	3.27	2.50	5.00
1860	4.30	3.50	5.00	1896	3.95	3.50	5.00
1861	5.36	4.50	6.00	1897	3.92	3.50	4.75
1862	4.58	4.00	6.00	1898	4.31	4.00	5.00
1863	5.04	4.00	7.00	1899	4.96	4.25	6.00
1864	6.45	5.50	8.50				
1865	4.62	4.00	6.00	10-yr. av.	3.78		
1866	5.18	4.00	6.00				
1867	3.74	3.00	4.50	1900	4.88	4.50	6.00
1868	3.22	3.00	4.00				
1869	3.28	2.50	4.00				
10-yr. av.	4.57						

A. Jöhr, *Die Schweizerischen Notenbanken 1826–1913*. Zurich, 1915, pp. 504ff. Rates charged by banks of issue at Geneva, Basel, Zurich, and St. Gallen.

from an extreme annual average of 6.45% in 1864 to 2.88% in 1884. Other European rates also were declining sharply.

During the last decade of the century Swiss rates took an independent course, rising to average 3.78% while rates in all the other principal countries declined further. Switzerland did not experience the sustained extremely low short-term rates that prevailed in most European countries in the late nineteenth century.

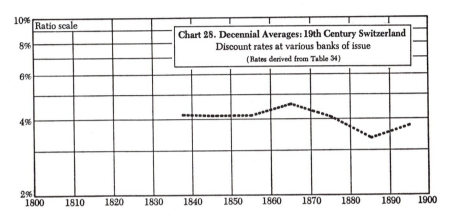

Chart 28. Decennial Averages: 19th Century Switzerland
Discount rates at various banks of issue
(Rates derived from Table 34)

SWEDISH INTEREST RATES

In 1812 Sweden joined Russia in the coalition against Napoleon and acquired Norway in the final peace settlement. Throughout the remainder of the nineteenth century Sweden was involved in no wars. The chief political problem was the union with Norway, which, however, was not dissolved until 1905 and then without armed conflict.

During the second half of this century the Swedish constitution was revised to provide a popular government and a limited monarchy. During the last three decades, Sweden, which had been primarily agricultural, enjoyed a rapid commercial development. However, during this century Sweden was never an international financial center. The Bank of Sweden (*Riksbank*), in spite of its long history from 1656, antedating the Bank of England, did not become a true central bank until 1897. (472) The history of Swedish interest rates in this century is confined to rates charged by the Bank of Sweden and the effective rates of interest paid by the government on its long-term and short-term loans.

In Chapter XII, Table 17 reviewed the rates of interest that the Bank of Sweden was permitted by legislative action to charge during the seventeenth and eighteenth centuries. Apparently the rate had been forced down late in the eighteenth century from 6 to 3% at a time when other European rates were rising.

TABLE 35

INTEREST RATES IN SWEDEN: NINETEENTH CENTURY

Year	Rates Charged by Bank of Sweden		Effective Rate on Bonds Issued by the State, %		Year	Rates Charged by Bank of Sweden		Effective Rate on Bonds Issued by the State, %	
	Annual Average, %	Range,* %	Long term	Short term		Annual Average, %	Range, %	Long term	Short term
1816		6			1877	5.49	5–6		
1824		5			1878	5.83	5.5–6	4.90 (4s)	
1830		4–6			1879	5.46	5–6		4.50 (4½s)
1835		4–6							
					10-yr. av.	5.00		4.91	
1854	(4.50)	4–5							
1855	(4.50)	4–5	4.00 (4s)		1880	4.33	4–5	3.57 (3½s)	
1856	5.00	5			1881	4.00	4		
1857	5.00	5			1882	4.46	4–4.5		
1858	5.80	5–6	5.27 (4½s)		1883	4.75	4.5–5		
1859	5.67	5–6			1884	4.49	4–5		
	5.09 6-yr. av.		4.64		1885	4.50	4.5		
					1886	4.10	4–4.5	3.86 (3½s)	
					1887	4.00	4	3.71 (3.60s)	
1860	6.00	6	5.00 (4½s)		1888	3.56	3.5–4	3.79 (3s)	
1861	5.77	5–6	5.17		1889	3.55	3.5–4		
1862	5.14	5–6			10-yr. av.	4.17		3.73	
1863	6.00	6		5.11 (5s)					
1864	6.00	6	5.32 (4½s)		1890	4.48	4–6	3.64 (3½s)	
1865	5.51	5–6		8.11 (6s)	1891	4.90	4.5–5.5		
1866	6.33	6–7	5.59 (5s)		1892	4.75	4.5–5.5		4.64 (4s)
1867	5.00	4.5–6		5.76 (5s)	1893	4.21	4–5		
1868	4.84	4.5–5	5.96 (5s)		1894	4.00	4	3.66 (3s)	
1869	4.73	4.5–5		5.36 (5s)	1895	4.00	4		
10-yr. av.	5.53		5.41	6.06	1896	3.78	3.5–4.5		
					1897	4.59	4.5–5		
1870	4.50	4.5	5.20 (5s)		1898	4.88	4–5.5		
1871	4.28	4–4.5			1899	5.89	5.5–6	3.76 (3½s)	
1872	4.00	4	4.85 (4s)						
1873	4.52	4–5.5			10-yr. av.	4.55		3.68	
1874	5.11	5–5.5							
1875	5.50	5.5	4.76 (4½s)		1900	5.87	5.5–6	3.82 (3½s and 4s)	
1876	5.30	5–5.5	4.87 (4½s)						

* From 1856 the bank was free to set rates between 4% and 6% (later 7%). Earlier rates were set by legislation, and the range is for varied types of loans. After 1856 rates are ranges for the type of loan commanding the lowest rate.

SOURCES

Sveriges Riksbank, *Statistika Tabeller* 1668–1924, 1931, p. 139.
Riksgoldskontoret's Year Book, 1940–1941, p. 53.

A discount rate of 6% in 1816 is the earliest nineteenth-century quotation. A rate of 5% is quoted for 1824 without the implication that these rates prevailed in the intervening years. In 1830 rates of 4–6% are quoted, depending on the type of collateral: 4% for loans on gold, silver, and real estate; 5% for loans on government paper and deposit receipts; and a rate up to 6% for loans on bills. Similar rates are quoted for 1835 and 1841, while a range of 4–5% is quoted for 1845, 1848, 1851, and 1854. These rates were set by legislation, but in 1856 the bank was set free to vary its rates from 4 to 6% (later to 7%). The subsequent variations of the discount rate of the Bank of Sweden are presented in Table 35 and Chart 29, together with a weighted annual average of these rates.

Swedish discount rates remained relatively high throughout this century. The average for the later 1850's was 5.09%, and for the 1860's it was even higher at 5.53%. In 1866 a rate as high as 7% was once quoted and the low for the decade was 4½%. Thereafter rates declined to an average of 5% in the 1870's and 4.17% in the 1880's. Like Swiss rates, and unlike

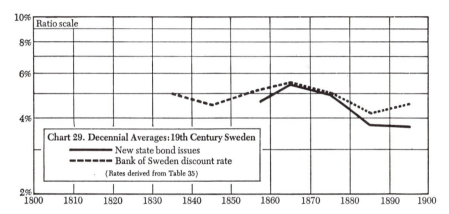

Chart 29. Decennial Averages: 19th Century Sweden
——— New state bond issues
------ Bank of Sweden discount rate
(Rates derived from Table 35)

other European rates, the Swedish discount rate tended to rise during the last decade, the average moving up from 4.17 to 4.55%. This was far above most other European short-term rates. At no time did the Swedish discount rate decline even near to the very low levels which at times prevailed elsewhere. Furthermore, Swedish discount rates remained always above the rates quoted on long-term obligations of the government.

Swedish government bonds are not quoted here at market rates of interest. Only their nominal and effective rates at time of flotation are quoted. The earliest bond quotation is for 1855 when 4s were sold at 100 to yield 4% at a time when the discount rate ranged from 4% to 5%. By 1858, when the discount rate was up to 5–6%, the government sold 4½s, to yield 5.27%. A rate as high as 8.11% was paid by the government in 1865 on a short-term issue of 6s, but no such high rate was paid on long-term bonds. The highest long-term rate was 5.96%, in 1868, on an issue of 5s. By 1875 long 4½s were sold, to yield 4.76%, and by 1890 long 3½s were sold, to yield only 3.64% when the discount rate was 4%. This was the low rate recorded for Swedish government bond offerings in this century. In the last decade bond offering yields apparently remained at around their lows, although the discount rate was tending to move moderately higher.

Chapter XVI

The United States in the Eighteenth and Nineteenth Centuries

BACKGROUND AND INTEREST RATES
DURING THE COLONIAL AND REVOLUTIONARY PERIODS

The American colonies were outposts of an old civilization. Their physical environment was primitive, but their political and financial traditions were not. Therefore, the history of colonial credit and interest rates is not a history of innovation but rather a history of adaptation.

The colonists from England brought with them seventeenth-century English attitudes toward credit and interest. Commercial loans at interest were considered entirely moral and legal and a normal part of business life. Personal debt for consumption was frowned upon as imprudent. Moderate interest rates were desirable, while high interest rates were usurious and were forbidden by law. The English usury laws had established the legal maximum at 6%. This 6% tradition crossed the Atlantic and in most of the states survived until the 1950's. The colonies also adopted the harsh English laws in favor of creditors. This combination of rigorous enforcement of debt and legal maximum rates of interest comes down from Hammurabi through Rome, through seventeenth-century England, to the modern United States. The different Greek tradition of laissez faire was revived by seventeenth-century Holland and adopted by nineteenth-century England.

Interest rate legislation in the colonies was by no means uniform, nor are state usury laws uniform today. In 1661 Massachusetts fixed the legal maximum rate at 8%; in 1692 Maryland adopted 6%. A 6% legal maximum was soon established in most of the colonies. In Virginia 5% became the maximum. (473) While such legislation does not tell what the prevailing rates of interest were in the colonies, it does indicate the rates that leading citizens considered normal or reasonable. According to Benjamin Franklin, commercial interest rates in Pennsylvania in the latter half of the eighteenth century were between 6% and 10%. (473)

Hard money was very scarce throughout the early colonial period. There was no domestic mining of gold or silver. European coins were brought over in small quantities by colonists, but were soon shipped home in return for needed manufactures. (474) American communities were largely self-sufficient. Nevertheless, some goods, such as metal products, salt, paper, medicines, and ammunition had to be bought; the cost of such purchases is estimated at $10–$50 a year per family. (475) Exports did not equal imports, and hence there was a drain of specie out of the colonies.

As a consequence, both barter and the use of commodities for money were common in the early colonial period. Indian shells were used for money. Later, certain staple commodities were declared by law to be legal tender in payment of debts: corn, cattle, furs in New England, and tobacco and rice in the South. Taxes were often payable in commodities at full valuations, and warehouse receipts for such commodities passed for currency. One Harvard student, later president of the college, settled his tuition bill with "an old cow" in the manner of the Homeric Greeks. (476) The total supply of specie existing in the colonies has been estimated at around $1,000,000 in 1700, and $12,000,000 in 1775. (477)

The adverse balance of trade with Europe was in part financed by credit obtained from British merchants. Southern planters and other men of substance generally did their banking in London. Foreign bills of credit on London passed as a substitute for currency.

The extreme scarcity of specie led to many expedients, but not to a record of very high interest rates. High rates no doubt existed in commercial and personal transactions. But high interest rates were vigorously opposed by colonial law and custom and were therefore negotiated secretly and have not come down to us. Many very high rates will be reported from the Western frontier and from nineteenth-century money markets, but few from the colonial period. Instead, the colonies resorted to experiments with paper currency and bills of credit at legal rates of interest.

In experimenting with paper money, the colonists were only following a European example. Bank notes became officially recognized in England in the 1690's with the funding of the British national debt through the new Bank of England. In the 1720's the South Sea Bubble in England and the Mississippi Bubble in France were both based on paper-money schemes. The colonists were thus not departing from respectable tradition. There were few practical alternatives. The consequences of paper money were favorable in England, disastrous in France, and unsatisfactory in the colonies. The relative merits of paper money and metallic money became a lively subject of economic and political debate in this country, which lasted throughout the nineteenth century. The related controversy of low vs. high interest rates is still with us.

In 1690 Massachusetts put out the first regularly authorized issue of bills of credit. It was for military expenses in a war against French Canada. The bills were payable in one year and were acceptable for taxes at a premium. The issue was later enlarged and redemption postponed to six years and then to thirteen years. (478) The bills drove specie out of circulation. Bills emitted by the Carolinas, Massachusetts, Rhode Island, and Connecticut depreciated as much as 90%. Bills of other states, however, fared much better.

There were no organized private banking institutions in the colonies. Most sizable loan transactions were negotiated in London, and this is one reason why there is little independent history of colonial interest rates. However, some indication of the rates that the colonists believed to be reasonable is obtainable from the history of a few loan banks established by the colonial governments. In 1711 and 1714 Massachusetts issued bills of credit to certain local merchants and charged them 5% interest. In Pennsylvania public outcry against interest of 8%, which was generally charged by private bankers, led to the establishment in 1722 of a loan office. This bank loaned its bills of credit to citizens at 5%, secured by land and repayable in twelve equal annual installments. This and a similar Philadelphia fund set up in 1739 were successful and useful. (479) In 1755, Virginia's first issue of bills carried 5% interest; Georgia's first issue was loaned out on good security at 6%. (478)

These rates of interest were not market rates. The need for these government institutions must have arisen from a lack of private credit at rates this low. To understand the attitude of the colonists toward the level of interest rates, it should be recalled that the mid-eighteenth century was a period of very low Dutch and English interest rates. The British government had refunded its debt at 3% in 1751, and good commercial loans in Holland were procurable at 2–3% per annum. The colonies maintained close economic ties with Europe. Commerce between colonies was small, but foreign trade with Europe and with Spanish America was large and lucrative. The Southerners and the New Englanders judged the level of their own interest rates by European standards.

These traditions of moderate interest rates and paper money had a profound effect on Revolutionary war finance. The Continental Congress voted an issue of paper money in 1775 within a week of the beginning of the war. This issue was to be redeemed by the states in four to six years. During the next four years, forty emissions totaling $240 million were authorized, and in addition the states put out $209 million of paper notes, a total of $449 million, or $150 for each member of the population. (480) In contrast, the whole circulating specie was estimated at around $12 million. Depreciation set in early but did not go to extremes until 1779 when the value of Continental currency in specie declined from 8 to 1 in January to 38 to 1 in November. In 1781 it was valued at 100 to 1 and later at much less. In the funding act of 1790 Continental money was received in subscription for new government stock at 100 to 1.

In spite of this enormous issue of noninterest-bearing debt, it is estimated that the American people sold to their government only $41 million specie value of commodities in exchange for the entire issue of this paper. Although the war was won and a new nation created, the unfavorable consequences of this experiment with unrestricted paper money was long remembered. It created a respect for hard money that influenced American finance and politics for two centuries.

The first interest-bearing domestic loan by the Continental Congress was attempted a year and a half after the war had begun. In 1776 Congress authorized a loan of $5 million at 4% payable in three years. The rate was too low, and in 1777 the rate was increased to 6%, but only $3.8 million was subscribed. Thereafter, Congress offered to pay interest in foreign funds derived from a French loan. This offer proved attractive, since the loan could be purchased in paper currency, and $63 million was subscribed, of which the specie value was only $7.7 million. (481) Because of this important inducement the 6% rate cannot be judged an acceptable market rate of interest, but it was evidently conventional and no more was paid. After 1782 the interest on the debt was not met, and certificates of interest were issued receivable for taxes. All of these loans were refunded in 1790 at par plus accrued interest into the securities of the new United States government.

Funds to finance the Revolution were also obtained abroad, as detailed on Table 36. Until 1782 these loans were in effect political subsidies. By 1782 it was seen in Holland that American victory was assured. Confidence in the political integrity of the new regime and appreciation of the immense resources of the new nation led to a favorable nominal interest rate of 5%. However, large discounts, or commissions, demanded by the Dutch bankers, and specified in the table, substantially increased the interest cost of these loans. These rates, however,

TABLE 36

PRINCIPAL FOREIGN LOANS OF THE AMERICAN
REVOLUTIONARY GOVERNMENT AND ITS SUCCESSORS

Year	Millions of Dollars	From	Nominal Rate, %	Net Price after Agent's Commission	Maturity	Effective Yield to Average Maturity, %
1778	3.2	France	5	100	3–15 years after peace	5.00
1781	1.8	France	4	100	1797–1802	4.00
1782	2.0	Holland	5	$95\frac{1}{2}$	1793–97	5.50
1784	0.8	Holland	4	$95\frac{1}{2}$	1801–07	4.33
1790	1.2	Holland	5	92	1802–06	5.85
1791	2.4	Holland	5	92	1802–06	5.90
1791	1.2	Holland	4	89	1802–06	5.17
1792	1.2	Holland	4	90	1803–07	5.05
1794	1.2	Holland	5	92	1805–09	5.90

were a part of the interest rate history of the creditor countries and do not indicate market rates of interest in America.

The peace of 1783 was followed by years of deep depression. The disappearance of the inflated paper money and the loss of wartime demand for goods led to a collapse of prices. Furthermore, the essential export trade now had to compete in world markets without the advantages that it previously enjoyed as part of the British mercantile system. The government of the Confederation could not even meet its own small expenses. Interest on its domestic and foreign debt went largely unpaid.

The average nominal interest charge on the domestic debt of the Confederation was 5.40% in 1783. This moderate rate does not give a true picture of the government's credit. The finances of the nation were chaotic. Expenditures were authorized without the power to tax. Government credit sank so low that by 1787 certified interest-bearing claims against it were worth less than fifteen cents on the dollar. (482) At 4% this would be an effective interest rate of more than 26%, and at 6% it would be more than 40% current return, plus capital gains if the certificates were eventually honored.

In spite of the great potential economic strength of the new country, its financial and political system broke down completely in 1786. Credit at home and abroad was no longer available. The impossibility of government without money, credit, or power led to the Constitutional Convention of 1787 and a new nation in 1789.

TABLE 37

SUMMARY OF COLONIAL AND REVOLUTIONARY INTEREST RATES

Time	Description	Rate, %	Sources
Seventeenth and eighteenth centuries	Legal maxima in various colonies	5–8	(473)
1711–14	Massachusetts bills of credit loaned to merchants at	5	(479)
Early eighteenth century	Pennsylvania merchants loan at	8	(479)
1722–39	Pennsylvania loan office provides credit at	5	(479)
1755	Virginia issues bills of credit at	5	(478)
1755	Georgia issues bills of credit at	6	(478)
Eighteenth century, second half	Prevailing interest rates in Philadelphia according to Franklin	6–10	(473)
1777	Continental Congress borrows its own paper money at	6	(481)
1783	Average nominal interest charge on domestic debt	5.40	(482)
1787	Estimated current rate on defaulted government credit certificates selling at 15¢ on the dollar, if honored	26–40	(482)

POLITICAL AND ECONOMIC BACKGROUND, 1789–1900

From 1789 to 1815 the new United States of America was deeply involved in a succession of European wars and crises which began with the French Revolution and ended with Waterloo. Caught between English and French ambitions, and with its sympathy and interest divided between these two world powers, the United States was finally involved on the losing side in the War of 1812. During these first twenty-six years, foreign political affairs exerted a dominant influence on American finance. During the succeeding one hundred years, the political events that influenced American finance were usually domestic.

The dominating domestic political event of this century was the Civil War, which profoundly affected the history of national finance and of interest rates. Since it had no European repercussions of importance, it helped to create a pattern of American nineteenth-century interest rates somewhat different from the common European pattern.

European economic events, however, powerfully influenced the money markets of the United States. The alternating periods when European capital was poured out lavishly or was withheld or withdrawn often called the turn of American markets. Therefore, had it not been for the Civil War, it seems probable that the trends of American interest rates in the nineteenth century would have closely resembled the general European trends.

The economic history of the United States in the nineteenth century is sometimes described in textbooks as a succession of excesses and calamities. Booms are pictured in terms of wild speculation, knavery, and irresponsible finance. These were regularly succeeded by panics, during which the financial structure collapsed and the fruits of lifetimes of sober toil were swept away. Then ensued hard times and depression; the nation groaned under unsalable surpluses. There followed expensive experiments by governments and new excesses by infatuated capitalists, new speculative excitement; the precepts of wisdom and experience were laughed at; and then followed another sad day of reckoning. After shivering through the story of an entire century of such economic follies and retributions, one might expect by 1900 to view the shrunken and dilapidated wreckage of the hopeful young nation of 1800. But lo and behold! The erstwhile agricultural outpost had become a giant among industrial nations, almost ready to assume financial, economic, and political leadership among the greatest nations on earth.

The ups and downs of the American economy in the nineteenth century were certainly severe. As they had an important influence on the trend of interest rates, they will be summarized here, if possible without ex post facto lectures on right living.

During the European wars of 1792 to 1815, American farm prices rose rapidly and remained abnormally high. This gave the new nation a pros-

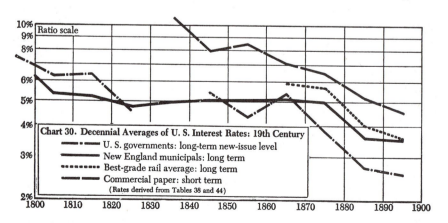

Chart 30. Decennial Averages of U. S. Interest Rates: 19th Century
— · — U. S. governments: long-term new-issue level
——— New England municipals: long term
·········· Best-grade rail average: long term
——— Commercial paper: short term
(Rates derived from Tables 38 and 44)

perous start. Staples increased 75–100% in price in terms of specie, some rising almost to modern levels. There were temporary dips in 1802–1803 and during the embargoes of 1808–1809, but general prosperity was the rule. Cotton growing became big business, with the price rising from 16 to 44 cents a pound. Northern manufacturers took advantage of the wars abroad to replace imported manufactures.

The War of 1812–1814 created financial stress and political misfortune, but it did not mark the end of this first period of prosperity. After 1815 Europe, newly released from conflict, continued to demand American produce. The "Era of Good Feeling" that followed 1815 came to an end with the panic of 1819. The postwar decline in European prices then finally spread to America. American staples dropped 50% in price, back to the level of 1792. (483) Rents were cut in half, and commercial paper rates rose to 36% in Boston. By 1823 conditions were back to normal. Business fluctuations were thereafter moderate for a decade, with minor pressures in 1825, 1828, and 1831.

In 1833 another boom began. The states pledged their credit to finance canal construction and turnpikes; railroad construction began in earnest; and there was speculation in Western lands. Commodity prices rose moderately. Government funds were transferred to private banks, and state bank notes flooded the country. Foreign capital poured in freely.

The crisis of 1837 was one of the country's four great economic catastrophes. Its immediate causes were financial trouble in England, crop failures in 1835 and 1837, and a fall in the price of cotton. The government suddenly reversed its land policy and required prompt payment for public lands in hard money instead of state bank notes. Security prices declined and banks suspended specie payments.

Although specie payments were generally resumed in 1839, depression continued for years, banks continued to fail, some states defaulted on their public improvement bonds, and commodity prices fell. It was not until 1845 that a substantial business recovery occurred. Prices rose somewhat. The Mexican War of 1846 created no serious pressures. The European financial disturbances of 1847–1848 led to only a brief setback. Following the California gold strike of 1848, there was a period of great prosperity. Banking expanded and prices rose. There was another and greater land boom and railroad construction became massive. (484) A brief panic on the New York Stock Exchange in 1854, accompanied by tight money and failures, did not spread out to depress the general economy.

The panic of 1857 was in part a reflection of economic disturbances in Europe. There was a sharp decline in security prices and fourteen railroads went into bankruptcy. Money became very tight and banks again suspended specie payments. In 1858 recovery was rapid and the country was prosperous up to the tragic events of 1860–1861.

During the first sixty years of the nineteenth century the population of the United States had increased from about 4 million to 32 million, or eightfold. (485) An index of commodity prices had risen from 140 (1910–1914 = 100) in 1800 to 175 in 1816, declined to 108 in 1820, and thereafter fluctuated erratically, declining further to 95 in 1860. (486) The opening of the West had been the dominant force stimulating the nation's economy.

The Civil War brought the usual economic stimulations and dislocations of a great conflict. War finance led to a suspension of specie payments and a huge emission of short-term government securities and legal tender notes. Paper currency depreciated so that $1 in gold equaled $1.30 in paper in 1862 and a high of $2.33 in 1864. With victory, gold was back to $1.50 in 1865, $1.30 in 1866, and $1.15 in 1871, but did not return to $1 until specie payments were resumed in 1879—an interval of seventeen years. (487) The business recession in 1865–1867 was brief. Railroad construction was resumed, and postwar prosperity assumed boom proportions and lasted until 1873.

The panic of 1873 ushered in another major depression. Jay Cooke & Co., the financiers of the Civil War, failed as a result of involvement in financing the Northern Pacific Railroad. The banks suspended specie payments, security prices collapsed, and the New York Stock Exchange was closed for ten days. One fifth of the railroad mileage in the United States was sold under foreclosure. Financial scandals connected with the financing of the Union Pacific shook confidence.

In 1879 crop failures in Europe and heavy gold imports into the United States led to an abatement of financial pressures and the beginning of business recovery. The government assured convertibility of its paper money at par and re-established a de facto gold standard. Railroad construction was resumed on a large scale. In 1884 there was a sharp financial panic, during which call money went briefly to 3% a day; but there were no cumulative effects, and in 1885 business revived. (488) The years 1887–1893 were years of prosperity and unprecedented railroad construction. The opening of the West was no longer the dominant stimulant to the economy, but the rate of growth was unabated. Speculation and promotions were on the grand scale.

The panic of 1893 was marked by a collapse of the stock market and 600 bank failures. The Baring crises had led British investors to sell American securities and withdraw gold. The gold standard was considered to be in danger, and confidence in the Treasury position was undermined by the dissipation of the surplus. There were serious labor troubles, an agricultural depression, and agitation for free silver. Railroad bankruptcies again became common. The government responded with strong measures to reassure foreigners of the integrity of the dollar: silver purchase legislation was repealed, and the government borrowed heavily to buy gold. By 1897 commodity prices finally stabilized after thirty-three years of intermittent decline. Foreign demand revived. Gold reserves increased. Business improved, and a period of prosperity began that was to last until 1903, and in fact, with only small reactions in 1903, 1907, 1910, and 1913, until 1920.

During the period from 1860 to 1900 the population of the United States increased from 32 million to 80 million; this was twenty times the population of 1800. (485) The commodity-price index had risen from 95 in 1860 to 195 in 1864 (in paper money) and then declined almost steadily to 70 in 1896, recovering to 91 in 1900. At the end of the century it was some 35% below its level in 1800.

MONEY AND BANKING

Few chapters in the economic history of the young nation are more astonishing to the orderly mind than the story of its monetary and banking legislation. The Constitution gave to Congress the power "to coin money and regulate the value thereof." All money, however, was not coined money. The Supreme Court declared in 1839 that "the right to issue bank notes was at common law an occupation open to all men." The states might, if they wished, restrain and regulate their citizens in pursuit of this attractive occupation, but the federal government was not to be concerned. Monetary authority was thus divided: hard money was controlled by the federal government; paper money, by private concerns regulated at the discretion of each of many states with which the federal government was free to compete. Successful merchants had to become connoisseurs of bank notes, accepting only the best at par.

Although the new country freely copied many English commercial and financial institutions and drew on Europe's centuries of experience in credit forms and banking techniques, it accepted only briefly the power and guidance of a central bank. The first Bank of the United States, 1791–1811, and the second Bank of the United States, 1817–1836, were deeply involved in politics, just as was the Bank of England in its youth. The Bank of England's friends, however, remained in power long enough to permit it to become a dominant factor in finance and an invaluable aid to any government. The friends of the two Banks of the United States held insufficient tenure. Finance itself was less important and less respected in the new nation, and centralized power of all sorts was suspect. Even at the present time there are not one but dozens of American banking systems.

The bankers of London were also merchants. They insisted that their prime short bills must always have a market—at a price—and they always had one, thanks to the Bank of England. In the United States no one undertook this responsibility for the community as a whole until the twentieth century. The decentralized nineteenth-century money markets lacked a common pool of reserve funds, an instrument of national monetary policy, and a lender of last resort. In consequence there were weird fluctuations in the rates on short-term market paper, far wider than any reported from European centers. As late as 1899 call money on the New York Stock Exchange ranged from a low of 1% per annum to a high of 186% per annum. In contrast, in the same year the yields of prime long-term American corporate and municipal bond averages ranged from 3.07% low to 3.23% high.

The financial vicissitudes of the Civil War and the aroused spirit of nationalism led directly to the organization of the National Banking System. A uniform circulation was desired. In 1862, 1496 banks were circulating notes under the laws of twenty-nine states, all different. Some states chartered many kinds of banks. Seven thousand different kinds of notes circulated, aside from counterfeits. There were 5500 varieties of altered and fraudulent notes. (489) When the issue of United States notes in 1862 was followed by a decline in the specie value of all paper money, the blame was placed on bank notes rather than on government notes. It was argued that a currency secured solely by government bonds would improve public credit and encourage national union.

In 1863 an act was approved to provide a national currency secured by a pledge of United States securities. Nationally chartered banks, upon depositing United States bonds with the Treasury, could receive from it and issue notes up to 90% of the market or par value of the bonds, whichever was lower. The system at first developed slowly. In 1864 a new law provided convenient provisions for the conversion of state banks into national associations. In 1865 a law taxed the issue of state banks at 10% and thus forced state bank notes into retirement.

After the war was over the new National Banking System dominated the currency and the market for government bonds. However, after 1882 the application of a chronic Treasury surplus to the reduction of the national debt reduced the volume of bonds that could be held by the banks to secure circulation, while at the same time individuals, trustees, and corporations were seeking to buy government bonds for investment. The bonds advanced to such high premiums that it became unprofitable for the banks to retain them even with the circulation privilege; as a consequence note circulation declined. The redemption yields of some bonds were at times negative, even when short-term interest rates were very high. Congress was urged to accept other forms of bank assets as security for the currency or to fund high-rate government bonds into new issues at low nominal rates running for long periods of time and not subject to redemption.

The last two decades of the century were marked by a succession of political battles involving the currency and the banking system. Recurrent periods of monetary scarcity and abundance, with extreme volatility in the money markets and frequent financial crises, were unsatisfactory to all parties. Basic reform, however, was postponed by the political nature of the issues. It was not until the twentieth century that the Federal Reserve Act finally provided for a pooling of bank reserves, a truly uniform currency, a responsible monetary authority, and a potential lender of last resort.

The Treasury throughout the nineteenth century had, as it has today, many powers to influence bank reserves and the money market without the aid of a central bank. By shifting its balances between its subtreasuries and the banks, it could tighten or ease the banking position. Its choice of financing surpluses or deficits through, or outside of, the banking system had similar monetary effect. It could starve or feed the money market. The Treasury occasionally used these powers to alleviate crises, but its moves were always subject to political considerations and were of an improvised character. It assumed no responsibility for an orderly money market, and it developed no systematic program of smoothing out the pressures on the market.

HIGH-GRADE BOND YIELDS

No single security or group of securities provides a continuously satisfactory index of the going rate of interest for best American long-term bonds throughout the nineteenth century. At times, United States government bond yields offer a good indication of the level and trends of market rates. At other times only choice municipal and state bonds provide a usable index of the level and trends of the market. Late in the century the best long-term railroad bonds achieved such high quality and respect as to provide a good index of prime market yields.

Table 38 below summarizes the yields on new issues and seasoned issues of longer-term United States government bonds which are presented in later tables in greater detail. It also summarizes the yields of New England municipal bonds from 1798 and the yields of a railroad bond average from 1857. In addition, it includes a series on real estate mortgage yields from 1879.

The principal data in the table are pictured on Chart 31. The chart and table suggest that during a part of the century these various series agree in substance on the trend of long-term interest rates and that they

TABLE 38

SUMMARY OF LONG-TERM HIGH-GRADE AMERICAN
BOND YIELDS: NINETEENTH CENTURY

| Year | Federal Government Bonds | | New England Municipal Bond Yields, %* | High-Grade Railroad Bond Yields, % | New York City Real Estate Mortgages, % |
	New Issue Yields, %	Selected Market Yields, %			
1798		7.56	6.30		
1799	8.00	7.42	6.16		
		7.49 2-yr. av.	6.23		
1800	7.34	6.94	6.13		
1801		6.44	5.63		
1802		6.02	5.25		
1803		6.16	5.06		
1804		6.29	5.14		
1805		6.38	5.36		
1806		6.14	5.32		
1807	6.00	6.08	5.29		
1808		5.96	5.19		
1809		5.85	5.02		
10-yr. av.		6.23	5.33		
1810		5.82	5.02		
1811		5.95	5.09		
1812	6.00	6.12	5.13		
1813	6.83	6.30	5.03		
1814	7.50	7.64	5.26		
1815	7.00–7.75	7.30	5.29		
1816		7.25	5.72		
1817		5.86	5.27		
1818		5.78	5.08		
1819		5.90	5.17		
10-yr. av.		6.39	5.20		
1820	5.00–5.88	5.16	5.00		
1821	4.25–4.50	4.57	4.93		
1822		4.65			
1823		4.72	5.00		
1824	4.50	4.25	4.52		
1825	4.50	4.32	4.52		
1826		4.50			
1827		4.37	4.61		
1828		4.48			
1829		4.50	4.77		
10-yr. av.		4.55	4.77 7-yr. av.		

TABLE 38 (*Continued*)

Year	Federal Government Bonds		New England Municipal Bond Yields, %*	High- Grade Railroad Bond Yields, %	New York City Real Estate Mort- gages, %
	New Issue Yields, %	Selected Market Yields, %			
1830		4.37	4.90		
1831		4.41			
1832		4.45	5.00		
1833			4.87		
1834			4.87		
1835			4.83		
1836			4.96		
1837			4.95		
1838			5.01		
1839			5.21		
10-yr. av.			4.95		
1840			5.07		
1841	5.50–6.00		4.99		
1842	6.00–6.14	6.07	4.95		
1843	4.82–4.95	5.03	4.88		
1844		4.85	4.84		
1845		5.16	4.86		
1846	6.00	5.50	4.92		
1847	5.88	5.77	5.14		
1848	5.76	5.71	5.31		
1849		5.16	5.31		
10-yr. av.		5.41 8-yr. av.	5.02		
1850		4.58	5.13		
1851		4.47	5.08		
1852		4.39	4.98		
1853		4.02	4.99		
1854		4.14	5.13		
1855		4.18	5.16		
1856		4.11	5.10		
1857		4.30	5.19 *	6.97	
1858	4.36–4.81	4.32	5.03	6.50	
1859		4.72	4.81	6.22	
10-yr. av.		4.33	5.06		
1860	4.92	5.57	4.79	6.04	
1861	6.73	6.45	5.04	6.33	
1862	6.00	6.25	4.91	5.52	
1863	6.00	6.00	4.37	4.77	
1864	5.00–5.60	5.10	4.80	4.83	
1865	4.62–5.42	5.19	5.51	6.02	
1866	4.62–5.42	5.17	5.50	6.37	
1867	5.16	4.97	5.34	6.32	
1868	5.61	4.62	5.28	6.26	
1869	5.87	4.07	5.37	6.55	7.00
10-yr. av.		5.34	5.10	5.90	

287

TABLE 38 (*Continued*)

Year	Federal Government Bonds		New England Municipal Bond Yields, %*	High-Grade Railroad Bond Yields, %	New York City Real Estate Mortgages, %
	New Issue Yields, %	Selected Market Yields, %			
1870		4.24	5.44	6.41	
1871	5.00	4.18	5.32	6.35	
1872		3.70	5.36	6.18	
1873		3.51	5.58	6.20	
1874		3.42	5.47	5.91	
1875		3.30	5.07	5.45	
1876	4.50	3.66	4.59	5.16	
1877	4.50	3.81	4.45	5.18	
1878	4.00–4.50	3.97	4.34	5.11	
1879		3.96	4.22	4.77	5.92
10-yr. av.		3.75	4.98	5.67	
1880		3.63	4.02	4.46	5.78
1881	3.50	3.13	3.70	4.13	5.80
1882	3.00	2.91	3.62	4.20	5.65
1883		2.88	3.63	4.23	5.43
1884		2.76	3.62	4.15	5.35
1885		2.68	3.52	3.98	5.20
1886		2.43	3.37	3.81	5.10
1887		2.32	3.52	3.80	5.14
1888		2.27	3.67	3.69	5.20
1889		2.13	3.45	3.51	5.13
10-yr. av.		2.71	3.60	4.00	5.38
1890		2.37	3.42	3.68	5.45
1891	2.00	2.58	3.62	3.84	5.38
1892		2.73	3.60	3.72	5.20
1893		2.96	3.75	3.73	5.20
1894	2.98	2.72	3.70	3.62	5.16
1895	3.75	2.82	3.46	3.46	5.04
1896	3.52	3.06	3.60	3.50	5.12
1897		2.57	3.40	3.33	5.04
1898	3.00	2.50	3.35	3.26	4.96
1899		2.22	3.10	3.13	5.05
10-yr. av.		2.55	3.50	3.53	5.16
1900	2.00		3.15	3 18	5.17

* Before 1857, Massachusetts or Boston 5s; after 1857, Macaulay's *Average of New England Municipals.*
Sources
     See text and periodic tables which follow. Mortgages from *Real Estate Analyst,* by permission of copyright owners, Roy Wenzlick Research Corp. of St. Louis.

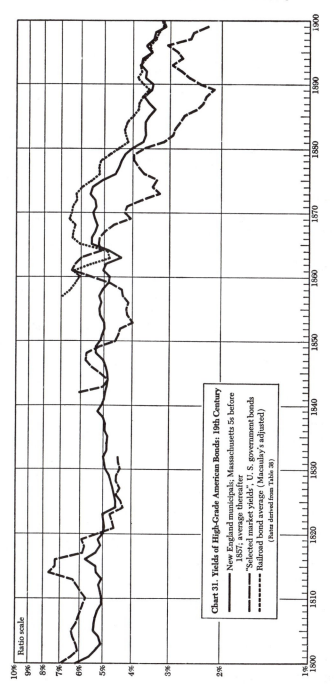

Chart 31. Yields of High-Grade American Bonds: 19th Century

New England municipals; Massachusetts 5s before 1857; average thereafter

"Selected market yields", U. S. government bonds

Railroad bond average (Macaulay's adjusted)

(Rates derived from Table 38)

Ratio scale

indicate a general level of long-term prime interest rates in a broad band. Several important distortions and inadequacies render certain of the series misleading at specific periods.

During and directly after the Civil War, United States government bond yields were distorted by gold premiums because they were quoted in greenbacks and might be paid in specie. Also, from the late 1860's on, the national banks bought government bonds at low yields to secure circulation, and this was later supplemented by Treasury purchases at large premiums. Therefore, market yields on governments must be disregarded altogether from 1863 until 1918 as a guide to American long-term interest rates. Furthermore, from 1825 to 1842 there were few government bond issues outstanding, and occasionally there were none.

New-issue yields of government bonds are supplemented in the table by a highly abbreviated estimate of market yields. This series is derived from average annual prices of those longer-term issues with the least discount or premium. Yields are selected to reflect what appears to be a realistic going average rate for the year. This attempt at selection, liable as it is to error, has resulted in a series that was usually close to new-issue yields until 1865.

Frederick R. Macaulay of the National Bureau of Economic Research (491) has provided several important interest rate averages, starting in 1857. Macaulay's New England municipal bond index is probably a good guide to the level and trend of American long-term high-grade bond yields at that time; tax exemption did not distort their yields as it does today. His adjusted railroad bond index is a rough but serviceable guide to prime corporate bond yields after 1885. Before 1857 municipal yields are represented here only by State of Massachusetts bonds, usually 5s, and City of Boston bonds, usually 5s. These are too few issues to provide anything but a very rough indication of the market.

In summary, from 1798 until 1863, the United States government bond yields for issues selling close to par provide the best available guide to market trends. After 1865, for two decades, the municipal average alone must be relied upon. After 1885, prime railroad bond yields were about the same as the municipal average yields and provide a usable index.

Most attempts to present a history of American bond yields date back only to specie resumption in 1879 or, at the earliest, to the 1850's. This may be because of these technical difficulties, which cast doubt on the adequacy of earlier data and on resulting yield calculations. There existed, however, from the days of Alexander Hamilton, an American investment market for long-term government and state obligations, with frequent quotations and with fluctuating prices and yields. It seems worthwhile, therefore, to accept the risk of inaccuracy and to attempt to approximate the market yields that prevailed for the best long-term American bonds throughout the nineteenth century.

SUMMARY OF NINETEENTH-CENTURY YIELD TRENDS

The simplest breakdown of the history of nineteenth-century American bond yields, as pictured in the chart, is into two easily distinguishable parts: (A) erratic fluctuations in a high but declining range from 1800 to 1870, and (B) a sustained decline in yields during the last three decades of the century. Both of these periods, however, can be subdivided.

A. The high-yield decades included three periods of declining yields and three periods of rising yields. Each of these fluctuations were far more pronounced in government yields than in New England municipal yields. They may be summarized as follows:

1. 1798 to 1810–1811. A decline in all yields, briefly interrupted by a small advance in 1805.

2. 1810–1811 to 1815–1816. A rise in all yields during the war, almost, but not quite, to their high levels of 1798.

3. 1815–1816 to 1825. A sharp decline in all yields to levels well below the lows of the first decade.

4. 1825 to 1842–1848. A gradual rise in municipal yields, even during the years when the federal debt was being paid off, followed by sharply higher yields for the first new federal issues. The high yields of the 1840's were well below 1810–1816 highs.

5. 1842–1848 to 1858. A decline in government yields to the low levels of the 1820's, but no pronounced trend in these municipal yields.

6. 1858 to 1861–1865. A sharp rise in government yields to wartime highs in 1861, which were nevertheless below their highs of 1814–1815 and 1798. A very irregular advance in municipal yields to levels approximating 1816 was interrupted by a sharp brief drop in 1863. There were conflicting trends in the different departments of the market during the Civil War.

B. The sweeping decline in yields after the Civil War started first in governments, moved much later to rails, and last to municipals. The special factors then helping governments and the credit risk present in railroad bonds suggest that municipals were then the best guide to prime market yields. If so, this great bull market in prime American bonds can be dated from 1873. It lasted for more than twenty-five years. This bull market can be subdivided into three parts:

1. 1873 to 1886. A sharp decline in all yields. The 3½% level which became general for municipals was far below any yields attained in the first seven decades of the century.

2. 1886 to 1893. A small, irregular advance in yields which remained in a very low band. Best-grade rails now for the first time seemed to command truly high-grade prices.

3. 1893 to 1899. A renewed decline in municipal and corporate bond yields to 3–3¼%, which were approximately their low yields until the 1930's.

Chart 32, which compares the yields on British consols with Ameri-

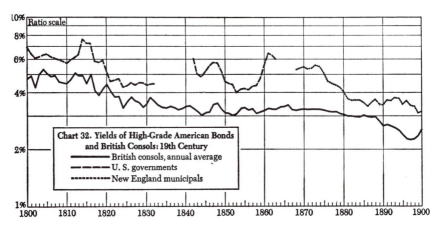

Chart 32. Yields of High-Grade American Bonds and British Consols: 19th Century
———— British consols, annual average
— — — U. S. governments
∙∙∙∙∙∙∙∙∙∙ New England municipals

can long-term bonds, reveals similarities and differences. Yields in both countries declined very substantially during the century as a whole. British yields were always below American yields.

During the period of the Napoleonic Wars, of which our War of 1812 may be considered a part, both British and American yields were in their high range for the century. Yields in both countries declined after 1815. After 1825–1830 American yields tended to rise sharply, while British yields declined further. This created a very wide differential from the 1830's through the 1870's, which, no doubt, encouraged heavy British investment in American securities. British yields rose only a trifle during our Civil War period, when American yields rose substantially.

After 1870 both markets again moved together in a manner that has continued most of the time ever since. While yields in both countries declined sharply during the last three decades of the century, the American decline was far larger than the British decline, especially in the 1870's. The gap was then partly closed. However, American yields did not reach the low level of British yields in the nineteenth century and, indeed, did not decline below British yields until after World War I.

DETAILED HISTORY OF TREASURY FINANCE AND
HIGH-GRADE BOND YIELDS

1790–1809. Alexander Hamilton's famous refunding, approved by Congress in 1790 and carried out successfully in 1791–1794, was based on the creation of three new bond issues: (492)

1791–1794—$30.0 million	"6s of 1790," redeemable at the pleasure of the government at 100 in an amount not exceeding 2% a year.
$14.6 million	"Deferred 6s of 1790," paying 6% after 1800, same redemption terms.
$19.7 million	"3s of 1790," redeemable at the pleasure of the government at 100.

$64.3 million

These securities were offered par-for-par to holders of the debt issued by the Congress during the Revolutionary War and the Confederation and to holders of state debts incurred for national purposes. Holders of Congressional debt received two thirds of principal in the 6s of 1790 and one third in the Deferred 6s of 1790, and thus received average interest of 4% to 1800 and 6% thereafter. Their claims for unpaid interest were met with the 3s of 1790 par-for-par. Holders of approved state debts received four ninths in the 6s of 1790, two ninths in the Deferred 6s of 1790, and three ninths in the 3s of 1790. The securities accepted in exchange for these new issues had sold at large discounts. Therefore, a market rate of interest cannot be inferred for the years 1790–1794 from these nominal rates.

The conversion was not forced. It was generally believed that the market rate of interest would fall as the public credit rose. (493) All of the old debt was redeemable at the pleasure of the government, whereas the new 6s could not be redeemed faster than 2% a year; therefore the conversion appealed to the self-interest of creditors. The national revenues and proceeds of the sale of Western lands were pledged to the payment of interest on these domestic issues subject only to the servicing of the $12 million of foreign debt, which was always regarded as having a prior claim.

During the period 1791–1801 Treasury surpluses exceeded deficits. In 1792 a regular sinking fund was established by Hamilton as a device to improve the credit of the government and raise the price of its securities. (494) Appropriations were made and a commission appointed to borrow money and make purchases in the market. "It ought to be the policy of the government," said Hamilton, "to raise the value of stock to its true standard, as fast as possible. When it arrives at that point, foreign speculations . . . will become beneficial." While few market quotations on the new government securities are available until 1798, Hamilton's statement implies that the 6% bonds stood below par in their earlier years. A price of 70 is reported for 1791, to yield 8.57%.

The favorable financial position of the Treasury was changed in 1797–1799 when an undeclared naval war with France required the creation of a military establishment. A new loan was authorized in 1798. It was sold for cash in 1799 and 1800 and bore the highest nominal rate for a long-term government bond in our history until recently:

1799–$5.0 million "8s of 1798," redeemable in 1809;* sold at 100 = 8%.
1800–$1.5 million "8s of 1800," redeemable in 1809;* sold at 105¾ = 7.34%.†

Market prices for government bond issues are reported from 1798. (495) In 1798–1799, as Table 39 reveals, the market for federal government bonds was depressed. This was ascribed to public expectation of war and invasion. The 6s of 1790 sold as low as 75, to yield 8%. These prices explain the Treasury's use of a rate as high as 8% for its new issues in 1799 and 1800.

In 1798 the 3s of 1790 were selling in a range of 42½–50, to provide a current yield of 6–7.07%. This was about 110 basis points lower yield than the 6s of 1790 and 150 basis points average below the yield of the new 8s. Such differentials suggest an investor preference for low-rate discount securities; just such a preference has been noticed in most European countries. The 3s provided an assured continuity of income at a good rate while early retirement was expected for the 8s and did in fact occur, and the 6s would probably be paid off at 2% a year. It was the intention of the new nation to pay off its debts regardless of terms, and it did so.

In 1799 and 1800 the bond market improved. The second issue of 8s was floated at a good premium and sold up to 110. The 6s and the 3s rose 4–7 points. In 1802 the market reached a temporary high, declined until 1805, and then recovered to a new high in 1809. There was a suc-

---

* Although these 8% loans are officially described as "redeemable after fifteen years," the redemption date is here stated as 1809 because the act says "bearing interest at 8% . . . until December 31, 1808, and thereafter during the pleasure of Congress, until redeemed." The bonds were in fact redeemed in 1809.

† Yield on the 8s at premiums is figured on the assumption of redemption at the earliest possible time because of the high rate.

TABLE 39

PRICES AND YIELDS OF LONG-TERM HIGH-GRADE BONDS, 1798–1809

Year	U.S. 6s of 1790: Current Yields						U.S. 3s of 1790: Current Yields			
	Annual Average		Annual High Price	Yield, %	Annual Low Price	Yield, %	Annual Average		Annual	
	Price	Yield, %					Price	Yield, %	High Price	Low Price
1798	79⅜	7.56	83¾	7.16	75	8.00	46¼	6.47	50	42½
1799	82½	7.29	86¼	6.95	78¾	7.62	47½	6.31	50	45
		7.42 2-yr. av.						6.39 2-yr. av.		
1800	86⅜	6.94	91½	6.56	81¼	7.38	51	5.97	54½	47½
1801	93¼	6.44	100	6.00	86½	6.93	56¼	5.33	60	52½
1802	99¾	6.02	102	5.87	97½	6.16	63	4.76	67	59
1803	97½	6.16	100	6.00	95	6.31	59½	5.05	62	57
1804	95¼	6.29	96½	6.22	94	6.39	58	5.16	59	57
1805	94¼	6.38	97	6.19	91½	6.56	55¼	5.43	57½	53
1806	97¾	6.14	100	6.00	95½	6.28	60½	4.96	64	57
1807	98¾	6.08	101½	5.91	96	6.26	63¼	4.74	65	61½
1808	100¾	5.96	103½	5.80	98	6.12	64½	4.66	65¼	63½
1809	102½	5.85	104	5.76	101	5.94	66¼	4.53	67½	65
10-yr. av.		6.22						5.06		

Year	U.S. 8s of 1798–1809: Redemption Yields				Massachusetts 5s: Current Yields					
	Annual Average		Annual High Price	Annual Low Price	Annual Average		Annual High Price	Yield, %	Annual Low Price	Yield, %
	Price	Yield, %			Price	Yield, %				
1798					79½	6.30	81½	6.12	77½	6.45
1799	104	7.42	106	102	81¼	6.16	82½	6.08	80	6.25
						6.23 2-yr. av.				
1800	107	6.93	110	104	81⅝	6.13	83¼	6.00	80	6.25
1801	110½	6.31	115	106	88¾	5.63	92½	5.40	85	5.89
1802	112½	5.80	114	111	95¼	5.25	100	5.00	90½	5.52
1803	109¾	6.03	112½	107	98½	5.06	100	5.00	97	5.15
1804	107½	6.22	109	106	97¼	5.14	98	5.10	96½	5.18
1805	105¼	6.50	106½	104	93¼	5.36	96½	5.18	90	5.55
1806	105	6.12	106	104	94	5.32	98	5.10	90	5.55
1807	103	6.37	105	101	96	5.21	98	5.10	94	5.32
1808	101¾	6.12	102½	101	96¼	5.19	99½	5.02	93	5.38
1809	Paid in 1809	6.30 9-yr. av.			99½	5.02	100	5.00	99	5.04
						5.33 10-yr. av.				

SOURCES
High and low prices from Joseph G. Martin, *Martin's Boston Stock Market*, Boston, 1886, p. 127,

cession of government surpluses, and debt was rapidly reduced from a high of $86 million in 1804 to $57 million in 1809. The foreign debt was all paid off. In 1809 both issues of 8s were paid off at 100. The 8% had been good while it lasted. This was a decade of sharply declining bond yields.

These early issues of long-term domestic government bonds did not offer investors a clear privilege of demanding the return of their principal at a specified future maturity date in the modern manner. Redemption of principal was a right of the debtor, and the debtor usually had to waive this right for a fixed number of years to make the securities acceptable. This was the European principle of perpetual funded debts, dating back to the medieval census annuities. Loans to a foreign country, however, usually specified a maturity date at which the debtor must pay. Short-term loans of the government also often specified a maturity. While the maturity provisions of long-term American government loans were lacking or were ambiguously worded, almost all issues were in fact redeemed at, or a few years after, earliest redemption date.

For these years the market prices and current yields of State of Massachusetts 5% bonds are available and may be compared with the yields on federal government bonds. There was no government issue with the same nominal rate; therefore precise comparison of yields is not always possible. However, the lower yield for the Massachusetts 5s in periods when the United States 6s of 1790 sold at heavy discounts, as well as when the 6s sold at par, suggests that the new national government had not yet achieved the credit standing of the venerable state. The year-to-year price trend of the Massachusetts bonds was the same as the trend of federal government bonds. Indeed, the yields of all four issues quoted in the table fluctuated together in spite of very different terms and levels; this indicates that we are reviewing a true market for long-term debt instruments.

1810–1829. In spite of the recurrent Treasury surpluses of the first decade and a remarkable record of debt retirement, the Treasury and the financial markets of the United States were not well prepared to finance the War of 1812. In 1811 the first Bank of the United States was deprived of its charter, and the government, with its funds transferred to state banks, enjoyed no sure source of credit. The war was politically unpopular in wealthy states, and Congress refused to vote adequate taxes to support the new war debt. Caught between limitations placed by Congress on the rates and prices of its loans and the reluctance of investors to buy, the Treasury was ultimately forced to accept very unfavorable terms.

TABLE 40

PRICES AND YIELDS OF LONG-TERM HIGH-GRADE BONDS, 1810–1829

Year	U.S. 6s of 1790: Current Yields						U.S. 3s of 1790: Current Yields			
	Annual Average		Annual High Price	Yield, %	Annual Low Price	Yield, %	Annual Average		Annual	
	Price	Yield, %					Price	Yield, %	High Price	Low Price
1810	103	5.82	104	5.76	102	5.87	65¾	4.55	67½	64
1811	100¾	5.95	104	5.76	97½	6.15	62	4.84	66	58
1812	98	6.12	101	5.93	95	6.30	59	5.10	62	56
1813	95	6.30	100	6.00	90	6.68	55¼	5.43	57½	53
1814	78½	7.64	92	6.52	65	9.22	51¾	5.85	53¾	49
1815	85½	7.02	90	6.68	81	7.41	47¼	6.33	51	44
1816	88¾	6.75	97½	6.15	80	7.50	54½	5.52	61	48
1817	102¼	5.86	108¼	5.52	96	6.25	65½	4.56	70	61
1818	103¾	5.78	106¼	5.62	101	5.94	67½	4.45	71	64
1819	101½	5.90	103	5.82	100	6.00	65	4.61	68	62
10-yr. av.		6.33						5.14		
1820	105	5.71	108	5.53	102	5.87	67½	4.45	70	65
1821	109¼	5.49	112	5.36	106¼	5.64	74¾	4.04	79¼	69
1822	106½	5.63	111	5.40	102	5.87	76	3.95	79	73

Year	U.S. 6s of 1814–1827									
	Annual Average			Annual						
	Price	Current Yield, %	Redemp. Yield, %	High Price	Low Price					
1823	106¼	5.64	4.27	109	103½		75¼	3.96	79	72¼
1824	108¾	5.52	2.94	112	105¼		84½	3.56	90	79
1825	106½	5.62	2.65	111	102		87½	3.43	90	85
1826	103½	5.79	3.10	106	101		83	3.62	86	80
1827	103¾	5.77	2.20 *	106	101½		84¼	3.57	88	80½
1828	103¼	5.80	2.65 *	106	100½		85	3.54	87	83
1829	102⅞	5.85	3.30 *	104¾	100½		86⅝	3.47	89¼	84
			Paid in 1831					3.76		
10-yr. av.								Paid in 1833		

War finance was divided between issues of short-term Treasury notes and issues of long-term bonds. All save the small denominations of notes bore interest, and this was usually at 5.40%. The notes were made fundable into government bonds, and after the war they were rapidly funded. (496)

Table 40 shows that the market for government securities remained

TABLE 40 (*Continued*)

Year	U.S. 7s of 1815–1824					U.S. 5s of 1821–1835				
	Annual Average			Annual		Annual Average			Annual	
	Price	Curr. Yield, %	Redemp. Yield, %	High Price	Low Price	Price	Curr. Yield, %	Redemp. Yield, %	High Price	Low Price
1810										
1811										
1812										
1813										
1814										
1815										
1816	96½	7.25	7.54	102	91					
1817	106¾	6.55	5.92	111½	102					
1818	107½	6.50	5.68	110	105					
1819	105	6.66	6.00	106½	103½					
1820	108	6.46	5.16	110½	105½					
1821	110⅜	6.32	4.15	111¾	109	106⅞	4.57	4.34	108 †	105⅛ †
1822	106¼	6.62	4.74	108½	104					
1823	103¼	6.76	5.20 Paid in 1825	104	102½	105¼	4.72	4.42		105¼
	U.S. 4½s of 1824–1832									
1824	105¾	4.25	3.66	105¾		112	4.46	3.66	112	
1825	104	4.32	3.85	104		106½	4.67	4.20	108	105
1826	100	4.50	4.50	102	98	103½	4.81	4.39	107	100
1827	102¼	4.37	4.00	103½	101	108	4.62	3.82	108	
1828	100⅛	4.49	4.45	102	98¼	105½	4.72	4.10	108	103
1829	100	4.50	4.50	102	98	103⅜	4.82	4.35	105¾	101
			Paid in 1834					4.15 8-yr. av. Paid in 1834–35		

around its 1809 highs in 1810 and 1811 in spite of the war clouds. In 1812 in a lower market the government floated its first bond issue for new cash in many years:

1812—$8.1 million "6s of 1812," redeemable in 1825; sold at 100 = 6%.

In 1813 the bond market declined a few points further. With difficulty the treasury obtained the permission of Congress to sell bonds below par and then made the mistake of promising buyers of the first discount 6s that they would get the benefit of any lower prices subsequently accepted. Now investors had a near-term interest in a further decline in the market. Three issues of 6s were sold under this authorization as follows:

TABLE 40 *(Continued)*

Year	Annual Average Price	Annual Average Yield, %	Annual High Price	Yield, %	Annual Low Price	Yield, %
			Massachusetts 5s: Current Yields			
1810	99½	5.02	100	5.00	99	5.04
1811	98¼	5.09	100½	4.98	96	5.21
1812	97¼	5.13	99½	5.02	95	5.26
1813	99¼	5.03	101	4.95	97½	5.12
1814	95	5.26	101	4.95	89	5.61
1815	94½	5.29	101	4.95	88	5.68
1816	87½	5.72	91	5.50	84	5.95
1817	95	5.27	100	5.00	90	5.56
1818	98½	5.08	100	5.00	97	5.15
1819	96¾	5.17	98½	5.08	95	5.27
10-yr. av.		5.20				
1820	100	5.00	103	4.86	97	5.15
1821	101½	4.93	103	4.86	100	5.00
			Paid in 1822			
			Boston City 5s: Sold in 1823 @ 100			
1824	110¼	4.54	110¼	4.54		
1825	110½	4.52	110½	4.52		
1826						
1827	108½	4.61	109	4.59	108	4.63
1828						
1829	104½	4.77	104½	4.77		

* Figured as 1 year to maturity.
† New issue prices.
SOURCE
High and low prices from Martin, *op. cit.*, p. 127.

1813	—$18.1 million	"6s of 1813 1st Loan," redeemable in 1826; sold at 88 = 6.83% current yield.
1813–1814	—$ 8.5 million	"6s of 1813, 2nd Loan," redeemable in 1826; sold at 88¼ = 6.80% current yield.
1814	—$15.4 million	"6s of 1814," redeemable in 1827; sold at 80 = 7.50% current yield.

The last loan created trouble. Some of it was even sold for state bank notes worth only 65 in specie, and this was a yield of 9.25%. Earlier subscribers hastened to demand supplementary stock for the difference.

In 1814 the 6s of 1790 declined to a low of 65, to yield 9.22%. These years saw the highest yields for long-term American government bonds in the nineteenth century. Few apparently believed that in three years the 6s would be up from 65 to 108, and that in 20 years virtually the entire national debt would be paid off.

In 1815, with the news of peace, the market improved for a while. In this year the Treasury undertook to fund its notes by offering two long-term issues to noteholders at curiously contrasting terms:

To holders of notes under $100 denomination:
1815–$ 9.0 million   "7s of 1815," redeemable after 1824; sold at
100 = 7%.
To holders of larger notes:
1815–$12.3 million   "6s of 1815," redeemable after 1825; sold at
$95\frac{1}{4}$ = 6.31%.

The relationship of these yields to prevailing market yields of 6.68–7.41% suggests that the prices received by the Treasury were in reality lower than $95\frac{1}{4}$ and 100. Treasury notes which were accepted in payment were selling at times as low as 75–90. (497) If we accept the low market value of the notes as the price of the bonds, the new issues were sold to yield:

1815–7s of 1815 at 75–90, to yield 9.31–7.75%.
1815–6s of 1815 at $95\frac{1}{4}$% of 75–90, to yield 8.22–7.00%.

In 1816 the market was still depressed with the new 7s of 1815 selling at a low of 91, to yield 7.69%. In 1817 the real postwar market recovery occurred. The 6s of 1790 sold up 16–28 points, and the new 7s of 1815 sold up 20 points to $111\frac{1}{4}$, to yield 5.30%.

Such prices above 100 for government bond issues without fixed maturity dates make it difficult to be sure just what yield buyers expected to receive from any given bargain. Some of the yields in the table are current yields arrived at by simply dividing rate by price; other yields are figured to earliest redemption. Most bonds were redeemable at a future date at the pleasure of the government, but there was no certainty of redemption; such issues provided a speculative rate of return. Thus the 6s of 1814–1827 sold in 1824 at a high of 112; this was a current yield of 5.36%, but in the event of redemption in 1827 at 100 it was a yield of only 1.85%. For such issues the tables provide both current yields and yields to earliest redemption and thus reveal the speculative choices offered to the investor. For ascertaining the going rate of long-term interest, new issues or seasoned issues selling at around 100 and not redeemable are far more reliable than high-premium issues.

The year 1819 was marked by an industrial and commercial crisis which had little adverse effect on the bond market. Three small loans floated in 1820–1821, principally to permit the continued redemption of high rate war loans, provide an interesting clue to investor preference in a rising bond market. These were:

1820–$1.0 million "5s of 1820," redeemable in 1832; sold at 100 = 5%.
1820–$2.0 million "6s of 1820," redeemable at pleasure of United States; sold at 102 = 5.88%.
1821–$4.7 million "5s of 1821," redeemable in 1835; sold at 105⅛ = 4.50%, and at 108 = 4.25%.

The yield was highest for the issue with early redemption risk and much lower for those with later redemption risks.

In 1824–1825 the market reached its high prices for this decade. The Treasury then undertook a refunding to reduce the interest charges on the war debt. This was in the form of three 4½% issues which may be combined as follows:

1824–1825–$14.5 million "4½s of 1824," redeemable in 1832–1834; at 100 = 4.50%.

This was the last long-term financing until 1841. The problem of the government now was how to disburse its surplus.

From 1825 through 1829 the bond market declined moderately. Something like 4½% seemed like a going rate for bonds with an early redemption risk. By 1835 the debt was entirely paid off.

During the years from 1810 to 1829 the current yields on bonds of the State of Massachusetts and of the City of Boston, also given in Table 40, fluctuated far less than the yields on federal government securities. Since these local issues had 5% nominal rates and in the decade 1820–1829 commanded premiums, their yields were probably kept up by fear of redemption. But in the lower markets of 1810–1819 discounts were usual, and these provided a true yield that was always far below the yield on Treasury 6s and sometimes below the yield on Treasury 3s.

Allowing for distortions due to rate differences and premiums, it seems that Massachusetts bonds suffered from the War of 1812 far less than treasury bonds and recovered less with peace. The yield and price differences were not very large in the 1820's, suggesting that the popularity of the national government securities may by then have approximated that of Massachusetts and the City of Boston securities.

1830–1859. The history of the national debt during this thirty-year period may be divided into three parts: (a) redemption of the entire remaining debt, 1830–1835; (b) no debt, 1835–1842; and (c) creation of a new debt, 1842–1859. The total national debt from 1800 fluctuated as follows:

Year	Millions of Dollars	Year	Millions of Dollars
1800	83	1840	3
1804	86	1850	63
1810	53	1851	68
1820	91	1857	28
1830	48	1860	64
1835	0		

During the period of final debt redemption, 1830–1835, the trend of government bond yields was downward, as might be expected. Examination of the market for City of Boston 5s which ranged between 4.79 and 5.02% suggests that the true level of market yields may have changed very little during this period, and that the low redemption yields on premium governments reflected merely the possibility that they might not be redeemed promptly.

By January of 1835 the debt was wiped out. From 1835 to 1841 there were no government bonds outstanding and hence no government bond yields for history to record. However, issues of the City of Boston and the State of Massachusetts were quoted regularly, and these yields may be taken as a help in judging market levels and trends. The possibility of special privileges and the effects of local financial preferences make it impossible to draw firm conclusions on national market trends from the prices of one or two local issues.

Boston yields were about the same in 1835, when the federal debt was wiped out, as they were in 1830; this reinforces the view that there was little change in going rates of long-term interest during this five-year period of debt redemption. During the years 1835–1841, when there were no treasury issues outstanding, the yields on local issues rose. A rise in market yields is also suggested by the fact that the first government financing in 1841–1842 took the form of 6s, while the issues redeemed in 1830–1835, which commanded premiums, were mostly 5s and 4½s.

This seven-year debtless interval was in fact one of great financial disturbance. The second Bank of the United States had lost its charter, and federal deposits had been transferred to state banks. A period of wild speculation had ended in the collapse of 1837, which had been succeeded by a heavy depression. Treasury surpluses quickly gave way to deficits.

From 1837 to 1841 the Treasury financed its deficits entirely through the sale of about $40 million of notes without recourse to long-term loans. The idea of a new national debt for peacetime purposes met widespread political opposition; the notes were considered a temporary expedient. With a change in administration in 1841 a new policy of funding notes into longer-term bonds was inaugurated. The first loan, which was redeemable in only three years, was not a success and had to be broken up into two parts:

1841—$3.2 million 5½s of 1841, redeemable in 1845; sold at 100 = 5.50%.

2.4 million 6s of 1841, redeemable in 1845; sold at 100 = 6.00%.

Soon thereafter a loan was floated with the unusually long redemption term of twenty years and met with success:

1842—$8.3 million "6s of 1842," redeemable in 1863; sold from 97½ = 6.14% to 100 = 6.00%.

Between 1842 and 1843 a striking improvement occurred in the bond market. The Treasury took advantage of this good market to float another long-term loan at very much more satisfactory terms:

1843—$7.0 million "5s of 1843," redeemable in 1853; sold from 101 = 4.95% to 103¾ = 4.82% current.

A period of Treasury surpluses was again at hand. Many state banking systems had been put on a firm foundation. The Independent Treasury System was inaugurated to protect the government from losses due to bank failures. Thereafter the power to shift Treasury funds between the vaults of the banks and those of the subtreasuries provided a de facto weapon of monetary policy which was not fully recognized or systematically used.

Between 1844 and 1846 the bond market declined. The Mexican War of 1846–1848 brought further long-term loans. The Treasury offered three issues for cash, two with unusually long twenty-year terms, and achieved heavy oversubscription:

1846—$ 5.0 million "6s of 1846," redeemable in 1856; sold at 100 = 6%.

1847— 28.2 million "6s of 1847," redeemable in 1868; sold at 102 = 5.88%.

1848— 16.0 million "6s of 1848," redeemable in 1868; sold at 104 = 5.76%.

TABLE 41

Prices and Yields of Long-Term High-Grade Bonds: 1830–1859

Year	U.S. 3s of 1790: Current Yields				U.S. 5s of 1821–1835				
	Annual Average		Annual		Annual Average			Annual	
	Price	Yield, %	High Price	Low Price	Price	Curr. Yield, %	Redemp. Yield, %	High Price	Low Price
1830	92¼	3.25 *	95½	89	105¼	4.72	3.82	108½	102
1831	94	3.19	95½	92½	104¾	4.76	3.71	106½	103
1832	98	3.06	100	96	104	4.80	3.57	105	103
1833		Paid			101¾	4.92	4.04	103	100½
1834					100½	4.97	4.45	101	100
							3.92 5-yr. av.		
1835							Paid		
1836									
1837									
1838									
1839									

Year	U.S. 6s of 1842–1863						
	Annual Average			Annual High Price	Current Yield, %	Annual Low Price	Current Yield, %
	Price	Current Yield, %	Redemption Yield, %				
1840							
1841							
1842	98¾	6.07	6.12	100	6.00	97½	6.14
1843	112⅛	5.32	5.03	118¾	5.04	105	5.71
1844	114⅛	5.24	4.85	115	5.21	113¼	5.27
1845	109¾	5.47	5.16	114	5.25	105½	5.68
1846	105½	5.68	5.50	112	5.33	99	6.06
1847	102½	5.85	5.77	108	5.56	97	6.18
1848	102⅞	5.84	5.71	108	5.56	97¾	6.13
1849	108⅜	5.54	5.16	111¾	5.35	105	5.71
8-yr. av.			5.41				

Year	U.S. 6s of 1848–1868						
1850	117¼	5.10	4.58	122	4.91	112½	5.31
1851	118¼	5.05	4.47	122½	4.90	114	5.26
1852	118⅜	5.06	4.39	121	4.96	115¾	5.18
1853	122	4.91	4.02	124	4.83	120	5.00
1854	119⅝	5.02	4.14	123¼	4.86	116	5.17
1855	118	5.08	4.18	120	5.00	116	5.17
1856	117¾	5.09	4.11	119	5.04	116½	5.15
1857	114¾	5.22	4.30	118½	5.06	111	5.41
1858	113½	5.29	4.32	116	5.17	111	5.41
1859	109¼	5.49	4.72	111	5.41	107½	5.57
10-yr. av.			4.33				

TABLE 41 (*Continued*)

Year	Boston City 5s: Current Yields				Massachusetts 5s: Current Yields					
	Annual Average		Annual High Price	Annual Low Price	Annual Average		Annual High Price	Yield, %	Annual Low Price	Yield, %
	Price	Yield, %			Price	Yield, %				
1830	102	4.90	102							
1831										
1832	100	5.00		100						
1833	102½	4.87	102½							
1834	102½	4.87	102½							
1835	103¼	4.83	107	99½						
1836	100¾	4.96	106½	95						
1837	101	4.95	102½	99½	98⅝	5.07	103½	4.83	93¾	5.06
1838	99⅞	5.01	102	97¾	101½	4.92	103	4.86	100	5.00
1839	96	5.21	97	95	98¾	5.06	100	5.00	97½	5.13
9-yr. av.		4.95								
1840	98¾	5.07	99½	98	98⅜	5.08	99	5.05	97¾	5.12
1841	100¼	4.99	100½	100	92⅜	5.41	99¼	5.04	86	5.81
1842	101	4.95	102	100	88⅜	5.65	92	5.43	84¾	5.90
1843	102¼	4.88	104½	100	95⅛	5.25	104	4.81	86¼	5.79
1844	103⅜	4.84	105¼	101½	102⅞	4.87	104½	4.79	101¼	4.94
1845	103	4.86	106	100	103½	4.84	104	4.81	103	4.86
1846	101½	4.92	105	98	100	5.00	103	4.86	97	5.14
1847	97¼	5.14	103½	91	94	5.34	98	5.10	90	5.55
1848	94¼	5.31	97½	91	90¾	5.52	93¾	5.35	88¼	5.66
1849	94¼	5.31	96½	92	93½	5.36	95	5.26	92	5.43
10-yr. av.		5.02				5.23				
1850	97½	5.13	100	95	97½	5.13	100	5.00	95	5.26
1851	98½	5.08	100	97	98¾	5.07	100	5.00	97½	5.13
1852	100½	4.98	101	100	99¼	5.04	100½	4.98	98	5.10
1853	100¼	4.99	101½	99	100	5.00	100½	4.98	99½	5.04
1854	97½	5.13	101	94	97¾	5.12	100½	4.98	95	5.26
1855	97	5.16	100	94	97¾	5.12	99	5.05	96½	5.18
1856	98	5.10	99½	96½	97	5.16	99	5.05	95	5.26
1857	95½	5.24	99	92	95½	5.24	99	5.05	92	5.43
1858	98¼	5.09	101½	95	98½	5.08	101	4.95	96	5.20
1859	101	4.95	102	100¼	100¾	4.97	101½	4.92	100	5.00
10-yr. av.		5.09				5.09				

* If redemption in 1833 had been certain, yield at 92¼ was 5.85%.
SOURCE
High and low prices from Martin, *op. cit.*, p. 127.

In 1849 the market began a sharp recovery which continued until 1853–1856. The 6s of 1848–1868 in 1853 sold at an average price of 122. It is small wonder that the twenty-year 6s were regretted by the Treasury and prized by investors.

The panic of 1857 brought failures among banks and railroads. Note circulation, which had more than trebled in fourteen years, declined by a fourth in one year. Treasury surpluses ceased and again there were deficits. These weakened the Treasury position just when the catastrophe of the Civil War was approaching. In 1858 the Treasury, for the first time in ten years, had recourse to the bond market for cash:

1858—$20.0 million "5s of 1858," redeemable in 1874; sold from 102 = 4.81% to 107 = 4.36% to redemption.

During these last few years before the Civil War, a market decline occurred in premium governments, but during the same period the Boston and Massachusetts 5s advanced 3 or 4 points, coming up to a yield of around 5%.

1860–1879.[*]   During the Civil War, when the national debt rose from $60 million to $2,675 million, high-grade bond yields increased sharply, but did not reach the high levels of the War of 1812. The impact of the Civil War on the bond market was probably softened by the wealth and

[*] NOTE: The record of American high-grade bond yields was distorted during the Civil War and its aftermath by two complicating influences:

1. The depreciation of the legal tender paper currency in which all bond quotations were recorded led to an understatement of yields from currency quotations. The value of a gold dollar in terms of paper currency fluctuated as follows: (490)

Year	Low	High	Year	Low	High
1861	$1.00		1870	$1.11	$1.21
1862	1.01	$1.32	1871	1.09	1.15
1863	1.25	1.60	1872	1.09	1.14
1864	1.55	2.33	1873	1.09	1.18
1865	1.36	2.16	1874	1.10	1.13
1866	1.27	1.52	1875	1.12	1.17
1867	1.35	1.43	1876	1.09	1.14
1868	1.34	1.45	1877	1.03	1.07
1869	1.21	1.39	1878	1.00	1.02

Most bond issues were assumed to be payable in coin, but the contract was not always explicit. There were doubts during the war whether the government would, or, in fact, could, ever repay in coin. All bond issues were, in fact, redeemed as agreed, even those paid off during the war. Therefore, issues redeemed during the years of high gold prices received premiums in currency, and those paid off later, when gold was cheaper, received smaller premiums or none. A calculation of yields based on currency prices understates the hoped-for rate of return, but a calculation based on gold prices might overstate the rate of return, because the price of gold at redemption date was unknown and redemption date itself was at the option of the government and, therefore, unknown. Fortunately there were bond issues outstanding that were not redeemable for a great many years and, therefore, provide a better guide to bond yields. All, however, were helped after 1862 by the hope for a gold profit. Therefore, the tables of bond yields for the years 1863 to 1870 do not provide a reliable picture of long-term interest rates.

2. The National Banking Acts of 1863–1865 provided that government bonds could and must be used to secure bank notes. The national banking system eventually created a demand for government bonds which by the mid-1870's put government bond prices up to levels where their yields were far below acceptable rates of long-term interest. Fortunately, however, there is a good history of high-grade municipal bond yields covering the last half of the century and of high-grade corporate bond yields covering the last two or three decades. With their help the level and trends of high-grade long-term interest rates can be traced.

prosperity of the North and by heavy issues of noninterest-bearing legal tender notes.

During 1860 the country expected war. Government bonds declined six points or more in price, but an annual average of New England municipals improved a trifle in price, and an average of railroad bond prices also rose. In September of 1860 the government tried to finance at rates not too much higher than in 1859, but the loan was not well taken:

1860—$7.0 million   "5s of 1860," redeemable in 1871; sold at 101 = 4.92%.

The elections of November, 1860, gave a severe shock to public and private credit. Loan contraction and the withdrawal of Southern balances brought financial panic. (498) The Treasury was forced to issue one-year notes at rates of 10–12%, its highest rate for the war, and perhaps for the century. Additional bids for these notes, ranging from 15 to 36% interest, were rejected. The Treasury 5s of 1858–1874 dropped from 104½ to 89.

By the time of Lincoln's inauguration on March 4, 1861, some measure of confidence was restored to the market. For the financing of the war, Congress approved the flotation of three-year 7.30% notes, or twenty-year bonds at rates not to exceed 7%. Some $123 million of the 7.30% notes were subscribed, largely by banks. When the government attempted to remove the proceeds in specie to the subtreasuries, the banks could not stand the drain, and in December, 1861, they suspended specie payment. The Treasury also floated long-term loans as follows:

1861, February—$18.4 million   "6s of February, 1861," redeemable in 1881; sold at 89 = 6.73%.
1861, July— $50.0 million   "6s of July, 1861," redeemable in 1881; sold at 89¼ = 6.70%.

The year 1861 witnessed the low point of the bond market during the war. The old 6s of 1848–1868 sold down to a low of 86 to yield 6.98% currently. Municipal and railroad bonds also declined sharply in price.

In 1862 the form in which the war was to be financed became clear. Borrowing was to be divided between (a) long-term loans, usually with early redemption privilege; (b) interest-bearing short-term notes, temporary loans, or certificates of deposit; and (c) noninterest-bearing legal tender notes. During the entire war period of 1861–1865 these forms of credit provided funds as follows: (499)

Long-term loans	$1,044 million
Interest-bearing notes	890
Temporary loans	208
Noninterest-bearing notes	481
	$2,623 million

The notes were often made convertible into long-term bonds. Although the notes were not usually payable in specie, the bonds into which they were convertible were considered to be payable in specie. Notes were receivable at the Treasury for taxes and dues, except for customs. Bonds were made exempt from local taxation. The Treasury found that a large volume of outstanding convertible notes facilitated the flotation of bonds, and that the depreciation of the currency at times had the same effect. Most bond issues took the form of 6s redeemable in five years and due in twenty years; these were the famous 5–20s of which several series were floated. They were sold for cash or exchanged for Treasury notes.

At first these 6% 5–20s sold poorly. Outstanding 6s were usually selling well below par. The military news in 1862 was adverse. Out of an authorized amount of $515 million, the Treasury sold only $23.7 million of such bonds in 1862 as follows:

1862–$23.7 million   "6% 5–20s of 1862," redeemable in 1867, due in 1882, exempt from local taxes; sold at about 100 = 6.00%.
   (An additional $491 million of this issue was sold in 1863 and 1864.)

During the crucial year of 1862 the bond market declined no further. In fact the average price of the 6s of 1848–1868 rose three points to 96, New England municipals advanced in price, and railroad bonds advanced sharply. The war no doubt was good for railroad credit. Railroad bonds were not yet high-grade securities.

In 1863 the Congress gave the Treasury great latitude in the sale of bonds or notes. It also passed the National Banking Act, which provided for a large future market for government bonds. There was increasing confidence in victory. Finally a different method of bond selling was adopted. Instead of asking banks for bids, the Treasury employed an experienced investment banker, Jay Cooke, as agent, at a commission of ⅜ of 1%. Cooke employed 2500 subagents.

TABLE 42

Prices and Yields of Long-Term High-Grade Bonds: 1860–1879

Year	U.S. 6s of 1848–1868					U.S. 6s of 1861–1881				
	Annual Average			Annual		Annual Average			Annual	
	Price	Curr. Yield, %	Redemp. Yield, %	High Price	Low Price	Price	Curr. Yield, %	Redemp. Yield, %	High Price	Low Price
1860	102¾	5.86	5.57	109½	96					
1861	93	6.45		100	86	89½	6.70		95¾	83
1862	96	6.25		107⅛	85	97⅝	6.12		107¼	87½
1863	100	6.00	6.00	107	93	101¼	5.92	5.89	110¾	91¾
1864	125⅞	4.75	neg.	145	106¾	110	5.45	5.07	118	102
1865	122½	4.89	neg.	135	110	108	5.56	5.24	112⅜	103½
1866	128	4.69	neg.	142	114	109¼	5.49	5.11	114¾	103¾
1867	132½	4.53	neg.	138	127	110	5.45	5.00	113¼	106½
1868	137	4.38	neg.	142	132	113¼	5.29	4.62	118⅛	108⅜
1869			Paid in gold			118	5.09	4.07	125	111
1870						115⅜	5.20	4.24	118½	112⅜
1871						114¾	5.22	4.18	119⅜	110¼
1872						117½	5.12	3.70	120⅝	114¼
	U.S. Refunding 4½s of 1891									
1873						117¼	5.12	3.51	123⅛	111½
1874						119⅜	5.03	2.91	122⅛	116⅝
1875						122¼	4.90	2.03	126¼	118¼
1876	109⅝	4.10	3.66	111⅜	108	122⅛	4.91	1.40	128¾	115½
1877	106⅛	4.23	3.93	109	103⅛	112⅝	5.32	2.65	115¾	109½
1878	103½	4.35	4.15	105¼	101⅞	108	5.55	3.20	110¾	105⅜
1879	106	4.23	3.87	107⅞	104	105⅞	5.66	2.95	107⅝	104⅛
	U.S. 5s of 1858–1874					U.S. 5s of 1864–1874 (10–40s)				
1860	96⅞	5.16		104½	89					
1861	86	5.81		97	75					
1862	87⅞	5.74		97½	78					
1863	93¼	5.33		101	85½					
1864	103½	4.82	4.56	112	95	98	5.10		103½	92½
1865	98¾	5.06		105	92½	96¼	5.19		102⅞	89¾
1866	99½	5.03		106½	92½	96½	5.17		103¼	90
1867	107	4.67	3.85	112	102	100¾	4.97	4.87	104	97½
1868	115½	4.32	2.22	123	108	105	4.76	4.05	109⅝	100¼
1869	117½	4.25	1.36	123	112	110¾	4.52	2.67	116½	105
1870	109⅝	4.56	2.45	114	105¼	109¼	4.56	2.55	114	104¾
1871	107½	4.64	2.40	110	105	110	4.54	1.55	113¼	106¾
1872			Paid in gold, 1874			110⅝	4.53	neg.	113⅝	107⅝
1873						110½	4.53	neg.	116⅛	105
1874						113¾	4.40	neg.	116⅜	111¼
1875						116¾	4.28	neg.	119¾	113¾
1876						116½	4.29	neg.	121¾	111½

TABLE 42 (*Continued*)

Year	U.S. Refunding 4s of 1907					U.S. 5s of 1864–1874 (10–40s)				
	Annual Average			Annual		Annual Average			Annual	
	Price	Curr. Yield, %	Redemp. Yield, %	High Price	Low Price	Price	Curr. Yield, %	Redemp. Yield, %	High Price	Low Price
1877	103½	3.87	3.81	106	101	111	4.51	neg.	114⅞	107⅜
1878	101¼	3.95	3.97	102¾	99¾	106¾	4.70	neg.	109⅜	103⅞
1879	101⅝	3.94	3.96	104¼	99	104⅛	4.80	neg. Re-deemed	108⅜	100

Year	New England Municipal Bond Yields			Adjusted Average of Higher-Grade Railroad Bond Yields		
	Annual Average, %	Low Quarter, %	High Quarter, %	Annual Average, %	Low Month, %	High Month, %
1860	4.79	4.77	4.81	6.04	5.81	6.44
1861	5.04	4.88	5.27	6.33	6.10	6.49
1862	4.91	4.51	5.23	5.52	4.94	6.14
1863	4.37	4.20	4.46	4.77	4.44	5.03
1864	4.80	4.67	5.06	4.83	4.36	5.19
1865	5.51	5.15	5.74	6.02	5.40	6.41
1866	5.50	5.23	5.75	6.37	6.16	6.61
1867	5.34	5.25	5.41	6.32	6.25	6.41
1868	5.28	5.24	5.37	6.26	6.17	6.44
1869	5.37	5.31	5.46	6.55	6.42	6.72
10-yr. av.	5.10			5.90		
1870	5.44	5.40	5.51	6.41	6.30	6.65
1871	5.32	5.24	5.43	6.35	6.25	6.42
1872	5.36	5.31	5.46	6.18	6.07	6.26
1873	5.58	5.51	5.67	6.20	6.06	6.50
1874	5.47	5.41	5.64	5.91	5.70	6.08
1875	5.07	4.87	5.33	5.45	5.30	5.63
1876	4.59	4.47	4.77	5.16	5.09	5.24
1877	4.45	4.38	4.52	5.18	5.11	5.26
1878	4.34	4.30	4.38	5.11	5.03	5.16
1879	4.22	4.15	4.28	4.77	4.66	4.92
10-yr. av.	4.98			5.67		

Sources

For government quotations, *The Financial Review Annual*, 1921, Wm. B. Dana Co., pp. 221–232.

New England municipal and high-grade railroad bond averages from Frederick R. Macaulay, *The Movements of Interest Rates, Bond Yields and Stock Prices*, New York, 1938, National Bureau of Economic Research, pp. A142ff., A174ff.

In 1863 greenback prices in all departments of the bond market improved substantially. The year 1864 saw gold rise to its wartime high of $2.33 in greenbacks. As a consequence the greenback prices of gold bonds of short redemption date rose to large premiums, although the redemption gold price and redemption policy were unknown. As an example, the 6s of 1848–1868 rose from a low of 93 in 1863 to a high of 145 in 1864. These bonds were in fact redeemed in 1869 in gold, but in gold worth about $1.25 in greenbacks, not $2.33.

Longer-term government bond prices also rose to premiums in 1864. The municipal and railroad bond average prices declined in sharp contrast to the speculative rise in government bond prices.

In 1864, although the war was approaching its end, it had only been half financed. The Treasury was able to sell a large volume of bonds, but not at such favorable terms as the market price of its seasoned issues might suggest. Early in the year another $100 million of the 5–20s of 1862 were sold and then a new longer issue was sold as follows:

1864–$75 million   "6s of 1863," redeemable in 1881, tax-exempt; sold at 104.45 = 5.60%.

The Treasury soon made an attempt to sell 5s, which met with a lukewarm reception. In order to attract investors to the lower rate the Treasury extended the term to redemption from five to ten years and the maturity from twenty to forty years:

1864–$73 million   "5%, 10–40s of 1864," redeemable 1874, due in 1904, tax-exempt; sold at 100 = 5%.

(In 1865 $123 million more were sold at prices up to 107 = 4.62%.)

In 1865, with peace and victory, the gold price declined to as low as $1.36. The prices of bonds of all kinds also declined. Governments averaged 2–5 points lower. Railroad bonds fell precipitately, the average yield moving from 4.83% in 1864 to 6.02% in 1865. Railroad bonds did not recover until 1879; the end of wartime prosperity had an adverse effect on railroad credit. In 1865 the Treasury returned to a 6% coupon on its long-term bonds and promoted a vigorous program of debt funding. New issues sold in 1865–1866 were:

1865   –$125 million   "6% 5–20s of 1864," redeemable in 1869, due in 1884, tax-exempt; sold at 102½ average price = 5.42% to redemption.

1865–66–$203 million   "6% 5–20s of 1865," redeemable in 1870, due in 1885, tax-exempt; sold at 102½ average price = 5.42% to redemption.

At this time a determined effort was begun to contract the currency and return to a gold standard. Political opposition, postwar economic disturbances and the great depression of 1873–1877 postponed the resumption of specie payments until 1879. Nevertheless, success was in sight and the gold premium declined almost steadily from 1866. Reorganization of the currency and funding of the debt were both greatly facilitated by the growth of the new national banking system.

During the years 1866–1870 the bond market as a whole remained depressed. Outstanding governments, however, rose steadily in price, as they were attractive to the new national banks. The early government refunding offerings were generally at yields well above market yields as follows:

1867–1868—$333 million   "Consol 6s of 1865," redeemable in 1870, due in 1885; sold at $103\frac{5}{8}$ = 5.16% to redemption.
1868–1869—$379 million   "Consol 6s of 1867," redeemable in 1872, due in 1887; sold at $101\frac{5}{8}$ = 5.61% to redemption.
1869— $ 42 million   "Consol 6s of 1868," redeemable in 1873, due in 1888; sold at $100\frac{1}{2}$ = 5.87% to redemption.

The bond market of the 1870's can be divided into two parts: (a) the first four years, when all bond prices except governments remained depressed, and (b) the next six years, when most bond prices rose. During this decade the Treasury made important progress in refunding its 6% issues at lower rates. European government bond yields were then in the range of 3–4%; it was felt that our 6% was discreditable and operated unfavorably on industrial and real estate investment. The Refunding Act of 1870 authorized 5% bonds redeemable in 10 years, $4\frac{1}{2}$% bonds redeemable in fifteen years, and 4% bonds redeemable in 30 years, all payable in coin and exempt from national and local taxes, none to be sold for less than 100 in gold. The longer the term to possible redemption the lower was the rate of interest; this was in keeping with investor preference at the time. In this way long-term issues were created which were difficult to retire out of the large surpluses soon to accrue to the Treasury. These refunding bonds eventually sold up to premiums of over 25%. Repayment was promised in "coin" and not in gold, which opened the way for the silver controversy of the last decades of the century.

The refunding program was delayed by the economic disturbances following the panic of 1873. Only the 5% issue was floated before 1877. This was successfully offered in exchange for redeemable 6s:

1871–1876—$517 million   "5s of 1881," redeemable in 1881; sold at 100 = 5%.

After 1874 all departments of the bond market rose in a prolonged advance which was to last for twenty-five years. Between 1874 and 1879 the New England municipal yield average moved from 5.64 to 4.15% and the railroad bond yield average from 5.70 to 4.66%. The United States 6s of 1861–1881 often sold at yields of 1–2% to redemption because of the circulation privilege. In 1876 the Treasury offered its next great refunding issue:

1876–1878—$250 million   "4½s of 1891," redeemable in 1891, tax-exempt; sold at 100 = 4.50%.

As early as 1876 these bonds sold as high as 111⅜ and averaged 109⅝, to yield 4.10% current and 3.66% to earliest redemption.

In 1878–1879 the gold premium vanished and specie payments were resumed. The Treasury offered its last great postwar refunding loan:

1878–1880—$739 million   "4s of 1907," redeemable in 1907, tax-exempt; sold at 100 = 4%.

Thereafter until 1917 most new Treasury issues were to be 2s or 3s bought to secure national bank notes.

1880–1900. During the last two decades of the nineteenth century, long-term high-grade bond yields in the United States declined almost steadily. The nation entered its first period of low long-term interest rates. They reached a range of 3–3½% for best long corporate and mu-

NOTE: The Confederate States (500) financed 60% of their war expenditures by paper money, 5% by taxation, and 30% by sales of bonds. In 1861 an issue of 8% long-term bonds was floated at 100 and in 1862 an issue of 6% bonds was floated, redeemable at the option of the holders. In 1863 the privilege of using paper currency to buy bonds was limited so that bonds purchased with certain notes before April 20 would yield 8%; thereafter until August, 7%; thereafter nothing. Later note issues were limited to purchase of 7% or 6% or 4% bond issues. In 1864 there was a forced conversion of currency into 4% bonds and a tax of 10% a month on large bills that had not been converted. Some market prices of the 8% Confederate bond issue of 1861 in terms of paper currency reflect the depreciation of the currency as follows:

December 1861	100
1862	103–104
1863	109–200
1864	130–172

In 1863 an issue of "Cotton Loan" 6s was floated at home and abroad, payable in cotton at 8 pence a pound.

Specie prices of Confederate 8s were quoted as low as 10 in 1863 and 5 in 1864–1865; subsequently they became valueless.

nicipal bonds at the same time that yields in most European nations were at even lower levels. Holland had first experienced such low rates in the seventeenth century, England in the early eighteenth century, and Europe generally in the mid-nineteenth century. Now "Dutch finance" crossed the Atlantic.

The United States, with the Civil War behind it, was approaching the status of a great financial power in its own right. It no longer had to pay high interest rates for foreign capital. Commodity prices were falling here, as they were in Europe, and there was an enormous growth of capital investment. A de facto gold standard was established. While short-term American interest rates continued their wild gyrations, occasionally soaring to high levels such as 186% in 1899, and declining to low levels such as 1% in the same year, long-term prime bond yields became stable and low in the European manner.

This well-defined decline in bond yields dates from 1873–1875. The New England municipal average stood at 5.67% in 1873, at 4.15% in 1879, at 3.35% in 1889, and at a low of 3.07% in 1899. The railroad average stood at 6.50% high in 1873, at 4.66% in 1879—still well above municipal yields—3.48% by 1889—now close to municipal yields and hence thoroughly respectable—and as low as 3.07% in 1899.

This twenty-five-year bull bond market brought impressive capital gains only to those who were lucky enough to hold truly long-term bonds of high quality. High-coupon callable governments had been called away. Many railroad bonds had defaulted and many others had matured. Only a few high-grade bond issues had long enough redemption terms to permit the full benefit to investors from the dramatic decline in yields. Some examples of the change in yields and of market appreciation of corporate bonds are shown in the accompanying table:

Issues	1870–1873	1899
Lowest yielding issues:		
Lehigh Valley 1st 6s–1898	93 = 6.58%	—
N. Y. Central 1st $3\frac{1}{2}$s–1997	—	$111\frac{1}{2}$ = 3.12%
Morris & Essex 7s–1914	97 = 7.42	142 = 3.41
Lehigh Valley 2nd 7s–1910	98 = 7.08	130 = 3.70
Chicago & Northwest 7s–1915	83 = 8.57	145 = 3.34

Such declines in yield would have created capital gains of 100% or more if they had applied to perpetual low-coupon bonds. In Europe just such capital gains had accrued to perceptive investors who had insisted on discount bonds and had avoided maturity or redemption privileges. Almost all American owners of high-coupon Civil War governments had long since lost their bonds through redemption. Most state, city, and corporate bonds had been redeemable or had had medium maturity. The nominal rates quoted in the municipal markets of the 1870's were usually 5s, 6s, and 7s, but by 1900 they were 3s and 4s.

Investors at this time began to seek long-term noncallable bonds. It was toward the turn of the century that many of today's 100-year maturity non-callable railroad bond issues were floated.

During the two decades 1880–1900 very high premiums for government bonds were the rule. The national debt was reduced from $1,919 million in 1880 to $838 million in 1893. The national banks bought bonds to secure circulation. The new 4½s of 1891, floated in 1877–1879 at 100, rose to an average price of 114¾ by 1882, where their yield was only 2.65% to redemption; there was no gold premium and redemption seemed assured. In 1887 they sold at 118½ high to yield nothing to redemption. It was a scarcity market aggravated by huge Treasury surpluses, some of which were used to buy in Treasury bonds at high premiums.

During this period almost all of the high-coupon government debt was redeemed and new issues were floated to refund a part of it as follows:

1881–$178 million　"Continued 3½s," redeemable at pleasure of the United States, tax-exempt; sold at 100 = 3.50%.

1882–$305 million　"3s of 1882," redeemable when no issues with higher rates were outstanding, exempt from local taxes; sold at 100 = 3%.

1891–$ 25 million　"Funded 2s," redeemable at pleasure of the United States, tax-exempt; sold at 100 = 2%.

Monetary policy was still a political issue. Tariff legislation, commercial disturbances here and abroad, and fear of silver legislation, led after 1891 to a loss of gold. The panic of 1893 created a heavy Treasury deficit in 1894. The government responded by reaffirming the gold standard, repealing silver purchase legislation, and selling new bonds to finance the purchase of gold. As Congress would not authorize a new bond issue, the Treasury was forced to finance under old authorizations at high nominal rates as follows:

1894–　　　$100 million　"5s of 1904," redeemable in 1904, tax-exempt; sold at 117.22 = 2.98% to redemption.

1895–1896–$162 million　"4s of 1925," redeemable in 1925, tax-exempt; sold at 104½ = 3.75% to 111.17 = 3.52%.

TABLE 43

Prices and Yields of Long-Term High-Grade Bonds: 1880–1900

Year	U.S. Refunding 4½s of 1891					U.S. Refunding 4s of 1907				
	Annual Average			Annual		Annual Average			Annual	
	Price	Curr. Yield, %	Redemp. Yield, %	High Price	Low Price	Price	Curr. Yield, %	Redemp. Yield, %	High Price	Low Price
1880	109½	4.11	3.45	112⅝	106⅜	106¼	3.76	3.63	113⅝	103
1881	113⅞	3.96	2.90	116½	111⅛	115⅜	3.46	3.13	118⅝	112⅜
1882	114¾	3.93	2.65	116½	112⅞	119¼	3.35	2.91	121¾	117¼
1883	113⅝	3.97	2.60	115	112¼	119⅞	3.32	2.88	125⅛	118½
1884	112½	4.00	2.55	114⅞	110	121½	3.29	2.76	124⅞	118½
1885	112¾	3.99	2.22	113½	112	122¼	3.17	2.68	124⅜	121½
1886	112	4.02	1.95	114	109⅞	126¼	3.16	2.43	129⅜	123
1887	113¼	3.98	1.10	118½	108	127⅛	3.14	2.32	129⅝	124½
1888	107⅞	4.17	1.80	109⅜	106⅜	127¾	3.13	2.27	130	123¾
1889	106⅞	4.22	1.04	109	104¾	127⅞	3.14	2.13	129⅞	126¼
		Paid in 1891–1892								
	U.S. Funded 2s (Redeemable at pleasure of U.S.)									
1890						122¾	3.26	2.37	126½	121½
1891						118½	3.38	2.58	122	116
1892						115⅝	3.46	2.73	118⅛	114
1893	97½	2.05		99¾	95¼	111⅞	3.56	2.96	115	108
1894						114	3.51	2.72	116	112½
1895	96¾	2.07		97	96½	112	3.56	2.82	113½	110
1896	93½	2.14		96	91	108¾	3.78	3.06	112½	106
1897	98⅜	2.03		98½	98¼	112⅝	3.54	2.57	115	111⅜
1898	98¾	2.02		99½	98	111½	3.58	2.50	114¾	107
1899	100½	1.98		102	99	113	3.54	2.22	115½	112
1900	100⅜	1.98		100½	100¼	115⅛	3.47	1.70	118½	114

Year	New England Municipal Bond Yields			Adjusted Average of High-Grade Railroad Bond Yields		
	Annual Average, %	Low Quarter, %	High Quarter, %	Annual Average, %	Low Month, %	High Month, %
1880	4.02	3.94	4.20	4.46	4.18	4.64
1881	3.70	3.65	3.84	4.13	4.04	4.22
1882	3.62	3.60	3.70	4.20	4.16	4.23
1883	3.63	3.62	3.67	4.23	4.18	4.25
1884	3.62	3.59	3.65	4.15	4.06	4.25
1885	3.52	3.46	3.60	3.98	3.83	4.11
1886	3.37	3.36	3.42	3.81	3.64	3.77
1887	3.52	3.41	3.75	3.80	3.70	3.85
1888	3.67	3.61	3.74	3.69	3.64	3.74
1889	3.45	3.35	3.59	3.51	3.48	3.60
10-yr. av.	3.60			4.00		
1890	3.42	3.34	3.54	3.68	3.59	3.83
1891	3.62	3.59	3.67	3.84	3.75	3.90
1892	3.60	3.58	3.66	3.72	3.68	3.75
1893	3.75	3.61	3.89	3.73	3.70	4.05
1894	3.70	3.65	3.75	3.62	3.51	3.73
1895	3.46	3.46	3.47	3.46	3.39	3.57
1896	3.60	3.43	3.72	3.50	3.44	3.69
1897	3.40	3.35	3.43	3.33	3.25	3.41
1898	3.35	3.19	3.61	3.26	3.17	3.38
1899	3.10	3.07	3.14	3.13	3.07	3.23
10-yr. av.	3.50			3.53		
1900	3.15			3.18	3.15	3.20

Sources

For government quotations, *The Financial Review Annual*, *op. cit.*, pp. 221–232.

New England municipal and high-grade railroad bond averages from Macaulay, *op. cit.*, pp. A142ff., A174ff.

The Spanish American War of 1898 resulted in another bond issue but did not interrupt the advance of the bond market. A $200 million issue of 3s brought subscriptions of $1,400 million from 320,000 subscribers:

1898—$198 million "3s of 1908," redeemable in 1908, due in 1918; sold at 100 = 3%.

SHORT-TERM INTEREST RATES

Nowhere in this history is the sharp distinction between short-term market rates of interest and long-term bond yields more clearly illustrated than in the United States of the nineteenth century. Good commercial paper fluctuated from 3½ up to 36% early in the century; and call money, from ½ to 186% or higher late in the century. This range was wider even than that reported in medieval Antwerp in the fifteenth and sixteenth centuries. It was far wider than the range of American bond yields. It was a wider range than can be explained merely by the youth of the country. Primitive nations often had high rates, but reported no such volatility on best credits. These high rates were not consistent with the 6% American tradition.

These high short-term interest rates can be explained in part, at least, by the predicament of a financial economy which lacked an organized money market. Most borrowers depended on their personal banking connections and did not pay these high rates. The stranger who sought accommodation in the open market when neighbors were hard pressed was mercilessly made to pay for money to tide him over for a few days.

Data on short-term American interest rates are infrequent early in the century. Table 44 below presents a series on New England commercial paper from 1831 to 1856 and thereafter a series on New York City choice commercial paper. Both are in terms of annual highs, lows, and averages. The table also presents a series on call money rates on the New York Stock Exchange from 1857 in terms of monthly averages. When they are available, the extreme high and low hourly quotations on call money are added to the monthly average rates. Annual averages of both series are pictured in Chart 33. The table also includes the rate paid to regular depositors by the Bowery Savings Bank of New York from 1835.

The pattern of short-term rates from 1830, as suggested by the decennial averages in Chart 30 and by the annual averages in Chart 33, was different from the pattern of long-term bond yields. The Civil War did not bring a peak in these short rates. Financial panics were invariably marked by peak short rates. These peaks became successively lower.

TABLE 44

SHORT-TERM AMERICAN INTEREST RATES: NINETEENTH CENTURY

Year	Commercial Paper			Call Money				Savings Bank Rate: Regular Deposits
	Annual Average	Low	High	Annual Average	Monthly Average		Extreme Quotations	
					Low	High		
1819			36.00					
1830								
1831	6.12	5.50	7.00					
1832	6.25	6.00	7.00					
1833	7.83	5.50	15.00					
1834	14.70	8.00	24.00					
1835	7.00	5.00	10.00					5.00
1836	18.00	10.00	36.00					5.00
1837	14.25	6.00	32.00					5.00
1838	9.04	6.00	18.00					5.00
1839	12.58	6.00	36.00					
9-yr. av.	10.64							
1840	7.75	5.00	12.00					5.00
1841	6.80	6.00	12.00					5.00
1842	8.08	6.00	12.00					5.00
1843	4.41	3.50	6.00					5.00
1844	4.87	4.00	5.50					5.00
1845	4.71	5.00	6.00					5.00
1846	8.33	6.00	12.00					5.00
1847	9.59	6.00	18.00					5.00
1848	15.10	12.00	18.00					5.00
1849	10.25	7.00	15.00					6.00
10-yr. av.	7.99							
1850	8.04	6.50	10.50					6.00
1851	9.66	6.00	16.00					6.00
1852	6.33	5.50	9.00					5.00
1853	10.25	6.00	18.00					5.00
1854	10.37	7.00	18.00					5.00

TABLE 44 (*Continued*)

Year	Commercial Paper			Call Money					Savings Bank Rate: Regular Deposits
	Annual Average	Low	High	Annual Average	Monthly Average		Extreme Quotations		
					Low	High			
1855	8.92	6.00	15.00						5.00
1856	8.83	7.00	12.00						5.00
1857	11.56	7.90	24.00	9.33	6.60	18.00			5.00
1858	4.81	3.64	7.50	4.15	3.50	6.50			5.00
1859	6.14	4.62	7.04	5.43	4.31	6.38			5.00
10-yr. av.	8.49			6.30 3-yr. av.					
1860	7.31	5.40	12.90	5.97	4.75	7.25			5.00
1861	6.70	5.50	8.00	5.75	4.50	6.50			5.00
1862	5.32	4.50	6.30	5.23	4.00	6.50			5.00
1863	5.65	5.20	6.80	6.19	5.20	7.00			5.00
1864	7.36	5.60	9.20	6.58	5.60	7.00			5.00
1865	7.77	6.70	9.00	6.17	4.90	7.00			5.00
1866	6.33	5.25	7.37	5.04	4.13	6.38	3.70	6.50	5.00
1867	7.32	6.50	8.56	6.25	4.25	10.76		11.45	6.00
1868	7.28	5.72	10.00	7.51	3.50	17.03		35.00	6.00
1869	9.66	7.69	11.94	10.21	5.63	23.67		30.10	6.00
10-yr av.	7.07			6.50					
1870	7.23	5.46	9.00	5.70	4.20	11.45	4.00	18.40	6.00
1871	6.98	4.90	10.03	5.56	2.80	12.36	2.55	18.15	6.00
1872	8.63	6.00	11.62	8.34	3.65	20.06		58.65	6.00
1873	10.27	6.44	16.50	14.25	3.80	61.23		360.00	6.00
1874	5.98	5.44	7.44	3.44	2.50	5.50	2.00		6.00
1875	5.44	4.31	6.61	3.11	2.19	5.17	1.00	6.00	6.00
1876	5.13	3.60	6.44	3.34	1.70	5.83	1.00	7.50	6.00
1877	5.01	4.00	7.25	3.88	1.75	6.10	1.00	8.65	6.00
1878	4.82	3.60	5.85	4.23	1.75	9.76	1.00		5.00
1879	5.14	3.81	6.25	5.46	2.95	12.34	1.50	45.80	5.00
10-yr. av.	6.46			5.73					

TABLE 44 (*Continued*)

| Year | Commercial Paper | | | Call Money | | | | | Savings Bank Rate: Regular Deposits |
| | Annual Average | Low | High | Annual Average | Monthly Average | | Extreme Quotations | | |
					Low	High			
1880	5.23	4.44	6.00	4.86	2.50	11.20	1.50	22.00	5.00
1881	5.36	3.50	6.30	5.73	3.15	15.91	2.00	50.12	4.00
1882	5.64	4.62	6.75	4.70	3.00	7.80	1.50	30.00	4.00
1883	5.62	4.78	6.38	3.72	2.00	10.38	1.00	25.00	4.00
1884	5.21	4.62	5.95	3.03	1.44	14.98	0.50	1080.00	4.00
1885	4.05	3.50	4.69	1.68	1.19	2.75	0.50	10.00	4.00
1886	4.77	3.85	6.06	4.02	2.06	8.70	1.00	28.69	4.00
1887	5.73	4.81	6.94	5.01	3.56	7.20	1.00	33.26	4.00
1888	4.91	4.08	5.60	2.52	1.44	4.13	1.00	8.00	4.00
1889	4.85	3.85	6.09	4.50	2.31	8.30	1.00	30.00	4.00
10-yr. av.	5.14			3.98					
1890	5.62	5.00	7.33	5.84	4.25	11.63	2.00	186.00	4.00
1891	5.46	4.83	5.83	3.42	2.13	4.50	1.00	25.00	4.00
1892	4.10	2.95	5.50	3.08	1.40	6.81	1.00	40.00	4.00
1893	6.78	3.66	10.88	4.58	1.16	8.88	0.75	74.00	4.00
1894	3.04	2.76	3.48	1.07	1.00	1.44	0.50	3.00	4.00
1895	2.83	2.62	4.75	1.88	1.03	4.56	0.75	100.00	4.00
1896	5.82	3.73	8.36	4.28	1.94	11.13	1.00	127.00	4.00
1897	3.50	3.00	4.19	1.77	1.19	2.92	1.00	5.50	4.00
1898	3.83	3.12	5.75	2.17	1.25	2.97	1.00	6.00	4.00
1899	4.15	2.90	5.88	5.08	2.47	11.13	1.00	186.00	3.50
10-yr. av.	4.51			3.32					
1900	4.38	3.68	5.05	2.94	1.30	5.13	1.00	25.00	3.50

SOURCES

Commercial paper: 1830–1857, Bigelow's Boston first class 3–6 mos., quoted by Macaulay, *op. cit.,* p. A248; from 1857, New York City choice 60–90-day monthly averages from Macaulay, *op. cit.,* p. A142ff.

Call money: New York Stock Exchange, high and low monthly averages from Macaulay, *op. cit.,* p. A142. Other quotations are extremes without uniform quality standards quoted from various sources, including *The Financial Review Yearbook, op. cit.;* Owens and Hardy, *Interest Rates and Stock Speculation,* Washington, 1930, p. 145; Martin, *op. cit.;* National Monetary Commission, Vol. XXI, *op. cit.,* pp. 119–138; Wright, *op. cit.,* pp. 472, 872.

Savings bank rate from the records of the Bowery Savings Bank of New York City.

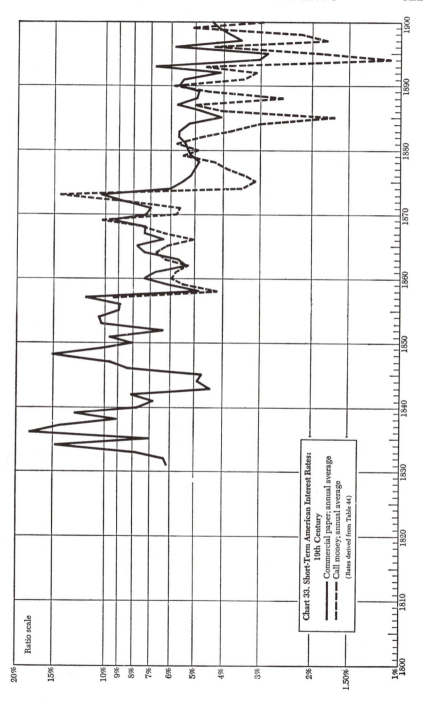

Chart 33. Short-Term American Interest Rates:
19th Century
—— Commercial paper; annual average
----- Call money; annual average
(Rates derived from Table 44)

Short-term rates had been averaging sharply lower for several decades before the 1870's, when long-term yields began their decisive decline.

Decennial averages of annual averages of these short-term rates were as follows:

Years	Commercial Paper	Call Money
1831–1839	10.64 (9 yrs.)	
1840–1849	7.99	
1850–1859	8.49	
1860–1869	7.07	6.50
1870–1879	6.46	5.73
1880–1889	5.14	3.98
1890–1899	4.51	3.32

This table reveals a tendency for short rates to decline at least from the 1830's. The decline was steady from the 1850's to the end of the century. It shows that call money averaged well below commercial paper in spite of occasionally much higher call money rates.

The decennial averages in Chart 30 indicate that short-term rates as measured by commercial paper averaged far above prime long-term bond yields throughout the nineteenth century. The gap tended to narrow in the 1850's and 1860's. Such averaging, although essential to establish usual relationships and trends, conceals an important characteristic of the market—the relative stability of long rates as contrasted with the extreme volatility of short rates, which ranged far above and far below long rates. This contrast was noted for Britain. It was far more extreme in the United States.

In Europe during the easy-money decades at the close of the nineteenth century, there was in many countries a prolonged period when short rates averaged below long rates. In the United States, although long prime bond yields achieved lows close to 3% and averaged 3½% for one decade, short rates did not hold at levels below long rates for any length of time and, indeed, averaged much higher. It was not until the organization of a central bank and a modern money market that low bond yields in the United States were regularly accompanied by even lower short-term money market rates of interest.

RISK RATES AND ECCENTRIC LOCAL RATES

The American frontier of the nineteenth century provided a colorful interest-rate history. The data are haphazard and disorganized and insufficient to permit a chronological and geographical presentation. The range is enormous; the relevancy to the main stream of interest rate history is slight. Some samples are provided by way of contrast and to illustrate once again the narrowness of the concept of market rates of interest on prime credits.

The Western frontier was not inhibited, as the early American colonies seem to have been, by the English tradition of moderate interest rates or by the 6% convention brought to New England by its early settlers. The West did not enjoy the access to the London money market that colonial merchants and planters maintained; in fact, it enjoyed only limited access to eastern American money markets. Money was scarce, opportunity was great, and local debtors paid accordingly.

California, as usual, set some records which are hard to duplicate elsewhere. The transition from Mexican to American ownership was complicated by the economic effects of the gold rush. After 1849 the price of California cattle multiplied and then collapsed. The Mexican owners of the great cattle ranches of southern California found themselves fabulously wealthy, borrowed freely by mortgaging their ranches, and with the collapse they generally lost their ranches. The lenders were often French, Swiss, German, and Yankee speculators. The following examples may be cited: (501)

In 1850 in San Diego, D. J. Bandini borrowed $10,000 at 4% a month, or 48% a year.

Judge B. D. Hayes, of southern California, paid 60% a year on a $500 note.

In 1850, Joaqim Ruiz mortgaged his 8100 acres in southern California to Abel Stearns for $600 at 60% a year. (502)

In 1852, D. Valenzuela defaulted on two mortgages totaling $2200 on which interest had accrued at 96% a year.

In 1854, J. R. Yarba mortgaged 17,000 acres in southern California for $5500 at 60% annual interest.

In 1854, José Sepulveda owed $7000 at rates varying between 48 and 84% a year.

In 1859, San Francisco hypothecated local government revenues for a loan of $250,000 at 24% a year.

In 1859, the city of Los Angeles sold 20-year public improvement bonds which paid 1% a month, or 12% a year.

In 1861, J. Verdigo mortgaged his ranch for $3445 at 3% a month, which after nine years raised his debt to $58,750. He lost the ranch.

From 1848 until 1868, commercial interest rates in California were quoted as high as 120% a year, but usually stood at 24–36% a year.

In 1860, savings banks in California paid 15% interest. (503)

By 1877 southern California mortgage rates had declined, and the normal rate was down to 12% a year. (502)

In Milwaukee during the 1840's a moderate rate of interest for bank loans and personal loans was 10–12% per annum. (504) A business loan to one prominent enterprise is reported there at 10% in 1859 and a substantial bank loan at 10% in 1871. By 1873–1893 such rates were quoted at 7–10% per annum.

In Indiana there was no legal limit to the rate of interest until 1833. The common rate by contract is quoted at about 50% per annum during the early decades of the century. (505)

In Utah in the 1850's and 1860's Brigham Young set the rate of interest paid by the Zion's Savings and Trust Company at 10%.

In 1879 Wyoming banks customarily charged 12% a year for mortgages and for ordinary trade credit; in fact, this was sometimes deducted in advance. (506) Between 1885 and 1890, however, the Stock Growers National Bank of Cheyenne charged an average of only 9% on loans to a prominent rancher. (507) At about this period the city of Sedalia, Missouri, floated a bond issue at 10%. (508)

In the 1880's, in Colorado, 12% was a usual rate for a bank to charge. (509) In 1879, a Montana banker pointed out that "18% was the lowest rate known in Montana." By 1884 he said that his rates were down to 12–15% and the longest term was six months. (510)

The early financial history of several states was in sharp contrast to the dull stability that has been recorded for obligations of the state of Massachusetts. When several states that had guaranteed railroad and other private obligations in the 1840's defaulted, this affected the credit of all states. Examples of large fluctuations are:

Illinois 6s declined from 62½ to 14½ in 1841–1842; the yields rose from 9.60 to 41.0% current. They recovered in 1843 to 45, and by 1853 they were up to 92½, or 6.49%, an appreciation from their lows of 550% odd.

Indiana 5s declined from 73 in 1841 to 16½ in 1842 (6.85% and 31%), thus maintaining a market premium over Illinois bonds. They recovered to a price of 102 in 1852.

Kentucky 6s during the difficult years of the 1840's never sold below 72, or 8.35%, and after 1845 generally sold at premiums that ran up to 113, to yield 5.30%. Sometimes they sold to yield less than bonds of the state of Massachusetts.

Ohio 6s of 1860 declined from 97 to 48½ in 1842, to yield 12.3% current; they recovered to 101½ in the following year.

Pennsylvania 5s declined to 40 in 1842, to yield 12½%; they recovered
to 80 in 1844.

Virginia 6s, as might be expected, declined sharply during the Civil
War. They dipped from 95 in 1860 to 36 in 1861, to yield 16⅔%,
and recovered to 65½ in 1862 and 75 in 1863. In the postwar period, however, they declined to 41 in 1867, 28 in 1874, and 22 in
1876.

California 7s benefited from the Civil War premium on gold. They
rose from a low of 71½, or 9.80% current in 1861, to 116½ high in
1862 and 167 high in 1864. California had gold and paid in gold.
By 1873 these bonds were back to 101.

By the 1890's the market for state and city securities had become a
relatively humdrum affair. State of Maine 3s of 1921 fluctuated between
93 and 101 during the years 1891–1897. Massachusetts 3s of 1923 at the
same time sold in a range of 95–100½, and Connecticut 3½s of 1903
sold in a range of 99–103¼. Bonds with high nominal rates commanded
big premiums: Springfield Water 7s of 1903 sold at 137 in 1890, a yield
of 3.45% to maturity. Southern bonds yielded more: in 1890 Alabama 4s

		Yield, %
1849	Federal bonds	5.16
	Massachusetts bonds	5.31
	N.Y. & Erie 1st 7s of 1868, high price	6.60
	N.Y. & Erie 2nd 7s of 1859, low price	9.60
1854	Federal bonds	4.11
	Massachusetts bonds	5.10
	N.Y. Central 6s of 1883, low price	7.54
	Michigan Central 8s of 1882 low price	8.72
1857	Federal Bonds	4.30
	New England municipals	5.30
	Higher-grade railroad average	6.97
	N.Y. Central 6s of 1883, low price	9.85
	Michigan Central 8s of 1882, low price	11.60
1875	New England municipals	5.33
	Higher-grade railroad average	5.45
	N.Y. & Erie 1st 7s of 1897, high price	6.57
	Chicago & Northwest 7s of 1915, low price	7.97
1890	New England municipals	3.34
	High-grade railroad average	3.68
	Pennsylvania R.R. 6s of 1910, low price	3.77
	Nashville, Chattanooga & St. Louis 7s of 1913, low price	5.22
	Oregon Short Line 6s of 1922, low price	6.35

of 1920 fluctuated between 93 and 104¾, and North Carolina 4s of 1910 between 95¾ and 103.

A few railroad bonds began to be quoted in the 1840's. At first their maturity was usually relatively short—ten or twenty years. Later in the century maturity ran out to fifty years, and by the end of the century 100 years became popular. A few examples, as shown in the table on page 325, confined to respectable credits and compared with high-grade bond yields will indicate the scope of the market.

PART FOUR

Europe and North America Since 1900

This history of interest rates now reviews our own century. From 1900 to 1989, we find the lowest interest rates and the highest interest rates in modern history for prime marketable credit instruments in the leading financial centers. The peak bond yields of the seventeenth, eighteenth, and nineteenth centuries did not even come near the peak yields of the twentieth century. The lowest rates of the twentieth century were likewise well below the earlier low rates.

It might have been supposed that the spectacular growth of the credit markets in the United States and elsewhere and the simultaneous improvement in market technology and economic know-how would have led to a more stable range of interest rates. Quite the opposite occurred. The larger, more efficient credit markets served the free world's economies well for many decades, but at length their seeming ability to provide unlimited sums on request was overexploited. The very efficiency of the credit markets served to finance an unprecedented inflation, which in former times would have been checked earlier by the imperfections of the credit markets themselves. Politicians generally could not curb the pressures for expansion and social expenditures. Ultimately only the discipline of the marketplace, in the form of punitive interest rates, checked the spiraling inflation.

It has often been said that twentieth-century technological progress has not been matched by political progress. Until the 1970's it was certainly not matched by financial novelties. During the seventeenth, eighteenth, and nineteenth centuries the medieval census annuity, the deposit, the special partnership, and the bill of exchange were developed into modern credit instruments convenient alike to debtor and to creditor, to government, to entrepreneur, and to investor and were adaptable to purposes of war and to purposes of peace. The first half of the twentieth century witnessed few fundamental changes in credit forms. It did, however, give rise to development of a vast structure of investing institutions capable of mobilizing the savings of individuals and business firms. It also began to develop an efficient international market structure capable of financing the largest worldwide enterprises. After the long decline in interest rates during the Middle Ages, a range of rates emerged in the eighteenth and nineteenth centuries for the best credits in the most advanced countries that until the 1960s usually proved adequate for the purposes of the modern world. Interest rates during much of the twentieth century at times reached new lows and new highs; but most of the time they fluctuated in this traditional range.

In contrast, the quarter-century after 1965 witnessed a marked change of direction—if not a discontinuity—with these long-enduring developments. In these years, interest rates in all major market economies soared to levels unprecedented in modern history, as inflation raged and international monetary arrangements were revamped. Commodity price shocks led to a slowing down of the long post-World War II economic expansion and to stagflation, as the combination of stagnant real GNP and rising inflation came to be called. In a further break with the past, a host of financial innovations appeared and flourished. Among these in the United States were negotiable certificates of deposit, floating-rate bank loans, Euro-currency obligations, variable-rate mortgages, money-market funds, interest-rate futures, zero-coupon bonds, options traded on exchanges, NOW (negotiable order of withdrawal) accounts, foreign currency futures, mortgage pass-through securities, home equity lines of credit, cash management/sweep accounts, and Individual Retirement Accounts (IRAs). A new and increasingly sophisticated financial world came into being, but for all its sophistication it was not obviously more stable than the world it replaced.

The nineteenth century after 1815 has been described as a century of relative peace in Europe, economic growth, hard money, and declining interest rates. Of these attributes, only economic growth has been carried forward. The twentieth century thus far has been a century of unprecedented warfare, economic growth, soft money, and erratic interest rates. Inflations, wars, and social changes have threatened, but have not destroyed, the centuries-old pattern of saving and investing in strong capitalist economies. The ability and desire of seventeenth-century Dutch burghers to provide for emergencies, for their families, and for their retirement by systematic saving and investing at interest has spread throughout the social structure of the Western world. Rich and poor alike now aspire to retire at a suitable age and live on an income derived, explicitly or implicitly, from savings accumulated either by the individual or by the society as a whole.

As this history of interest rates approaches the markets of today, three changes in the plan of presentation seem appropriate. First, less background description of major political and economic events and of standard credit forms need be provided because contemporaries will be familiar with them. Second, the history will be able to quote a greater variety of rates over a wider geographic area, while still placing its emphasis on the principal long- and short-term market rates of interest on best credits in the most advanced commercial countries. Third, the mainstream of this history will shift to the United States, as has the mainstream of the market.

During the eighteenth century and even more so in the nineteenth century, Great Britain occupied such a dominant position in world trade and finance that the London market appropriately received a large share of attention. It was even used as a norm for measuring interest-rate levels and trends in other countries. In the course of the twentieth century, leadership in finance shifted to the United States. Britain, in spite of two desperate wars, a currency that has at times been devalued and nonconvertible, and a loss of empire, has retained an important role in international trade and finance. However, the United States, in spite of its greater self-sufficiency and its early desire to avoid international commitments, became the chief source of international capital and the largest market where savers met investors.

Yet the United States, during its period of world-wide financial leadership after 1914, did not aim at or achieve that financial stability based on hard currency that Britain achieved in the long period of her dominance. A larger degree of self-sufficiency and a tradition of populism led to overexpansion and devaluation and to emphasis on stimulating consumption rather than production, which permitted a world-wide spiraling inflation. In the midst of this inflation, the United States government in 1981 cut tax rates substantially but not its expenditures. As a result, large federal budget deficits persisted through the 1980's, and the U.S. national debt more than tripled. At the same time, the United States made an abrupt transition from being the world's largest international creditor to being its largest international debtor. Whether these recent trends will last and whether, if they last, they will prove to be consistent with continued U.S. financial leadership are open questions.

Candidates for future financial leadership are not difficult to identify. Western Europe (including Britain), having recovered from the great wars of the first half of the century and formed into an integrated European Community, could reassume the dominant position it held in international finance during previous centuries. Japan, Asia's high-growth, high-saving economic giant and international creditor, is another candidate.

The successes and calamities of nations and of the community of nations as they occurred in this century are accurately pictured, in the pages that follow, in the fever charts of interest rates. Wars, depressions, inflations, and a variety of lesser influences have all left their marks on the historical record.

Chapter XVII

The United States in the Twentieth Century: 1900–1945

POLITICAL BACKGROUND

Four political events during the eventful first ninety years of this century may be singled out for their dominant effect on all American affairs: (a) World War I, 1914–1918; (b) the New Deal, 1933–1938; (c) World War II, 1939–1945; and (d) the Cold War, 1947–1989(?). Three economic events must also be mentioned for their effect on interest rates: (a) the organization of the Federal Reserve System, 1914–1917; (b) the Great Depression of 1929–1939; and (c) the great inflation that started in 1965. The years through World War II are covered in detail in this chapter, and the years since 1945 in the next.

Interest rates throughout history have been a subject of political and doctrinal controversy, and so they are today. During the twentieth century, many persons, impressed by the success of science in controlling the physical environment, have urged the advantages of also controlling the economic environment. The old liberal doctrines of laissez faire have given ground in most countries of the world and were at times abandoned altogether in some. When this happened, however, it soon became apparent that controlling an economy, unlike controlling the physical environment, required controlling possibly uncooperative groups of people. Trying to do this, especially in peacetime, met with very understandable opposition wherever freedom is a political tradition, and, as the 1980s demonstrated, even where it is not. Various compromises have been achieved, based largely on the degree of control that peoples have been willing to accept or unable to avoid. But the issue of government controls, though much better understood now than it was a few decades ago, remains far from settled. It is important to this history because interest rates are among those prices most directly influenced by governments. No doubt the ultimate verdict of history will associate some part of the very wide swings of interest rates during recent decades with political doctrine. No doubt also the political issue of high or low interest rates will survive to occupy frequent headlines in the decades to come and will have its share in determining the future pattern of markets.

Social priorities in the United States, Britain, and elsewhere shifted during the 1930's and 1940's. Economic stability based on a hard currency took second place, and full employment and growth took first place. For a time in the 1950's it looked as though by a miracle we could enjoy both, but in the later 1960's and 1970's, a real testing forced the United States and most of the free world to choose. The sad result was an inflationary spiral that varied from country to country, depending in part on local priorities and productivity. The people of the United States suffered their first bouts of peacetime spiraling inflation. Whether this experience will lead in the decades ahead to a healthier balance of priorities remains to be seen.

The organization of the Federal Reserve System in 1914–1917 permitted government to influence interest rates by methods that had long been used in Europe. It made a basic change in the structure of the American money market. By pooling bank reserves and creating lenders of last resort, the legislation put an end to those erratic upswings in short-term market rates of interest that had recurred whenever immediate and pressing demands for loans exceeded available funds. Not only were the seasonal fluctuations in rates smoothed out, so that short-term debtors no longer stood in fear of the demands of farmers each fall, or of the demands of the Christmas trade, or of dividend dates, but also pressures during business crises were prevented from reaching panic proportions. Short-term rates still rose and fell with supply and demand for credit, but a ceiling was provided. Funds were always (or nearly always) available for short periods at a price.

When the Federal Reserve System was planned, it was expected primarily to serve trade by providing a flexible currency through dealing in short-term business obligations. World War I soon followed, however, and a huge new government debt altered the structure of the money market and enhanced the political responsibilities of the Federal Reserve System. Over the next few decades, government debt replaced commercial paper in the portfolios of member banks and in the portfolios of the Reserve Banks. The New Deal, the Great Depression, and World War II augmented this trend. At the same time, very low interest rates to promote full employment became a political objective. In the 1950's, the central banks here and abroad reverted to flexible interest-rate policies of a traditional sort.

The banking resources of the economy were increased after World War I by large imports of gold. This increase occurred so soon after the organization of the Federal Reserve System that it is impossible to ascribe the lower subsequent range of short-term interest rates wholly to the new system. This history shows, however, that before 1921 short American interest rates usually averaged well above the yields on best long-term bonds, while after 1921 short interest rates have usually averaged below long-term bond yields— often far below. On balance, the influence of the Federal Reserve System in its early decades served to lower interest rates below what they otherwise would have been, both in periods of falling and in periods of rising interest rates.

THE INVESTMENT MARKET

At the turn of the century the American investment market dealt chiefly in the following types of loans and securities: corporate bonds, state and municipal bonds, federal government bonds, short-term loans, real estate mortgages, and stocks. These continue to be the chief investment media. These basic instruments were all developed in earlier centuries and have been altered little in their fundamentals; nevertheless, certain changes in the market structure since 1900 may be noted:

1. The undated perpetual bonds of the early nineteenth century and the noncallable 100-year corporate bonds so popular in 1900 all but vanished. Investors became maturity-conscious; the early concept of a permanent annuity lost its appeal. A sinking fund was sometimes considered an added attraction, and call prices unfavorable to investors were often accepted passively. Investors, in other words, evinced a livelier desire to secure the repayment of their principal and less concern for an assured income. Conversely, corporate debtors wished to retain control of their capital structures by call and sinking-fund options or by serial maturities. Few in the 1990's would think of committing themselves or their successors to receive or make a payment in the year 2361 or the year 2862; these are the maturity dates of two noncallable railroad bonds issued before 1900. Up to the 1960's, most new corporate bond issues matured in twenty to forty years. However, in the 1970's and 1980's, following major declines in bond prices and rises in yields to new highs, many investors began to insist on shorter maturities of five to ten years. This, of course, was a great hardship to some corporations since the money earned by the new funds often could not amortize the debt in so short a period of time. Nevertheless, many such issues were marketed be-

cause there often was no other way to obtain needed funds, especially to refund excessive short-term debt.

2. On the other hand, the nineteenth-century American concept that the
national debt is temporary and must all be redeemable and redeemed at an
early date has changed. Like the Europeans, Americans have become recon-
ciled to a permanent national debt. They have come to measure its burden
not in terms of principal but in terms of interest, its inflationary effects, and
the undesirable competition (crowding out) it provides to private borrowers.
The Treasury has even sold long-term bonds without early-redemption privilege. More important, however, a large part of the national debt has been
created at short term and has remained unfunded. Much of this short debt is
held by banks and corporations, whose business always requires a sizable
amount of short-term investments. With the assurance of a steady demand of
these holders, the government has usually been able to treat its floating debt
as a permanent liability. Some of the distinction between short-term and
long-term debt has thus been obscured. The smooth functioning of the modern banking system has seemed to provide an assurance, not only to government but to all with high credit ratings, that they can always borrow if they
need to do so. Many besides the government have been encouraged to borrow at short term who in an earlier age would have borrowed at long term
just to be sure the funds would be available if needed. The dangers of this
procedure became sadly evident in the 1970's, when certain borrowers, such
as Penn Central and New York City, suddenly found the refunding market
closed to them. Nonetheless, the soaring national debt of the 1980's continued to diminish the importance of the traditional market for long-term
corporate bonds.

3. The progressive income tax created a special demand for tax-exempt
state and municipal bonds, which rendered them no longer a good index of
prevailing yields. It also encouraged the creation of new debt, discouraged
the creation of new equities, and modified the significance of market yields
to taxable borrowers and to taxable lenders. It concentrated the market for
taxable bonds in the hands of institutions that are not subject to the full income tax and in the hands of low-bracket individual investors. It also stimulated the search for capital gains. These tax laws therefore served to reduce
the demand for corporate and government bonds and thus increased their
yield.

4. The concept of social security, which long antedates the legislation of
the 1930's, created an army of investing institutions, which grew so large that
they have tended to supplant the individual private investor in the security
markets. The safety and convenience of the contracts offered to savers by
these institutions often seemed more important than the rate of return, especially during periods when all interest rates were low and public distrust

was widespread. The insured checking account proved so convenient that it often commanded a negative return in the form of service charges. Life insurance, which permits the instant creation of an estate at small immediate cost, attracted vast funds away from higher-yielding investments. The tax-sheltered pension fund, the immediate cost of which is rarely apparent to the beneficiaries, attracted billions of dollars with little initial reference to the rate of return to be earned on the principal. Only in periods of high interest rates have these institutions seemed to compete with one another or with the bond market on the basis of return. Differing requirements, differing legislation, and differing tax status determined their investment policies and directed their funds into limited investment areas often regardless of rate. In this way captive buyers were created. The effect in the 1950's was a compartmentalization of the investment markets and a very erratic correlation of the yields of competing investment media. From the 1960's through the 1980's, however, as yields rose, competition among institutions became severe, and indeed private investors transferred funds from institutions to direct market investment. One result of this was the deregulation of various financial markets that had been heavily regulated since the 1930's. Thus market compartmentalization was reduced or eliminated as everyone sought the best income wherever it was to be found.

5. After World War II, credit of all sorts proliferated, especially consumer and mortgage credit, and there were some modifications of existing credit instruments. New federal agencies used "moral obligation" notes, mostly to promote the real estate mortgage market, and these new issues often exceeded in volume the new financing of the Treasury itself. Since the yields of these agency issues usually substantially exceeded the yields of Treasury obligations, critics wondered why the Treasury itself did not undertake this financing at lower cost. Federal agency financing was often the chief cause of higher and higher bond yields. Also several government agencies guaranteed various private obligations in the name of the federal government. In the corporate sector many forms of lease obligations were developed, and at times equity participations, called "kickers," were added to bond issues. Corporate equity financing itself was moderate or negligible until the late 1960's as corporate management sought "performance" and often achieved it; by the mid-1980's more corporate stock was retired than issued, reflecting low share prices, mergers, and leveraged buy-outs.

A SUMMARY OF THE TRENDS OF HIGH-GRADE BOND YIELDS IN THE TWENTIETH CENTURY

Long-term trends of the yields of best-quality long-term American bonds in the twentieth century can best be described in terms of the history of prime long-term corporate bond yields. Long-term government bonds were

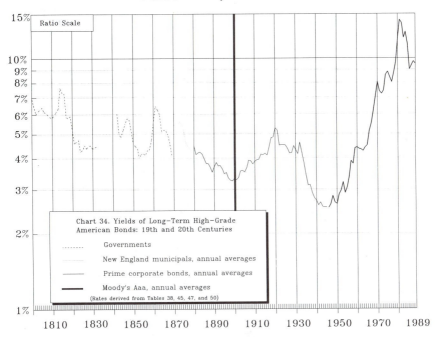

Chart 34. Yields of Long–Term High–Grade
American Bonds: 19th and 20th Centuries

.... Governments

New England municipals, annual averages

Prime corporate bonds, annual averages

Moody's Aaa, annual averages

(Rates derived from Tables 38, 45, 47, and 50)

often not outstanding. Tax advantages and other privileges often distorted the yields of both government and municipal bonds.

The charts of prime long-term American corporate bond yields during the first eight decades of the twentieth century describe a gigantic letter *N* with its final upstroke to 1981 rising high above its earlier peak. After 1981, yields—despite a substantial decline—remained, as the 1990's began, at levels not seen in this century before 1974. Around the turn of the century, as shown in Chart 34, yields, after declining for more than twenty-five years, turned up. They rose most of the time for twenty years and reached the high point—since the 1870s—in 1920. Thereafter, yields turned down, declined most of the time for twenty-six years, and reached their all-time lows in 1946. Then they turned up and rose again most of the time for thirty-five years in the largest and longest of all bear bond markets, which appears to have reached its final peak yields in 1981. This pattern of the bond market during the first ninety years of the twentieth century permits it to be conveniently described in three well-distinguished segments: (a) the first bear bond market, 1899–1920; (b) the great bull bond market, 1920–1946; and, in the following chapter, (c) the greatest of all bear bond markets, 1946–1981. Not yet well distinguished is the bull market that began in 1982. Only time and events will tell whether it represents the start of a secular bull market or something else.

Each of the two world wars occurred just before a major turning point in the history of bond yields. World War I was accompanied by high and rising yields, and so was every earlier great war of modern times. The point of highest bond yields up to the 1960's occurred two years after World War I ended. World War II, in contrast, was accompanied by low and declining bond yields; the war ended one year before the point of lowest bond yields in this century. For those who have been impressed by the regular coincidence of interest-rate peaks with wars over several centuries, World War II presented a notable exception, both here and in Europe. On the other hand the Cold War, or armed truce, which closely followed World War II, was a basic inflationary force and was accompanied by the largest rise in American bond yields and fall in American bond prices in this record. As the 1980s ended, signs of the ending of the Cold War were evident. An end to the Cold War would increase the likelihood that peak yields of the greatest bear market in bonds were reached in 1981.

In 1900 or thereabouts the best corporate bonds sold to yield around 3.25%. At least one new issue came to market to yield as low as 3%, and governments (which enjoyed the privilege of backing national bank note circulation) often sold to yield less than 2%. The best municipal issues carried 3% coupons.

In 1920, in sharp contrast, the best corporate bonds sold to yield 5.56%, the highest yields since the 1870s. High-grade municipals yielded as much as 5.25%, and governments of medium maturity, which no longer enjoyed the circulation privilege but were partially tax-exempt, sold to yield on average as high as 5.67%.

In 1946 the lowest bond yields in history were reached. Prime corporate bonds averaged a yield as low as 2.37%; one issue of long taxable government bonds sold to yield as little as 1.93%; the best long municipal bonds sold to yield less than 1%.

By 1959 yields were again very high, although not so high as they were in 1920 or during the Civil War. Seasoned corporate bonds of best quality sold to yield a monthly average of 4.65%, and new issues, as much as 5.62%. Long governments sold to yield as much as 4.50% and medium-term governments to yield above 5%. Prime municipals sold to yield 3.65%, which, if allowance is made for the value of tax exemption, equated to yields of 6–7% or more for taxable bonds. During only a very few years since the 1870's had prime long American bonds sold to yield as much.

And yet at these 1959 peak yields, the great bear bond market, which began in 1946, was less than halfway in both time and scope to its 1981 low prices and high yields. The latter part of the great bear bond market, which ran from the mid-1960's through 1981, was barely longer than the first part, as illustrated in Chart 34, but it was much more spectacular and newsworthy because its yields were unprecedented in modern experience. One after the other, each bear phase made new history. At their 1981 peaks, seasoned prime long corporate bonds were selling to yield 15.50%. Commercial paper yields reached 16.66%, three-month Treasury bills sold to yield about 16.30%, and the Federal Reserve's discount rate was raised to 14%. The annual average of the prime rate in 1981 was 18.87%.

A SUMMARY OF THE TRENDS OF HIGH-GRADE BOND YIELDS IN THE NINETEENTH AND TWENTIETH CENTURIES

Five great secular cycles of long-term American bond yields can be discerned in the history of annual averages from 1798, shown in Chart 34. These are summarized in the table below.

BOND YIELDS: 1798–1981

	Annual Average Yields			Change		Duration in Years
	Peak, %	Trough, %	Peak, %	In Basis Points	In %	
Governments*						
1798	7.56?					
1810		5.82		−174	−23	12
1814			7.64	+182	+31	4
				+8		16
1814	7.64					
1824		4.25		−339	−44	10
1842			6.07	+182	+43	18
				−157		19
1842	6.07					
1853		4.02		−205	−34	11
1861			6.45	+243	+61	8
				+38		19
1861	6.45					
Corporates						
1899		3.24		−321	−50	38
1920			5.27	+203	+63	21
				−118		59
1920	5.27					
1946		2.53		−274	−52	26
1981			14.17	+1164	+460	35
				+890		61

*Selected market yields from Tables 38, 45, and 50.

These five "great cycles," or "secular trends," reveal no uniformity of timing or scope. The longest bull market by far was that lasting from 1861 to 1899. The longest bear market was that lasting from 1946 to 1981.

Between 1946 and 1981, prime corporate bond yields rose to a level much higher than had ever before prevailed. This raised the question of whether the long suprasecular decline in American interest rates, which was noticeable during the nineteenth century, taken in the large, and which continued during the first half of the twentieth century, may have ended. If so, the turning point in 1946 was more fundamental than the secular turning points in 1899 and 1920; secular increases in yields in the future would average larger than secular declines; each generation would experience higher average yields and would come to look upon low interest rates as old-fashioned, spasmodic, or transitory freaks. A review of the record by itself, however, suggests no such conclusions. It hardly seems necessary to add that the record is not by itself predictive, and that future economic and political events will alone answer this question.

Chart 34, which is based on annual averages, shows that the peak yields of 1959–1960 were below the peak yields of 1920, which in turn were below those of the Civil War, which in their turn were below the peaks in 1814 and probably earlier. Similarly, the yields in periods of low yield in 1810, 1824, 1853, 1899, and 1946 became progressively lower. In the limited sense, then, of comparing extremes, the suprasecular trend of bond yields was downward until the 1960's.

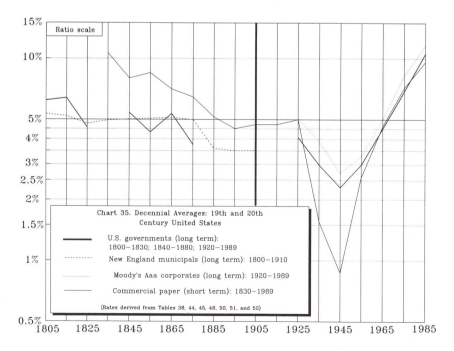

Chart 35. Decennial Averages: 19th and 20th Century United States

U.S. governments (long term): 1800–1830; 1840–1880; 1920–1989

New England municipals (long term): 1800–1910

Moody's Aaa corporates (long term): 1920–1989

Commercial paper (short term): 1830–1989

(Rates derived from Tables 38, 44, 45, 48, 50, 51, and 52)

Such comparisons, however, may put too much stress on peaks and troughs; these extremes were often transitory and not representative of prevailing interest rates. A better long-term guide is provided by decennial averages. Chart 35 presents decennial averages of several American interest-rate series for the nineteenth and twentieth centuries. Because of the distortions affecting U.S. governments between the 1870's and the 1920's, mainly their use by national banks as backing for bank note currency, they have been omitted for that period. Municipals have been omitted for years after 1900 because of the distortion of tax exemption.

This chart clearly reveals the long suprasecular decline in prime interest rates, both long term and short term, in the United States from the earliest time until the 1940s. It also emphasizes the sharp reversal in trend that occurred in the 1950's, which carried long yields (but not, by a small margin, short-term commercial paper rates) to new high decennial averages in the 1980's.

DETAIL OF THE FIRST BEAR BOND MARKET: 1899–1920

The absolute low of American bond yields until the 1930's occurred in 1899. The average yields of New England municipal bonds and best corporate bonds then stood at 3.07–3.20%. This was two years after the low yields were reached in England and most other European countries. By 1899 most European interest rates were rising rapidly, but no pronounced uptrend became noticeable in the United States until 1902.

Some examples from the period 1897–1901 that illustrate the level of the market for the best bonds at the extreme of this first period of low yields are shown in tabular form below.

1897–1901 High Prices and Low Yields

Issue	Due	Price	Yield, %
Pennsylvania R.R. General 6s	1910	130½	2.97
Rome, Watertown & Ogdensburg 5s	1922	129	3.20
Lake Shore & Michigan Southern 3½s	1997	109¾	3.18
N.Y. Central & Hudson River 3½s	1997	112	3.11
Chicago & North Western 3½s	1987	109¾	3.17
Chicago, Burlington & Quincy (Ill. Div.) 3½s	1949	104	3.33
West Shore 4s	2361	114¾	3.48
State of Maine 3s	1921	99	3.06
State of Massachusetts 3s	1923	99½	3.03
State of Massachusetts 3½s	1923	109	3.00
City of Boston 4s	1923	112	3.31
City of Detroit 4s	1920	109½	3.40
City of St. Louis 4s	1918	109	3.40

During the first decade of the twentieth century, U.S. government bonds were still supported, as in the late nineteenth century, by the circulation privilege, which permitted banks in the National Banking System to issue bank notes secured by government bonds. Governments therefore sold at such high premiums that they did not compete in the investment markets. In 1900–1902, for example, U.S. 2s of 1930 sold up to 109⅝, to yield 1.55%; the 4s of 1925 sold in a range of 136½–137⅞ and usually yielded less than 2%.

Although this was a period of very low bond yields, it was not a period of very low short-term interest rates. Prime 4- to 6-month commercial paper averaged 5.71%, 5.40%, and 5.81% in the first three years of the century. Call loans on the New York Stock Exchange were quoted as low as 1% and as high as 75%.

The bear bond market of 1899–1920 can be subdivided into three major price declines interspersed by two rallies. These are summarized in terms of a monthly average of prime corporate bond yields and a corresponding bond price index in the table below.

The first price decline, 1899–1907, was very large, accounting for almost half of the gross decline, but it was spread over a period of nine years. From 1907 to 1917, the fluctuations in price were smaller. Finally, the three years from January 1917, through May 1920, contained more than half of the twenty-one-year aggregate bear market. This three-year decline amounted to 23.6% in price; such a drop in the market had not been experienced for

THE BEAR BOND MARKET: 1899-1920

Dates of Price Trends	Duration		Yield, % (from Table 45)	Yield Change, Basis Points*	Price Change of a Constant 30-Year 3¼s Bond, Points
	Yrs.	Mos.			
1. Jan. 1899					
Decline to Nov. 1907	8	10	3.20–4.21	+101	−17½
Advance to Feb. 1909	1	3	−3.77	−44	+7⅞
	10	1		+57	−10⅛
2. Feb. 1909					
Decline to Sept. 1915	6	7	3.77–4.30	+53	−8½
Advance to Jan. 1917	1	4	−3.98	−32	+4½
	7	11		+21	−4
3. Jan. 1917					
Decline to May 1920	3	4	3.98–5.56	+158	−20⅜ (23.6s)
Total change: Jan. 1899–May 1920	21	4	3.20–5.56	+236	−34½ (points and s)

*1 basis point = .01s in yield.

fifty-six years, or since the first year of the Civil War. It approximated the demoralized decline of the market for government bonds that occurred late in the War of 1812.

During the first two decades of this century, American prosperity suffered no major setback. Commodity prices rose throughout this period. The B.L.S. Index of Wholesale Prices, which had declined from 285 during the Civil War to 100 in 1896, advanced to 150 by 1910 and to 340 by 1920—a level somewhat above the Civil War peak and about equal to the 1814 peak. This was the most sustained rise in the price level in the history of the United States up to that time.(511)

Chart 36 and Tables 45 and 46 suggest that the bond market was firm in 1900 and 1901. In 1902 prime bond yields began to rise. This was a period of great prosperity and speculation. The rise in yields continued into the panic of late 1907, when no call money was offered at all for one day and the rate rose from 1 to 125%—the last call rate over 30% in this history. The decline in prime bond prices averaged about 12 points in 1907 alone.

Bond yields declined in the postpanic years 1908 and 1909 and thereafter rose gradually. In 1913, a sharper rise carried yields back to their 1907 highs. By this time 80% of the government debt of $965 million was owned by national banks as security for bank notes. There were ever-recurrent threats of currency shortage because the debt was being reduced. The lessons of 1907 and earlier periods, however, had at last led to legislation setting up a central banking system that would manage a flexible currency sensitive to commercial demands rather than to the fiscal position of the Treasury.

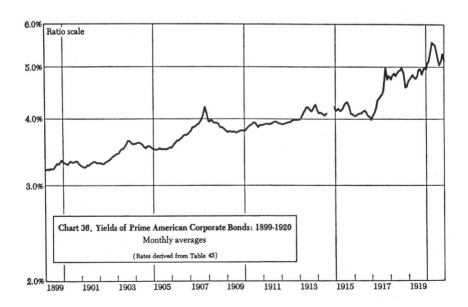

Chart 36. Yields of Prime American Corporate Bonds: 1899-1920
Monthly averages
(Rates derived from Table 45)

TABLE 45

CORPORATE AND MUNICIPAL LONG-TERM BOND YIELDS: 1899–1920

Year	Prime Corporate Bonds, % Yield													High-Grade Municipal Bonds, % Yield				
	Annual Average	Jan.	Feb.	Mar.	Apr.	May	June	July	Aug.	Sept.	Oct.	Nov.	Dec.	New England, Ann. Avg.	H.G. Bond Buyer, Ann. Avg.	Standard & Poor's Ann. Avg.	Standard & Poor's Low	Standard & Poor's High
1899	3.24	3.20	3.20	3.21	3.20	3.22	3.21	3.22	3.26	3.29	3.28	3.31	3.34					
1900	3.31	3.31	3.30	3.29	3.28	3.31	3.32	3.31	3.31	3.32	3.32	3.29	3.27	3.15	3.25	3.12	3.08	3.13
1901	3.28	3.26	3.25	3.24	3.25	3.28	3.27	3.29	3.31	3.32	3.32	3.30	3.30	3.12	3.10	3.13	3.08	3.19
1902	3.34	3.30	3.30	3.29	3.29	3.31	3.32	3.33	3.35	3.37	3.40	3.41	3.43	3.21	3.18	3.20	3.15	3.25
1903	3.55	3.43	3.45	3.49	3.52	3.51	3.55	3.59	3.64	3.64	3.60	3.58	3.59	3.37	3.30	3.38	3.26	3.49
1904	3.57	3.59	3.60	3.61	3.60	3.59	3.57	3.54	3.53	3.55	3.55	3.54	3.53	3.45	3.40	3.45	3.39	3.52
1905	3.51	3.51	3.50	3.50	3.51	3.52	3.51	3.51	3.51	3.51	3.51	3.53	3.54	3.43	3.48	3.40	3.37	3.44
1906	3.65	3.53	3.55	3.59	3.61	3.64	3.64	3.66	3.69	3.72	3.73	3.73	3.75	3.60	3.43	3.57	3.44	3.70
1907	3.92	3.77	3.80	3.85	3.85	3.87	3.90	3.90	3.95	3.99	4.06	4.21	4.10	3.90	3.67	3.86	3.68	4.17
1908	3.90	3.96	3.95	3.99	3.96	3.93	3.93	3.92	3.88	3.85	3.85	3.83	3.81	4.02	3.87	3.92	4.79	4.17
1909	3.78	3.79	3.77	3.78	3.78	3.77	3.78	3.77	3.77	3.78	3.79	3.80	3.80	3.85	3.76	3.79	3.72	3.85
10-yr. av.	3.47													3.51	3.44	3.48		
1910	3.87	3.79	3.80	3.82	3.86	3.88	3.90	3.93	3.92	3.88	3.86	3.89	3.89	4.00	3.91	3.97	3.87	4.04
1911	3.93	3.89	3.90	3.91	3.91	3.90	3.91	3.91	3.93	3.94	3.94	3.92	3.92	4.00	3.98	3.98	3.96	4.01
1912	3.95	3.91	3.90	3.91	3.92	3.92	3.94	3.94	3.96	3.98	3.98	3.98	3.99	4.07	4.01	4.03	3.99	4.09
1913	4.14	3.99	4.00	4.07	4.12	4.16	4.21	4.21	4.17	4.13	4.17	4.23	4.24	4.40	4.45	4.22	4.08	4.36
1914	4.11	4.16	4.10	4.11	4.09	4.08	4.06	4.09					4.22	4.37	4.16	4.12	4.09	4.17
1915	4.18	4.17	4.15	4.19	4.14	4.15	4.19	4.25	4.28	4.30	4.21	4.08	4.08		4.24	4.16	4.02	4.23
1916	4.10	4.06	4.05	4.07	4.09	4.09	4.19	4.12	4.14	4.12	4.07	4.04	4.04		4.05	3.93	3.84	3.99
1917	4.41	3.98	4.05	4.10	4.19	4.32	4.36	4.41	4.45	4.54	4.98	4.73	4.81		4.23	4.21	3.82	4.51
1918	4.82	4.79	4.75	4.82	4.87	4.81	4.87	4.92	4.93	4.98	4.86	4.59	4.61		4.57	4.50	4.36	4.59
1919	4.84	4.71	4.75	4.79	4.83	4.77	4.76	4.80	4.95	4.96	4.83	4.94	4.99		4.50	4.46	4.43	4.53
10-yr. av.	4.23														4.21	4.15		
1920	5.27	4.95	5.10	5.11	5.32	5.56	5.52	5.50	5.36	5.18	5.03	5.13	5.30		4.97	4.98	4.53	5.28

Annual high and low corporate yields are underlined.

SOURCES

Corporate bonds: Durand, *Basic Yields of Corporate Bonds* for 30-year prime corporate bonds each February, with monthly fluctuations interpolated from Macaulay's *Adjusted Railroad Bond Average.*

Municipals: New England municipals from Macaulay, *op. cit.*, pp. A14ff. Bond Buyer High-Grade and Standard & Poor's from those publications.

TABLE 46

Prices and Yields of Long-Term U.S. Government Securities: 1900–1920

Year	Consol 2s of 1930 *†				4s of 1907 *†				4s of 1925 *†			
	Annual Average		High	Low	Annual Average		High	Low	Annual Average		High	Low
	Price	Red. Yield, %			Price	Red. Yield, %			Price	Red. Yield, %		
1900	104	1.82	105	103⅛	115⅛	1.70	118½	114	136⅜	2.12	136⅜	138⅝
1901	107⅜	1.67	109½	105¼	112⅞	1.72	115¼	112	138⅜	1.98	139⅞	136⅞
1902	108¾	1.62	109⅝	107¾	110½	1.81	113	108¾	138⅛	1.93	139¾	136½
1903	107⅜	1.66	108¾	106	110⅜	1.34	112	109¼	135⅞	1.97	137½	134¼
1904	105⅜	1.74	106¼	104½	106¾	1.68	108	104½	132½	2.08	134	130⅞
1905	104¼	1.79	105⅜	103¼	104⅝	1.63	105⅞	103½	132⅜	2.03	134½	130¼
1906	104⅛	1.78	105¼	103	102⅞	1.11	104⅞	101⅞	130⅞	2.03	132¼	129⅜
1907	105¼	1.73	106¼	104¼	101	1.07	101⅞	100⅞	123¾	2.33	130½	117
1908	104	1.77	104⅛	104					122⅛	2.39	123½	120¾
1909	101⅜	1.92	103	100¼					118½	2.57	121	116
					Panama Canal 3s of 1961 *§							
						Mat. Yield, %						
1910	100½	1.97	100¾	100¼					115⅛	2.76	115¾	114½
1911	100⅞	1.94	101¾	100⅛	102⅜	2.92	103	101¾	115	2.70	116⅜	113¾
1912	101	1.93	101⅜	100¾	101¾	2.93	102	101⅜	114	2.71	114¾	113¼
1913	98⅜	2.11	101¼	95½	101	2.96	103⅛	99	111¾	2.83	114½	109
1914	97⅞	2.16	99	96¾	101⅝	2.93	102½	100¾	111⅜	2.79	113¼	109½
1915	98⅛	2.14	99	97¼	101⅜	2.94	102	100¾	110½	2.79	111½	109½
1916	100	2.00	100½	99½	102½	2.90	103¼	101⅞	111⅜	2.57	112½	110¼
1917	98¼	2.16	99¾	96¾	93½	3.27	102¾	84	107½	2.95	111⅛	104
1918	98	2.19	98⅞	97¼	85¼	3.69	85½	85	106	3.05	107	105
1919	99⅛	2.09	100¼	98	89¼	3.49	91	87½	105⅜	3.02	106⅝	104¼
1920	100¾	1.95	101	100½	84½	3.74	89¼	79½	105⅛	2.90	106¼	104

Prices and Yields of War Loans

Year	1st Liberty 3½s, 1932–1947 *§				3rd Liberty P.T.E. 4¼s, 1928 §				4th Liberty P.T.E. 4¼s, 1933–1938 §			
	Annual Average		High	Low	Annual Average		High	Low	Annual Average		High	Low
	Price	Mat. Yield, %			Price	Mat. Yield, %			Price	Mat. Yield, %		
1917	99⅛	3.55	100⅜	98								
1918	99⅞	3.51	102½	97¼	96½	4.69	99⅛	94	96	4.56	98⅛	94
1919	99⅝	3.52	101	98¼	94⅞	4.96	96⅝	93¼	93⅜	4.79	95¾	91
1920	94¾	3.82	100½	89⅛ ‖	90⅜	5.76	95	85⅝ ¶	87½	5.32	93	82 **

* Tax-exempt. † Circulation privilege § No circulation privilege. P.T.E. partially tax-exempt; see text.
‖ To yield 4.18%. ¶ To yield 6.58%. ** To yield 5.82%.
Source: *The Financial Review Annual*, 1921, *op. cit.*, pp. 221–232.

The outbreak of war in 1914 caught the market by surprise. A sudden wave of international liquidation converged on the New York market, and the Stock Exchange closed from July 31 to December 12, 1914. Money stringency in New York was alleviated by the issuance of emergency currency that had been authorized by the Aldrich-Vreeland Act of 1908. Call money did not rise above 10%. Late in 1914 the Federal Reserve Banks opened their doors. When the Stock Exchange reopened, bond prices were only a few points lower than when the exchange closed, and they quickly recovered most of this loss. The war began with prime corporate and municipal bonds averaging around 4.25% in yield.

Bond yields tended to decline in 1915–1916. The new Federal Reserve System quickly mobilized a large part of the banking reserves of the country and stood ready to provide additional reserves at a rediscount rate, which was brought down in 1914–1916 from 6 to 3%. Average commercial paper rates declined from 6.20% in 1913 to 3.84% in 1916. Call money averaged 1.92% in 1915, and the new five-year 5% joint gold loan to Britain and France was quoted to yield 6.35%; Canadian 5s were quoted to yield 4.50%, and Philippine 4s, to yield 4%.(512)

Treasury financing before 1917 was chiefly by means of bonds that could be held by banks to secure bank notes. The principal long-term new issues, all tax-exempt and all with the circulation privilege unless otherwise noted, are given in the table below.

1900–1907	$646 million	"2s consols of 1930," redeemable after 1930; sold at 100 = 2.00s. (to refund 5s of 1904 and 4s of 1907, etc.)
1906	30 million	"Panama Canal 2s," redeemable after 1916, due 1936; sold at 104 = 1.56s*
1907	24 million	"Panama Canal 2s," redeemable after 1916, due 1936; sold at 103 = 1.63s*
1908	30 million	"Panama Canal 2s," redeemable after 1918, due 1938; sold at $102\frac{3}{8}$ = 1.74s*
1911	50 million	"Panama Canal 3s," due 1961, no circulation privilege; sold at $102\frac{5}{8}$ = 2.90s.
1916	29 million	"Conversion 3s," two series due 1946 and 1947, no circulation privilege; sold at $103\frac{1}{2}$ = 2.82s.
1917		Same series, issued in exchange for 2s circulation bonds; sold at $94\frac{1}{2}$ = 3.28s.

*Redemption yield.

The entry of the United States into the war in April 1917, was marked by an immediate large decline in the bond market. The prime corporate bond yields rose from 3.98% in January to 4.98% in October. Even though the Federal Reserve held its rediscount rate at 3–3.50%, commercial paper rates rose from an average of 3.84% in 1916 to an average of 5.07% in 1917.

Long-term Treasury war financing in 1917 took the form of the following two issues, each of which was convertible into such higher-rate bonds as might be issued during the war:

1917	$2.0 billion	"First Liberty Loan 3½s," redeemable in 1932, due 1947, tax-exempt; sold at 100 = 3.50%.
	3.8 billion	"Second Liberty Loan 4s," redeemable in 1927, due 1942, partially tax-exempt (P.T.E.: partially tax-exempt government bonds were exempt from the normal income tax but subject to the surtax); sold at 100 = 4%.

These new issues were successfully sold with the aid of patriotic appeals and bank credit. They served to re-establish a wide public market for government bonds. Their rates, however, did not long remain competitive. When the tax-exempt First Liberty Loan 3½s were offered at 100, the yields on the best tax-exempt state and municipal bonds rose from 3.82% to 4.51%. The tax-exempt Panama Canal 3s of 1961 declined 17 points in the market, to yield 3.74%. The Liberty 3½s themselves promptly declined to 98, to yield 3.61%.

The Second Liberty Loan 4s, because they were only partially tax-exempt (P.T.E), had to compete with prime corporate bonds for the funds of many investors. These bonds were declining rapidly in price and selling to yield 4.98% and up. The Second Liberty Loan 4s themselves promptly declined to 97. When doubt was expressed about the adequacy of these rates, Charles G. Dawes, chairman of the Liberty Loan Drive, replied, "Anybody who declines to subscribe for that reason, knock him down." Members of the Stock Exchange declared that anybody who sold Liberty Bonds below par should be condemned as unpatriotic.(513)

In 1918, with the end of the war, the market rallied sharply for just two months. However, the government had to pay more than 4% on its new issues. These were both 4¼s, and even that rate was not long competitive with the market. Both issues sold at discounts as large as 6 points soon after trading began. The strong appeal to the investor's hope for postwar capital gains, which had dominated English financing during the Napoleonic Wars and later and much American financing during the Civil War, was evidently not a part of Treasury policy during the world wars of this century.

The new issues of 1918 were:

1918	$4.2 billion	"Third Liberty 4¼s," due 1928, P.T.E.; sold at 100 = 4.25%.
	7.0 billion	"Fourth Liberty 4¼s," redeemable after 1933, due 1938, P.T.E.; sold at 100 = 4.25%.

were the last long-term issues of the war and the last, except for re-
~~ing issues, until the 1930's.

~ 1919, the first full year of peace, the bond market lost its small rally and
~eclined to approximately the lows of 1918. A brief postwar business boom
was accompanied by rising commodity prices, which were now up to 272% of
those of 1913—a rise even greater than that of the Civil War period. In this
one peacetime year, American bank loans rose 23%.(514) In November 1919,
the rediscount rate was raised to 4¾%. Call money averaged 10.89% in one
month. The Treasury's chief financing was at medium term. It took the form
of $3.8 billion of "Victory Loan 4¾% notes," redeemable in 1922 and due in
1923, P.T.E., sold at 100 to yield 4.75%.

The crisis that drove the bond market down sharply occurred in early
1920. The Federal Reserve Banks raised their rediscount rates to 7% and
held them there throughout the year of heavy deflation that followed. Commercial paper averaged 7.50% for the year, its highest annual average until
1969. Call money touched 25% and averaged 7.74%. The Treasury issued
six-month certificates at 5.75% and twelve-month certificates at 6%, and
these sold to yield as much as 7.75%. The yield curve became sharply negative: the shorter the maturity, the higher the yield.

From January to May of 1920, the average of prime corporate bond yields
rose from 4.95 to 5.56%, the highest yield of the century until 1967. Market
liquidation, however, was centered in Liberty Bonds. It is estimated that of
18 million original subscribers to Liberty Bonds, 14 million sold out.(515)
Price fluctuations of as much as 11½% occurred in thirty days. The first 3½s
of 1947 declined from 100 to 89⅛, to yield 4.18%, tax-exempt; the comparatively short-term Third 4¼s of 1928 declined from 95 to 85⅝, to yield
6.58%, P.T.E.; and the longer Fourth 4¼s of 1938 declined from 94 to 82, to
yield 5.82%, P.T.E. A representative group of high-grade corporate bond
issues at their low prices of this decade are shown in the table below.

1920 Low Prices and High Yields

Issue	Due	Price	Yield, s
N.Y. Central 3½s	1997	63	5.60
Lake Shore & Mich. Southern 3½s	1997	65	5.43
Pennsylvania 4½s	1960	84	5.48
Morris & Essex 3½s	2000	63½	5.57
Norfolk & Western 4s	1996	70½	5.72
Union Pacific 4s	1947	77	5.67
Central R.R. of N.J. 5s	1987	91	5.52
Atchison, Topeka & Santa Fe Gen. 4s	1995	71½	5.62

DETAIL OF THE GREAT BULL BOND MARKET: 1920–1946

For twenty-six years after May of 1920, interest rates tended to decline and high-grade bond prices to rise most of the time (see Chart 37 and Tables 47 and 48). This decline in interest rates is sometimes dated from 1933–1934, when the dollar was devalued in terms of gold. The charts clearly show, however, that the decline began thirteen or fourteen years earlier—in 1920. By 1928, almost one-half of the gross twenty-six-year decline in yields and more than one-third of the gross twenty-six-year advance in bond prices had taken place.

This, the United States's greatest bull bond market, can be arbitrarily divided, for convenience of description, into three periods of price advance, interrupted by two important setbacks, as shown in the following table:

THE BULL BOND MARKET: 1920-1946

Dates of Price Trends	Duration		Yield, s (from Table 47)	Yield Change, Basis Points*	Price Change of a Constant 30-Year 5½s Bond, Points
	Yrs.	Mos.			
1. May 1920					
Advance to Jan. 1928	7	8	5.56–4.04	−152	+25⅛
Decline to Sept. 1929	1	8	–4.59	+55	−10⅝
	9	4		−97	+14½
2. Sept. 1929					
Advance to May. 1931	1	8	4.50–3.99	−60	+11¾
Decline to June 1932	1	1	–4.83	+84	−15⅞
	2	9		+24	−4½
3. June 1932					
Advance to Apr. 1946	13	10	4.83–2.37	−246	+56⅝
Total change: May 1920–April 1946	25	11	5.56–2.37	−319	+67*

*Points and percent.

The average of long-term prime bond yields in 1920 reached a peak above any attained for at least forty-five years earlier and forty-seven years later, a total span of ninety-two years. The decennial average of prime bond yields for the 1920's was the highest in the eight decades of which it occupied approximately the center.

The depression of 1920–1921 was one of the very few modern depressions during which interest rates did not decline importantly while business was

Chart 37
Yields of Prime American Corporate Bonds: 1920-1946
Monthly averages
(Rates derived from Table 47)

declining. Rates did decline after May of 1920, but only moderately. The Federal Reserve Banks maintained their 7% crisis rate unchanged until the sweeping deflation of 1920–1921 was about completed. In this one year, Reserve Bank credit declined from $3.5 billion to $1.5 billion, commodity prices declined almost 50%, and industrial production declined one-third. At last, after the spring of 1921, the rediscount rate was reduced in a series of steps from 7 to 4%. The crisis was over. Business, although still depressed, improved.

A really important decline in corporate bond yields began in June of 1921. In fifteen months, yields moved from close to the highs to close to the lows of the 1920s. The average yield of long-term P.T.E. governments declined from its 1921 high of 5.27% to a 1922 low of 4.12%. Fourth Liberty 4¼s of 1933–1938 were up from 82 in 1920 to 101¾ in 1922. The entire postwar decline in the bond market was erased in about a year. The Treasury enjoyed a surplus, and the war debt was reduced. Treasury long-term financing during the 1920s was confined to refunding issues at almost steadily declining yields as shown below.

1922	$0.8 billion	"4¼s of 1947–1952"	P.T.E. at 100 = 4.25%
1924	1.1 billion {	"4s of 1944–1954"	P.T.E. at 100 = 4.00
1925		"4s of 1944–1954"	P.T.E. at 100½ = 3.96
1926	0.5 billion	"3¾s of 1946–1956"	P.T.E. at 100½ = 3.72
1927	0.5 billion	"3⅜s of 1943–1947"	P.T.E. at 100½ = 3.33
1928	0.4 billion	"3⅜s of 1940–1943"	P.T.E. at 100 = 3.37
Thereafter none until 1931			

Dates are earliest redemption date and maturity date.

From 1922 on, this decade was characterized by rising prosperity except in the field of agriculture. Commodity prices declined. The total of private debt approximately doubled. Nevertheless, American savings not only financed this credit expansion but also permitted the purchase of some $4.5 billion of foreign long-term securities and after 1925 financed stock market speculation.

Throughout the boom years after 1922, bond yields fluctuated in a moderate range. Short-term rates became far lower than they had ever been during pre-World War I periods of prosperity. In early 1928, however, there began a brief period of rising interest rates, which lasted until the fateful autumn of 1929. Between January of 1928 and August of 1929, the rediscount rate was raised four times, moving from 3½ to 6%. Call money rose from 3½ to 20%. Prime corporate bond yields rose moderately, from 4.04% in January of 1928 to a high of 4.59% in September of 1929, the high point for five years past and two years to come.

With the collapse of the stock market in the autumn of 1929, pressures on the money market immediately relaxed, interest rates declined precipitately, and the bond market started to rise. The prime corporate bond yield average moved from 4.59% in September 1929 to 3.99% in May of 1931. The rediscount rate by mid-1930 was down to 3%, and by mid-1931 it was down to 1½%. Call money declined from 20% to a 1931 low of 1%. All this was very different from the tight money depression of 1920–1921, with its persistent 7% rediscount rate. The Federal Reserve System was leaning against a very big wind indeed, or so it seemed if one ignored the collapse of the money stock and the price level. In 1931 the Treasury resumed its long-term financing, after a lapse of three years, and took full advantage of the lower interest rates then prevailing:

1931, March	$0.6 billion	"3⅜s of 1941–1943," P.T.E., sold at 100 = 3.37%.
1931, June	0.8 billion	"3⅛s of 1946–1949," P.T.E., sold at 100 = 3.12%.
1931, September	0.8 billion	"3s of 1951–1955," P.T.E., sold at 100 = 3.00%.

The last issue was unfortunately timed on the eve of a crisis. Allotments ranged up to 100%, the first quotations were at 99⅝, and within four months the bonds sold down to 82⅛, to yield 4.24%.

In late 1931, foreign crises and devaluations, the collapse of the banking system, and distrust of the dollar brought on an export of gold. The Federal Reserve met this crisis in traditional fashion by raising interest rates. Again, as in 1920–1921, there was an official policy of deflation in the midst of depression. The Fed now leaned not against but with a wind that became a hurricane, and in doing so it assumed a posture that was very difficult to

TABLE 47
CORPORATE AND MUNICIPAL LONG-TERM BOND YIELDS: 1920–1946

Year	An-nual Aver-age	Jan.	Feb.	Mar.	Apr.	May	June	July	Aug.	Sept.	Oct.	Nov.	Dec.
					Prime Corporate Bonds, s Yield								
1920	5.27	4.95	5.10	5.11	5.32	5.56	5.52	5.50	5.36	5.18	5.03	5.13	5.30
1921	5.16	5.13	5.17	5.23	5.26	5.29	5.42	5.28	5.20	5.14	5.12	4.92	4.78
1922	4.49	4.71	4.71	4.65	4.55	4.51	4.49	4.39	4.33	4.30	4.38	4.44	4.41
1923	4.51	4.39	4.61	4.54	4.58	4.52	4.56	4.58	4.57	4.61	4.64	4.62	4.65
1924	4.51	4.63	4.66	4.66	4.63	4.59	4.52	4.46	4.50	4.50	4.48	4.49	4.51
1925	4.50	4.51	4.50	4.48	4.47	4.42	4.43	4.47	4.53	4.49	4.51	4.49	4.46
1926	4.36	4.43	4.40	4.41	4.36	4.32	4.33	4.35	4.37	4.37	4.36	4.33	4.32
1927	4.18	4.30	4.30	4.26	4.21	4.19	4.23	4.23	4.19	4.15	4.11	4.06	4.04
1928	4.19	4.04	4.05	4.06	4.08	4.13	4.23	4.30	4.36	4.31	4.30	4.27	4.34
1929	4.47	4.38	4.42	4.46	4.46	4.48	4.53	4.56	4.52	4.59	4.56	4.46	4.43
10-yr. av.	4.56												
1930	4.31	4.42	4.40	4.33	4.38	4.35	4.32	4.27	4.21	4.14	4.12	4.16	4.22
1931	4.15	4.10	4.10	4.10	4.08	3.99	4.01	4.00	4.04	4.08	4.29	4.42	4.66
1932	4.61	4.64	4.70	4.60	4.76	4.77	4.83	4.73	4.48	4.40	4.41	4.44	4.33
1933	4.19	4.14	4.15	4.32	4.49	4.34	4.18	4.11	4.06	4.08	4.09	4.23	4.19
1934	3.83	4.07	3.99	3.93	3.86	3.82	3.74	3.74	3.79	3.86	3.79	3.70	3.66
1935	3.44	3.57	3.50	3.46	3.45	3.46	3.43	3.40	3.43	3.44	3.44	3.38	3.33
1936	3.11	3.26	3.20	3.14	3.12	3.09	3.07	3.09	3.10	3.07	3.05	3.01	2.95
1937	3.12	2.97	3.08	3.21	3.25	3.20	3.17	3.15	3.13	3.14	3.14	3.09	3.06
1938	2.90	3.04	3.03	3.01	3.03	2.95	2.94	2.92	2.92	2.92	2.88	2.83	2.81
1939	2.77	2.75	2.75	2.74	2.75	2.71	2.71	2.69	2.72	3.03	2.91	2.77	2.72
10-yr. av.	3.64												
1940	2.70	2.71	2.70	2.66	2.65	2.72	2.75	2.71	2.69	2.64	2.64	2.62	2.62
1941	2.59	2.66	2.65	2.63	2.64	2.61	2.58	2.54	2.53	2.54	2.52	2.51	2.60
1942	2.66	2.62	2.65	2.67	2.63	2.63	2.63	2.61	2.61	2.60	2.61	2.59	2.61
1943	2.55	2.60	2.57	2.57	2.56	2.56	2.53	2.51	2.52	2.54	2.53	2.54	2.58
1944	2.54	2.57	2.56	2.55	2.54	2.54	2.53	2.52	2.53	2.55	2.56	2.58	2.56
1945	2.54	2.54	2.53	2.52	2.51	2.52	2.51	2.53	2.55	2.54	2.53	2.54	2.54
1946	2.45	2.46	2.39	2.38	2.37	2.41	2.41	2.41	2.43	2.50	2.53	2.53	2.58
7-yr. av.	2.58												

Annual high and low yields are underlined.

TABLE 47 (*Continued*)

Year	High-Grade Municipal Bonds, % Yield								
	Prime New Issues			Moody's Aaa			Bond Buyer, High Grade		
	Annual Average	Low	High	Annual Average	Low	High	Annual Average	Low	High
1920		4.80	4.80				4.97	4.53	5.25
1921		4.70	5.00				5.02	4.48	5.16
1922		3.80	4.30				4.19	4.05	4.37
1923		3.80	4.15				4.23	4.10	4.38
1924		3.70	4.15				4.19	4.07	4.35
1925		3.75	4.05				4.09	3.98	4.23
1926		3.80	4.10				4.08	4.05	4.13
1927		3.70	4.00				3.97	3.91	4.10
1928		3.65	3.95				3.98	3.83	4.15
1929		3.95	4.10				4.29	4.13	4.47
10-yr. av.		3.97	4.26				4.30		
1930		3.65	4.10				4.08	6.92	4.25
1931		3.20	3.85				3.88	3.60	4.23
1932		3.15	3.95				4.33	4.02	4.66
1933		3.05	3.85				4.30	3.81	4.90
1934		2.90	3.85				3.73	3.38	4.50
1935		2.35	3.00				2.99	2.79	3.30
1936		2.25	2.65				2.63	2.35	2.84
1937		2.35	3.00	2.50	2.18	2.81	2.67	2.35	2.90
1938		2.30	2.60	2.24	2.14	2.45	2.58	2.42	2.75
1939		1.75	2.10	2.07	1.90	2.32	2.42	2.26	2.94
10-yr. av.		2.70	3.30				3.36		
1940	1.60	1.60	2.00	1.83	1.56	2.06	2.20	1.82	2.66
1941	1.82	1.35	1.80	1.52	1.39	1.71	1.80	1.57	2.13
1942	1.47	1.70	2.00	1.63	1.54	1.84	1.88	1.72	2.19
1943	1.15	1.25	1.75	1.38	1.25	1.56	1.58	1.35	1.80
1944	1.05	1.10	1.20	1.16	1.14	1.21	1.34	1.30	1.44
1945	1.12	0.95	1.20	1.08	0.95	1.22	1.21	1.06	1.43
1946		0.90	1.50	1.10	0.91	1.38	1.23	1.04	1.66
7-yr. av.		1.26	1.64	1.39			1.61		

SOURCES

Corporate bonds: Durand, *op. cit.*, for thirty-year prime corporate bonds each February, with monthly fluctuations interpolated from Macaulay's *Adjusted Railroad Bond Average*, through 1936, and thereafter from *Moody's Aaa Public Utility Average*.

Municipals: *Moody's Aaa* and *Bond Buyer High Grade* averages are from those publications. The new issue yields through 1940 are derived principally from thirty-year New York State offerings and, in the absence of new issues, from market quotations. After 1940, new-issue yields are derived from a privately prepared series reflecting the twenty-year maturity yields of all substantial prime issues which sold reasonably well.

TABLE 48

Prices and Yields of Long-Term U.S. Government Securities: 1920–1946

Year	Yield Average of Long Governments,* %			4th Liberty 4$\frac{1}{4}$s, 1933–1938 P.T.E.				3$\frac{3}{8}$s, 1943–1947 P.T.E.			
	Annual Average	Monthly Low	Monthly High	High Price	Mat. Yield,† %	Low Price	Mat. Yield,† %	High Price	Mat. Yield,† %	Low Price	Mat. Yield,† %
1920	5.32	4.93	5.67	93	4.82	82	5.82				
1921	5.09	4.47	5.27	98$\frac{1}{8}$	4.41	85$\frac{1}{2}$	5.57				
1922	4.30	4.12	4.50	101$\frac{3}{4}$	4.04	95$\frac{1}{4}$	4.62				
1923	4.36	4.32	4.40	99$\frac{1}{4}$	4.32	96$\frac{1}{4}$	4.53				
1924	4.06	3.87	4.30	103	3.86	98$\frac{1}{4}$	4.42				
1925	3.86	3.79	3.96	103$\frac{1}{8}$	3.78	101$\frac{5}{8}$	4.02				
1926	3.68	3.56	3.77	103$\frac{1}{2}$	3.65	101$\frac{7}{8}$	3.96				
1927	3.34	3.17	3.51	104$\frac{3}{8}$	3.50	103$\frac{3}{8}$	3.68	103$\frac{1}{8}$	3.13	100$\frac{1}{4}$	3.36
1928	3.33	3.17	3.48	104	3.48	103$\frac{1}{8}$	4.23	103$\frac{3}{8}$	3.10	98$\frac{1}{4}$	3.51
1929	3.60	3.35	3.74	101$\frac{3}{4}$	3.76	98$\frac{1}{4}$	4.49	100$\frac{1}{4}$	3.35	95$\frac{3}{8}$	3.72
10-yr. av.	4.09										
1930	3.29	3.19	3.43	103$\frac{3}{4}$	2.87	100$\frac{7}{8}$	3.92	102$\frac{3}{4}$	3.10	99	3.45
1931	3.34	3.13	3.93	105$\frac{1}{4}$	2.05	98$\frac{1}{2}$	4.51	103$\frac{1}{2}$	3.02	90$\frac{5}{8}$	4.21
1932	3.68	3.35	4.26	104$\frac{1}{4}$	0	98$\frac{1}{4}$	4.60	102$\frac{1}{2}$	3.10	87$\frac{5}{8}$	4.55
1933	3.31	3.19	3.53		First call			102$\frac{7}{8}$	3.05	97$\frac{1}{8}$	3.63
1934	3.12	2.92	3.50					105$\frac{1}{2}$	2.67	98$\frac{3}{4}$	3.50
1935	2.79	2.69	2.88					108	2.27	103$\frac{7}{8}$	2.86
1936	2.65	2.51	2.80					2$\frac{3}{4}$s, 1956–1959, P.T.E.			
1937	2.68	2.46	2.76					103$\frac{1}{2}$	2.52	98	2.87
1938	2.56	2.48	2.65					103$\frac{1}{2}$	2.51	100$\frac{1}{2}$	2.72
1939	2.36	2.13	2.65					109	2.12	99$\frac{1}{8}$	2.81
10-yr. av.	2.98			2$\frac{1}{2}$s, Sept., 1967–1972 Bank Eligible, Taxable							
1940	2.21	1.89	2.39					111$\frac{1}{4}$	1.92	103$\frac{3}{4}$	2.47
1941	1.95	1.85	2.10	103$\frac{5}{8}$	2.31	100	2.50	112	1.82	106$\frac{3}{4}$	2.23
1942	2.46	2.43	2.50	101$\frac{1}{2}$	2.42	100	2.50	110	1.94	107$\frac{3}{8}$	2.16
1943	2.47	2.45	2.49	101$\frac{1}{4}$	2.43	100$\frac{1}{4}$	2.49	112$\frac{1}{2}$	1.70	108$\frac{3}{8}$	2.04
1944	2.48	2.30	2.50	100$\frac{3}{4}$	2.46	100$\frac{1}{4}$	2.49	112$\frac{1}{4}$	1.60	110$\frac{3}{4}$	1.75
1945	2.37	2.30	2.45	108$\frac{7}{8}$	1.99	100$\frac{3}{4}$	2.46	115$\frac{1}{4}$	1.24	112$\frac{1}{8}$	1.61
1946	2.19	2.17	2.44	109$\frac{5}{8}$	1.93	104$\frac{5}{8}$	2.22	116$\frac{1}{2}$	1.10	111$\frac{1}{2}$	1.48
7-yr. av.	2.30										

* *Banking and Monetary Statistics*, a publication of the Federal Reserve Board, Washington, D.C., 1943. Thereafter, Federal Reserve *Bulletins*. Based on yield of all P.T.E.'s of over eight years' term through 1925; thereafter, over twelve years' term. After 1941, an average of long taxable issues.

† Yield at premiums figured to earliest redemption.

maintain. In the face of heavy bank liquidation, the bond market suddenly ended its two-year advance and turned sharply lower. Between May of 1931 and the low in June 1932, the prime corporate average moved from 3.99 to 4.83%. This was a somewhat higher yield than was reached at the 1929 high, and in this sense the entire bond market advance of 1929–1931 has been called a false start.

The bond market decline of 1931–1932 turned out to be a sharp, brief interruption of a secular advance in the bond market that had proceeded most of the time for twelve years and had fourteen more years to go. The intense phase of the decline lasted only four to nine months. Most of the ground lost was regained in the next six months. Although there were moderate price reactions in 1933 (the bank holiday), 1934, 1937 (doubled reserve requirements), and 1939 (war in Europe), the bond market advanced most of the time from June of 1932 to April of 1946.

In 1932 short-term interest rates also resumed their decline. In that year, call money declined to 1%, and commercial paper declined to 1½%. Treasury bills at 0.08% entered that wonderland of nominal yields that from time to time has been the dream of both entrepreneurs and social reformers.

In February of 1934 the average of corporate bond yields declined below 4%. By December of 1934 this average stood at 3.66%. By March of 1936 it reached its previous all-time low, which had occurred in 1899. By December of 1936 it stood at 2.95%, a new low.

During the years 1932–1936 business recovered substantially and commodity prices rose 35%. Unemployment, however, was still high, and confidence in credit continued to be low. Risk rates of interest were very high. A large volume of refugee gold was imported from Europe. Short-term interest rates declined further, some to nominal levels: commercial paper to 0.75%, bankers' acceptances to 0.16%, and Treasury bills to an 0.06–0.23% monthly range, with occasional lower rates. This was a period of active speculation in government bonds, encouraged by the Treasury's efforts to achieve low yields and its frequent deficit financing. The Treasury's new longer-term issues are shown in tabular form below.

1933	$1.4 billion	"$3\frac{1}{4}$s of 1943–1945" P.T.E. at $101\frac{1}{2}$ = 3.07%
1934	1.5 billion	"$3\frac{1}{4}$s of 1944–1946" P.T.E. at 100 = 3.25
1934	1.0 billion	{ "3s of 1946–1948" P.T.E. at 100 = 3.00
1934		"3s of 1946–1948" P.T.E. at $103\frac{1}{4}$ = 2.67
1934	0.5 billion	"$3\frac{1}{8}$s of 1949–1952" P.T.E. at 100 = 3.12
1935	2.6 billion	{ "$2\frac{7}{8}$s of 1955–1960" P.T.E. at 100 = 2.87
1935		"$2\frac{7}{8}$s of 1955–1960" P.T.E. at $103\frac{3}{8}$ = 2.79
1935	1.2 billion	"$2\frac{3}{4}$s of 1945–1947" P.T.E. at 100 = 2.75
1936	1.2 billion	"$2\frac{3}{4}$s of 1948–1951" P.T.E. at 100 = 2.75
1936	1.6 billion	"$2\frac{3}{4}$s of 1951–1954" P.T.E. at 100 = 2.75
1936	1.0 billion	"$2\frac{3}{4}$s of 1956–1959" P.T.E. at 100 = 2.75
1936	1.8 billion	"$2\frac{1}{2}$s of 1949–1953" P.T.E. at 100 = 2.50

In late 1936 the Federal Reserve Board, fearful of rising commodity prices and the inflationary potential of the swollen gold reserve, announced a doubling of commercial bank reserve requirements, to take place in stages in early 1937. This new policy was followed by a sharp six-point decline in the bond market. The episode was brief. By July 1937, bond prices were again rising, and short-term rates were declining. By the fall the stock market was declining sharply, and fears of inflation evaporated as recession set in. A new period of even lower bond yields began, which was to last for nine years.

By June of 1938 the average of corporate bond yields was down to a new low, at 2.94%. Short-term rates were down, some also at new lows. Treasury bill yields were sometimes quoted at 0.001% and occasionally sold at negative yields because they were exempt from the personal property taxes of some states. The lowest yields for short-term obligations occurred during 1938–1941, although the lowest long-term bond yields occurred five to eight years later in 1946.

A section of the next chapter will record some of the very high risk rates of interest that simultaneously prevailed during these years. It was a period when a large part of the liquid capital of the country attempted to crowd into the always limited area of riskless investment. The sharp recession of 1937–1938 had destroyed the last hopes of some of the most stubborn optimists that 1932 was only a traditional cyclical crisis and that the United States would, as always, recover to resume its climb to new heights of prosperity. This pessimism was not altogether dispelled for over fifteen years.

The outbreak of war in Europe brought a brief sharp decline in the bond market, but no noticeable repercussion in the money market. Between July and September of 1939, the prime corporate bond price average declined 6½%. By December of 1939, all or almost all of this price decline was regained.

The early years of war brought a gradual further decline in prime corporate bond yields. The decline in prime municipal yields was larger because taxes rose, increasing the value of tax exemption. Treasury longer-term financing during 1938–1940 was also at declining yields, as shown in tabular form below.

1938	$0.5 billion	"$2\frac{1}{2}$s of 1948"	P.T.E. at 100 = 2.50%
1938	0.9 billion	"$2\frac{3}{4}$s of 1958–1963"	P.T.E. at 100 = 2.75
1938	1.2 billion	"$2\frac{1}{2}$s of 1950–1952"	P.T.E. at 100 = 2.50
1938	1.5 billion	"$2\frac{3}{4}$s of 1960–1965"	P.T.E. at 100 = 2.75
1939	1.1 billion	"$2\frac{1}{4}$s of 1951–1953"	P.T.E. at 100 = 2.25
1940	0.7 billion	"$2\frac{1}{4}$s of 1954–1956"	P.T.E. at 100 = 2.25
1940	0.7 billion	"2s of 1953–1955"	P.T.E. at 100 = 2.00
1941, Mar.	1.0 billion	"$2\frac{1}{2}$s of 1952–1954"	Fully taxable at 100 = 2.50
1941, June	1.5 billion	"$2\frac{1}{2}$s of 1956–1958"	Fully taxable at 100 = 2.50
1941, Oct.	2.7 billion	"$2\frac{1}{2}$s of 1967–1972"	Fully taxable at 100 = 2.50

In early 1941, when the United States was rearming, new legislation provided that new issues of government bonds would be fully taxable. When these were experimentally introduced, they commanded a yield 0.50% higher than the lowest-yielding new issue of P.T.E. bonds. However, some part of this differential was probably due to novelty, as the market for government bonds (as for corporate bonds) was largely in the hands of nontax-paying institutions.

Pearl Harbor brought a moderate decline in the corporate and government bond markets—much less than the one that had followed the outbreak of war in 1939. The corporate bond price average declined 4 points and Government bonds declined about 2 points. Prime municipals, with tax-exemption threatened by war sentiment, declined an average of 11 points in price. After recovering from this brief decline, prime corporate and government bond prices remained approximately stable during the war, while municipals advanced sharply to new high prices.

Treasury war finance was based on a fixed schedule of yields. The Federal Reserve Banks bought whatever securities were required to maintain this schedule. Three-month Treasury bills were at $\frac{3}{8}$% (and were largely bought by Federal Reserve Banks), one-year Certificates of Indebtedness were at $\frac{7}{8}$%, short bonds were at 2%, longer bonds were at $2\frac{1}{4}$%, and twenty-five-to-thirty-year bonds were at $2\frac{1}{2}$%. The last were not at first eligible for ownership by commercial banks. The Treasury's principal long-term offerings, all fully taxable, were:

1942	$ 1.5 billion	"$2\frac{1}{4}$s of 1952–1955" Fully taxable at	100 = 2.25%
1942	2.1 billion	"$2\frac{1}{2}$s of 1962–1967" Fully taxable at	100 = 2.50
1942	2.8 billion	"$2\frac{1}{2}$s of 1963–1968" Fully taxable at	100 = 2.50
1943	7.7 billion	"$2\frac{1}{2}$s of 1964–1969" (2 series) taxable at	100 = 2.50
1944	3.8 billion	"$2\frac{1}{4}$s of 1956–1959" Fully taxable at	100 = 2.25
1944	5.2 billion	"$2\frac{1}{2}$s of 1965–1970" Fully taxable at	100 = 2.50
1944	3.5 billion	"$2\frac{1}{2}$s of 1966–1971" Fully taxable at	100 = 2.50
1945	8.8 billion	"$2\frac{1}{4}$s of 1959–1962" (2 series) taxable at	100 = 2.25
1945	19.7 billion	"$2\frac{1}{2}$s of 1967–1972" (2 series) taxable at	100 = 2.50

After 1945, no new long-term bonds were offered for eight years. Memories of the 18-point market decline of Liberty Bonds after World War I were vivid at the outset of World War II. Skepticism as to the ability of the Treasury to finance a war at $2\frac{1}{2}$% was widespread. But the amount of savings of individuals and corporations was enormous during the wartime prosperity because incomes were high while expenditures and investment were restricted. Alternative "safe" investments were scarce, and safety was demanded because it was generally expected that prosperity would end with the end of the war. With the passage of the war years, confidence grew in the ability of the government to maintain low interest rates and bond yields. If this could and would be done, some investors argued, there was no reason to accept less than 2½%, even when investing short-term funds. Long bonds pegged at 100 were not only considered safe for short-term funds, but it was believed that, as they became shorter, they must rise in the market, first to a 2¼% yield and finally to a ⅞% yield, because shorter bonds commanded these lower yields. Thus they would provide capital gains. This was called "riding the yield curve"; it became a profitable sport for private and institutional investors.

When the war ended, some people thought that the Treasury would not always be offering as much as 2½%. Perhaps rates as high as 2½% would vanish forever. Therefore, in 1945, after the war ended, purchases of the last issues of 2½s approached $20 billion. The Treasury indeed stopped issuing new bonds altogether. The wartime "ineligibles," or "tap" 2½s, as they were called from their ineligibility for commercial banks and the unlimited size of offerings during drives, rose in the market in early 1946 to 106⅛, to yield 2.12%, while the bank-eligible 2½s of 1967–1972 rose to 109⅝, to yield 1.93%. This was the great crest of a twenty-six-year bull bond market. American prime corporate bond yields declined to 2.37%. American bond yields had at last dropped below the extreme low yields at the crest of the market for British funds reached fifty years earlier.

Municipals, spurred by shrinking supply and rising taxes, rose even more steeply in price. Long-maturity prime municipals reached a yield of only 0.90% at the 1946 highs; this represented a four-year price appreciation of about 21%. Thus a bull market was superimposed on a bull market. A price index of 4% thirty-year prime municipals (with constant maturity) had fluctuated over the years as follows

From	80 in 1920
up to	110 in 1931
down to	90 in 1932
up to	140 in 1937
down to	124 in 1937
up to	165 in 1941
up to	178 in 1946

Although the price advance from 1920 or from 1932 of good-quality, long-term, noncallable taxable bonds was less than the price advance of similar municipals, it was very considerable. Most corporate bonds had been called, or had defaulted, or had lost their credit standing. Those few, mostly rails, that suffered none of these shortcomings served their owners well. A few examples are shown in the table below.

Bond Issue		1920 Low	1932 Low	1946 High
Atchison General	4s of '95	$71\frac{1}{2}$	80	141
Norfolk & Western	4s '96	$70\frac{1}{2}$	$83\frac{1}{2}$	143
Chesapeake and Ohio	$4\frac{1}{2}$s '92	$70\frac{1}{2}$	$77\frac{1}{2}$	$151\frac{1}{8}$
Northern Pacific	4s '97	$70\frac{5}{8}$	$71\frac{3}{4}$	$127\frac{3}{4}$
Hocking Valley	$4\frac{1}{2}$s '99	$62\frac{1}{4}$	$69\frac{1}{4}$	150
Atchison Adjustment	4s '95	$64\frac{1}{8}$	$70\frac{1}{2}$	$131\frac{1}{4}$

SHORT-TERM INTEREST RATES: 1900–1945

Table 49 lists short-term American interest rates from 1900 to 1945. It includes seven types of money-market rates: (a) prime four- to six-month commercial paper rates in terms of annual averages, monthly high averages, and monthly low averages; (b) prime sixty- to ninety-day commercial paper rates until 1936 in terms of annual averages; (c) call loan rates in terms of annual averages, monthly high and low averages, and extreme quotations; (d)

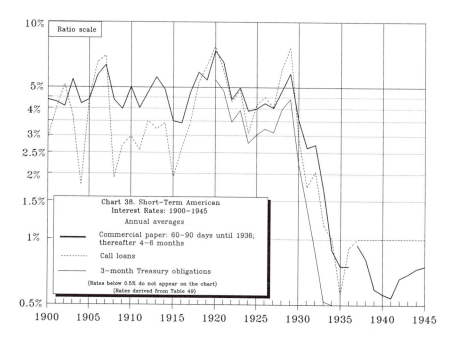

Chart 38. Short–Term American Interest Rates: 1900–1945

Annual averages

——— Commercial paper: 60–90 days until 1936; thereafter 4–6 months

·········· Call loans

——— 3–month Treasury obligations

(Rates below 0.5% do not appear on the chart)
(Rates derived from Table 49)

TABLE 49
Short-Term American Interest Rates: 1900–1945

Year	Prime Commercial Paper, %					Call Loans, %				
	4–6 Months			60–90 Days, Annual Average	Annual Average	Monthly Average		Extreme Quotations	
	Annual Average	Monthly Average							
		Low	High			Low	High		
1900	5.71	5.00	6.60	4.38	2.94	1.30	5.13	1.00	25.00
1901	5.40	4.83	5.79	4.28	4.00	2.00	6.88	1.00	75.00
1902	5.81	5.25	6.93	4.09	5.15	2.38	10.80	2.00	35.00
1903	6.16	5.60	6.75	5.44	3.71	2.03	6.00	1.00	15.00
1904	5.14	4.63	5.75	4.21	1.78	0.90	3.13	0.50	6.00
1905	5.18	4.71	6.75	4.40	4.44	2.05	16.50	1.50	125.00
1906	6.25	5.75	7.21	5.68	6.54	2.97	14.00	1.50	60.00
1907	6.66	5.71	7.33	6.34	7.01	2.31	21.00	1.00	125.00
1908	5.00	4.25	6.70	4.37	1.92	1.06	4.75	0.75	20.00
1909	4.69	4.15	5.98	3.98	2.71	1.81	5.03	1.00	7.00
10-yr. av.	5.60			4.72	4.02				
1910	5.72	5.16	6.31	5.02	2.98	1.55	4.72	1.00	14.00
1911	4.75	4.28	5.25	4.02	2.57	2.28	4.03	1.00	5.00
1912	5.41	4.50	6.50	4.75	3.52	2.28	6.50	1.50	20.00
1913	6.20	5.50	6.66	5.58	3.22	2.25	4.63	1.00	10.00
1914	5.47	4.28	7.60	4.89	3.43	1.78	6.25	1.37	10.00
1915	4.01	3.45	4.38	3.50	1.92	1.78	2.13	1.00	3.00
1916	3.84	3.50	4.38	3.43	2.62	1.88	4.44	1.50	15.00
1917	5.07	3.98	5.75	4.73	3.43	2.05	5.16	1.50	10.00
1918	6.02	5.83	6.22	5.86	5.28	4.10	6.00	2.00	6.00
1919	5.37	5.13	5.88	5.40	6.32	4.64	10.89	2.00	30.00
10-yr. av.	5.19			4.72	3.53				
1920	7.50	6.00	8.13	7.38	7.74	6.96	9.94	5.00	25.00
1921	6.62	5.13	7.88	6.53	5.97	4.97	7.26	3.50	9.00
1922	4.52	4.13	5.00	4.41	4.29	3.72	4.90	2.75	6.00
1923	5.07	4.50	5.38	4.98	4.86	4.32	5.11	3.50	6.00
1924	3.98	3.13	4.88	3.90	3.08	2.00	4.39	2.00	5.75
1925	4.02	3.63	4.38	3.99	4.18	3.32	5.32	2.00	6.00

TABLE 49 (*Continued*)

Year	Prime Commercial Paper, %					Call Loans, %				
	4-6 Months			60-90 Days, Annual Average	Annual Average	Monthly Average		Extreme Quotations		
	Annual Average	Monthly Average								
		Low	High			Low	High			
1926	4.34	4.00	4.63	4.23	4.50	3.81	5.16	3.00	6.00
1927	4.11	4.00	4.25	4.02	4.06	3.60	4.38	3.50	5.50
1928	4.85	4.00	5.63	4.81	6.04	4.24	8.60	3.50	12.00
1929	5.85	5.00	6.25	5.78	7.61	4.83	9.23	4.50	20.00
10-yr. av.	5.09			5.00	5.23				
1930	3.59	2.88	4.88	3.56	2.94	2.00	4.64	1.50	6.00
1931	2.64	2.00	4.00	2.63	1.74	1.45	2.70	1.00	3.50
1932	2.73	1.50	3.88	2.72	2.05	1.00	2.65	1.00	3.50
1933	1.73	1.25	3.00	1.66	1.16	0.75	3.32	0.75	5.00
1934	1.02	0.88	1.50	0.89	1.00	1.00	1.00		1.00
1935	0.76	0.75	0.88	0.75	0.56	0.25	1.00	0.25	1.00
1936	0.75	0.75	0.75	0.75	0.91	0.75	1.00	0.75	1.00
1937	0.94	0.75	1.00		1.00	1.00	1.00	1.00	1.00
1938	0.81	0.63	1.00		1.00	1.00	1.00	1.00	1.00
1939	0.59	0.56	0.69		1.00	1.00	1.00	1.00	1.00
10-yr. av.	1.56				1.34				
1940	0.56	0.56	0.56		1.00	1.00	1.00	1.00	1.00
1941	0.54	0.50	0.56		1.00	1.00	1.00	1.00	1.00
1942	0.66	0.56	0.69		1.00	1.00	1.00	1.00	1.00
1943	0.69	0.69	0.69		1.00	1.00	1.00	1.00	1.00
1944	0.73	0.69	0.75		1.00	1.00	1.00	1.00	1.00
1945	0.75	0.75	0.75		1.00	1.00	1.00	1.00	1.00
6-yr. av.	0.66				1.00				

TABLE 49 (*Continued*)

Year	Prime Bankers' Accept-ances, 90 Days, Annual Average, %	Prime Corp. Bonds, 1-Year Maturity, Feb. Average, %	3-Month Treasuries (Bills After 1931), %			Rediscount Rate of the Federal Reserve Bank of New York, %		
			Annual Average	Monthly Average		Annual Average	Low	High
				Low	High			
1900		3.97						
1901		3.25						
1902		3.30						
1903		3.45						
1904		3.60						
1905		3.50						
1906		4.75						
1907		4.87						
1908		5.10						
1909		4.03						
10-yr. av.		3.98						
1910		4.25						
1911		4.09						
1912		4.04						
1913		4.74						
1914		4.64				5.50	5.00	6.00
1915		4.47				4.13	4.00	5.00
1916		3.48				3.66	3.00	4.00
1917		4.05				3.05	3.00	3.50
1918	4.19	5.48				3.87	3.50	4.00
1919	4.37	5.58				4.12	4.00	4.75
10-yr. av.	4.28	4.48				4.06		
1920	6.06	6.11	5.42	4.50	5.88	6.48	4.75	7.00
1921	5.28	6.94	4.83	3.90	5.67	5.88	4.50	7.00
1922	3.51	5.31	3.47	3.13	3.90	4.21	4.00	4.50
1923	4.09	5.01	3.93	3.65	4.22	4.45	4.00	4.50
1924	2.98	5.02	2.77	1.90	3.76	3.66	3.00	4.50
1925	3.29	3.85	3.03	2.61	3.65	3.44	3.00	3.50
1926	3.59	4.40	3.23	2.93	3.58	3.83	3.50	4.00
1927	3.45	4.30	3.10	2.68	3.39	3.79	3.50	4.00

TABLE 49 (*Continued*)

Year	Prime Bankers' Accept- ances, 90 Days, Annual Average, %	Prime Corp. Bonds, 1-Year Maturity, Feb. Average, %	3-Month Treasuries (Bills After 1931), %			Rediscount Rate of the Federal Reserve Bank of New York, %		
			Annual Average	Monthly Average		Annual Average	Low	High
				Low	High			
1928	4.09	4.05	3.97	3.27	4.70	4.54	3.50	5.00
1929	5.03	5.27	4.42	3.03	5.09	5.21	4.50	6.00
10-yr. av.	4.14	5.03	3.82			4.55		
1930	2.48	4.40	2.23	1.40	3.39	3.00	2.00	4.50
1931	1.57	3.05	1.40	0.48	3.25	2.12	1.50	3.50
1932	1.28	3.99	0.88	0.08	2.68	2.83	2.50	3.50
1933	0.63	2.60	0.52	0.10	2.29	2.50	2.00	3.50
1934	0.25	2.62	0.26	0.07	0.67	1.54	1.50	2.00
1935	0.13	1.05	0.14	0.06	0.21	1.50	1.50	
1936	0.16	0.61	0.14	0.08	0.23	1.50	1.50	
1937	0.43	0.69	0.45	0.10	0.70	1.29	1.00	1.50
1938	0.44	0.85	0.05	0.01	0.10	1.00	1.00	
1939	0.44	0.57	0.02	0.01	0.06	1.00	1.00	
10-yr. av.	0.78	2.04	0.61			1.83		
1940	0.44	0.41	0.01	Neg.	0.07	1.00	1.00	
1941	0.44	0.41	0.10	Neg.	0.30	1.00	1.00	
1942	0.44	0.81	0.33	0.21	0.37	1.00	1.00	
1943	0.44	1.17	0.37	0.37	0.37	1.00	1.00	
1944	0.44	1.08	0.37	0.37	0.37	1.00	1.00	
1945	0.44	1.02	0.37	0.37	0.37	1.00	1.00	
6-yr. av.	0.44	0.82	0.26			1.00		

TABLE 49 (*Continued*)

Year	Prime Rate for Commercial Loans, Annual Average, %	Average Business Loan Rates Charged by Commercial Banks, Annual Average, %	Savings Bank Dividend Rate, Jan. 1, %	Demand Deposits Maximum Rate paid by New York Clearinghouse Banks, %	
				Low	High
1900			3.50		
1901			4.00		
1902			4.00		
1903			3.50		
1904			3.50		
1905			4.00		
1906			3.50		
1907			4.00		
1908			4.00		
1909			4.00		
10-yr. av.			3.80		
1910			3.50		
1911			3.50		
1912			3.50		
1913			3.50		
1914			3.50		
1915			3.50		
1916			3.50		
1917			4.00		
1918			4.00	2.00	
1919			4.00	2.00	2.25
10-yr. av.			3.65		
1920		6.58	4.00	2.25	
1921		6.68	4.00	2.25	
1922		5.53	4.00	2.00	2.35
1923		5.52	4.00	2.00	
1924		5.10	4.00	2.00	
1925		4.98	4.00	2.00	
1926		5.08	4.00	2.00	
1927		4.96	4.00	2.00	

TABLE 49 (*Continued*)

Year	Prime Rate for Commercial Loans, Annual Average, %	Average Business Loan Rates Charged by Commercial Banks, Annual Average, %	Savings Bank Dividend Rate, Jan. 1, %	Demand Deposits Maximum Rate paid by New York Clearinghouse Banks, %	
				Low	High
1928		5.38	4.00	2.00	
1929		6.02	4.50	2.00	
10-yr. av.		5.58	4.05		
1930		4.85	4.50	1.50	2.00
1931		4.30	4.00	1.00	1.50
1932		4.71	3.50	0.50	1.00
1933		4.27	3.00	0.00	1.00
1934	1.50	3.45	3.00	none thereafter	
1935	1.50	2.93	2.50		
1936	1.50	2.68	2.00		
1937	1.50	2.59	2.00		
1938	1.50	2.53	2.00		
1939	1.50	2.78	2.00		
10-yr. av.	1.50	3.51	2.85		
1940	1.50	2.63	2.00		
1941	1.50	2.54	2.00		
1942	1.50	2.61	2.00		
1943	1.50	2.72	2.00		
1944	1.50	2.59	1.50		
1945	1.50	2.39	1.50		
6-yr. av.	1.50	2.58	1.83		

SOURCES

Commercial paper 4–6 months, call loan averages, bankers' acceptances, short treasuries, rediscount rates, business loans: from Federal Reserve Board publications.

Call loans extremes of fluctuations are for loans without uniform standards; quoted from various sources, including the Library of the New York Stock Exchange, Commercial paper, 60–90 days: Macaulay, *op. cit.*, p. A142ff.

Prime corporate bonds: from Durand's *Basic Yields, op. cit.* Savings bank rate on regular deposits: from the records of the Bowery Savings Bank of New York City.

Demand deposit rate: privately compiled.

Prime rate: from Standard & Poor's publications.

market rates on short-term Treasury certificates, during 1920–1931 and three-month Treasury bills from 1931 in terms of annual averages and monthly highs and lows; (e) the rediscount rate on prime paper of the Federal Reserve Bank of New York in terms of annual averages and annual highs and lows; (f) prime ninety-day bankers' acceptance rates from 1918 in terms of annual averages; and (g) basic yields (Durand's) for one-year prime corporate bonds for February of each year. The table also presents a few other series of short rates not so closely connected with the money market: the prime rate for commercial loans from 1934, average business loan rates, a savings bank dividend rate (not a true interest rate), and demand deposit rates from 1918 to 1933. The commercial paper, call loan, and short-term Treasury rates are pictured in Chart 38 on page 357.

Although these money-market rates usually rose and fell at the same time, and although all were rates on prime loans of one year or less in duration, they often differed strikingly from one another. Some examples of annual averages that illustrate the differences are shown in tabular form below.

Year	4–6 Month Com-mercial Paper, %	Call Loans, %	Treasury Bills, %	Rediscount Rate, %	Bankers' Accept-ances, %
1900	5.71	2.94			
1904	5.14	1.78			
1908	5.00	1.92			
1914	5.47	3.42		5.50	
1917	5.07	3.43		3.05	
1920	7.50	7.74	5.43	6.48	6.06
1925	4.02	4.18	3.03	3.44	3.29
1929	5.85	7.61	4.42	5.21	5.03
1932	2.73	2.05	0.88	2.83	1.28
1935	0.76	0.56	0.14	1.50	0.13
1939	0.59	1.00	0.02	1.00	0.44
1945	0.75	1.00	0.37	1.00	0.44

The wide differences in the rates on loans of similar quality and short term again caution the analyst against engaging in generalities about "the level of the short-term rate of interest." A market preference for shorter or longer maturity does not explain most of the differences between, for example, four- to six-month commercial paper and one-day call loans. The differences were not due primarily to differences in either maturity or quality. The differences in these rates often arose from the structure of the money market and the convenience of the instrument and carried only a narrow technical significance.

Over the decades there have been important shifts in the relative importance of these various forms of short-term credit. In the nineteenth century, commercial paper dominated the market. Late in the century, call loans grew rapidly in importance as a more convenient form of secondary bank reserve. Call loan rates, although very volatile, averaged far below commercial paper rates during the late nineteenth century and early twentieth century, probably largely because of this convenience. By 1920, however, daily balances could be settled at the Federal Reserve Banks. Call loan rates in the 1920s rose approximately to the level of commercial paper rates and often higher. This was in part because short prime commercial paper could be rediscounted at the newly organized Federal Reserve Banks and security loans could not, and in part because the volume of call loans grew enormously in the late 1920s and the volume of commercial paper did not. Corporations in the United States, as in Britain, tended then to borrow more against lines of credit at their own banks and less in the commercial paper market.

In the 1930's, both the commercial paper market and the call loan market shrank in significance. Call loans never recovered their importance, partly because of strict margin-requirement rules. Treasury bills, however, have dominated the money markets both here and abroad since the 1930's. Their rates in the 1930's fell far below those of other short-term credit forms, sometimes to negative yields when investors or institutions wanted to report money at work rather than idle balances.

At the beginning of the century, commercial paper rates were high by pre-1970 standards, and call money rates, while very volatile, were also often high. Before the establishment of the Federal Reserve System, it was not unusual for commercial paper to run up to 18 or 36% for a few days and for call money briefly to exceed 100%.

The average of four- to six-month commercial paper rates actually declined from the first decade of the century to the second and from the second decade to the third. Call money rates also declined from the first decade to the second, but rose in the third decade. In contrast, one-year prime corporate bond yields rose with long-term bond yields during the first and second decades, but rose even further during the third decade. These contrasts are probably largely explained by the fact that the new Federal Reserve System helped the commercial paper market more than it helped these other short markets.

In the 1930's all short-term rates declined sharply. Most of them went to nominal levels below 1% as the protracted Depression discouraged borrowing. In the early 1940's most short rates began to rise gradually but remained very low. The Treasury restricted non-war-related borrowing and pegged short-term government borrowing rates at the low levels of the 1930's.

Chapter XVIII

The United States in the Twentieth Century: 1946–1990

POLITICAL AND ECONOMIC BACKGROUND

The period from World War II to 1990 divides into two eras roughly equal in length but of marked contrast in economics and finance. From the war's end through the mid-1960's, the United States was preeminent among nations. The American economy experienced stable economic growth with minimal inflation, aided the recovery of war-torn Europe, led the Western alliance in keeping a lid on the Cold War, assisted the efforts of the less developed countries to raise their economic levels, and prepared to land humans on the moon. Talk of "the American century" was common. During the later 1960's the American century began to unravel. The remainder of the period to 1990 would be one of an unpopular war in Asia, social dissent, political scandals, a more stagnant and unstable economy, monetary instability, large budget and trade deficits that returned the country to a debtor status internationally, and, above all, a great and protracted inflation of prices. All of these developments had profound and unprecedented effects on the interest rates.

DETAIL OF THE SECOND BEAR BOND MARKET: 1946–1981

The greatest of all secular bear bond markets, which began in April of 1946, and probably ended in September 1981, carried prime long American corporate bond yields from their lowest recorded yields to their highest. The yield index rose from 2.46 to 15.49% for seasoned prime issues and up to 16.5% (industrials) and 18.0% (utilities) for high-quality new issues. This was a yield increase of 1303 basis points on seasoned issues, and 1981 peak yields were more than six times greater than 1946 low yields. The great bear market lasted some thirty-five years, by far the longest duration for a bear bond market in U.S. history. If a constant maturity thirty-year 2½% bond had been available throughout this second bear market of the century, its price would have declined from 101 in 1946 to 17 in 1981, or 83%. In contrast, in the first bear bond market of the century, 1899 to 1920, the same bond would have declined 35% in price. The recent bear bond market seemed to have much more social and economic significance than that of all earlier bear bond markets. In all the others, bond yields stayed within the traditional band that had prevailed for centuries. This time they broke decisively out of that band.

The bear bond market of 1946–1981 can be subdivided into seven major price declines interspersed by six rallies. These are summarized in terms of the monthly average of prime corporate bond yields and a corresponding price index for a constant maturity 2½% bond in the table on page 368.

The economic climate during the postwar period from 1946 to the mid-1960's was favorable, often exuberant. It was not until 1958 that inflationary expectations became highly articulate, and then for a while there developed something like a flight from bonds and from the dollar into gold, foreign currencies, or equities. By 1961, stability was restored, and the inflation rate was negligible for the next five years. In 1965, however, a dangerous inflationary spiral began and with it a superboom that was only briefly interrupted by a recession in 1970. Wage and price controls imposed in 1971 and relaxed in 1973 had no lasting effect on the price level. Inflation reached double digits in 1974, in part because of a steep increase in oil prices put into effect by the OPEC cartel in late 1973. It spread through most of the free world. At times it seemed that no government could command a political majority in favor of effective anti-inflation measures. The recession of 1974–1975 reduced the inflation from double digits to under 6% in 1975–1976, but this was merely a temporary lull as inflation marched back up to double digit levels during 1979–1981. Another steep increase in oil prices in 1979 again contributed to the price upsurge. A brief recession in 1980 had almost no impact on the inflation. The term "stagflation" came into general use as a result of the experiences of 1973–1975 and 1980–1982. The optimistic economic climate of the initial postwar decades gave way to a deepening pessimism in the 1970's and early 1980's. Interest rates advanced to their highest levels in the American record, leading to a severe recession in 1981–1982, after which inflation retreated to annual rates of 3 to 5% during the remainder of the 1980's. Interest rates and yields also retreated, but remained,

THE BEAR BOND MARKET: 1946–1981

Dates of Price Trends	Duration		Yield, % (from Table 50)	Yield Change, Basis Points	Price Change of a Constant 30-Year 2½% Bond, Points
	Yrs.	Mos.			
Initial date: Apr. 1946					Initial price: 100⅞
1. Decline to Aug. 1948	2	4	2.46–2.84	+38	−7¾
Advance to Jan. 1950	1	5	−2.57	−27	+5⅜
	3	9		+11	−2⅜
2. Decline to June 1953	3	5	−3.40	+83	−15⅜
Advance to Apr. 1954		10	−2.85	−55	+9⅞
	4	3		+28	−5½
3. Decline to Sept. 1957	3	5	−4.12	+127	−20¾
Advance to May 1958	0	8	−3.57	−55	+8¼
	4	1		+72	−12½
4. Decline to June 1970	1	5	−4.57	+100	−14
Advance to Feb. 1963	3	4	−4.19	−38	+4⅞
	4	9		+62	−9⅛
5. Decline to Oct. 1960	7	4	−8.48	+429	−37⅛
Advance to Jan. 1972	1	7	−7.19	−129	+9¾
	8	11		+300	−27⅜
6. Decline to Oct. 1974	2	9	−9.27	+208	−14⅜
Advance to Sept. 1977	2	11	−7.92	−135	+8⅝
	5	8		+73	−5⅞
7. Decline to Sept. 1981	4	0	−15.49	+757	−21
Total change: Apr. 1946–Sept. 1981	35	5		+1303	−83¾ (−83%)
					Final price: 17⅛

at the close of the 1980's, at levels not seen in the American markets before 1974 (see Chart 39 and Tables 50 and 51).

During the first segment of the bear bond market, 1946–1948, the corporate bond average declined about 10% in price; the government bond average, reflecting the continued pegging policy of the Treasury and the Federal Reserve, declined only 7½%, while the prime municipal average declined 23%. Municipal yields more than doubled. Large new municipal issues over-

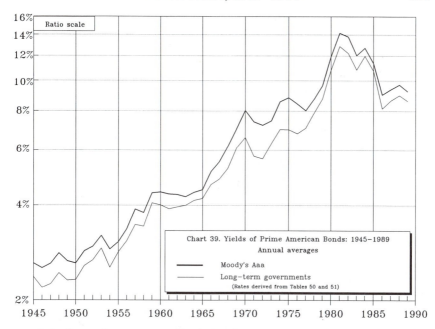

Chart 39. Yields of Prime American Bonds: 1945–1989
Annual averages

——— Moody's Aaa

——— Long–term governments
(Rates derived from Tables 50 and 51)

taxed the limited resources of high-bracket investors and forced the market to seek a wider clientele. After the surprise election victory of the Democrats in November 1948, and after signs of faltering in business, all bond prices recovered.

Bond prices again began to decline in January of 1950. During the first six months of the Korean War, June–December 1950, the bond market paused as if to consider whether the new war meant a return to wartime austerity and low interest rates or whether inflation would be allowed to push interest rates up. Municipal prices rose sharply in expectation of high taxes and wartime controls on expenditures. The Korean War in fact broke the grip with which the government had for eight years controlled the market for its own bonds. Although President Truman threw the prestige of his office behind the demand of the Secretary of the Treasury that government bonds be supported at par, in February–March of 1951, the Treasury and the Federal Reserve Board reached an accord that ended the policy of rigid support. Following the accord, long governments declined 4–7 points in the market, prime corporate bonds declined 7 points, and municipals declined 13%.

The elections of 1952 brought a renewed wave of business exuberance and a shift to the right in fiscal and monetary policy. The stage was set for another decline in the bond market, which came in the spring of 1953. The rediscount rate was raised to 2%, its highest level since 1933. The bill rate rose to 2.23%. The Reserve Banks put pressure on member banks to reduce their large rediscounts. On one occasion there was some difficulty in securing

TABLE 50
CORPORATE AND MUNICIPAL LONG-TERM BOND YIELDS: 1946–1989

Year	Annual Average	Prime Corporate Bonds, s Yield											
		Jan.	Feb.	Mar.	Apr.	May	June	July	Aug.	Sept.	Oct.	Nov.	Dec.
1946	2.53	2.54	2.48	2.47	2.46	2.51	2.49	2.48	2.51	2.58	2.60	2.59	2.61
1947	2.61	2.57	2.55	2.55	2.53	2.53	2.55	2.55	2.56	2.61	2.70	2.77	2.86
1948	2.82	2.86	2.85	2.83	2.78	2.76	2.76	2.81	2.84	2.84	2.84	2.84	2.79
1949	2.66	2.71	2.71	2.70	2.70	2.71	2.71	2.67	2.62	2.60	2.61	2.60	2.58
4-yr. av.	2.66												
1950	2.62	2.57	2.58	2.58	2.60	2.61	2.62	2.65	2.61	2.64	2.67	2.67	2.67
1951	2.86	2.66	2.66	2.78	2.87	2.89	2.94	2.94	2.88	2.84	2.89	2.96	3.01
1952	2.96	2.98	2.93	2.96	2.93	2.93	2.94	2.95	2.94	2.95	3.01	2.98	2.97
1953	3.20	3.02	3.07	3.12	3.23	3.34	3.40	3.28	3.24	3.29	3.16	3.11	3.13
1954	2.90	3.06	2.95	2.86	2.85	2.88	2.90	2.89	2.87	2.89	2.87	2.89	2.90
1955	3.06	2.93	2.93	3.02	3.01	3.04	3.05	3.06	3.11	3.13	3.10	3.10	3.15
1956	3.36	3.11	3.08	3.10	3.24	3.28	3.26	3.28	3.43	3.56	3.59	3.69	3.75
1957	3.89	3.77	3.67	3.66	3.67	3.74	3.91	3.99	4.10	4.12	4.10	4.08	3.81
1958	3.79	3.60	3.59	3.63	3.60	3.57	3.57	3.67	3.85	4.09	4.11	4.09	4.08
1959	4.38	4.12	4.14	4.13	4.23	4.37	4.46	4.47	4.43	4.52	4.57	4.56	4.58
10-yr. av.	3.30												
1960	4.41	4.61	4.56	4.49	4.45	4.46	4.45	4.41	4.28	4.25	4.30	4.31	4.35
1961	4.35	4.32	4.27	4.22	4.25	4.27	4.33	4.41	4.45	4.45	4.42	4.39	4.42
1962	4.33	4.42	4.42	4.39	4.33	4.28	4.28	4.34	4.35	4.32	4.28	4.25	4.24
1963	4.26	4.21	4.19	4.19	4.21	4.22	4.23	4.26	4.29	4.31	4.32	4.33	4.35
1964	4.40	4.37	4.36	4.38	4.40	4.41	4.41	4.40	4.41	4.42	4.42	4.43	4.44
1965	4.49	4.43	4.41	4.42	4.43	4.44	4.46	4.48	4.49	4.52	4.56	4.60	4.68
1966	5.13	4.74	4.78	4.92	4.96	4.98	5.07	5.16	5.31	5.49	5.41	5.35	5.39
1967	5.51	5.20	5.03	5.13	5.11	5.24	5.44	5.58	5.62	5.65	5.82	6.07	6.19
1968	6.18	6.17	6.10	6.11	6.21	6.27	6.28	6.24	6.02	5.97	6.09	6.19	6.45
1969	7.03	6.59	6.66	6.85	6.89	6.79	6.98	7.08	6.97	7.14	7.33	7.35	7.72
10-yr. av.	5.01												
1970	8.04	7.91	7.93	7.84	7.83	8.11	8.48	8.44	8.13	8.09	8.03	8.05	7.64
1971	7.39	7.36	7.08	7.21	7.25	7.53	7.64	7.64	7.59	7.44	7.39	7.26	7.25
1972	7.21	7.19	7.27	7.24	7.30	7.30	7.23	7.21	7.19	7.22	7.21	7.12	7.08
1973	7.44	7.15	7.22	7.29	7.26	7.29	7.37	7.45	7.68	7.63	7.60	7.67	7.68
1974	8.57	7.83	7.85	8.01	8.25	8.37	8.47	8.72	9.00	9.24	9.27	8.89	8.89
1975	8.83	8.83	8.62	8.67	8.95	8.90	8.77	8.84	8.95	8.95	8.86	8.78	8.79
1976	8.43	8.60	8.55	8.52	8.40	8.58	8.62	8.56	8.45	8.38	8.32	8.25	7.98

TABLE 50 (*Continued*)

Year	Annual Average	Jan.	Feb.	Mar.	Apr.	May	June	July	Aug.	Sept.	Oct.	Nov.	Dec.
					Prime Corporate Bonds, s Yield								
1977	8.02	7.96	8.04	8.10	8.04	8.05	7.95	7.94	7.98	7.92	8.04	8.08	8.19
1978	8.73	8.41	8.47	8.47	8.56	8.69	8.76	8.88	8.69	8.69	8.89	9.03	9.16
1979	9.63	9.25	9.26	9.37	9.38	9.50	9.29	9.20	9.23	9.44	10.13	10.76	10.74
10-yr. av.	8.23												
1980	11.94	11.09	12.38	12.96	12.04	10.99	10.58	11.07	11.64	12.02	12.31	12.97	13.21
1981	14.17	12.81	13.35	13.33	13.88	14.32	13.75	14.38	14.89	15.49	15.40	14.22	14.23
1982	13.79	15.18	15.27	14.58	14.46	14.26	14.81	14.61	13.71	12.94	12.12	11.85	11.83
1983	12.04	11.79	12.01	11.73	11.51	11.46	11.74	12.15	12.51	12.37	12.25	12.41	12.57
1984	12.71	12.20	12.08	12.57	12.81	13.28	12.55	13.44	12.87	12.66	12.63	12.29	12.13
1985	11.37	12.08	12.13	12.56	12.23	11.72	10.94	10.97	11.05	11.07	11.02	10.55	10.16
1986	9.02	10.05	9.67	9.00	8.79	9.09	9.13	8.88	8.72	8.89	8.86	8.68	8.49
1987	9.38	8.36	8.38	8.36	8.85	9.33	9.32	9.42	9.67	10.18	10.52	10.01	10.11
1988	9.71	9.88	9.40	9.39	9.67	9.90	9.86	9.96	10.11	9.82	9.51	9.45	9.57
1989	9.26	9.62	9.64	9.80	9.79	9.59	9.10	8.93	8.96	9.01	8.92	8.89	8.86
10-yr. av.	11.34												

Year	Medium-Grade Corporate Bonds, % Yield, Annual Average	Aaa Utility Bonds, Prime New Issues, % Yield		
		Annual Average	Low	High
1946	3.05			
1947	3.24			
1948	3.47			
1949	3.42			
4-yr. av.	3.30			
1950	3.24			
1951	3.41			
1952	3.52			

TABLE 50 (*Continued*)

Year	Medium-Grade Corporate Bonds, % Yield, Annual Average	Aaa Utility Bonds, Prime New Issues, % Yield		
		Annual Average	Low	High
1953	3.74			
1954	3.51			
1955	3.53			
1956	3.88			
1957	4.71			
1958	4.73			
1959	5.05			
10-yr. av.	3.93			
1960	5.19	4.63	4.19	4.93
1961	5.08	4.35	4.05	4.62
1962	5.02	4.19	4.12	4.40
1963	4.86	4.21	4.08	4.35
1964	4.83	4.34	4.25	4.39
1965	4.87	4.50	4.30	4.84
1966	5.67	5.43	4.78	5.85
1967	6.23	5.82	5.18	6.59
1968	6.94	6.50	6.18	6.93
1969	7.81	7.71	6.98	8.82
10-yr. av.	5.65			
1970	9.11	8.68	7.93	9.25
1971	8.56	7.62	7.28	8.04
1972	8.16	7.31	7.09	7.45
1973	8.24	7.74	7.38	8.36
1974	9.5	9.33	8.12	10.38
1975	10.61	9.40	8.97	9.68
1976	9.75	8.48	7.94	8.82
1977	8.97	8.19	8.07	8.34
1978	9.49	8.96	8.68	9.28
1979	10.69	10.03	9.48	11.42
10-yr. av.	9.31			
1980	13.67	12.74	11.73	14.51
1981	16.04	15.56	14.12	17.21
1982	16.11	14.41	11.70	15.93
1983	13.55	12.73	11.92	13.29
1984	14.19	13.81	12.88	15.00

TABLE 50 (*Continued*)

Year	Medium-Grade Corporate Bonds, % Yield, Annual Average	Aaa Utility Bonds, Prime New Issues, % Yield		
		Annual Average	Low	High
1985	12.72	12.06	10.91	13.17
1986	10.39	9.61	9.08	10.74
1987	10.58	9.96	8.82	11.07
1988	10.83	10.20	9.75	10.61
1989	10.18	9.79	9.28	10.37
10-yr. av.	12.83	12.09		

| Year | High-Grade Municipal Bonds, % Yield | | | | | | | | |
| | Prime New Issues | | | Moody's Aaa | | | Bond Buyer, High Grade | | |
	Annual Average	Low	High	Annual Average	Low	High	Annual Average	Low	High
1946	1.12	0.90	1.50	1.10	0.91	1.38	1.23	1.04	1.66
1947	1.46	1.35	1.80	1.45	1.35	1.69	1.63	1.56	1.85
1948	1.91	1.70	2.15	1.87	1.75	1.96	2.16	2.00	2.25
1949	1.65	1.60	1.70	1.66	1.61	1.71	1.92	1.84	1.99
4-yr. av.	1.54			1.52			1.74		
1950	1.52	1.40	1.65	1.57	1.42	1.66	1.74	1.58	1.86
1951	1.79	1.40	2.00	1.60	1.30	1.78	1.75	1.43	2.02
1952	2.02	1.85	2.25	1.79	1.67	1.99	1.98	1.84	2.20
1953	2.45	2.25	2.75	2.31	2.04	2.64	2.50	2.21	2.85
1954	2.32	2.15	2.45	2.03	1.93	2.18	2.24	2.10	2.37
1955	2.34	2.25	2.40	2.17	2.06	2.29	2.33	2.24	2.50
1956	2.54	2.30	2.85	2.50	2.19	3.04	2.62	2.34	3.10
1957	3.05	2.70	3.25	3.10	2.79	3.43	3.15	2.89	3.43
1958	2.87	2.65	3.30	2.92	2.69	3.28	3.05	2.80	3.51
1959	3.31	3.10	3.65	3.35	3.06	3.60	3.43	3.15	3.70
10-yr. av.	2.42			2.33			2.48		
1960	3.40	3.10	3.65	3.26	2.99	3.53	3.37	3.12	3.65
1961	3.38	3.25	3.40	3.27	3.12	3.37	3.35	3.16	3.44
1962	3.21	3.10	3.35	3.03	2.88	3.26	3.10	2.92	3.28
1963	3.19	3.10	3.30	3.06	2.93	3.18	3.10	2.95	3.24

TABLE 50 (*Continued*)

Year	High-Grade Municipal Bonds, % Yield								
	Prime New Issues			Moody's Aaa			Bond Buyer, High Grade		
	Annual Average	Low	High	Annual Average	Low	High	Annual Average	Low	High
1964	3.26	3.20	3.35	3.09	2.99	3.16	3.15	3.06	3.25
1965	3.32	3.15	3.50	3.16	2.97	3.39	3.21	2.99	3.47
1966	3.72	3.45	4.10	3.67	3.40	3.93	3.72	3.43	4.14
1967	3.91	3.30	4.30	3.74	3.38	4.15	3.87	3.32	4.37
1968	4.40	3.90	4.90	4.20	4.00	4.50	4.33	3.96	4.72
1969	5.71	4.80	6.35	5.45	4.58	6.50	5.60	4.68	6.74
10-yr. av.	3.75			3.59			3.68		
1970	6.35	5.25	6.95	6.12	5.81	6.81	6.12	5.02	7.00
1971	5.55	5.15	6.25	5.22	4.75	5.75	5.25	4.75	6.04
1972	5.20	5.00	5.30	5.04	4.84	5.23	5.05	4.78	5.35
1973	5.20	5.00	5.50	4.99	4.76	5.26	5.09	4.87	5.45
1974	5.90	5.05	6.50	5.89	5.03	6.65	5.93	5.04	6.71
1975	6.59	6.30	7.00	6.42	5.96	6.67	6.62	5.94	7.23
1976	6.02	5.50	6.40	5.66	5.07	6.22	6.18	5.59	7.64
1977	5.45	5.30	5.60	5.20	5.07	5.31	5.36	5.20	5.57
1978	5.75	5.40	6.15	5.52	5.11	5.91	5.70	5.36	5.98
1979	6.18	5.85	7.00	5.92	5.54	6.50	6.13	5.81	6.91
10-yr. av.	5.82			5.60			5.74		
1980	8.15	7.20	9.20	7.85	6.58	9.44	8.15	6.85	9.68
1981	10.81	9.40	12.75	10.43	8.98	12.05	10.79	9.27	12.58
1982	11.32	9.60	12.75	10.88	9.15	12.30	11.44	9.70	12.89
1983	9.15	9.00	9.60	8.80	8.28	9.34	9.22	8.56	9.63
1984	9.80	9.40	10.75	9.61	9.00	10.10	9.98	9.34	10.64
1985	8.95	8.30	9.50	8.60	7.98	9.18	9.10	8.34	9.78
1986	7.57	6.80	8.85	6.95	6.19	7.74	7.25	6.61	8.24
1987	7.83	6.75	8.90	7.14	6.05	7.90	7.45	6.43	8.41
1988	7.57	7.20	7.85	7.36	7.05	7.56	7.57	7.22	7.85
1989				7.00	6.72	7.40	7.12	6.75	7.62
10-yr. av.	9.02 (9-yr. av.)			8.46			8.81		

SOURCES

Prime and medium-grade corporates and prime new issues of Aaa utilities: Moody's Aaa and Baa and Aaa utilities from Federal Reserve, *Banking and Monetary Statistics 1941–1970* (1976); Federal Reserve, *Annual Statistical Digest*, and *Federal Reserve Bulletin*.

Municipals: Moody's Aaa from same sources as for corporates. Prime new issues and bond buyer high grade from the Salomon Brothers publication, *An Analytical Record of Yields and Yield Spreads* (July 1989 and updates).

TABLE 51
Prices and Yields of Long-Term U.S. Government Securities: 1946–1989

Year	Annual Average	Jan.	Feb.	Mar.	Apr.	May	June	July	Aug.	Sept.	Oct.	Nov.	Dec.
					Yield Average of Long Governments, %								
1946	2.19	2.21	2.12	2.09	2.08	2.19	2.16	2.18	2.23	2.28	2.26	2.25	2.24
1947	2.25	2.21	2.21	2.19	2.19	2.19	2.22	2.25	2.24	2.24	2.27	2.36	2.39
1948	2.44	2.45	2.45	2.44	2.44	2.42	2.41	2.41	2.45	2.45	2.45	2.44	2.44
1949	2.31	2.42	2.39	2.38	2.38	2.38	2.38	2.27	2.24	2.22	2.22	2.20	2.19
4-yr. av.	2.30												
1950	2.32	2.20	2.24	2.27	2.30	2.31	2.33	2.34	2.33	2.36	2.38	2.38	2.39
1951	2.57	2.39	2.40	2.47	2.56	2.63	2.65	2.63	2.57	2.56	2.61	2.66	2.70
1952	2.68	2.74	2.71	2.70	2.64	2.57	2.61	2.61	2.70	2.71	2.74	2.71	2.75
1953	2.92	2.80	2.83	2.89	2.97	3.12	3.13	3.04	3.05	3.01	2.87	2.86	2.79
1954	2.54	2.69	2.62	2.53	2.48	2.54	2.55	2.47	2.48	2.52	2.54	2.57	2.59
1955	2.84	2.68	2.77	2.78	2.82	2.81	2.82	2.91	2.95	2.92	2.87	2.89	2.91
1956	3.08	2.88	2.85	2.93	3.07	2.97	2.93	3.00	3.17	3.21	3.20	3.30	3.40
1957	3.47	3.34	3.22	3.26	3.32	3.40	3.58	3.60	3.63	3.66	3.73	3.57	3.30
1958	3.43	3.24	3.26	3.25	3.12	3.14	3.19	3.36	3.60	3.75	3.76	3.70	3.80
1959	4.07	3.90	3.92	3.92	4.01	4.08	4.09	4.11	4.10	4.26	4.11	4.12	4.27
10-yr. av.	2.99												
1960	4.01	4.37	4.22	4.08	4.17	4.16	3.99	3.86	3.79	3.82	3.91	3.93	3.88
1961	3.90	3.89	3.81	3.78	3.80	3.73	3.88	3.90	4.00	4.02	3.98	3.98	4.06
1962	3.95	4.08	4.09	4.01	3.89	3.88	3.90	4.02	3.97	3.94	3.89	3.87	3.87
1963	4.00	3.88	3.92	3.93	3.97	3.97	4.00	4.01	3.99	4.04	4.07	4.10	4.14
1964	4.15	4.15	4.14	4.18	4.20	4.16	4.13	4.13	4.14	4.16	4.16	4.12	4.14
1965	4.21	4.14	4.16	4.15	4.15	4.14	4.14	4.15	4.19	4.25	4.27	4.34	4.43
1966	4.66	4.43	4.61	4.63	4.55	4.57	4.63	4.74	4.80	4.79	4.70	4.74	4.65
1967	4.85	4.40	4.47	4.45	4.51	4.76	4.86	4.86	4.95	4.99	5.18	5.44	5.36
1968	5.25	5.18	5.16	5.39	5.28	5.40	5.23	5.09	5.04	5.09	5.24	5.36	5.65
1969	6.10	5.74	5.86	6.05	5.84	5.85	6.06	6.07	6.02	6.32	6.27	6.51	6.81
10-yr. av.	4.51												
1970	6.59	6.86	6.44	6.39	6.53	6.94	6.99	6.57	6.75	6.63	6.59	6.24	5.97
1971	5.74	5.91	5.84	5.71	5.75	5.96	5.94	5.91	5.78	5.56	5.46	5.44	5.62
1972	5.63	5.62	5.67	5.66	5.74	5.64	5.59	5.57	5.54	5.70	5.69	5.50	5.63
1973	6.30	5.94	6.14	6.20	6.11	6.22	6.32	6.53	6.81	6.42	6.26	6.31	6.35

TABLE 51 (*Continued*)

Year	Annual Average	Jan.	Feb.	Mar.	Apr.	May	June	July	Aug.	Sept.	Oct.	Nov.	Dec.
					Yield Average of Long Governments, %								
1974	6.99	6.56	6.54	6.81	7.04	7.07	7.05	7.18	7.33	7.30	7.22	6.93	6.78
1975	6.98	6.68	6.61	6.73	7.03	6.99	6.86	6.89	7.06	7.29	7.29	7.21	7.17
1976	6.78	6.94	6.92	6.87	6.73	6.99	6.92	6.85	6.79	6.70	6.65	6.62	6.39
1977	7.06	6.68	7.15	7.20	7.14	7.17	6.99	6.97	7.00	6.94	7.08	7.14	7.23
1978	7.89	7.50	7.60	7.63	7.74	7.87	7.94	8.09	7.87	7.82	8.07	8.16	8.36
1979	8.74	8.43	8.43	8.45	8.44	8.55	8.32	8.35	8.42	8.68	9.44	9.80	9.59
10-yr. av.	6.87												
1980	10.81	10.03	11.55	11.87	10.83	9.82	9.40	9.83	10.53	10.94	11.20	11.83	11.89
1981	12.87	11.65	12.23	12.15	12.62	12.96	12.39	13.05	13.61	14.14	14.13	12.68	12.88
1982	12.23	13.74	13.63	12.98	12.84	12.67	13.32	12.97	12.15	11.48	10.51	10.18	10.33
1983	10.84	10.37	10.60	10.34	10.19	10.21	10.64	11.10	11.42	11.26	11.21	11.32	11.44
1984	11.99	11.29	11.44	11.90	12.17	12.89	13.00	12.82	12.23	11.97	11.66	12.25	11.21
1985	10.75	11.15	11.35	11.78	11.42	10.96	10.36	10.51	10.59	10.67	10.56	10.08	9.60
1986	8.14	9.51	9.07	8.13	7.59	8.02	8.23	7.85	7.72	8.08	8.04	7.81	7.67
1987	8.64	7.60	7.69	7.62	8.31	8.79	8.63	8.70	8.97	9.58	9.61	8.99	9.12
1988	8.98	8.82	8.41	8.61	8.91	9.24	9.04	9.20	9.33	9.06	8.89	9.07	9.13
1989	8.58	9.07	9.16	9.33	9.18	8.95	8.40	8.19	8.26	8.31	8.15	8.03	8.02
10-yr. av.	10.38												

SOURCES
Federal Reserve sources, as given in Table 50.

enough bidders to cover the Treasury's weekly bill issue. Public statements assured the market of the new government's tight money policies. While government bonds were declining 6 points, the Treasury offered its first long-term bond issue since 1945 and its last for two years to come:

1953 $1.6 billion   "3¼s of 1978–1983," fully taxable at 100 = 3.25%.

The new issue immediately declined to 98½, to yield 3.34%. Between January and the lows of June 1953, the corporate bond average declined 6½% in price, and the municipal average declined 10⅛%.

In July of 1953, a small business recession set in, monetary policy relaxed, and the bond market began a sharp ten-month rally. By April of 1954, the corporate bond price average had recovered 12%, and the U.S. 2½s of 1967–1972 had advanced from 89¾ to 100⅞; this price was above the pre-accord support level, but was achieved without support. The low rates and high bond prices of the early postwar years had returned—but only briefly.

In the early months of 1955, as business recovered, bond prices again began to fall. In February and July the Treasury again issued long-term bonds:

1955 　$2.7 billion (two issues) 　"3s of 1995," fully taxable at 100 = 3%.

In April of 1956, a sharper decline in the bond market began. Business then entered a traditional capital-goods boom that lasted until late 1957. The rise in consumer credit broke previous records. The decline in the corporate bond price average from April 1954, to September 1957, amounted to some 22%; this was about as large as the largest previous cyclical decline, that of 1917–1920. Prime municipal prices declined about 21%. The U.S. 3¼s of 1978–1983 declined from a high of 112⅜ in 1954 to a low of 92⅜ in 1957, a gross decline of nearly 18%. The bill rate rose from 0.65% in 1954 to 3.59% in 1957.

During 1957 the Treasury offered two small new long-term bond issues:

1957, Oct. $0.7 billion 　"4s of 1969," fully taxable at 100 = 4.00%.
1957, Dec. 0.7 billion 　"3⅞s of 1974," fully taxable at 100 = 3.87%.

In late 1957, the decline in the bond market was suddenly and sharply reversed. A decline in the stock market was followed by signs that the business boom was faltering. In November the Federal Reserve Banks signaled a reversal of policy by reducing the rediscount rate. In two to four months the corporate bond price index rose 12½%, Treasury 3¼s of 1978–1983 rose 12%, and the municipals index rose 13% in price. The bill rate declined to 0.88%. In early 1958 the Treasury took advantage of the better market by selling:

1958, Feb. 　$1.7 billion 　"3½s of 1990," fully taxable at 100 = 3.50%.
1958, June 　 1.1 billion 　"3¼s of 1985," fully taxable at 100½ = 3.23%.

Just as the business recession of 1957–1958 was sharp but brief, so the bond market rally of 1957–1958 was also sharp and very brief. The price recovery was about as large as that of 1953–1954, but it was all accomplished in two to four months, as contrasted with the seventeen months' recovery of 1948–1950 and the ten months' recovery of 1953–1954.

The first half of 1958 was characterized by unprecedented speculation in government bonds. In May and June of 1958, early signs of business recovery caught bond speculators by surprise, and the brief, intense bond market boom collapsed. The prospect of a large Treasury deficit in a period of recovery induced expectations of inflation at home and fear for the dollar abroad. Investors looking to the lessons of the past staged a flight from dollars to property and from bonds to stocks. U.S. 3¼s of 1978–1983 declined from 103⅜, or 3.07%, in early 1958, to 82⅞, or 4.42%, in late 1959. The average of corporate bond prices declined about 18%, to yield 4.57%. This decline lasted one year and five months. It penetrated deeply down toward the historic lows of the market since specie resumption in 1879. Only in the crisis years around 1920 and 1932 had yields of prime corporate and government bonds averaged much higher. If allowance is made for the value of tax exemption, prime municipal yields had never been higher.

In 1959 the rediscount rate rose to 4%, its high since 1930; commercial paper rates rose to 4.88%; call money rose to 5½% (in early 1960); and Treasury ninety-day bills rose to 4.57%, with some longer bills up to well over 5%. Short- and medium-term bonds were again yielding more than were long-term bonds. The Treasury considered itself limited by law to a 4¼% maximum yield on long-term financing. Nevertheless, it managed to sell three small long-term bond issues:

1959	$0.9 billion	"4s of 1980," fully taxable at 99 = 4.06%.
1959	0.6 billion	"4s of 1969," reopened, fully taxable at 100 = 4.00%.
1960	0.5 billion	"4¼s of 1975–1985," fully taxable at 100 = 4.25%.

The sequence of coupons employed by the Treasury for its long-term bond financing after World War II contrasts as follows with the sequence employed by the Treasury in the earlier postwar boom period of the 1920's:

1922–1931	4¼%, 4%, 3¾%, 3⅜%, 3⅜%, 3⅛%, 3%
1953–1960	3¼%, 3%, 4%, 3⅞%, 3½%, 3¼%, 4%, 4%, 4¼%

In October of 1959, the corporate and municipal bond price averages reached their lows and then turned up. Government bond prices turned up in January of 1960. A hesitant and irregular price advance continued to mid-1960 and was resumed in early 1961. By 1961 the price recovery was almost as large as that of 1957–1958, but it was accompanied by doubts and hesitation, and at no time did it attract the speculative following of early 1958. The market had learned to expect high and rising yields and to regard declining or moderate yields as temporary manifestations of transitory business recessions. Nevertheless, the business recovery of 1961–1962 did not bring high yields.

Instead, from 1961 until 1965, there followed the most unusual period of stability in the postwar period. Prime corporate bond yields remained close to 4.50% for five years. Short-term rates, which had declined sharply in 1960 (three-month bills from 4.52 to 2.19%), began to rise in 1961 and rose sharply in 1963 and 1964, but long bond yields did not rise significantly with them. During these years the Treasury made a strong effort to extend the maturity of its debt and sold the following long-term bond issues, all fully taxable, many as exchanges or prefundings:

1961	$1.3 billion	"3½s of 1980"	at	$91\frac{3}{8}$ = 4.16%
	1.3 billion	"3½s of 1990"	at	$90\frac{7}{8}$ = 4.28
	1.2 billion	"3½s of 1998"	at	$88\frac{1}{2}$ = 4.10
1962	0.6 billion	"4s of 1980"	at	$99\frac{1}{2}$ = 4.64
	0.9 billion	"3½s of 1990"	at	$90\frac{7}{8}$ = 4.21
	0.9 billion	"3½s of 1998"	at	$88\frac{3}{4}$ = 4.19
	0.4 billion	"4¼s of 1987–1992"	at 101	= 4.19
	? billion	"4s of 1980"	at	$99\frac{1}{2}$ = 4.07
1963	0.3 billion	"4s of 1988–1993"	at	$99\frac{7}{8}$ = 4.61
	1.1 billion	"4s of 1986"		
	1.6 billion	"4⅛s of 1989–1994"	at	$100\frac{1}{2}$ = 4.10
1964	0.7 billion	"4¼s of 1975–1985"	at 100	= 4.25
	3.5 billion	"4¼s of 1987–1992"	at 100	= 4.25

These were the last long-term Treasury financings until 1971.

An entirely new and revolutionary phase of bond market history began in 1965. The Great Society program was under way, and business was assured that never again would even the smallest recession be permitted. And many believed just this. There seemed to be no more risk. Besides this already inflationary setting, the war in Vietnam was escalating.

The new "era" began quietly enough in 1965 with a continued rise in short-term interest rates, which carried three-month Treasury bills from 3.81% up to 4.47%. The Federal Reserve was exerting mild pressure, and the discount rate had been raised from 3.50 to 4% in late 1964. Nevertheless, bond yields remained almost unchanged until late in the year. Then suddenly the market collapsed, led by a sharp decline in the bellwether, the recently issued Treasury 4¼s of 1987–1992. New utility yields rose from 4.40 to 4.90%, and long government yields rose from 4.22 to 4.50%, thus exceeding their 1959 peak yields. Market psychology, which had clung to traditional benchmarks, was shattered, and the stage was set for a major bear market.

The year 1966 was a dress rehearsal for disaster. New issue high-grade public utility bond yields started at 4.90% and broke through 6%, while seasoned issue yields rose above 5.50%. Treasury bill rates rose to 5.59%, and municipal yields soared. Late in the summer, there was distress liquidation and extreme pressure on the money market. In response to this threat, the Federal Reserve temporarily eased its pressure, and the bond market staged a mild rally, which lasted five months.

The year 1967 made 1966 look tame. The mini-rally that had begun in October of 1966 lasted only until February of 1967. People began to think that the bond market was a thing of the past. The market declined almost steadily throughout the year. Corporate new issue yields moved up from 5.05 to 6 to 6.90%. The magic 6% defense was broken wide open. Seasoned prime corporate bond yields rose from 5.03 to 6.19%. Long government yields rose from 4.47 to 5.64%. Prime long municipal yields rose from 3.35 to 4.30%. These represented price declines of 15 to 20% in one year. This upsurge in long yields in 1967 was not caused by or accompanied by a corresponding rise in short-term interest rates; indeed, during 1967, the discount rate was temporarily lowered from 4½ to 4%, the federal funds rate declined over 100 basis points, and the Treasury bill rate declined and recovered, closing 1967 about unchanged. The problem was largely psychological. At this time a new market force made itself felt: Private investors began to withdraw money from institutions and buy high-yielding bonds. They were destined to be a basic market force in the years to come. At the time, this disintermediation, as the bypassing of financial institutions came to be called, was a counter-force to the panic psychology of many institutions. Later and on a larger scale, disintermediation would cause many problems for these institutions and their regulators.

The year 1968 was one of zigzag in the long-term taxable markets. Yields declined again, rose, declined and rose again, closing somewhat higher than at the close of 1967. Long municipal yields rose more than did those of taxable bonds, and short-term interest rates soared.

The year 1969 saw all yields rise steeply—in some cases to the largest annual rise in basis points on the record. New issue prime utility yields rose from around 7 to around 9%, a then unprecedented level in the history of the American long-term bond market. Seasoned prime long corporate bond yields rose from 6.59 to 7.72%, lagging new issues by a large amount. Long governments, in the absence of new issues, also lagged, their yield rising from 6.05 to 6.83%, while prime municipal yields soared from 4.90 to 6.60%. Federal funds rose from 6 to over 9%, and the discount rate was pegged at 6%. The backdrop for this market turbulence was a dangerous business boom, widespread speculation, and a sharp rise in inflation and, especially, inflationary expectations.

The small recession of 1969–1970, brought about a general decline in short-term interest rates. The three-month Treasury bill rate dropped from 8 to about 5%. This decline began at the start of 1970 and ran almost continuously throughout, and all short-term rates behaved similarly. The long-term bond market in 1970, however, followed a very different pattern: Long bond yields continued to rise during the first half-year, peaked in June 1970, and then declined, closing the year well below the opening. The Penn Central bankruptcy was quickly effective in cooling the inflationary boom psychology. Seasoned prime long corporate bond yields opened the year at 7.91%, rose to a peak of 8.48%, and closed the year at 7.64%.

Yields declined a little bit further in 1971, stabilized in 1972, and started going up again in 1973. These were years of force-fed business recovery and wage/price controls, which masked a continuing high and rising inflation rate. Short-term rates again followed a different course from long-term ones. They declined further in 1971 and started going up again in late 1972, some time before long yields started going up.

The year 1973 witnessed the crest of the great boom but by no means the crest of bond yields or of the rate of inflation. The recession that started in November 1973 was based on scarcities in supply, not lack of demand. That came in 1974. Inventory-building of panic proportions in 1973 created a vast demand for credit—the beginning of one more big upsurge in all interest rates. In 1973, three-month Treasury bills rose from 5.12% to a high of 9.05%, declined briefly to 7%, and then rose in 1974 to a historic peak of 9.74%. The federal funds rate rose in 1973 from 5.44 to 11% and in mid-1974 crested at 13¾%. The discount rate rose in 1973 from 4½ to 7½% and crested in 1974 at 8%.

In the long-term market, seasoned prime long corporate yields rose in 1973 from 7.15 to 7.68% and then crested in October 1974 at 9.27%, not long after President Nixon resigned amid scandal. The rates on high-grade new long corporate issues rose in 1973 from 7.35 to 8.50% and crested in late 1974 at 10.50%. Long government yields rose in 1973 from 5.95 to 7.97% and then crested in 1974 at 8.75%. On the other hand, prime long municipals remained relatively firm in 1973, close to 5¼%, and in 1974 rose to 6.80%, peaking in 1975 at around 7.00%. Thus the peak of yields occurred not in a boom, but in the midst of a very serious recession—a recession that for a while was accompanied by a record rate of inflation. It was not until the inflation rate came down sharply in 1975 that bonds did better.

In 1975 the recession grew more severe and then in April bottomed out, and the recovery began. Short-term interest rates, which had declined in late 1974, came down sharply in 1975. Treasury bill rates sank to close to 5% in 1975 and 1976. The short market was again well within its traditional range but by no means close to levels typical during previous recessions. The long-term market again behaved differently: Yields remained very high throughout 1975 in spite of the recession and sharply lower short rates. The yields on prime long seasoned corporate bonds declined modestly from their then all-time peak of 9.27% in October 1974 to average 8.83% in 1975 before commencing a gradual retreat to a low of 7.92% in September 1977.

It is at this point, the mid-1970's, that the bond market began to be dominated by a new and dynamic force. The budget deficit of the federal government leapt to a record level of $69.4 billion in 1975 (calendar year, national income and product accounts measure). Although the deficit, in the typical pattern of recovery and expansion after a recession, did decline somewhat between 1975 and 1979, it returned to near 1975 levels in 1980 and 1981 (recession years) before climbing steeply to $145.9 billion in 1982, another recession year. After the recessions of the early 1980's, the deficit, in a departure from past norms, did not decline in recovery and expansion. Instead, it rose to a record $206.9 billion in 1986 and stayed at or above the 1982 level during the last years of the 1980's. The impetus for this unprecedented result was a major cut in tax rates in the early 1980's, a policy initiative of the Reagan administration, without corresponding cuts in government spending. As a result of these deficits, federal debt in the hands of the public increased from $344 billion in 1974 to $709 billion in 1980 and to $2200 billion in 1989.

As noted above, between 1964 and 1971, the Treasury issued no long-term bonds. Annual issues commenced in 1971, but the outstanding stock of marketable government bonds actually continued to decline through 1974, as more bonds matured than were issued and the Treasury relied increasingly on shorter-term bills and notes to finance its then-modest deficits. That trend changed in 1975, when the outstanding stock of marketable long-term governments began to increase. Between 1974 and 1989, as the national debt soared, the marketable proportion consisting of bonds increased from one-eighth to one-sixth, an absolute rise from $33 billion to over $300 billion. The table on the next two pages lists the chief long-term issues of 1971–1989, a few of which were exchange offerings without a cash price. Because of the frequency of the Treasury's trips to the bond market in these two decades, the progression of coupon rates and average new issue yields provides a fairly accurate portrayal of the dramatic moves of the long-term market in these years.

Interest rates, both long and short, declined moderately during 1976, the year of lowest inflation since 1972. The following year, 1977, was one of contrasts. Prime corporate bond yields were remarkably stable from month to month; they touched a low of 7.92% in September, which was to prove the low point of the corporate market between early 1974 and the 1990's, and averaged only 23 basis points higher in December than in January. Long-term governments rose somewhat more over the course of the year, narrowing the spread between corporates and governments. Short-term rates, in contrast, rose some 150 to 200 basis points in 1977, as the recovery continued and inflation increased.

In 1978, inflation (CPI, December to December) reached 9%, and all interest rates rose. Long-term rates rose 75–100 basis points, with governments leading the rise as Treasury bond auctions increased in frequency and amounts raised. Short-term rates soared during the year; Treasury bills rose 260–270 basis points from January to December, while six-month commercial paper climbed from 6.79 to 10.43%.

The years 1979–1982 were remarkable and unprecedented in the long history of American money and capital markets. Inflation (CPI, annual averages) reached double-digit levels in the three years 1979–1981. In the markets, interest rates and yields were relatively stable, albeit at high levels,

1971	$1.8 billion	"6⅛s of 1986"			
1972	2.6 billion	"6⅜s of 1982"	at 100.60	=	6.29%
1973	2.3 billion	"6⅜s of 1984"			
	0.6 billion	"6¾s of 1993"	at 99.50	=	6.79
	0.7 billion	"7s of 1993–1998"	98.75	=	7.11
	0.5 billion	"7½s of 1988–1993"	95.00	=	8.00
	0.3 billion	"7½s of 1988–1993"	101⅝	=	7.35
1974	0.3 billion	"7½s of 1988–1993"	at 100.50	=	7.46
	0.6 billion	"8½s of 1994–1999"	102⅞	=	8.23
	0.9 billion	"8½s of 1994–1999"	98.75	=	8.63
	0.9 billion	"8½s of 1994–1999"	103.00	=	8.21
1975	0.9 billion	"7⅞s of 1995–2000"	at 99.25	=	7.95
	1.2 billion	"8¼s of 1990"	99.50	=	8.30
	1.6 billion	"8¼s of 2000–2005"	99.50	=	8.30
	1.1 billion	"8⅜s of 1995–2000"	99.25	=	8.44
	1.2 billion	"8⅜s of 1995–2000"	101.50	=	8.23
1976	0.6 billion	"8¼s of 2000–2005"	at 101.75	=	8.09
	0.9 billion	"7⅞s of 1995–2000"	96.73	=	8.19
	1.6 billion	"8s of 1996–2001"	99.89	=	8.01
	1.0 billion	"7⅞s of 1995–2000"	100.79	=	7.80
1977	1.1 billion	"7⅝s of 2002–2007"	at 99.94	=	7.63
	1.9 billion	"7⅝s of 2002–2007"	98.25	=	7.77
	1.5 billion	"7¼s of 1992"	99.61	=	7.29
	1.2 billion	"7⅝s of 2002–2007"	98.94	=	7.72
	1.5 billion	"7⅝s of 2002–2007"	99.26	=	7.94
1978	1.5 billion	"7⅞s of 1993"	at 99.32	=	7.95
	2.0 billion	"8¼s of 2000–2005"	100.13	=	8.23
	2.4 billion	"8⅜s of 1995–2000"	99.02	=	8.47
	1.8 billion	"8⅝s of 1993"	99.92	=	8.63
	2.1 billion	"8⅜s of 2003–2008"	99.40	=	8.43
	1.5 billion	"8⅝s of 1993"	99.84	=	8.64
	2.4 billion	"8¾s of 2003–2008"	98.85	=	8.86
1979	1.5 billion	"9s of 1994"	at 99.96	=	9.00
	2.8 billion	"8¾s of 2003–2008"	97.05	=	9.03
	1.5 billion	"9s of 1994"	98.79	=	9.14
	2.2 billion	"9⅛s of 2004–2009"	98.94	=	9.23
	1.5 billion	"8¾s of 1994"	99.47	=	8.81
	2.4 billion	"9⅛s of 2004–2009"	102.13	=	8.92
	1.5 billion	"10⅛s of 1994"	99.62	=	10.17
	2.0 billion	"10⅜s of 2004–2009"	99.41	=	10.44
1980	1.5 billion	"10½s of 1995"	at 99.20	=	10.60
	2.0 billion	"11¾s of 2005–2010"	99.26	=	11.84
	1.5 billion	"12⅝s of 1995"	99.49	=	12.69
	2.0 billion	"10s of 2005–2010"	98.88	=	10.12
	1.5 billion	"10⅜s of 1995"	99.66	=	10.42
	1.5 billion	"10⅜s of 2004–2009"	96.91	=	10.71
	1.5 billion	"11½s of 1995"	99.17	=	11.61
	2.0 billion	"12¾s of 2005–2010"	99.54	=	12.80

Year	Amount	Security	Price	Yield
1981	1.5 billion	"$11\frac{3}{4}$s of 2001"	at 99.41	= 11.82%
	2.6 billion	"$12\frac{3}{4}$s of 2005–2010"	100.43	= 12.68
	1.8 billion	"$13\frac{3}{8}$s of 2001"	99.31	= 13.21
	2.3 billion	"$13\frac{7}{8}$s of 2006–2011"	99.19	= 13.99
	1.8 billion	"$13\frac{3}{8}$s of 2001"	99.38	= 13.45
	2.3 billion	"$13\frac{7}{8}$s of 2006–2011"	99.47	= 14.98
	1.8 billion	"$15\frac{3}{4}$s of 2001"	99.70	= 15.78
	2.0 billion	"14s of 2006–2011"	99.30	= 14.10
1982	1.8 billion	"$14\frac{1}{4}$s of 2002"	at 99.90	= 14.25
	2.6 billion	"14s of 2006–2011"	96.08	= 14.56
	2.8 billion	"$11\frac{5}{8}$s of 2002"	99.50	= 11.68
	3.2 billion	"$10\frac{3}{8}$s of 2007–2012"	99.23	= 10.46
	3.0 billion	"$10\frac{3}{4}$s of 2003"	99.94	= 10.75
1983	3.9 billion	"$10\frac{3}{8}$s of 2007–2012"	at 94.40	= 11.01
	3.9 billion	"$10\frac{3}{8}$s of 2007–2012"	100.78	= 10.29
	3.5 billion	"$11\frac{1}{8}$s of 2003"	99.18	= 11.22
	4.9 billion	"12s of 2008–2013"	99.36	= 12.08
	3.5 billion	"$11\frac{7}{8}$s of 2003"	99.74	= 11.90
	4.7 billion	"12s of 2008–2013"	101.55	= 11.80
	3.8 billion	"$11\frac{7}{8}$s of 2003"	99.31	= 11.95
1984	5.2 billion	"12s of 2008–2013"	at 100.98	= 11.88
	5.0 billion	"$13\frac{1}{4}$s of 2009–2014"	99.49	= 13.32
	5.0 billion	"$13\frac{3}{4}$s of 2004"	99.85	= 13.76
	5.1 billion	"$12\frac{1}{2}$s of 2009–2014"	99.84	= 12.52
	4.0 billion	"$11\frac{5}{8}$s of 2004"	99.47	= 11.69
	6.0 billion	"$11\frac{3}{4}$s of 2009–2014"	99.35	= 11.83
	4.3 billion	"$11\frac{5}{8}$s of 2004"	98.13	= 11.86
1985	6.2 billion	"$11\frac{1}{4}$s of 2015"	at 99.83	= 11.27
	4.3 billion	"12s of 2005"	99.62	= 12.04
	6.4 billion	"$11\frac{1}{4}$s of 2015"	98.82	= 11.38
	4.5 billion	"$10\frac{3}{4}$s of 2005"	99.93	= 10.75
	7.2 billion	"$10\frac{5}{8}$s of 2015"	99.69	= 10.66
	6.9 billion	"$9\frac{7}{8}$s of 2015"	99.46	= 9.93
	4.8 billion	"$9\frac{3}{8}$s of 2006"	99.47	= 9.43
1986	7.3 billion	"$9\frac{1}{4}$s of 2016"	at 99.70	= 9.28
	9.3 billion	"$7\frac{1}{4}$s of 2016"	98.56	= 7.37
	9.0 billion	"$7\frac{1}{4}$s of 2016"	95.52	= 7.63
	9.4 billion	"$7\frac{1}{2}$s of 2016"	99.53	= 7.54
1987	9.5 billion	"$7\frac{1}{2}$s of 2016"	at 100.08	= 7.49
	9.4 billion	"$8\frac{3}{4}$s of 2017"	99.90	= 8.76
	9.1 billion	"$8\frac{7}{8}$s of 2017"	99.84	= 8.89
	4.9 billion	"$8\frac{7}{8}$s of 2017"	100.84	= 8.79
1988	8.8 billion	"$8\frac{7}{8}$s of 2017"	at 102.53	= 8.51
	8.7 billion	"$9\frac{1}{4}$s of 2018"	99.54	= 9.17
	9.0 billion	"9s of 2018"	98.97	= 9.10
1989	9.6 billion	"$8\frac{7}{8}$s of 2019"	at 99.64	= 8.91
	9.6 billion	"$8\frac{7}{8}$s of 2019"	97.55	= 9.11
	9.8 billion	"$8\frac{1}{8}$s of 2019"	99.83	= 8.14
	10.1 billion	"$8\frac{1}{8}$s of 2019"	102.875	= 7.87

during the first half of 1979. Prime corporate yields advanced above their 1974 peak from March to May but then retreated to beginning-of-year levels. From July through September, however, most short-term rates rose more than 100 basis points, and an atmosphere of crisis pervaded the markets both in the United States and abroad. It was at this point that the Federal Reserve, under its newly appointed chairman, Paul Volcker, announced an altered approach to monetary policy. The new policy called for the Fed to target monetary aggregates and let interest rates seek whatever levels they would as the markets balanced demand and supply. The ensuing three years witnessed unprecedented volatility of rates and yields, and their climb in late 1981 to the highest levels in U.S. history.

The yield fluctuations of 1979–1982 are evident in Chart 40. There were two periods of rapidly advancing yields and two periods of decline, with successive highs and lows above the previous ones. Prime corporate yields rose from 9.93% in September 1979 to 12.96% in March 1980, declined to 10.58% in June 1980, advanced to the record level of 15.49% in September 1981, and then retreated to 11.0% in November 1982. In the same periods, the composite average of long-term government yields advanced from 8.68 to 11.87%, declined to 9.40%, then rose to a September 1981 peak of 12.92%, and finally fell to 10.18% in November 1982. These years witnessed a mini-recession in 1980, along with a short-lived policy initiative of the Car-

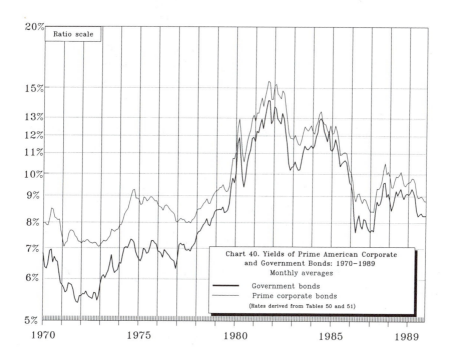

Chart 40. Yields of Prime American Corporate and Government Bonds: 1970–1989
Monthly averages
Government bonds
Prime corporate bonds
(Rates derived from Tables 50 and 51)

ter administration to restrain interest rates and the growth of credit, and then a severe recession in 1981–1982, which bottomed out in November 1982 with the unemployment rate in double digits. For this history, one event in the long-term market stands out: at the peak of yields in the fall of 1981, the U. S. government borrowed money for twenty years by issuing 15¾% bonds, which sold at just under par to yield 15.78%. This stands as the highest bond yield the government had to pay in the two-century history of the republic.

Fluctuations in short-term rates, as is typical, were even more pronounced than those in long yields in these years. With its emphasis on controlling monetary aggregates from October 1979 forward, the Federal Reserve had to control bank reserves. The key Federal funds rate, the rate on overnight interbank loans of reserves, was stable at around 10% in the first half of 1979. It raced up to a monthly average of 17.61% in April 1980, retreated to 9.03% in July, and then rose to 18.90% in December. In 1981, the Federal funds rate averaged 16.38%, reaching a peak of 19.10% in June. Eighteen months later, December 1982, at the close of the 1981–1982 recession, the funds rate was down to 8.95%. The commercial bank prime rate peaked at 21½% in December 1980 (annual average of 18.87% in 1981), and three-month Treasury bills peaked at 16.30% in May 1981 (annual average of 14.03% in 1981).

At the end of 1982, there began a sustained economic expansion which carried through the 1980's. Although the money and capital markets became less turbulent in these years than they had been in 1979–1982, the financial legacy of 1979–1982 continued to be present in the form of continuing federal budget deficits, bank and savings and loan (S & L) failures, the less developed countries (LDCs) debt crisis, and a stock market advance to record levels but punctuated by price crashes the likes of which had not previously been seen in the post-World War II era. Despite these problems, the trend of interest rates and yields after 1981 was downward. Reduced rates of inflation and inflationary expectations were an important contributor to declining rates. Nonetheless, the 1980's ended with rates and yields at levels seldom seen before 1974.

From the recession and postrecession lows of late 1982 and early 1983, a vigorous economic recovery coupled with a small rise in rates of inflation propelled market rates and yields upward until mid-1984. The peaks reached then were considerably below those of late 1981, and they were followed by steep declines lasting until early 1987. Prime corporate bond yields advanced from a low of 11.46% in May 1983 to 14.40% in June 1984 before falling to 8.36% in early 1987. The composite index of long governments rose from 10.2 to 13%, and then declined to 7.6 in the same period. In the middle of the 1984–1987 rate decline, the OPEC cartel became unglued in

December 1985, and oil prices collapsed on world markets. This helped to make the 1986 rate of inflation the lowest in two decades, as did a moderating rate of real economic expansion.

By early 1987, the effect of markedly lower oil prices on inflation had ended, and the price level started once again to advance at rates typical of 1983–1985. The Federal Reserve, worrying about a potentially overheating economy, allowed Federal funds rates to rise 120 basis points from February to October 1987, and the entire structure of rates and yields rose sharply. Prime corporate yields, for example, rose from 8.36% in March to 10.52% in October, and the composite of long governments advanced from 7.6 to 9.6%. The stock market peaked out at a then-record level in late August, before crashing more than 20 percent on October 19, 1987. After the crash, yields declined into early 1988 as the Federal Reserve provided liquidity to shell-shocked markets. It is worth noting that the October 1987 yield peak was well below that of June 1984, which in turn was well below that of September 1981. Although yields remained high by historical standards, the long post-World War II bear market in bonds appeared to have ended in 1981.

Yields rose from post-crash lows in 1988, peaking in August; then fell until November; and then rose again until March 1989, before declining for the remainder of the year. Peak yields in 1988 were below those of 1987, and those in 1989 were below those of 1988. This could be taken as further evidence that the great bear bond market was dead and gone, but it was also consistent with slower economic growth and fears in 1989 that a recession was around the corner after a seven-year expansion. Most short rates were higher in 1988–1989 than in 1986–1987, as the Federal Reserve continued its battle to keep a lid on, if not actually reduce, the persistent inflation of the quarter-century 1965–1989.

SHORT-TERM INTEREST RATES: 1946–1989

Table 52 presents the major short-term American interest-rate series from 1946 through 1989. Most of the 1900–1945 series from Chapter XVII are continued, and several new ones are introduced: (a) federal funds, a key rate for understanding Federal Reserve policy, from 1955 through 1989, in terms of annual averages and monthly highs and lows; (b) one-year Treasury notes/bonds; (c) the three-month Eurodollar rate; and (d) large negotiable certificate of deposit (CD) rates in the secondary market.

Three of the most important short-term rates are plotted in Chart 41. During and immediately after World War II, the Federal Reserve pegged three-month Treasury bills at ⅜% per year in order to aid the Treasury in war financing and to keep down the costs of servicing the federal debt. In the early postwar years, especially when price controls were removed, an ob-

TABLE 52
Short-Term American Interest Rates: 1946–1989

Year	Prime Commercial Paper, %				Federal Funds, %			Prime Bankers' Acceptances, 90 Days, Annual Average, %	1-Year Treasuries, Annual Average, %
	4–6 Months			60–90 Days, Annual Average	Annual Average	Monthly Average			
	Annual Average	Monthly Average							
		Low	High			Low	High		
1946	0.81	0.75	1.00					0.61	0.82
1947	1.03	1.00	1.19					0.87	0.88
1948	1.44	1.31	1.56					1.11	1.14
1949	1.48	1.33	1.56					1.12	1.14
4-yr. av.	1.19							0.93	1.00
1950	1.45	1.31	1.73					1.15	1.26
1951	2.16	1.86	2.31					1.60	1.73
1952	2.33	2.31	2.38					1.75	1.81
1953	2.52	2.25	2.75					1.87	2.07
1954	1.58	1.31	2.11			0.90	1.26	1.35	0.92
1955	2.18	1.47	2.99		1.78	1.35	2.48	1.71	1.89
1956	3.31	3.00	3.63		2.73	2.44	2.96	2.64	2.83
1957	3.81	3.63	4.10		3.11	2.90	3.50	3.45	3.53
1958	2.46	1.50	3.49		1.57	0.63	2.72	2.04	2.09
1959	3.97	3.26	4.88		3.30	2.40	4.00	3.49	4.11
10-yr. av.	2.58				2.50			2.11	2.22
1960	3.85	3.23	4.91		3.22	1.98	3.99	3.51	3.55
1961	2.97	2.72	3.19		1.96	1.16	2.54	2.81	2.91
1962	3.26	3.16	3.36		2.68	2.14	2.94	3.01	3.02
1963	3.55	3.25	3.96		3.18	2.90	3.50	3.36	3.28
1964	3.97	3.88	4.17		3.50	3.36	3.85	3.77	3.76
1965	4.38	4.25	4.65		4.07	3.90	4.32	4.22	4.09
1966	5.55	4.82	6.00		5.11	4.42	5.77	5.36	5.17
1967	5.10	4.65	5.73		4.22	3.88	5.00	4.75	4.84
1968	5.90	5.50	6.25		5.66	4.60	6.12	5.75	5.62
1969	7.83	6.53	8.84		8.22	6.30	9.19	7.61	7.06
10-yr. av.	4.64				4.18			4.42	4.33

TABLE 52 (*Continued*)

Year	Prime Commercial Paper, %				Federal Funds, %			Prime Bankers' Acceptances, 90 Days, Annual Average, %	1-Year Treasuries, Annual Average, %
	4–6 Months			60–90 Days, Annual Average	Annual Average	Monthly Average			
	Annual Average	Monthly Average							
		Low	High			Low	High		
1970	7.72	5.73	8.78		7.18	4.90	8.98	7.31	6.90
1971	5.11	4.19	5.75		4.66	3.71	5.57	4.85	4.88
1972	4.69	3.93	5.45		4.43	3.29	5.33	4.47	4.96
1973	8.15	5.78	10.23		8.73	5.94	10.78	8.08	7.31
1974	9.87	7.83	11.72		10.50	8.53	12.92	9.92	8.18
1975	6.33	5.79	7.30		5.82	5.20	7.13	6.30	6.76
1976	5.35	4.70	5.94		5.04	4.65	5.29	5.08	5.88
1977	5.60	4.74	6.64		5.54	4.61	6.56	5.54	6.09
1978	7.99	6.79	10.43		7.93	6.70	10.03	8.06	8.34
1979	10.91	9.71	13.26		11.19	10.01	13.78	10.99	10.67
10-yr. av.	7.17				7.10			7.06	7.00
1980	12.29	8.03	16.50		13.36	9.03	18.90	12.72	12.05
1981	14.76	11.96	16.66		16.38	12.37	19.10	15.32	14.78
1982	11.89	8.50	14.27		12.26	8.95	14.94	11.89	12.27
1983	8.89	8.15	9.68		9.09	8.51	9.56	8.90	9.57
1984	10.16	8.55	10.94		10.23	8.38	11.64	10.14	10.89
1985	8.01	7.38	9.23		8.10	7.53	8.58	7.92	8.43
1986	6.39	5.61	7.62		6.80	5.85	8.14	6.39	6.46
1987	6.85	5.76	7.96		6.66	6.10	7.29	6.75	6.77
1988	7.68	6.58	8.97		7.57	6.58	8.76	7.56	7.65
1989	8.80	7.93	9.97		9.21	8.45	9.85	8.87	8.53
10-yr. av.	9.57				9.97			9.65	9.74

TABLE 52 (*Continued*)

Year	3-Month Treasuries (Bills After 1931), %			Rediscount Rate of the Federal Reserve Bank of New York, %		
	Annual Average	Monthly Average		Annual Average	Low	High
		Low	High			
1946	0.37	0.37	0.37	1.00	1.00	
1947	0.59	0.37	0.94	1.00	1.00	
1948	1.04	0.97	1.15	1.35	1.25	1.50
1949	1.10	0.98	1.16	1.50	1.50	
4-yr. av.	0.78			1.21		
1950	1.22	1.09	1.37	1.60	1.50	1.75
1951	1.55	1.39	1.73	1.75	1.75	
1952	1.77	1.57	2.13	1.75	1.75	
1953	1.93	1.40	2.23	2.00	2.00	
1954	0.95	0.65	1.21	1.58	1.50	2.00
1955	1.75	1.18	2.56	1.92	1.50	2.50
1956	2.66	2.31	3.23	2.79	2.50	3.00
1957	3.28	3.10	3.59	3.12	3.00	3.50
1958	1.84	0.88	2.81	2.12	1.75	3.00
1959	3.40	2.71	4.57	3.38	2.50	4.00
10-yr. av.	2.04			2.20		
1960	2.93	2.27	4.43	3.50	3.00	4.00
1961	2.38	2.27	2.62	3.00	3.00	3.00
1962	2.78	2.69	2.95	3.00	3.00	3.00
1963	3.16	2.90	3.52	3.23	3.00	3.50
1964	3.54	3.46	3.84	3.54	3.50	4.00
1965	3.95	3.80	4.37	4.04	4.00	4.50
1966	4.85	4.50	5.36	4.50	4.50	4.50
1967	4.30	3.53	4.96	4.24	4.00	4.50
1968	5.33	4.97	5.94	5.15	5.00	5.50
1969	6.64	6.01	7.81	5.85	5.50	6.00
10-yr. av.	3.99			4.01		
1970	6.42	4.87	7.87	5.94	5.00	5.75
1971	4.33	3.38	5.39	4.88	4.50	5.25
1972	4.07	3.20	5.07	4.50	4.50	4.50
1973	7.03	5.41	8.67	6.44	5.00	7.50
1974	7.84	7.12	8.96	7.83	7.50	8.00

TABLE 52 (*Continued*)

Year	3-Month Treasuries (Bills After 1931), %			Rediscount Rate of the Federal Reserve Bank of New York, %		
	Annual Average	Monthly Average		Annual Average	Low	High
		Low	High			
1975	5.80	5.23	6.44	6.33	6.00	7.25
1976	4.98	4.36	5.41	5.50	5.50	6.00
1977	5.27	4.54	6.19	5.46	5.25	6.50
1978	7.22	6.31	9.12	7.46	6.50	9.50
1979	10.04	9.05	12.07	10.28	9.50	12.00
10-yr. av.	6.30			6.46		
1980	11.51	7.00	15.66	11.77	10.00	13.00
1981	14.08	10.93	16.30	13.41	12.00	14.00
1982	10.69	7.75	13.78	11.02	8.50	12.00
1983	8.63	7.86	9.39	8.50	8.50	8.50
1984	9.58	8.16	10.49	8.75	8.00	9.00
1985	7.48	7.01	8.92	7.67	7.50	8.00
1986	5.97	5.18	7.04	6.78	5.50	7.50
1987	5.78	5.45	6.40	5.66	5.50	6.00
1988	6.67	5.69	8.07	6.20	6.00	7.50
1989	8.11	7.63	8.82	7.00	7.00	7.00
10-yr. av.	8.85			8.68		

Year	Prime Rate for Commercial Loans, Annual Average, %	Average Business Loan Rates Charged by Commercial Banks, Annual Average, %	Insured Savings & Loan Dividend Rate, Annual Average, %	Eurodollar 3-month Interbank Rate, Annual Average, %	Certificates of Deposit, Secondary Market, Annual Average, %
1946	1.50	2.34	2.31		
1947	1.51	2.28	2.34		
1948	1.83	2.57	2.43		
1949	2.00	2.68	2.52		
4-yr. av.	1.71	2.47	2.40		

TABLE 52 (*Continued*)

Year	Prime Rate for Commercial Loans, Annual Average, %	Average Business Loan Rates Charged by Commercial Banks, Annual Average, %	Insured Savings & Loan Dividend Rate, Annual Average, %	Eurodollar 3-month Interbank Rate, Annual Average, %	Certificates of Deposit, Secondary Market, Annual Average, %
1950	2.05	2.79	2.55		
1951	2.75	3.11	2.62		
1952	3.00	3.49	2.75		
1953	3.17	3.69	2.87		
1954	3.06	3.61	2.95		
1955	3.41	3.70	3.01		
1956	3.77	4.20	3.13		
1957	4.17	4.62	3.37		
1958	3.85	4.34	3.49		
1959	4.48	5.00	3.66		
10-yr. av.	3.37	3.86	3.04		
1960	4.83	5.20	3.86		
1961	4.50	5.00	3.90	3.60	
1962	4.50	5.00	4.08	3.73	
1963	4.50	5.00	4.17	3.91	
1964	4.50	5.00	4.19	4.31	3.91
1965	4.54	5.10	4.23	4.83	4.35
1966	5.62	6.00	4.48	6.12	5.47
1967	5.62	6.00	4.68	5.46	5.02
1968	6.31	6.68	4.71	6.36	5.86
1969	7.90	8.21	4.81	9.76	7.77
10-yr. av.	5.28	5.72	4.31	5.34	5.40
1970	7.87	8.48	5.14	8.52	7.56
1971	5.75	6.32	5.30	6.58	4.99
1972	5.30	5.82	5.37	5.41	4.67
1973	8.02	8.30	5.51	9.28	8.41
1974	10.69	11.28	5.96	11.04	10.24
1975	7.88	8.65	6.21	7.03	6.44
1976	6.84	7.52	6.31	5.58	5.27
1977	6.82	7.83	6.39	6.03	5.64
1978	9.06	9.81	6.56	8.78	8.22
1979	12.67	13.18	7.29	11.96	11.22
10-yr. av.	8.09	8.72	6.00	8.02	7.27

TABLE 52 (*Continued*)

Year	Prime Rate for Commercial Loans, Annual Average, %	Average Business Loan Rates Charged by Commercial Banks, Annual Average, %	Insured Savings & Loan Dividend Rate, Annual Average, %	Eurodollar 3-month Interbank Rate, Annual Average, %	Certificates of Deposit, Secondary Market, Annual Average, %
1980	15.27	15.17	8.78	13.07	14.00
1981	18.87	19.54	10.71	15.91	16.79
1982	14.86	14.69	11.19	12.27	13.12
1983	10.79	10.64	9.71	9.56	9.07
1984	12.04	12.02	9.93	10.73	10.37
1985	9.93	11.93	9.03	8.28	8.05
1986	8.33	8.04	7.84	6.71	6.51
1987	8.21	8.04	6.92	7.06	6.87
1988	9.32	9.18	7.20	7.85	7.73
1989	10.87	11.04	7.70	9.16	9.09
10-yr. av.	11.85	12.03	8.90	10.06	10.16

SOURCES

Prime commercial paper, federal funds, bankers' acceptances, 1-year Treasuries, 3-month bills, rediscount rate, Eurodollar 3-month interbank rate, and certificate of deposit rate from Federal Reserve sources given in Table 50.

Insured savings and loan dividend rate (cost of funds) from publisher of Federal Housing Administration, Federal Home Loan Bank Board, and Office of Thrift Supervision.

vious conflict emerged between a monetary policy to promote price-level stability and one to minimize the Treasury's cost of servicing the debt. The conflict was resolved by the Treasury–Federal Reserve accord of March 1951, which freed the Fed from the obligation to support government security prices. By the mid-1950's, the chief short-term rates were in tandem and moving up secularly, albeit with fluctuations related to the business cycle, toward the great peak of 1981. Earlier in the century, structural characteristics of the money market led to striking differences in short-term rates; such differences have been less noticeable in recent decades. The Fed came to implement its policy in the market for federal funds, overnight loans of reserve funds between banks, and the other major short-term markets followed the federal funds market.

Although short-term and long-term rates generally move together over long periods of time, with the amplitude of short-rate movements typically

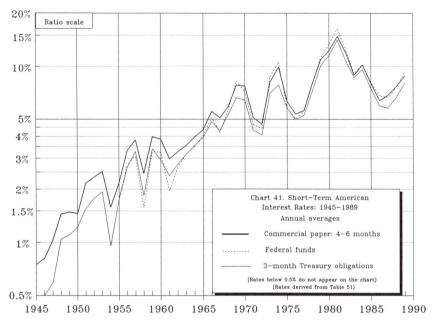

Chart 41. Short-Term American
Interest Rates: 1945–1989
Annual averages

——————— Commercial paper: 4–6 months

············· Federal funds

——————— 3-month Treasury obligations

(Rates below 0.5% do not appear on the chart)
(Rates derived from Table 51)

exceeding that of long rates, there are some interesting exceptions. In the late 1980's, for example, short-term rates moved up rather sharply compared to long-term rates, narrowing the long-short spread. The Federal Reserve battled inflation by keeping short rates relatively high; to some extent its success in this battle was evident in moderate to declining long rates.

THE TERM STRUCTURE OF INTEREST RATES

Ideally, the term structure of interest rates should compare yields simultaneously prevailing on different maturities of obligations of the same issuer. U.S. government securities fit this specification, but suffer from certain drawbacks when the concern is with long periods of history. The government has not always been an active and regular participant in the credit markets, and it has not always issued obligations with a full range of maturities. Furthermore, yields of governments have sometimes been pegged, as during and after World War II. That is why previous editions of this work concentrated on the term structure of prime corporate yields. Since the 1950's, however, the market in governments has not suffered from the aforementioned drawbacks; indeed, it has become the dominant and pacesetting component of the U.S. debt market. Twentieth-century term structure can therefore be best studied by looking at both the corporate and the government markets.

Tables 53A and 53B provide two measures of term structure. For the period 1900–1975, Table 53A presents Durand's basic yields of corporate

TABLE 53A

YIELDS BY MATURITY—BASIC YIELDS OF PRIME CORPORATE BONDS:
1900–1975 (FEBRUARY DATA)

Feb.:	Years to Maturity						
	1	5	10	15	20	25	30
1900	3.97	3.36	3.30	3.30	3.30	3.30	3.30
1901	3.25	3.25	3.25	3.25	3.25	3.25	3.25
1902	3.30	3.30	3.30	3.30	3.30	3.30	3.30
1903	3.45	3.45	3.45	3.45	3.45	3.45	3.45
1904	3.60	3.60	3.60	3.60	3.60	3.60	3.60
1905	3.50	3.50	3.50	3.50	3.50	3.50	3.50
1906	4.75	3.67	3.55	3.55	3.55	3.55	3.55
1907	4.87	3.87	3.80	3.80	3.80	3.80	3.80
1908	5.10	4.30	4.02	3.95	3.95	3.95	3.95
1909	4.03	3.97	3.91	3.86	3.82	3.79	3.77
10-yr. av.	3.98	3.63	3.57	3.56	3.55	3.55	3.55
1910	4.25	4.10	3.99	3.92	3.87	3.83	3.80
1911	4.09	4.05	4.01	3.97	3.94	3.92	3.90
1912	4.04	4.00	3.96	3.93	3.91	3.90	3.90
1913	4.74	4.31	4.12	4.06	4.02	4.00	4.00
1914	4.64	4.45	4.32	4.22	4.16	4.12	4.10
1915	4.47	4.39	4.31	4.25	4.20	4.17	4.15
1916	3.48	4.03	4.05	4.05	4.05	4.05	4.05
1917	4.05	4.05	4.05	4.05	4.05	4.05	4.05
1918	5.48	5.25	5.05	4.91	4.82	4.77	4.75
1919	5.58	5.16	4.97	4.87	4.81	4.77	4.75
10-yr. av.	4.48	4.38	4.28	4.22	4.18	4.16	4.15
1920	6.11	5.72	5.43	5.26	5.17	5.12	5.10
1921	6.94	6.21	5.73	5.46	5.31	5.22	5.17
1922	5.31	5.19	5.06	4.95	4.85	4.77	4.71
1923	5.01	4.90	4.80	4.73	4.68	4.64	4.61
1924	5.02	4.90	4.80	4.73	4.69	4.67	4.66
1925	3.85	4.46	4.50	4.50	4.50	4.50	4.50
1926	4.40	4.40	4.40	4.40	4.40	4.40	4.40
1927	4.30	4.30	4.30	4.30	4.30	4.30	4.30
1928	4.05	4.05	4.05	4.05	4.05	4.05	4.05
1929	5.27	4.72	4.57	4.49	4.45	4.43	4.42
10-yr. av.	5.03	4.89	4.76	4.69	4.64	4.61	4.59

TABLE 53A (*Continued*)

Feb.:	Years to Maturity						
	1	5	10	15	20	25	30
1930	4.40	4.40	4.40	4.40	4.40	4.40	4.40
1931	3.05	3.90	4.03	4.08	4.10	4.10	4.10
1932	3.99	4.58	4.70	4.70	4.70	4.70	4.70
1933	2.60	3.68	4.00	4.07	4.11	4.14	4.15
1934	2.62	3.48	3.70	3.83	3.91	3.96	3.99
1935	1.05	2.37	3.00	3.23	3.37	3.46	3.50
1936	0.61	1.86	2.64	2.88	3.04	3.14	3.20
1937	0.69	1.68	2.38	2.72	2.90	3.01	3.08
1938	0.85	1.97	2.60	2.81	2.91	2.97	3.00
1939	0.57	1.55	2.18	2.50	2.65	2.72	2.75
10-yr. av.	2.04	2.95	3.36	3.52	3.61	3.66	3.69
1940	0.41	1.28	1.95	2.34	2.55	2.65	2.70
1941	0.41	1.21	1.88	2.28	2.50	2.61	2.65
1942	0.81	1.50	2.16	2.47	2.61	2.64	2.65
1943	1.17	1.71	2.16	2.45	2.61	2.65	2.65
1944	1.08	1.58	2.20	2.54	2.60	2.60	2.60
1945	1.02	1.53	2.14	2.45	2.55	2.55	2.55
1946	0.86	1.32	1.88	2.26	2.35	2.40	2.43
1947	1.05	1.65	2.08	2.30	2.40	2.46	2.50
1948	1.60	2.03	2.53	2.66	2.73	2.77	2.80
1949	1.60	1.92	2.32	2.54	2.62	2.68	2.74
10-yr. av.	1.00	1.57	2.13	2.43	2.55	2.60	2.63
1950	1.42	1.90	2.30	2.40	2.48	2.54	2.58
1951	2.05	2.22	2.39	2.51	2.59	2.63	2.67
1952	2.73	2.73	2.73	2.81	2.88	2.94	3.00
1953	2.62	2.75	2.88	2.97	3.05	3.11	3.15
1954	2.40	2.52	2.66	2.78	2.88	2.95	3.00
1955	2.60	2.70	2.80	2.88	2.95	3.00	3.04
1956	2.70	2.78	2.86	2.93	2.99	3.04	3.09
1957	3.50	3.50	3.50	3.50	3.50	3.60	3.68
1958	3.21	3.25	3.33	3.40	3.47	3.54	3.61
1959	3.67	3.80	4.03	4.10	4.10	4.10	4.10
10-yr. av.	2.69	2.82	2.95	3.03	3.09	3.15	3.19

Feb.:	Years to Maturity						
	1	5	10	15	20	25	30
1960	4.95	4.73	4.60	4.55	4.55	4.55	4.55
1961	3.10	3.75	4.00	4.06	4.12	4.16	4.22
1962	3.50	3.97	4.28	4.37	4.40	4.41	4.42
1963	3.25	3.77	3.98	4.05	4.10	4.14	4.16
1964	4.00	4.15	4.25	4.29	4.33	4.33	4.33
1965	4.15	4.29	4.33	4.35	4.35	4.35	4.35
1966	4.95	4.95	4.90	4.85	4.80	4.78	4.75
1967	5.29	5.28	5.23	5.08	5.00	4.95	4.95
1968	6.24	6.24	6.20	6.08	6.00	5.99	5.93
1969	7.05	7.05	7.05	6.95	6.77	6.60	6.54
10-yr. av.	4.65	4.82	4.88	4.86	4.84	4.83	4.82
1970	8.15	8.10	8.00	7.75	7.60	7.60	7.60
1971	4.60	5.88	7.05	7.12	7.12	7.12	7.12
1972	4.25	6.50	7.05	7.08	7.05	7.03	7.01
1973	6.25	6.85	7.05	7.15	7.20	7.20	7.20
1974	7.26	7.47	7.67	7.78	7.80	7.80	7.80
1975	7.55	7.70	8.00	8.25	8.35	8.35	8.35
6-yr. av.	6.34	7.08	7.47	7.52	7.52	7.52	7.51

SOURCES

1900–1942: David Durand, *Basic Yields of Corporate Bonds, 1900–1942*, National Bureau of Economic Research, Technical Paper 3 (1942).

1943–1947: David Durand and Willis J. Winn, *Basic Yields of Bonds, 1926–1947: Their Measurement and Patterns*, National Bureau of Economic Research, Technical Paper 6 (1947).

1948–1952: *The Economic Almanac, 1953–1954* (New York: Thomas Y. Crowell Company, 1953).

1953–1958: David Durand, "A Quarterly Series of Corporate Basic Yields, 1952–57, and Some Attendant Reservations," *Journal of Finance*, Vol. VIII, No. 3 (Sept. 1958).

1959–1975: Estimates prepared by Sidney Homer using methods similar to Durand's; see concluding section of this chapter for description.

TABLE 53B
YIELDS BY MATURITY—U.S. GOVERNMENT BONDS: 1950–1989
(FEBRUARY DATA)

Feb.:	Years to Maturity						
	1	2	3	5	10	20	30
1950	1.17	1.23	1.29	1.45	1.98	2.29	
1951	1.52	1.60	1.63	1.75	2.32	2.45	
1952	1.77	1.99	2.12	2.22	2.50	2.73	
1953	2.12	2.21	2.28	2.42	2.65	2.79	
1954	1.13	1.32	1.53	1.99	2.49	2.64	2.91
1955	1.28	1.87	2.12	2.33	2.55	2.74	2.98
1956	2.48	2.55	2.60	2.63	2.78	2.80	2.87
1957	3.28	3.36	3.39	3.35	3.28	3.19	3.25
1958	1.98	2.37	2.64	2.76	2.97	3.28	3.32
1959	3.40	3.68	3.82	3.88	3.89	3.95	3.97
10-yr. av.	2.01	2.22	2.34	2.48	2.74	2.89	3.22
1960	4.44	4.58	4.69	4.82	4.51	4.39	4.34
1961	2.77	3.18	3.42	3.69	3.85	3.91	3.95
1962	3.22	3.57	3.75	3.95	4.12	4.15	4.16
1963	3.04	3.20	3.37	3.68	3.86	3.97	4.01
1964	3.77	3.92	3.98	4.05	4.15	4.16	4.19
1965	3.94	3.97	4.02	4.08	4.19	4.18	4.18
1966	4.81	4.87	4.92	4.93	4.67	4.58	4.54
1967	4.62	4.61	4.61	4.60	4.50	4.44	4.42
1968	5.30	5.37	5.41	5.47	5.47	5.37	5.29
1969	6.30	6.23	6.17	6.07	6.00	6.00	6.00
10-yr. av.	4.22	4.35	4.43	4.53	4.53	4.52	4.51
1970	8.11	8.12	8.16	8.16	7.50	6.84	6.82
1971	4.31	4.59	5.23	5.73	5.99	5.97	5.95
1972	4.20	4.85	5.24	5.67	6.19	5.90	5.89
1973	6.08	6.23	6.32	6.41	6.49	6.85	6.89
1974	7.10	6.79	6.79	6.82	6.93	7.38	7.39
1975	6.14	6.92	6.90	7.20	7.00	7.64	7.95
1976	5.48	6.35	6.88	7.40	7.38	7.85	8.01
1977	5.50	6.13	6.49	6.91	7.40	7.68	7.74

TABLE 53B (*Continued*)

Feb.:	Years to Maturity						
	1	2	3	5	10	20	30
1978	7.22	7.40	7.51	7.68	7.89	8.09	8.12
1979	10.12	9.60	9.19	8.94	8.92	8.84	8.80
10-yr. av.	6.43	6.70	6.87	7.09	7.17	7.30	7.36
1980	12.32	11.73	11.10	11.09	11.11	11.11	11.08
1981	13.92	13.26	12.91	12.73	12.64	12.40	12.23
1982	14.05	14.17	14.23	14.09	14.19	14.17	13.88
1983	8.92	9.59	9.98	10.44	10.75	11.08	11.18
1984	9.76	10.54	10.78	11.31	11.59	11.77	11.73
1985	9.15	9.99	10.29	10.80	11.07	11.30	11.19
1986	7.55	7.94	8.14	8.59	9.04	9.41	9.33
1987	5.92	6.33	6.42	6.73	7.17	7.74	7.51
1988	6.68	7.27	7.49	7.82	8.31	8.53	8.50
1989	9.02	9.10	9.11	9.04	8.98	8.92	8.83
10-yr. av.	9.73	9.99	10.05	10.26	10.49	10.64	10.55

SOURCES

1950–1969: Salomon Brothers, *An Analytical Record of Yields and Yield Spreads* (1989).

1970–1989: Federal Reserve, *Annual Statistical Digest* and *Federal Reserve Bulletin*, supplemented by Salomon Brothers, *op cit.*

bonds, which give a February yield for every important maturity (516). For 1950–1989, Table 53B presents U.S. government security yields, also for February, and a similar but not identical series of maturities. Table 54 lists, for corporates during 1900–1955 and governments during 1956–1989, the differentials between yields of one- and ten-year maturities, the ten- and twenty-year and the twenty- and thirty-year differentials, and the gross differential between one- and thirty-year bonds. In addition, it compares prime commercial paper rates with long-term corporate yields (Moody's Aaa), and three-month Treasury yields with the composite yields of long-term Treasury bonds.

The data on the term structure of yields are charted in four ways. Chart 42 pictures the corporate bond yield differentials between one- and ten-year, ten- and twenty-year, twenty- and thirty-year, and one- and thirty-year maturities at each February since 1900. It shows that much the greater part of

TABLE 54
YIELD DIFFERENTIALS IN BASIS POINTS ACCORDING TO MATURITY: 1900–1989

Year	Long U.S. Governments vs. 3-Month Governments, Annual Average	Prime 30-Year Corporate Bond Yields vs. Commercial Paper Rates, February Averages	Prime Corporate Bonds, February Averages			
			10-Year vs. 1-Year Maturity	20-Year vs. 10-Year Maturity	30-Year vs. 20-Year Maturity	30-Year vs. 1-Year Maturity
1900		−110	−67	0	0	−67
1901		−44	0	0	0	0
1902		−70	0	0	0	0
1903		−103	0	0	0	0
1904		−118	0	0	0	0
1905		−28	0	0	0	0
1906		−148	−120	0	0	−120
1907		−214	−107	0	0	−107
1908		−111	−108	−7	0	−115
1909		27	−12	−9	−5	−26
10-yr. av.		−92	−41	−2	−0	−44
1910		−64	−26	−12	−7	−45
1911		−16	−8	−7	−4	−19
1912		15	−8	−5	−1	−14
1913		−90	−62	−10	−2	−74
1914		25	−32	−16	−6	−54
1915		40	−16	−11	−5	−32
1916		93	57	0	0	57
1917		−4	0	0	0	0
1918		−93	−43	−23	−7	−73
1919		−43	−61	−16	−6	−83
10-yr. av.		−14	−20	−10	−4	−34
1920	−10	−123	−68	−26	−7	−101
1921	26	−258	−121	−42	−14	−177
1922	83	−17	−25	−21	−14	−60
1923	43	−7	−21	−12	−7	−40
1924	129	−12	−22	−11	−3	−36
1925	83	−12	65	0	0	65
1926	45	25	0	0	0	0
1927	24	14	0	0	0	0
1928	−64	43	0	0	0	0
1929	−82	−114	−70	−12	−3	−85
10-yr. av.	28	−46	−26	−12	−5	−43

TABLE 54 (*Continued*)

Year	Long U.S. Governments vs. 3-Month Governments, Annual Average	Prime 30-Year Corporate Bond Yields vs. Commercial Paper Rates, February Averages	Prime Corporate Bonds, February Averages			
			10-Year vs. 1-Year Maturity	20-Year vs. 10-Year Maturity	30-Year vs. 20-Year Maturity	30-Year vs. 1-Year Maturity
1930	106	−22	0	0	0	0
1931	194	160	98	7	0	105
1932	280	82	71	0	0	71
1933	279	277	140	11	4	155
1934	286	228	108	21	8	137
1935	265	275	195	37	13	245
1936	251	245	203	40	16	259
1937	223	233	169	52	18	239
1938	251	200	175	31	9	215
1939	234	219	161	47	10	218
10-yr. av.	237	190	132	25	8	164
1940	220	214	154	60	15	229
1941	185	209	147	62	15	224
1942	213	202	135	45	4	184
1943	210	196	99	45	4	148
1944	211	191	112	40	0	152
1945	200	180	112	41	0	153
1946	182	170	102	47	8	157
1947	174	158	103	32	10	145
1948	140	138	93	20	7	120
1949	121	118	72	30	12	114
10-yr. av.	186	178	113	42	8	163
1950	110	117	88	18	10	116
1951	102	70	34	20	8	62
1952	91	63	0	15	12	27
1953	101	68	26	17	10	53
1954	160	132	26	22	12	60
1955	109	88	20	15	9	44

TABLE 54 (*Continued*)

Year	Long U.S. Governments vs. 3-Month Governments, Annual Average	Prime 30-Year Corporate Bond Yields vs. Commercial Paper Rates, February Averages	U.S. Government Bonds, February Averages			
			10-Year vs. 1-Year Maturity	20-Year vs. 10-Year Maturity	30-Year vs. 20-Year Maturity	30-Year vs. 1-Year Maturity
1956	42	5	30	2	7	39
1957	19	8	0	−9	6	−3
1958	159	133	99	31	4	134
1959	67	41	49	6	2	57
10-yr. av.	96	73	26	14	10	50
1960	108	56	7	−12	−5	−10
1961	152	138	108	6	4	118
1962	117	107	90	3	1	94
1963	84	71	82	11	4	97
1964	60	43	38	1	3	42
1965	26	11	25	−1	0	24
1966	−22	−42	−14	−9	−4	−27
1967	53	41	−12	−6	−2	−20
1968	−9	28	17	−10	−8	−1
1969	−58	−80	−30	0	0	−30
10-yr. av.	51	37	23	−4	−2	17
1970	19	32	−61	−66	−2	−129
1971	141	228	168	−2	−2	164
1972	156	252	199	−29	−1	169
1973	−73	−71	41	36	4	81
1974	−85	−130	−17	45	1	29
1975	121	250	86	64	31	181
1976	181	308	190	47	16	253
1977	179	242	190	28	6	224
1978	70	74	67	20	3	90
1979	−133	−128	−120	−8	−4	−132
10-yr. av.	58	106	74	14	5	93
1980	−52	−35	−121	0	−3	−124
1981	−116	−59	−128	−24	−17	−169
1982	162	190	14	−2	−29	−17

TABLE 54 (*Continued*)

Year	Long U.S. Governments vs. 3-Month Governments, Annual Average	Prime 30-Year Corporate Bond Yields vs. Commercial Paper Rates, February Averages	U.S. Government Bonds, February Averages			
			10-Year vs. 1-Year Maturity	20-Year vs. 10-Year Maturity	30-Year vs. 20-Year Maturity	30-Year vs. 1-Year Maturity
1983	223	315	183	33	10	226
1984	247	255	183	18	−4	197
1985	327	336	192	23	−11	204
1986	217	263	149	37	−8	178
1987	286	253	125	57	−23	159
1988	231	303	163	22	−3	182
1989	47	35	−4	−6	−9	−19
10-yr. av.	157	186	76	16	−10	82

SOURCES

Governments: Federal Reserve sources given in Tables 48 and 51.

Corporates: Basic yields (Durand) given in Table 53 (1900–1945) and Moody Aaa given in Table 50.

Commercial paper: Macaulay, *op cit.*, p. A152 for 60- to 90-day prime through 1936; thereafter, Federal Reserve sources given in Table 50, for 4- to 6-month or 6-month prime.

the total yield differentials created by maturity occurred between one and ten years, and almost all the rest, between ten and twenty years. The trend of the differentials was usually in the same direction but not always.

Charts 43A and 43B picture the resulting pattern of yields, called yield curves, at selected dates. Each curve connects the simultaneous yields of bonds maturing in from one to thirty years as of the inscribed date. Some curves are relatively flat; that is, yields were roughly the same for all maturities (for example, 1918 and 1989). Some were positive; that is, yields increased as maturity lengthened (1941 and 1984). And some were negative; that is, yields decreased as maturities lengthened (1921 and 1981).

During the nineteenth century, four- to six-month commercial paper rates averaged far higher than did prime long-term bond yields (see decennial Chart 35 in Chapter XVII). This relationship prevailed during the first three decades of the twentieth century, but thereafter bond yields averaged higher than did commercial paper rates. Similarly the yield curves of prime corporate bonds tended to be negative (long-term yields below short-term

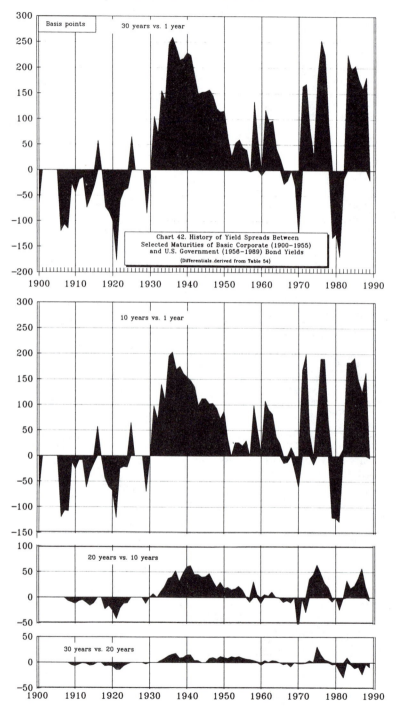

Basis points

30 years vs. 1 year

Chart 42. History of Yield Spreads Between
Selected Maturities of Basic Corporate (1900–1955)
and U.S. Government (1956–1989) Bond Yields
(Differentials derived from Table 54)

10 years vs. 1 year

20 years vs. 10 years

30 years vs. 20 years

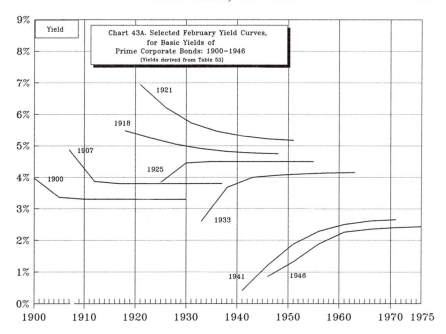

Chart 43A. Selected February Yield Curves, for Basic Yields of Prime Corporate Bonds: 1900–1946 (Yields derived from Table 53)

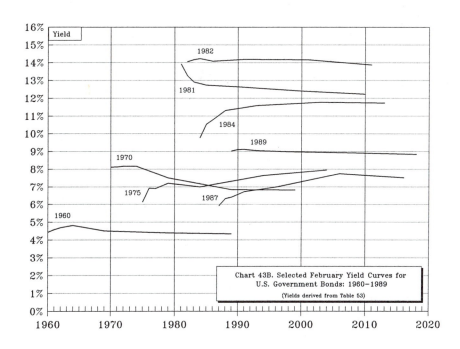

Chart 43B. Selected February Yield Curves for U.S. Government Bonds: 1960–1989 (Yields derived from Table 53)

yields) most of the time from 1900 until 1930; when the curves were not negative, they were usually flat. In only two years before 1930 (1916 and 1925) was the curve positive (long-term yields above short-term yields).

After 1930, positive yield curves were the rule until 1960. The differential grew enormous in the mid-1930's, when short rates were nominal and long rates were low. Short-term yields reached their extreme low points in 1940–1941 and rose thereafter, whereas long-term bond yields continued to decline until 1946. Thus, from 1940 until 1946, there occurred one of those rare periods when short and long rates moved in opposite directions for several years. After 1946 the differential declined almost steadily and finally, in 1960, became negative in another period of what were then considered high interest rates. After 1960, yield spreads became more erratic than they had been earlier in the century. After 1964 the yield curve became negative, sometimes sharply negative. Then suddenly in 1971 it became sharply positive and tended to remain positive until the late 1970's except in the period of extreme market pressure in 1974. This positive curve is sometimes interpreted to mean a market forecast of still higher yields to come. Such a forecast proved to be correct as yields advanced to record levels in 1979–1981, during which time negative yield curves were common. Until 1989, when the curve became flat, it was generally positive, except that thirty-year yields were often less than twenty-year yields.

Finally, Charts 44A and 44B present in three-dimensional perspectives all

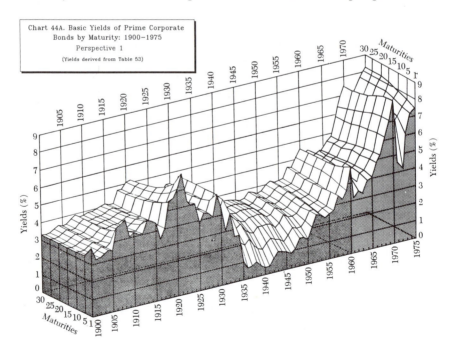

Chart 44A. Basic Yields of Prime Corporate
Bonds by Maturity: 1900–1975
Perspective 1
(Yields derived from Table 53)

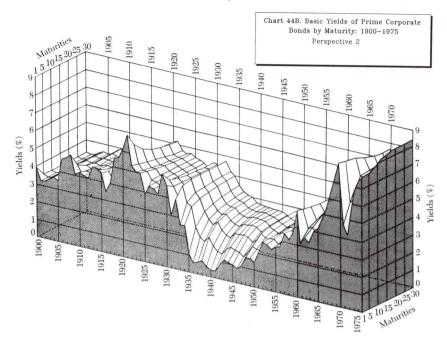

Chart 44B. Basic Yields of Prime Corporate
Bonds by Maturity: 1900–1975
Perspective 2

the corporate bond yield curves linked together to show the history of the yields of each maturity from 1900 to 1975, and Charts 45A and 45B present, in slightly different perspectives, U.S. government bond yield curves from 1950 to 1989. The shortest maturity yields are nearest to the reader, and the longest maturity yields are at the back of each chart. All the other maturity yields range in between. Chart 44A proceeds from 1900 to 1975, and in it the great decline in longer yields from 1930 to 1940 is hidden from the eye. Chart 44B charts the same data from a different point of view, which reveals those parts hidden in Chart 44A. Charts 45A and 45B accomplish the same for governments from 1950 to 1989, although it should be noted that yields at all maturities shown were not available throughout the period. Three variables are simultaneously pictured: yield, maturity, and time. These charts suggest a riptide as the powerful currents of rising or falling interest rates cut across very powerful currents of change in the relationship of long-term to short-term interest rates.

The construction of these smooth yield curves proceeding from very short maturities to very long maturities runs the risk of concealing the very fundamental difference between short-term loans and long-term loans. This is because there is no precise maturity at which short ends and long begins. Historically, we have seen that long-term and short-term loans had very different origins and histories. Medieval financiers would have been surprised at any attempt to link together their bills of exchange with permanent in-

Chart 45A. Yields of U.S. Government
Securities by Maturity: 1950–1989
Perspective 1
(Yields derived from Table 53)

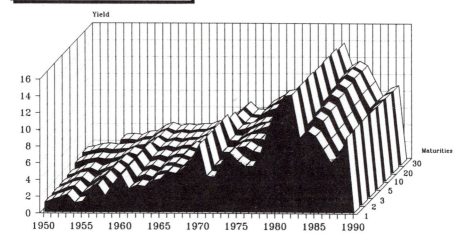

Chart 45B. Yields of U.S. Government
Securities by Maturity: 1950–1989
Perspective 2

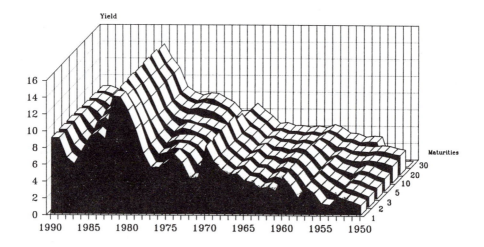

come contracts, such as their perpetual annuities. The essence of the bill of exchange was the repayment of principal; the annuity often contemplated no repayment of principal.

These maturity curves thus are the result of grouping together and comparing the rates prevailing in a number of very different markets or submarkets (517), which were not always alike in their investment attributes and hence were subject to different supply and demand schedules. These schedules overlap sufficiently so that there is a tendency for short, medium, and long rates to move in the same direction most of the time, but no tendency at all for them to move by similar amounts. Over the ninety Februaries covered by the data in Table 53, the one-year and the thirty-year rates have generally risen and fallen together. Corporate one-year and thirty-year yields moved in opposite directions during only seven of the years 1900–1975. Over the shorter period 1955–1989, U.S. government one-year and thirty-year yields also moved in opposite directions in seven years.

The timing of lows and highs has usually been similar for rates on both long and short maturities. There were, however, a few important exceptions. The low rates for shorts came in 1939–1942, but the lows for longer maturities tended to appear about 1946 or even as late as 1950. The high yields for every maturity in the first half of the century were in 1918–1922; in the second half, they were in 1980–1982.

HIGH-GRADE NEW ISSUE YIELDS AND YIELD SPREADS

The trend and level of the corporate bond market have been described throughout this chapter in terms of market yields of seasoned issues rather than new issue yields. A review of the market, however, requires some chronicling of the yields of new issues. Table 55, which presents a sampling of new issue yields of prime corporate bonds, is based on a selection of high-quality issues. The yields, until 1946, are not necessarily representative and are not sufficiently numerous or uniform to provide an index of new issue yields. From 1946 through 1989, however, they are based on comparable averages of Aa public utility long-term new issue yields derived from all important new issues in this category.

The table shows the yield at the offering date of one or two of the lowest-yielding prime large new issues of straight long-term corporate bonds for almost every year until 1946. It excludes convertible issues, serial issues, and issues with special features. Each offering yield is compared in the table with the simultaneous yield of the average of prime thirty-year seasoned corporate bonds. For years after 1920, comparison is also made with the simultaneous yield of longer governments. The differentials are called yield spreads.

Because the new issues are not averages or uniformly selected before

TABLE 55
EXAMPLES OF TERMS, YIELDS, AND YIELD SPREADS OF NEW ISSUES OF HIGH-GRADE CORPORATE BONDS: 1900–1989

Date	Terms of New Issues			Yield Spreads, Basis Points	
	Rate, %	Maturity	Yield at Offering, %	From Seasoned Corporate Yields	From Government Bond Yields*
1900 April	$3\frac{1}{2}$	2000	3.00	−28	
1902 April	$3\frac{1}{2}$	1952	3.22	−7	
1903 January	$3\frac{1}{2}$	1952	3.34	−9	
1905 June	$3\frac{1}{2}$	1946	3.50	−1	
1908 August	4	1948	4.05	+17	
1909 January	4	1933	3.84	+5	
1911 March	4	1943	3.89	−2	
1914 May	4	1987	4.22	+14	
1915 January	$3\frac{1}{2}$	2000	4.21	+4	
1915 January	$4\frac{1}{2}$	1960	4.31	+14	
1916 October	4	1951	4.11	+4	
1917 January	4	1948	4.14	+16	
1918 December	5	1968	5.04	+43	
1919 April	$4\frac{1}{2}$	1957	5.25	+42	+53
1920 December	5	1952	6.06†	+76†	+66†
1922 January	5	1941	4.92	+21	+47
1922 June	5	1937	5.00†	+51†	+55†
1923 March	$4\frac{1}{2}$	1973	4.69	+15	+31
1924 October	4	1943	4.81	+33	+94
1925 May	4	1955	4.55	+13	+68
1927 March	$4\frac{1}{2}$	1977	4.65	+39	+128
1927 December	4	2003	4.32	+26	+115
1928 December	$4\frac{1}{2}$	1958	4.69	+35	+124
1929 October	5	1941	5.00	+44	+139
1930 May	5	1970	4.86	+51	+155
1931 January	$4\frac{1}{2}$	1981	4.45	+35	+125
1932 April	$4\frac{1}{2}$	1961	5.00	+24	+116
1932 July	5	1962	5.30	+57	+160
1935 May	4	1965	3.94	+48	+115
1935 July	$3\frac{1}{2}$	1965	3.30	−10	+51
1936 May	$3\frac{1}{2}$	1966	3.17	+8	+24
1938 August	$3\frac{1}{2}$	1968	3.01	+9	+29
1939 June	3	1969	2.75	+4	+34
1940 December	$2\frac{3}{4}$	1970	2.52	−10	+33
1941 November	$2\frac{3}{4}$	1971	2.55	+4	+15
1942 June	3	1972	2.79	+16	+29

TABLE 55 (*Continued*)

Date	Terms of New Issues			Yield Spreads, Basis Points	
	Rate, %	Maturity	Yield at Offering, %	From Seasoned Corporate Yields	From Government Bond Yields*
1944 September	3	1974	2.71	+16	+16
1945 December	$2\frac{3}{4}$	1985	2.65	+11	+14
1946 Annual av.	$2\frac{5}{8}$	1976	2.57	+12	+27
1947	$2\frac{3}{4}$	1977	2.76	+19	+43
1948	3	1978	3.05	+23	+58
1949	$2\frac{3}{4}$	1979	2.79	+11	+42
1950	$2\frac{3}{4}$	1980	2.71	−1	+33
1951	$3\frac{1}{8}$	1981	3.09	+13	+49
1952	$3\frac{1}{4}$	1982	3.19	+12	+50
1953	$3\frac{1}{2}$	1983	3.49	+18	+42
1954	3	1984	3.03	+5	+33
1955	$3\frac{1}{4}$	1985	3.22	+9	+35
1956	$3\frac{3}{4}$	1986	3.71	+31	+64
1957	$4\frac{5}{8}$	1987	4.61	+61	+113
1958	$4\frac{1}{8}$	1988	4.08	+28	+61
1959	$4\frac{3}{4}$	1989	4.74	+26	+66
1960	$4\frac{3}{4}$	1990	4.73	+32	+66
1961	$4\frac{1}{2}$	1991	4.52	+17	+58
1962	$4\frac{3}{8}$	1992	4.36	+8	+30
1963	$4\frac{3}{8}$	1993	4.33	+10	+25
1964	$4\frac{1}{2}$	1994	4.46	+5	+25
1965	$4\frac{5}{8}$	1995	4.57	+8	+31
1966	$4\frac{1}{2}$	1986	5.45	+27	+73
1967	$5\frac{7}{8}$	1987	5.57	+33	+93
1968	$6\frac{5}{8}$	1998	6.61	+46	+121
1969	$7\frac{3}{4}$	1999	7.75	+71	+147
1970	$8\frac{7}{8}$	2000	8.83	+76	+201
1971	$7\frac{3}{4}$	2001	7.74	+50	+162
1972	$7\frac{1}{2}$	2002	7.45	+34	+150
1973	$7\frac{3}{4}$	2003	7.74	+28	+74
1974	$10\frac{1}{2}$	2004	10.50	+57	+175
1975	$9\frac{1}{2}$	2005	9.51	+90	+126
1976	$8\frac{3}{4}$	2006	8.69	+57	+72
1977	$8\frac{1}{4}$	2007	8.28	+54	+56
1978	9	2008	9.06	+42	+60
1979	$10\frac{1}{8}$	2009	10.10	+53	+85
1980	$13\frac{1}{2}$	2010	13.11	+61	+175
1981	$16\frac{1}{8}$	2011	16.12	+126	+245
1982	$15\frac{3}{8}$	2012	15.33	+82	+203

TABLE 55 (*Continued*)

Date	Terms of New Issues			Yield Spreads, Basis Points	
	Rate, %	Maturity	Yield at Offering, %	From Seasoned Corporate Yields	From Government Bond Yields*
1983	12¼	2013	12.47	+23	+102
1984	13⅜	2014	13.61	+30	+107
1985	12	2015	11.94	+25	+86
1986	9¾	2016	9.36	−19	+134
1987	9⅝	2017	9.63	−7	+108
1988	10	2018	9.97	+11	+105
1989					

*After 1928, yield spreads from governments are adjusted for difference in maturity; before 1928, spreads are from average of long government yields. Before 1941 yields are for partially tax exempts (PTE) and afterwards for taxable governments.

†Quality less than that of other issues.

Sources

New-issue prices and yields were derived from securities manuals and periodicals. The one or two issues a year that are quoted before 1946 are insufficient to give a complete picture of the market. The examples were among the lowest-yielding, important, regular long-term corporate bond issues at the time of offering. After 1946, comprehensive new-issue averages from *An Analytical Record of Yields and Yield Spreads* (published by Salomon Brothers) are used.

1946, accurate trends cannot be read from their yields, and precise relationships cannot be generalized from these yield spreads. The table, however, does suggest some tendencies for spreads to be wide at times and narrow at other times and for new issue yields to be much more volatile than even seasoned issue yields.

Table 56 contains columns comparing the yields of prime seasoned thirty-year corporate bonds and long governments. The spreads show less volatility than that of the new issue spreads, but similar trends. Other columns compare the yields of the high-grade municipal bond averages and the simultaneous yields of the prime seasoned corporate bond averages. The municipal-corporate relationships are pictured in Chart 46. Municipal yields tended to be low (and municipal bond prices high) relative to corporates in periods when average marginal federal income tax rates were high because municipal interest was tax exempt. The effects of tax bracket creep during the inflationary 1970's are evident in Chart 46, as are the Reagan tax cuts in

TABLE 56
Yield Differentials Between Long-Term Government, Corporate, and Municipal Bonds: 1900–1989

Date	Prime 30-Year Corporate Bonds vs. Government Bonds, Annual Averages		Long-Term Municipal Bonds vs. Prime 30-Year Corporate Bonds, Annual Averages	
	Yield Spreads, Basis Points	Corporate Yields as % of Government Yields	Yield Spreads, Basis Points	Municipal Yields as % of Corporate Yields
1900			−6	98
1901			−18	94
1902			−16	95
1903			−25	93
1904			−17	95
1905			−3	99
1906			−22	94
1907			−25	93
1908			−3	99
1909			−2	99
10-yr. av.			−13	96
1910			+4	101
1911			+5	101
1912			+6	102
1913			+31	108
1914			+5	102
1915			+6	102
1916			−5	99
1917			−18	96
1918			−25	95
1919			−34	93
10-yr. av.			−3	99
1920	−5	99	−47	91
1921	+7	101	−31	94
1922	+19	105	−44	91
1923	+15	104	−53	88
1924	+45	111	−59	87
1925	+64	116	−60	87
1926	+68	118	−41	91
1927	+84	125	−33	92
1928	+86	126	−39	91
1929	+87	126	−45	90
10-yr. av.	+47	113	−45	90

TABLE 56 (*Continued*)

Date	Prime 30-Year Corporate Bonds vs. Government Bonds, Annual Averages		Long-Term Municipal Bonds vs. Prime 30-Year Corporate Bonds, Annual Averages	
	Yield Spreads, Basis Points	Corporate Yields as % of Government Yields	Yield Spreads, Basis Points	Municipal Yields as % of Corporate Yields
1930	+102	131	−44	90
1931	+81	125	−62	85
1932	+93	125	−106	78
1933	+88	127	−74	82
1934	+71	123	−46	87
1935	+65	123	−76	81
1936	+46	118	−66	78
1937	+44	117	−44	86
1938	+34	113	−45	84
1939	+41	117	−85	70
10-yr. av.	+67	122	−65	82
1940	+49	122	−90	67
1941	+64	132	−99	62
1942	+20	108	−84	68
1943	+8	103	−108	58
1944	+6	102	−139	45
1945	+17	107	−149	41
1946	34	116	−143	43
1947	36	116	−116	56
1948	38	116	−95	66
1949	35	115	−100	62
10-yr. av.	14	114	−45	57
1950	32	114	−105	60
1951	54	123	−126	56
1952	39	115	−117	60
1953	52	119	−89	72
1954	−2	99	−87	70
1955	22	108	−89	71
1956	28	109	−86	74
1957	42	112	−79	80
1958	36	110	−87	77
1959	31	108	−103	76
10-yr. av.	33	112	−97	70
1960	40	110	−115	74
1961	45	112	−108	75
1962	38	110	−130	70

TABLE 56 (*Continued*)

Date	Prime 30-Year Corporate Bonds vs. Government Bonds, Annual Averages		Long-Term Municipal Bonds vs. Prime 30-Year Corporate Bonds, Annual Averages	
	Yield Spreads, Basis Points	Corporate Yields as % of Government Yields	Yield Spreads, Basis Points	Municipal Yields as % of Corporate Yields
1963	26	107	−120	72
1964	25	106	−131	70
1965	28	107	−133	70
1966	47	110	−146	72
1967	66	114	−177	68
1968	93	118	−198	68
1969	93	115	−158	78
10-yr. av.	50	111	−142	72
1970	145	122	−192	76
1971	165	129	−217	71
1972	158	128	−217	70
1973	114	118	−245	67
1974	158	123	−268	69
1975	185	127	−241	73
1976	165	124	−277	67
1977	96	114	−282	65
1978	84	111	−321	63
1979	89	110	−371	61
10-yr. av.	136	120	−263	68
1980	113	110	−409	66
1981	130	110	−374	74
1982	156	113	−291	79
1983	120	111	−324	73
1984	72	106	−310	76
1985	62	106	−277	76
1986	88	111	−207	77
1987	74	109	−224	76
1988	73	108	−235	76
1989	68	108	−226	76
10-yr. av.	96	109	−288	75

SOURCES

Corporate yields are 30-year Durand's basic yields to 1945, from second edition (1977) of this HISTORY, Table 49, and Moody's Aaa, 1946–1989, from Table 50. Municipals are bond buyer, high grade to 1920, New York State to 1940, and long-term prime new issues to 1945, from Tables 45 and 47, and Moody's Aaa, 1946–1985, from Table 50. Governments are P.T.E. to 1941 and taxable thereafter, from Tables 46, 48, and 51.

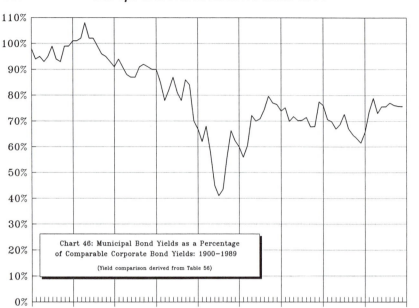

Chart 46: Municipal Bond Yields as a Percentage
of Comparable Corporate Bond Yields: 1900-1989

(Yield comparison derived from Table 56)

the 1980's. Relative to corporates, the former increased the demand for municipals and reduced their relative yield, while the latter had the opposite effect.

RISK RATES

Although prime bond yields usually ranged between 2.50 and 5% during the first sixty-five years of the twentieth century in the United States, investors were offered a wealth of opportunities to work their money harder. There is no precise way of comparing the differential between prime rates and risk rates over a period of time, because there is no precise way of measuring risk. Risk is subjective, not objective. A rough approach to measuring the subjective hopes and fears of investors is provided by Chart 47, which measures the yield difference between bonds rated prime or Aaa at the time of quotation and bonds rated medium grade or Baa. The enormous rise in the differentials during the Depression of the 1930's is apparent, as are the low differentials in the 1920's and especially in recent years.

A few examples of high bond yields offered to American investors are provided by the tables below. The first table reports the offering yields on some new issues of foreign bonds during the 1920's. The second table reports market yields at the low prices of the 1930's from seasoned standard and respectable domestic corporate bond issues that did not default. The first table

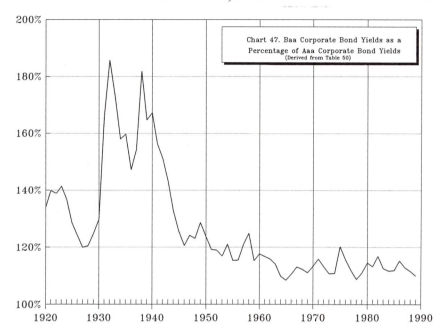

Chart 47. Baa Corporate Bond Yields as a
Percentage of Aaa Corporate Bond Yields
(Derived from Table 50)

SELECTED NEW FOREIGN BOND ISSUES IN NEW YORK, 1916–1928, WITH OFFERING PRICE AND YIELD

Year	Issue	Coupon, %	Maturity Date	Price	Maturity Yield, %
1916	Imperial Russian Government	$5\frac{1}{2}$	1921	$94\frac{3}{4}$	6.75
1922	City of Berlin	6	1958	95	6.36
1922	Serbs, Croats, and Slovenes	8	1962	$95\frac{1}{2}$	8.40
1923	Bolivia	8	1947	101	7.90
1925	Antioquia, Colombia	7	1945	90	8.00
1925	Belgium, Kingdom of	7	1955	98	6.65
1925	Poland, Republic of	8	1950	95	8.45
1925	Saõ Paulo, Brazil	8	1950	$99\frac{1}{2}$	8.04
1926	Baden Municipal	7	1951	93	7.62
1927	British & Hungarian Bank	$7\frac{1}{2}$	1962	$98\frac{3}{4}$	7.54
1927	Agricultural Mortgage Bank, Colombia	6	1947	92	6.72
1927	Colombia, Republic of	6	1961	$92\frac{1}{2}$	6.55
1928	Peru, Republic of	6	1961	91	6.65
1928	Chile, Republic of	6	1961	94	6.45

SELECTED HIGH MARKET YIELDS ON BONDS IN GOOD STANDING AT THE
LOW PRICES OF THE 1930's

Issue	Coupon, %	Maturity Date	Low Price	Maturity Yield, %
Atchison, Topeka & Santa Fe Conv.	4	1955	60	7.60%*
Bell Telephone of Canada (U.S. $ Pay)	5	1960	79	6.70*
Dominion of Canada (U.S. $ Pay)	3	1967	59	6.10*
Central Pacific R.R. 1st Ref.	4	1949	48½	10.60*
C.B.&Q. R.R. 1st Ref.	4½	1977	65	7.20*
Elmira & Williamsport (Penn. R.R. Gtd.)	5	2862	75	6.65†
Great Northern R.R. Ref.	4½	1977	34	13.40†
Kansas Gas & Elec. Deb.	6	2022	61¼	9.80*
Lorillard	5	1951	76½	7.28*
New York Central Ref.	4½	2013	31	15.00†
Northern Pacific Ref.	6	2047	45	13.30†
Ohio Power Deb.	6	2024	70	8.55*
Penn. Gas & Elec. 1st & Ref.	5	1958	50	10.60*
Pennsylvania R.R. Gen.	5	1968	54½	9.45*
Rochester Gas & Elec. General	4½	1977	75	6.20*
San Joaquin Light & Power	6	1952	88	7.15*
Southern Pacific Deb.	4½	1969	29	15.40†
Southern Pacific 1st Ref.	4	1955	50	9.25*

*Yield to maturity.
†Current yield.

illustrates a type of popular conventional risk, which usually invited disappointment, and the second table illustrates some unpopular unconventional opportunities, which involved little risk and brought large reward.

Not included in the second table are some examples from a long list of bonds that defaulted in the 1930's. Many of them sold at nominal prices. Examples are Missouri Pacific Convertible Debenture 5½s of 1949, low price ½; Missouri Pacific Refunding 5s of 1965, low price 12½; Central of Georgia 5½s of 1959, low price ¾; Chicago, Rock Island & Pacific Refunding 4s of 1934 (Rocky Reefers), low price 4. Most issues of this type recovered handsomely in the 1940's and reached values equal to many times these market lows. Prime corporate bond issues, in contrast, were never seriously depressed in the 1930s. The average yield of prime rails never exceeded 4.83% during that decade.

During speculative periods of the late 1960's, those who sought high yields generally demanded equity "kickers" on their bond investments or extrapolated handsome performance from stock portfolios. Private investors generally favored prime bonds, municipal or corporate. In the early 1970's such high yields were provided by prime bonds that the market for risk bonds was all but ignored. Furthermore, the severe liquidity crisis, illustrated by the Penn Central bankruptcy and the New York City defaults of the mid-1970s created a new investor conservatism.

As yields rose to record levels in the late 1970's and early 1980's, the long-term corporate bond market as a whole diminished in importance, especially relative to the U.S. governments market, which was fed by rising fiscal deficits. Corporations, along with state and municipal governments, increased their reliance on short- and medium-term borrowing at the expense of long-term bonds. The quality distribution of corporate bond issues also declined, as fewer and fewer issues merited top grade and more and more were of medium and lower grade. (518) Lower yields in the mid- and later 1980's revived the bond market somewhat, but it was a far different and more heterogeneous market in emphasis from the traditional high-grade market of earlier decades. Stimulated by a mergers/acquisitions/corporate take-over/leveraged buy-out mania on the part of borrowers, and by a yearning for the high yields offered in the early 1980's on the part of investors, issues of low-grade debt ("junk bonds") proliferated. These offered yields several hundred basis points over those of high-quality issues. At the end of the decade, several issuers of junk bonds ran into difficulty in meeting their obligations, and it remained to be seen if this high-risk sector of the market would be able to weather the less inflationary environment shaping up for the 1990's.

 ### REAL ESTATE MORTGAGES

Interest rates on real estate mortgages were usually higher than interest rates on prime marketable obligations until the 1970's. According to some theorists, most interest rates higher than prime rates are risk rates, but this explanation of the yield differential ignores costs, liquidity, convenience, and tradition. An example entirely within the field of unquestioned credits was provided by Federal Housing Administration mortgages issued in the 1950's under the Capehart Amendment. They were assumed by one department of the U.S. government and insured by an agency of the United States. These mortgages sold in early 1960 to yield 5.25% when at the same time marketable government bonds of similar term were selling to yield 4.25%. There was no risk implicit in this 100 basis point differential and, indeed, very little cost. The differential was due to institutional causes: convenience and liquidity. The "Capehart mortgages" had a poor secondary market; they were available only in large pieces, usually $1 million or more, and their purchase involved some sophisticated negotiation and paperwork. Risk is far from being the only explanation of higher than prime interest rates.

In the post-World War II era, U.S. government credit was extended to eliminate the risk from a wide variety of private credit instruments, many in the form of mortgages. A number of federal agencies bought mortgages, and those agencies resold their own paper or guaranteed the mortgages and sold them publicly. The mortgage market, with this aid, was able to absorb a disproportionate volume of the total savings of the country.

Table 57 lists some real estate mortgage rates in the United States. Several of these rates are portrayed in Chart 48. The farm mortgage rate is a blend rate of all outstanding issues, and therefore adjusts only gradually to the new issue rate trend. The table of decennial averages below shows how sluggishly conventional U.S. mortgage rates responded to changes in prime corporate bond yields before the 1970s; during the 1970's and 1980's, the relative gap between mortgage rates and bond yields narrowed, and the two series moved together. Since 1970 or so, mortgage rates have adjusted fairly quickly to changes in other yields, as the table also indicates.

DECENNIAL AVERAGES OF MORTGAGE RATES AND
CORPORATE BOND YIELDS: 1900–1989

Decade	Conventional U.S. Mortgages, %	Prime Corporate Bonds, %	Mortgage Rates as Share of Prime Bond Yield, %
1900–1909	5.35	3.47	155
1910–1919	5.51	4.23	130
1920–1929	5.89	4.56	128
1930–1939	5.40	3.64	148
1940–1949	4.85	2.61	185
1950–1959	5.22	3.33	156
1960–1969	6.47	4.94	131
1970–1979	8.93	8.23	109
1980–1989	12.68	11.40	111

As this table shows, mortgage rates averaged far above corporate bond yields in the easy-money period of the 1940's and also in the 1950's. As yields rose in the 1960's, the yield spread in favor of mortgages came down sharply, and in the 1970's and 1980's it was nearly eliminated. Indeed, at times in the 1970's and 1980's, seasoned corporate bond yields exceeded some mortgage yields, while new issue corporate bond yields were far above high-grade mortgage yields. This big change in yield relationship was one of the most significant changes in recent decades. Why should savings institutions insist on mortgages if they yield less than prime corporate bonds, much less if the expenses of a mortgage portfolio are taken into account? Hence government agencies intervened to permit the mortgage market to tap the money market and the bond market. Because of this intervention, even the massive failures of savings and loan institutions at the end of the 1980's had minimal impact on mortgage rates.

TABLE 57
U.S. Conventional Real Estate Mortgage Rates: 1900–1989

Year	Manhattan/ HUD, Annual Average, %	Contract Rate, Annual Average, %	New Home Mortgage Yields, Annual Average, %	Farm, Annual Average, %
1900	5.17			
1901	5.11			
1902	5.09			
1903	5.18			
1904	5.35			
1905	5.50			
1906	5.68			
1907	5.45			
1908	5.60			
1909	5.35			
10-yr. av.	5.35			
1910	5.35			6.0
1911	5.47			6.0
1912	5.46			6.1
1913	5.50			6.1
1914	5.58			6.1
1915	5.60			6.1
1916	5.50			6.2
1917	5.47			6.1
1918	5.55			6.1
1919	5.65			6.1
10-yr. av.	5.51			6.1
1920	5.75			6.1
1921	5.97			6.2
1922	5.95			6.3
1923	5.91			6.4
1924	5.92			6.3
1925	5.90			6.3
1926	5.89			6.2
1927	5.88			6.1
1928	5.85			6.1
1929	5.92			6.0
10-yr. av.	5.89			6.2
1930	5.95			6.0
1931	5.75			6.0

TABLE 57 (*Continued*)

Year	Manhattan/ HUD, Annual Average, %	Contract Rate, Annual Average, %	New Home Mortgage Yields, Annual Average, %	Farm, Annual Average, %
1932	5.77			6.0
1933	5.60			6.0
1934	5.45			5.8
1935	5.26			5.5
1936	5.09			5.1
1937	5.11			4.9
1938	5.00			4.7
1939	5.05			4.6
10-yr. av.	5.40			5.5
1940	5.03			4.6
1941	4.90			4.5
1942	4.98			4.4
1943	4.77			4.4
1944	4.71			4.4
1945	4.70			4.5
1946	4.74			4.5
1947	4.80			4.5
1948	4.91			4.5
1949	4.93			4.5
10-yr. av.	4.85			4.5
1950	4.95			4.5
1951	4.93			4.6
1952	5.03			4.6
1953	5.09			4.7
1954	5.15			4.7
1955	5.18			4.7
1956	5.19			4.7
1957	5.42	5.79		4.7
1958	5.58	5.75		4.8
1959	5.71	5.92		4.9
10-yr. av.	5.22	5.82		4.7
1960	6.30	5.98		5.0
1961	6.97	5.93		5.1
1962	5.93	5.81		5.2
1963	5.81	5.84		5.3

TABLE 57 (*Continued*)

Year	Manhattan/ HUD, Annual Average, %	Contract Rate, Annual Average, %	New Home Mortgage Yields, Annual Average, %	Farm, Annual Average, %
1964	5.80	5.78	5.3	
1965	5.83	5.76	5.4	
1966	6.40	6.14	5.4	
1967	6.53	6.33	5.4	
1968	7.12	6.83	5.5	
1969	7.99	7.66	5.7	
10-yr. av.	6.47	6.21		5.3
1970	8.52	8.27	8.45	5.8
1971	7.75	7.60	7.74	6.0
1972	7.64	7.45	7.60	6.1
1973	8.30	7.78	7.95	6.4
1974	9.22	8.71	8.92	6.6
1975	9.10	8.75	9.01	7.0
1976	8.99	8.76	8.99	7.6
1977	8.95	8.80	9.01	7.6
1978	9.68	9.30	9.54	7.4
1979	11.15	10.48	10.77	7.9
10-yr. av.	8.93	8.59	8.80	6.2
1980	13.95	12.25	12.65	8.3
1981	16.52	14.16	14.74	9.1
1982	15.79	14.47	15.12	9.7
1983	13.43	12.20	12.66	9.7
1984	13.80	11.87	12.37	9.6
1985	12.28	11.12	11.58	9.4
1986	10.07	9.82	10.16	9.1
1987	10.17	8.94	9.31	9.0
1988	10.30	8.81	9.18	9.5
1989	10.22	9.76	10.11	9.4
10-yr. av.	12.68	11.34	11.79	9.3

SOURCES

Manhattan mortgage rates from second edition of this HISTORY, Table 56; from 1970 on, this series is the federal government's HUD series from Federal Reserve, *Annual Statistical Digest* and *Federal Reserve Bulletin*. Conventional contract rates and new home mortgage yields also from same Federal Reserve sources. Farm mortgage rates (a blend of rates on all outstanding mortgages) are from *Historical Statistics of the United States, Statistical Abstract of the United States;* and USDA, *Agricultural Statistics.*

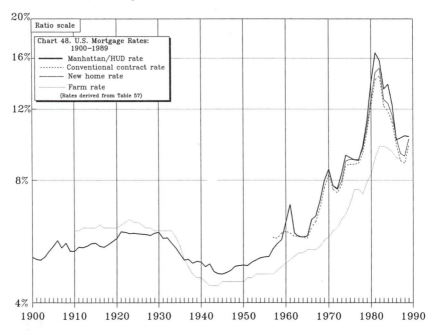

Chart 48. U.S. Mortgage Rates: 1900–1989

Before the 1960's, relative stability at a high level was characteristic of rates, such as mortgage rates, that involve large servicing costs and heavy responsibilities for the creditor. These costs and responsibilities rarely change with interest rates. Great-grandfather and -grandmother may have invested in mortgages on their neighbors' farms. If so, they drove around to collect the payments and watched their neighbors' crops and their neighbors' personal habits closely. They earned a good part of their extra mortgage income. It was always much easier to deposit money in a savings account than to own and service a portfolio of home mortgages—hence the difference in rate, only in part, perhaps in small part, due to risk and in large part attributable to cost and convenience.

As the mortgage market came more nearly to resemble the bond market in recent decades, however, mortgage rates were no longer quite as stable relative to bond rates as they once were. In the great advance and decline of rates between 1965 and 1989, the time pattern of mortgage rates was almost the same as that of bond yields.

CONSUMER CREDIT RATES AND LEGAL LIMITS

Home mortgage rates, although above prime rates of interest, have been below the prevailing rates of interest on most forms of consumer credit with relatively short maturity. This apparently has been true over the centuries. During the Middle Ages, relatively modest rates often prevailed for long-term loans secured by farms or estates, but pawnshop rates were much higher, including even those charged by the publicly endowed pawnshops. The reason for the higher rates was probably not primarily that the risk of making short loans on valuable security was greater than the risk of making long-term loans on homes, but rather that the cost of making many small short loans was very large. (519)

Modern usury statutes usually authorize two rates of interest on commercial lending: a legal rate that an obligation is assumed to bear in the absence of an agreed rate of interest and a maximum rate that may be charged by agreement. Related provisions govern real estate and consumer loans. In the mid-1950's the legal rate was 4% in one state, 5% in five states, 6% in forty states, and 7% in four states. A majority still clung to the 6% tradition of the Stuart kings. Ten states set the maximum rate to be the same as the legal rate; thirty-three set the maximum rate above the legal rate; and four states had no maximum. The penalties for usury varied from none to forfeiture of excessive interest, loss of principal, or even fines and imprisonment. Corporate debtors generally were not protected by usury statutes. Commissions, brokerage, and legal fees were often permitted as supplements to maximum payments.

During the recent decades of rising interest rates, many states have raised legal limits sharply, and in other ways liberalized their usury statutes. By the mid-1980's, the legal rate was still 5% in five states, 6% in fifteen states and the District of Columbia, 7–10.5% in twenty-one states, 12–18% in nine states, and unlimited in one state (Idaho). Maximum allowed rates set by contract or agreement were generally higher and sometimes indexed to another rate, for example, 5% above the Federal Reserve discount rate (Alaska and Arkansas), 6% above six-month Treasury bills (North Carolina), and 6% above the New York City bank prime rate (Montana). Twelve states had no limit on contract rates, and another thirteen had no limit on contract rates for loans above a certain minimum amount. Several states put into their laws a statement that rates greater than 45% per year were considered "extortionate" or "unconscionable."

The old statutes, which were usually written in the nineteenth century, did not contemplate modern consumer credit. Under them, there was often no legitimate capital available for small personal loans to urban workers. Many of these workers were driven to illegal loan sharks. This was a situation that has been reported repeatedly from the earliest chapters of this history. In ancient Babylonia, Greece, and Rome and in Europe during the Middle Ages the provision and regulation of consumer credit was a pressing political and social issue.

Legislation in the twentieth century has provided for small personal loans through regulated institutions at higher rates of interest than were permitted by the usury laws. In addition, purchases of consumer goods may legally be financed at higher rates of interest through sales finance companies, which buy time payment notes at a discount from dealers. Effective rates of interest on installment loans in the late 1950's were permitted up to 12–24% a year. Commercial banks, likewise, were permitted to extend consumer credit at rates as high as 7–14% (520) and sometimes higher. In 1960, statutory limits for interest on the smallest personal finance loans, usually of $300 or less, ranged from 30 to 48% in most American states, with 36% the most common legal maximum.

The statutory limit for larger loans made by small loan companies, usually about $1000, generally ranged from 8 to 36% per annum. Pawnshops in New York were permitted to charge 3% a month for the first six months and 1½% a month for the next six months, or 27% for the first year. In Pennsylvania the pawnshop rate was 3% a month on merchandise and 1½% a month on jewelry. New Jersey permitted 2% a month, or 24% a year. Modern forms of consumer credit outmoded the pawnshops, which became of far less relative importance than in the past.

These modern rates of interest on consumer credit must recall a number of earlier chapters of this history. The 20% legal limit of Babylonia, the 24% rate charged in Ptolemaic Egypt, and the 8–12% legal limits of Rome were within our modern range for consumer credit; so was the 15% charged by the charitable pawnshops of the Middle Ages.

So-called "truth in lending" legislation, passed early in the 1970's for the first time, required lenders to provide borrowers with the true annual percentage rate of interest implicit in consumer and other forms of credit. This has made it possible to gather and publish nationwide data on the average rates charged on important categories of consumer credit. Table 58 and

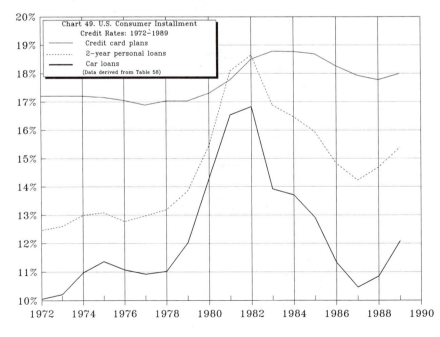

Chart 49. U.S. Consumer Installment Credit Rates: 1972–1989
——— Credit card plans
············ 2–year personal loans
——— Car loans
(Data derived from Table 58)

TABLE 58
U.S. CONSUMER CREDIT COMMERCIAL BANK RATES:
1972–1989

Year	% Yield		
	New Automobiles (36–48 months)*	Personal Loans (24 months)	Credit Card Plans
1972	10.05	12.46	17.21
1973	10.21	12.60	17.21
1974	10.97	12.99	17.21
1975	11.36	13.08	17.16
1976	11.07	12.77	17.05
1977	10.92	12.97	16.89
1978	11.02	13.19	17.03
1979	12.02	13.85	17.03
8-yr. av.	10.95	12.99	17.10
1980	14.30	15.47	17.31
1981	16.54	18.09	17.78
1982	16.83	18.65	18.51
1983	13.92	16.88	18.78
1984	13.71	16.47	18.77
1985	12.91	15.94	18.69
1986	11.33	14.82	18.26
1987	10.46	14.23	17.93
1988	10.85	14.68	17.78
1989	12.07	15.44	18.02
10-yr. av.	13.29	16.07	18.18

* 1972–1982, 36 months; 1983–1989, 48 months.

SOURCES
Federal Reserve, *Annual Statistical Digest* and *Federal Reserve Bulletin*.

Chart 49 present several such average annual rates from 1972 through 1989. The pattern of new automobile and personal loan rates conforms in general to the pattern of money and bond market rates over this period, but these rates behave more sluggishly than do the open market rates, being slower to rise when market rates are trending up and slower to fall when market rates fall. Credit card plan rates, in contrast, on average moved barely at all in relation to other rates during a period that witnessed the greatest fluctuations in money and bond market rates in U.S. history. Some of what was said earlier about the reasons for the relative stability of mortgage rates, at least before government intervention and securitization, applies also to consumer credit. The published rates contain large cost components that do not vary much, even as open market rates swing up and down. That is an important part of the explanation of why consumer credit rates are both higher and more stable over time than market rates.

LOAN SHARKS

As in ancient Athens, and in all other periods of history, there has been no limit to the charges made by loan sharks. The better class of modern loan shark skirts the law by buying salaries or selling overpriced merchandise. A prevailing rate of 240%, running up to 1500% per annum, on loans of this type was suggested during the Great Depression by a survey in those states that did not license consumer credit companies. (521) These were short loans and were usually negotiated at weekly or monthly rates, which are here converted to annual rates. The conversion of rates quoted for a few days or weeks into annual rates is statistically necessary for comparative purposes but can give a distorted picture of such transactions as they are viewed by debtor and by creditor.

Earlier in the twentieth century, a favorite rate for illegal small loans in American cities seems to have been $1 a week for loans of $5. Needy workers might borrow $5 on Saturday and promise to repay $6 on payday, which would be Friday of the next week. They would no doubt consider that the loan had financed a "spree" or a visit to the doctor at a cost of an extra $1. Our mathematics tells us that they pay 20% a week, or 1040% a year. If they renewed the loan weekly or, more likely, repaid each Friday and reborrowed each Saturday, they did in fact pay $52 a year for the use of $5. During the 1950's loan shark prosecutions in New York County repeatedly revealed just this rate of interest.

In the 1920's, a group of clerks in the financial district of New York made a regular business of lending to other clerks on these terms: $5 on Monday for $6 on Friday. In 1960 a criminal information (similar to an indictment) against a loan shark ring in New York, which for ten years had loaned to taxi drivers, mentioned an average loan of $100 with the recipient paying $120 at the end of a week plus $25 a week for any longer term or in case of arrears. This is again a rate of 1040% a year, uncompounded plus penalties, bringing it up to a theoretical 1295% a year. In the 1930's and earlier, blacks in the South were said to pay twice this New York loan shark rate; $7 on Friday for the use of $5 for any part of a week. This was an annual rate of 2080%. (522)

Larger illegal loans, as might be expected, commanded lower rates. A Senate investigation was once told of a group of New York racketeers who loaned to other gangsters sums totaling at least $300,000 at various rates of interest quoted as 30%, 47%, 65%, 73%, 104%, 173%, and 198% per annum. (523)

Similar rates on such transactions have been reported in the press in recent decades. Apparently this type of interest rate does not rise and fall with the money market.

REAL INTEREST RATES

The rise of interest rates and market yields to record levels in the 1970's and early 1980's cannot be understood without reference to inflation and the economic concept of real interest rates. If a lender considers that a 4% real return, that is, a 4% gain in purchasing power or in dollars of constant value, is required in order to justify lending $100 for one year, then that lender will demand a nominal interest rate of 14.4% if the expected rate of inflation in that year is 10%. Then, supposing that the expected inflation is realized, the loan repayment of $114.40 a year later will consist of $110 repayment of principal, which is equivalent to the $100 principal before the price level rose 10%, and $4.40, equivalent to $4 of interest before the 10% rise of prices. In this example, the nominal, or market, rate of interest is 14.4%, and the real, or inflation-adjusted, rate of interest is 4%. (524)

Before the rise of inflation that began in the later 1960's, the real rate of interest was a concept confined almost exclusively to the academic world. Apart from wartime episodes inflation was neither a notable occurrence in economic life nor a major concern of investors. Indeed, those who lived through the Depression of the 1930's were likely to view deflation as much more of a threat and, therefore, to take a somewhat positive view of small year-to-year increases in the price level as long as the economy was prosperous. Since the 1960's, however, higher and often rising rates of inflation have served to propel the concept of real rates of interest to the forefront of lender and borrower thinking. The effect of inflationary expectations on market rates and yields has become evident and pronounced. (525)

Because the real rate of interest depends on the expected inflation, it cannot be directly observed. The theoretical concept is often roughly approximated as a market, or nominal, rate less the expected rate of inflation, and sometimes—after the fact—the real rate is crudely calculated by subtracting the actual rate of inflation from the prevailing nominal rate of interest, or market yield. More sophisticated modelers of expectations usually assume that expected future rates of inflation are formed by current and/or recent past inflation rates. There is thus no real rate of interest to be discovered; there are merely a variety of attempts approximately to measure it.

The results of one such attempt to approximate the real interest rate in the United States since 1857 are presented in the table on page 430 and in Chart 50. The table gives the annual average nominal yield of corporate bonds and estimates of the average real interest rate and expected inflation, by decades from 1857 to 1989. Real rates in the table are calculated by subtracting expected inflation from nominal rates, which is only a rough approximation.

ESTIMATED REAL INTEREST RATES

Decade	Nominal Rate, Annual Average, %*	Expected Inflation, %[†]	Real Interest Rate, Annual Average, %
1857–1859	9.84	0.64	9.19
1860–1869	8.00	5.80	2.20
1870–1879	7.41	−3.22	10.64
1880–1889	5.14	−0.97	6.12
1890–1899	4.51	−1.23	5.75
1900–1909	4.16	0.82	3.34
1910–1919	4.77	3.73	1.04
1920–1929	5.08	3.00	2.08
1930–1939	3.89	−2.12	6.01
1940–1949	2.71	4.49	−1.78
1950–1959	3.31	2.65	0.66
1960–1969	5.02	1.81	3.20
1970–1979	8.24	5.97	2.27
1980–1989	11.32	6.63	4.69

*Nominal interest rates are bond yields derived from Macaulay, *op. cit.*, table A10, for the period 1857–1918, and from Moody's Aaa corporate series, 1919–1989, as given in Federal Reserve publications.

[†]Expected inflation is estimated by a weighted average of Consumer Price Index inflation rates during the seven previous years, with a weight of 0.33 for the previous year and weights declining by 30% per year for previous years 2 through 7. The data were analyzed by Professor Jack W. Wilson of North Carolina State University. Note that expected inflation is not the same as the actual inflation rate of a decade; the expected inflation estimate is influenced by actual inflation rates of the prior decade.

It is apparent from the table that real interest rates were generally higher in the nineteenth than in the twentieth century. It is also apparent that real rates vary widely from decade to decade and (see Chart 50) from year to year. Even in the twentieth century, the ten-year averages vary from +6.01 to −1.78. There is little basis for the widespread belief that the real interest rate is 2 to 3% in twentieth-century America. (526) There is a basis in the estimates for the widespread contention that real rates were high in the 1980's, but they seem to have been no higher than they were in the 1930's and in much of the previous century. The extreme swings in real rates shown in Chart 50 resulted mainly from extreme swings in inflation (or deflation) rates connected with wars or depressions. Before the 1970's nominal rates were much more stable than either inflation or real rates.

The connection of historical fluctuations in real rates with wars and depressions goes far toward explaining why the concept of real interest rates

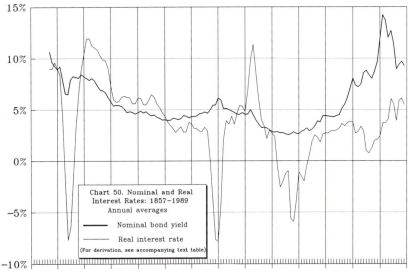

Chart 50. Nominal and Real
Interest Rates: 1857–1989
Annual averages

——————— Nominal bond yield

——————— Real interest rate

(For derivation, see accompanying text table)

was largely ignored until recent times. Indeed, there was no mention of the concept in the first two editions of this HISTORY or in most academic and financial community discussions. Wars and depressions—along with their inflationary or deflationary effects—were either unexpected or considered to be temporary, or both. Once they were over, a reasonably stable price level was expected to return. The experience of the gold standard before the 1930's and the gold exchange standard and the Bretton Woods system before the 1970's served in general to reinforce these expectations.

What changed during the 1970's and 1980's was that persistent inflation came to be expected, an expectation that was reinforced by the cutting of the old ties of the dollar and other currencies to gold. As rates of inflation rose, so—with a lag—did bond yields and short-term rates. And as rates of inflation came down, so—again with a lag—did market rates and yields. In this new financial and economic environment, there is much more risk and uncertainty about the future value of money. An investor considering the purchase of a twenty- or thirty-year bond knows its current market yield, but to estimate its real yield to maturity requires forecasting the average rate of inflation for the next twenty or thirty years. That is a highly uncertain matter, depending as much or more on future politics than on economics. This uncertainty transformed the long-term, fixed-interest bond from the conservative investment it had been for much of U.S. history into a risky, rather speculative investment.

During the 1970's and 1980's, an increasingly widespread understanding of the concept of real interest rates and of the risks of traditional lending and investment in an uncertain inflationary environment had a number of consequences for interest rates, market yields, and credit instruments. To compensate for increased risk and uncertainty of inflation, lenders and investors demanded what appeared to be higher real rates of interest. Borrowers, attempting to avoid getting locked into costly long-term commitments in case the inflation rate turned out to be less than expected, turned increasingly to shorter-term financing. These behaviors diminished the relative importance of the traditional long-term bond markets and fixed interest rate bonds after the mid-1970's.

Another consequence was increased discussion of and the actual appearance of inflation-indexed bonds. The British government, beginning in 1981, made the greatest use of this innovation, as will be discussed in the next chapter. The U.S. government considered issuing inflation-indexed bonds in 1981 but did not issue any. Starting in 1982, interest rates and bond yields began to decline, which removed some of the pressures building for the innovation. A few U.S. financial institutions nonetheless issued inflation-indexed instruments in the 1980's. These paid a constant real rate of interest plus the rate of inflation as measured by the Consumer Price Index. (527)

The inflation-indexed bond made few inroads in the United States for another reason besides the decline of yields. Variable- or floating-rate instruments—loans, notes and mortgages—came in as another way to cope with market fluctuations and inflation. The interest rate on such instruments was linked to other key interest rates, such as U.S. government bill, note, and bond rates, or the London Inter-Bank Offered Rate (LIBOR), a rate akin to the U.S. Federal Funds rate, in the Eurodollar market. To the extent that such key interest rates follow inflation rates, there is little difference between variable- or floating-rate financing and inflation indexing.

A NOTE ON CORPORATE BOND YIELD AVERAGES AND INDICES

The prevailing market yields for the best bonds of well-defined types and terms are usually known within a narrow range each day by contemporary bond dealers and professional investors. Nevertheless, the construction of a time series tracing the history of these market yields over long periods presents difficulties. Economists sometimes ask the impossible: a series of yields or interest rates over long periods of time derived from instruments of substantially identical terms and quality that fulfill the same economic function in the same way in one decade as in another. The objectives of some forms of economic analysis require just this uniformity. In real life it often does not exist, even from year to year.

At the outset of this history, it was made clear that the security behind the rates quoted for various times or places could not always be uniform. Such comparability over time as the principal series provide is derived from the attempt to compare rates on only the most highly regarded credits of their type at each time and place. The lowest acceptable market yields at one point of time are compared with the lowest acceptable market yields at another point of time, provided that terms are similar and prices are not distorted by extraneous circumstances. These "prime rates" are treated as comparable limits.

An important attempt was made by Frederick R. Macaulay to construct an American corporate bond yield average free from changes in the average quality of the bond issues composing the average. His adjusted average of high-grade railroad bond yields, 1857–1937 (528), was quoted in our nineteenth-century tables. The objective, however, should not be taken literally. No railroad bonds were likely to exist in 1860 of quality equal to that carried by dozens in 1900 and 1925. Macaulay collected monthly prices and yields of all the principal railroad bond issues from 1857, discarded those that were of short maturity or otherwise unsuitable, and constructed an unadjusted average as a chain index of yields down to 1937. These were typical yields, and not high-grade yields. Then, by studying the scatter between the lower and higher yields, he constructed his adjusted average to reflect the yields of best-quality bonds. This highly theoretical average, over most of its life, usually came close to the actual going yields commanded by the best railroad bonds, although at times it ranged slightly below the lowest prevailing yields.

From 1900 to 1958, updated here to 1975, the best index of prime corporate bond yields classified by years to maturity is provided by David Durand's *Basic Yields of Corporate Bonds.* (529) It was constructed on an entirely different principle from that of averaging. The market yields of all the principal high-quality corporate bond issues of all maturities were plotted as of each February on a scatter chart. Those with disqualifying characteristics, such as price above call, active sinking fund, convertibility, and so on, were discarded. A freehand curve was then drawn through the clusters of lowest yields at each maturity. This curve provided an index of the yields of the most highly regarded bonds in each maturity. The method was unsatisfactory only in maturity ranges where there was a scarcity of prime bond issues; this was sometimes the case with short-maturity corporate bonds. There has always, however, been an ample number of representative long-term bond issues. It must be understood that in periods of sharply rising yields, low-coupon, deep-discount issues usually provide lower yields than those of high-coupon issues. It is these low yields that the Durand series will report, which makes it less satisfactory for the high-yield environment of the 1970's and 1980's. Durand's basic yields for thirty-year corporate bonds are quoted in all the 1900–1945 corporate tables of Chapter XVII, and the complete series is provided here in Table 53. For years from 1945 to 1989, Moody's Aaa corporate index is given in Table 50. It is quite similar to the

Durand series in the years of their overlap, even though it is not precisely a thirty-year index. Since the 1950's, the homogeneous U.S. government market has provided the best indicator of yields by maturity. These data for each February are reported also in Table 53.

Since Durand's basic yields are calculated only for the first quarter of each year or for February, they do not provide monthly fluctuations. In the monthly tables, therefore, the February basic yields have been adjusted for monthly fluctuations by interpolation from Macaulay's adjusted average for years until 1930, and for years thereafter from the monthly fluctuations of Aaa and Aa utility averages. The Moody's Aaa series is available monthly.

Most attempts at constructing bond yield averages encounter certain difficulties, the chief of which are described here.

1. Changes in the number of outstanding bond issues. An average of the ten best railroad bonds, for example, might at one time represent one-tenth of the suitable active issues; and at another time it might represent half of all suitable active issues and hence lose something in relative quality.

2. Quality standards if specific issues are averaged. Several railroad bonds that in the 1920's received the highest agency ratings and were included in the highest grade averages defaulted in the 1930's. Many others—indeed, most—lost status without default. It was evidently impossible to eliminate such issues sufficiently far in advance of their deterioration to prevent the averages themselves from losing status. Thus, many averages in the early 1930's drifted far above the true going market for prime corporate bond yields.

3. Maturity. Most averages used to contain a variety of maturities and discarded only truly short bonds. In the early part of this century and in the mid-1920's, when there was little or no yield difference between, say, fifteen-year and forty-year bonds, this was not a handicap. However, in 1920, when medium-term bonds sold to yield much more than longs, the presence of a few ten- to twenty-year maturities in an average would raise its yield above the going yields of truly long-term bonds. Conversely, when in the 1930's the yield curve became sharply positive, the presence of shorter maturities depressed the average yield. The same problem persisted through the 1950's. Later, in periods when high rates brought negative yield curves, the presence in an average of medium-term bonds served to exaggerate its fluctuations. In general, however, yield spreads have not typically been large for ten- to thirty-year issues in the homogeneous U.S. government market.

4. Call prices. In the high bond markets of the 1930's and 1940's, there were times when most prime corporate bonds sold up near call price or above call price. Averages based on such issues would then stand at yields above the going rate.

5. Quotation. Many seasoned corporate bonds become very inactive. Stock Exchange quotations used by some averages, based on a unit of one bond, gave a poor clue to the true level of the market.

6. Sinking funds. In the lower bond markets of recent decades, when the bond market included a large number of high-quality industrial issues with big sinking funds selling at large discounts, industrial bond yield averages would sometimes be depressed far below the going yields that investors were willing to accept. Agencies that must present averages made up entirely of industrial bonds found it difficult not to understate the level of market yields.

7. Coupon. High-coupon corporate and government bonds often yield much more than do otherwise identical low-coupon bonds, especially in periods of low prices.

Most of these difficulties are reasonably well overcome by Durand's method of creating his basic yield index for corporate bonds. Since the 1970's, U.S. Treasury and Federal Reserve publications have reported "constant maturity" yield series for government securities for a number of maturities ranging from one to thirty years. These are derived by techniques similar to those used by Durand.

Since the 1930's, techniques for deriving indices of yields have improved. Credit ratings became very severe, and the issues in the prime market became much more uniform. In the higher markets of the 1930's and 1940's, call price became the chief problem and seemed to keep some yield averages a trifle above prevailing market yields for bonds unaffected by call. Differences, however, were slight. From the 1940's to the 1970's (when the Durand series ends), the Durand series and Moody's Aaa corporate series, as noted, are quite similar.

In the high-yield era of the 1970's and 1980's, the chief problem in constructing bond averages derived from large differences in yields between low-coupon bond issues and identical higher-coupon issues. Indeed, the most sensitive of all yields, the new issue yields, were almost always well above similar seasoned issue yields. The only complete solution is to construct a series of averages for different coupon groups, as well as for different maturity groups. Such a series of monthly high-grade bond yield averages, some of which go back to 1946, can be found in the Salomon Brothers publication *An Analytical Record of Yields and Yield Spreads*.

Chapter XIX

England in the Twentieth Century

There is an old saying to the effect that in France the more things change, the more they stay the same, whereas in England the more things stay the same, the more they change. England lost much of its reputation for financial stability and leadership in the twentieth century. The financial consequences of the two world wars played a role in this, as did England's ardent pursuit of full employment at almost any cost for much of the post-World War II decades. Nonetheless, there were small signs of the old capacity for leadership. English long-term interest rates peaked in the 1970's, well before the early 1980's peaks in other large industrial nations. Having suffered the most from interventionist and questionable full-employment policies, England was one of the first to back off from them. Another sign of innovative leadership in finance was the government's introduction of inflation-indexed bonds beginning in 1981, an official and explicit recognition of the consequences of inflation for interest rates.

Their fondness for tradition will, we hope, lead the British people to forgive us for maintaining our own tradition of referring to their country as England rather than the more comprehensive and accurate Great Britain or United Kingdom.

POLITICAL AND ECONOMIC BACKGROUND

The financial history of England during the first six decades of the twentieth century was dominated by World Wars I and II. Both of these wars required financial mobilization on a scale hitherto unknown. Although victorious in both wars, England lost its position as the dominant political and financial power in the world, but nevertheless retained large financial resources and commercial and political power. In the 1960's and 1970's, however, a highly unstable political situation developed, with a series of weak or minority governments. Voter support was purchased by large social expenditures unmatched by increased production. The result was a flight of capital, a massive increase in the national debt, a loss of monetary reserves, a loss of exports, a rise in imports, huge international borrowings, a disastrous inflation, and an unprecedented rise in interest rates. At times it seemed to many as though internal victory in this class war was more important than national survival. The later 1970's and 1980's brought more conservative, or neo-liberal and monetarist, approaches to economic policy. The inflation rate of the 1980's fell to approximately one-half of what it had been in the 1965–1980 period.

Up to 1960 the English national debt had been largely a war debt. The increase from 1945 to 1960 had been small, but thereafter the increase was very large and was supplemented by heavy borrowings by local authorities and public corporations. If the debt of all government agencies is included, total public debt almost doubled after 1965 and reached £61 billion in 1975. It nearly doubled again in the next five years, reaching £117 billion in 1980. The rate of increase of total public debt slowed thereafter, but nonetheless reached £205 billion in 1987. The official national debt traced the following course in the twentieth century:

BRITISH NATIONAL DEBT

Year	Billions of Pounds
1900	0.6
1914	0.7
1920	7.9
1930	7.6
1939	8.3
1945	22.4
1960	28.0
1970	34.1
1975	45.5
1980	94.2
1987	191.3

The century opened with the Boer War, 1899–1902, which increased the debt but created very little economic strain. The first decade was marked by a mobilization of the power of labor and by social legislation, such as old-age pensions, health and unemployment insurance, and the income tax. The establishment of the Entente Cordiale with France in 1904 and naval rivalry

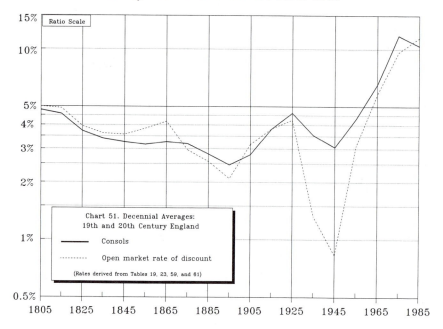

Chart 51. Decennial Averages:
19th and 20th Century England

—————— Consols

············· Open market rate of discount

(Rates derived from Tables 19, 23, 59, and 61)

with Germany foreshadowed the calamities of the next decade, but the period was one of peace and prosperity. The pound sterling was "as good as gold," a true international currency. The accumulation of English capital and the difficulty of finding profitable outlets for it in England led to increased foreign investment, which rose to more than one-quarter of the national wealth. (530) Commodity prices, which had reached a low in 1896, rose irregularly, but by an aggregate of 40%, between 1896 and 1914. (531) English prosperity suffered only minor interruptions. Interest rates rose almost steadily during the eighteen years before World War I and continued to rise during the war and for two years after its end (see Chart 51).

World War I, 1914–1918, took the world's markets by surprise and created a wave of liquidation. In time it became a contest between the resources of the Central Powers blockaded in Europe and those of most of the rest of the world. The necessary mobilization of resources set a precedent for government intervention in economic affairs that has enhanced the economic role of the English government and most other governments ever since. Although English taxes were trebled, only 28% of war expenditures came from taxes. The national debt rose elevenfold, and bank deposits rose by about 450%. In spite of the tremendous inflation resulting from the war and measured by a 130% rise in commodity prices, the English were determined and were able, with the aid of American credits and tight controls, to maintain the exchange rate of the pound sterling reasonably close to its gold parity.

Immediately after World War I, the course of the English economy was similar to that of the United States economy: a short, sharp boom in 1919–1920 and a sharper depression in 1920–1921, during which English unemployment rose to 10%. The subsequent recovery in England, however, was not so rapid as that of the United States. Foreign markets had been lost and exports were down to 50% of their prewar total. (532) World-wide protective tariffs hindered British trade. The English government struggled throughout the 1920's to bring back the pound sterling to prewar parity and to hold it there. This made the recovery of foreign markets difficult. Interest rates were kept near high wartime levels.

The crash of the American stock market in 1929 brought large declines on the London Exchange and started a wave of credit liquidation throughout the world. American capital, which had financed an important part of world trade in the 1920's, was no longer available. Commodity prices in England declined 24% from 1929 through 1931. Liquidation and deep depression led many countries to abandon their recently restored gold standards, and this put pressure on the London money market. The insolvency of the Austrian Creditanstalt in 1931 led to a financial crisis throughout Europe. In September 1931, England abandoned the gold standard and set the pound to fluctuate with supply and demand. It declined from $4.86 to $3.49, or almost 30%. By the end of 1932, thirty-five countries had left the gold standard, and only the United States, France, Switzerland, the Netherlands, and Belgium remained to form the "gold block." During the next few years devaluation became general. The United States devalued the dollar in 1933–1934, and the pound rose to $5.

Immediately after England abandoned the gold standard, English monetary policy was reversed. Interest rates were quickly pushed down, and every effort was made to encourage production and consumption. The risk of inflation seemed remote. The economic effects of these new policies, however, were obscured by a rash of small wars and political crises that upset ordinary peacetime economies. The German denunciation of the Treaty of Versailles in 1934, the Italian-Ethiopian conflict of 1935–1936, the Spanish Civil War of 1936–1939, the reoccupation of the Rhineland in 1936, and the fear of a new world war wrought havoc with international trade, budgets, and economic readjustment. During these years English trade revived, but prosperity and stability did not return. A very large part of the gold reserves of the world fled to the United States.

World War II, 1939–1945, was the first to deserve the name "total war." Budgetary expenditures of belligerent states for war materials have been estimated at $1154 billion. (533) The English financial mobilization was probably more rigorous than that of any other belligerent power. The nation expended 54% of its national income on war in 1944–1945. The government's expenditures increased from £1147 million in 1938–1939 to £6190 million in 1944–1945.

The outbreak of the war in 1939 did not come as a surprise. The markets had long been prepared for it and were very liquid. There was no financial panic such as had occurred in 1914. Detailed plans had been made in England for economic mobilization. It was fully realized that economic resources would play a large part in determining the outcome of the war. Consumers were rationed, prices were controlled, exports and imports were regulated for national purposes, and the foreign assets of nationals were mobilized. The investment markets were tightly controlled, and interest rates were not allowed to rise as they had risen in World War I. Instead of paying 4½–5% interest for war loans as in 1915–1917, England now fought a 3% war. Between 1939 and 1946, whenever market yields on government bonds were not frozen, they tended to decline.

High taxes paid for 48.5% of the total expenditures of the government, a far higher percentage than the 28.5% of World War I. (534) The national debt increased by £14 billion, or 175%, as compared with the 1100% increase in a much smaller debt during World War I. In spite of active and successful campaigns to sell government bonds to the public, inflation was not avoided, but it was held within reasonable bounds during the war. Note circulation rose 160%, bank deposits rose 145%, and wholesale prices rose 74% between 1939 and 1945.

England drew heavily on her foreign assets to finance essential imports. She also lost an important part of her export markets. Total "disinvestment" overseas was £3.9 billion, and England came out of the war a net debtor. Thus, she required much larger exports than before the war to balance her international accounts.

After World War II, financial demobilization and the struggle to gain national solvency were complicated by ideological and political differences of opinion. Some of the wartime controls were looked upon by the Labour party as good in themselves and suitable for a peacetime economy. Subsidies, rationing, price controls, the control of investment, and the level of the rate of interest became political issues, to which was added public ownership of heavy industry. In 1946 a Labour government depressed interest rates to levels below their lows of the 1930's and issued long-term 2½% bonds at par. Soon, however, it became evident that the public was more interested in spending some of its enforced wartime savings than in investing new savings at 2½% before taxes. At the same time, large new issues of government securities were required to finance nationalized industries or to exchange for the stock of newly nationalized industries. The Labour party retreated from its low interest rate policy and the retreat was hastened by a succession of crises in the balance of payments. The Cold War forbade a full, rational settlement of international problems, on which England, more than most countries, depended for her prosperity. Large dollar credits were quickly used up. In 1949 the pound, which had been stabilized during the war at $4, was devalued to $2.80. Thus, during the first six decades of the twentieth century, the pound lost 42% of its dollar value. This was much less of a loss than that suffered by many other currencies. In 1967, another devaluation reduced the pound to $2.40. After being allowed to float in 1972, the pound declined further, to below $2.

During the years after 1949, the pound was held at its reduced value, but only by weathering a succession of new crises in the reserves of gold and dollars. Nevertheless, large international debts were steadily liquidated. The country turned politically conservative in the 1950's, and most wartime controls were eventually eased or abandoned. There was a return to monetary orthodoxy, and with it, a reduction in the excessive liquidity of the economy. Bank-rate and other credit controls were used vigorously to offset cyclical trends of business and to maintain the gold reserves. A very large part of the floating debt was funded. High bond yields became a deliberate objective of the government policy.

These traditional defenses of the pound, however, did not go to the heart of the problem. Huge social expenditures were demanded by the public, and at the same time the productivity of British industry declined. After 1965 a world-wide inflation got under way, and it soon became worse in England than in other industrial nations. The English people simply could not agree on a rational strategy to control it. The oil embargo accentuated the crisis. The money supply escalated at an impossible rate, and the government borrowed large sums abroad. Membership in the Common Market did not solve these problems. Finally, however, general suffering from a runaway inflation seemed to create a better political climate, and steps were announced to reduce consumption and encourage production. In the 1980's, the conservative Thatcher government pursued policies similar to those of the Reagan administration in the United States.

A SUMMARY OF LONG-TERM INTEREST RATES

The course of long-term English interest rates in the twentieth century, as shown in Chart 52, described a letter *M*, in much the same manner as did the course of the American long-term interest rates, but with a much larger upsweep at the end, reaching higher levels than had ever before prevailed—for example 18% for consols. The rates rose almost steadily from 1896 to 1920, declined very irregularly from 1920 to 1946, rose with a few cyclical interruptions from 1946 to 1974, and then declined (with an interruption in 1980–1981) to the end of the 1980's.

Chart 52 includes a summary of long-term yields back to 1750. It is evident that the pattern of the twentieth century has been very different from the patterns of the eighteenth and nineteenth centuries. The course of the eighteenth-century market resembled the letter *U:* Rates declined almost steadily during the first half of the century (not shown) and rose in a very

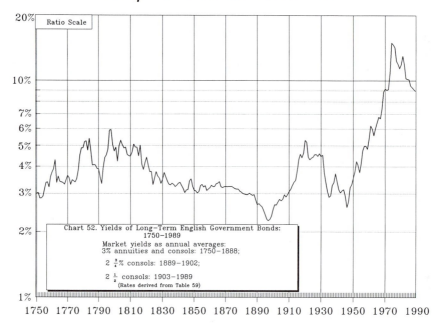

Chart 52. Yields of Long–Term English Government Bonds: 1750–1989
Market yields as annual averages:
3% annuities and consols: 1750–1888;
2 ¾% consols: 1889–1902;
2 ½ consols: 1903–1989
(Rates derived from Table 59)

jagged manner during the second half, not returning, however, to earlier highs. The nineteenth-century pattern was one of almost steady decline. Viewing this history from the vantage point of 1900, the English investor could have been justified in thinking that in peacetime bond yields usually declined. When the first nine decades of the twentieth century are added to the chart, however, the visual impression of preponderant decline vanishes. The high yields of 1974 were far above those of 1920, and of the 1790's; the low yields of 1935 and 1946 were above the low yields of 1896. The impression was one of oscillation for more than 200 years in a band bounded by 6% and 2.25%. Events since 1960, however, have again radically altered the pattern of the chart. Yields not only moved up out of this historical band, bounded by a high of 6%, but in a few years rose to more than twice that level. After 1974, yields declined but remained well above the historical band as the 1990's opened. For this century to date, the suprasecular trend of prime long English yields has been clearly up.

TECHNICAL NOTES ON BRITISH GOVERNMENT BOND YIELDS

The history of the yields of British funds in the twentieth century can no longer be based solely on consol yields. The reliance on the yield of one issue was permissible during a good part of the eighteenth century and most of the nineteenth century, when consols comprised a very large part of the national debt. The world wars of the twentieth century, however, were financed by a great variety of bond issues with all sorts of rates and terms. Some were undated; some had long, some had medium, and some had short maturity dates; most had a date of redemption and a more distant date of maturity. The old concept of perpetual funded debt was gradually replaced by a concept of funding and refunding. Investors sought an eventual return of their principal at the risk of losing income, and the government ceded this right. The most notable example of the change was the giant issue of War Loan 5s floated in 1917, due in 1947, and redeemable in only twelve years, that is, in 1929. The privilege of calling this issue at an early date handsomely compensated the Treasury for the high rate; in 1932 the bonds were refunded into the War Loan perpetual 3½s.

Most of these issues with higher nominal rates commanded higher yields in the market most of the time than the yields of the consol 2½s. The market yields of consols seemed permanent, and their appreciation possibilities were larger than the appreciation possibilities of higher-priced issues. This was important in a country with a high income tax and no capital gains tax. During the 1970's, however, when consols sank in price to below 25, the old dreams of capital gains seemed to fade, the low coupon became unpopular, and at times consols sold to yield more than did high-coupon issues. The yield on consols after 1918, therefore, can no longer be taken as typical of the market, although the difference usually was not large.

In Table 59, prices and yields of consols are given for the sake of continuity. These consol yields are supplemented by a band of yields bounded by two series that give the simultaneous lowest and highest interest yields of all British government securities with maturities of thirty years or more on each December 31. This band should satisfactorily picture the trend and level of long-term English government bond yields.

One complication involves the speculative yields provided during the high bond markets of the 1930's and 1940's by premium issues, which might or might not be called at the earliest redemption date. The band of yields is based on the assumption that premium issues will be redeemed as soon as possible. The table provides, as an alternative calculation, maximum current yields of bonds selling at premiums. These were yields that might be realized if interest rates rose and these issues were not called. Just this happened. These higher current yields in the 1930's and 1940's were so much above the market that they cannot be considered as the prevailing rates on long-term bonds that investors expected to receive. They are listed in the table, but are not included in the corresponding graph in Chart 53.

COMPARISON WITH UNITED STATES BOND YIELDS

Chart 53 pictures this band of December 31 yields on long British government bonds and compares them with the annual average of yields of American prime corporate bonds. Comparison with U.S. government bond yields would be preferable, but the circulation privilege before 1917, partial

TABLE 59
Prices and Yields of Long-Term British Government Securities: Twentieth Century

Year	2½% Consols						Yield Range of All Issues 30 Years or Longer as of Dec. 31		
	Annual Average		Annual High		Annual Low		Low Yield, %	High Yield, %	Maximum Current Yield of Premium Issues, %
	Price	Yield, %	Price	Yield, %	Price	Yield, %			
1900	$99\frac{5}{8}$	2.54	$103\frac{1}{4}$	2.44	$96\frac{3}{4}$	2.62	2.57	2.82	
1901	$94\frac{3}{16}$	2.67	$97\frac{7}{8}$	2.57	91	2.77	2.67	2.82	
1902	$94\frac{1}{2}$	2.66	$97\frac{7}{8}$	2.57	$92\frac{1}{8}$	2.73	2.69	2.80	
1903	$90\frac{15}{16}$	2.75	$93\frac{5}{8}$	2.68	86	2.92	2.84	2.88	
1904	$88\frac{3}{8}$	2.83	$91\frac{1}{4}$	2.74	85	2.94	2.83	2.92	
1905	$89\frac{13}{16}$	2.78	$91\frac{13}{16}$	2.73	$87\frac{1}{2}$	2.86	2.79	2.91	
1906	$88\frac{3}{8}$	2.83	91	2.75	$85\frac{9}{16}$	2.92	2.90	2.98	
1907	$84\frac{3}{16}$	2.97	$87\frac{3}{8}$	2.86	$80\frac{3}{4}$	3.10	2.97	3.04	
1908	$86\frac{1}{4}$	2.90	$88\frac{3}{8}$	2.83	$83\frac{5}{16}$	3.00	2.97	3.04	
1909	$83\frac{7}{8}$	2.98	86	2.91	$82\frac{1}{16}$	3.05	3.01	3.08	
10-yr. av.		2.79						2.82	2.93
1910	$81\frac{3}{16}$	3.08	$83\frac{1}{4}$	3.00	$78\frac{3}{8}$	3.19	3.15	3.23	
1911	$79\frac{3}{8}$	3.15	$82\frac{3}{16}$	3.05	$76\frac{3}{8}$	3.27	3.24	3.38	
1912	$76\frac{1}{4}$	3.28	$79\frac{3}{16}$	3.16	$72\frac{1}{2}$	3.45	3.32	3.50	
1913	$73\frac{3}{4}$	3.39	$75\frac{5}{8}$	3.31	71	3.52	3.48	3.67	
1914	$72\frac{1}{4}$	3.46	$77\frac{11}{16}$	3.22	$69\frac{1}{4}$	3.61	3.65	3.65	
1915	$65\frac{1}{2}$	3.82	$68\frac{3}{4}$	3.64	57	4.38	4.22	4.58	
1916	58	4.31	$61\frac{1}{4}$	4.05	$56\frac{3}{4}$	4.41	4.52	5.00	
1917	$54\frac{9}{16}$	4.58	$56\frac{3}{8}$	4.43	$50\frac{1}{8}$	4.99	4.58	5.00	
1918	$56\frac{13}{16}$	4.40	$63\frac{1}{4}$	3.95	$53\frac{1}{2}$	4.67	4.23	4.51	
1919	$54\frac{1}{8}$	4.62	60	4.17	$49\frac{7}{8}$	5.01	4.87	5.49	
10-yr. av.		3.81						3.93	4.20
1920	47	5.32	52	4.81	$43\frac{5}{8}$	5.73	5.55	5.97	
1921	48	5.21	$50\frac{3}{4}$	4.93	$44\frac{2}{5}$	5.60	4.99	5.39	
1922	$56\frac{7}{16}$	4.43	$60\frac{1}{4}$	4.15	$49\frac{3}{8}$	5.04	4.48	4.75	
1923	58	4.31	60	4.17	$54\frac{5}{8}$	4.58	4.49	4.66	
1924	$56\frac{15}{16}$	4.39	$58\frac{7}{8}$	4.25	$54\frac{3}{8}$	4.60	4.37	4.64	
1925	$56\frac{7}{16}$	4.43	$58\frac{3}{8}$	4.28	$54\frac{1}{4}$	4.61	4.55	4.87	
1926	$54\frac{15}{16}$	4.55	$56\frac{7}{16}$	4.43	$53\frac{1}{2}$	4.67	4.62	4.76	

TABLE 59 (*Continued*)

Year	$2\frac{1}{2}\%$ Consols						Yield Range of All Issues 30 Years or Longer as of Dec. 31		
	Annual Average		Annual High		Annual Low		Low Yield, %	High Yield, %	Maximum Current Yield of Premium Issues, %
	Price	Yield, %	Price	Yield, %	Price	Yield, %			
1927	$54\frac{13}{16}$	4.56	$56\frac{1}{8}$	4.45	$53\frac{3}{4}$	4.65	4.41	4.73	
1928	$55\frac{15}{16}$	4.47	$56\frac{15}{16}$	4.39	$54\frac{3}{4}$	4.57	4.37	4.66	
1929	$54\frac{3}{8}$	4.60	$56\frac{3}{8}$	4.42	52	4.81	4.60	4.92	
10-yr. av.		4.63					4.64	4.94	
1930	56	4.46	$59\frac{1}{4}$	4.22	$52\frac{3}{4}$	4.74	4.27	4.44	
1931	$55\frac{3}{16}$	4.53	$60\frac{7}{8}$	4.11	$49\frac{1}{2}$	5.05	4.57	5.07	
1932	$66\frac{1}{2}$	3.76	$78\frac{1}{8}$	3.18	$54\frac{3}{8}$	4.60	3.37	3.62	3.77
1933	74	3.38	$77\frac{1}{4}$	3.24	$70\frac{1}{4}$	3.56	3.37	3.48	3.66
1934	$81\frac{3}{16}$	3.08	$93\frac{1}{4}$	2.68	$73\frac{15}{16}$	3.38	2.72	3.02	3.40
1935	$86\frac{1}{2}$	2.89	$94\frac{3}{8}$	2.65	80	3.13	2.88	3.13	3.48
1936	85	2.94	$87\frac{1}{4}$	2.87	$82\frac{1}{4}$	3.04	2.96	3.17	3.54
1937	$76\frac{1}{4}$	3.28	$84\frac{13}{16}$	2.95	$73\frac{3}{8}$	3.42	3.37	3.43	3.64
1938	74	3.38	$79\frac{3}{16}$	3.16	64	3.91	3.56	3.62	
1939	$67\frac{1}{4}$	3.72	$71\frac{1}{8}$	3.51	61	4.10	3.65	3.77	3.87
10-yr. av.		3.54					3.47	3.68	
1940	$73\frac{1}{2}$	3.40	77	3.25	$68\frac{1}{8}$	3.67	3.25	3.44	3.62
1941	$79\frac{7}{8}$	3.13	$82\frac{7}{8}$	3.02	$76\frac{3}{4}$	3.26	3.03	3.19	3.58
1942	$82\frac{1}{2}$	3.03	$83\frac{5}{8}$	2.99	81	3.09	3.03	3.18	3.62
1943	$80\frac{5}{8}$	3.10	$83\frac{1}{4}$	3.00	$78\frac{1}{4}$	3.19	3.14	3.23	3.65
1944	$79\frac{5}{8}$	3.14	$82\frac{1}{4}$	3.04	$78\frac{11}{16}$	3.18	3.07	3.18	3.62
1945	$85\frac{5}{8}$	2.92	$92\frac{13}{16}$	2.69	$91\frac{9}{16}$	3.06	2.74	2.91	3.62
1946	$96\frac{3}{16}$	2.60	$99\frac{5}{8}$	2.51	$81\frac{1}{8}$	3.08	2.53	2.67	3.44
1947	$90\frac{1}{2}$	2.76	$99\frac{1}{8}$	2.52	80	3.12	3.00	3.05	3.69
1948	$77\frac{7}{8}$	3.21	$83\frac{3}{16}$	3.01	$74\frac{1}{2}$	3.36	3.13	3.19	3.65
1949	$75\frac{3}{4}$	3.30	$81\frac{15}{16}$	3.05	$65\frac{1}{8}$	3.84	3.56	3.81	3.94
10-yr. av.		3.06					3.05	3.19	
1950	$70\frac{3}{8}$	3.55	$74\frac{11}{16}$	3.35	$68\frac{1}{8}$	3.67	3.53	3.73	3.90
1951	66	3.79	$71\frac{1}{2}$	3.50	$60\frac{1}{8}$	4.16	4.06	4.44	
1952	$59\frac{1}{8}$	4.23	62	4.03	55	4.55	4.27	4.61	

TABLE 59 (*Continued*)

Year	$2\frac{1}{2}\%$ Consols						Yield Range of All Issues 30 Years or Longer as of Dec. 31		
	Annual Average		Annual High		Annual Low		Low Yield, %	High Yield, %	Maximum Current Yield of Premium Issues, %
	Price	Yield, %	Price	Yield, %	Price	Yield, %			
1953	$61\frac{1}{4}$	4.08	$64\frac{1}{4}$	3.83	$58\frac{3}{8}$	4.28	3.89	4.27	
1954	$66\frac{1}{2}$	3.76	$69\frac{3}{4}$	3.58	$58\frac{3}{8}$	4.28	3.81	4.15	
1955	60	4.17	$66\frac{1}{2}$	3.76	$54\frac{7}{8}$	4.56	4.39	4.50	
1956	$52\frac{3}{4}$	4.74	$56\frac{3}{4}$	4.41	$49\frac{7}{8}$	5.01	4.90	5.08	
1957	$50\frac{1}{4}$	4.98	$55\frac{11}{16}$	4.49	45	5.56	5.41	5.62	
1958	$50\frac{1}{4}$	4.98	$52\frac{13}{16}$	4.73	$46\frac{3}{4}$	5.35	4.89	5.20	
1959	$51\frac{7}{8}$	4.82	$53\frac{5}{8}$	4.66	$48\frac{5}{8}$	5.14	4.99	5.40	
10-yr. av.		4.31					4.41	4.70	
1960	$46\frac{3}{8}$	5.40	$49\frac{3}{4}$	5.02	$43\frac{7}{8}$	5.71	5.68	6.07	
1961	$40\frac{3}{8}$	6.20	$44\frac{1}{16}$	5.70	$36\frac{1}{8}$	6.92	6.48	6.83	
1962	$41\frac{3}{4}$	5.98	$45\frac{3}{4}$	5.46	$37\frac{15}{16}$	6.59	5.38	5.79	
1963	$44\frac{3}{4}$	5.58	$47\frac{1}{8}$	5.30	$40\frac{7}{8}$	6.11	5.60	6.00	
1964	$41\frac{1}{2}$	6.03	$43\frac{5}{8}$	5.73	$39\frac{1}{2}$	6.33	6.17	6.54	
1965	39	6.42	$41\frac{3}{8}$	6.04	$36\frac{3}{4}$	6.80	6.37	6.64	
1966	$36\frac{3}{4}$	6.80	$39\frac{3}{16}$	6.38	$34\frac{1}{4}$	7.30	6.59	6.93	
1967	$37\frac{3}{8}$	6.69	$39\frac{7}{8}$	6.27	$34\frac{3}{8}$	7.27	6.93	7.26	
1968	$33\frac{1}{2}$	7.39	$35\frac{13}{16}$	6.98	$30\frac{3}{8}$	8.23	7.79	8.24	
1969	$28\frac{1}{4}$	8.88	$31\frac{1}{4}$	8.00	$25\frac{7}{16}$	9.83	8.36	8.36	
10-yr. av.		6.54					6.54	6.87	
1970	$27\frac{1}{4}$	9.16	$30\frac{1}{8}$	8.30	25	10.00	9.25	9.93	
1971	$27\frac{5}{8}$	9.05	$30\frac{1}{4}$	8.26	$25\frac{1}{16}$	9.97	7.65	8.66	
1972	$27\frac{1}{2}$	9.11	$30\frac{13}{16}$	8.11	25	10.00	9.05	9.99	
1973	$23\frac{1}{4}$	10.85	$26\frac{1}{4}$	9.52	$19\frac{7}{16}$	12.96	11.06	12.45	
1974	$16\frac{3}{4}$	14.95	$20\frac{7}{16}$	12.23	$13\frac{7}{8}$	18.02	16.02	17.72	
1975	$17\frac{1}{4}$	14.66	$18\frac{3}{8}$	13.60	$14\frac{1}{8}$	17.70	14.31	15.18	
1976	17.6	14.25	19.1	13.12	16.6	15.05	13.46	16.03	
1977	20.43	12.31	24	10.41	17.3	14.49	10.98	15.48	
1978	21	11.93	23.9	10.47	19.8	12.65	11.06	13.22	
1979	22.1	11.39	23.6	10.60	20	12.53	11.68	14.72	
10-yr. av.		11.77					11.45	13.34	

TABLE 59 (*Continued*)

Year	2½% Consols						Yield Range of All Issues 30 Years or Longer as of Dec. 31		
	Annual Average		Annual High		Annual Low		Low Yield, %	High Yield, %	Maximum Current Yield of Premium Issues, %
	Price	Yield, %	Price	Yield, %	Price	Yield, %			
1980	21.1	11.88	22.4	11.26	19.7	12.72	13.07	14.70	
1981	19.3	13.01	20.8	12.02	17.7	14.14	13.64	15.95	
1982	21.4	11.90	25.7	9.73	18	13.89	10.50	15.65	
1983	24.5	10.24	25.4	9.83	23	10.96	10.29	11.60	
1984	24.7	10.16	25.5	9.82	23	10.89	10.23	11.67	
1985	24.8	10.11	25.6	9.87	23.9	10.46	10.22	11.06	
1986	26.4	9.47	28.9	8.54	24.1	10.36	8.76	10.80	
1987	26.8	9.31	28.3	8.80	24.6	9.82	8.82	10.09	
1988	27.4	9.12	27.8	8.93	26.6	9.33	9.12	9.60	
1989	27.8	8.97	29.2	8.56	26.6	9.42	9.15	9.88	
10-yr. av.		10.42					10.38	12.10	

SOURCES

Great Britain, Central Statistical Office, *Annual Abstract of Statistics* and *Financial Statistics*.
Warren & Pearson, *op. cit.*, p. 273.
Bankers Almanac (London: Thomas Skinner & Co.).
The Economist.
United Nations Statistical Year Book.
Quotation sheets of the firms Pember & Boyle and of Kitcat & Aitken.

tax exemption from 1917 to 1941, and the frequent lack of new long-term U.S. government bond issues deprive us of a usable series for several decades. The series on prime American corporate bond yields is reasonably uniform, and the bonds included in the series were of very high quality. The comparison, however, of American corporate bond yields with the yields of the bonds of other governments, which is made throughout this part of the history, must be judged for what it is. If a comparable series of very long American government yields existed, it would average at least slightly below the yields of these American corporate bonds, as has been shown by the yield spread studies of the American market in Chapter XVIII.

Viewed broadly, both the English and the American bond markets followed the same pattern in the twentieth century. English yields started

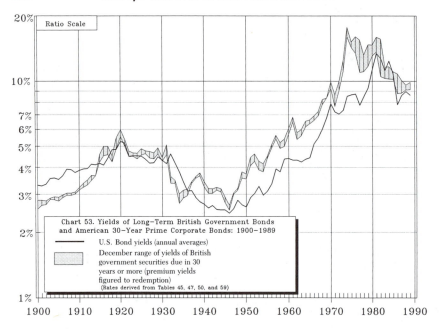

Chart 53. Yields of Long-Term British Government Bonds and American 30-Year Prime Corporate Bonds: 1900–1989

——— U.S. Bond yields (annual averages)

December range of yields of British government securities due in 30 years or more (premium yields figured to redemption)
(Rates derived from Tables 45, 47, 50, and 59)

rising in 1896, and American yields started rising in 1899. Both reached their highs in 1920 and their next lows in 1946, and both rose most of the time from 1946 to 1981, although the peak in Britain came in 1974. In both countries, therefore, there was a major bear bond market until 1920, a bull bond market from 1920 to 1946, and a second and much larger bear bond market after 1946 lasting until the 1980's. In spite of the disruption of the international gold standard and interruptions of a smooth flow of international investment between these two countries, the trends of their bond yields were usually in the same direction. In fact, the correlation over long periods of time was much closer in the twentieth century than it was in the nineteenth century.

English government bond yields started the century well below American corporate bond yields. In 1897 the low yields were 2.21% for British consols and 3.25% for American prime corporate bonds—a difference of over 100 basis points. By 1900, since English yields had risen rapidly and American yields had not, the difference was down to about 50 basis points. Some such differential held for fourteen years, but in 1915 it vanished altogether. English government bond yields averaged above American corporate bond yields most of the time from 1915 to 1932. From 1932 to 1936, English yields were again lower, but after 1937 they were consistently higher until the 1980's, when they became similar to the American yields. The differential thus has been quite variable.

A DETAILED HISTORY OF LONG-TERM BRITISH GOVERNMENT BOND YIELDS

During the sixteen years before World War I broke out, English bond yields rose most of the time. By 1907 consols yielded more than 3% for the first time since 1888. This represented a peacetime price decline of 29%, or almost half of the total decline from the highs of 1897 to the lows of 1920. By 1912, consols were down to 72½, to yield 3.45%, a yield that had not been much exceeded since 1848, and was well above the decennial average yields of seven of the decades of the nineteenth century. The price decline from 1897 to 1912 was almost 60% of the total 1897–1920 decline, which is so often attributed largely to the war.

The first year of World War I brought with it only a moderate further price decline, but in 1915, and again in 1917, the market fell away sharply. War financing was at 3.96% in 1914, 4.50% in 1915, and 5.33% in 1917. After a sizable rally in 1918, English bonds again declined in 1919 and 1920, when consols reached their low at 43⅝, to yield 5.73%, and other issues sold to yield 6% and more.

The price decline of consols from the high of 1897 to the low of 1920 was 70¼ points, or 62%. This was the largest price decline in their history until 1961, when a new low price was reached. The 1920 yield was, however, well below the all-time high yield (until 1961) of 6.35%, reached in 1798 when the price of the old 3% consols got down to 47¼. In 1920, short rates were also at their highest for the century until 1961. The bank rate ranged between 6% and 7%, and the open market rate of discount averaged 6.38%.

The entire decade of the 1920's was marked by a long struggle to regain lost financial prestige by restoring the pound to prewar parity. In spite of stable or declining commodity prices and large unused resources, interest rates were held at a high level for more than ten years. The bank rate averaged 4.82% during the decade, its highest decennial average since the Napoleonic Wars. Consols averaged 4.63%, which was their highest decennial average since 1820. The decade of the 1920's was, in fact, unique in the record for its high interest rates in time of peace, although its high rates were far exceeded after 1961. It was a decade of unemployment and social unrest. War debts and reparations distorted the flow of commerce, and American credit only postponed the day of reckoning.

In 1922, consols recovered 10 points or so from their extreme low of 1920. They advanced a trifle further in 1923, and then tended to decline through 1929. The relatively short-term giant issue of War Loan 5s held the market down. New long-term government financing after 1921 was at 4.71–5.00% during a period when the United States was refunding at as low as 3⅜%. A strong effort was made to attract international funds to England by means of high interest rates, but in the face of international unsettlement and American stock speculation, the effort did not achieve its ends.

The crisis of 1931–1932 brought, first of all, higher interest rates, and then a plunge of all rates to low levels. The trouble was largely of foreign origin. England had experienced very little of a boom in the late 1920's. The American stock market collapse, the rash of bank failures in America and Europe, the rush for liquidity, and the liquidation of foreign balances all put unbearable pressure on the newly convertible pound. The bank rate was pushed up from 2½ to 6% in 1931, and consols declined 10 points, to 49½, to yield 5.05%—still well above 1920 low prices.

In late 1931, the pound was set loose from gold, and monetary policy was reversed. In 1932, the bank rate was brought down to its traditional low of 2%. It was held there, except for a brief rise in 1939, for eighteen years. The open market rate of discount declined in 1931–1932 from 5.88% to 0.68%, and stayed down. The 2½% consols rose in a few months from 49½, or 5.05%, to 78½, or 3.18%—their high price since 1912. This was a price rise of 58%. In 1932, the giant 5% War Loan was redeemed and successfully converted into an issue of War Loan 3½s at a price of 99, to yield 3.54%. The new loan was not redeemable until 1952, and, in the ancient tradition, it was perpetual unless the government chose to redeem.

England was again in a period of easy money. Long yields did not decline to the lows of the late nineteenth century, but short-term interest rates got down to new lows. The economic and political environments however, were sadly different from what they had been in the easy-money decades of the nineteenth century. At home there was unemployment and depression; abroad, a new war was visibly approaching.

English bond yields had followed a very similar pattern to that of American bond yields throughout the 1920s. They diverged sharply from 1931 through 1939, and thereafter again for some time followed the trends of American bond yields. In America yields rose in 1932, and thereafter declined almost steadily until 1946. In England yields started to decline a year earlier, in 1931, reached a low in 1935, rose until 1939, and thereafter resumed their decline, reaching their lows for the period in 1946. The chief difference was that American yields did not share noticeably in the 1935–1939 rise of English yields.

By 1935 consols were up to 94⅜, to yield 2.65%. They had not stood so high since 1902. By 1939, when World War II broke out, consols had declined to 61, to yield 4.10%. This was just about their low price during the first year of World War I.

It soon became evident that this was not going to be another 5% war. The bank rate was pegged at 2%, and the open market rate of discount remained around 1%. Government bond issues were offered at a monotonous 3%, and even these were callable in a comparatively few years. Long bonds recovered in the market to 3.03–3.19% in 1941 and stayed in about that range until 1945.

In 1945–1946, the bond market in England, as in America, celebrated the peace by one final sharp thrust upward. The market reached new high prices in America, but in England it stopped 14 points short of its nineteenth-century highs. In America this final crest of the wave seemed to be in part a natural expression of market optimism. In England it was based on the official policy of a new Labour government and was enforced by every monetary tool. Rising bond prices, however, did not catch the fancy of English investors or speculators. Consols were forced up from 81½, or 3.06%, in 1945 to a high of 99⅝, or 2.51%, in 1946. They had not touched par since 1900, and they did not quite touch par in 1946. The government floated a new issue of 2½% undated Treasury stock at 100, the "Daltons," which were said to be preferable to redeemable consols because they could not be redeemed until 1975.

In 1946 began the long retreat of the English bond market, which lasted, with occasional cyclical interruptions, until 1974. English monetary policy maintained very low short-term rates until 1952 and attempted to support the bond market. Nevertheless, long-term investors turned their backs on government bonds. They missed the attraction of the potential capital gains that they had enjoyed after the Napoleonic Wars and of the high yields that they had enjoyed after World War I. In 1947, consols were back to 80. In 1948 consols declined to 74½, to yield 3.36%. In 1949, the pound was devalued, and consols declined to 65⅛, to yield 3.84%. In 1950, the market did a little better. In 1951, however, consols were down to 60⅛, to yield 4.16%.

In 1952, there was a revival of monetary orthodoxy. Short-term rates were deliberately raised for the first time in twenty-one years as part of an official attack on inflation and in defense of the monetary reserves. The bank rate was put up from 2% to 4%, and the government issued new 4¼% bonds, to yield 4.31%. Consols declined to 55, to yield 4.55%. The market was again in a high range of yields, similar to the range of the 1920's and above the range of any other extended period since 1820. These proved to be the low prices and high yields for three years to come. In 1953 and 1954, there was an interim period of easier money coinciding with a small business recession and an easy-money period in the United States. Consols rose from 55 to 69¾, an advance of over 25%.

In 1955, interest rates again rose and the bond market declined quickly to new postwar lows. The Suez Crisis followed, and in 1957 there was a dangerous run on the pound. Government policy now swung the full circle and was prepared to use every weapon of traditional monetary policy to repress inflation and restore foreign confidence. The gold reserves were fortified by enormous foreign credits, and the bank rate in 1957 was moved up to the crisis rate of 7% for the first time since 1920. The open market rate of discount rose to 6.81%. In 1958 the government financed with 5¼% and 5½%

bonds at discount. Consols declined to 45 in 1957, where their yield was 5.56%. They were almost, but not quite, down to the earlier low of 43⅝ reached in 1920. Confidence in the pound was restored, and reserves rose.

In 1958, another brief recession occurred and brought the usual decline in interest rates. Consols rose to a high of 53⅝ in 1959, to yield 4.66%, a gain of 19% from 1957 lows.

In 1959, a Conservative victory at the polls was followed by a strong revival in business and a large expansion in bank credit. The balance of payments position weakened, and the authorities took measures to ward off a return of inflation. The bank rate was raised to 6% in 1960 and to 7% in 1961. Long-term bond yields were deliberately raised by large-scale funding. Consols declined in 1961 to a new all-time low of 36¼, to yield 6.90%. Thereafter, they recovered 25% in price to 45, to yield 5.55%.

In 1964 a sharp rise in short-term interest rates began with the bank rate up from 4 to 7%. However, consols declined in price only moderately. In 1965 the rise in short rates continued, but consols again declined only moderately. These were only the opening years of a period of great economic instability and inflation around the world. The dollar became suspect. A great boom was under way in the United States, which was to have devastating effects around the world and to put great strain on the international position of both the dollar and the pound. The 1970's brought devaluations and floating currencies. Short rates in London rose almost steadily from 1965 to the highs in 1974. The bank rate rose from 7% to a high of 13%; the bill rate, from 7% to a high of 15½%.

In the long market, although consols touched a new low price in 1966, the big rise in yields did not get under way until 1968. Consols fell from around 40 in 1967, to yield 6¼%, to a low of about 14 in 1974, to yield 18%. The Treasury financed with long-term bonds featuring 13¼% coupons. There were doubts about the viability of the entire British economy—and, more important, about its political structure. The rate of inflation was out of hand, at times exceeding 30%. This rise in British yields greatly exceeded the rise in yields in the United States and in all other major industrial nations. The decline in consols from 1964 to 1974 was from 43⅝ to 13⅞, or 29¾ points, or about 66%. During this period their yield about trebled.

After 1974, British long yields remained high compared both to their previous history and to contemporaneous long yields in other large nations. But unlike yields in these other countries, which rose to new all-time peaks in the early 1980's, the 1974 peak in Britain held. British long yields declined moderately until 1978 or 1979, and then rose moderately to 1981. In 1981, however, peak yields were well below those of 1974. Consols yielded about 14% at their 1981 low prices, compared to 18% in 1974, and other long issues yielded less than 16%, instead of nearly 18% as in 1974. In this sense, England turned the corner toward lower yields before other countries did.

After 1981, British long yields generally followed the declining pattern evident in U.S. and other nations' yields during the 1980's.

The table below gives the low and high nominal yields of British government long-term securities by decade in the twentieth century. The peak nominal yield came in 1977 with a 15½% Treasury Loan maturing in 1998. When one considers how high British long yields had risen in conjunction with (as noted earlier) how rapidly the national debt was growing in the 1970's and 1980's, it is evident that the government was under severe pressure to reduce its financing costs. The short-term market offered limited opportunity to cut these costs because British short-term rates (see the next section) were generally as high as or higher than long-term rates in these years.

RANGE OF NOMINAL YIELDS ON
PRINCIPAL LONG-TERM BRITISH
GOVERNMENT SECURITIES:
1900–1989

Decade	Low Coupon, %	High Coupon, %
1900–1909	$2\frac{3}{4}$	$2\frac{3}{4}$
1910–1919	$3\frac{1}{2}$	5
1920–1929	$3\frac{1}{2}$	5
1930–1939	$2\frac{1}{2}$	$4\frac{1}{2}$
1940–1949	$2\frac{1}{2}$	3
1950–1959	3	$5\frac{1}{2}$
1960–1969	5	$8\frac{3}{4}$
1970–1979	$7\frac{3}{4}$	$15\frac{1}{2}$
1980–1989	8	14

SOURCES

THIS HISTORY, 2nd ed., table 58, supplemented by Central Statistical Office, *Statistical Abstract*, and the London *Times*.

It was in this situation of financial desperation that the British government in 1981 introduced on a large scale the inflation-indexed bond. (535) This was a financial innovation of considerable importance even though it failed to catch on in other leading countries where the government's financial situation was less desperate than in Britain. These bonds offered to pay a fixed real rate of interest and to increase the principal value (and ultimate redemption value) each year at the rate of inflation. Initially the real yield at issue was less than 3%, although it rose to the 3–4% range along with real rates in the rest of the world in the mid- and later 1980's. Inflation was measured by the change in Britain's retail price index, to which the bond values were linked. Hence, they are often termed "index-linked gilts," "gilts" being short for gilt-edged bonds, as the English call their government's fixed-interest securities.

The advantage to the British government in issuing inflation-indexed bonds was at times considerable. In the mid-1980's, it could borrow on index-linked gilts at a real rate of about 3%. At that time the inflation rate was about 5%, so the cost of financing was about 8% compared to new issue yields of 12–13% on non-indexed gilts. The advantage to the bond-buying investor is, of course, elimination of the risk of the real return's being ravaged by unanticipated inflation, as happened to so many investors around the world in the twentieth century.

Table 60 gives the annual ranges of high and low prices and the approximate real yield ranges of several issues of index-linked gilts in the 1980's. The steady rise in market value of these bonds stands in marked contrast to the behavior of traditional non-indexed, fixed-yield bond prices in recent decades of high inflation. The real yields also fluctuate, but in a much narrower range than have nominal yields of traditional bonds. The British innovation

TABLE 60

PRICES AND REAL YIELDS OF REPRESENTATIVE BRITISH GOVERNMENT INDEX–LINKED BONDS: 1981–1989

Year	2s of 1996			2s of 2006			$2\frac{1}{2}$s of 2011		
	Price Range		Real Yield Range, %	Price Range		Real Yield Range, %	Price Range		Real Yield Range, %
	High	Low		High	Low		High	Low	
1981	$100\frac{3}{4}$	$90\frac{1}{2}$	2–2.8	$92\frac{1}{4}$	$86\frac{3}{8}$	2.6–2.7			
1982	108	93	2–2.3	$104\frac{1}{4}$	88	2.2–3.0	$106\frac{1}{2}$	90	2.6–3.0
1983	$111\frac{3}{4}$	$99\frac{3}{8}$	2.5–3.5	$107\frac{1}{4}$	$94\frac{3}{4}$	2.4–3.2	$109\frac{1}{2}$	97	2.5–3.1
1984	$111\frac{1}{2}$	$98\frac{3}{4}$	3.6–4.2	$104\frac{1}{4}$	$90\frac{1}{4}$	3.2–3.5	$106\frac{3}{4}$	$91\frac{3}{4}$	3.1–3.5
1985	$114\frac{1}{2}$	108	3.7–4.3	107	99	3.3–3.9	$108\frac{1}{2}$	$100\frac{3}{4}$	3.2–3.7
1986	122	$108\frac{3}{4}$	3.8–4.2	$110\frac{1}{2}$	$96\frac{3}{4}$	3.8–3.9	$111\frac{1}{2}$	97	3.6–3.7
1987	$130\frac{3}{8}$	$117\frac{7}{8}$	3.1–3.9	113	$94\frac{3}{4}$	3.3–4.1	$113\frac{1}{2}$	$93\frac{1}{8}$	3.2–4.0
1988	142	$127\frac{5}{8}$	2.9–3.4	$120\frac{7}{8}$	110	3.7–3.8	118	$99\frac{5}{8}$	3.7–3.8
1989	$155\frac{3}{8}$	$139\frac{1}{8}$	n.a.	$131\frac{1}{2}$	$117\frac{5}{8}$	n.a.	128	$114\frac{1}{2}$	n.a.

SOURCES

The London *Times*. The real yield range is based on yields prevailing at the beginning of each quarter of each year, and is therefore only an approximation.

has much to recommend it, and it remains to be seen whether circumstances will lead to its acceptance on a wider scale.

SHORT-TERM INTEREST RATES

Short-term English interest rates are represented here by the rates on only two of the many forms of short-term credit. Table 61 and Chart 54 include the bank rate and the open market rate of discount in terms of annual averages and extremes of fluctuations. The open market rates are the rates on three-month bankers' bills or three-month bankers' acceptances and have been selected because of their long continuity over two centuries, not because they are today more representative of the London money market than other types of short-term rates. Other important short-term money-market rates are Treasury bill rates and the day-to-day, or call money, rates. The open market rate of discount and the three-month Treasury bills tend to be similar, while the call money rate tends to be lower than both.

The table and chart suggest that short-term rates followed a somewhat different pattern during the first nine decades of the twentieth century from the pattern of long-term government bonds yields. The principal difference was that the low short-term rates of the 1930's and 1940's averaged far below the low short rates of earlier easy-money periods, whereas the low long-term bond yields of the 1930's and the 1940's were above earlier low bond yields.

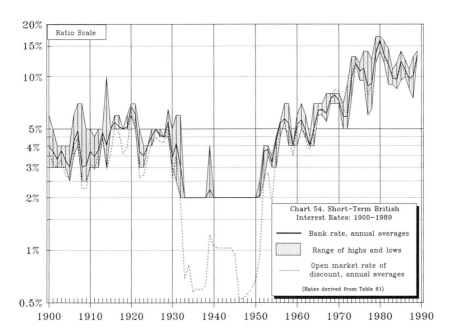

Chart 54. Short–Term British Interest Rates: 1900–1989

— Bank rate, annual averages

Range of highs and lows

.... Open market rate of discount, annual averages

(Rates derived from Table 61)

TABLE 61
Short-Term British Interest Rates: Twentieth Century

Year	Bank Rate, %			Open Market Rate of Discount, %			Differential of Maximum Long Government Bond Yield over Open Market Rate of Discount, Basis Points
	Average	Low	High	Average	Low	High	
1900	3.94	3	6	3.70	2.61	4.03	−88
1901	3.72	3	5	3.17	2.32	4.15	−35
1902	3.33	3	4	2.97	2.49	3.90	−17
1903	3.75	3	4	3.40	2.42	4.00	−52
1904	3.30	3	4	2.68	2.05	3.25	+24
1905	3.01	2.5	4	2.63	1.75	3.98	+28
1906	4.27	3.5	6	4.04	3.15	5.85	−106
1907	4.88	4	7	4.46	3.26	6.45	−142
1908	3.00	2.5	7	2.26	1.28	4.19	+78
1909	3.10	2.5	5	2.26	1.36	4.23	+82
10-yr. av.	3.63			3.16			−23
1910	3.72	3	5	3.18	2.07	4.42	+5
1911	3.47	3	4.5	2.92	2.03	3.80	+46
1912	3.78	3	5	3.63	2.86	4.85	−13
1913	4.77	4.5	5	4.37	3.71	4.91	−70
1914	4.03	3	10	2.93	2.00	5.21	+72
1915	5.00	5	5	3.64	1.38	5.19	+94
1916	5.47	5	6	5.20	4.56	5.58	−20
1917	5.15	5	6	4.77	4.60	5.11	+23
1918	5.00	5	5	3.58	3.49	4.01	+93
1919	5.15	5	6	3.95	3.21	5.80	+154
10-yr. av.	4.55			3.82			+38
1920	6.71	6	7	6.38	5.58	6.77	−41
1921	6.10	5	7	5.19	3.56	6.70	+20
1922	3.71	3	5	2.63	1.89	3.58	+212
1923	3.49	3	4	2.71	1.99	3.31	+195
1924	4.00	4	4	3.44	3.01	3.79	+120
1925	4.56	4	5	4.14	3.58	4.77	+73
1926	5.00	5	5	4.46	4.25	4.76	+30
1927	4.65	4.5	5	4.24	3.88	4.32	+49
1928	4.50	4.5	4.5	4.16	3.82	4.39	+50
1929	5.49	4.5	6.5	5.26	4.32	6.15	−34
10-yr. av.	4.82			4.26			+68
1930	3.41	3	5	2.56	2.07	4.06	+188
1931	4.13	2.5	6	3.61	2.11	5.88	+146

TABLE 61 (*Continued*)

Year	Bank Rate, %			Open Market Rate of Discount, %			Differential of Maximum Long Government Bond Yield over Open Market Rate of Discount, Basis Points
	Average	Low	High	Average	Low	High	
1932	3.01	2	6	1.87	0.68	5.56	+175
1933	2.00	2	2	0.69	0.42	1.16	+279
1934	2.00	2	2	0.82	0.47	1.01	+220
1935	2.00	2	2	0.58	0.36	0.74	+255
1936	2.00	2	2	0.60	0.55	0.87	+257
1937	2.00	2	2	0.59	0.55	0.74	+284
1938	2.00	2	2	0.63	0.53	0.99	+299
1939	2.24	2	4	1.22	0.55	3.48	+255
10-yr. av.	2.48			1.32			+236
1940	2.00	2	2	1.04	1.03	1.09	+240
1941	2.00	2	2	1.03	1.03	1.03	+216
1942	2.00	2	2	1.03	1.03	1.03	+215
1943	2.00	2	2	1.03	1.03	1.03	+220
1944	2.00	2	2	1.03	1.03	1.03	+215
1945	2.00	2	2	0.95	0.53	1.03	+196
1946	2.00	2	2	0.53	0.53	0.53	+214
1947	2.00	2	2	0.53	0.53	0.53	+252
1948	2.00	2	2	0.56	0.54	0.56	+263
1949	2.00	2	2	0.60	0.56	0.62	+321
10-yr. av.	2.00			0.83			+235
1950	2.00	2	2	0.67	0.62	0.69	+306
1951	2.07	2	2.5	0.92	0.69	1.50	+352
1952	3.71	2.5	4	2.70	1.50	3.00	+191
1953	3.81	3.5	4	2.78	2.19	3.00	+149
1954	3.18	3	3.5	1.84	1.60	2.19	+231
1955	4.31	3	4.5	3.75	2.02	4.22	+75
1956	5.37	4.5	5.5	5.05	4.22	5.34	+3
1957	5.71	5.5	7	4.98	4.04	6.81	+64
1958	5.37	4	7	4.75	3.34	6.51	+45
1959	4.00	4	4	3.49	3.28	3.72	+191
10-yr. av.	3.95			3.09			+161
1960	5.29	4	6	5.05	4.14	5.76	+102
1961	5.65	5	7	5.44	4.35	6.91	+139
1962	4.85	4.5	6	4.31	3.81	5.69	+148
1963	4.00	4	4.5	3.79	3.56	3.91	+221

TABLE 61 (*Continued*)

Year	Bank Rate, %			Open Market Rate of Discount, %			Differential of Maximum Long Government Bond Yield over Open Market Rate of Discount, Basis Points
	Average	Low	High	Average	Low	High	
1964	5.05	4	7	4.77	3.87	6.81	+177
1965	6.40	6	7	6.37	5.87	6.81	+27
1966	6.47	6	7	6.41	5.87	6.97	+52
1967	6.15	5.5	8	6.02	5.31	7.75	+124
1968	7.46	7	8	7.38	6.94	7.75	+86
1969	7.84	7	8	8.41	7.25	8.75	−5
10-yr. av.	5.92			5.80			+99.3
1970	7.25	7	8	8.19	8.00	8.75	+174
1971	5.91	5	7	6.44	4.34	8.00	+222
1972	5.91	5	9	6.18	4.36	8.75	+381
1973	9.86	7.5	13	10.49	7.69	14.13	+196
1974	11.94	12	13	13.04	11.79	15.56	+468
1975	10.75	9.5	12	10.61	9.44	12.44	+457
1976	11.12	9.5	14	11.23	8.50	14.78	+480
1977	8.83	6	14	7.79	4.53	13.52	+769
1978	9.13	6.5	12.5	8.98	5.98	12.50	+424
1979	13.74	12	17	13.45	11.16	16.88	+127
10-yr. av.	9.44			9.64			+369.8
1980	16.27	14	17	15.84	13.63	17.78	−114
1981	13.28	12	16	13.17	11.47	15.94	+228
1982	11.87	9	14.5	11.52	8.56	14.69	+413
1983	9.81	9	11	10.35	8.88	11.03	+125
1984	9.69	8.5	12	9.39	8.38	11.63	+228
1985	12.22	9.5	14	11.71	9.56	13.56	−65
1986	10.88	10	12.5	10.50	9.28	12.75	+30
1987	9.75	8.5	11	9.36	8.22	10.75	+73
1988	10.12	7.5	13	9.94	7.34	12.69	−34
1989	13.23	13	14	12.78	12.38	13.69	−240
10-yr. av.	11.71			11.46			+64.4

SOURCES
   Great Britain, Central Statistical Office, *Annual Abstract of Statistics* and *Financial Statistics*.
   An unpublished paper by Eugene A. Birnbaum, International Monetary Fund, 1958.
   IMF, *International Financial Statistics*.
   The Federal Reserve Bulletin.
   Bank of England, *Quarterly Bulletin*.

The annual average of the open market rate fell below 1% in only two years in the nineteenth century. In the twentieth century, it averaged below 1% for thirteen years. The decennial averages of the 1930's and 1940's were far below any earlier decennial averages. Another major difference is that English short rates peaked in 1980, six years after the peak in long rates. Furthermore, in the 1980's short rates remained well above pre-1970 levels, whereas long rates retraced most of their post-1970 rise.

The decennial averages of short-term rates pictured in Chart 51 rose in the first three decades of the century, but the rise was not larger than the rise of long rates. The high bond yield decade of the 1920's was not notable for high short rates. In the 1930's and 1940's, short rates were most of the time far lower than during any earlier decades. In the 1950's, when all rates rose, short rates on the average were below their levels during earlier high interest rate periods, but long rates were close to their highest levels and actually went to new highs in 1961. Thereafter, short rates were about stable until 1964, and then rose with few interruptions almost steadily until 1981. The levels of the 1970's and 1980's were far above any earlier peak short-term English interest rates.

SHORT-TERM INTEREST RATES COMPARED WITH LONG-TERM INTEREST RATES

Table 61 also lists the differentials between the highest yields of long-term English government bonds and the annual averages of open market rates of discount. This column shows the highly erratic nature of the relationship between this short rate and the yield on long-term government bonds.

The decennial average chart (Chart 51) pictures the trend of both short and long rates of interest over a long period of time. It shows that short rates averaged above consol yields from 1800 through the 1860's; averaged below consol yields in the late, easy-money decades of the nineteenth century; and averaged above consol yields early in the twentieth century; and averaged below consol yields in the 1920's and far below consol yields in the 1930's and 1940's. In the 1950's and 1960's, the spread tended to narrow, but short rates did not return to an average above that of long rates until the 1980's.

Chapter XX

Europe in the Twentieth Century: France, the Netherlands, Belgium, Germany, Italy

This chapter surveys the twentieth-century interest-rate history of the five Western European nations that, along with tiny Luxembourg, formed the European Economic Community, or Common Market, in 1957. These countries formed the core of the European Community, which plans nearly complete economic integration in 1992. Britain, covered in the previous chapter, joined the European Community in 1973. Denmark and Ireland also joined in 1973, followed by Greece in 1981, and Spain and Portugal in 1986. These later joiners of the Economic Community, with the exception of Greece, are surveyed in the next chapter, along with non-members Switzerland, Austria, Sweden, Norway, and Turkey. The interest-rate histories shed light on questions of financial integration within the European Community, and between it and its European neighbors as well as the rest of the world.

FRANCE

France survived the crises of the first nine decades of the twentieth century largely at the expense of its *rentiers* and other holders of franc assets. The history of the dollar exchange value of the franc may be roughly summarized as follows:

Years		Value of French Franc in U.S. Cents
1900–1918		20.0 – 18.0
1920–1922		9.1 – 6.0
1923–1926		6.0 – 2.5
1926–1933	Franc stabilized	4.0
1934–1936	Dollar devalued	6.7
1936–1940		6.7 – 2.0
1940–1945		2.0
1946–1947		0.83
1948–1957		0.29
1958–1990	(old franc)	0.25– 0.17

This loss of more than 99% of the dollar value of the franc, most of which occurred before 1958, does not tell the whole story of the *rentier*'s woe. The dollar itself was devalued several times, and, in addition, the purchasing power of the dollar declined sharply. The contrast with the stability of the franc in the nineteenth century is striking.

French political history in the twentieth century was dominated by the world wars that shaped the history of the entire civilized world. Victorious at great sacrifice in World War I, France played a passive role in World War II, but nevertheless emerged a part of the victorious alliance. France's political instability, recurrent throughout the nineteenth century and, indeed, since Louis XVI, continued throughout the first six decades of the twentieth century. This perhaps explains the failure of such a rich and unusually prosperous nation, victorious in its wars and possessed of large physical and financial resources, to maintain the value of its currency. During the period 1960–1990, however, France has enjoyed a much larger measure of political stability, and this has helped to restrain her inflation and sustain the value of the franc.

Long-Term French Interest Rates. Chart 55 shows decennial averages for long and short interest rates in nineteenth- and twentieth-century France. In view of France's turbulent monetary and financial history in the preceding fifty years, it is surprising to find that up to 1960 so little had changed in the structure of French interest rates. French *rentes* fluctuated in the first six decades of the twentieth century within their nineteenth-century range. Both the discount rate of the Bank of France and the open market rate of discount in Paris ranged below their nineteenth-century averages. At times, however, the rates alone did not tell the whole story. In periods of pronounced inflation, loans at quoted rates could not be readily obtained. The government often experienced great difficulty in funding and refunding its

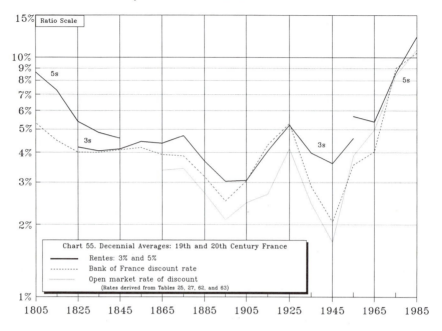

Chart 55. Decennial Averages: 19th and 20th Century France
——— Rentes: 3% and 5%
---------- Bank of France discount rate
——— Open market rate of discount
(Rates derived from Tables 25, 27, 62, and 63)

debt, even at high rates, and, partly as a consequence, offered index bonds tied to the price of stocks or to gold or carrying other inducements.

In the 1950's, yields were approximately stable in a range then considered high. In the early 1960's, yields tended to decline. After the crisis of 1968, however, French bond yields rose with most others, reaching extreme highs at nearly 17% in 1981.

Table 62 traces the history of long-term French interest rates partly in terms of the 3% *rentes* because they provide a continuous series from 1825. Chapter XIV contained this series and also an alternative series of prices and yields of 5% *rentes* from 1797 to 1852. Table 62 also provides a series on a new issue of 5% *rentes* from 1949 to the 1980's. These market yields, which are calculated as simple current yields, were always higher for issues with a higher nominal rate and higher price; therefore, the yields of the 5s cannot be compared with the yields of the 3s, although both series indicate different trends. The index bonds with special redemption features, issued by the government since World War II, have not been included in the table and charts because a true interest rate is not obtainable from them. For years starting in 1970, a new series of French bond yields is presented, comprising of an average of long-term governments calculated by yield to maturity. These generally sold to yield somewhat more than did the *rentes*.

In the 1950's, France issued some bonds indexed to foreign currencies, to gold, and to equities. The importance of these index bonds to this history

TABLE 62
PRICES AND YIELDS OF LONG-TERM FRENCH GOVERNMENT SECURITIES: TWENTIETH CENTURY

Year	3% Perpetual *Rentes*					
	Annual Average		Annual High		Annual Low	
	Price	Yield, %	Price	Yield, %	Price	Yield, %
1900	$100\frac{3}{4}$	2.98	$102\frac{3}{8}$	2.94	$99\frac{1}{8}$	3.04
1901	$101\frac{1}{8}$	2.96	$102\frac{1}{2}$	2.90	$99\frac{7}{8}$	3.01
1902	$100\frac{1}{4}$	2.99	102	2.96	$98\frac{1}{2}$	3.06
1903	$98\frac{1}{4}$	3.06	$100\frac{1}{8}$	2.99	$96\frac{1}{4}$	3.12
1904	96	3.11	$99\frac{1}{8}$	3.02	94	3.20
1905	$99\frac{1}{8}$	3.03	$100\frac{1}{2}$	2.98	$97\frac{3}{4}$	3.10
1906	$97\frac{3}{4}$	3.08	$99\frac{7}{8}$	3.01	$94\frac{7}{8}$	3.14
1907	$94\frac{7}{8}$	3.16	$96\frac{1}{4}$	3.12	$93\frac{3}{4}$	3.26
1908	$95\frac{7}{8}$	3.13	$97\frac{5}{8}$	3.10	$94\frac{1}{8}$	3.15
1909	$97\frac{3}{4}$	3.07	$99\frac{1}{4}$	3.04	$96\frac{1}{4}$	3.12
10-yr. av.		3.06				
1910	$97\frac{3}{4}$	3.06	$99\frac{1}{4}$	3.05	$96\frac{1}{2}$	3.11
1911	$95\frac{1}{2}$	3.14	$97\frac{1}{2}$	3.10	$93\frac{1}{2}$	3.16
1912	$91\frac{3}{8}$	3.27	$95\frac{5}{8}$	3.15	$88\frac{1}{4}$	3.36
1913	$87\frac{1}{8}$	3.44	$90\frac{3}{4}$	3.30	$83\frac{1}{2}$	3.54
1914	$77\frac{3}{8}$	3.78	$88\frac{1}{2}$	3.40	$70\frac{1}{4}$	4.22
1915	$68\frac{3}{4}$	4.36	$73\frac{3}{4}$	4.01	$63\frac{3}{4}$	4.71
1916	$62\frac{1}{2}$	4.80	$64\frac{5}{8}$	4.55	$60\frac{3}{8}$	4.92
1917	$60\frac{5}{8}$	4.95	$62\frac{3}{4}$	4.80	$58\frac{1}{2}$	5.15
1918	$60\frac{7}{8}$	4.94	$64\frac{1}{4}$	4.55	$56\frac{3}{4}$	5.30
1919	$62\frac{1}{4}$	4.82	$65\frac{1}{8}$	4.52	$59\frac{3}{8}$	5.08
10-yr. av.		4.06				
1920	$56\frac{1}{2}$	5.30	$60\frac{1}{8}$	4.98	53	5.62
1921	$56\frac{1}{2}$	5.30	$59\frac{1}{2}$	5.02	$53\frac{5}{8}$	5.58
1922	$59\frac{5}{8}$	5.05	$64\frac{1}{8}$	4.55	54	5.52
1923	$55\frac{5}{8}$	5.42	$59\frac{1}{8}$	5.02	51	5.97
1924	$53\frac{1}{8}$	5.58	59	5.04	48	6.12
1925	$47\frac{1}{8}$	6.37	$51\frac{3}{4}$	5.78	$42\frac{1}{2}$	7.00
1926	$50\frac{1}{4}$	6.15	$56\frac{3}{8}$	5.30	$44\frac{1}{4}$	6.96
1927	$65\frac{1}{2}$	4.60	$72\frac{1}{4}$	4.15	$58\frac{3}{4}$	5.05
1928	69	4.35	$75\frac{7}{8}$	3.98	$62\frac{1}{4}$	4.80
1929	$74\frac{3}{8}$	4.08	$76\frac{1}{4}$	3.94	72	4.22
10-yr. av.		5.22				

TABLE 62 (*Continued*)

Year	3% Perpetual *Rentes*					
	Annual Average		Annual High		Annual Low	
	Price	Yield, %	Price	Yield, %	Price	Yield, %
1930	$87\frac{1}{4}$	3.44				
1931	$86\frac{1}{4}$	3.48	$88\frac{1}{4}$	3.40	79	3.80
1932	$78\frac{1}{8}$	3.84	$83\frac{1}{8}$	3.61	$73\frac{3}{8}$	4.09
1933	$68\frac{1}{2}$	4.38	$70\frac{1}{4}$	4.27	$67\frac{1}{8}$	4.47
1934	$72\frac{1}{2}$	4.14	$78\frac{1}{2}$	3.82	$65\frac{3}{4}$	4.56
1935	$77\frac{3}{8}$	3.88	$79\frac{1}{8}$	3.79	$71\frac{3}{4}$	4.18
1936	$69\frac{1}{2}$	4.32	$74\frac{3}{4}$	4.01	$65\frac{3}{4}$	4.56
1937	$70\frac{1}{4}$	4.27	72	4.17	$69\frac{1}{8}$	4.34
1938	$74\frac{1}{4}$	4.04	$87\frac{3}{4}$	3.42	$87\frac{1}{4}$	4.44
1939	$75\frac{1}{2}$	3.97	$82\frac{5}{8}$	3.63	$67\frac{1}{4}$	4.46
10-yr. av.		3.98				
1940	$73\frac{7}{8}$	4.06	$74\frac{5}{8}$	4.02	$69\frac{5}{8}$	4.31
1941	94	3.19				
1942	$95\frac{1}{2}$	3.14				
1943	$96\frac{1}{2}$	3.11				
1944	$99\frac{5}{8}$	3.01				
1945	$100\frac{3}{8}$	2.99	$104\frac{1}{8}$	2.87	99	3.04
1946	$94\frac{5}{8}$	3.17	99	3.04	$89\frac{1}{4}$	3.35
1947	$76\frac{3}{4}$	3.91	$90\frac{1}{8}$	3.34	67	4.48
1948	$64\frac{7}{8}$	4.62	$75\frac{1}{8}$	4.00	60	5.00
1949	$62\frac{3}{4}$	4.78	$76\frac{3}{8}$	3.95	$58\frac{1}{4}$	5.15
10-yr. av.		3.60				
1950	$59\frac{3}{4}$	5.02	$63\frac{7}{8}$	4.70	$55\frac{1}{2}$	5.41
1951	$56\frac{1}{4}$	5.31	$59\frac{3}{4}$	5.02	$52\frac{3}{4}$	5.70
1952	$62\frac{1}{4}$	4.81	72	4.17	$52\frac{3}{4}$	5.70
1953	$60\frac{7}{8}$	4.93	$63\frac{3}{4}$	4.71	$58\frac{1}{8}$	5.16
1954	$66\frac{1}{4}$	4.53	$73\frac{1}{8}$	4.10	$59\frac{1}{4}$	5.07
1955	$70\frac{1}{2}$	4.25	$75\frac{7}{8}$	3.96	65	4.62
1956	$65\frac{3}{8}$	4.59	$71\frac{7}{8}$	4.18	$59\frac{1}{4}$	5.07
1957	$58\frac{1}{8}$	5.16	$61\frac{7}{8}$	4.86	$54\frac{5}{8}$	5.49
1958	$76\frac{5}{8}$	3.92	$98\frac{1}{8}$	3.06	$54\frac{5}{8}$	5.49
1959	88	3.41	$92\frac{3}{4}$	3.24	$83\frac{1}{4}$	3.61
10-yr. av.		4.59				
1960	$84\frac{7}{8}$	3.54	$90\frac{7}{8}$	3.30	$78\frac{7}{8}$	3.82
1961	$78\frac{1}{2}$	3.81	$82\frac{5}{8}$	3.64	$75\frac{1}{4}$	3.98

TABLE 62 (*Continued*)

| Year | 3% Perpetual *Rentes* | | | | | |
| | Annual Average | | Annual High | | Annual Low | |
	Price	Yield, %	Price	Yield, %	Price	Yield, %
1962	$81\frac{1}{4}$	3.70	$84\frac{7}{8}$	3.53	$77\frac{1}{2}$	3.87
1963	82	3.66	$87\frac{1}{2}$	3.43	$76\frac{1}{4}$	3.94
1964	$73\frac{3}{4}$	3.84	$78\frac{7}{8}$	3.80	$68\frac{3}{4}$	4.36
1965	$71\frac{1}{4}$	4.20	74	4.05	$68\frac{3}{8}$	4.39
1966	66	4.55	$72\frac{5}{8}$	4.13	$59\frac{3}{8}$	5.05
1967	$63\frac{1}{4}$	4.75	$66\frac{1}{2}$	4.51	60	5.00
1968	61	4.90	65	4.62	$57\frac{1}{8}$	5.25
1969	$62\frac{7}{8}$	4.80	$66\frac{5}{8}$	4.50	$59\frac{1}{8}$	5.08
10-yr. av.		4.18				
	Government Bond Yield					
1970		8.06		n.a.		n.a.
1971		7.74		n.a.		n.a.
1972		7.35		7.16		7.72
1973		8.25		7.63		8.90
1974		10.49		9.44		11.83
1975		9.49		8.59		10.68
1976		8.25		7.50		8.86
1977		8.77		6.80		9.94
1978		8.96		8.33		9.61
1979		9.48		7.86		11.46
10-yr. av.		8.68				
1980		13.03		11.75		13.72
1981		15.79		12.28		16.84
1982		15.69		14.82		16.06
1983		13.63		13.11		14.39
1984		12.54		11.23		12.96
1985		10.94		10.67		11.44
1986		8.44		7.67		10.26
1987		9.43		8.55		10.66
1988		9.06		8.62		9.86
1989		8.89		8.45		9.44
10-yr. av.		11.74				

TABLE 62 (*Continued*)

Year	5% Perpetual *Rentes* of 1949					
	Annual Average		Annual High		Annual Low	
	Price	Yield, %	Price	Yield, %	Price	Yield, %
1949	$79\frac{3}{4}$	6.28	84	5.95	$75\frac{3}{4}$	6.60
1950	$76\frac{5}{8}$	6.52	$83\frac{1}{2}$	5.99	$75\frac{7}{8}$	6.59
1951	$76\frac{1}{2}$	6.54	$83\frac{1}{4}$	6.00	76	6.58
1952	$89\frac{1}{4}$	5.60	$100\frac{1}{2}$	4.98	$76\frac{1}{4}$	5.56
1953	$92\frac{3}{8}$	5.41	$99\frac{3}{8}$	5.03	$89\frac{3}{8}$	5.51
1954	93	5.38	$99\frac{7}{8}$	5.01	92	5.45
1955	96	5.21	101	4.95	93	5.37
1956	$94\frac{5}{8}$	5.28	$100\frac{1}{4}$	4.99	$90\frac{1}{4}$	5.55
1957	$84\frac{1}{2}$	5.92	$94\frac{5}{8}$	5.26	$81\frac{1}{4}$	6.15
1958	88	5.68	$100\frac{3}{4}$	4.96	$79\frac{7}{8}$	6.26
1959	$94\frac{7}{8}$	5.27	106	4.71	91	5.50
10-yr. av.		5.68				
1960	$97\frac{1}{8}$	5.15	$105\frac{1}{4}$	4.75	$94\frac{1}{4}$	5.31
1961	$98\frac{5}{8}$	5.07	$103\frac{3}{4}$	4.82	$97\frac{1}{4}$	5.13
1962	$99\frac{3}{8}$	5.03	$102\frac{5}{8}$	4.87	$97\frac{1}{8}$	5.15
1963	$100\frac{5}{8}$	4.97	104	4.81	$98\frac{1}{4}$	5.09
1964	$98\frac{1}{2}$	5.08	$100\frac{5}{8}$	4.97	$93\frac{1}{4}$	5.36
1965	$94\frac{7}{8}$	5.27	$98\frac{3}{8}$	5.08	$91\frac{3}{8}$	5.47
1966	$92\frac{5}{8}$	5.40	$95\frac{5}{8}$	5.23	$88\frac{5}{8}$	5.64
1967	$88\frac{3}{8}$	5.66	$91\frac{7}{8}$	5.44	84	5.95
1968	$85\frac{3}{8}$	5.86	$87\frac{3}{8}$	5.72	$83\frac{3}{8}$	6.00
1969	$77\frac{3}{4}$	6.43	$84\frac{3}{8}$	5.93	$73\frac{5}{8}$	6.80
10-yr. av.	$93\frac{3}{8}$	5.39				
1970	$66\frac{1}{8}$	7.56	$71\frac{3}{4}$	6.97	$64\frac{3}{8}$	7.77
1971	$65\frac{3}{4}$	7.61	$68\frac{1}{8}$	7.34	$64\frac{1}{8}$	7.80
1972	$69\frac{3}{4}$	7.17	$71\frac{1}{2}$	6.99	$68\frac{1}{4}$	7.32
1973	$63\frac{5}{8}$	7.86	68	7.35	$60\frac{5}{8}$	8.24
1974	$60\frac{1}{8}$	8.33	$66\frac{1}{2}$	7.52	$55\frac{1}{4}$	9.06
1975	58	8.60	61	8.20	55	9.10
1976	$52\frac{1}{8}$	9.60				
1977	$51\frac{1}{4}$	9.76				
1978	53	9.43				
1979	$48\frac{1}{2}$	10.31				
10-yr. av.		8.62				

TABLE 62 (*Continued*)

| Year | 5% Perpetual *Rentes* of 1949 | | | | | |
| | Annual Average | | Annual High | | Annual Low | |
	Price	Yield, %	Price	Yield, %	Price	Yield, %
1980	44⅛	11.32				
1981	37⅞	13.20				
1982	34¾	14.56				
1983	39	12.81				
1984	43⅜	11.52				
1985	51	9.80				
1986						
1987						
1988						
1989						
6-yr. av.		12.20				

SOURCES

Leonidas J. Louchitch, *Des Variationes du Taux de l'Intérêt en France de 1800 à Nos Jours* (Paris: Libraire Felix Alcan, 1930).

League of Nations, *Statistical Year Book, 1939–1940*, p. 224.

United Nations, *Monthly Bulletin of Statistics.*

IMF, *International Financial Statistics.*

Annuaire Statistique de la France.

OECD, *Financial Statistics Monthly.*

lies in two circumstances: They provided an escape from the franc, and this tended to depress the price of the *rentes.* Conversely, however, holders of *rentes* were at times offered the privilege of converting all or part of their holdings into index bonds, and these conversion offers raised the price of the *rentes.* Since conversion offers were sporadic, they created a large difference between annual high prices, when they were in effect, and annual low prices, when they were not. Therefore, after 1950 these average yields of *rentes* must be regarded as often reflecting yields below those acceptable without special inducements. New issue yields were often far above the market yield of seasoned *rentes.*

Chart 56, which links the twentieth century with the nineteenth century, shows how the erratic but persistent nineteenth-century decline of French bond yields became in the twentieth century a series of wide swings. Their

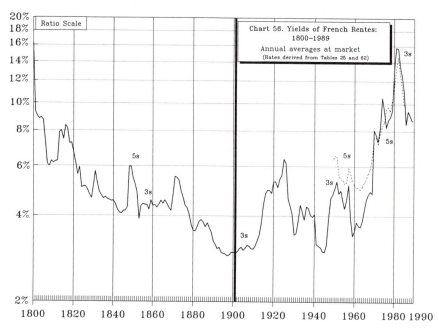

Chart 56. Yields of French Rentes:
1800–1989

Annual averages at market
(Rates derived from Tables 25 and 62)

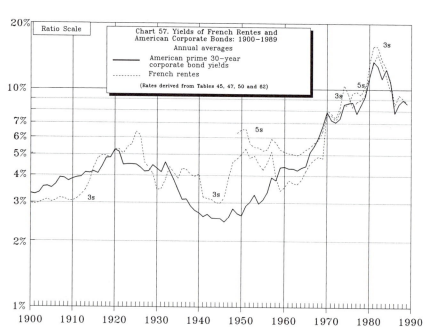

Chart 57. Yields of French Rentes and
American Corporate Bonds: 1900–1989

Annual averages

American prime 30–year
corporate bond yields

French rentes

(Rates derived from Tables 45, 47, 50 and 62)

range was very similar, however, to the range of 1800–1900. The wartime low yield of the 1940's was only a trifle above the lows of the 1890's. The high yield of the 3s in 1925 was moderately above their high yield in 1871–1872, and the high yield of the 5s in 1950 was moderately above the high of the 5s in 1848. At no time, until the 1970s, did the recorded yields return to the highs of the Napoleonic period; in the early 1980's they even approached the high yields of the demoralized markets at the end of the French Revolution.

The manner in which the trends of French bond yields in the twentieth century resembled yield trends in the United States is indicated by Chart 57. Such international comparisons are only relative to changes over time and not to absolute levels. For example, the French *rentes* were exempt from income tax while the American corporate bonds were not.

The French government bond yields started the century well below the American corporate bond yields. During the first decade French yields remained stable and low, while American yields were rising rapidly. During the decade of World War I, French yields rose sharply; by 1916 they considerably exceeded the American yields, but after the great 1917–1920 rise in the latter, the French *rentes* yielded about the same as did prime American corporate bonds. At the 1920 high point of American yields, the French, American, and English markets were quoted very closely together, as follows:

	1920 High Yields, %*
American corporate bonds	5.56
French 3% *rentes*	5.62
British 2½% consols	5.73

*The annual average charts do not picture these monthly high yields.

After 1920, the trend of French yields diverged from the trends of American and British yields (see Charts 53 and 57). That year was by no means the turning point in the French bond market as it was elsewhere. For the next five years, France struggled with inflation and until 1926 was unable to find a government strong enough to settle the urgent financial and political problems left by the war. The 3% *rentes* declined in price another 22% between 1920 lows and 1925 lows, while American and English bond prices were recovering. The 3% *rentes* reached a price of 42½ in 1920, to yield 7%. Their aggregate price decline from 1900 to 1925 was 57½%. This was about the same as the decline of British consols from 1900 to 1920, but greatly exceeded the decline in the American thirty-year bond index. The relationships of yields at their highs in 1925 had changed importantly:

	1925 High Yields, %
American corporate bonds	4.53
British consols	4.61
French 3% *rentes*	7.00

The year 1925 was the turning point of the French market. The currency was stabilized, and a stronger government made at least temporary arrangements to settle pressing international problems. The price of *rentes* soared as France entered an easy-money period six years before England and America entered their easy-money periods. By 1930, 3% *rentes* were up to an average price of 87¼, to yield 3.44%, although new-issue yields were higher. They had appreciated over 100% since 1925. The *rentiers* were winning back a little of their losses. The entire wartime decline in *rentes* had been made up. France briefly occupied the position of England in the late nineteenth century—a citadel of hard money and low interest rates. In 1930 average yields were as follows:

	1930 Average Yields, %
French 3% *rentes*	3.44
American corporate bonds	4.31
British consols	4.46

This period of low French bond yields was brief. The financial crises of 1930 and 1931 were not French crises, but they brought French yields up. When after 1931 American and British yields plunged, the yields on 3% French *rentes* rose further and stabilized at around 4%, while new issues yielded above 5%. France had devalued her currency in 1925–1926 and was determined not to devalue again. Throughout the 1930's, France struggled unsuccessfully to defend the franc in the face of world-wide depression and the looming prospect of war. By 1939 France was again a country of relatively high yields, as shown by the following table:

	1939 Average Yields, %
American corporate bonds	2.77
British consols	3.72
French 3% *rentes*	3.97 (new issue 5.10%)

During World War II, including the Occupation, the market for French *rentes* was quoted at high prices and low yields. From 1941 through 1945, the 3% *rentes* sold at close to 100. This meant that their yield was close to its all-time low. It was still, however, well above American wartime yields and about the same as the English 3% rate for war finance. It has been pointed out that such comparisons are only relative: Differences in tax privileges and in the structures of these markets forbid absolute comparison of one market with the others.

Immediately after the Liberation in 1945, *rentes* dropped sharply in price, and French yields began to rise at the same time that American and British yields began their long rise. French yields at first rose much faster than did American yields or even English yields. The franc fell almost steadily in world markets, and a succession of French governments sought in vain to stabilize it. By 1949, the 3% *rentes* were down to 58¼, to yield 5.25%; and by 1951, they were down to 52¾, to yield 5.70%. These yields were not, however, as high as the 7% yield of 1925.

In 1948–1949, a new issue of straight 55 perpetual *rentes* was floated at 100, to yield 5%. It carried no amortization privileges, but it carried a pledge that its rate of interest would be increased if the state floated future loans at a rate above 5½%. It also carried a right to subscribe to future loans. People over sixty who had long been holders of the 3% rentes were given the right to convert into this issue of 5% *rentes*.

In 1949, the new 5% *rentes* sold as low as 75¾, to yield 6.60%. Simultaneously, the 3% *rentes* sold no lower than 58¼, to yield 5.15%. The wide discrepancy illustrates the effect not only of discount but of other benefits, such as conversion offers at 100, which would help the 3s more than the 5s. In fact, after 1949 the continued inflation and the complicated and novel devices employed by the government to finance its deficits distorted the yields of all *rentes* so much that these tables have little significance in establishing either level or trend during the 1950's. We cannot conclude that the rates quoted here would have prevailed if holders had not expected advantageous exchange offers.

There is no doubt, however, that by 1950 French yields had risen sharply and were high by comparison with earlier French yields and with yields in other countries. The relationship among 1950 average yields was as follows:

	1950 Average Yields, %
American corporate bonds	2.62
British consols	3.55
French 5% *rentes*	6.52

This was the widest differential between French yields and other yields. During the 1950's while American and English bond yields were rising rapidly, the market yields on French *rentes* tended to decline, although they rose briefly in 1957–1958 and remained in a high range. By 1959, the 5s were quoted as high as 106, or 4.71%, an appreciation of about 40% during a period when the exchange value of the franc fell moderately, but to new lows, and then was stabilized. In 1959 the relationship to other yields was as follows:

	1959 Average Yields, %
American government bonds	4.07
British consols	4.82
French 5% *rentes*	5.27 (new issue 6%)

The international differentials had closed remarkably since 1950. The French-American spread came down from 390 basis points to 91 basis points, and the French-British spread, from 297 basis points to 45 basis points. By 1960–1961, British yields actually ranged above French yields.

The decline in the French yields in the 1950's must be interpreted partly in the light of the new index bonds and the privilege of converting *rentes* into them. Two important index issues may be mentioned:

1952–1958: The "Pinay" $3\frac{1}{2}$s, due 2012, redeemable by the government after 1970, exempt from income and inheritance taxes, amortized semiannually from 1953 to 2012 by drawings based on the free market value of a 20-franc gold piece, offered at 100 = 3.50%.

Year	*Price* of "Pinay" $3\frac{1}{2}$s	
	High Price	Low Price
1956	112	97
1960	119	105
1965	140	137
1970	172	141
1973	300	196 (refunded at $251\frac{1}{2}$)

1957: Index 5s payable in equal semiannual installments, 1958 through 1967, at a price determined by multiplying the nominal value of each bond by an index of common stock prices of the preceding year divided by the index of 1956, offered at 100 = 5%.

Year	High Price	Yield, %	Low Price	Yield, %
1957	103	4.86	$97\frac{7}{8}$	5.24
1958	111	4.51	$95\frac{3}{8}$	5.25
1959	$118\frac{7}{8}$	4.22	$106\frac{3}{8}$	4.70
1960	$119\frac{1}{2}$	4.19		

Among the conversion offers that lifted the prices of the *rentes* was the privilege offered at one time in 1958 to holders of the 5% *rentes* of 1949 to convert 100% into the "Pinay" gold 3½s and to holders of the 3% *rentes* to convert 50% of their holdings into the "Pinay" gold 3½s. As the "Pinay" 3½s then ranged in the market from 97¼ to 106½, it is not surprising that the 5s moved up in that year to a high of 98⅛ in 1958. In fact, in 1959 the 3s did not sell below 83¼, or 3.61%, which was far below the rate of long-term interest on other issues.

In the 1960's French bond yields declined for five years and then rose. By 1969, following on the crisis of 1968, the *rentes* sold to yield over 6.5%. This was approximately the same peak reached in the crises of 1925 and 1950, and above all other yields of the *rentes* since 1820. Nevertheless, yields continued to rise. By 1970 long-term government bond yields were up to 8%. Inflation was intense, currencies were uncertain, and interest rates were rising almost everywhere. French long-term yields peaked with most others in 1981, and then came down with them. At the peaks, as the following table shows, French bond yields were far above U.S. bond yields as well as the yields of British consols. The latter, however, had yielded considerably more than had French bonds at the previous interest rate peak in 1974.

	1981 Average Yields, %
American government bonds	12.87
British consols	13.01
French government bonds	15.79

The French government has outstanding a long list of obligations with a wide variety of maturities, redemption terms, and conversion privileges. The range of yields at any one time can be wide. In spite of these complications and the consequent impossibility of settling on one series of yields as representing the going rate of long-term French interest, it is probably true to assert that French yields declined in the late 1950's and in the early 1960's and thereafter rose steadily to the early 1980's. The yield pattern of the 1970's and 1980's was similar to those of the United States and other Western European nations.

Short-Term French Interest Rates. Short-term French interest rates are presented in Table 63 and Chart 58 in two groups: the discount rate of the Bank of France in terms of annual average and annual range; and, in the same terms, a succession of series called the open market rate of discount from 1900 to 1914, the private discount rate from 1925 through 1939, and day-to-day money (call money) or the money-market rate since 1940. These are not precisely comparable. They are, however, sufficient to indicate market trends.

These short-term French rates remained low during the first decade of the

TABLE 63
Short-Term French Interest Rates: Twentieth Century

Year	Discount Rate of Bank of France, %			Open Market Rate of Discount, %		
	Annual Average	Annual Low	Annual High	Annual Average	Annual Low	Annual High
1900	3.21	3	4.5	3.04	2.62	4.19
1901	3.00	3	3	2.41	1.69	2.85
1902	3.00	3	3	2.39	1.89	2.97
1903	3.00	3	3	2.70	2.22	2.84
1904	3.00	3	3	2.14	1.14	2.81
1905	3.00	3	3	2.11	1.34	3.06
1906	3.00	3	3	2.68	2.25	2.98
1907	3.46	3	4	3.35	3.00	3.84
1908	3.04	3	3.5	2.14	1.15	3.41
1909	3.00	3	3	1.75	1.12	2.78
10-yr. av.	3.07			2.47		
1910	3.00	3	3	2.39	2.00	2.91
1911	3.12	3	3.5	2.61	2.12	3.50
1912	3.38	3	4	3.12	2.56	3.88
1913	4.00	4	4	3.82	3.56	4.00
1914	4.54	3.5	6	2.87	2.75	3.52
1915	5.00	5	5			
1916	5.00	5	5			
1917	5.00	5	5			
1918	5.00	5	5			
1919	5.00	5	5			
10-yr. av.	4.30			2.96 (5-yr. av.)		
1920	5.75	5	6			
1921	5.79	5.5	6			
1922	5.10	5	5.5			
1923	5.00	5	5			
1924	5.92	5.5	7	Private Discount Rate, %		
1925	6.58	6	7	5.69	4.78	6.40
1926	6.50	6	7.5	5.66	4.25	7.25
1927	5.33	4	6.5	2.91	1.82	4.99
1928	3.54	3.5	4	3.02	2.62	3.41
1929	3.50	3.5	3.5	3.47	3.37	3.50
10-yr. av.	5.30			4.15		
1930	2.75	2.5	3.5	2.35	2.03	3.38
1931	2.13	2	2.5	1.56	1.06	1.90

TABLE 63 (*Continued*)

Year	Discount Rate of Bank of France, %			Private Discount Rate, %		
	Annual Average	Annual Low	Annual High	Annual Average	Annual Low	Annual High
1932	2.50	2.5	2.5	1.30	0.91	1.75
1933	2.50	2.5	2.5	1.63	1.12	2.26
1934	2.63	2.5	3	2.02	1.44	2.75
1935	3.50	2.5	6	3.24	1.79	5.89
1936	4.04	2	6	3.68	1.96	5.60
1937	3.92	2	6	3.83	2.22	5.20
1938	2.79	2.5	3	2.76	2.23	3.25
1939	2.04	2	2.5	2.05	1.88	2.70
10-yr. av.	2.88			2.44		
				Day-to-Day Money, %		
1940	2.00	2	2	1.72	1.25	1.94
1941	1.81	1.7	2	1.67	1.50	1.94
1942	1.75	1.75	1.75	1.62	1.42	1.74
1943	1.75	1.75	1.75	1.65	1.61	1.73
1944	1.75	1.75	1.75	1.64	1.49	1.73
1945	1.63	1.63	1.63	1.37	0.74	1.65
1946	1.63	1.63	1.63	1.31	1.19	1.36
1947	2.19	1.75	3	1.57	1.39	2.12
1948	2.98	2.5	4	2.09	2.00	2.84
1949	3.00	3	3	2.26	2.03	2.55
10-yr. av.	2.05			1.69		
1950	2.54	2.5	3	2.43	2.18	2.70
1951	2.79	2.5	4	2.70	2.45	3.50
1952	4.00	4	4	3.85	3.50	4.00
1953	3.83	3.5	4	4.04	3.75	4.34
1954	3.25	3	3.5	3.59	3.29	3.82
1955	3.00	3	3	3.16	2.99	3.27
1956	3.00	3	3	3.18	2.95	3.71
1957	4.17	3	5	5.35	3.52	7.94
1958	4.88	4.5	5	6.48	5.17	10.04
1959	4.08	4	4.5	4.07	3.67	4.39
10-yr. av.	3.55			3.89		
1960	3.90	3.5	4	4.08	3.70	4.53
1961	3.50	3.5	3.5	3.65	3.51	3.91
1962	3.50	3.5	3.5	3.61	3.46	3.98
1963	3.58	3.5	4	3.98	3.13	5.26

TABLE 63 (*Continued*)

Year	Discount Rate of Bank of France, %			Day-to-Day Money, %		
	Annual Average	Annual Low	Annual High	Annual Average	Annual Low	Annual High
1964	4.00	4	4	4.70	4.13	6.18
1965	3.63	3.5	4	4.17	3.77	4.62
1966	3.50	3.5	3.5	4.79	3.83	5.68
1967	3.50	3.5	3.5	4.77	4.29	5.57
1968	4.42	3.5	6	6.21	4.75	9.16
1969	6.83	6	8	8.96	7.88	9.55
10-yr. av.	4.04			4.89		
1970	7.66	7	8	8.68	7.30	10.21
1971	6.50	6.5	6.75	5.84	5.27	6.46
1972	7.15	5.75	7.5	4.95	3.75	7.31
1973	8.92	7.5	11	8.91	7.22	11.52
1974	12.16	11	13	12.91	11.83	13.84
1975	9.54	8	12	7.92	6.45	11.42
1976	9.08	8	10.5	8.56	6.36	10.44
1977	10.08	9.5	10.5	9.07	8.30	9.94
1978	9.50	9.5	9.5	7.98	6.67	10.18
1979	9.50	9.5	9.5	9.04	6.64	12.17
10-yr. av.	9.01			8.39		
1980	9.50	9.5	9.5	11.85	10.74	12.96
1981	15.74	10.75	22	15.30	10.74	19.93
1982	15.21	12.5	17.5	14.87	12.88	16.81
1983	12.30	12	12.5	12.53	12.27	12.84
1984	11.44	10.75	12	11.74	10.95	12.48
1985	9.78	8.75	10.55	9.93	8.98	10.67
1986	7.46	7	8.7	7.74	7.05	8.84
1987	7.60	7.25	8 5	7.98	7.36	8.90
1988	7.21	6.75	7.7	7.52	7.11	8.20
1989	8.64	8.25	9.5	9.07	8.31	10.48
10-yr. av.	10.49			10.85		

*As of the end of February 1981, the rate is that at which the Bank of France discounts Treasury bills for 7 to 10 days.

SOURCES

R.G. Hawtrey, *A Century of Bank Rate* (London: Longmans, Green & Co., 1938).

United Nations, *Monthly Bulletin of Statistics*.

Federal Reserve, *Banking and Monetary Statistics* (1976), *Annual Statistical Digest*, and *Federal Reserve Bulletin*.

IMF, *International Financial Statistics*.

OECD, *Financial Statistics Monthly*.

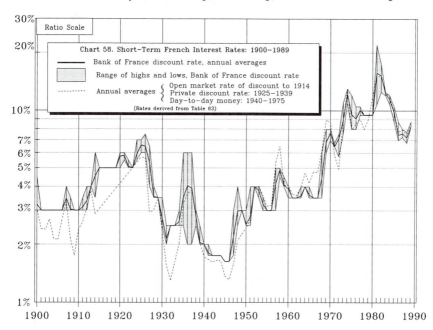

Chart 58. Short-Term French Interest Rates: 1900–1989
—— Bank of France discount rate, annual averages
▨ Range of highs and lows, Bank of France discount rate
Annual averages { Open market rate of discount to 1914 / Private discount rate: 1925–1939 / Day-to-day money: 1940–1975
(Rates derived from Table 63)

twentieth century, as did French bond yields. A sharp rise in the second decade was followed by a further rise in short rates in the 1920's. The Bank of France discount rate got up to 7½% and the private discount rate got up to 7¼% in 1926. By 1931, however, the bank discount rate was down to 2%, and by 1932 the private discount rate was down to 0.91%. By the mid-1930's, easy money had vanished; the bank discount rate was up to 6%, and the private discount rate rose at one time to 5.89%. Low short rates returned during World War II, when the bank discount rate was pushed down to a new low of 1⅝%.

The postwar history of French short-term interest rates was different from the postwar history of long-term French bond yields. Both rose, but by 1951 the discount rate was up to only 2½–4%, while bond yields were above 6%. In the 1950's, short rates continued to rise, while bond yields fluctuated erratically and then declined. By 1958, short rates were at a peak, with the bank discount rate up to 5% and day-to-day money briefly up to 10.04% and averaging 6.48%. Short rates came down sharply with bond yields in 1959, and they remained low until the 1968 crisis. Then in 1970, 1974, and 1981, short rates rose to new peaks, each higher than the previous one. The 1980's saw rates decline considerably despite the fact that French inflation was barely lower than it had been from 1965 to 1980.

In France, open market short-term interest rates averaged below the quoted yields of *rentes* throughout the twentieth century, as they had during the latter decades of the nineteenth century. The difference was small in the second decade; it was unusually large in the 1940's and 1950's, but since then it has again become small. The following table of decennial averages may be used to compare French long-term rates with French short-term rates, and both with American and English rates.

COMPARISON OF DECENNIAL AVERAGE RATES OF INTEREST

Decade	American Commercial Paper, %	English Open Market, %	French Open Market and Day-to-Day Money, %	American Corporate Bonds, %	English Consols, %	French 3% Rentes to 1950; 5% Rentes, thereafter, %
1880–1889	5.14	2.57	2.71	4.00	2.97	4.01
1890–1899	4.51	2.09	2.09	3.53	2.47	2.98
1900–1909	4.72	3.16	2.47	3.47	2.79	3.06
1910–1919	4.72	3.82	3.97 est.	4.23	3.81	4.06
1920–1929	5.00	4.26	4.66 est.	4.56	4.63	5.22
1930–1939	1.56	1.32	2.44	3.64	3.54	3.98
1940–1949	0.87	0.83	1.69	2.61	3.06	3.60
1950–1959	2.58	3.09	3.88	3.33	4.31	5.68
1960–1969	4.63	5.80	4.90	4.94	6.53	5.39
1970–1979	7.17	9.44	8.39	8.23	11.77	8.68
1980–1989	9.57	11.71	10.79	11.34	10.42	11.74

THE NETHERLANDS

In the twentieth century the Netherlands held to its long tradition of political and financial stability. Neutral and prosperous during World War I, the country was overrun during World War II and soon thereafter lost the greater part of its empire. As a trading nation, it could not escape the effects of the violent political and economic disturbances that brought a succession of crises to its large neighbors. The value of the guilder, which was stable in the nineteenth century, fluctuated in the twentieth century.

Long-Term Dutch Interest Rates. Chart 59 shows long and short decennial averages for the nineteenth and twentieth centuries. In the twentieth century interest rates were more stable in the Netherlands than in the United States, England, France, and most other countries. Table 64 presents long-term Dutch government bond yields, largely in terms of the same series of 2½% perpetual bonds that was carried through the nineteenth century from 1814. This issue has been selected for its long continuity and freedom from risk of redemption. Its yields, however, are not always typical of the yields available in the market for long-term Dutch government bonds because they tend, as in most countries, to be lower than the yields on bonds with higher

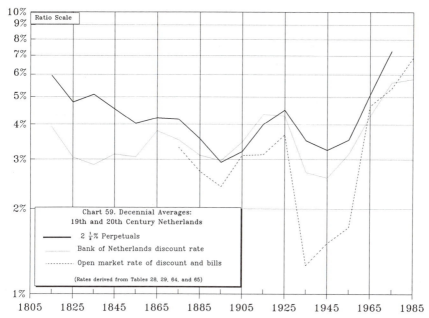

Chart 59. Decennial Averages:
19th and 20th Century Netherlands

——— 2 ½% Perpetuals

——— Bank of Netherlands discount rate

·········· Open market rate of discount and bills

(Rates derived from Tables 28, 29, 64, and 65)

nominal rates. They do, however, provide an adequate picture of the trend of Dutch bond yields. The table also presents for years from 1950 to 1985 an annual average of an issue of 3¼% bonds due in 1998. These tended to yield 10 to 50 basis points more than the 2½s yielded. The differential widened during the periods of higher yields and became small during periods of lower yields. For years since 1970, a new and more representative series is added; it is composed of long-term government bonds.

Chart 60 pictures the annual high, low, and average yields of the perpetual 2½s from 1814 to 1989. The pattern of fluctuation was similar to those of the other countries reviewed, but there were some important differences. Similar was the decline of rates throughout the second half of the nineteenth century, the rise from 1896 to 1920, the decline to 1938–1945, and the rise since 1945. These long-term Dutch interest rates just about touched their lows of the 1890's in 1938 and again in 1946, while the 1935–1946 lows of American long rates were well below their nineteenth-century lows. One noticeable difference is that Dutch long-term rates in the 1950's did not rise to levels near their 1920 highs, while rates in many other countries did. The impression up to 1960 given by Chart 60 is that of oscillations in a narrowing range, with a firm minimum around 2.75% and a declining maximum: 8.20% in 1814; 7.35% in 1831 and 1848; 6.10% in 1920, and 3.81% in 1951. After 1955, however, Dutch long-term bond yields rose sharply, as did yields in all countries, about doubling from 1955 to 1968 and nearly doubling again between 1968 and 1981, when they reached 11.55%. Thus the age-long pattern

TABLE 64
Prices and Yields of Long-Term Dutch Government Securities: Twentieth Century

Year	$2\frac{1}{2}$% Perpetual Debt of the Central Government						$3\frac{1}{2}$s Due 1998, Annual Average, Yield to Maturity, %	Government Bond Yield, Annual Average, %
	Annual Average		Annual High		Annual Low			
	Price	Yield, %	Price	Yield, %	Price	Yield, %		
1900	76	3.29	$82\frac{1}{2}$	3.03	75	3.34		
1901	$77\frac{1}{8}$	3.24	81	3.09	$76\frac{1}{2}$	3.27		
1902	$82\frac{1}{2}$	3.07	85	2.94	80	3.12		
1903	$80\frac{3}{8}$	3.11	$82\frac{3}{4}$	3.02	78	3.21		
1904	79	3.12	$80\frac{1}{2}$	3.10	$79\frac{7}{8}$	3.13		
1905	$78\frac{3}{4}$	3.16	$80\frac{1}{8}$	3.12	$77\frac{3}{4}$	3.22		
1906	$75\frac{1}{2}$	3.17	$80\frac{1}{2}$	3.10	$76\frac{7}{8}$	3.25		
1907	$75\frac{1}{2}$	3.31	78	3.21	$72\frac{3}{4}$	3.44		
1908	$76\frac{1}{2}$	3.31	$77\frac{1}{2}$	3.23	74	3.38		
1909		3.27	80	3.12	$75\frac{1}{2}$	3.31		
10-yr. av.		3.21						
1910	$74\frac{5}{8}$	3.35	$77\frac{3}{8}$	3.23	$72\frac{1}{2}$	3.45		
1911	71	3.52	$73\frac{3}{8}$	3.41	$68\frac{1}{4}$	3.66		
1912	$67\frac{3}{8}$	3.71	71	3.52	$65\frac{1}{8}$	3.84		
1913	$71\frac{1}{2}$	3.50	$77\frac{7}{8}$	3.21	$64\frac{1}{2}$	3.88		
1914	$71\frac{3}{4}$	3.49	$77\frac{7}{8}$	3.21	65	3.85		
1915	$63\frac{1}{4}$	3.95	77	3.25	59	4.24		
1916	$61\frac{1}{8}$	4.09	$65\frac{1}{2}$	3.82	56	4.46		
1917	$60\frac{5}{8}$	4.12	63	3.97	59	4.24		
1918	$55\frac{1}{4}$	4.52	$60\frac{1}{8}$	4.16	$49\frac{3}{4}$	5.02		
1919	50	5.00	$55\frac{7}{8}$	4.47	44	5.68		
10-yr. av.		3.93						
1920	45	5.56	$49\frac{3}{8}$	5.06	41	6.10		
1921	48	5.21	$53\frac{1}{4}$	4.69	$42\frac{5}{8}$	5.87		
1922	$51\frac{1}{2}$	4.86	$57\frac{3}{4}$	4.33	$48\frac{5}{8}$	5.14		
1923	54	4.63	$58\frac{1}{4}$	4.29	$50\frac{3}{8}$	4.96		
1924	$53\frac{1}{8}$	4.70	$55\frac{1}{8}$	4.54	$48\frac{1}{2}$	5.15		
1925	$59\frac{3}{4}$	4.18	$64\frac{1}{8}$	3.90	$55\frac{1}{2}$	4.50		
1926	$62\frac{1}{2}$	4.00	$64\frac{3}{4}$	3.86	$61\frac{1}{4}$	4.08		
1927	$62\frac{3}{8}$	4.01	$64\frac{1}{2}$	3.88	$60\frac{1}{2}$	4.13		
1928	$64\frac{1}{2}$	3.88	$65\frac{3}{4}$	3.80	$62\frac{3}{8}$	4.01		
1929	$63\frac{1}{2}$	3.94	65	3.85	60	4.17		
10-yr. av.		4.50						
1930	$65\frac{5}{8}$	3.81	68	3.68	$62\frac{1}{8}$	4.02		
1931	$64\frac{3}{4}$	3.86	$70\frac{3}{8}$	3.55	$51\frac{5}{8}$	4.84		
1932	$64\frac{1}{4}$	3.89	$71\frac{5}{8}$	3.49	$54\frac{3}{8}$	4.60		

TABLE 64 (*Continued*)

Year	$2\frac{1}{2}$% Perpetual Debt of the Central Government						$3\frac{1}{2}$s Due 1998, Annual Average, Yield to Maturity, %	Government Bond Yield, Annual Average, %
	Annual Average		Annual High		Annual Low			
	Price	Yield, %	Price	Yield, %	Price	Yield, %		
1933	68	3.68	$71\frac{1}{2}$	3.50	$62\frac{3}{4}$	3.98		
1934	$74\frac{5}{8}$	3.35	$80\frac{3}{8}$	3.11	$69\frac{7}{8}$	3.58		
1935	$72\frac{7}{8}$	3.43	$82\frac{3}{4}$	3.02	67	3.73		
1936	$75\frac{1}{4}$	3.32	$86\frac{7}{8}$	2.88	$71\frac{3}{4}$	3.48		
1937	$79\frac{7}{8}$	3.13	$85\frac{1}{2}$	2.92	77	3.25		
1938	$83\frac{5}{8}$	2.99	$91\frac{3}{4}$	2.72	75	3.33		
1939	$70\frac{1}{4}$	3.56	83	3.01	61	4.10		
10-yr. av.		3.50						
1940	$62\frac{3}{4}$	3.98	$70\frac{3}{8}$	3.55	$56\frac{3}{8}$	4.43		
1941	68	3.68	$76\frac{3}{4}$	3.26	62	4.03		
1942	$77\frac{7}{8}$	3.21	81	3.09	$72\frac{1}{2}$	3.45		
1943	$80\frac{3}{8}$	3.11	$85\frac{7}{8}$	2.91	$78\frac{7}{8}$	3.19		
1944	$80\frac{7}{8}$	3.09	$85\frac{1}{2}$	2.92	$80\frac{7}{8}$	3.09		
1945	$83\frac{1}{4}$	3.01	$84\frac{1}{2}$	2.96	82	3.05		
1946	$83\frac{5}{8}$	2.99	$91\frac{7}{8}$	2.72	81	3.09		
1947	$81\frac{5}{8}$	3.06	$83\frac{1}{2}$	2.99	$80\frac{1}{8}$	3.12		
1948	$80\frac{7}{8}$	3.09	$82\frac{1}{8}$	3.04	$80\frac{3}{4}$	3.11		
1949	$80\frac{1}{8}$	3.12	$81\frac{1}{8}$	3.08	$77\frac{7}{8}$	3.22		
10-yr. av.		3.23						
1950	$80\frac{1}{4}$	3.12	$81\frac{1}{2}$	3.07	$78\frac{1}{4}$	3.19	3.28	
1951	$73\frac{1}{4}$	3.42	$77\frac{7}{8}$	3.23	$65\frac{5}{8}$	3.81	3.88	
1952	$73\frac{3}{8}$	3.41	$77\frac{5}{8}$	3.22	69	3.62	3.95	
1953	$78\frac{3}{8}$	3.18	80	3.12	$76\frac{1}{2}$	3.27	3.43	
1954	$79\frac{1}{8}$	3.16	$81\frac{3}{4}$	3.06	$76\frac{1}{2}$	3.27	3.31	
1955	$78\frac{3}{8}$	3.18	$81\frac{3}{4}$	3.06	75	3.33	3.26	
1956	$72\frac{7}{8}$	3.42	$79\frac{3}{4}$	3.13	66	3.79	3.84	
1957	$61\frac{3}{4}$	4.05	$70\frac{3}{8}$	3.55	$53\frac{1}{4}$	4.69	4.58	
1958	$61\frac{1}{4}$	4.07	$65\frac{1}{2}$	3.82	$56\frac{3}{4}$	4.41	4.32	
1959	60	4.17	$64\frac{3}{8}$	3.89	$56\frac{5}{8}$	4.42	4.12	
10-yr. av.		3.52					3.80	
1960	$58\frac{1}{2}$	4.26	60	4.16	$57\frac{1}{4}$	4.35	4.20	
1961	61	4.11	$63\frac{7}{8}$	3.92	58	4.31	3.91	
1962	$57\frac{1}{2}$	4.35	60	4.16	55	4.54	4.21	
1963	56	4.45	60	4.16	52	4.80	4.22	
1964	53	4.70	$55\frac{1}{4}$	4.53	51	4.90	4.92	
1965	$49\frac{1}{2}$	5.05	53	4.70	46	5.55	5.21	
1966	$43\frac{5}{8}$	5.70	$46\frac{5}{8}$	5.40	41	6.08	6.24	
1967	$45\frac{5}{8}$	5.50	$47\frac{1}{4}$	5.30	$43\frac{1}{2}$	5.71	6.00	

TABLE 64 (*Continued*)

Year	2½% Perpetual Debt of the Central Government						3½s Due 1998, Annual Average, Yield to Maturity, %	Government Bond Yield, Annual Average, %
	Annual Average		Annual High		Annual Low			
	Price	Yield, %	Price	Yield, %	Price	Yield, %		
1968	41⅝	6.00	44¼	5.65	39	6.40	6.22	
1969	36½	6.85	40	6.25	33	7.51	7.84	
10-yr. av.		5.10					5.30	
1970	34¾	7.20	37⅞	6.60	31⅛	8.00	7.85	8.22
1971	38⅜	6.50	40¾	6.15	36	6.91	7.05	7.35
1972	37½	6.65	39⅞	6.25	35	7.10	6.67	6.88
1973	33½	7.45	36⅝	6.80	30¼	8.20	7.31	7.72
1974	30¼	8.20	34¾	7.20	25¾	9.80	9.20	9.83
1975	32½	7.71	35½	7.05	29½	8.50	7.96	8.79
1976							8.10	8.95
1977							7.30	8.10
1978							6.70	7.74
1979							7.07	8.78
10-yr. av.							7.52	8.24
1980							7.84	10.21
1981							8.46	11.55
1982							6.77	10.10
1983							5.66	8.61
1984							5.55	8.33
1985							4.81	7.34
1986								6.35
1987								6.38
1988								6.29
1989								7.22
10-yr. av.							6.52	8.24

SOURCES

The Netherlands, Central Bureau of Statistics, *Statistical Yearbook of the Netherlands*.
IMF, *International Financial Statistics*.
Morgan Guaranty Trust Company, *World Financial Markets*.
OECD, *Financial Statistics Monthly*.

of fluctuation in a band was decisively broken, and Dutch yields reached their highest recorded level for several centuries.

No precise series of long-term Dutch interest rates has been presented for the years before 1814. However, scraps of information on long-term Dutch annuity rates were reported in earlier chapters back to the sixteenth century.

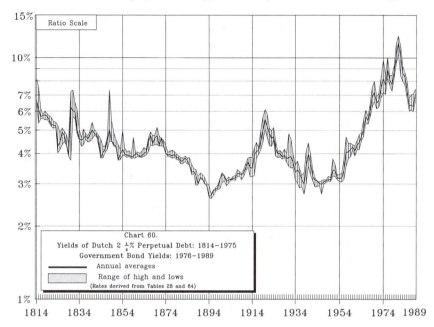

Chart 60.
Yields of Dutch 2 ½% Perpetual Debt: 1814–1975
Government Bond Yields: 1976–1989
———— Annual averages
▒▒▒▒ Range of high and lows
(Rates derived from Tables 28 and 64)

Since the Dutch Republic was a pioneer in developing low European interest rates, the following attempt at generalizing these early scraps of information and combining them with more precise data on modern rates seems
worth the risk of error. The lowest yield quotations available for long-term
Dutch debt instruments over the centuries are shown in the table below.

LOWEST REPORTED DUTCH LONG-TERM
INTEREST RATES

		%
Sixteenth century	First half	8.33
	Second half	6.16
Seventeenth century	First half	5.00
	Second half	3.00
Eighteenth century	First half	3.00
	Second half	2.50
Nineteenth century	First half	3.75
	Second half	2.60
Twentieth century	First half	2.72
	Second half	3.06

If such a table can be taken as a rough guide, it appears that twentieth-
century low rates in Holland were not much below the lows reported for the
eighteenth century. In every other country examined, nineteenth- or twentieth-century low rates were well below earlier low rates. It is not necessary

to claim valid comparability of these early scraps with modern quotations to conclude that Dutch rates were very low, very early, and that the low-yield periods of the nineteenth and twentieth centuries were not novel to the Dutch, as they were to the Americans and to most other peoples. As for high yields, which are sometimes hard to trace during periods of invasion and crisis, no rates higher than 8% are reliably reported during several centuries, and 8% was reached only during the Napoleonic invasion. By comparison, the 1981 peak was about 12%.

Another view of the trends of Dutch long-term interest rates in the twentieth century is obtained from Chart 61, which compares yields on the long-term Dutch government bonds with yields on American corporate bonds. The yields on these Dutch government bonds in the early twentieth century were usually below the American corporate bond yields, above British consol yields, and close to the yields on French *rentes*. The Dutch yields rose during the first two decades with the other yields. By 1920 they were slightly higher than the American yields, about equal to the French yields, and below the English yields. In the 1920's Dutch yields did not rise further, as did French yields; they declined with, but much more than, American and English yields. They fell below 4% in 1925 and stayed there. There was no flurry in 1929 and only a brief rise in 1931. During the early 1930's the Dutch yields remained well below the American yields. However, they did not decline as sharply as did English and American yields after 1931, nor did they go so low in 1935 and 1946. When, after 1937, American yields plunged below 3%,

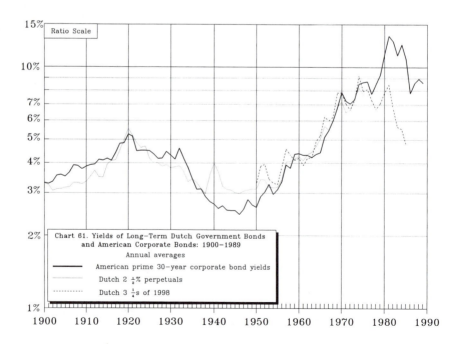

Chart 61. Yields of Long-Term Dutch Government Bonds and American Corporate Bonds: 1900–1989
Annual averages
——— American prime 30-year corporate bond yields
- - - Dutch 2 ½% perpetuals
· · · · · Dutch 3 ¼s of 1998

Dutch yields rose with other European yields until the outbreak of World War II. During the period of occupation, Dutch yields declined again to 3%, just as English and French yields declined during the war, but remained far above American yields.

After 1946, Dutch yields, like all other yields, rose, but far less than the yields in many other countries. For a few years after the war, perpetual 2½s were supported by the privilege of turning them in as payment of temporary war taxes. By 1959, these Dutch yields were roughly the same as the American yields and were far below English and French yields.

After 1960, Dutch yields almost paralleled the huge rise in American yields to the mid-1970's. From then until the end of the 1980s, Dutch yields were noticeably below American yields. The gap was quite large for the Dutch 3¼s shown in Chart 61 but was also present in the case of other Dutch yields.

Short-Term Dutch Interest Rates. Dutch short-term interest rates are presented in Table 65 in two groups: (a) the discount rate of the Bank of the Netherlands in terms of annual average and range of fluctuation; and (b) the market rate of discount in Amsterdam, or the private discount rate, 1900–1912, 1915–1941, and the rate on three-month Treasury bills, 1945–1989, all in terms of annual average and annual high and low. The discount rate continued to be a penalty rate, as it was in the nineteenth century, and the open market rates often were below it; in easy-money periods they were far below it. These short rates are pictured in Chart 62.

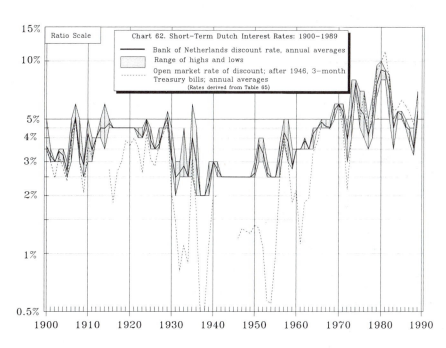

Chart 62. Short-Term Dutch Interest Rates: 1900-1989
Bank of Netherlands discount rate, annual averages
Range of highs and lows
Open market rate of discount; after 1946, 3-month Treasury bills; annual averages
(Rates derived from Table 65)

TABLE 65
SHORT-TERM DUTCH INTEREST RATES: TWENTIETH CENTURY

Year	Discount Rate of Netherlands Bank, %			Market Rate of Discount in Amsterdam, %		
	Annual Average	Annual Low	Annual High	Annual Average	Annual Low	Annual High
1900	3.61	3.5	5	3.44		
1901	3.23	3	3.5	3.00		
1902	3.00	3	3	2.47		
1903	3.40	3	3.5	3.19		
1904	3.23	3	3.5	2.77		
1905	2.68	2.5	3	2.39		
1906	4.11	3	5	3.77		
1907	5.10	5	6	4.86		
1908	3.38	3	5	3.01		
1909	2.88	2.5	3	2.07		
10-yr. av.	3.46			3.10		
1910	4.23	3	5	3.64		
1911	3.45	3	4	3.17		
1912	4.00	4	4	3.91		
1913	4.50	4	5			
1914	4.48	3.5	6			
1915	4.75	4.5	5	2.76	2.44	3.09
1916	4.50	4.5	4.5	1.84	1.03	2.60
1917	4.50	4.5	4.5	2.68	1.58	3.78
1918	4.50	4.5	4.5	2.99	2.23	3.72
1919	4.50	4.5	4.5	3.87	3.57	4.18
10-yr. av.	4.34			3.11		
1920	4.50	4.5	4.5	3.65	3.08	4.22
1921	4.50	4.5	4.5	3.99	3.59	4.42
1922	4.27	4	4.5	3.55	2.75	4.34
1923	4.02	4	4.5	2.62	2.93	4.28
1924	4.94	4.5	5	4.19	2.88	5.19
1925	3.90	3.5	4.5	3.10	2.14	3.72
1926	3.50	3.5	3.5	2.84	2.19	3.39
1927	3.71	3.5	4.5	3.67	2.97	4.50
1928	4.50	4.5	4.5	4.23	3.97	4.46
1929	5.10	4.5	5.5	4.82	3.52	5.37
10-yr. av.	4.29			3.67		
1930	3.23	3	4.5	2.08	1.31	2.99
1931	2.48	2	3	1.47	1.05	2.76

TABLE 65 (*Continued*)

Year	Discount Rate of Netherlands Bank, %			Market Rate of Discount in Amsterdam, %		
	Annual Average	Annual Low	Annual High	Annual Average	Annual Low	Annual High
1932	2.65	2.5	3	0.81	0.37	2.24
1933	2.85	2.5	4.5	1.10	0.37	3.54
1934	2.50	2.5	2.5	0.89	0.50	2.07
1935	4.02	2.5	6	3.18	0.58	5.48
1936	2.92	2	4.5	1.64	0.76	3.92
1937	2.00	2	2	0.19	0.13	0.52
1938	2.00	2	2	0.15	0.13	0.32
1939	2.33	2	3	1.10	0.13	2.94
10-yr. av.	2.70			1.26		
1940	3.00	3	3	1.96	1.35	2.25
1941	2.75	2.5	3	2.00	1.88	2.25
1942	2.50	2.5	2.5			
1943	2.50	2.5	2.5			
1944	2.50	2.5	2.5	3-Month Treasury Bills, %		
1945	2.50	2.5	2.5			
1946	2.50	2.5	2.5	1.20	0.90	1.52
1947	2.50	2.5	2.5	1.35	0.93	1.72
1948	2.50	2.5	2.5	1.30	1.03	1.56
1949	2.50	2.5	2.5	1.27	1.07	1.43
10-yr. av.	2.58			1.51		
1950	2.62	2.5	3	1.40	1.20	1.57
1951	3.71	3	4	1.36	1.16	1.55
1952	3.33	3	4	1.08	0.84	1.40
1953	2.63	2.5	3	0.57	0.03	0.93
1954	2.50	2.5	2.5	0.55	0.23	0.88
1955	2.50	2.5	2.5	0.96	0.75	1.49
1956	3.12	2.5	3.75	2.38	1.32	3.48
1957	4.26	3.75	5	4.06	3.47	4.87
1958	3.83	3	5	3.01	2.26	4.43
1959	2.87	2.75	3.5	1.85	1.61	2.52
10-yr. av.	3.14			1.72		
1960	3.50	3.5	3.5	2.14	1.51	2.53
1961	3.50	3.5	3.5	1.12	0.77	1.74
1962	3.88	3.5	4	1.85	1.02	2.46
1963	3.50	3.5	3.5	1.94	1.67	2.25

TABLE 65 (*Continued*)

Year	Discount Rate of Netherlands Bank, %			3-Month Treasury Bills, %		
	Annual Average	Annual Low	Annual High	Annual Average	Annual Low	Annual High
1964	4.21	3.5	4.5	3.37	2.31	4.26
1965	4.50	4.5	4.5	3.83	3.05	4.29
1966	4.83	4.5	5	4.74	4.32	5.00
1967	4.58	4.5	5	4.58	4.47	4.87
1968	4.54	4.5	5	4.44	4.19	4.65
1969	5.58	5	6	5.55	4.90	6.00
10-yr. av.	4.26			3.36		
1970	6.00	6	6	5.97	5.75	6.00
1971	5.46	5	6	4.34	3.59	5.60
1972	3.92	3	4.5	2.16	0.70	3.61
1973	5.50	4	8	4.07	1.22	6.41
1974	7.75	7	8	6.90	6.00	7.50
1975	5.63	4.5	7	4.91	2.60	6.60
1976	5.29	4	7	6.80	2.50	14.50
1977	4.13	3.5	5	4.01	2.75	6.38
1978	4.96	4	6.5	5.49	4.10	9.50
1979	7.58	6.5	9.5	8.90	6.75	14.00
10-yr. av.	5.62			5.36		
1980	9.00	8	10	9.87	8.00	10.87
1981	8.83	8	9	11.23	8.75	15.25
1982	6.96	5	8.5	7.74	5.63	9.63
1983	4.50	3.5	5	5.48	4.50	6.50
1984	5.46	5	5.5	5.73	5.38	6.12
1985	5.25	5	5.5	6.30	5.69	7.00
1986	4.58	4.5	5	5.86	4.75	6.88
1987	4.40	3.75	4.5	5.40	4.75	5.94
1988	3.54	3.25	4.5	4.68	4	5.56
1989	5.92	5	7	6.69	6.44	7
10-yr. av.	5.84			6.90		

SOURCES

Federal Reserve, *Banking and Monetary Statistics* (1943, 1976), *Annual Statistical Digest*, and *Federal Reserve Bulletin*.

Morgan Guaranty Trust Company, *World Financial Markets*.

Kurt Eisfeld, *Das Niederlaendische Bankwesen* (1916), Vol. II, p. 40.

The Netherlands, Central Bureau of Statistics, *Statistical Yearbook of the Netherlands*.

IMF, *International Financial Statistics*.

OECD, *Financial Statistics Monthly*.

Short-term Dutch open market rates at the beginning of the twentieth century were rising. However, they were moderate, like other European short rates, and unlike American commercial paper rates, which were high. Aside from a flurry in 1906–1907, which also occurred in other countries, the Dutch open market rates stayed moderate until 1910. During World War I, in spite of an increase in the discount rate, which was finally pegged at 4½%, the open market rate fell at one time to below 2%. In 1920, it rose only to 4.22% when the English open market rate rose above 6%. Clearly, short-term interest rates in the Dutch money market remained low, far below those of the belligerents. Dutch bond yields, in contrast, rose at their 1920 highs above 6%. The German inflation of 1920–1923 created few repercussions in the Dutch money market, which remained relatively stable in the 1920's. Average rates were then at their highest since the 1860's, but they were well below the English and French short-term rates.

In the 1930's, Dutch short rates declined sharply, as did short rates in other countries. They ran up sharply in 1935, and then declined to new lows. During World War II, Dutch short rates remained low. After the war and through the devaluation of 1949, the Dutch official discount rate was held at 2½%, and open market rates were permitted to decline to around 1%. This resembled the postwar English policy of very low short-term rates and contrasted with rising short rates in France and in America.

It was in the 1950's that the Dutch money market contrasted most strikingly with other money markets. Short rates stayed low after a flurry in 1951 and rose only moderately in another flurry in 1956–1957. In 1957, the discount rate got up briefly to 5% when the British bank rate was at 7%. The Dutch bill rate averaged 3% when open market rates in Britain averaged 5% and those in France averaged over 6%. Soon after 1957, the Dutch open market rate declined again, to below 2%. Short open market Dutch rates averaged 1.72% in the 1950's, when English open market rates averaged above 3%, French open market rates averaged nearly 4%, and American commercial-paper rates averaged 2.58%.

Clearly, the Dutch were clinging to the advantages, such as they were, of low interest rates. They were permitting their larger neighbors to resort to the weapon of tight money against the postwar inflation and thus help keep Dutch prices down. Holland did not abandon its ancient tradition of low interest rates. This policy was maintained into the 1960's and, indeed, until inflation got out of hand in 1973. The Dutch decennial average for Treasury bills was 3.36% for the 1960's, as compared to 3.97% in the United States, 4.90% in France, and 5.80% in England. An annual average of 2% occurred as late as 1972. Then came the first oil price shock. In 1974, the Dutch discount rate reached 8%, and the short rate peaked at 7.50%. In 1980, the discount rate hit 10%, and short rates rose to 15.25% in 1981. In the mid- to late 1980's, however, Dutch short rates were back in the range that prevailed earlier in the century.

The Dutch short-term open market rates quoted have averaged far below the Dutch bond yields quoted at all times during the nineteenth and twentieth centuries. The differential was larger and more persistent than in other countries. Low short-term rates of interest were a distinguishing characteristic of the early Dutch market, which was still evident in the 1980's.

BELGIUM

The history of Belgian interest rates during the first half of the twentieth century was interrupted by two world wars, during both of which Belgium became an occupied country. The "perpetually neutral state" of 1831 was restored to its historical role as Europe's favorite battlefield. The nation could neither avoid nor influence constructively the political and economic struggles between her great neighbors.

The Belgian franc fluctuated very closely with the French franc until after World War II, losing 90% of its dollar value. Thereafter, it approximately held its dollar value, while the French franc lost another 90% of its dollar value. However, in spite of such financial calamities and finally the loss of its African empire, Belgium grew industrially and in times of peace achieved a high level of commercial prosperity.

Long-Term Belgian Interest Rates.   The Belgian long-term interest rates shown in Table 66 and Charts 63, 64, and 65 include the yields of the same Belgian *rentes* that have been reported from 1830. The 2½% and 3% *rentes*

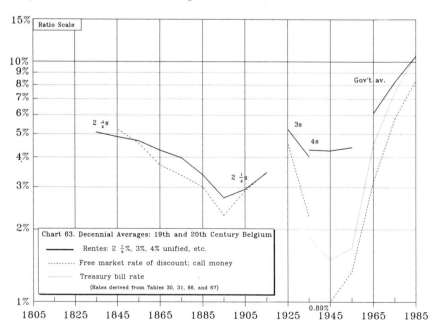

Chart 63. Decennial Averages: 19th and 20th Century Belgium
——— Rentes: 2 ½%, 3%, 4% unified, etc.
·········· Free market rate of discount; call money
——— Treasury bill rate
(Rates derived from Tables 30, 31, 66, and 67)

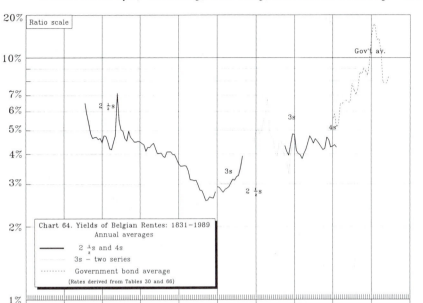

Chart 64. Yields of Belgian Rentes: 1831–1989
Annual averages

——— $2\frac{1}{2}$s and 4s

········· 3s – two series

·········· Government bond average

(Rates derived from Tables 30 and 66)

are carried on the tables up to 1914. No data are available for the war years. A new series of 3% *rentes* covers the years 1919 through 1939, and a series of 4% *rentes* ("unified debt," no maturity) covers the years 1935 to 1960. In 1960, a new series begins, an average of all bonds with a maturity of over five years.

The securities with the higher nominal rates, as usual, yielded more. None of the issues studied sold for long over their face value. There is available to us no single Belgian series as reliable in describing the going rate of long-term interest as were British consols in the eighteenth and nineteenth centuries, the band of British long-term yields, and the American corporate bond yield averages in the twentieth century.

The trend of long-term Belgian interest rates was similar to the general trend in the other countries reviewed during the first two decades of the twentieth century: Yields rose sharply after 1910. In the 1920's the Belgian market diverged from the American, English, and Dutch markets and followed the French market: Yields rose further until 1925, as the two francs were under attack, and fell sharply after 1926, following devaluation and stabilization. In the 1930's the Belgian market continued to follow the French rather than the American, British, and Dutch markets. In spite of very low short-term interest rates, bond yields did not then fall to very low levels. Belgian yields rose sharply from 1937 to 1940. During World War II, they declined, as did yields in other countries, but not far. After the war Belgian yields as described by the 4s formed a unique pattern. They did not rise

TABLE 66
PRICES AND YIELDS OF LONG-TERM BELGIAN GOVERNMENT SECURITIES: TWENTIETH CENTURY

Year	Annual Averages					
	$2\frac{1}{2}$% Rentes		3% Rentes		4% Unified Debt (No Maturity), P.T.E.	
	Price	Yield, %	Price	Yield, %	Price	Yield, %
1900	$85\frac{5}{8}$	2.92	$95\frac{1}{4}$	3.15		
1901	86	2.91	$97\frac{3}{4}$	3.08		
1902	$88\frac{1}{8}$	2.84	$99\frac{5}{8}$	3.01		
1903	$90\frac{1}{8}$	2.77	$99\frac{5}{8}$	3.01		
1904	$87\frac{5}{8}$	2.85	$99\frac{5}{8}$	3.01		
1905	87	2.88	$99\frac{5}{8}$	3.01		
1906	$85\frac{3}{4}$	2.92	$99\frac{5}{8}$	3.01		
1907	$82\frac{5}{8}$	3.03	$97\frac{3}{4}$	3.07		
1908	$79\frac{3}{8}$	3.14	$95\frac{1}{4}$	3.17		
1909	$80\frac{3}{8}$	3.11		3.15		
10-yr. av.		2.94		3.07		
1910	$77\frac{3}{4}$	3.22	$93\frac{3}{4}$	3.20		
1911	$76\frac{7}{8}$	3.25	$89\frac{7}{8}$	3.34		
1912	$71\frac{3}{8}$	3.50	$83\frac{3}{8}$	3.60		
1913	$63\frac{3}{4}$	3.92	$76\frac{5}{8}$	3.90		
4-yr. av.		3.47		3.51		
			3% Rentes, 2nd Series			
1919			$67\frac{3}{4}$	4.43		
1920			$60\frac{5}{8}$	4.95		
1921			59	5.08		
1922			$61\frac{3}{4}$	4.86		
1923			$59\frac{3}{8}$	5.05		
1924			$54\frac{5}{8}$	5.49		
1925			51	5.88		
1926			$44\frac{5}{8}$	6.72		
1927			$58\frac{7}{8}$	5.10		

TABLE 66 (*Continued*)

| Year | Annual Averages | | | | | |
| | 2½% Rentes | | 3% Rentes, 2nd Series | | 4% Unified Debt (No Maturity), P.T.E. | |
	Price	Yield, %	Price	Yield, %	Price	Yield, %
1928	$63\frac{7}{8}$	4.70				
1929	$64\frac{3}{4}$	4.63				
10-yr. av.				5.25		
1930			$74\frac{3}{8}$	4.03		
1931			$76\frac{1}{2}$	3.92		
1932			$67\frac{1}{8}$	4.47		
1933			$66\frac{1}{8}$	4.54		
1934			$73\frac{1}{8}$	4.10		
1935			$76\frac{1}{2}$	3.92	$92\frac{5}{8}$	4.32
1936			$80\frac{1}{4}$	3.74	$97\frac{7}{8}$	4.09
1937			$90\frac{1}{8}$	3.33	$101\frac{1}{2}$	3.94
1938			$75\frac{1}{2}$	3.97	$91\frac{5}{8}$	4.36
1939			$68\frac{5}{8}$	4.37	$82\frac{3}{4}$	4.83
10-yr. av.				4.04		4.31 (5-yr. av.)
1940					$83\frac{1}{8}$	4.81
1941					$96\frac{7}{8}$	4.13
1942					$99\frac{5}{8}$	4.01
1943					$101\frac{1}{8}$	3.96
1944					$104\frac{5}{8}$	3.82
1945					$99\frac{3}{4}$	4.01
1946					$95\frac{7}{8}$	4.17
1947					90	4.44
1948					$84\frac{1}{4}$	4.75
1949					87	4.60
10-yr. av.						4.27
1950					$90\frac{1}{2}$	4.42
1951					$86\frac{5}{8}$	4.62
1952					$88\frac{5}{8}$	4.51
1953					$90\frac{7}{8}$	4.40
1954					$93\frac{5}{8}$	4.27

TABLE 66 (*Continued*)

Year	Annual Averages					
	2½% *Rentes*		3% *Rentes*, 2nd Series		4% Unified Debt (No Maturity), P.T.E.	
	Price	Yield, %	Price	Yield, %	Price	Yield, %
1955	96⅛	4.16				
1956	95	4.21				
1957	85¼	4.69				
1958	87½	4.57				
1959	93⅝	4.27				
10-yr. av.						4.41
	Government Bond Average					
1960		5.55			93	4.30
1961		5.87			91¾	4.36
1962		5.18			93⅞	4.26
1963		5.28				
1964		6.45				
1965		6.44				
1966		6.65				
1967		6.68				
1968		6.55				
1969		6.55				
10-yr. av.		6.12				4.31 (3-yr. av.)
1970		7.81				
1971		7.35				
1972		7.04				
1973		7.44				
1974		8.68				
1975		8.54				
1976		9.05				
1977		8.80				

TABLE 66 (*Continued*)

Year	Annual Averages					
	Government Bond Average		3% *Rentes*, 2nd Series		4% Unified Debt (No Maturity), P.T.E.	
	Price	Yield, %	Price	Yield, %	Price	Yield, %
1978		8.45				
1979		9.51				
10-yr. av.		8.27				
1980		12.04				
1981		13.71				
1982		13.56				
1983		11.86				
1984		11.98				
1985		10.61				
1986		7.93				
1987		7.83				
1988		7.85				
1989		8.64				
10-yr. av.		10.60				

SOURCES

Bulletin de l'Institute des Sciences Economiques, Université Catholique de Louvain, August 1937, No. 4, pp. 435–36; and November 1933, no. 1, p. 104.

Banque National de Belgique, *Statistiques Economiques Belges, 1919–1928*, p. 36; *1929–1940*, pp. 74, 76; and *1941–1950*, p. 82.

IMF, *International Financial Statistics.*

OECD, *Financial Statistics Monthly.*

sharply from 1945 to the early 1960's, as did the yields in most other countries studied; they had not fallen very low. They simply fluctuated between 4.25% and 4.75% most of the time, when Dutch yields were rising from 3 to 4.40%, American yields were rising from 2.37 to 4.60%, British yields were rising from 2.50 to 7.00%, and French yields were rising from 3% to a high of 6.50%.

New Belgian government issues of medium term were offered at an average yield of 4.78% during the 1950's. They sometimes yielded over 5%. The lower yield of the 4s was in part due to the terms and privileges of the 4%

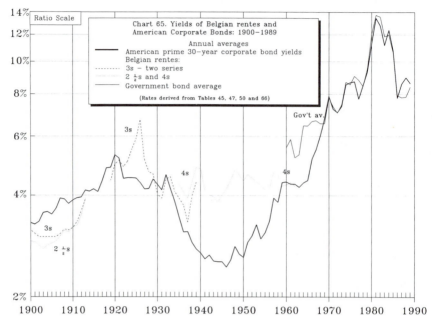

debt. However, unusual stability of bond yields and, indeed, unusual economic stability characterized Belgium in this second postwar period. This period of stability ended abruptly in 1964. Thereafter, yields rose sharply to 6.5%, stabilized there for several years, rose again in 1970 to about 7.50%, stabilized for three years, and then rose to an annual average of 8.68% in 1974. Belgian yields remained in a range of 8.5 to 9.0% from 1975 to 1978, and then climbed rapidly to peaks over 13.50% in 1981 and 1982. Thus their highs were below the American highs and far below the English and French highs. Yields then declined to around 8% in the later 1980's.

The comparison with American corporate bond yields in Chart 65 brings out the similarities and differences in the trends of Belgian yields in the twentieth century. Like most European yields, the Belgian yields started the century below the American yields and rose faster than the American yields. The crisis of high yields did not occur in Belgium in 1920, but, as in France, it occurred in 1925–1926. After 1926, Belgian yields fell to the American level or a little lower, whereas in France yields then fell far below the American level.

During the early 1930's, Belgian yields tended to fluctuate with American yields, but after 1937 Belgian yields rose far above American yields. In this they also followed the French pattern. After 1946, the difference from other trends became very striking. There was no great rise in the yield of the 4s from 1946 to 1960 such as there was in the yields of bonds in almost every other country studied. American yields rose and met the yield of the Belgian 4s in 1959. While other Belgian issues yielded more than the 4s, the uptrend in yields in the 1950's was unusually small. Thereafter, they rose steeply to 1981, almost exactly equaling the American yields, and then fell in tandem with American yields during the 1980's.

Short-Term Belgian Interest Rates.   In Table 67, Belgian short-term interest rates are represented by four series: (a) the official discount rate of the National Bank of Belgium; (b) the annual average and high and low of the free market rate of discount for commercial paper, 1900–1913, 1919–1940; (c) the annual average and high and low of call money, 1927–1989; and (d) the annual average and high and low of Treasury bills, 1937–1939, 1942–1989. These last were offered on tap by the Treasury at a fixed price; they were pegged at 1.31% from 1946 to 1956. These short rates are pictured in Chart 66 (see also Chart 63 for decennial averages).

Belgian short-term rates rose in the first two decades of the twentieth century. They reached their highs until the 1970's and 1980's along with French short rates in the crisis of 1925–1926, and not in 1920 as in America and Britain. In the 1930s Belgian short rates plunged below 1%, although Belgian bond yields stayed up. Short rates stayed down most of the time until 1946. Belgium even had a 1½% discount rate—a rate below the lowest British bank rate. After 1946 the call money and the bill rates remained very low, but the discount rates came up to 3% and 4% and stayed in that range most of the time until 1960. There was a sharp, brief rise to 4½% in 1957–1958, but no 6 or 7% crisis rate as in England.

In the 1960's short-term Belgian interest rates rose persistently but gradu-

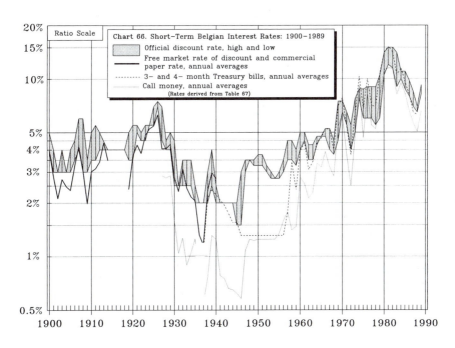

Chart 66. Short-Term Belgian Interest Rates: 1900–1989
Official discount rate, high and low
Free market rate of discount and commercial paper rate, annual averages
3– and 4– month Treasury bills, annual averages
Call money, annual averages
(Rates derived from Table 67)

TABLE 67
SHORT-TERM BELGIAN INTEREST RATES: TWENTIETH CENTURY

	Official Discount Rate, %			Free Market Rate of Discount, %			Call Money, %			4-Month Treasury Bills, %		
	Low	High	Annual Average	Low	High	Annual Average	Low	High	Annual Average	Low	High	
1900	4	5	3.94	3.62	4.75							
1901	3	4	2.81	2.50	3.50							
1902	3	3	2.12	2.12	2.12							
1903	3	4	2.72	2.50	3.12							
1904	3	3	2.47	2.25	2.75							
1905	3	4	2.36	2.12	2.75							
1906	3.5	4.5	3.24	2.97	3.62							
1907	4	6	4.17	3.56	4.62							
1908	3	6	3.04	1.93	5.19							
1909	3	3.5	1.98	1.87	2.12							
10-yr. av.	3.25		2.89									
1910	3.5	5	3.01	2.62	3.50							
1911	3.5	5.5	3.13	2.12	4.37							
1912	4	5	3.42	3.12	3.85							
1913			4.38	4.32	4.50							
1914	4	4	3.49									
1915	4	4	(4-yr.									
1916	4	4	av.)									
1917	4	4	Discount of Commercial Paper, %									
1918	4	4										
1919	3.5	5	2.39	2.00	2.88							
10-yr. av.	3.83 (9-yr. av.)											
1920	3.5	5.5	3.69	2.00	4.75							
1921	5	5.5	4.25	4.00	4.37							
1922	4.5	5	3.81	2.75	4.25							
1923	4.5	5.5	4.81	3.94	5.37							
1924	5.5	5.5	5.25	5.12	5.37							
1925	5.5	7	5.44	5.12	6.94							
1926	7	7.5	6.28	4.32	7.27							

TABLE 67 (*Continued*)

	Official Discount Rate, %			Discount of Commercial Papers			Call Money, %			4-Month Treasury Bills, %		
	Low	High	Annual Average	Low	High	Annual Average	Low	High	Annual Average	Low	High	
1927	4.5	7	4.05	3.79	4.25	2.85	1.68	4.02				
1928	4	4.5	4.06	3.87	4.40	2.78	1.71	3.64				
1929	4	5	4.30	3.96	4.94	2.85	2.11	3.48				
10-yr. av.	4.80		4.59			2.83 (3-yr. av.)						
1930	2.5	4.5	2.78	2.05	3.41	1.59	0.90	2.59				
1931	2.5	2.5	2.32	2.13	2.44	1.04	0.78	1.28				
1932	2.5	3.5	3.12	2.91	3.36	1.27	0.88	2.27				
1933	2.5	3.5	2.42	2.12	2.89	0.89	0.72	1.07				
1934	2.5	3.5	2.16	1.93	2.38	1.05	0.75	2.09				
1935	2	2.5	2.06	1.88	2.38	1.25	0.50	2.24				
1936	2	2	1.32	1.00	1.52	n.a.	n.a.	n.a.				
1937	2	2	1.16	1.00	1.78	0.55	0.50	0.78	1.07	0.74	1.89	
1938	2	3	2.35	1.50	3.26	0.76	0.50	1.45	2.12	1.41	2.85	
1939	2.5	4	2.96	1.98	4.28	1.31	0.50	2.20	2.38	1.56	2.75	
10-yr. av.	2.30		2.27			1.08 (9-yr. av.)			1.86 (3-yr. av.)			
1940	2	2.5	2.75	2.68	2.94	1.25	1.00	1.50				
1941	2	2				0.78	0.75	1.00				
1942	2	2				0.75	0.75	0.75	1.94	1.94	1.94	
1943	2	2				0.66	0.63	0.75	1.75	1.63	1.94	
1944	2	2				0.65	0.63	0.89	1.55	1.38	1.63	
1945	1.5	2				0.62	0.50	1.00	1.56	1.56	1.56	
1946	1.5	3				0.58	0.50	1.00	1.31	1.31	1.31	
1947	3	3.5				1.08	1.00	1.25	1.31	1.31	1.31	
1948	3.5	3.5				1.25	1.25	1.25	1.31	1.31	1.31	
1949	3.25	3.5				1.23	1.11	1.25	1.31	1.31	1.31	
	2.2											
10-yr. av.	2.28					0.89			1.51 (8-yr. av.)			

TABLE 67 (*Continued*)

	Official Discount Rate, %			Discount of Commercial Papers			Call Money, %			4-Month Treasury Bills, %		
	Low	High	Annual Average	Low	High	Annual Average	Low	High	Annual Average	Low	High
1950	3.25	3.75				1.25	1.25	1.25	1.31	1.31	1.31
1951	3.25	3.75				1.25	1.25	1.25	1.31	1.31	1.31
1952	3	3.25				1.25	1.25	1.25	1.31	1.31	1.31
1953	2.75	3				1.25	1.25	1.25	1.31	1.31	1.31
1954	2.75	2.75				1.25	1.25	1.25	1.31	1.31	1.31
1955	2.75	3				1.35	1.25	1.50	1.31	1.31	1.31
1956	3	3.5				1.58	1.46	1.70	1.31	1.31	1.31
1957	3.5	4.5				1.78	1.70	2.25	1.76	1.31	4.25
1958	3.5	4.5				1.41	1.11	2.08	3.40	2.50	4.25
1959	3.25	4				1.47	1.00	1.03	2.38	2.25	3.50
10-yr. av.	3.10					1.38			1.67		

										3-Month Treasury Bills, %		
1960	4	5				2.79	2.07	3.80	3.92	3.50	4.50
1961	4.5	5				2.56	2.25	2.90	4.38	4.00	4.50
1962	3.5	4.25				2.13	1.48	2.73	3.09	2.90	3.60
1963	3.5	4.25				2.29	1.76	2.87	3.42	3.00	4.10
1964	4.25	4.75				3.35	2.83	3.95	4.43	4.20	4.75
1965	4.75	4.75				3.19	2.23	3.98	4.62	4.50	4.80
1966	4.75	5.25				3.89	3.16	4.57	5.25	4.75	5.85
1967	4	5.25				3.19	2.53	3.71	5.18	4.40	5.75
1968	3.75	4.5				2.84	2.45	3.36	3.96	3.75	4.75
1969	4.5	7.5				5.40	3.16	7.46	7.08	5.40	8.50
10-yr. av.	4.15					3.16			4.53		
1970	6.5	7.5				6.26	5.30	6.74	7.80	6.95	8.50
1971	5.5	6.5				3.72	1.65	4.84	5.40	4.60	6.80
1972	4	5.5				2.51	1.69	3.70	3.75	3.45	4.80
1973	5	7.75				4.80	2.96	8.52	6.38	4.80	7.65
1974	7.75	8.75				9.24	7.94	10.34	10.30	7.65	11.75
1975	6	8.75				4.68	3.88	6.47	6.80	6.05	10.05
1976	6	9				8.31	3.99	15.52	10.00	6.05	13.40
1977	6	9				5.49	3.42	7.16	7.05	6.05	8.45

TABLE 67 (*Continued*)

	Official Discount Rate, %		Discount of Commercial Papers			Call Money, %			3-Month Treasury Bills, %		
	Low	High	Annual Average	Low	High	Annual Average	Low	High	Annual Average	Low	High
1978	5.5	9				5.23	3.63	7.56	7.05	5.60	9.15
1979	6	10.5				7.97	4.81	11.32	10.75	7.90	14.35
10-yr. av.	5.83					5.82			7.53		
1980	10.5	14				11.22	9.50	14.83	14.08	12.25	17.38
1981	12	15				11.47	8.98	16.44	15.21	12.37	17.19
1982	11.5	15				11.44	9.29	13.05	14.10	12.25	15.38
1983	9	14				8.18	5.85	11.28	10.56	9.25	13.63
1984	10	11				9.47	7.17	11.13	11.41	10.75	12.25
1985	8.75	11				8.27	6.60	9.45	9.59	8.68	10.75
1986	8	9.75				6.64	5.09	8.67	8.11	7.35	9.75
1987	7	8.5				5.67	4.61	6.90	6.51	6.65	7.75
1988	6.5	7				5.04	4.15	6.30	6.29	6.10	6.86
1989	8.25	10.25				7.02	5.37	8.55	8.68	7.58	10.04
10-yr. av.	9.15					8.44			10.45		

SOURCES

See sources for Table 66.

Unpublished statistics collected by the Studiedienst of the Krediet Bank of Belgium.

OECD, *Financial Statistics Monthly.*

ally until 1969, when the discount rate rose to 7½%. In the early 1970's rates declined sharply. The crisis came suddenly in 1973 and peaked in 1974, with bills yielding as high as 11¾% at one time. Except for brief episodes, short-term rates remained in a 5–10% range during the later 1970's, before climbing to unprecedented levels in the early 1980's. As in other countries, such as the United States, rates in Belgium declined considerably in the remainder of the 1980's, but remained at levels that would have been considered high at any time before 1970.

GERMANY

In the twentieth century, Germany made financial as well as political history. The story of the great inflation after World War I is well known; less well known is the fact that the Berlin Stock Exchange once quoted a market rate of interest on call loans in excess of 10,000% per annum.

In the nineteenth century, Germany had effectively adopted the Dutch-English system of mobilizing the savings of the people through issues of long-term bonds. The German people first bought the bonds of Prussia, Bavaria, Saxony, and a host of principalities, and when the unification came, they bought Imperial German bonds and the bonds of mortgage banks. During the last three decades of the nineteenth century and the first of the twentieth century, these savings financed an economic and military expansion almost without precedent.

Chart 67 shows long and short decennial averages in the nineteenth and twentieth centuries, and Chart 68 shows annual averages for long bond yields in these centuries. During 1870–1910, the decades of dynamic expansion, German government bond yields were actually declining. German yields did not decline as far as did British, Dutch, and French yields but were low enough to suggest that the savings of the people were keeping up with the financing requirements of a fast-growing economy. Germany was enjoying the benefits of that mighty weapon, a smooth annual accrual of new savings seeking investment in interest-bearing securities. In the years before 1914, German bond yields were similar to yields in the United States, another large and fast-growing nation during the period 1870–1914.

The two unsuccessful world wars of the twentieth century transformed Germany. After each war the German currency became all but worthless.

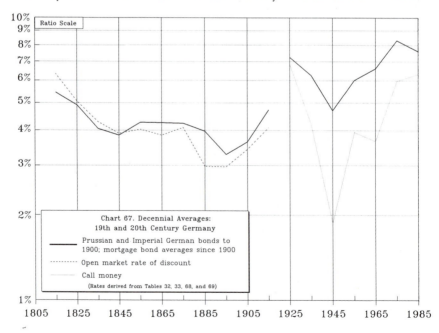

Chart 67. Decennial Averages:
19th and 20th Century Germany

——— Prussian and Imperial German bonds to 1900; mortgage bond averages since 1900

·········· Open market rate of discount

——— Call money

(Rates derived from Tables 32, 33, 68, and 69)

After World War II, the country was divided, heavily damaged, and occupied. It is not surprising, therefore, that the history of German interest rates since 1914 has at times been chaotic. All German interest rate series were frequently interrupted, and and there were periods for which quotations are mere formalities.

Since the 1960's, however, West Germany developed a powerful economy and enjoyed great prosperity. Furthermore, West Germany's international economic position was at times the strongest in the free world. Large surpluses in its international accounts contrasted with deficits in the United States, Britain, and elsewhere. West Germany experienced less inflation than did most other large economies in recent decades and became known as a paragon of monetary and price stability. This was often thought to reflect the German people's negative memories of the disasters earlier in the century. One result of the relatively conservative financial policies of the new Germany was that West German interest rates, particularly long-term rates, were above those in the United States for much of the postwar era. Since the mid-1970's, however, West German yields have generally been lower than American yields. The trend of West German interest rates in the second half of this century has therefore differed from that of most other Western nations. West German long-term rates were higher in the 1950's, rose less during the inflation-plagued 1960's and 1970's, and became lower than rates in nations such as the United States in the late 1970's and 1980's. West German short-term rates, while fluctuating from year to year, exhibit a generally flat long-term trend from the late 1940's to the late 1980's, in contrast to the sharply rising trend in many other countries during these four decades.

Long-Term German Interest Rates. To provide some picture of the long-term market rates of interest in Germany, several series are presented in Table 68. These are (a) yields of Imperial German 3s until 1908; (b) a computed average of high-grade bond yields from 1900 through 1921, 1924 through 1943, and 1948 through 1989; (c) an average of yields on long-term government loans from 1927 through 1944 and 1956 through 1989. Nominal rates on bonds on which the averages are based ranged widely, and call and redemption privileges were complex and various. The yields early in the century were no doubt comparable to the nineteenth-century yields. The yields after 1920 were hardly comparable from decade to decade, at least until the 1960's.

German yields in the twentieth century formed a pattern very different from the pattern in most other nations studied. They rose to four great crisis peaks in 1924, 1932, 1974, and 1981, each above the 10% level for long government bonds (see Chart 68). Between the peaks, German yields, of course, came down sharply, but they did not drop to the low levels that prevailed in most other countries until the late 1970's and 1980's, when West German bonds often were lower than elsewhere. Thus the low yields in the

TABLE 68

PRICES AND YIELDS OF LONG-TERM GERMAN GOVERNMENT SECURITIES: TWENTIETH CENTURY

Year	Imperial German 3s Annual Average		Annual Averages, %		Year	Imperial German 3s Annual Average		Annual Averages, %	
	Price	Yield, %	High-Grade Bond Yields	Government Loans		Price	Yield, %	High-Grade Bond Yields	Government Loans
1900	86¾	3.46	3.68		1925			8.45	
1901	89¼	3.36	3.65		1926			6.71	
1902	92¼	3.25	3.52		1927			5.93	6.97
1903	91½	3.28	3.53		1928			6.89	7.00
1904	90⅛	3.33	3.57		1929			7.27	7.01
1905	90⅛	3.33	3.57						
1906	87¾	3.42	3.63		10-yr. av.			7.25	6.99
1907	84¼	3.56	3.75					(8-yr. av.)	(3-yr. av.)
1908	83⅜	3.60	3.80						
1909			3.70		1930			7.24	7.21
					1931			7.33	12.47
10-yr. av.			3.64		1932			10.19	8.17
					1933			7.81	6.62
1910			3.76		1934			6.77	5.20
1911			3.79		1935			4.78	4.96
1912			3.91		1936			4.77	4.94
1913			4.09		1937			4.60	4.88
1914			5.06		1938			4.51	4.61
1915			5.06		1939			4.56	4.61
1916			5.10						
1917			5.11		10-yr. av.			6.26	6.37
1918			5.11						
1919			6.20		1940			4.49	3.92
					1941			4.40	3.69
10-yr. av.			4.72		1942			4.35	3.57
					1943			4.35	3.56
1920			6.34		1944				3.56
1921			6.45		1945				
1922					1946				
1923					1947				
1924			9.97		1948			5.39	

TABLE 68 (Continued)

Year	Imperial German 3s Annual Average		Annual Averages, %		Year	Imperial German 3s Annual Average		Annual Averages, %	
	Price	Yield, %	High-Grade Bond Yields	Government Loans		Price	Yield, %	High-Grade Bond Yields	Government Loans
1949			5.22		1969			7.02	6.84
10-yr. av.			4.70 (6-yr. av.)	3.66 (5-yr. av.)	10-yr. av.			6.61	6.59
					1970			8.14	8.33
					1971			8.28	7.99
1950			5.78		1972			8.36	7.87
1951			6.33		1973			9.59	9.33
1952			5.28		1974			10.73	10.38
1953			5.67		1975			9.00	8.48
1954					1976			8.20	7.80
1955					1977			6.60	6.20
1956			6.23	6.90	1978			6.40	5.80
1957			6.64	7.50	1979			7.70	7.40
1958			6.28	6.80					
1959			5.86	5.77	10-yr. av.			8.30	7.96
10-yr.av.			6.01 (8-yr. av.)	6.74 (4-yr. av.)	1980			8.70	8.50
					1981			10.60	10.40
					1982			9.10	9.00
					1983			8.00	7.90
1960			6.50	6.40	1984			7.80	7.80
1961			6.00	5.90	1985			7.00	6.90
1962			6.03	5.90	1986			6.10	5.90
1963			6.12	6.05	1987			5.90	5.80
1964			6.17	6.23	1988			6.10	6.10
1965			6.74	7.04	1989			7.00	6.80
1966			7.64	8.12					
1967			7.01	6.96	10-yr. av.			7.63	7.51
1968			6.84	6.45					

SOURCES

Dr. Herman Albert, *Geschichtliche Entwickelung des Zinsfusses in Deutschland, 1895–1908* (Leipzig: 1910), p. 36.

Averages 1910–1913, 1924–1930, 1926–1934, compiled by the National Bureau of Economic Research from various published sources.

Deutsche Bundesbank publications.

IMF, *International Financial Statistics*.

OECD, *Financial Statistics Monthly*.

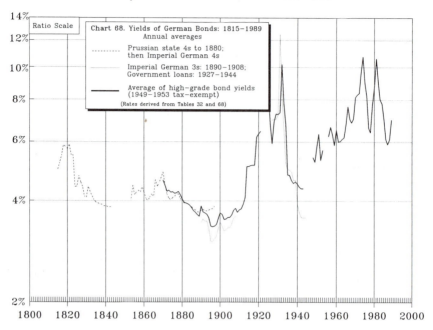

Chart 68. Yields of German Bonds: 1815–1989
Annual averages

.... Prussian state 4s to 1880; then Imperial German 4s

Imperial German 3s: 1890–1908; Government loans: 1927–1944

Average of high-grade bond yields (1949–1953 tax-exempt)

(Rates derived from Tables 32 and 68)

late 1930's and during World War II did not average below 3½%, and after World War II they were rarely below 6%. But in the 1980's, West German long yields averaged well *below* comparable American corporate and government yields.

Chart 69, which compares German yields with American yields, shows that, despite important gaps, German yields in the twentieth century were usually rising when American yields were rising and falling when American yields were falling, but with important exceptions. From 1900 to 1920, German yields rose with all others. German government bond yields started the century slightly above the American corporate bond yields. They rose with the American yields in the first decade and much faster in the second decade. A sharp rise in 1912 and 1913 is noticeable. They continued to rise from 1920 to 1925 during the period of great inflation. This was very different from the American, English, and Dutch declining trend during these inflationary years. In Germany, however, the inflation was much more extreme, and the rise in yields was larger. Unfortunately, no bond yields at all were computed by the sources quoted for the inflation years of 1922 and 1923, no doubt because of the chaotic state of the market and the currency. A 9.97% average and a high of 20% is computed for 1924, the first year of stabilization.

After a dip in 1924, German bond yields again rose rapidly. Only in Germany did the crisis of 1930–1932 bring extremely high yields. These were in the range of 10–12%, equal to or above those of 1924 but perhaps below the unreported inflation yields of 1923.

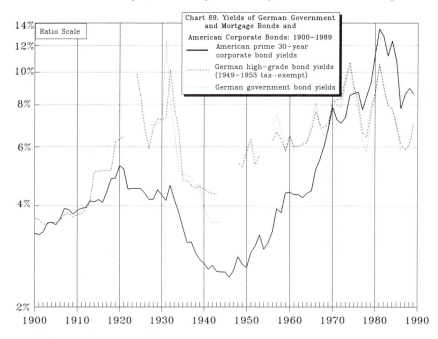

Chart 69. Yields of German Government and Mortgage Bonds and American Corporate Bonds: 1900–1989

After 1932, German yields came down sharply, just as did all other yields. Hitler's dictatorship enforced moderate, but not really low, interest rates. Vast new issues of government bonds, usually at 4½%, were sold to the people to finance roads, buildings, and weapons. During World War II, yields declined further, but remained far above the 2½% American level and the 3% English level.

After World War II, West German yields rose with all other yields. Following a statistical gap, they emerged in 1950 at around 6% and fluctuated between 5.50% and 6.50% during the 1950's. A wide variety of nominal rates, redemption terms, payment and tax provisions makes detailed yield quotations of little significance in this decade. Changes in tax status and the laws governing or controlling the market prevent comparison even from one year to the next. There is no doubt, however, that West German yields in the 1950's were very high in comparison with yields in other Western nations.

In 1950, West German prime long yields were 355 basis points higher than similar yields in the United States. By 1960 the differential had declined to 175 basis points. By 1970 the differential had vanished, and in the late 1970's and 1980's it became negative. Thus while West German yields were rising throughout the postwar years to 1981, as were all yields elsewhere, the West German rise was much less than in other countries because the yields started at a very high level.

The Inflation. The German inflation of 1923 has become the classic model of inflation in a modern industrial nation. As might be expected, it provides the historian of interest rates with a fine collection of unusual quotations. These deserve a few paragraphs of detailed description. (536)

In early 1922, the official discount rate of the Reichsbank was 5%. This had been the wartime rate. The inflation, which had proceeded for years in gradual form, then took hold, and the discount rate was successively raised to 7%, 8%, and 10%. This last was a traditional crisis rate used at times by the Bank of England and seen before in Germany only in the early nineteenth century. The high discount rate did not prove an effective deterrent to inflation. In January 1923, the official discount rate was raised to 12%, and in April, to 18%. At these rates, the Reichsbank made credit freely available, and the inflation proceeded unchecked. In August 1923, the Reichsbank announced a new form of discount: loans at "constant value." They were repayable at not less than four-fifths of the sterling exchange value of the sum lent. The discount rate of the Reichsbank for bills without this "constant value" clause was raised to 30% and then to 90%. It was put at 10% for bills with the "constant value" clause. The inflation continued.

At the height of the inflation in October 1923, the special paper used for printing the notes of the Reichsbank was being made in thirty paper mills. It was not sufficient. Between January and June of 1923, the circulation rose 800%, the cost of living rose 600%, and the value of the dollar expressed in marks rose from 3644 to 22,301. Between July and October of 1923, the currency circulation increased by 300,000%.

In 1922 the open market rate of discount in Berlin rose from 3¾% to 10½%. Our best indication of the open market rate in 1923 is the 10–90% level of the official mark discount rate, which was almost always a penalty rate above the open market rate. In September and October, however, daily money rates reached annualized levels of 1606% and 1825%. (537) At the peak of the inflation in November of 1923, call money on the Berlin Stock Exchange rose to a rate as high as 30% a day for loans not protected against mark depreciation. This was the annual rate of 10,950%.

In November and December of 1923, the mark was stabilized. Confidence, however, was not immediately restored. Call money was quoted in December at 3–5% per day, or 1095–1825% annual rate, for loans repayable in the new paper marks and the much lower rates of 1–1½% per month, or 12–18% annual rate, for loans guaranteed against the risk of currency depreciation. Even in 1914, when the mark was stable, loans payable in the new marks were quoted as high as 72% per annum, while loans payable in foreign currencies were at 15–16%. By October 1924, however, mark loans were down to 13% per annum, and foreign currency loans were down to 7.2% per annum.

During the period of preliminary stabilization in 1924, high-grade mortgage bonds, now with a "stable value" clause, were quoted to yield as high as 15–20%. The average of high-grade long bond yields for the year 1924 is computed at 9.97%.

By 1926 the discount rate had finally been brought down to 6%. Call money came down from 9.41% in October of 1925 to 5.64% in April of 1926. The range of mortgage bond yields came down from 8.02–9.64% in 1925 to 6.08–8.13% in April of 1926. The expenses of a mortgage loan (interest plus commissions and other expenses) came down from 15% of the nominal capital in 1925 to 10% in 1926.

The decline in interest rates of 1925–1927 did not last. A political and economic crisis was brewing. Efforts to restore normal interest rates to capital markets were not successful. Mortgage bonds at 7% had little appeal. Rates rose sharply in 1928 and 1929. By 1931, it was calculated that mortgage loans cost an average of 9.50%. Even in the absence of inflation, the discount rate of the Reichsbank rose to 15% in 1931, and the open market of discount rose to 10%.

Short-Term German Interest Rates.   Short-term German interest rates are presented in Table 69 in three series: (a) the official discount rate of the central bank in terms of annual average and range, 1900 through 1989; (b) the open market rate of discount in Berlin in terms of annual average and highs and lows of monthly averages, 1900 through 1959; and (c) call money in terms of annual average, 1925 through 1944, and 1950 through 1989, with some exceptionally high spot rates in 1923 and 1924. Chart 70 pictures these short-term rates.

The chart suggests the following generalizations: German short-term rates

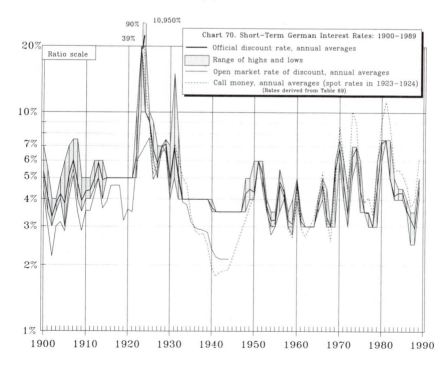

TABLE 69
SHORT-TERM GERMAN INTEREST RATES: TWENTIETH CENTURY

Year	Official Discount Rate, %			Open Market Rate of Discount, %			Call Money, %
	Annual Average	Annual Low	Annual High	Annual Average	Annual Low	Annual High	Annual Average
1900	5.33	5	7	4.41	3.63	5.63	
1901	4.10	3.5	5.5	3.06	2.13	4.13	
1902	3.32	3	4	2.19	1.5	3.63	
1903	3.84	3.5	4	3.01	1.89	3.89	
1904	4.22	4	5	3.14	2.25	4.25	
1905	3.82	3	6	2.85	1.75	5.38	
1906	5.15	4.5	7	4.04	3.13	6	
1907	6.03	5.5	7.5	5.12	4	7.38	
1908	4.76	4	7.5	3.52	2.25	6	
1909	3.93	3.5	5	2.86	1.75	4.63	
10-yr. av.	4.45			3.42			
1910	4.35	4	5	3.54	2.75	4.75	
1911	4.40	4	5	3.54	2.25	5	
1912	4.95	4.5	6	4.22	3	6	
1913	5.88	5	6	4.98	4.06	6	
1914	4.89	4	6	3.63	2	4	
1915	5.00	5	5	3.89	3.25	4.5	
1916	5.00	5	5	4.62	5.38	5.5	
1917	5.00	5	5	4.63	4.63	4.63	
1918	5.00	5	5	4.63	4.63	4.63	
1919	5.00	5	5	3.19	4.63	4.63	
10-yr. av.	4.95			4.09			
1920	5.00	5	5	3.59	3.25	4.25	
1921	5.00	5	5	3.49	3	4.5	
1922	6.31	5	10	5.94	3.75	10.5	
1923	38.68	10	90				10,950
1924	10.00	10	10				13 to 72
1925	9.15	9	10	7.62	6.75	8.31	8.96
1926	6.74	6	9	4.92	4.13	6.38	5.22
1927	5.82	5	7	5.49	4	7	5.88
1928	7.00	7	7	6.53	5.89	6.89	6.65
1929	7.11	6.5	7.5	6.87	5.5	7.5	7.50
10-yr. av.	10.08			6.29 (5-yr. av.)			6.84 (5-yr. av.)
1930	4.93	4	7	4.43	3.13	6.89	4.78
1931	6.91	5	15	6.78	4.63	10	7.23
1932	5.21	4	8	4.95	3.89	7	6.06

TABLE 69 (*Continued*)

Year	Official Discount Rate, %			Open Market Rate of Discount, %			Call Money, %
	Annual Average	Annual Low	Annual High	Annual Average	Annual Low	Annual High	Annual Average
1933	4.00	4	4	3.88	3.89	3.89	5.03
1934	4.00	4	4	3.77	3.5	3.89	4.64
1935	4.00	4	4	3.15	3	3.75	3.36
1936	4.00	4	4	2.96	2.89	3	2.87
1937	4.00	4	4	2.91	2.89	3	2.76
1938	4.00	4	4	2.88	2.89	2.89	2.79
1939	4.00	4	4	2.82	2.75	2.89	2.47
10-yr. av.	4.51			3.85			4.20
1940	3.67	3.5	4	2.36			1.95
1941	3.50	3.5	3.5	2.18			1.78
1942	3.50	3.5	3.5	2.13			1.85
1943	3.50	3.5	3.5	2.13			1.88
1944	3.50	3.5	3.5	2.13			1.91
1945	3.50	3.5	3.5				
1946	3.50	3.5	3.5				
1947	3.50	3.5	3.5				
1948	4.25	3.5	5				
1949	4.46	4	5				
10-yr. av.	3.69			2.19 (5-yr. av.)			1.87 (5-yr. av.)
1950	4.33	4	6				4.20
1951	6.00	6	6				6.02
1952	5.25	4.5	6	4.88	4.00	5.89	5.17
1953	3.71	3.5	4	3.63	3.00	4.25	3.58
1954	3.21	3	3.5	2.75	2.38	3.13	2.94
1955	3.21	3	3.5	3.00	2.38	3.63	3.13
1956	4.83	3.5	5.5	4.63	3.63	5.63	4.70
1957	4.33	4	4.5	4.13	3.38	4.75	4.08
1958	3.21	3	3.5	3.00	2.50	3.63	2.93
1959	3.08	2.75	4	3.00	2.13	3.89	2.67
10-yr. av.	4.12			3.63 (8-yr. av.)			3.94
1960	4.83	4	5				4.54
1961	3.17	3	3.5				2.96
1962	3.00	3	3				2.69
1963	3.00	3	3				2.97
1964	3.00	3	3				3.29
1965	3.71	3.5	4				4.11

TABLE 69 (*Continued*)

Year	Official Discount Rate, %			Open Market Rate of Discount, %			Call Money, %
	Annual Average	Annual Low	Annual High	Annual Average	Annual Low	Annual High	Annual Average
1966	4.67	4	5				5.34
1967	3.33	3	4.5				3.35
1968	3.00	3	3				2.58
1969	5.42	3	6				4.81
10-yr. av.	3.71						3.66
1970	6.87	6	7.5				8.65
1971	4.75	4	6				6.10
1972	3.42	3	4.5				4.30
1973	6.25	5	7				10.18
1974	6.88	6	7				8.86
1975	4.42	3.5	6				4.40
1976	3.50	3.5	3.5				3.90
1977	3.46	3	3.5				4.10
1978	3.00	3	3				3.40
1979	4.50	3	6				5.90
10-yr. av.	4.71						5.98
1980	7.25	6	7.5				9.10
1981	7.50	7.5	7.5				11.30
1982	5.00	5	7.5				8.70
1983	4.17	4	5				5.40
1984	4.29	4	4.5				5.50
1985	4.29	4	4.5				5.20
1986	3.58	3.5	4				4.60
1987	3.25	2.5	3.5				3.70
1988	2.96	2.5	3.5				4.00
1989	4.92	4	6				6.59
10-yr. av.	4.72						6.41

SOURCES

Arthur Spiethoff, *Die Wirtschaflichen Wechsellagen* (Zurich: 1955).

Federal Reserve, *Banking and Monetary Statistics* (1976), *Annual Statistical Digest*, and *Federal Reserve Bulletin*.

Open market rate of discount, 1900–1939, compiled by the National Bureau of Economic Research from various published sources.

IMF, *International Financial Statistics*.

Bank Deutscher Lander, *Statistical Manual*.

Constantine Bresciani-Turroni, *The Economics of Inflation* (New York: Barnes & Noble, 1973).

Morgan Guaranty Trust Company, *World Financial Markets*.

OECD, *Financial Statistics Monthly*.

were high in the first decade. The discount rate rose above 7% twice, and the open market rate got up to an annual average of 5%. World War I did not bring a rise in short-term interest rates; instead, they were stabilized at 5% or less. In 1920 there was no crisis marked by high rates, such as occurred in England and America; the crisis with its extraordinarily high rates came a few years later. After the inflation, short rates came down briefly in 1927, but quickly rose again and were very high in the early 1930's. Short-term rates came down in the 1930's but remained well above American and English short rates. Typically, the discount rate was 4%. Immediately after World War II, short rates rose to 5 or 6%. These rates, however, did not approach the inflation rates of the 1920's in spite of the new devaluation of the mark and the division and destruction of the country. During the 1950's, West German short rates declined irregularly at a time when short rates were rising in America and England. At times in the late 1950s, West German short-term interest rates actually reached levels below American short-term interest rates, although West German bond yields were far above American bond yields.

After 1960, the West German government and Bundesbank, the central bank, adopted a very dynamic interest-rate policy to cope with twin and conflicting objectives: to prevent a rapid rise in the international value of the mark and to control the rate of inflation. The official discount rate was moved frequently and substantially up and down: 3% low, 7½% high. Short-term rates averaged below 4% in the 1960's, about 6% in the 1970's, and somewhat over 6% in the 1980's. These West German rates were usually lower and more stable from year to year than short rates in most other nations.

German bond yields seem to have averaged above the German short rates quoted almost all the time since the 1850's. An exception probably was the inflation years of 1922–1923, when there were spectacular short rates. The differential widened in the 1930's and 1940's. It narrowed somewhat in the 1950's and 1960's but remained very wide, at about 300 basis points. In the 1970's and 1980's the differential narrowed further as short rates increased more than long rates did. The German money market recovered from the effects of two disastrous wars and two inflations more rapidly than did the German investment market for long-term bonds. In the 1970's and 1980's, West Germany's relative financial stability completed the recovery of the long-term market.

ITALY

Modern Italian interest-rate history is of more than ordinary interest because of the leading financial role Italian bankers played during the Middle Ages and because Italy has recently achieved a new importance in world financial markets. After the ruin of the Italian bankers in the sixteenth and seventeenth centuries, few Italian interest rates were reported. During long centuries there was no Italian nation. The new Kingdom of Italy, proclaimed in 1861 and firmly established in the 1870's, organized its financial affairs in the conventional European manner. After some decades of deficits and financial difficulties, the reforms of 1893–1896 balanced the budget, established the Bank of Italy, and reorganized the credit and monetary structure.

Table 70 starts with a few Italian government bond yields before 1924, based on high and low points in the market for 5% government bonds. The yields stood at 9.05% in 1873, fell to 5.40% in 1881, rose to 5.88% in 1883, declined to 5% in 1886, and rose again to 7.55% in 1894 at a time of crisis and reforms. These were far above the bond yields then prevailing in European and American financial centers. After 1894, however, Italian yields came down steadily: 4.90% in 1902, 4.80% in 1905, and 3.86% in 1912, based on a new issue of government 3½s. This was close to the range of government bond yields elsewhere. The yield spread of Italian government bond yields above British consol yields at these dates was as follows:

Year	Basis Points	Year	Basis Points
1873	+578	1894	+496
1881	+249	1902	+233
1883	+286	1905	+194
1886	+207	1912	+ 70

Italian yields rose from 1881 to 1894, when other European yields were falling to all-time lows. They fell sharply from 1894 to 1912, when other European yields were rising. Domestic events evidently had greater influence than did foreign interest-rate trends. After 1912, the trend of bond yields in Italy tended to conform to the general Western pattern.

In the twentieth century, Italy suffered from two great wars and postwar inflations. It was a member of the winning coalition in one war and of the losing coalition in the next, but win or lose, both wars were followed by currency debasement and high interest rates. The Italian lira lost more than 99% of its dollar value in the course of the twentieth century to 1960, about the same as the loss sustained by the French franc. Italian bond yields, however, began the twentieth century far above French bond yields and ended the 1950's not very far from French bond yields.

Table 70 provides annual Italian interest rates from 1924. It includes the official discount rate, 1924–1989; a private discount rate, 1924–1939; the rate on Treasury bills, 1952–1971 and 1974–1989; and yields on a series of 5% government bonds from 1937 through 1940 and 1950 through 1969, a series of 3½% government bonds from 1924 through 1953, and an average of relatively long-term government bonds from 1970 through 1989. The dis-

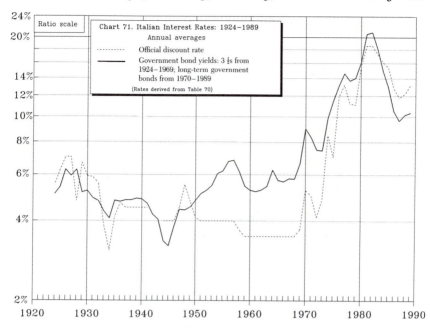

Chart 71. Italian Interest Rates: 1924–1989
Annual averages

- - - - - - - Official discount rate
——————— Government bond yields: 3 ½s from
1924–1969; long-term government
bonds from 1970–1989
(Rates derived from Table 70)

count rate and government bond yields are portrayed in Chart 71.

The table and chart show a swift rise of yields in 1925 and 1926, when the inflation was finally checked and the currency was stabilized. Thereafter, yields declined to 1934, and then rose. During World War II, yields declined to 3.22%, a very low rate for Italy and not far above the wartime 3% of England. High yields returned rapidly after 1945. Bond yields were up to 5.73% (for 5s) in 1950 and 6.81% by 1957. They had come down to 5.24% by 1960. Italian government bond yields, until 1960, remained well above English and American yields as illustrated by the decennial averages in the table below; but in 1959–1961 they declined to levels below the rising

DECENNIAL AVERAGES OF GOVERNMENT BOND YIELDS

Years Averaged	Italy, %	England, %	United States, %
1920–1929	5.68 (6 yr.)	4.63	4.09
1930–1939	4.74	3.54	3.34
1940–1949	4.16	3.06	2.31
1950–1959	6.12	4.31	2.99
1960	5.24	5.40	4.01
1960–1969	5.70	6.53	4.51
1970–1979	10.91	11.77	6.87
1980–1989	14.42	10.42	10.40

TABLE 70
Italian Interest Rates: Annual Averages, Late Nineteenth and Twentieth Centuries

Year	Official Discount Rate, %	Private Discount Rate, %	Government Bond Yields, %	
			$3\frac{1}{2}$s	5s
1873				9.05
1881				5.40
1883				5.88
1886				5.00
1894				7.55
1902				4.90
1905				4.80
1912			3.86	
1924	5.50	5.37	5.07	
1925	6.25	7.40	5.38	
1926	7.00	8.45	6.28	
1927	7.00	7.72	5.94	
1928	4.77	5.46	6.27	
1929	6.66	6.86	5.14	
6-yr. av.	6.20	6.88	5.68	
1930	5.93	5.93	5.21	
1931	5.88	5.91	4.90	
1932	5.56	5.80	4.77	
1933	3.85	3.87	4.35	
1934	3.10	3.10	4.09	
1935	4.16	4.17	4.79	
1936	4.69	4.70	4.74	
1937	4.50	4.80	4.81	5.46
1938	4.50	5.00	4.81	5.41
1939	4.50	5.00	4.88	5.49
10-yr. av.	4.67	4.83	4.74	5.45 (3-yr. av.)
1940	4.50		4.85	5.51
1941	4.50		4.67	
1942			4.24	
1943			4.06	
1944	4.00		3.36	
1945	4.00		3.22	
1946	4.00		3.81	

TABLE 70 (*Continued*)

Year	Official Discount Rate, %	Treasury Bills, %	Government Bond Yields, %	
			$3\frac{1}{2}$s	5s
1947	4.50		4.43	
1948	5.50		4.40	
1949	4.75		4.52	
10-yr. av.	4.47 (8-yr. av.)		4.16	
1950	4.12		4.79	5.73
1951	4.00		5.08	6.11
1952	4.00	2.75	5.23	5.90
1953	4.00	2.75	5.46	6.06
1954	4.00	2.75		6.06
1955	4.00	2.75		6.20
1956	4.00	2.75		6.74
1957	4.00	2.75		6.81
1958	3.70	2.45		6.16
1959	3.50	2.25		5.43
10-yr. av.	3.93	2.65 (8-yr. av.)	5.14 (4-yr. av.)	6.12
1960	3.50	3.63		5.24
1961	3.50	3.63		5.18
1962	3.50	3.60		5.26
1963	3.50	3.59		5.43
1964	3.50	3.63		6.26
1965	3.50	3.63		5.72
1966	3.50	3.58		5.65
1967	3.50	3.58		5.81
1968	3.50	3.56		5.79
1969	3.71	3.99		6.64
10-yr. av.	3.52	3.64		5.70
			Long-Term Government Bonds	
1970	5.25	6.78	9.01	
1971	5.00	6.21	8.34	
1972	4.13		7.47	
1973	4.83		7.42	

TABLE 70 (*Continued*)

Year	Official Discount Rate, %	Treasury Bills, %	Long-Term Government Bonds
1974	8.50	13.50	9.87
1975	7.00	10.14	11.50
1976	11.90	10.51	13.08
1977	13.20	13.15	14.62
1978	11.20	11.44	13.70
1979	11.10	13.53	14.05
10-yr. av.	8.21	10.66 (8-yr. av.)	10.91
1980	15.50	15.94	16.11
1981	18.60	19.63	20.58
1982	18.60	19.35	20.90
1983	17.30	17.81	18.02
1984	16.10	15.33	14.95
1985	15.40	13.85	13.00
1986	12.83	11.55	10.52
1987	11.79	10.73	9.65
1988	12.21	11.15	10.16
1989	13.33	12.30	11.61
10-yr. av.	15.17	14.76	14.55

SOURCES

W. L. Raymond, *American and Foreign Investment Bonds* (Boston: Houghton-Mifflin, 1916), p. 77, for 1873–1912.

Federal Reserve, *Banking and Monetary Statistics* (1943, 1976), *Annual Statistical Digest*, and *Federal Reserve Bulletin*.

League of Nations, *Statistical Year Book, 1939–40*, pp. 220, 221.

IMF, *International Financial Statistics*.

Eurostat Review.

Morgan Guaranty Trust Company, *World Financial Markets*.

OECD, *Financial Statistics Monthly*.

English yields. In the 1970's, the Italian yields peaked below the British yields but remained well above yields in the United States. During the 1980's, Italian inflation remained at the double-digit levels of 1965–1980, whereas inflation was reduced sharply in Britain and somewhat in the United States. As a result, Italian yields rose absolutely and relatively.

Table 70 and Chart 71 indicate that short-term Italian interest rates were also relatively high during most of the period reviewed. During the 1950's, however, the Italian discount rate was held stable during a period when most other countries were permitting the boom to force up short-term rates of interest. Thus, the international position of the Italian discount rate changed from high to average to low. In 1958 and 1959, it was lowered from 4% to 3½%, where at times it stood below the comparable rate in the United States and far below that in England. In the late 1950's, therefore, the interest-rate trend in Italy tended to break away from the rising trend elsewhere—it declined. Bond yields remained relatively high, but short rates became relatively low. In the 1960's, the Italian official discount rate continued low, in contrast to sharp increases elsewhere; it averaged below the United States rate and far below the British rate. In the 1970's, however, the Italian discount rate at last joined the world-wide procession to high rates. The advance of rates continued into the 1980's, a decade that saw Italian interest rates move to very high levels and then decline, but the decline was less than in most other Western nations. The change in short rates is illustrated by the following table of decennial averages:

DECENNIAL AVERAGES OF DISCOUNT RATES

Years Averaged	Italy, %	England, %	United States, %
1920–1929	6.20 (6 yr.)	4.82	4.55
1930–1939	4.67	2.48	1.83
1940–1949	4.46 (8 yr.)	2.00	1.09
1950–1959	3.93	3.95	2.20
1960	3.50	5.29	3.50
1960–1969	3.52	5.72	4.01
1970–1979	8.21	9.44	6.46
1980–1989	15.15	11.71	8.65

Chapter XXI

Europe in the Twentieth Century: Switzerland, Austria, Scandinavia, Ireland, Iberia, and Turkey

The European and Mediterranean countries reviewed in this chapter were all either a part of the Western European community of nations or were closely associated with it financially. The recent history of interest rates on their more conventional forms of credit was importantly influenced by the mainstream of Western interest-rate history, which was described and analyzed in Chapters XVII–XX. Except for Switzerland and possibly Sweden, however, these countries exerted little influence upon that mainstream.

The interest rates presented here for those countries are usually those on the conventional sort of loans modeled after the principal credit forms in the large financial centers: typically the official discount rates and market yields on government bonds. Almost all modern nations report such rates systematically to the International Monetary Fund, and this is the source of most of the data in this chapter. They do not report, and this history does not include, the truly indigenous rates of interest paid locally by most workers, bankers, and entrepreneurs. In these countries there no doubt exists a colorful but untold history of local interest rates that is different from the history of the rates quoted here.

Little attempt is made here to study the credit structures of these countries or to bring out the local conditions that have influenced the level of the interest rates reported. Because of the small size of many of these markets and the consequent ease with which rates can be influenced by local customs and regulations, it is difficult to draw generalizations from the levels and trends of the bond yields and interest rates reported here.

SWITZERLAND

Switzerland has enjoyed unusual political and economic stability for more than a century and a half. Beleaguered but unmolested by two world wars, the small nation became a symbol of neutrality, monetary and price stability, and a safe haven for capital. Through an elaborate system of numbered bank accounts, Swiss bankers protected and invested the funds of Swiss and foreign customers, whose identities they sometimes did not know. These large funds could not find adequate outlet in Swiss securities, but were invested abroad in the name of Swiss bankers. They moved from market to market according to the strength of the currencies and the opportunities for income or profit.

The Swiss franc has been correspondingly stable in a century of inflations and devaluations. It was devalued only once, and this was in 1936 at a time when France and all the "gold bloc" countries finally devalued. The Swiss devaluation was less than that of the dollar, which had occurred earlier, and, as a consequence, the Swiss franc up to 1970 was worth over 23 U.S. cents, as compared to 20 U.S. cents in 1900. In the years of inflation and floating exchange rates since 1973, the Swiss franc has risen sharply in value and stood at 65 U.S. cents as the 1990's opened. Swiss per capita product, measured in dollars, surpassed that of the United States to become the highest in the world.

At the beginning of the twentieth century, Switzerland was a country of relatively high interest rates. During and after World War I, Swiss bond yields rose more and to higher levels than those of many belligerents. Even during the 1930's, Swiss interest rates continued to be higher than those in most leading financial centers. Following World War II, however, Switzerland became a country of low interest rates.

Swiss interest rates are presented in Table 71 in four series: (a) An annual average of the official discount rate from 1900 is presented. This continues a series previously presented from 1837. The Swiss National Bank was not established until 1907; earlier, discount rates were set by several banks of issue. (b) An annual average of the private discount rate is given for three-month bills, 1900–1975, and Treasury bill rates, 1980–1989. (c) An annual average of call money rates is listed intermittently from 1937; before 1950 these were interbank loans. (d) An annual average of government bond yields dates from 1907; before 1950, these were weighted averages of the

TABLE 71
SWISS INTEREST RATES: TWENTIETH CENTURY

Year	Official Discount Rate	Private Discount Rate, 3-Month Bills	Call Money	Government Bond Yield (Over 5 Years)	Year	Official Discount Rate	Private Discount Rate, 3-Month Bills	Call Money	Government Bond Yield (Over 5 Years)
	Annual Average, %					Annual Average, %			
1900	4.88	4.31			1930	2.89	2.01		4.12
1901	3.98	3.30			1931	2.03	1.44		3.86
1902	3.77	2.93			1932	2.00	1.52		3.80
1903	4.06	3.34			1933	2.00	1.50		4.02
1904	4.05	3.44			1934	2.00	1.50		4.16
1905	4.05	3.56			1935	2.33	2.20		4.64
1906	4.76	4.32			1936	2.30	2.06		4.43
1907	4.93	4.49		3.66	1937	1.50	1.03	1.00	3.41
1908	3.73	3.41		3.73	1938	1.50	1.00	1.00	3.24
1909	3.22	2.75		3.64	1939	1.50	1.08	0.50	3.76
10-yr. av.	4.14	3.59		3.68 (3-yr. av.)	10-yr. av.	2.01	1.53	0.83 (3 yr. av.)	3.94
1910	3.51	3.36		3.70	1940	1.50	1.36	1.72	4.06
1911	3.70	3.40		3.85	1941	1.50	1.25		3.39
1912	4.20	3.89		4.02	1942	1.50	1.25		3.15
1913	4.81	4.52		4.17	1943	1.50	1.25		3.32
1914	4.34	4.04		4.16	1944	1.50	1.25		3.27
1915	4.50	3.52			1945	1.50	1.25	1.00	3.29
1916	4.50	2.46		4.85	1946	1.50	1.25	1.00	3.10
1917	4.50	2.66		5.03	1947	1.50	1.28	1.11	3.17
1918	4.75	4.15		5.34	1948	1.50	1.56	1.50	3.42
1919	5.32	4.69		5.56	1949	1.50	1.55	1.12	2.94
10-yr. av.	4.41	3.67		4.52 (9-yr. av.)	10-yr. av.	1.50	1.33	1.24 (6-yr. av.)	3.31
1920	5.00	4.56		7.00	1950	1.50	1.50	0.96	2.67
1921	4.44	3.39		6.10	1951	1.50	1.50	1.13	2.95
1922	3.39	1.68		4.80	1952	1.50	1.50	1.05	2.84
1923	3.47	2.63		4.79	1953	1.50	1.50	1.01	2.55
1924	4.00	3.54		5.31	1954	1.50	1.50	1.03	2.62
1925	3.90	2.27		5.05	1955	1.50	1.50	1.38	2.97
1926	3.50	2.52		4.80	1956	1.50	1.50	1.45	3.11
1927	3.50	3.27		4.79	1957	2.16	2.18	1.80	3.64
1928	3.50	3.81		4.73	1958	2.50	2.50	1.19	3.19
1929	3.50	3.81		4.66	1959	2.04	2.10	1.01	3.08
10-yr. av.	3.82	3.10		5.20	10-yr. av.	1.72	1.73	1.20	2.96

TABLE 71 (*Continued*)

Year	Annual Average, % Official Discount Rate	Private Discount Rate, 3-Month Bills	Call Money	Government Bond Yield (Over 5 Years)	Year	Annual Average, % Official Discount Rate	Treasury Bills	Call Money	Government Bond Yield (Over 5 Years)
1960	2.00	2.00	1.10	3.09	1980	3.00	5.15	2.30	4.77
1961	2.00	2.00	1.03	2.96	1981	6.00	7.82	4.18	5.57
1962	2.00	2.00	1.33	3.12	1982	4.50	3.87	2.09	4.83
1963	2.00	2.00	1.75	3.25	1983	4.00	3.04	2.42	4.52
1964	2.25	2.37	2.35	3.97	1984	4.00	3.58	1.97	4.70
1965	2.50	3.00	2.63	3.95	1985	4.00	4.15	1.97	4.78
1966	3.00	3.74	3.18	4.16	1986	4.00	3.54	1.78	4.29
1967	3.25	4.07	2.71	4.60	1987	2.50	3.18	1.37	4.12
1968	3.00	3.75	2.26	4.37	1988	3.50	3.01	2.46	4.15
1969	3.25	3.90	3.49	4.90	1989	5.08	6.35	6.46	5.20
10-yr. av.	2.53	2.88	2.18	3.84	10-yr. av.	4.06	4.37	2.70	4.69
1970	3.75	5.14	3.44	5.82					
1971	3.75	5.25	2.39	5.27					
1972	3.75	4.81	2.83	4.97					
1973	4.50	5.09	5.38	5.60					
1974	5.50	6.63	2.31	7.15					
1975	4.30	6.25	0.60	6.44					
1976	2.00		0.68	4.99					
1977	1.50		1.68	4.05					
1978	1.00		0.49	3.33					
1979	2.00		0.67	3.45					
10-yr. av.	3.21	5.53 (6-yr. av.)	2.05	5.11					

SOURCES
Swiss National Bank Statistics.
IMF, *International Financial Statistics*.
Federal Reserve Bulletin.
Morgan Guaranty Trust Company, *World Financial Markets*.
OECD, *Financial Statistics Monthly*.

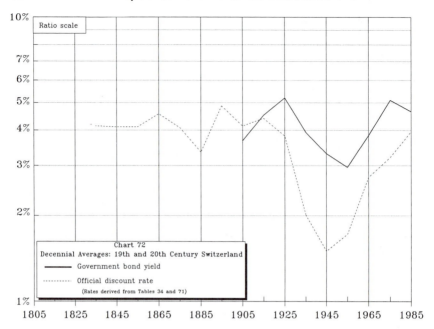

Chart 72
Decennial Averages: 19th and 20th Century Switzerland
——— Government bond yield
.... Official discount rate
(Rates derived from Tables 34 and 71)

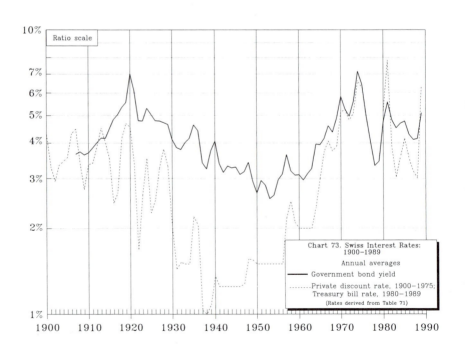

Chart 73. Swiss Interest Rates:
1900–1989
Annual averages
——— Government bond yield
.... Private discount rate, 1900–1975;
Treasury bill rate, 1980–1989
(Rates derived from Table 71)

yields to maturity of twelve government and Federal Railway bond issues with maturities of at least five years. This comparatively short term makes comparison with long yields in other countries difficult.

Chart 72 presents the decennial averages of the official discount rate since 1837 and of the government bond yields since 1907. Chart 73 presents the annual averages of the private discount rate, 1900–1975, Treasury bill rates, 1980–1989, and government bond yields since 1907.

At the start of this century, Swiss interest rates resembled German interest rates in that they were higher than those of most other European countries. The average of the official Swiss discount rates in 1900–1909 was 4.14%, when the English average was 3.63%, the Dutch average was 3.46%, and the French average was 3.05%. The average of Swiss government bond yields was 3.68% in 1907–1909, when the highest-yielding English government bonds yielded 3.05%, French *rentes* yielded 3.17%, and Dutch perpetuals yielded 3.30%. The Swiss bonds in this period yielded about the same as did the American corporate bonds. While these Swiss bonds were of shorter average term than the quoted bond issues of the other countries, this probably made little difference early in the century, but it affected comparisons in later periods of steep positive yield curves.

After the first decade, Swiss bond yields followed a very different trend from that of Swiss short-term rates. The bond yields rose steeply during World War I and remained relatively high most of the time until after World War II. The short-term interest rates rose very little during World War I and became relatively low soon thereafter. Swiss bond yields rose to an annual average of 7% in 1920, which was above the bond yields in the belligerent countries. In contrast, Swiss short rates at the 1920 peak were only 4.56–5.00%, which was below those of most other countries and far below Swiss bond yields. In this manner, Switzerland, just at the time of the peak bond yields, developed a sharp positive yield curve. It was the reverse of the negative curves in America and England. From 1910 to 1920, Swiss bond yields rose 330 basis points, while the Swiss private discount rate rose only 120 basis points. This episode provided an interesting exception to the rule that short-term interest rates fluctuate more than long-term interest rates do.

After 1920, Swiss bond yields declined, thus following the American, English, and Dutch markets rather than the French, Belgian, and German markets, where yields continued to rise until the stabilizations of 1923–1926. Swiss yields came down rapidly, and by 1930, at 4.12%, they approximated American and English yields.

During the 1930's, Swiss bond yields declined further, but not as much as American and English yields did. They fluctuated in a pattern more like the French one than like others, rising to 4.64% in 1935, when both the Swiss and French were struggling to avoid devaluation and when America and England, which had already devalued, were experiencing very low bond yields. Just before World War II, however, Swiss bond yields came down to new lows for the century at 3.24% and, after a flurry in 1939, remained close to 3.25% during the war. This was still above American and English wartime bond yields.

From 1900 to 1946, Swiss bond yields very broadly followed the American and English pattern: a sharp rise until 1920, and then a more or less steady decline until 1946. After 1946, however, Swiss bond yields followed an independent course: They did not rise as yields did elsewhere; rather, they fell. Until the 1960's there was no sustained postwar bear bond market in Switzerland as there was in many other countries. From 1946 to 1948, Swiss yields rose only a trifle. From 1948 to 1953, Swiss yields declined substantially. They reached their lows of the century at 2.55% annual average in 1953, far below American and other bond yields in that year. From 1953 to 1957, they did for a while share in the general rise in interest rates, rising to 3.64%. This, however, was only slightly above their 1948 level. From 1957 through 1961, Swiss bond yields fell again, to 2.96%. In the 1950's the Swiss decennial average of bond yields stood at its low point of this century.

In the 1960's Swiss bond yields crept up persistently but moderately, never reaching an average as high as 5%. In 1969 and 1970, however, they rose more rapidly, reaching an annual average of 5.82%. They then declined before peaking in 1974 at an annual average of 7.15%—well below that of most other countries. From 1974 to 1979, Swiss yields declined to less than half of their 1974 peak, as capital sought a safe haven from inflation. Yields then rose until 1981, but that peak was far below the 1974 peak, in contrast to virtually every other country. During the remainder of the 1980's Swiss yields were both low and stable relative to yields elsewhere.

Swiss short-term interest rates became relatively low much earlier in the century than did Swiss bond yields. The change became apparent during World War I. In 1916 the Swiss private discount rate came down to 2.46% annual average. In 1920 the official discount rate was held at 5% when the American rediscount rate and the English bank rate both rose to 7%. In the 1920's, Swiss short rates ranged around 3% when Swiss bond yields averaged above 5%. In the 1930's, Swiss short rates declined, as did those in other countries, but did not sink to nominal levels below 1%. Since World War II, Swiss short rates have risen, but have remained relatively low. The private discount rate averaged 1.73% during the 1950's, and the official discount rate was not put above 2.50%; in 1960 both were close to 2%. In the 1960's, Swiss short rates averaged below 3%. In the 1970's, they came up at times to 5% or so and in 1974 rose for a time to between 6% and 7%. Unlike long yields, Swiss short rates peaked in 1981 above 1974 levels, but soon fell to a 3–4% range for most of the 1980's. The decennial averages of Swiss short rates remained far below the low decennial average of Swiss bond yields and below short-term averages in other countries, but the long-short differential tended to narrow in the 1970's and 1980's.

AUSTRIA

Austrian interest rates are represented in Table 73 by the official discount rate from 1935 and the government bond yield from 1965. The history of interest rates in the Austro-Hungarian Empire in the nineteenth and early twentieth centuries is omitted because it closely paralleled German interest-rate history, was comparatively brief, and came to an end in 1918.

In the 1930's the official Austrian discount rate was pegged at 3.50%. After the end of World War II, this rate was resumed. In 1951, there was a return to a flexible monetary policy; the discount rate rose to the comparatively high level of 5.50% in 1952, but the average for the 1950's was only 4.52%, which was also the average for the 1960's. In the 1970's, the average rose to 5.13%. The Austrian discount rate reached a twentieth-century peak of 6.75% in 1980–1981, but the average for the 1980's fell back to 4.70%. Austrian government bond yields after 1965 followed the rising pattern seen elsewhere, but only once—in 1981—averaged above 10% in any year. Austria had become a country of stability and relatively low rates.

SWEDEN

Sweden, like Switzerland, was permitted by her belligerent neighbors to remain neutral and at peace during both of the great wars of the twentieth century. Sweden, however, did not enjoy Switzerland's economic stability. Although the dollar value of the krona survived World War I almost unimpaired, it shared in the general devaluations of 1931, 1949, and later.

In the nineteenth and early twentieth centuries, Swedish interest rates were higher than those of many European countries reviewed. In the 1930's and 1940's, Swedish interest rates declined with other rates. In the 1950's, Swedish rates rose somewhat less than did rates in most countries reviewed. The net result was that Swedish rates by 1960 were about average and were no longer above those of most other countries. After 1960, Swedish rates followed the pattern of most Western countries, with a few exceptions noted below.

Swedish interest rates are presented in Table 72 in three series: (a) the official discount rate charged by the Bank of Sweden in terms of an annual average and annual range; (b) the effective rates on new issues of long-term government bonds until 1945; and (c) the market yields of long-term government bonds from 1922 based on an annual average of the yield. Chart 74

TABLE 72
INTEREST RATES IN SWEDEN: TWENTIETH CENTURY

Year	Discount Rate Charged by Bank of Sweden, %			Effective Rate on Long-Term Loans Issued by the State		Market Yield on Long-Term Government Bonds, Annual Average, %
	Annual Average	Annual Low	Annual High	Yield, %	Coupon	
1900	5.87	5.50	6.00	3.82	$3\frac{1}{2}$s, 4s	
1901	5.46	5.00	6.00			
1902	4.51	4.00	5.00			
1903	4.50	4.50	4.50			
1904	4.61	4.50	5.00	3.64	$3\frac{1}{2}$s	
1905	4.72	4.50	5.50			
1906	5.20	5.00	5.50	3.64	$3\frac{1}{2}$s	
1907	6.10	5.50	6.50	3.77	$3\frac{1}{2}$s, 4s	
1908	5.88	5.50	7.00	3.87	$3\frac{1}{2}$s, 4s	
1909	4.69	4.50	5.50			
10-yr. av.	5.15			3.75 (5-yr. av.)		
1910	4.62	4.50	5.00			
1911	4.57	4.00	5.00	4.00	$3\frac{1}{2}$s, 4s	
1912	4.80	4.50	5.50			
1913	5.50	5.50	5.50	4.81	$4\frac{1}{2}$s	
1914	5.23	4.50	6.50	5.03	5s	
1915	5.51	5.50	6.00			
1916	5.23	5.00	5.50	5.10	5s	
1917	5.68	5.05	7.00	5.03	5s	
1918	5.93	6.50	7.00	5.36	5s	
1919	6.38	6.00	7.00	6.36	6s	
10-yr. av.	5.45			5.10 (7-yr. av.)		
1920	6.92	6.00	7.50			
1921	6.49	5.50	7.50	6.24	6s	
1922	4.84	4.50	6.00			4.82
1923	4.64	4.50	5.50	5.03	5s	4.86
1924	5.50	5.50	5.50	5.74	$5\frac{1}{2}$s	4.90
1925	5.21	4.50	5.50			4.83
1926	4.50	4.50	4.50			4.68
1927	4.17	4.00	4.50	4.58	$4\frac{1}{2}$s	4.58
1928	4.00	3.50	4.50			4.59
1929	4.75	4.50	5.50	4.57	$4\frac{1}{2}$s	4.56
10-yr. av.	5.10			5.23 (5-yr. av.)		4.73 (8-yr. av.)

TABLE 72 (*continued*)

Year	Discount Rate Charged by Bank of Sweden, %			Effective Rate on Long-Term Loans Issued by the State		Market Yield on Long-Term Government Bonds, Annual Average, %
	Annual Average	Annual Low	Annual High	Yield, %	Coupon	
1930	3.79	3.50	4.50	4.53	$4\frac{1}{2}$s	4.18
1931	4.16	3.00	8.00	4.36	4s	4.22
1932	4.50	3.50	6.00	4.60	$4\frac{1}{2}$s	4.32
1933	3.17	2.50	3.50	4.37	4s	4.02
1934	2.50	2.50	2.50	3.59	$3\frac{1}{2}$s	3.47
1935	2.50	2.50	2.50	2.82	$2\frac{1}{2}$s	3.19
1936	2.50	2.50	2.50			3.12
1937	2.50	2.50	2.50	3.05	3s	3.04
1938	2.50	2.50	2.50			2.34
1939	2.50	2.50	2.50	2.75	$2\frac{3}{4}$s	2.90
10-yr. av.	3.06			3.76 (8-yr. av.)		3.48
1940	3.29	3.00	3.50	4.05	4s	3.91
1941	3.21	3.00	3.50	4.03	4s	
1942	3.00	3.00	3.00	3.51	$3\frac{1}{2}$s	
1943	3.00	3.00	3.00	3.50	$3\frac{1}{2}$s	
1944	3.00	3.00	3.00	3.50	$3\frac{1}{2}$s	
1945	2.54	2.50	3.00			3.04
1946	2.50	2.50	2.50			3.01
1947	2.50	2.50	2.50			3.02
1948	2.50	2.50	2.50			3.08
1949	2.50	2.50	2.50			3.02
10-yr. av.	2.80			3.72 (5-yr. av.)		3.18 (6-yr. av.)
1950	2.54	2.50	3.00			3.11
1951	3.00	3.00	3.00			3.23
1952	3.00	3.00	3.00			3.28
1953	2.97	2.75	3.00			3.27
1954	2.75	2.75	2.75			3.24
1955	3.50	2.75	3.75			3.70
1956	3.79	3.75	4.00			3.75
1957	4.50	4.00	5.00			4.33
1958	4.66	4.50	5.00			4.33
1959	4.50	4.50	4.50			4.28
10-yr. av.	3.52					3.65

TABLE 72 (continued)

Year	Discount Rate Charged by Bank of Sweden, %			Effective Rate on Long-Term Loans Issued by the State		Market Yield on Long-Term Government Bonds, Annual Average, %
	Annual Average	Annual Low	Annual High	Yield, %	Coupon	
1960	4.98	4.50	5.00			4.56
1961	5.00	5.00	5.00			4.55
1962	4.33	4.00	5.00			4.40
1963	3.79	3.50	4.00			4.45
1964	4.50	4.00	5.00			4.80
1965	5.38	5.00	5.50			5.01
1966	5.79	5.50	6.00			5.75
1967	5.21	5.00	6.00			5.31
1968	5.42	5.00	6.00			5.90
1969	6.42	5.00	7.00			6.83
10-yr. av.	5.08					5.16
1970	7.00	7.00	7.00			7.39
1971	5.92	5.00	7.00			7.23
1972	5.00	5.00	5.00			7.29
1973	5.00	5.00	5.00			7.39
1974	6.17	5.00	7.00			7.79
1975	6.58	6.00	7.00			8.79
1976	6.29	5.50	8.00			9.28
1977	8.00	7.50	8.00			9.74
1978	6.92	6.50	7.50			10.09
1979	7.25	6.50	9.00			10.47
10-yr. av.	6.41					8.55
1980	10.00	10.00	10.00			11.74
1981	11.75	11.00	12.00			13.49
1982	10.17	10.00	11.00			13.04
1983	8.63	8.50	9.00			12.30
1984	9.08	8.50	9.50			12.28
1985	10.33	9.50	11.50			13.09
1986	8.13	7.50	9.50			10.26
1987	7.50	7.50	7.50			11.49
1988	8.13	7.50	8.50			11.20
1989	9.33	8.50	10.50			11.30
10-yr. av.	9.31					12.02

SOURCES

Sveriges Riksbank statistics.
IMF, International Financial Statistics.
Federal Reserve, Annual Statistical Digest.

Morgan Guaranty Trust Company, World Financial Markets.
OECD, Financial Statistics Monthly.

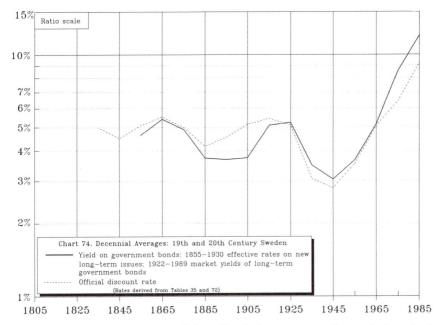

Chart 74. Decennial Averages: 19th and 20th Century Sweden
——— Yield on government bonds: 1855–1930 effective rates on new long–term issues; 1922–1989 market yields of long–term government bonds
·········· Official discount rate
(Rates derived from Tables 35 and 72)

pictures decennial averages of the official discount rate from 1830 and of long-term government bond yields from 1856. The same series are represented as annual averages from 1900 in Chart 75.

The annual averages of Swedish bond yields in general followed the American, English, and Dutch pattern throughout this century. They rose until 1920, fell until 1938–1948, and then rose again. The tendency toward relatively lower rates was by no means as pronounced as in Switzerland, but it was noticeable. It was a characteristic shared by these two prominent neutral countries.

Swedish government bond yields were above American corporate bond yields and far above most European government bond yields when the twentieth century began. They had come down to below 4% during the last few years of the nineteenth century, but there was no period of very low yields at the turn of the century such as was common elsewhere.

Swedish bond yields, insofar as they can be traced by the effective yields of new issues of long governments, rose late in the first decade and rose more sharply in the second decade. They reached highs in 1919–1921, just about when American, English, and Dutch yields reached a high point. The Swedish government then sold 6s at a discount. In the 1920's, Swedish bond yields declined sharply and steadily. By 1930, the government was selling 4½s, and the market yield of discount perpetuals was 4.18%.

After 1933, Sweden, like many other countries, adopted low interest rates as a matter of economic policy. The discount rate was put down to 2½%, and

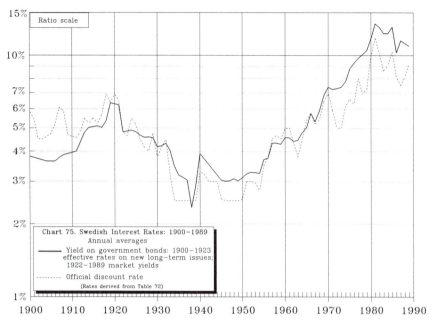

Chart 75. Swedish Interest Rates: 1900–1989
Annual averages
——— Yield on government bonds: 1900–1923
effective rates on new long–term issues;
1922–1989 market yields
········· Official discount rate
(Rates derived from Table 72)

the government floated 4s, then 3½s, and then 2½s. In 1938 the low annual
average yield of 2.34% was established in the open market. This turned out
to be the all-time low of Swedish bond yields. It came eight years before the
American and English markets reached their low yields for the century, and
it was below the English low yield of 1946. This was a brief episode for Sweden. During only two years have Swedish yields averaged below 3%. By
1940, the government was again issuing 4s. Later in the war it issued 3½s.

After World War II, there was a renewed period of low interest rates in
Sweden, which lasted to the mid-1950's. The discount rate was held at 2.50%
for five years, and the market yield on perpetual governments hovered
slightly above 3%. Following the devaluation of 1949, yields began a long,
slow rise that at first was more gradual than the rise in America or Britain. By
1953, the average yield was up to only 3.27%, and the discount rate was still
at 3% or lower. A sharper rise in Swedish interest rates began in 1955. Yields
rose to 4.33% in 1957. After two years of stability, they rose again to 4.60% in
1960. In these years Swedish government bond yields were close to the
yields of prime American corporate bonds and well below English government bond yields. From the early 1960's to the early 1980's Swedish bond
yields rose steadily and substantially, thus sharing the great bear market
with almost everyone else. The main difference is that in the Swedish bear
market, rallies were few and limited. Other countries reached a peak in
1974, and then experienced several years of lower yields before the new and
generally higher peak of 1981. But in Sweden there was no bond market

rally in the later 1970's, and in the 1980's yields declined less than they did elsewhere. The postwar bear bond market in Sweden on the whole was not quite as severe as that in America or England, and the rally after 1981 was also more limited.

The discount rate of the Bank of Sweden was relatively high throughout most of the twentieth century, as it was in the nineteenth century. It opened the century at 6% and reached a high of 7½% in 1920–1921. In the 1920's, it averaged over 5%, and in 1931, got up to 8%, a level not reached again until 1976. From 1933 to 1954, however, its range was usually 2.50–3.00%. After 1954, there came a gradual rise. In the 1960's, it averaged about 5%, but by 1969, it had risen to 7%. A decade later, the Swedish discount rate reached 9%. It peaked at 12% in 1981. In 1989 a discount rate of 9½% was higher than any Sweden had experienced from 1900 to 1979.

Persistent inflation almost certainly contributed to Sweden's historically high interest rates in the 1970's and 1980's, as it did elsewhere. Swedish consumer prices doubled from 1971 to 1979, and then doubled again from 1979 to 1988.

NORWAY

Norwegian interest rates are represented in Table 73 by the official discount rate and by government bond yields. The latter series is now derived from an average of bonds with a maturity of at least fifteen years. Before the 1960's, it was derived from the yield to maturity of an issue of 4s floated in 1955 and due in 1975; from 1946 through 1954 the yields were derived from an average of current yields of various 2½% bonds; from 1940 through 1946, from 3.6% bonds. These shifts in coupons make such a large difference in yield that the table presents an unsatisfactory picture of levels; however, it probably gives a fair indication of trends.

The table shows that since 1930 the trends of Norwegian interest rates have followed the English, American, and Dutch pattern but with a few important differences. Long-term and short-term Norwegian rates declined in the 1930's, became very low in the 1940's, and rose steadily from the 1950's through the late 1980's. In the 1930's, however, the decline in Norwegian bond yields was small. They remained relatively high. While Swedish government bond yields came down from 4.18% in 1930 to 2.34% in 1938, the Norwegian series declined from 5.05% to only 4.33% in the same period. In 1940 the Norwegian yields rose to 5.39%, the high until the 1970's. With the war and the occupation, a new series of bonds sold at moderate yields, around 3.50%. After the war, the easy-money policy then prevalent in Europe was adopted in Norway, and a new bond series provided yields around 2.50%—well below the Swedish level and even below the English level. It was not until 1955 that a large rise in bond yields began. A new issue of 4%

TABLE 73
AUSTRIAN, NORWEGIAN, DANISH, AND IRISH INTEREST RATES: ANNUAL AVERAGES, 1930–1989

Year	Austria		Norway		Denmark		Ireland	
	Official Discount Rate, %	Government Bond Yield, %	Official Discount Rate, %	Government Bond Yield, %	Official Discount Rate, %	Government Bond Yield, %	Official Discount Rate, %	Government Bond Yield, %
1930			4.53	5.05	4.19	4.71		
1931			4.65	5.01	4.22	4.66		
1932			4.68	5.02	4.50	4.84		
1933			3.70	4.95	3.17	4.01		
1934			3.50	4.67	2.50	3.94		
1935	3.50		3.50	4.44	2.86	4.20		
1936	3.50		3.53	4.52	3.56	4.38		
1937	3.50		4.00	4.46	4.00	4.48		
1938			3.51	4.33	4.00	4.27		
1939			3.83	4.58	4.08	4.66		
10-yr. av.	3.50 (3-yr. av.)		3.94	4.70	3.71	4.42		
1940			4.50	5.39	4.12	4.99		
1941			3.00	3.67	3.50	4.15		
1942			3.00	3.54	3.50	4.06	2.50	
1943			3.00	3.52	3.50	4.38	2.50	
1944			3.00	3.45	3.50	3.97	2.50	
1945	3.50		3.00	3.42	3.50	3.76	2.50	
1946	3.50		2.50	2.96	3.00	3.55	2.50	
1947	3.50		2.50	2.50	3.00	3.65	2.50	
1948	3.50		2.50	2.49	3.00	4.07	2.50	
1949	3.50		2.50	2.50	3.00	4.44	2.50	
10-yr. av.	3.50 (5-yr. av.)		2.95	3.34	3.36	4.10	2.50 (8-yr. av.)	
1950	3.50		2.50	2.58	3.62	4.53	2.50	
1951	3.87		2.50	2.74	4.50	5.14	2.50	
1952	5.50		2.50	2.74	4.50	5.29	3.50	4.53
1953	4.62		2.50	2.72	4.50	5.08	3.50	4.58
1954	3.62		3.50	2.69	4.75	5.24	3.00	4.42
1955	4.45		3.50	2.99	5.37	5.55	4.00	4.47
1956	5.00		3.50	4.31	5.50	5.71	5.00	5.29
1957	5.00		3.50	4.58	5.50	5.77	6.00	5.59
1958	5.00		3.50	4.76	5.00	5.24	4.25	5.61
1959	4.62		3.50	4.61	4.75	5.32	4.25	5.10
10-yr. av.	4.52		3.10	3.47	4.80	5.29	3.85	4.95 (8-yr. av.)

TABLE 73 (*continued*)

Year	Austria Official Discount Rate, %	Austria Government Bond Yield, %	Norway Official Discount Rate, %	Norway Government Bond Yield, %	Denmark Official Discount Rate, %	Denmark Government Bond Yield, %	Ireland Official Discount Rate, %	Ireland Government Bond Yield, %
1960	5.00		3.50	4.58	5.50	5.76	4.90	5.45
1961	5.00		3.50	4.64	6.50	6.02	5.42	6.04
1962	5.00		3.50	4.95	6.50	6.32	4.39	6.06
1963	4.71		3.50	4.96	5.50	6.44	3.93	5.48
1964	4.50		3.50	4.94	6.50	6.24	4.72	5.93
1965	4.50	6.52	3.50	4.99	6.50	7.35	6.10	6.24
1966	4.50	6.93	3.50	5.00	6.50	7.86	6.38	6.96
1967	4.18	7.24	3.50	5.00	7.50	8.17	7.78	6.99
1968	3.75	7.74	3.50	4.94	6.00	8.43	7.17	7.36
1969	4.08	7.52	3.83	5.12	9.00	9.34	8.25	9.71
10-yr. av.	4.52	7.19 (5-yr. av.)	3.53	4.91	6.60	7.19	5.90	6.62
1970	5.00	7.82	4.50	6.29	9.00	10.57	7.31	9.86
1971	5.00	7.71	4.50	6.40	7.50	10.67	4.81	8.48
1972	5.50	7.37	4.50	6.27	7.00	10.37	8.00	9.46
1973	5.50	8.25	4.50	6.19	9.00	11.08	12.75	12.33
1974	6.50	9.74	5.50	7.10	10.00	14.55	12.00	16.86
1975	6.00	9.61	5.00	7.29	7.50	13.10	10.00	14.64
1976	4.00	8.75	6.00	7.25	10.00	13.21	14.75	15.49
1977	5.50	8.74	6.00	7.39	9.00	13.38	6.75	11.30
1978	4.50	8.21	7.00	8.45	8.00	14.54	11.85	12.83
1979	3.75	7.96	9.00	8.59	11.00	15.82	16.50	15.07
10-yr. av.	5.13	8.42	5.65	7.12	8.80	12.73	10.47	12.63
1980	6.75	9.24	9.00	10.27	11.00	17.66	14.00	15.35
1981	6.75	10.61	9.00	12.31	11.00	18.92	16.50	17.26
1982	4.75	9.92	9.95	13.20	10.00	20.39	14.00	17.06
1983	3.75	8.17	9.43	12.86	7.00	14.46	12.25	13.90
1984	4.50	8.02	10.15	12.16	7.00	13.93	14.00	14.62
1985	4.00	7.77	10.60	12.89	7.00	12.01	10.25	12.64
1986	4.00	7.33	13.55	13.47	7.00	10.76	13.25	11.07
1987	3.00	6.91	13.86	13.56	7.00	11.10	9.25	11.27
1988	4.00	6.67	13.04	12.97	7.00	11.19	8.00	9.49
1989	5.50	7.10	10.56	10.75	7.00	10.48	8.40	8.66
10-yr. av.	4.70	8.17	10.91	12.44	8.10	14.09	11.99	13.13

SOURCES

Austria: IMF, *International Financial Statistics*.

Norway: *Ibid.*; and League of Nations, *Statistical Year Book, 1939–40*, p. 221.

Denmark: *Ibid.*, pp. 221 and 224; Morgan Guaranty Trust Company, *World Financial Markets*; and IMF, *International Financial Statistics*.

Ireland: *Ibid.*

bonds sold at discounts to yield as much as 4.76% annual average in 1958—a yield above that prevailing in Sweden but below the English level.

In the 1960's, Norwegian bond yields were stable. Then, with few interruptions, they rose to a peak of 13.56% in 1987, well after the 1981 peak elsewhere. The Norwegian government tended to follow a low interest rate policy in the face of a dangerous inflation, which delayed but hardly prevented yields from reaching record levels.

While Norwegian bond yields rose in the late 1950's in a manner similar to that of other bond yields, the official discount rate did not rise above 3½% until 1969, even though in 1957 the Swedish discount rate rose to 7%. Even in the 1970's, the Norwegian discount rate was moderate, averaging 5.65%.

DENMARK

Interest rates in modern Denmark are represented in Table 73 by the official discount rate and by a series of government bond yields. Since World War II, Denmark has suffered almost the same degree of inflation as have the other Scandinavian countries, although Denmark's inflation rate was somewhat higher than that of Norway and Sweden from the late 1960's to the early 1980's, when interest rates soared everywhere.

Denmark had comparatively high interest rates throughout the period 1930 to 1990. Unlike interest rates in Norway, those in Denmark tended to become comparatively higher. Throughout most of the 1930's, Denmark's discount rates and bond yields were below those of Norway, but above those of Sweden. In the 1940's, Denmark's rates were above those of both Norway and Sweden. From the 1950's to the 1980's, Denmark's rates rose faster than did most other rates and became far higher than those of Norway and Sweden. These comparisons are brought out by the decennial averages in Table 73.

The trend of Danish interest rates followed the general pattern. They tended to decline in the 1930's, but they never reached very low levels. The discount rate got down to 2.50% in 1934, and bond yields declined to slightly below 4%. In the late 1930's, Danish interest rates rose and reached, or exceeded, the high rates of 1930. During the 1940's, Danish rates declined again; the discount rate got down to 3%, and bond yields approached 3.50%. These rates were well above those of most other countries. In the 1950's, the Danish discount rate got up to 5.50%, and the bond yields often approached 6%—well above their level of 1930.

In the 1960's, Danish yields soared, rising to levels well above the very high English level. This was true of both long-term and short-term rates. In the 1970's, all Danish yields again rose steeply. The Danish discount rate reached a peak of 11% during 1979–1981. The peak in government bond yields came in 1982 and was above 20%. Long yields averaged higher than the extraordinarily high English yields and far above all other Scandinavian yields. The contrast with Norway's low yields was striking, at least until the mid-1980's, when, for the first time since 1940, Danish yields became lower than Norwegian yields.

IRELAND

Recent Irish interest rates are represented in Table 73 by two series, the official discount rate and government bond yields.

Very close financial ties have been maintained between Ireland and the United Kingdom. Although the Irish discount rate did not follow the English bank rate from year to year, its decennial average was nearly identical to Britain's in the 1950's and 1960's. In the 1970's and 1980's, however, Irish interest rates averaged even higher than English interest rates. The official discount rate rose to 12.75% in 1973, and further to 16.50% in 1979 and 1981, paralleling peaks in the English bank rate.

The Irish government bond yields reported were also close to English long-term bond yields in the 1950's and 1960's. Yields started up in 1965, in Ireland as elsewhere. From that time on, Irish bond yields generally ranged above English yields.

PORTUGAL

Portugal is an ancient trading nation, which must have a long and colorful interest-rate history, extending backward for many centuries. Unfortunately, organized data on early Portuguese interest rates are not available. Therefore Portuguese interest rates are represented in Table 74 only by two series, which start in 1930: the official discount rate and government bond yields. The latter are now based on an average of the yields of all bonds outstanding; up to 1973 they were based on 4% bonds due in 1980.

The pattern of these Portuguese interest rates was different from the general European pattern, especially after 1940. In 1930–1931, both the discount rate of 7.30–7.71% and the bond yields at 6.66% were very high. These rates declined in the 1930's, like rates in other countries, but did not become very low. During these years, an authoritarian government brought the country under tight economic control. It maintained unusual financial stability for several decades.

During World War II, the Portuguese government brought the official discount rate steadily down from 4 to 2% and held it there. Government bond yields came down from 3.97% annual average in 1939 to 2.76% annual average in 1944. After 1946, these yields remained relatively low through the early 1970's. They rose briefly to 3.92% in 1950, but came down again to 3.03% in 1956–1959, a trend quite the opposite from the rising trend that prevailed in most other countries. They rose moderately in the 1960's and a little further in the early 1970's, reaching 6%. At that time the authoritarian regime was replaced by a more democratic government. Portuguese interest

TABLE 74
PORTUGUESE, SPANISH, AND TURKISH INTEREST RATES:
ANNUAL AVERAGES, 1930–1989

Year	Portugal		Spain		Turkey	
	Official Discount Rate, %	Government Bond Yield, %	Bank of Spain Rate, %	Treasury Bill Rate, %	Official Discount Rate, %	Government Bond Yield, %
1930	7.71		5.73			
1931	7.30	6.66	6.24			
1932	6.63	6.03	6.41		7.52	
1933	6.07	4.78	6.00		5.75	
1934	5.48	4.00	5.91		5.50	
1935	5.00	4.05	5.27		5.50	
1936	4.67	3.65	5.00		5.50	
1937	4.25	3.61	4.87		5.50	
1938	4.00	3.74	4.37		4.75	
1939	4.00	3.97	4.00		4.00	
10-yr. av.	5.51	4.50 (9-yr. av.)	5.38		5.50 (8-yr. av.)	
1940	4.00	3.83	4.00		4.00	
1941	3.62	3.61	4.00		4.00	
1942	3.50	2.92	4.00		4.00	
1943	2.75	2.82	4.00		4.00	
1944	2.00	2.76	4.00		4.00	
1945	2.00	2.83	4.00		4.00	
1946	2.00	2.83	4.00		4.00	
1947	2.00	3.04	4.12		4.00	
1948	2.00	3.24	4.50		4.00	6.90
1949	2.00	3.76	4.00		4.00	6.84
10-yr. av.	2.59	3.16	4.06		4.00	
1950	2.00	3.92	4.00		4.00	6.52
1951	2.00	3.79	4.00		3.00	5.49
1952	2.00	3.48	4.00		3.00	4.95
1953	2.00	3.38	4.00		3.00	4.21
1954	2.00	3.27	3.87		3.00	4.81
1955	2.00	3.18	3.75		4.12	4.81
1956	2.00	3.03	4.00		5.62	4.82
1957	2.00	3.05	4.62		6.00	4.80
1958	2.00	3.03	5.00		6.00	4.72
1959	2.00	3.45	5.62		6.00	4.79
10-yr. av.	2.00	3.36	4.29		4.37	4.99

TABLE 74 (*continued*)

Year	Portugal		Spain		Turkey	
	Official Discount Rate, %	Government Bond Yield, %	Bank of Spain Rate, %	Treasury Bill Rate, %	Official Discount Rate, %	Government Bond Yield, %
1960	2.00	3.46	4.60		6.75	4.74
1961	2.00	3.82	4.60		8.25	4.77
1962	2.00	3.96	4.60		7.50	4.71
1963	2.00	4.18	4.60		7.50	4.64
1964	2.00	3.94	4.60		7.50	4.64
1965	2.17	3.88	4.60		7.50	4.63
1966	2.50	3.96	4.60		7.50	4.63
1967	2.50	5.00	5.10		7.50	4.56
1968	2.50	5.11	5.10		7.50	4.54
1969	2.73	5.15	5.10		7.50	4.02
10-yr. av.	2.24	4.25	4.75		7.50	4.59
1970	3.50	5.28	6.50		9.00	
1971	3.75	5.70	5.00		9.00	
1972	4.00	6.01	5.00		9.00	
1973	5.00	5.50	6.00		8.75	
1974	7.50	n.a.	7.00		9.00	
1975	6.50	n.a.	7.00		9.00	
1976	6.50	9.74	7.00		9.00	
1977	13.00	10.80	8.03		9.00	
1978	16.33	16.17	9.02	14.41	10.00	
1979	18.00	16.68	7.98	15.70	10.75	
10-yr. av.	8.41	9.49	6.85	15.06	9.25	
1980	18.00	16.68	10.90	15.70	26.00	
1981	18.00	16.71	10.51	15.80	31.50	
1982	18.75	16.79	18.40	15.70	31.50	
1983	23.17	19.22	21.40	19.80	48.50	
1984	25.00	21.50	12.50	13.43	52.00	
1985	23.50	20.75	10.50	10.90	52.00	
1986	17.00	n.a.	11.84	8.63	48.00	
1987	14.96	15.02	13.50	11.32	45.00	
1988	13.71	13.87	12.40	10.79	54.00	
1989	14.00	13.86	14.03	13.76	54.00	
10-yr. av.	18.61	15.44	13.60	13.58	44.25	

SOURCES

League of Nations, *Statistical Year Book, 1939–40*, pp. 221, 225.
IMF, *International Financial Statistics*.
Morgan Guaranty Trust Company, *World Financial Markets*.

rates quickly climbed to relatively high levels and remained high through the 1980's.

Before the revolution of the early 1970's, Portuguese stock prices, commodity prices, cost of living, and other economic indices were remarkably stable. The nation did not share in the growth prevalent elsewhere. The very small national debt scarcely increased at all, and most of it was owned outside the banking system. The interest-rate history of Portugal might be construed as representing an exception to the rule that relatively low bond yields have usually prevailed in the dominant financial centers. More likely, it represented the control of markets that is customary under authoritarian regimes. After the revolution, the markets were freer to respond to inflationary economic policies. Portuguese inflation rates have soared, and so have Portuguese interest rates.

SPAIN

Modern Spanish interest rates are represented in Table 74 by the official discount rate and, since 1978, the Treasury bill rate. Even in the centuries of its greatest power, Spain was never well developed financially. Other countries handled its banking. The country contributed little to the history of Renaissance interest rates. In modern times, Spain continued to isolate itself economically from neighboring economies. In the 1930's, after a long history of political instability, the country was subjected to an authoritarian form of government and a controlled economy. Therefore Spain's interest rates lack the economic significance of interest rates in other countries. As in Portugal, the authoritarian regime gave way to a more democratic government in the 1970's. Interest rates have since become more indicative of supply and demand in free markets.

The Spanish discount rate was very high in the 1930's, about the highest of any country covered by this history in that decade, which in Spain was a period of civil war. It came down steadily, however, from 6.41% annual average in 1932 to 4% in 1939. The Spanish Civil War did not seem to interrupt the decline. Nonetheless, the rate averaged more than twice the official discount rates then prevailing in England and the United States.

From 1939 to 1953, the Spanish discount rate was held at 4% almost without interruption. This was then a comparatively high rate. In 1955, when rates elsewhere were rising, it was brought down to 3.75%. This was its lowest point of the period 1930–1989. In 1957–1960, it rose steadily and rapidly in a period of economic reform.

The rise of the Spanish discount rate in the late 1950's contrasted sharply with the stability of Portugal's 2% discount rate. There were other contrasts. In this decade, Spain's cost of living doubled while Portugal's cost of living rose only 9%. The dollar value of the Spanish peseta fell by 50–75%, while the dollar value of the Portuguese escudo was unchanged. These contrasts are significant because both economies were controlled by authoritarian governments.

During the 1960's, The Bank of Spain's discount rate was held at 4.6% through 1967, and then began to rise, reaching 7% in 1974–1976. Thereafter, under freer markets, it climbed rapidly, especially between 1981 and 1983, when it more than doubled, reaching a peak of 21.40%. Since the restoration of democratic governments, the rate of inflation in Spain has been lower than in Portugal, and Spanish interest rates generally have also been lower than Portuguese rates.

TURKEY

Turkish interest rates are represented in Table 74 by the official discount rate from 1932 and by two series of government bond yields from 1948 to 1969. The first series, which ends in 1952, is based on market yields to maturity of an issue of 7s due in 1965. The second series, which begins in 1953, is based on yields to maturity of an issue of 5s due in 1972. No bond yields have been reported since 1969.

Throughout this period, Turkey reported high interest rates by European standards. This was especially true in the most recent two decades of extremely high inflation in the country.

The Turkish discount rate declined from 7.52% annual average in 1932 to 4% in 1939; it stayed at 4% in the 1940's, came down to 3% in 1951–1954, and then moved up rapidly to 6% in 1957 and 9% in 1961. While this decline and recovery of the discount rate followed the European pattern, Turkish government bond yields took a different trend: They declined almost steadily from 1948 to 1953. Some part of this decline was no doubt due to a shift in the nominal rate in 1952–1953, but the mere fact of a 7% nominal rate's giving way to a 5% nominal rate suggests declining yields, and the yields of both series tended to decline from year to year. After 1953, bond yields rose, and then stabilized at levels well below the discount rate.

During the 1950's, Turkey was financially unstable. In ten years, the lira lost two-thirds of its dollar value and 60% of its purchasing power. A strong government was unable to stabilize the backward agricultural economy of the country. As in Spain, the currency lost value, and the discount rate rose. Nevertheless, Turkish bond yields declined.

In the 1960's, the official discount rate was pegged for many years at 7½%, an unusually high level at the time. In 1970, it came up to 9%, and it rose to 10.75% in 1979. This increase did not fully reflect rising inflation in Turkey, where the price level in 1979 was more than seven times its level in 1970. The 1980's were a different matter. The discount rate jumped to 26% in 1980 and stood at 54% in 1989. In 1988 the Turkish price level was nearly twenty times its level in 1979. These interest and inflation rates were unusually high and altogether atypical of the general European pattern.

Chapter XXII

Canada in the Twentieth Century

Canada provides very little autonomous interest-rate history. In the nineteenth century, there was little or no organized bond market in Canada. The country was then being developed by foreign capital, chiefly English. A period of very rapid growth from 1900 until World War I was also financed largely by the influx of some $2.5 billion of foreign capital, over half of it from London. After 1914, Canada turned briefly to New York to help finance war requirements. When the United States entered the war in 1917, Canada was for the first time forced to rely on her own financial resources. (538)

Canada's war effort was large. She supplied some 640,000 troops for World War I, which cost her $1.5 billion. The Victory Loan campaigns at 5% and 5½% led to the development of a domestic bond market. In the drive of October 1918, more than 1 million people subscribed $700 million. Before this time, Dominion of Canada bonds were largely sterling obligations, and their rates belong to the history of the English market rather than to that of the Canadian market. Although there was a local market for Canadian provincial obligations before World War I and a local market for Dominion obligations after World War I, both markets were very limited until World War II.

A Canadian money market was an even later development. The Bank of Canada was not organized until 1935. It was not until the 1950's that a modern money market based on a day-to-day credit was organized. Canada, which achieved a large measure of political independence in 1867, when the British North America Act created the Dominion, was late in achieving financial independence. No doubt the enormous opportunities afforded for profitable investment in Canada so far exceeded the local savings of a small population that dependence on foreign capital seemed natural and inevitable.

The lack of an early Canadian interest-rate history is no doubt due to the same conditions that deprived the American colonies of much of an interest-rate history. The land was primitive, but the people were not. They brought with them the sophisticated financial techniques of modern Europe and employed them as rapidly as their financial resources would permit. In the meantime, they financed in London and New York. When local Canadian markets and rates of interest finally emerged, they provided no novelties. The credit forms were the familiar ones of Europe and America. The range of interest rates, similar to that of the other countries studied, tended to be moderately higher than interest rates in the United States. Canada has been accorded a separate chapter here, not because her interest rate history has been novel or important, but because her markets are now rapidly achieving independence and importance.

Before the organization of the Dominion, Canadian sterling obligations sold at high yields in the London market. In 1860 Canada Consolidated Sterling 5s were floated in London, to yield 5.12%, which was 191 basis points more than the prevailing yield on British consols. A few years later British Columbia and Vancouver Island brought out sterling 5s. After 1867, the obligations of the new Dominion commanded lower yields. Quotation on a sterling issue of Canada 5s due in 1903, and not guaranteed by the government of the United Kingdom, provided market yields as follows, at annual high prices: (539)

Year	Yield of Canada (£)5s of 1903, %	Yield Spread in Basis Points Above British Consols
1871	4.70	150
1872	4.50	147
1873	4.50	130
1874	4.45	125
1875	4.45	131
1876	4.07	139
1877	4.43	135
1878	4.40	134
1879	4.27	126
1880	4.05	107
1881	3.93	102

Lesser Canadian administrative units paid higher rates in London. In 1874 Quebec sold its first debt issue; these were sterling bonds offered to yield

5.17%. In 1874 the city of Toronto sold sterling 6s, and in 1877 British Columbia sold sterling 6s. In 1879 Quebec floated its first U.S. dollar loan; these were 5s due in 1908, offered to yield 5%, at a time when U.S. government bonds were yielding 3.96%, New England municipals were yielding 4.22%, and best American corporate bonds were yielding 4.77%.

Between 1880 and 1900, high-grade bond rates declined in London, and Canadian credit improved further. In 1900 an issue of Canadian sterling perpetual 3s was selling in London at a small premium to yield 2.97%, which was only 53 basis points more than the yield of consols. The yields of this sterling issue are reported in Table 75 as an indication of the rates of interest Canada paid abroad on its best credits. Although an undeveloped country, Canada was enjoying the low rates of interest then prevailing in London. These sterling yields were a part of the history of English interest rates, not of Canadian interest rates; they should not be linked with, and compared to, later Canadian internal yields as though they formed a continuous history. Until a market developed in 1920 for Dominion internal obligations, a history of Canadian bond yields must rely on the yields of internal provincial bonds.

The history of Canadian interest rates in the twentieth century is summarized in Table 75. Prime bond yields are represented by two series, neither of which covers the entire period, but which, taken together, provide a reasonable indication of levels and trends: (a) annual average yields of the "most popular" bond issues of the province of Ontario from 1900 through 1943; and (b) annual average yields of long-term Dominion bonds from 1920 through 1989. The table also contains annual averages from 1917 through 1989 of Canadian real estate mortgage rates. These correspond roughly with trust company mortgage rates but were often half a percent or so above life insurance mortgage rates. Short-term Canadian interest rates are represented by three series: (a) annual averages of the discount rate of the Bank of Canada from 1935; (b) annual averages of the Treasury bill tender rate from 1934, which covered all bills until 1955, and after that year covered only three-month bills; and (c) annual averages of the yields of two-year Dominion bonds from 1925.

Chart 76 pictures the decennial averages of the province of Ontario bond yields and of the Dominion long-term bond yields. Chart 77 compares annual averages of prime U.S. corporate bond yields with annual averages of province of Ontario bond yields from 1900 through 1943 and of Dominion bond yields from 1935 through 1989.

The use of Ontario bond yields as a substitute for Dominion bond yields at times when Dominions were not available is justified by the very high credit standing of the province. In years when both yields were available, the difference was rarely large, and its variations were probably due largely to differences in coupon and maturity or temporary differences in supply. The

Chart 76. Decennial Averages: 20th Century Canada
——— Province of Ontario bonds
············ Dominion of Canada long−term bonds
(Rates derived from Table 75)

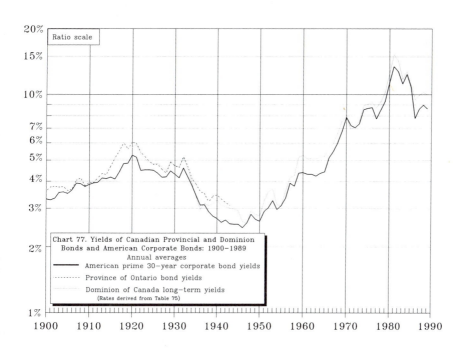

Chart 77. Yields of Canadian Provincial and Dominion
Bonds and American Corporate Bonds: 1900−1989
Annual averages
——— American prime 30−year corporate bond yields
············ Province of Ontario bond yields
Dominion of Canada long−term yields
(Rates derived from Table 75)

TABLE 75
CANADIAN INTEREST RATES: TWENTIETH CENTURY

Year	Province of Ontario Bonds, Annual Average, %	Dominion of Canada		Real Estate Mortgages, Annual Average, %	Bank of Canada Discount Rate, Annual Average, %	Treasury Bill Rate, Annual Average, %	Dominion 2-Year Bonds, Annual Average, %
		% Sterling Perpetuals, Annual Average, %	Long-Term Canadian Dollar Bonds, Annual Average, %				
1900	3.61	2.97					
1901	3.77	2.98					
1902	3.79	2.93					
1903	3.76	2.95					
1904	3.78	3.09					
1905	3.63	3.04					
1906	3.67	3.05					
1907	4.04	3.09					
1908	4.14	3.14					
1909	3.81	3.27					
10-yr. av.	3.80	3.05					
1910	3.95	3.28					
1911	3.94	3.27					
1912	4.14	3.32					
1913	4.34	3.56					
1914	4.29						
1915	4.68						
1916	5.12						
1917	5.51			7.64			
1918	6.01			7.76			
1919	5.63			7.51			
10-yr. av.	4.76	3.36 (4-yr. av.)		7.64 (3-yr. av.)			
1920	6.04		5.77	8.07			
1921	5.96		5.88	8.35			
1922	5.43		5.34	8.07			
1923	5.19		5.05	7.72			
1924	4.94		4.90	7.54			
1925	4.77		4.81	7.15			4.59
1926	4.79		4.84	6.99			4.83
1927	4.54		4.65	6.88			4.74
1928	4.37		4.48	7.08			4.64
1929	4.89		4.93	7.10			5.46
10-yr. av.	5.09		5.07	7.50			4.85 (5-yr. av.)
1930	4.71		4.73	6.99			
1931	4.63		4.65	6.84			

TABLE 75 (Continued)

Year	Province of Ontario Bonds, Annual Average, %	Dominion of Canada % Sterling Perpetuals, Annual Average, %	Dominion of Canada Long-Term Canadian Dollar Bonds, Annual Average, %	Real Estate Mortgages, Annual Average, %	Bank of Canada Discount Rate, Annual Average, %	Treasury Bill Rate, Annual Average, %	Dominion 2-Year Bonds, Annual Average, %
1932	5.21		5.14	6.60			
1933	4.68		4.55	6.84			
1934	4.11		3.91	6.43		2.65	
1935	3.88		3.39	6.05	2.50	1.49	
1936	3.59		2.97	5.80	2.50	0.84	1.28
1937	3.52		3.17	5.75	2.50	0.72	1.37
1938	3.22		3.09	5.87	2.50	0.59	1.14
1939	3.42		3.16	6.01	2.50	0.71	1.51
10-yr. av.	4.10		3.88	6.32	2.50 (5-yr. av.)	1.17 (6-yr. av.)	1.33 (4-yr. av.)
1940	3.46		3.28	5.90	2.50	0.70	1.48
1941	3.32		3.10	5.85	2.50		1.40
1942	3.20		3.06	5.76	2.50		1.48
1943	3.11		3.01	5.61	2.50		1.52
1944			2.99	5.33	1.50		1.46
1945			2.93	5.27	1.50	0.36	1.39
1946			2.61	5.28	1.50	0.39	1.39
1947			2.56	5.32	1.50	0.41	1.43
1948			2.93	5.42	1.50	0.41	1.41
1949			2.82	5.63	1.50	0.48	1.65
10-yr. av.	3.27 (4-yr. av.)		2.93	5.54	1.90	0.46 (5-yr. av.)	1.46
1950			2.78	5.64	1.62	0.55	1.82
1951			3.24	5.89	2.00	0.80	2.31
1952			3.59	6.40	2.00	1.07	2.69
1953			3.68	6.64	2.00	1.69	3.25
1954			3.14	6.71	2.00	1.44	2.25
1955			3.08	6.54	2.10	1.62	2.21
1956			3.61	6.71	3.12	2.92	3.61
1957			4.17	7.47	4.01	3.76	4.50
1958			4.26	7.27	2.50	2.25	n.a.
1959			5.17	7.39	5.06	4.81	n.a.
10-yr. av.			3.67	6.67	2.64	2.09	2.26 (8-yr. av.)
1960			5.26	6.75	3.57	3.32	3.96
1961			5.08	6.71	3.09	2.82	3.59
1962			5.09	6.50	4.89	4.60	4.28
1963			5.07	6.35	3.88	3.38	4.21

TABLE 75 (*Continued*)

Year	Province of Ontario Bonds, Annual Average, %	Dominion of Canada		Real Estate Mortgages, Annual Average, %	Bank of Canada Discount Rate, Annual Average, %	Treasury Bill Rate, Annual Average, %	Dominion 2-Year Bonds, Annual Average, %
		% Sterling Perpetuals, Annual Average, %	Long-Term Canadian Dollar Bonds, Annual Average, %				
1964			5.19	6.25	4.04	.74	4.41
1965			5.22	6.25	4.29	3.73	4.52
1966			5.74	6.83	5.17	5.00	5.38
1967			5.96	7.34	5.00	4.60	5.29
1968			6.67	8.64	6.79	5.27	6.37
1969			7.58	9.40	7.46	7.19	7.24
10-yr. av.			5.69	7.10	4.82	4.37	4.93
1970			7.91	10.06	7.13	5.99	6.32
1971			6.95	9.04	5.13	3.56	4.93
1972			7.23	8.95	4.75	3.56	5.54
1973			7.56	9.40	6.13	5.47	6.54
1974			8.90	10.06	8.50	7.83	8.03
1975			9.04	11.00	8.50	7.40	7.40
1976			9.18	11.72	8.50	8.87	8.11
1977			8.70	10.36	7.50	7.33	7.33
1978			9.27	10.29	10.75	8.67	8.75
1979			10.21	11.40	14.00	11.68	10.75
10-yr. av.			8.50	10.23	8.09	7.04	7.37
1980			12.48	13.97	17.26	12.80	12.44
1981			15.22	18.06	14.66	17.72	15.96
1982			14.26	16.85	10.26	13.64	13.82
1983			11.79	11.05	10.04	9.30	9.40
1984			12.75	12.00	10.16	11.06	11.67
1985			11.04	10.31	9.49	9.43	10.12
1986			9.52	10.15	8.49	8.97	9.09
1987			9.95	9.85	8.66	8.14	9.19
1988			10.22	10.73	11.17	9.48	9.68
1989			10.18	12.93	12.26	12.00	10.76
10-yr. av.			11.74	12.59	11.25	11.25	11.21

SOURCES

Canada, Central Statistical Office, *Monthly Bulletin of Statistics.*
Bank of Canada, *Review.*
League of Nations, *Statistical Year Book, 1939–40*, p. 223.
Canada, Report of Official Board of Enquiry, *Cost of Living* (1915).
IMF, *International Financial Statistics.*
Morgan Guaranty Trust Company, *World Financial Markets.*
OECD, *Financial Statistics Monthly.*

credit of the Dominion itself has rested more upon the economy of Ontario than has the credit of the government of the United States rested upon the economy of any one state.

Chart 77 suggests that the trends of Canadian bond yields in the twentieth century ran closely parallel to the trends of bond yields in the United States. Canadian yields, however, were almost always higher than U.S. yields. Canadian yields fluctuated much more in harmony with American yields than with English yields. English yields gained on American yields, especially from 1900 to 1915 and from 1934 to 1975. Canadian yields did not gain on American yields, although the spread widened in periods of high yields.

During these nine decades, there was a major shift in the relationship of Canadian to English yields. The Canadian yields, which in the first decade averaged 87 basis points above the English ones, averaged only 15 basis points above the English yields in the 1920's. They averaged slightly below the English yields during the 1940's, although part of this change may have been due to difference in maturity of the series used. During most of the 1950's, Canadian yields were far below English yields, although in 1955, and briefly again in 1960, the Canadian yields rose to English levels. In the 1960's, these Canadian yields averaged over 100 basis points below English yields, while during the crisis years of the 1970's, English yields soared, but Canadian yields rose much less and averaged nearly 500 basis points below English yields. During the bear bond markets of the 1960's, Canadian yields rose on average somewhat more than did yields in the United States and averaged a wide 68 basis points higher, well above their previous yield premium. In the 1970's, however, Canadian yields rose less than did U.S.

DECENNIAL AVERAGES OF LONG-TERM BOND YIELDS

Decade	Canada: Ontario to 1939; Dominions after 1939, %	England: Highest-Yielding Long Governments, %	United States: Prime Corporate Bonds, %	Canadian vs.	
				English	U.S.
1900–1909	3.80	2.93	3.47	+87	+33
1910–1919	4.76	4.20	4.23	+56	+53
1920–1929	5.09	4.94	4.56	+15	+53
1930–1939	4.09	3.68	3.64	+41	+45
1940–1949	2.93	3.19	2.61	−26	+32
1950–1959	3.67	4.70	3.30	−103	+37
1960–1969	5.69	6.87	5.01	−118	+68
1970–1979	8.49	13.34	8.23	−485	+26
1980–1989	11.74	12.10	10.20	−36	+154

yields, and the spread became at times nominal. In the 1980's, the spread between Canadian and American yields widened sharply, while Canadian advantage over Britain nearly disappeared. The decennial averages in the table on page 549 illustrate these shifts in international relationships.

Until the 1980's, there was little shift in the Canadian-U.S. differential. The change that occurred in the Canadian-English differential reflected the change that occurred in the U.S.-English differential. The Canadian-U.S. differential, however, was highly variable from year to year. Starting the century at +30 basis points, it almost vanished in 1906–1911, and then rose to over 100 basis points at times in 1916–1922. It declined in the 1920's and vanished in the mid-1930's. During World War II, it returned to about its average for the century, at 40 basis points, but immediately after the war, it again almost vanished. In the 1950's it fluctuated widely, approaching zero in periods of high and rising yields. These trends continued in the 1960's, but, as we have seen, the spreads were greatly reduced in the 1970's. They widened sharply in the 1980's, when Candian yields rose much more than did American yields. In other words, the direction of these two markets was usually the same, but the yield range of the Dominion bonds has been much larger than the yield range of the American prime corporate bonds.

Canadian short-term interest rates have little significance for this history. No organized money market was developed until the 1950's, and even then it was small and experimental. Canadian bill rates, like other bill rates, were very low in the late 1930's and the 1940's. Two-year bond yields were far above Treasury bill rates. Neither rate, however, was representative. Most Canadian businesses could borrow only at their banks and usually paid 4–5% or more. When a money market was developed in the mid-1950's, it was often thin and very volatile. At times little money was offered. At one time in 1959, because of usury laws, when the bill rate rose above 6%, banks found it difficult to make further loans. The Canadian bill rate has ranged from far above the U.S. bill rate to sometimes below the U.S. bill rate. The two money markets, like the two bond markets, have tended to move in the same direction, but the Canadian range has been larger and the Canadian short rates have usually been higher.

Chapter XXIII

Summary and Analysis of Interest Rates in Europe and North America Since 1700

Interest-rate statistics from shortly after 1700 in England and from 1800 in many countries are adequate to provide market trends from year to year. When these data are collated and viewed in perspective, a clearly discernible pattern of fluctuations emerges, first in one country and then in many countries, which is unambiguous and highly informative. The major political and economic events of two or three centuries may be observed in terms of their impact on various rates of interest. The result is a fever chart of the economic and political health of nations. Although economists and historians do not always agree on how to read the chart, especially on how to define normality, the extremes stand out, the direction of change is plain, and political and economic calamities are often recognizable at sight. The optimum rates of interest that signify economic and political health remain controversial.

THE DATA

Interest-rate history can be based on continuous series of annual or monthly statistics only from the early eighteenth century to the present and then only for England. The fact that precise statistics begin in eighteenth-century England and not in seventeenth-century Holland is probably an accidental by-product of early financial journalism and later statistical research. A daily market existed for the securities of the Dutch Republic throughout the eighteenth century, and probably through much of the seventeenth century, but prices and yields are not yet available in consecutive series. It is probable that a methodical study of the seventeenth- and eighteenth-century Dutch archives would prove a valuable contribution to financial history, correcting the estimates used here and providing a close view of the actual origin of the modern funded debt and of the first modern experience with low interest rates.

The modern annual interest-rate averages presented in the foregoing chapters are adequate to define interest-rate trends in many countries. They leave no doubt that in specific years and decades interest rates on credits of a designated type within a certain country were rising and in other years or decades were falling. The statistics, furthermore, usually tell the amount of the rise or of the fall.

The level of interest rates is a more complex concept than the trend of interest rates. This becomes apparent when two levels are compared over long periods of time or from one country to another, or at one time and place arising from loans of different types. Differences in taxation, in market structure, in prospects of redemption or of conversion, or in cost of acquisition, to name only a few variable influences, challenge any dogmatic deductions about relative levels merely because the interest rates quoted in one market are higher, lower, or identical with those in another market. There is no doubt that at specific times interest rates are rising and at other times rates are falling; but interpretation may be required when economic conclusions are drawn from the fact that one rate is equal to, above, or below, another rate at different times or places or for different types of loans.

In this history, no attempt is made at such interpretation. Only the raw statistics are offered and analyzed. Rates are presented and compared in a purely statistical manner: 5% is always said to be exactly 50 basis points higher than 4½%, regardless of surrounding circumstances that may have made a 4½% yield, say, from one contract more valuable than a 5% yield from another contract. The trends and levels of raw interest rate quotations provide only the beginning of a study of interest rates, but they do provide an essential point of departure for adjustments and interpretations.

Each market is described here by means of a very few series of interest rates, although most markets were highly complex and the few rates quoted in series do not give a complete picture of the rate structure. Only the English market for long-term government bonds during most of the eighteenth and nineteenth centuries can be well summarized by one series of rates, the yield of consols. Gross rates of interest are presented throughout, although these often were gross of tax advantages, tax penalties, redemption or refunding prospects, and other circumstances that might have added to or subtracted from the promised and realized yields.

In this chapter, the data presented in the preceding chapters are simplified further because in this way some useful generalizations concerning trends and patterns can be derived. Only one long-term series and one short-term series for each country are presented in the summary Tables 76 and 77. These rates are presented only as fifty-year minima and as decennial averages. No attempt, therefore, can be made from these tables at cyclical analysis, which requires monthly quotations. The trends analyzed in this summary are all secular or suprasecular trends.

The interest-rate histories summarized in this chapter are those of nine countries: England, France, Holland, Belgium, Germany, Switzerland, Sweden, the United States, and Canada. Although all countries at all times have had an interest-rate history, usually unrecorded, modern commerce and, especially, modern finance have become fully developed in only a few nations. In these nations, markets for credit instruments have been most fully recorded. The mainstream of interest-rate history is here defined, perhaps arbitrarily, as proceeding from ancient Greece and Rome through medieval Florence, Venice, and Genoa to medieval Antwerp and Lyons, thence through the Dutch Republic to England, and thence to most of modern Western Europe and North America. The emergence of Japan as an economic power, and the relatively recent liberalization of Japan's financial policies, including deregulation and the development of open markets, likely means that Japan is now entering the mainstream of interest rate history.

Table 76 brings forward from Table 11, Chapter X, the lowest long-term rates there tabulated for each country by half-centuries from 1200 through 1700. To these old interest rates the modern long-term rates are added in two ways: in the form of half-century lows (usually the lowest decennial average) and also in the form of all decennial averages. These various series are not based on identical credit instruments, but all are in varying degrees of long maturity. The data in Table 76 are analyzed and charted in several ways in an effort to summarize (a) the trends of long-term interest rates; and (b) the differences in the trends between these various countries.

THE SUPRASECULAR TRENDS OF MEDIEVAL AND MODERN LONG-TERM INTEREST RATES BY FIFTY-YEAR PERIODS

There was sufficient similarity in the long interest rate trends of all of these markets to encourage an attempt at generalization. This has been done in Chart 78, not by averaging but by linking together by half-centuries the lowest reported long rates in any one of these nine countries. It has been the point of view of this history that the wide band of simultaneous interest rates has just one specific boundary, its minimum. Sometimes the minimum boundary is higher or lower than at other times, and this is a reasonable way to define a trend. The chart applies this principle internationally. For years after 1700, the minima used are the lowest decennial averages, whenever they are available.

TABLE 76

Review of Medieval and Modern Western European and American Long-Term Interest Rates

Period	Minimum Rates on Best Credits by Half-Centuries*										
	Eng-land	France	Dutch Repub-lic, Holland	Spanish Nether-lands, Bel-gium	Ger-many	Sweden	Spain	Swit-zerland	Italy	Canada	United States
13th century											
1st half				8.00							
2nd half		14.00		8.00					6⅝		
14th century											
1st half				8.00					4⅞		
2nd half				8.00					5¼		
15th century											
1st half		10.00		8.00			4.00		6.00		
2nd half		10.00		8.00	5.00		4.00		5.00		
16th century											
1st half	10.00	8¼	8⅓	4.00	4.00				4.00		
2nd half	10.00	8⅓	6⅛	4.00	4.00				4.00		
17th century											
1st half	8.00	8⅓	5.00								
2nd half	4.00	5.00	3.00								
18th century											
1st half	3.05	5.00	3.00		4.00			5.00	4.00		
2nd half	3.13	5.00	2.50		4.00			4.00	4.00		
19th century											
1st half	3.26	4.06	4.53	4.43	3.84						4.55
2nd half	2.47	3.03	2.93	2.71	3.53	3.68					3.23
20th century											
1st half	2.79	3.06	3.20	2.94	3.64	3.04		3.31		2.93	2.31
2nd half	4.31	5.39	3.52	4.41	6.01	3.65		2.96		3.67	2.99

Period	Decennial Averages*								
	Eng-land	France	Holland	Belgium	Ger-many	Sweden	Swit-zerland	Canada	United States
18th century									
1st decade	7.00								
2nd decade	6.00								
3rd decade	3.40								
4th decade	3.05								
5th decade	3.22								
6th decade	3.13								
7th decade	3.59								
8th decade	3.75								
9th decade	4.64								
10th decade	4.54	14.00	6.42						7.49
19th century									
1st decade	4.80	8.66							6.23
2nd decade	4.57	7.29	5.95		5.45				6.39

TABLE 76 (*Continued*)

Decennial Averages*

Period	Eng-land	France	Holland	Belgium	Ger-many	Sweden	Swit-zerland	Canada	United States
3rd decade	3.72	4.21	4.79		4.91				4.55
4th decade	3.40	4.06	5.11	5.05	4.05				4.95
5th decade	3.26	4.14	4.53	4.43	3.84				5.41
6th decade	3.16	4.45	4.02	4.25	4.08	4.64			4.33
7th decade	3.27	4.37	4.21	3.62	4.03	5.41			5.34
8th decade	3.19	4.71	4.17	3.72	4.29	4.91			4.98
9th decade	2.97	3.68	3.55	3.38	3.82	3.73			3.60
10th decade	2.47	3.03	2.93	2.71	3.53	3.68			3.23
20th century									
1st decade	2.97	3.06	3.20	2.94	3.64	3.74	3.86	3.80	3.17
2nd decade	3.81	4.06	4.00		4.72	5.10	4.52	4.76	3.93
3rd decade	4.63	5.22	4.50	5.25	7.25	4.72	5.20	5.07	4.26
4th decade	3.54	3.98	3.50	4.04	6.26	3.48	3.94	3.88	3.34
5th decade	3.06	3.60	3.24	4.27	4.70	3.04	3.31	2.93	2.31
6th decade	4.31	5.68	3.52	4.41	6.01	3.65	2.96	3.67	2.99
7th decade	6.54	5.39	5.30	6.12	6.59	5.16	3.84	5.68	4.51
8th decade	11.77	8.68	8.24	8.27	7.96	8.55	5.11	8.49	6.87
9th decade	10.42	11.74	8.24	10.60	7.63	12.02	4.69	11.74	10.38

*Lowest decennial average where available; otherwise, lowest reported rate. Lowest yield or yields underlined for each period of time.

Key to Table 76

England: 13th–17th centuries: lowest reported private mortgage rates. 18th–20th centuries: decennial average of annuity and consol yields at market.

France: 13th–18th centuries: lowest reported rates on census annuities and *rentes*. 19th–20th centuries: decennial average of governments at market.

Holland: 13th–18th centuries: lowest reported rates on government annuities. 19th–20th centuries: decennial average of governments at market.

Spanish Netherlands and Belgium: 13th–16th centuries: rates for Spanish Netherlands; lowest reported rates on census annuities. 19th–20th centuries: decennial average of Belgian governments at market.

Germany: 15th–16th centuries and 18th century: lowest reported rates on census annuities. 19th–20th centuries: decennial average of long-term government bonds, including mortgage bonds at market.

Sweden: 1850–1920: decennial average of offering yields of new issues of long-term government bonds. 1920–1989: decennial average of government bond yield at market.

Switzerland: 18th century: lowest reported rates for census annuities. 1900–1989: decennial average of government bond yields at market, 5-year maturity or over.

Italy: 13th and 14th centuries: lowest market yield of Venetian *prestiti*. 15th and 16th centuries: lowest reported rates for census annuities.

Canada: 1900–1920: decennial average of market yields on province of Ontario bonds. 1920–1989: decennial average long-term Dominion bonds.

United States: Decennial average of market yields of long government bonds 1798–1829, of prime municipals 1830–1839, of long government bonds 1840–1869, of prime municipals 1870–1889, thereafter to 1939 of prime long corporate bonds adjusted to theoretical taxable government bond yields by subtraction of 30 basis points throughout. After 1940, average of long taxable governments.

A few of the "decennial averages" in this table cover less than 10 years because of the lack of data. These are so designated in the individual country tables from which this table is derived.

Rates are derived from previous country tables.

The suprasecular trends of ancient interest rates were charted and discussed in terms of national minima in Chart 1. Chart 2C traced medieval long-term rates in terms of half-century minima; the lines were determined by the rates in first one country and then by the rates in another, whichever was lowest. The same technique of following minimum rates from country to country is informative for modern times and is employed in Chart 78. The following countries reported lowest long-term interest rates by half-centuries:

Thirteen century—First half	Spanish Netherlands
Second half	Italy
Fourteenth century—First half	Italy
Second half	Italy
Fifteenth century—First half	Spain
Second half	Spain
Sixteenth century—First half	Spanish Netherlands—Germany—Italy
Second half	Spanish Netherlands—Germany—Italy
Seventeenth century—First half	Holland
Second half	Holland
Eighteenth century—First half	Holland—England
Second half	Holland
Nineteenth century—First half	England
Second half	England
Twentieth century—First half	The United States
Second half	Switzerland

The solid line in Chart 78 extends Chart 2C by half-centuries through the second half of the twentieth century. It does, indeed, tell a story. It shows that the tendency of long-term interest rates to decline, evident during the Middle Ages, has continued through modern centuries. Although the decline has decelerated, it has not yet been reversed for a period longer than half a century. Temporary reversals are observable from the second half of the sixteenth to the first half of the seventeenth century and from the second half of the eighteenth to the first half of the nineteenth century. It appears that the first four decades of the second half of the twentieth century represent another trend reversal. Only time will tell whether this is a reversal and, if so, whether it will be temporary, as were earlier reversals. Otherwise, the half-century trend of the minimum rates has been downward or flat for seven centuries. The largest declines occurred during the early thirteenth and early fourteenth centuries and during the seventeenth century. The lowest level in this history was reached during the mid-twentieth century, when the decennial average of long U.S. taxable government bonds fell to yield slightly less than the late nineteenth-century low decennial average yields for British consols.

Chart 1 provided a very rough sketch of the trends of minimum ancient

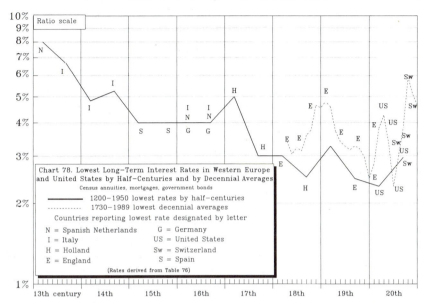

Chart 78. Lowest Long–Term Interest Rates in Western Europe and United States by Half–Centuries and by Decennial Averages
Census annuities, mortgages, government bonds
——————— 1200–1950 lowest rates by half–centuries
.... 1730–1989 lowest decennial averages
Countries reporting lowest rate designated by letter
N = Spanish Netherlands   G = Germany
I = Italy   US = United States
H = Holland   Sw = Switzerland
E = England   S = Spain
(Rates derived from Table 76)

Greek and Roman interest rates. Those were mostly traditional rates on short-term loans and thus were very different from modern long-term yields. A saucer-shaped pattern was followed by interest rates during the history of each ancient civilization. Rates declined during the early centuries of development and expansion, bottomed out in the centuries of commercial activity, and finally rose again with the disintegration of social and commercial life. Chart 78, which is based on long-term interest rates in those nations forming what is often called Western civilization, reveals what could be the first part of a similar saucer.

In this context the sharp rise in interest rates during recent decades is indeed alarming. The averages for the 1970's range from 5.11% low (Switzerland) to 11.77% high (England). Even the lowest of these averages, the Swiss, is a breakthrough to a level far above any earlier highs on the chart (remember that these are all decennial or fifty-year minima) back to the thirteenth century. The slightly lower Swiss average for the 1980's, 4.66%, the lowest of the lows for that decade, is the highest low since the first decade of the nineteenth century, when England was embroiled in the Napoleonic Wars. Moreover, five of the nine countries had higher average yields in the 1980's than in the 1970's. It is too early to know whether these recent high rates will last long enough to provide a trend, but those who commonly assume a range of, say, 5 to 10% in the decades to come are asserting a recent major turning point in the suprasecular downtrend of long-term yields since the Middle Ages.

Minimum rates on "normal safe loans" in Greece came down from 16% at the dawn of Greek financial history in the sixth century B.C. to a low of 6%

during the Hellenistic period of the fourth, third, and second centuries B.C. Minimum rates on "normal safe loans" in Rome came down from an 8⅓% legal limit in the earliest period of the Republic to 4% during the first century of the Empire. Minimum rates on best long-term credits in the Western world were first quoted at 8% in the thirteenth century and came down to about 5% in the fourteenth century, 4% in the fifteenth century, 3% in the seventeenth century, 2½% in the eighteenth and nineteenth centuries, and 2⅓% or lower in the mid-twentieth century. The modern range has been well below the ancient range. The low long-term yields of the mid-twentieth century were without precedent. So were the recent high yields. This means that the band of fluctuation has widened remarkably in our century; so far, it, indeed, has at least doubled.

Charts 1, 2C, and 78 can give a false impression of exact knowledge, which does not exist. The discovery of a lower prevailing rate for any half-century other than the one employed would alter the shape of the curve. The disqualification of one of the minimum rates employed would alter the shape of the curve. The charts have nevertheless been presented because the story they tell seems correct in general and because they facilitate a review of the broad sweep of interest rates over history.

The assertion that there has been a long history of declining interest rates since the twelfth century does not rest upon the choice of statistics in Table 76 or on the particular method employed in creating Chart 78. There is ample evidence that interest rates declined on the average in the late Middle Ages and Renaissance. There is no doubt about the 3% rate for British consols in the eighteenth century and no doubt that this was well below fourteenth- and fifteenth-century long-term interest rates. There is no doubt that the 2.47% decennial average for consols in the late nineteenth century was a new low for English rates and that the 2.31% average rate for long taxable U.S. governments in the fifth decade of the twentieth century was a new low for American rates. There were periods of easy money in the distant past—the downtrend has not been smooth—but twentieth-century lows have been below earlier lows, and twentieth-century highs have been above earlier highs.

THE SECULAR TRENDS OF MODERN LONG-TERM INTEREST RATES

The arrangement of the statistics in a succession of fifty-year minima obscures many very large fluctuations within these fifty-year periods. The latter are traced in Table 76 and Chart 78 by a series based on minimum decennial averages from 1730. These are only English decennial averages until 1790.

This decennial-average series shows that the suprasecular downtrend of interest rates during the last two centuries has been interrupted by three periods of secular increase: one during the late eighteenth century; the next during the early twentieth century; and the third following World War II. The annual data from which each decennial average was computed show that, beginning in 1737, there was a period of sixty-one years when minimum yields usually rose; then ninety-nine years when minimum yields usually declined; then twenty-three years of rise; then twenty-six years of decline; and finally twenty-eight years of rise, from 1946 to 1974, when Swiss yields peaked, although in most other countries the peak came in 1981. The decennial and annual lows were progressively lower. The lows of the twentieth century, however, were not very far below the lows of the nineteenth century.

The annual dates and rates at the turning points in these great secular fluctuations up to 1974 were as follows:

		Annual Averages, %	Monthly Averages, %
1737	England: low yield	2.83	2.80
1798	England: high yield	5.94	6.35
1897	England: low yield	2.25	2.21
1920	U.S.: high yield	5.32	5.67
1946	U.S.: low yield	2.19	2.08 (1.93 for one long issue)
1974	Swiss: high yield	7.15	7.40

This table provides the following time spans and yield fluctuations:

		By Annual Averages, Basis Points	By Monthly Highs or Lows, Basis Points
61 years	Rise in yields	+311	+355
99 years	Decline in yields	−369	−414
23 years	Rise in yields	+307	+345
26 years	Decline in yields	−313	−359 (374)
28 years	Rise in yields	+496	+532

In 1946 another secular rise in long-term bond yields began in most countries, which lasted until 1981. In some countries, the rise was very large and carried yields up to new all-time highs. In other countries, the rise was less.

The higher yields of the 1970's and 1980's have made an impression on the decennial averages. They have broken the trend of lower highs and lower lows that lasted from the beginning of the eighteenth to the middle of the twentieth century.

COMPARATIVE TRENDS OF MODERN LONG-TERM INTEREST RATES

Table 76 shows that the trends of bond yields in the countries studied have usually been in the same direction, but that there have been great differences in the size of fluctuations from country to country. Hence, the relationships of one country's rates to most other countries' rates have fluctuated widely. Chart 79 attempts to picture the fluctuations of these differentials since 1800 in six of the nations. Absolute differentials have little significance because of differences in currencies, terms, tax status, and other circumstances. However, changes in the differentials are meaningful.

In calculating the differentials between the rates in the six countries, there is danger of producing a statistical jungle. This can be avoided by comparing each to a common norm. The charts attempt just this by using the lowest long-term yield in any of these countries at each period of time as the norm with which to compare the rates in each country. Just one series of differentials is therefore charted for each country: the difference between its decennial average rates and the simultaneous lowest decennial average. These differentials are expressed in terms of basis points.

The left-hand panels cover the decennial differentials of the three countries that in turn since 1800 have had the lowest yields—England, the United States, and Holland. The chart does not show the rapid emergence of the English market in the early eighteenth century, when, during three decades, English rates declined from almost the highest to almost the lowest. With the Napoleonic Wars, the Dutch market was demoralized, and English rates, although high, became the lowest then recorded. England thereafter provided the norm of lowest rates until the twentieth century. After the wars of the twentieth century, England became a country of high bond yields, as by the 1980's did France and the United States.

American yields during the first half of the nineteenth century were relatively high and fluctuated much more widely than did the English norm. After the Civil War, American yields declined much more than did English yields. The rise of the United States in the late nineteenth century and early twentieth century to a position of financial leadership brought with it the lowest bond yields. The change is plainly visible on the chart, as is the dramatic reversal since the 1950's that carried U.S. yields from virtually the lowest to among the highest of the six countries.

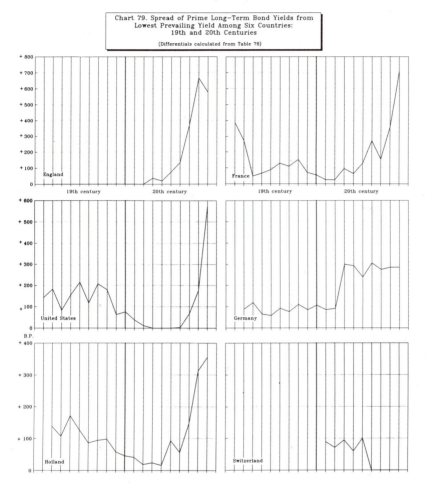

Chart 79. Spread of Prime Long–Term Bond Yields from Lowest Prevailing Yield Among Six Countries: 19th and 20th Centuries

(Differentials calculated from Table 76)

During the nineteenth century, Dutch yields, which had become very high by 1800, declined almost steadily and much faster than did the English norms. By World War I, the Netherlands was again close to being the country of lowest yields, but fell away again during and after World War II to a position of relatively moderate yields—below English yields but above American yields until the 1980's, and well above Swiss yields since the 1950's.

The right-hand panels trace the decennial differentials for the two great continental belligerents, France and Germany, and for a notable neutral, Switzerland. The chart shows the rapid recovery of the demoralized French market toward the norm in the first three decades of the nineteenth century.

After 1830, the performance of the French markets was much worse than that of the English and most other markets for forty years. After the War of 1870, the French market again gained on the English norm. By the turn of the century, France had become a country of relatively low yields. After World War I, however, the French market lost ground steadily, even more rapidly than did the English market. After World War II, France became a country of very high yields.

German yields remained relatively high throughout the nineteenth century, although they declined with English yields. The rapid rise of Germany as a world power after 1870 was not accompanied by a larger than average decline in bond yields. After World War I and the first German inflation, German yields became very high. After World War II, West Germany often reported the highest bond yields until the 1970's, when the rapid rise of yields in England, France, and Holland transformed West Germany into a country of relatively low yields, although considerably above the low Swiss yields. Since 1920, German yields have consistently averaged 2½ to 3% above the lowest prevailing yields. It is a comment on events elsewhere that this consistency transformed Germany from a country of relatively high to one of relatively low yields.

Swiss bond yields began the twentieth century well above the norm; they were about as high as German bond yields. Swiss yields remained relatively high until World War II. Thereafter, the Swiss average approximated that of the United States, and then became by far the lowest of all the countries studied. Although recent Swiss yields have been at the high end of the range of lowest prevailing yields since the late seventeenth century, Switzerland is the only country in recent times to stay within that range. Long-term yields in all the other countries have soared far above this historical range.

TRENDS OF MODERN SHORT-TERM INTEREST RATES

The level of short-term interest rates within a country is even more difficult to define than the level of long-term interest rates because there are many types of prime short-term credit instruments, their rates differ widely, and they are often governed by banking legislation. The trends, however, are usually unambiguous. For the same reasons, short-term rates in different countries usually are not comparable, though trends in differentials can be stated with some precision.

Table 77 summarizes short-term interest rates in these nine Western countries in the same manner that Table 76 summarized long-term bond yields in the same countries. Only one short rate is quoted for each country for each period of time. The nature of the series used in the table is not uniform from country to country or over time in one country, as the notes below the table indicate.

TABLE 77
Review of Medieval and Modern Western European and American Short-Term Interest Rates

Period	Minimum Rates on Best Credits by Half-Centuries*									
	England	France	Dutch Republic. Holland	Spanish Netherlands. Belgium	Germany	Sweden	Switzerland	Italy	Canada	United States
13th century										
1st half				10.00				20.00		
2nd half		15.00		10.00				8.00		
14th century										
1st half		15.00		10.00				7.00		
2nd half		15.00		10.00				5.00		
15th century										
1st half	10.00			5.00	5.00			5.00		
2nd half	10.00			5.00	5.00			5.00		
16th century										
1st half		5.00		4.00	4.50			4.00		
2nd half		8.00		6.25	5.00			5.00		
17th century										
1st half	6.00		6.00							
2nd half	3.00 [a]		1.75			6.00				
18th century										
1st half	3.00 [b]	4.00	1.75			4.00				
2nd half	5.00 [a]	4.00	2.00			3.00				
19th century										
1st half	3.57 [b]	4.00 [a]	2.87	3.71	3.90	4.00	4.11			7.99
2nd half	2.09 [b]	2.09 [b]	2.40	2.29	2.97	4.17	3.35			4.51
20th century										
1st half	0.83 [b]	1.69	1.26	1.83	2.18	2.80	1.33		1.90	0.87
2nd half	3.09	3.88	1.72	2.65	3.66	3.52	1.73		2.09	2.58

Period	Decennial Averages*								
	England	France	Holland	Belgium	Germany	Sweden	Switzerland	Canada	United States
19th century									
1st decade	5.00 [b]	5.32 [a]							
2nd decade	4.90	4.49	3.91		6.33				
3rd decade	3.95	4.01	3.05	3.71	5.07				
4th decade	3.62	4.00	2.87	4.67	4.28		4.14		10.64
5th decade	3.57	4.10	3.13	4.25	3.90		4.11		7.99
6th decade	3.84	4.20	3.06	4.59	4.03	5.09	4.11		8.49
7th decade	4.18	3.37 [b]	3.79	3.72	3.84	5.53	4.57		7.07
8th decade	2.96	3.43	3.31	3.36	4.09	5.00	4.08		6.46
9th decade	2.57	2.71	2.72	3.01	2.98	4.17	3.35		5.14
10th decade	2.09	2.09	2.40	2.29	2.97	4.55	3.78		4.51

TABLE 77 (*Continued*)

Period	Decennial Averages*								
	Eng- land	France	Holland	Belgium	Ger- many	Sweden	Swit- zerland	Canada	United States
20th century									
1st decade	3.16	2.47	3.10	2.89	3.42	5.15	3.68		4.72
2nd decade	3.82	2.68	3.12	3.47	4.09	5.44	3.67		4.72
3rd decade	4.26	4.15	3.67	4.59	6.28^c	5.10	3.10		5.00
4th decade	1.32	2.44	1.26	2.26	3.85	3.06	1.53	2.50	1.56
5th decade	0.83	1.69	1.51	1.83^d	2.18^e	2.80	1.33	1.90	0.87
6th decade	3.09	3.88	1.72	2.65^d	3.62	3.52	1.73	2.09	2.58
7th decade	5.80	4.89	3.36	4.53	3.66	5.08	2.88	4.36	4.64
8th decade	9.64	8.39	5.36	7.53	5.98	6.41	4.57^f	8.09	7.17
9th decade	11.46	10.85	6.90	10.45	6.41	9.31	4.37	11.25	9.57

*Lowest decennial average where available; otherwise, lowest reported rate. Lowest yield or yields underlined for each period of time.

^{a}Official discount rate.

^{b}Free open market.

^{c}1925–1929.

^{d}For these dates no open market rates are available; these are rates estimated from earlier and later relationships between open market and official discount rates.

^{e}1940–1944.

^{f}Decade average incorporates market rate estimated as official discount rate plus $1\frac{1}{2}$% for years 1976–1979.

KEY TO TABLE 77

England: 15th century and 1st half 17th century: lowest reported commercial loan rates. 2nd half 17th century and 2nd half 18th century: lowest bank rate. 1st half 18th century: lowest open market rates. 19th and 20th centuries: decennial averages of open market rates.

France: 13th, 14th, 16th, and 18th centuries: lowest reported commercial loan rates. 1st 7 decades of 19th century: average of official discount rate. 1870–1939: decennial averages of open market rates. 1939–1989: decennial averages of day-to-day money.

Holland: 17th and 18th centuries: lowest reported commercial loan rates. 1814–1872: decennial averages of official discount rate. 1873–1941: decennial averages of open market rates. 1946–1989: decennial averages of 3-month Treasury bills.

Spanish Netherlands and Belgium: 13th to 16th centuries: lowest reported commercial loan or open market rate. 1823–1849: decennial averages of official discount rate. 1850–1939: decennial averages rates. 1942–1989: decennial averages of 4-month Treasury bills.

Germany: 15th and 16th centuries: lowest reported commercial loan rates. 1814–1989: decennial averages of open market rates.

Sweden: 17th, 18th, and 19th centuries to 1854: lowest official discount rate. 1855–1979: decennial averages of official discount rate.

Switzerland: 1837–1899: decennial averages of official discount rates. 1900–1989: decennial averages of private discount rate for 3-month bills. 1980–1989: Treasury bill rate.

Canada: 1934–1989: decennial averages of official discount rates.

United States: 1831–1989: decennial averages of commercial paper rates.

A few of the averages in this table cover less than ten years because of lack of data. These are so designated in the individual country tables from which this table is derived.

Rates derived from previous regional tables.

THE SUPRASECULAR TREND OF MEDIEVAL AND MODERN
SHORT-TERM INTEREST RATES BY FIFTY-YEAR PERIODS

Chart 80 summarizes the trend over seven centuries of the minimum short-term interest rates from Table 78. This is done on the same principles that were used in Chart 78 to summarize the data on minimum long-term interest rates.

A broad picture of a declining trend of minimum short-term commercial rates is clear from the chart. The fifty-year minima were generally stable or declining except during the financial calamities commencing in the late sixteenth and late eighteenth centuries.

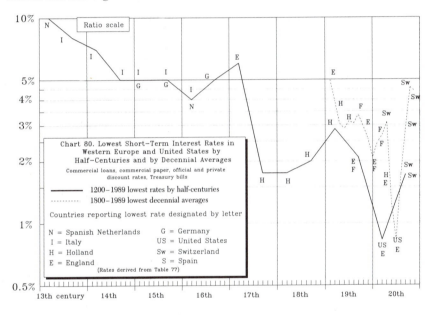

Chart 80. Lowest Short–Term Interest Rates in Western Europe and United States by Half–Centuries and by Decennial Averages
Commercial loans, commercial paper, official and private discount rates, Treasury bills

———— 1200–1989 lowest rates by half-centuries
- - - - - - - 1800–1989 lowest decennial averages

Countries reporting lowest rate designated by letter

N = Spanish Netherlands   G = Germany
I = Italy   US = United States
H = Holland   Sw = Switzerland
E = England   S = Spain
(Rates derived from Table 77)

A comparison of the summary of short-term rates on Chart 80 with the summary of long-term rates on Chart 78 reveals differences. Both series tended to decline most of the time after 1200, but the short rates declined both further and more irregularly. The short-term rates started higher and ended lower than the long-term rates. They were above long rates in the thirteenth, the early fourteenth, and the fifteenth centuries, were equal in the early sixteenth century, rose more than did long rates in the late sixteenth and early seventeenth centuries, and came down during the late seventeenth century much more than did long rates. They have usually been below long rates ever since. In the twentieth century much more than in any other century, the short rates averaged far below the long rates.

THE SECULAR TRENDS OF MODERN SHORT-TERM
INTEREST RATES

Chart 80 also pictures the lowest decennial average of short rates for each decade since 1800. The countries reporting lowest short-term decennial averages were not always the same as the countries reporting lowest long-term decennial averages. Both lists are as follows:

Decade	Lowest Long-Term	Lowest Short-Term
1800–1809	England	England
1810–1819	England	Holland
1820–1829	England	Holland
1830–1839	England	Holland
1840–1849	England	Holland
1850–1859	England	Holland
1860–1869	England	France
1870–1879	England	England
1880–1889	England	England
1890–1899	England	England, France
1900–1909	England	France
1910–1919	England	France
1920–1929	United States	Switzerland
1930–1939	United States	Holland, England
1940–1949	United States	England, United States
1950–1959	Switzerland, United States	Switzerland, Holland
1960–1969	Switzerland	Switzerland
1970–1979	Switzerland	Switzerland
1980–1989	Switzerland	Switzerland

The United States appears only once as reporting the lowest average short rates for a decade. England reported lowest short rates much less often than it reported lowest long rates. France and Holland reported lowest short rates at times when their long rates were far from the lowest. The contrast suggests a difference between modern short-term market rates of interest and modern long-term bond yields. Short rates far more than long rates are a function of monetary policy, officially organized market machinery, and the technical structure of each market. Long rates in large and relatively free markets over long periods probably better reflect the economic behavior and investment preferences of large numbers of people acting without guidance, compulsion, or organization.

In the nineteenth century the decennial series of short rates followed a secular pattern very similar to that of the decennial series of long rates: Both declined most of the time and by about the same amount. The mid-century interruption, however, was larger for short rates than for long rates.

In the twentieth century, the long-term and short-term secular fluctuations were similar in time, but were different in extent: Short rates rose less in the first three decades and declined much more in the fourth and fifth decades. During the four decades after 1950, short rates typically rose more than did long rates.

COMPARATIVE TRENDS OF MODERN SHORT-TERM INTEREST RATES

Table 77 includes such a wide variety of short-term credit instruments that charting of differentials is impractical. It indicates, however, that in the nineteenth century the English short-term rates were often not the lowest although the English long rates were always the lowest. Dutch short rates averaged far below English short rates during much of the nineteenth century, and then at the turn of the century French short rates averaged below English short rates. English short rates, however, fell very rapidly in the fourth and fifth decades of the twentieth century and briefly became the lowest short rates. They were about the same as American short rates in the 1940's at a time when English bond yields were far above American bond yields. After 1950 English short rates rose far more than did those of other countries and became comparatively very high. Historically, England was often the country with lowest bond yields, but far less frequently was it the country with lowest short-term interest rates.

American short-term interest rates declined much more than did those of other countries during the nineteenth and the first half of the twentieth centuries. During this period they declined from the highest to the lowest among the nine countries. The American short rates, however, were usually far from the lowest. After 1950, they averaged well above Swiss and Dutch short rates, and since the 1960's, West German short rates also have averaged below American.

For most of the past four centuries, Holland's short-term interest rates remained at or fairly close to the lowest. The Dutch differential widened moderately in the late nineteenth century and during World War II. In fourteen decades out of the last eighteen, Dutch short rates have been below English short rates, and in all but one decade for which comparison is possible they have been below American short rates. French short rates were relatively high in the eighteenth and the first half of the nineteenth century. Soon thereafter they became the lowest in Europe. French bond yields in this period were always above English bond yields, but French money market rates were often below English money market rates. After World War I, however,

French short rates, like French bond yields, became relatively high, and since World War II, they have been relatively very high.

German short-term interest rates since 1800 were usually relatively high; they did not become relatively low in comparison with most other countries until the 1960's. During the first half of the nineteenth century, they came down much faster than others did, but from shortly after the formation of the Empire, the differential widened persistently. Even excluding the extraordinary inflation rates, the German short rates of the 1920's were the highest of all the nine countries. In the 1930's German short rates remained relatively high. After World War II, they rose considerably less than did short rates in most other countries and became, by the 1980's, among the lowest of any nation.

In the nineteenth century, Swiss short-term rates were relatively high. In the first half of the twentieth century, however, Swiss short-term rates declined in every decade. In the period after World War II, short rates in Switzerland rose relatively much less than elsewhere. From the 1950's through the 1980's, Swiss short rates have been the lowest in the Western world.

PART FIVE

Other Countries

Parts Two, Three, and Four have traced the course of what we have called the mainstream of interest-rate history. This arbitrary term has been used to describe the history of the principal credit markets of Western Europe and North America from their early beginnings during the Middle Ages down to the present day because out of these areas came the largest and most complex credit markets in the world. In a broad sense, the mainstream comprised a single entity, not so much because of the direct flow of funds from country to country, which was often imperfect or altogether suspended, but because the members of this group of important commercial nations had similarities of culture and historical origins that produced similarities of financial traditions and methods. Major world political and economic events affected each of these countries simultaneously and similarly, although in varying degrees.

Part Five will deal with the history of interest rates in a number of other nations. These histories are of two kinds. The first is the history of interest rates in countries such as Russia and China, which had autonomous credit traditions and interest-rate histories that were largely independent of the mainstream. Western financial influence penetrated both countries briefly in the nineteenth and early twentieth centuries, resulting in a few decades when their credit instruments and interest rates bore a close resemblance to those of the mainstream. These epochs, however, were transient. Soviet Russia developed credit instruments and interest rates based on techniques and economic principles that are quite different from those of the Western world. China had a long history of credit and interest rates quite separate and apart from Western influence; that tradition continued under the Communist regime after 1949. In recent years, however, Soviet and Chinese citizens have demonstrated an appreciation of Western traditions of democracy and markets.

The second kind of history in Part Five belongs to countries in Asia, Africa, and Latin America that have been heavily influenced by the mainstream of interest-rate history but because of remoteness, newness or size, have not themselves had a great influence on the course of the mainstream. Some, such as India, have indeed had a long autonomous credit history before modern times, but the then-prevailing interest rates are not available to us. Other countries, Australia and New Zealand, for example, are relatively new and undeveloped but have directly inherited Western financial traditions and methods.

Japan is unique among the countries covered in Part Five. Its credit traditions were separate from, but heavily influenced by, the Western world. Until recently, Japan has had little influence on the mainstream of interest-rate history. But its rapid development into a great industrial and trading nation suddenly made Japan's role in world financial markets intense. It is now very much a part of the mainstream.

The interest-rate history of most of these countries has not been traced back into earlier centuries, for which the data are usually not available. Quotations for much of the twentieth century, however, are both available and provided here. They illustrate the similarities and the wide range of differences in modern interest rates in many parts of the world. A number of these rates and bond yields are derived from very small and closely controlled markets and therefore lack the economic significance attributed to rates and yields in the world's great investment markets. No attempt has been made to discover and present the local laws or economic conditions that influenced these interest rates.

Chapter XXIV

Japan

During the two decades since 1970, Japan has emerged as a great financial power in the world. Its remarkable recovery after World War II was based upon a high rate of investment in manufacturing plant and equipment, and a high priority on exports. Export markets were—and are—especially important to Japan because exports provide the means to finance imports of raw materials in a nation that is relatively deficient in natural resources. In Japan's high-growth period from the 1950's to the 1970's, government policies designated a number of key industries for development, and then promoted them by means of protection from foreign competition and favorable financing. Among these were oil refining, petrochemicals, automobiles, industrial machinery, and electronics and electrical appliances.

In the high-growth period, Japan encouraged a high rate of personal savings by means of such devices as savings accounts that exempted interest earned from taxation. However, Japan's financial markets were much less developed than those of Western Europe and North America, and Japanese interest rates were comparatively high. The Japanese financial sector was segmented rather than integrated, interest rates were regulated, and financial interactions with the rest of the world were controlled. Japanese enterprises relied heavily on financial institutions, primarily banks, for external finance. Bond and money markets were almost insignificant.

Since the mid-1970's, a financial revolution has taken place in Japan. The advent of flexible exchange rates and the first oil shock in 1973—which led to high inflation, recession, and balance-of-payments problems in Japan, as elsewhere—strained the old, regulated financial system. The Japanese economy quite simply had become too large and too important internationally to continue with a heavily regulated and isolated financial system. Regulatory barriers became counterproductive, hindering Japan from taking advantage of profitable opportunities in finance both at home and in international markets. Realizing this, the Japanese liberalized and decontrolled much of their financial system after 1975. Active Japanese money and bond markets developed, and, along with Japan's stock market, were increasingly opened up to foreign participation. The bond market in particular developed because the Japanese government, beginning in 1975, ran large fiscal deficits financed by bond issues. (540) As the 1990's begin, the liberalization of finance in Japan is far from complete. But its effects have been remarkable. Japan is no longer a country of high interest rates. Indeed, during the 1980's Japan's interest rates became among the lowest of any country.

BACKGROUND

Japan abruptly entered the modern world in 1867, when the last Shogunate fell and political power, after a lapse of several centuries, was returned to the emperor. Under Emperor Meiji (1852–1912), the old feudal society was hastily modernized. The political and economic forms of Europe and America were imitated and adapted to Japanese requirements.

The Japanese civilization is ancient. Money, credit, and banking existed over the centuries. There is a long history of rice money, metallic money, and even some paper money. This history need not detain us, however, because we can discover no indication of the rates of interest that then prevailed. Japan, like China, was an agricultural country. Japan also imported many Chinese monetary and financial techniques. There is little evidence of early Japanese commercial credit markets, and it seems probable, therefore, that credit in early Japan, as in China, was primarily consumer credit and probably of short term and at high rates.

Soon after 1867, the Japanese made a close study of the banking systems of Europe and America. At first they modeled their new banking system on the then-new national banking system of the United States. (541) The resulting plethora of banks without a central bank proved unsuccessful, and in 1882 Japan adopted a banking system modeled on Western European systems. The Japanese organized a central bank, the Bank of Japan, which became a bankers' bank and the fiscal agent of the government. After 1900, however, the powers of the central bank were reduced; many other important banks sprang up, and the Bank of Japan lost control of the management of the currency and of the rate of interest. Unlike the bank rate in England, some of the rates charged by the Bank of Japan were below market rates. They were not penalty rates. The bank's loans were limited, not by rate, but by the security that the bank required and by the strict limits that the government put upon the volume of its loans.

Japan also quickly adopted almost all the credit instruments of the Western world. The government issued short-term and long-term bonds. These were bought and sold on public exchanges. Savings banks, credit unions, and insurance companies siphoned the savings of the people into long-term investments. Industry and commerce were financed at short term and at long term by a multiplicity of commercial banks and investment banks. As early as 1879, clearinghouses were organized.

Until quite recently, Japanese interest rates were high by Western standards. Although Japan had a 5% legal rate of interest, it had no usury laws, and bank loans usually commanded much higher rates. In Japan the central bank made loans at its stated discount rate only up to certain limited amounts. After these limits were reached, the rate rose. The lending rate, therefore, varied according to three variables: (a) the basic rate, (b) the type of loan, and (c) the amount of credit extended to each member bank. For most of Japan's modern history, there were few market borrowing and lending transactions outside the banking system; therefore, interest-rate quotations on long-term loans were few and did not have the basic significance that they have in Western countries. Bond prices and interest rates in the last few decades frequently were pegged or limited by decree, just as was done in wartime in Western countries. From World War II until the 1970's, government bond issues were few, and corporate issues tended to be bought and held by banks. Hence, corporate bonds differed little from long-term bank loans. (542)

INTEREST RATES

Table 78 is based on only a few of the wide variety of interest rates provided by modern Japan. The Bank of Japan alone quotes many different rates, as do other banks. The table provides the discount rate of the Bank of Japan and another series averaging the rates on actual loans at the Bank of Japan from 1883 through 1989. It also provides an average of the bank loan rate from 1937 through 1989, which was usually above the Bank of Japan's rates, and a call money, or money-market, series from 1937, which was relatively low until the 1950's. Longer-term bond yields are represented by government bonds and corporate debentures from 1930.

A rough picture of long-term trends and levels is provided by the decennial averages presented in tabular form below:

Year	Loans at Bank of Japan, Average of Annual Lows, %	Discount Rate of Bank of Japan, Average of Annual Lows, %	Bank Loan Rate, %	Call Money, %	Government Bonds, Average of Annual Averages or Lows, %	Corporate Debentures, Average of Annual Lows, %
1883–1889	6.50	6.73				
1890–1899	6.71	7.19				
1900–1909	7.34	7.81				
1910–1919	6.17	5.80				
1920–1929	7.07	7.05				
1930–1939	4.96	3.94	6.13*	2.57*	4.34	5.04
1940–1949	4.16	3.74	6.54	3.92	4.01	5.30
1950–1959	6.97	6.35	8.62	7.51[†]	5.99	8.37
1960–1969	7.19	5.99	7.79	7.77	6.68	7.99
1970–1979	6.81	5.25	7.61	7.27	6.99	7.74
1980–1989	5.26	4.28	6.47	6.07	5.91	6.33

*3 years.
[†] 6 years.

In the nineteenth century, Japanese short-term rates were high by European standards. Furthermore, contrary to the European trend, they tended to rise from the 1880's until the first decade of the twentieth century. Year-to-year changes were large. There were periods of lower rates, 4.75%, for example, in 1893, and frequent periods when rates exceeded 8–9%. Japan had a central bank, however, and it reported no crisis rates such as then recurred from time to time in the American call money market.

The World War I era witnessed a narrowing of the spread between Japanese and Western rates. Average short-term rates declined during the war and approached the higher part of the European ranges. This was just when European rates were rising. In the 1920's, these Japanese rates rose again. In the 1930's, they declined with Western rates, but never reached the low rates then common in Europe and America. The lowest reported Japanese rates in the 1930's were 2.51% for call money, 3.29% for the official discount rate, and a simultaneous 5.95% annual average of the bank loan rate. The lowest average rates for Japan reached during World War II were not very low. Bond prices and the discount rate were pegged for long periods in the Western manner, and market forces evidently were not permitted to act on the interest rate structure. Short-term rates of 3.10–3.65% were permitted during the war, as were government bond yields of 3.75% or so.

Directly after Japan's surrender in 1945 interest rates rose. They remained comparatively high until the 1970's, or throughout Japan's high-growth pe-

TABLE 78
JAPANESE INTEREST RATES: 1883–1989

Year	Loans at Bank of Japan		Discount Rate at Bank of Japan		Average Bank Loan Rate, %	Call Money, %	Corporate Debentures Yields		Long-Term Government Bond Yields	
	Low, %	High, %	Low, %	High, %			Low, %	High, %	Low, %	High, %
1883	7.99	7.99	8.03	8.40						
1884	7.99	9.02	7.30	9.49						
1885	7.01	10.00	7.67	10.22						
1886	5.00	7.01	5.48	7.67						
1887	5.51	5.99	6.02	6.57						
1888	5.80	6.79	6.02	7.30						
1889	6.21	7.01	6.57	7.67						
7-yr. av.	6.50	7.69	6.73	8.19						
1890	6.50	7.01	6.94	7.67						
1891	6.39	7.67	6.75	8.03						
1892	6.02	6.39	6.39	6.75						
1893	4.75	6.21	5.11	6.94						
1894	6.21	8.03	6.94	8.40						
1895	7.30	8.03	8.03	8.40						
1896	7.30	7.67	8.03	8.40						
1897	7.67	9.13	8.40	9.13						
1898	8.40	9.86	8.40	9.86						
1899	6.57	8.40	6.94	8.40						
10-yr. av.	6.71	7.84	7.19	8.20						
1900	8.03	9.86	8.03	9.86						
1901	2.86	2.86	2.86	2.86						
1902	6.94	9.86	7.30	9.86						
1903	6.21	6.94	6.94	7.30						
1904	6.21	7.67	6.94	8.40						
1905	7.67	8.40	8.40	9.13						
1906	6.94	8.40	7.67	9.13						
1907	6.94	8.03	7.67	8.40						
1908	8.03	8.03	8.40	8.40						
1909	6.57	8.03	6.94	8.40						
10-yr. av.	6.64	7.81	7.12	8.17						
1910	5.11	5.84	4.75	5.48						
1911	5.11	5.84	4.75	5.48						
1912	5.84	6.94	5.48	6.57						
1913	6.94	6.94	6.57	6.57						
1914	6.94	7.67	6.57	7.30						
1915	7.67	7.67	7.30	7.30						

TABLE 78 (*continued*)

Year	Loans at Bank of Japan		Discount Rate at Bank of Japan		Average Bank Loan Rate, %	Call Money, %	Corporate Debentures Yields		Long-Term Government Bond Yields	
	Low, %	High, %	Low, %	High, %			Low, %	High, %	Low, %	High, %
1916	6.21	7.67	5.84	7.30						
1917	5.48	6.21	5.11	5.84						
1918	5.48	6.94	5.11	6.57						
1919	6.94	8.76	6.57	8.03						
10-yr. av.	6.17	7.05	5.81	6.64						
1920	8.76	8.76	8.03	8.03						
1921	8.76	8.76	8.03	8.03						
1922	8.76	8.76	8.03	8.03						
1923	8.76	8.76	8.03	8.03						
1924	7.67	10.40	8.03	8.03						
1925	7.21	9.86	7.30	8.03						
1926	6.21	9.13	6.57	7.30						
1927	4.75	8.76	5.48	6.57						
1928	4.38	7.67	5.48	5.48						
1929	5.48	6.21	5.48	5.48						
10-yr. av.	7.07	8.71	7.05	7.30						
1930	5.48	5.66	5.11	5.48			6.36	6.62	5.50	5.72
1931	5.84	7.30	5.84	6.57			6.24	6.45	5.18	5.73
1932	5.11	7.30	4.38	5.89			6.49	7.00	5.47	6.02
1933	4.38	5.11	3.65	4.38			5.12	5.97	4.12	4.95
1934	5.11	5.29	3.65	3.65			4.60	4.78	4.12	4.12
1935	5.11	5.11	3.65	3.65			4.41	4.58	4.12	4.12
1936	4.75	5.11	3.29	3.65			4.38	4.38	3.70	3.91
1937	4.75	4.75	3.29	3.29	6.42	2.66	4.20	4.49	3.69	3.69
1938	4.56	4.75	3.29	3.29	6.24	2.51	4.31	4.33	3.69	3.69
1939	4.47	4.47	3.29	3.29	5.95	2.56	4.32	4.32	3.81	n.a.
10-yr. av.	4.96	5.49	3.94	4.31	6.20 (3-yr. av.)	2.58 (3-yr. av.)	5.04	5.29	4.34	4.20 (9-yr. av.)
1940	4.02	4.02	3.29	3.29	5.00	2.81	4.31	4.32	3.81	
1941	4.02	4.02	3.29	3.29	4.96	2.59	4.31	4.32	3.83	
1942	4.02	4.02	3.29	3.29	4.86	2.74	4.31	4.32	3.78	
1943	4.02	4.02	3.29	3.29		3.03	4.29	4.30	3.77	
1944	3.65	4.02	3.29	3.29		3.10	4.29	4.29	3.76	
1945	3.65	3.65	3.29	3.29	4.70	3.10	4.28	4.28	3.76	
1946	3.65	4.38	3.29	4.65	5.62	3.29	4.30	4.38	3.70	
1947	4.38	4.38	4.65	4.65	7.37	4.02	4.46	7.03	3.70	4.44

TABLE 78 (*continued*)

Year	Loans at Bank of Japan		Discount Rate at Bank of Japan		Average Bank Loan Rate. %	Call Money. %	Corporate Debentures Yields		Long-Term Government Bond Yields	
	Low. %	High. %	Low. %	High. %			Low. %	High. %	Low. %	High. %
1948	4.38	5.84	4.65	5.11	9.67	5.29	9.07	10.64	4.50	5.53
1949	5.84	5.84	5.11	5.11	10.10	6.21	10.02	10.83	5.52	5.54
10-yr. av.	4.16	4.42	3.74	3.93	6.54 (8-yr. av.)	3.62	5.36	5.87	4.01	5.17 (3-yr. av.)
1950	5.84	5.84	5.11	5.84	9.23	6.41	8.95	9.46	5.50	
1951	5.84	6.57	5.84	5.84	9.09	7.12	8.96	9.00	5.50	
1952	6.57	6.57	5.84	5.84	9.13	8.06	8.99	9.01	5.50	
1953	6.57	6.57	5.84	5.84	8.76	7.82	8.98	9.02	5.50	7.22
1954	6.57	6.57	5.84	5.84	8.76	7.66	9.00	9.04	6.32	6.63
1955	6.57	8.03	5.84	7.30	8.54	8.03	8.30	9.00	6.32	6.37
1956	8.03	8.03	7.30	7.30	8.16		7.38	7.97	6.34	
1957	8.03	9.13	7.67	8.39	8.16		7.37	7.91	6.32	
1958	8.03	9.13	7.30	8.39	8.40		7.88	7.90	6.32	
1959	7.67	8.03	6.94	7.30	7.97		7.89	7.92	6.32	
10-yr. av.	6.97	7.45	6.35	6.79	8.62	7.52 (6-yr. av.)	8.37	8.62	5.99	6.74 (3-yr. av.)
1960	8.03	8.40	6.94	7.30	8.24	8.40	7.85	8.50	6.43	6.43
1961			6.57	7.30	8.15	8.31	7.87	8.50	6.43	6.43
1962			6.57	7.30	8.34	8.79	7.90	8.75	6.43	6.43
1963			5.84	6.57	7.79	7.48	8.50	9.20	6.43	6.43
1964			5.84	6.57	7.90	10.02				
1965			5.48	6.21	7.80	6.87				
1966	6.98	7.21	5.48	5.48	7.48	8.84	7.51	7.84	6.80	6.80
1967	6.88	7.00	5.48	5.84	7.31	6.39	7.55	8.57	6.85	6.98
1968	7.04	7.23	5.84	6.21	7.46	7.88	8.03	8.22	7.01	7.05
1969	7.03	7.37	5.84	6.25	7.41	7.70	8.71	9.07	7.05	7.14
10-yr. av.	7.19 (5-yr. av.)	7.44 (5-yr. av.)	5.99	6.50	7.79	8.07	7.99 (8-yr. av.)	8.58 (8-yr. av.)	6.68 (8-yr. av.)	6.71 (8-yr. av.)
1970	7.38	7.47	6.00	6.25	7.66	8.28	9.03	9.39	7.14	7.21
1971	7.10	7.45	4.75	5.75	7.59	6.41	7.42	8.72	7.20	7.24
1972	6.33	7.08	4.25	4.75	7.05	4.72	6.63	7.19	6.39	7.16
1973	6.32	7.91	4.25	9.00	7.19	7.16	7.08	10.73	6.41	7.79
1974	8.08	9.55	9.00	9.00	9.11	12.54	10.70	12.52	8.79	10.02
1975	8.60	9.51	6.50	9.00	9.10	10.67	9.10	11.83	9.30	10.05

TABLE 78 (*continued*)

Year	Loans at Bank of Japan Low. %	Loans at Bank of Japan High. %	Discount Rate at Bank of Japan Low. %	Discount Rate at Bank of Japan High. %	Average Bank Loan Rate. %	Call Money. %	Corporate Debentures Yields Low. %	Corporate Debentures Yields High. %	Long-Term Government Bond Yields Low. %	Long-Term Government Bond Yields High. %
1976	7.96	8.23	6.50	6.50	8.26	6.98	8.59	9.07	6.36	8.79
1977	6.34	7.95	4.25	6.50	7.56	5.68	6.36	8.37	6.27	8.58
1978	5.50	6.29	3.50	4.25	6.31	8.36	5.59	6.38	5.97	6.21
1979	4.44	6.51	3.50	6.25	6.29	5.86	6.93	8.34	6.11	8.76
10-yr. av.	6.81	7.80	5.25	6.73	7.61	7.27	7.74	9.25	6.99	8.18
1980	6.71	9.40	6.25	9.00	8.32	10.93	8.12	9.50	8.50	10.30
1981	6.95	7.94	5.50	7.25	7.79	7.43	7.70	8.49	7.93	9.15
1982	6.28	6.77	5.50	5.50	7.23	6.94	7.34	8.10	7.50	8.53
1983	5.89	6.28	5.00	5.50	7.05	6.39	7.09	7.39	6.93	7.77
1984	5.70	5.81	5.00	5.00	6.66	6.10	6.21	7.16	6.30	6.94
1985	5.69	5.78	5.00	5.00	6.52	6.46	7.56	6.26	5.82	6.79
1986	4.35	5.70	3.00	5.00	5.91	4.79	5.14	6.70	4.61	5.81
1987	3.37	3.75	2.50	3.00	5.09	3.51	4.71	6.89	3.38	5.48
1988	3.37	3.38	2.50	2.50	4.93	3.62	4.62	5.06	3.90	4.83
1989	4.25	5.75	2.50	4.25	5.34	4.87	4.50	6.47	4.26	5.87
10-yr. av.	5.26	6.06	4.28	5.20	6.48	6.10	6.30	7.20	5.91	7.15

SOURCES

Phra Sarasas, *Money and Banking in Japan* (London: Heath Cranton, 1940), pp. 172ff.

Bank of Japan, *Economic Statistics of Japan.*

IMF, *International Financial Statistics.*

Morgan Guaranty Trust Company, *World Financial Markets.*

OECD, *Financial Statistics Monthly.*

riod. Between 1945 and 1949, the discount rate rose from 3.29 to 5.11% (annual lows), and the bank loan rate rose from 4.70 to 10.10% (annual average). Call money rose from 3.10 to 6.21%, and the yield of corporate debentures rose from 4.28 to 10.02%. The year 1949 marked the high point of postwar Japanese corporate debenture yields until 1973, but not of all short-term rates. By 1959 the Bank of Japan rates were well above their 1949 levels, but some other rates were lower.

In the 1960's, Japanese interest-rate trends were mixed. Government bond yields rose on average, while the yields on corporate debentures tended to decline a bit. Short-term rates were mixed. Call money rose briefly to over 10% in 1964 but soon came down below 6%. The discount rate of the Bank of Japan never rose to crisis levels, and its average for this decade was lower than in the 1950's.

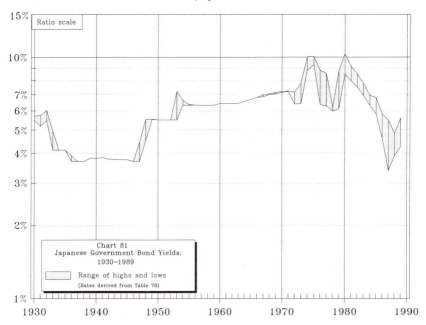

Chart 81
Japanese Government Bond Yields:
1930–1989

Range of highs and lows
(Rates derived from Table 78)

In the eventful 1970's, Japanese interest rates rose with those of all industrial nations. In the years 1973–1975 the discount rate at the Bank of Japan rose to 9%, call money reached 12.57%, corporate debentures reached 12.52%, and government bonds advanced to over 10%. Japan coped with an acute inflation and was using the traditional interest-rate tool. Chart 81 shows that Japanese government bond yields were stable but at a comparatively high level from the early 1950's to the early 1970's; these were regulated rates, and there was no open and active government bond market, such as existed in Western countries. The aftermath of the oil price shock sent yields soaring from 1973 until 1975. Japan's discount rate, shown in Chart 82, followed a similar course.

Then began the liberalization of the Japanese financial system. From 1975 until 1978, both bond yields and the discount rate fell to their lowest levels since the World War II era. In 1979, the second oil price shock began carrying both rates up, and by 1980, they had reached mid-1970's levels. In most other countries, however, the performance was worse, with interest rates in 1980–1981 moving well above 1974–1975 levels. Unlike these other countries, Japan avoided double-digit inflation and recession, although its growth rate slowed. After 1980, Japanese interest rates, long and short, declined considerably and became among the lowest in the world. Only Switzerland had lower rates. In 1989, Japanese rates rose somewhat, narrowing the gap in its favor with the main Western countries; the rise of Japanese rates continued into 1990.

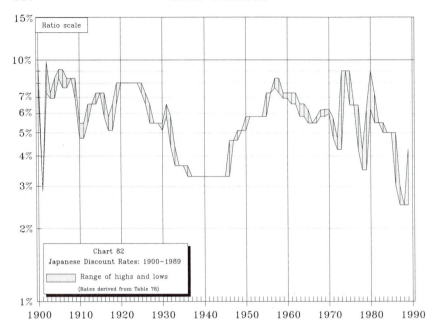

15%

Ratio scale

10%

7%
6%
5%

4%

3%

2%

Chart 82
Japanese Discount Rates: 1900–1989

Range of highs and lows
(Rates derived from Table 78)

1%

1900   1910   1920   1930   1940   1950   1960   1970   1980   1990

Short-Term Interest Rates. Trends of Japanese short-term market rates of interest have been different from trends of European and American rates over the past century. Short rates in Japan rose in the late nineteenth century, when the others' rates were declining; they declined in the period of World War I, when others' rates were rising. After the 1920's, the Japanese rates conformed slightly more to the general pattern: They declined with others in the 1930's and 1940's. After 1945, they rose with European rates and remained among the highest rates reported for a developed industrial and commercial nation until the mid-1970's. At that time, Japanese peak rates, both long and short, were well above U.S. rates but were far below the extraordinary English rates. Unlike most other countries, including the United States, Japan did not experience a rise of short-term rates to new highs after 1975. Indeed, the steep decline of Japan's short-term rates in the later 1980's resulted in rate levels that were the lowest in Japan's modern history since 1867.

Chapter XXV

The Old Sterling Area: Australia, New Zealand, South Africa, India, and Pakistan

The interest rates reviewed in this chapter are from countries as diverse in cultural traditions as any grouping in this history, but they were all bound until recent times by strong financial ties to England. Their interest-rate histories reflect little of their indigenous credit traditions but often reflect the fortunes of the sterling bloc and the leadership of the London money market. London's influence, however, was at times modified by local circumstances and local government policy. Furthermore, the many sterling crises of the postwar period resulted in weakening of the ties to London, as, of course, did Britain's entry into the European Community. The sterling area itself is now little more than a memory.

AUSTRALIA

The early English colonists in America and Canada did not develop local histories of credit and finance because they brought with them English mercantile traditions and financed much of their commerce in London. Australia was different: It was too far away. Furthermore, the original settlers of this penal colony did not enjoy a good credit standing at home. Therefore, a frontier credit market did develop and has been recorded.

For some time after 1788, when the first settlers arrived in Australia, a moneyless barter society prevailed. The colony was supposed to be self-sufficient. Government stores became trading centers and store receipts in time passed for money. The stores extended credit in kind and charged interest. (543)

In 1804 the governor, in a vain attempt to control the rate of interest, set 8% per annum as the maximum allowable on loans of either goods or money. This rate immediately became the minimum. (544) The governor soon raised the legal maximum to 10%, and this in turn became the minimum. Australian traders issued their own circulating notes, which sold at substantial discounts from scarce sterling notes; thus, a dual currency developed.

In 1817, the Bank of New South Wales was chartered and the indiscriminate issue of colonial currency was forbidden. As the bank at first paid no interest and merchants paid 8% interest on deposits, the new bank developed slowly. (545) It loaned at 10% and accepted store receipts at a discount as deposits, which it exchanged at maturity for Treasury bills. Its loans included mortgages on town property to run for not more than twelve months.

In the 1820's, seven other Australian banks were established. This competition brought the Bank of New South Wales's discount rate down from 10 to 8% in 1826, but in 1828, the rate was put up again to 10%. To obtain funds, certain of these banks paid 5% on six-month time deposits. A succession of booms and crises led to many bank failures.

In the 1830's, a number of English banks were established in Australia. English money sought investment there. English depositors received 5% pending permanent investment. (546) Overdrafts were allowed at 10%. In the late 1830's, competition forced the rates paid to depositors up to as high as 7% for deposits, subject to ten-day notice. (547) In 1841, the Derwent Bank in Tasmania received deposits in London at 8% and loaned the money in Tasmania on real estate mortgages at 12½%. This was a high point. In the 1840's, a slump brought down deposit rates to 3%. The lending rate, however, stayed at 10% or higher.

In 1819 the first Australian savings bank was organized. It paid interest at 7½% on deposits left for one year. (548) Deposits by convicts at the bank were mandatory. In 1832, the rate paid by the bank declined to 5%. This and other savings banks made mortgage loans at 10%.

During the early decades of the nineteenth century, bank loans in Australia commonly were at 10% but often were at 12½–15% and occasionally at 20%. In the late 1830's, mortgages were written at 10–20% interest for three- to ten-year terms. These, however, were "prime rates." Usury was common. Rates of 6⅔–7% a week are reported for short loans, which equaled 329–364% annual rate uncompounded. The conventional modern loan shark rate of 25% a week—equal to 1300% per annum—was also reported. (549)

By 1850, Australian "prime rates" had come down. The Savings Bank of New South Wales had reduced its deposit rate from 5 to 3⅓%; it loaned on mortgages at 8%. (550) Some other banks made mortgage loans at 7%. The commercial banks had reduced their rates on prime short loans from 10 to 6%, and some no longer paid any interest on demand deposits. Communications with London were improving, and the frontier penal colony was on its way to becoming a nation in its own right.

In 1851, gold was discovered in Australia. The discoveries were followed by a gold rush similar to California's, which had begun a few years earlier. In a decade Australia's population trebled, and wages and prices rose. (551) The gold boom arrested the decline of interest rates that had occurred before 1850. By the mid-1850's, the Savings Bank of New South Wales was again paying 5–6% on deposits. Sample mortgage rates at the Savings Bank remained in the earlier 7–8% range; banking expansion in the "golden decade" likely increased competition and narrowed intermediary spreads. In commercial banking, demand deposits earned from 0 to 3% in the third quarter of the nineteenth century, while banks in Sydney usually discounted bills at 5–7%, and those in Melbourne, at 6–9%. Overdraft rates ranged from 6–10% in Sydney and 6–12% in Melbourne. The commercial banking data are too scattered to support generalizations but appear to indicate no upward or downward trends in this period. (552)

For the Savings Bank of New South Wales, the deposit rate data are more complete. They indicate a level of 5–6% from the mid-1850's to 1894, and then a 3½ to 4% range until 1913, except for 1898 when the rate dipped to 3%. (553) Scattered mortgage rates for this bank were only a little higher, and so were likely rates on best credits. It thus appears that local bank interest rates in Australia barely declined in the late nineteenth century, while rates were falling in Europe and America. Most of the Australian decline came in the mid-1890's. From then to 1914, Australian rates rose very little, whereas the rise in Europe and America was greater.

Table 79 traces the history of market rates of interest in Australia since 1930. It provides two series: the market yields of short-term and of long-term government bonds. These were theoretical yields of two-year and of twelve-year bonds read from a schedule of the market yields of all taxable issues. The Reserve Bank of Australia did not quote a discount rate until 1970. During the 1970's, its low was 4.89% (1972), and its high, 14.82% (1976). In the 1980's, the low was 11.11% (1980), and the high, 16.93% (1986).

The interest rates quoted since 1930 were all within the range of Western European rates until the 1980's, when they became somewhat higher. The frontier had given way to a modern agricultural and industrial state with interest rates that were at times a trifle high, but not reminiscent of the primitive financial markets of the early nineteenth century.

After World War II, Australia suffered about the same degree of inflation as did the rest of the sterling area. Its postwar economic growth was very rapid, but did not lead to unusual rates of interest. The broad trends of Australian interest rates from the 1930's to the 1970's were similar to those of the

TABLE 79
AUSTRALIAN, NEW ZEALAND, AND SOUTH AFRICAN INTEREST RATES: ANNUAL AVERAGES, 1930–1989

Year	Australia Government Bonds Short Term, %	Australia Government Bonds Long Term, %	New Zealand Official Discount Rate, %	New Zealand Government Bonds, Long Term, %	South Africa Official Discount Rate, %	South Africa Government Bonds 3-Month Bills, %	South Africa Government Bonds Long Term, %
1930		5.12			5.87		
1931		5.55			5.32		
1932		6.06			5.77		
1933		4.42		3.94	3.82		
1934		3.75	4.00	3.53	3.50		
1935		3.35	3.79	3.33	3.50		
1936		3.58	2.42	3.72	3.50	0.75	
1937	3.44	3.88	2.00	3.61	3.50	0.75	3.20
1938	3.38	3.84	2.21	3.81	3.50	0.75	3.45
1939	3.84	3.91	3.68	4.24	3.50	0.75	3.70
10-yr. av.	3.55 (3-yr. av.)	4.35	3.02 (6-yr. av.)	3.74 (7-yr. av.)	4.18	0.75 (4-yr. av.)	3.45 (3-yr. av.)
1940		3.30	2.00	3.61	3.50	0.75	3.40
1941	2.38	3.23	1.50	3.37	3.12	0.75	3.00
1942	2.45	3.24	1.50	3.20	3.00	0.75	3.00
1943	2.48	3.23	1.50	3.18	3.00	0.75	3.00
1944	2.45	3.24	1.50	3.16	3.00	0.75	3.05
1945	2.48	3.25	1.50	3.18	3.00	0.74	3.05
1946	1.70	3.24	1.50	3.01	3.00	0.63	2.89
1947	2.12	3.17	1.50	3.02	3.00	0.63	2.63
1948	2.34	3.14	1.50	3.03	3.00	0.69	2.90
1949	2.00	3.12	1.50	3.00	3.12	0.87	3.33
10-yr. av.	2.27 (9-yr. av.)	3.22	1.55	3.18	3.07	0.73	3.03
1950	1.95	3.14	1.50	3.07	3.50	1.00	3.63
1951	2.01	3.53	1.50	3.08	3.50	1.00	3.60
1952	2.49	4.34	1.50	3.85	4.00	1.37	4.28
1953	3.07	4.48	1.50	4.01	4.00	1.69	4.50
1954	3.34	4.46	3.12	3.98	4.00	1.91	4.46
1955	3.79	4.52	5.25	4.15	4.25	2.51	4.33
1956	4.71	5.03	7.00	4.65	4.50	3.21	4.73
1957	4.57	5.02	7.00	4.82	4.50	3.25	4.75
1958	4.29	4.97	7.00	4.95	4.50	3.63	5.13
1959	3.99	4.92	6.75	4.85	4.00	3.45	5.25
10-yr. av.	3.42	4.44	4.21	4.14	4.08	2.30	4.47

TABLE 79 (*continued*)

Year	Australia Government Bonds		New Zealand		South Africa		
	Short Term, %	Long Term, %	Official Discount Rate, %	Government Bonds, Long Term, %	Official Discount Rate, %	Government Bonds 3-Month Bills, %	Government Bonds Long Term, %
1960	4.39	5.00	6.00	4.82	4.25	3.60	5.29
1961	4.99	5.27	7.00	5.08	4.75	4.25	5.77
1962	4.28	4.92	7.00	5.23	4.13	2.78	5.39
1963	3.81	4.58	7.00	5.15	3.50	1.99	4.75
1964	4.12	4.72	7.00	5.06	3.75	3.87	4.77
1965	4.85	5.21	7.00	5.10	4.92	4.04	5.60
1966	4.92	5.25	7.00	5.28	5.50	4.20	6.25
1967	4.55	5.25	7.00	5.51	6.00	4.86	6.50
1968	4.81	5.21	7.00	5.59	5.80	4.90	6.50
1969	5.25	5.81	7.00	5.54	5.50	4.62	6.50
10-yr. av.	4.60	5.12	6.90	5.24	4.81	3.91	5.73
1970	6.26	6.72	7.00	5.51	5.50	4.39	7.15
1971	6.14	6.87	7.00	5.52	6.50	5.38	8.38
1972	4.91	5.99	6.00	5.52	6.00	5.30	8.35
1973	6.30	7.11	6.00	5.80	3.78	3.18	7.83
1974	9.33	9.07	7.00	6.09	6.48	5.43	8.96
1975	8.46	9.75	7.00	6.33	7.42	6.12	9.71
1976	8.69	10.18	8.50	8.34	8.28	7.44	10.44
1977	9.74	10.28	10.00	9.23	8.41	7.87	11.01
1978	8.80	9.06	10.50	9.97	7.87	7.81	10.40
1979	9.62	9.76	13.00	12.04	4.70	5.26	9.26
10-yr. av.	7.83	8.25	8.50	7.74	6.38	5.83	9.10
1980	11.50	11.65	14.00	13.29	6.54	4.65	10.09
1981	13.76	13.96	13.00	12.83	14.54	9.80	12.99
1982	15.18	15.35	13.00	12.91	14.35	15.59	13.51
1983	12.84	14.33	7.50	12.18	17.75	13.45	12.67
1984	12.25	13.83	13.50	12.57	20.75	19.33	15.23
1985	14.03	14.10	19.80	17.71	13.00	17.56	16.79
1986	13.97	13.56	24.60	16.52	9.50	10.43	16.37
1987	13.17	13.47	18.55	15.69	9.50	8.71	15.30
1988	12.18	12.32	15.10	13.11	14.50	13.54	16.37
1989	15.28	13.79	14.75	12.91	16.17	16.47	17.01
10-yr. av.	13.42	13.55	15.06	13.68	12.86	11.58	14.29

SOURCES
League of Nations, *Statistical Year Book, 1939–40*, pp. 221, 225.
IMF, *International Financial Statistics.*

entire sterling area and indeed to those of most of the Western nations. Australian rates declined in the 1930's, moved even lower in the 1940's, and rose sharply in the 1950's and in the 1970's. They rose very sharply in the 1980's when the Australian price level more than doubled.

In 1930–1932 Australian long-term government bond yields rose from 5.12 to 6.06% annual average. These rates compared with 4.73–5.14% for Canadian government bonds and 4.46–4.53% for English government bonds. Long-term Australian bond yields were then above those of the other principal Commonwealth countries and those of the United States. In the 1930's, Australian long-term yields averaged above other Commonwealth yields, but were not as high as yields in a number of European countries, such as Norway and Italy. Long Australian yields came down substantially, however, and reached 3.35% in 1935. During World War II, they ranged close to 3.25%, when English yields ranged close to 3%. They remained low until 1951, but then they rose rapidly and reached an annual average of 5.03% in 1956. This was well above simultaneous Canadian government bond yields, then at 3.61%, and moderately above English government bond yields, then at 4.74%. In 1957–1960, however, Australian long-term bond yields declined slightly, while English and Canadian yields rose further. By 1960, Australian yields were no longer very high in relation to those of most other Commonwealth countries. They were well below English yields and above U.S. yields. In the 1960's, a decade of relatively low inflation, Australian yields increased only modestly and became relatively low. In the 1970's, a decade of high inflation, but less than that in England, Australian yields rose steeply to peak at 10.28%, still far below English yields. The 1980's reversed this situation; Australian yields soared while England's moderated somewhat, although they averaged higher than in the 1970's. These comparisons are brought out by the following tabulation of decennial averages:

DECENNIAL AVERAGES OF GOVERNMENT BOND YIELDS AND DISCOUNT RATES

Years Averaged	Long Government Bond Yields, %						
	Australia	New Zealand	South Africa	Canada	India	England	United States
1930–1939	4.35	3.74 (7 yrs.)	3.45 (3 yrs.)	3.88	3.35 (6 yrs.)	3.54	2.98
1940–1949	3.22	3.18	3.04	2.93	3.15	3.06	2.31
1950–1959	4.45	4.13	4.50	3.67	3.74	4.31	2.99
1960–1969	5.12	5.24	5.73	5.68	4.84	6.53	4.51
1970–1979	8.25	7.74	9.10	8.50	5.97	11.77	6.87
1980–1989	13.55	13.68	14.29	11.74	n.a.	10.42	10.40

DECENNIAL AVERAGES OF GOVERNMENT BOND YIELDS
AND DISCOUNT RATES (*Continued*)

Years Averaged	Official Discount Rates, %						
	Australia	New Zealand	South Africa	Canada	India	England	United States
	(2 yr. gov'ts)						
1930–1939	3.55	3.01 (6 yrs.)	4.19	2.50	4.05	2.48	1.83
1940–1949	2.29	1.55	3.08	1.90	3.00	2.00	1.09
1950–1959	3.41	4.21	4.07	2.64	3.60	3.95	2.20
1960–1969	4.60	6.90	4.81	4.77	4.81	5.92	4.01
1970–1979	7.83	8.50	6.38	8.09	7.80	9.44	6.46
1980–1989	13.42	15.06	12.86	11.23	9.90	11.71	8.50

NEW ZEALAND

Table 79 contains two interest-rate series for New Zealand starting in 1933: the official discount rate and a series of yields on long-term government bonds. The latter was based since 1954 on averages of bonds maturing in ten years or more; earlier, it was based on yields of the comparatively short 3s of 1960–1963.

The trends of government bond yields in New Zealand from 1933 to 1970 ran parallel to the trends of Australian government bond yields. These New Zealand yields were usually a little lower than the Australian yields presented in the table. In the mid-1930's, the New Zealand bond yields got down to 3.33% annual average, rose in 1939 to 4.24%, and declined again during the war to 3.01–3.20%, close to English bond yields. The Commonwealth's easy-money policy held New Zealand's yields down after the war, but in 1952 they started to rise. They reached a 4.01% average in 1953, and a 5.54% average in 1969. After 1969, New Zealand bond yields followed a remarkably independent course. They rose very little during the early 1970's, when most other yields were soaring and when the New Zealand discount rate was held at 7%. From 1975 to 1980, New Zealand's discount rate and bond yields doubled. A few years of stability were then followed by a period of tight money and very high rates in 1985–1987, after which yields fell to levels roughly equal to those that prevailed at the beginning of the 1980's.

The table of decennial averages presented in the Australian section above shows that New Zealand bond yields, which represented obligations of medium term, averaged moderately above English yields (for undated obligations) in the 1930's and 1940's and below English yields from the 1950's through the 1970's. In the 1980's, interest rates soared in New Zealand, as in Australia, and averaged well above English rates.

THE UNION OF SOUTH AFRICA

South African interest rates since 1930 are represented in Table 79 by three series: annual averages of official discount rates, of Treasury bill rates, and of the yields from long-term government bonds. The bond yields were based on yields to maturity of 4¼s of 1974 from 1954 to 1959; the earlier yields were based on the 3s of 1960–1970. Yields for years since 1960 were derived from an average of long-term bonds. South African bond yield trends followed closely those of the general Commonwealth. They were low in the late 1930's, declined further in the 1940's, and rose sharply in the 1950's. In the late 1930's, South African bond yields, at 3.20–3.70%, were lower than most Commonwealth bond yields. In the 1940's, they declined to a 3.04% average, or about the same as the English average and below many others. In contrast, in the 1950's, they averaged above the others, although they did not reach the peaks that English bond yields reached in 1957 and 1961. In the 1960's, South African long-term bond yields rose from about 5.50 to 6.50%, where they were well above most other Commonwealth yields but far below English yields. In the 1970's, yields rose further, peaking at around 11%—still well below the English peak rate but above most others. Yields rose through the 1980's, a period of political turmoil and growing international abhorrence of the white regime's policies toward the native black majority.

During these decades, the South African discount rate shifted its relative position from high to moderate to very high. In the 1930's, it did not decline below 3.50%, and in the 1940's, it did not decline below 3%. However, in the 1950's, its rise was moderate; the high was 4.50%. In fact, the reserve position of the sterling bloc was then defended, insofar as interest rates were employed in defense, almost entirely in London, where the reserves of the bloc were held. Other sterling bloc countries, such as South Africa, lacking international money markets, did not compete with the mother country in an effort to attract short-term balances. Therefore, short-term interest rates in South Africa and some other sterling bloc countries remained well below long-term bond yields during years of credit stringency, when English, New Zealand, and Canadian short-term rates sometimes rose well above their bond yields. In the 1960's, short-term South African rates remained low, averaging 3.91% for Treasury bills. In the stringencies of the 1970's, they rose only modestly, averaging less than 6%, but during the 1980's South Africa became a country of relatively high interest rates and bond yields.

TABLE 80
INDIAN AND PAKISTANI INTEREST RATES: ANNUAL AVERAGES, 1930–1989

Year	India				Pakistan	
	Official Discount Rate, %	Treasury Bills, %	Call Money, %*	Government Bond Yields, Long Term, %	Call Money, %†	Government Bond Yields, Long Term, %
1930	5.89	5.26				
1931	7.09	6.41				
1932	5.03	4.14				
1933	3.56	1.46				
1934	3.50	1.72		3.39		
1935	3.45	1.48		3.54		
1936	3.00	0.72		3.16		
1937	3.00	0.90	0.44	3.26		
1938	3.00	1.33	0.63	3.20		
1939	3.00	2.03	1.26	3.56		
10-yr. av.	4.05	2.55	0.78 (3-yr. av.)	3.35 (6-yr. av.)		
1940	3.00	1.21	0.68	3.61		
1941	3.00	0.76	0.28	3.33		
1942	3.00	0.86	0.29	3.45		
1943	3.00	0.96	0.25	3.20		
1944	3.00	0.57	0.25	3.11		
1945	3.00	0.39	0.25	3.10		
1946	3.00	0.43	0.49	2.79		
1947	3.00	0.44	0.49	2.86		
1948	3.00	0.49	0.51	2.97		2.91
1949	3.00	0.52	0.67	2.99	0.50	2.81
10-yr. av.	3.00	0.66	0.42	3.14		
1950	3.00		0.58	3.11	1.02	2.96
1951	3.50		0.98	3.28	1.02	2.98
1952	3.50	2.14	2.03	3.69	2.10	2.98
1953	3.50	2.42	2.21	3.64	1.01	3.06
1954	3.50	2.60	2.45	3.65	1.30	3.14
1955	3.50		2.59	3.72	1.45	3.15
1956	3.50		3.21	3.93	2.04	3.14
1957	4.00		3.71	4.14	2.06	3.20
1958	4.00		2.96	4.18	1.62	3.20
1959	4.00		2.74	4.05	1.66	3.25
10-yr. av.	3.60		2.35	3.74	1.53	3.11
1960	4.00		3.71	4.06	3.42	3.50
1961	4.00		4.35	4.11	3.87	3.69

TABLE 80 (*Continued*)

Year	India				Pakistan	
	Official Discount Rate, %	Treasury Bills, %	Call Money, %*	Government Bond Yields, Long Term, %	Call Money, %†	Government Bond Yields, Long Term, %
1962	4.00		3.71	4.36	3.36	3.81
1963	4.50		3.78	4.68	3.01	3.93
1964	4.63		3.97	4.73	3.59	3.90
1965	5.92		6.27	5.33	5.86	4.20
1966	6.00		4.36	5.55	4.70	4.48
1967	5.00		5.71	5.52	6.57	4.47
1968	5.00		3.79	5.07	6.24	4.76
1969	5.00		3.91	5.00	5.40	5.21
10-yr. av.	4.81		4.36	4.84	4.60	4.20
1970	5.00		5.68	5.00	5.50	5.50
1971	6.00		6.30	5.64	6.60	5.76
1972	6.00		4.69	5.65	5.34	5.76
1973	7.00		6.64	5.65	6.51	5.76
1974	9.00		13.52	6.03	10.33	5.77
1975	9.00		10.40	6.35	9.87	5.77
1976	9.00		11.28	6.29	9.37	9.04
1977	9.00		10.18	6.32	10.87	9.27
1978	9.00		8.05	6.37	10.41	9.48
1979	9.00		8.47	6.45	8.83	9.75
10-yr. av.	7.80		8.52	5.98	8.36	7.19
1980	9.00		7.24	6.71	8.63	11.20
1981	10.00		8.61	7.15	9.27	9.40
1982	10.00		7.27	7.59	9.51	9.36
1983	10.00		8.30	7.99	8.15	9.31
1984	10.00		9.95	8.65	9.97	9.25
1985	10.00		10.00	8.99	8.13	9.19
1986	10.00		9.97		6.59	n.a.
1987	10.00		9.83		6.25	8.26
1988	10.00		9.74		6.32	8.32
1989	10.00		11.12		6.29	8.19
10-yr. av.	9.90		9.20	7.85 (6-yr. av.)	7.91	8.25 (9-yr. av.)

*Interbank loans in Bombay.

†Interbank loans in Karachi.

SOURCES

League of Nations, *Statistical Year Book, 1939–40*, pp. 221, 225.

IMF, *International Financial Statistics*.

INDIA

India's ancient civilization has financial traditions very different from those of Western Europe. Its own autonomous history of credit and interest rates is unfortunately not available to this history. The modern Indian interest rates, quoted here in Table 80, were all a part of that segment of the Indian economy that reflected the influence of English finance and of modern Western commercial customs. Recent Indian market rates of interest are represented in Table 80 by four series: the official discount rates, rates on Treasury bills until 1955, rates on interbank or money-market loans (call money) in Bombay, and long-term government bond yields until 1986.

These modern Indian interest rates not only were within the familiar range of Western European rates in the twentieth century, but were often in the lower part of that range. When India achieved her political independence, European and Indian interest rates were low. India, faced with a vast program of capital expenditures, did not permit these demands to be reflected in high interest rates. Perhaps this was because so much of the capital expenditures had to be financed abroad. The postwar growth of the Indian economy has been rapid by such standards as the index of industrial production. Foreign and domestic resources have been expended and foreign loans incurred in large volume, but before 1971 the pressures of growth were not allowed to create a disruptive inflation, an abnormal growth in money supply, or strong pressures on the interest-rate structure. During the 1970's and 1980's, however, inflation grew more serious, and short-term interest rates rose sharply, while long-term interest rates rose more moderately.

The trends of these Indian interest rates from 1930 to 1990 were similar to the general European trends. Rates declined in the 1930's, declined further in the 1940's, rose gradually in the 1950's and 1960's, and rose more rapidly in the 1970's and 1980's. The official discount rate came down from an annual average of over 7% in 1931 to 3% in 1936, where it remained until 1950. After 1950, when all Commonwealth rates began to rise, the Indian discount rate went along, reaching 6% in 1966, 9% in the 1970's, and 10% in the 1980s. Thus, like the official discount rate of most Commonwealth countries, the Indian discount rate moved in a narrower range than that of the English bank rate.

Indian government bond yields were also relatively low during these early decades compared both to yields elsewhere and, more recently, to short-term rates in India. After 1933, they came down to 3.35% average, or about the same yield as was provided by English long-term bonds. In the mid-1940's they declined further. After independence, however, England's and India's yields diverged. English bond yields rose in one of their historic fluctuations from about the lowest to the highest of any major country. Indian bond yields rose much less and soon stood 100–150 basis points below

English bond yields. By 1960, these Indian government bond yields, at 4–4.1%, were often below American government bond yields and were far below the government bond yields in the other Commonwealth countries. In the 1960's, Indian bond yields averaged about 5%. In 1974–1975, the yields averaged slightly over 6%, which was well below U.S. yields and less than half the level of English yields. Yields approached 9% by the mid-1980's, still relatively low. Short-term Indian rates rose steeply in 1974, call money reaching 13.5%, but rates were lower during the next fifteen years. It seems that in India the negative yield curve between short-term rates and long-term yields was often extraordinarily large.

PAKISTAN

Table 80 presents Pakistani interest rates in two series: call money at Karachi and a series on government bond yields since 1948. Pakistani rates followed a pattern similar to that of Indian rates in that bond yields were usually very low compared to those of most other countries, while short rates behaved more like those of other countries. Both series, however, rose less than did comparable series for most European and North American countries in the 1970's and 1980's.

Chapter XXVI

Russia

BACKGROUND

The financial history of Russia is a history of chronic currency debasement. In the sixteenth century, the government recoined foreign money at a profit of 100%. In 1645–1676, the government managed to turn copper coins worth 5 rubles into coins with a nominal value of 312 rubles, which soon had to be devalued. In 1689–1725, the silver ruble was debased about 42%. In 1769, a paper assignat was introduced; by 1810, it had depreciated 75% in terms of silver rubles. In 1839, a silver standard was adopted, and assignat rubles were officially devalued by 71%. The Crimean War, 1853–1856, led to a new cycle of inflation. It was not until 1897, when a gold standard was introduced, that the country enjoyed a stable currency, but it lasted less than twenty years. (554)

World War I and the Revolution of 1917 led to a period of unprecedented inflation. By 1917, the ruble had lost 75% of its 1913 foreign-exchange value; by 1920, it had lost 99.9% of its 1913 foreign-exchange value. The commodity price index rose 5800% between 1913 and 1918 and rose 4.9 million% between 1913 and 1921. (555) The currency was reformed in 1921, when one new "1921" ruble was exchanged for ten thousand czarist rubles. Another devaluation occurred in 1922 in the ratio of one new "1922" ruble for a hundred "1921" rubles. This was not the end. In 1923, the rate of inflation increased; at one time the ruble was depreciating at the rate of 5% an hour. (556) In 1924, temporary stability was achieved after another devaluation. In all, fifty billion of czarist rubles were exchanged for one new "1924" ruble. After 1924, prices continued to rise, but at an orderly rate; for example, free market bread rose 40% in 1928 and another 119% in 1929. Rationing and price controls, however, obscured the changes in the value of the currency after 1924. Finally, in 1936, a period of real stability was achieved. This, however, was soon followed by World War II, another inflation, and other "reforms" of the currency. Prices fell from the late 1940's to the early 1950's, after which there was some evidence of a measure of price stability. But these were administered prices rather than market-determined prices.

Russian economic history falls into three parts. First, there were long centuries of medieval feudalism, during which a backward manorial economy was little concerned with commercial credit and money markets. This condition lasted well into the nineteenth century. Second, there was a brief period during the late nineteenth century when Russia attempted to develop a modern industrial and capitalistic economy in the manner of Western Europe; this lasted perhaps eight decades. Third, there followed seven decades of socialism under Communist direction. As the 1990's open, major changes in economic relationships in Soviet Russia appear to be on the horizon.

No history of interest rates is reported for the long centuries of Russian serfdom. Credit was confined largely to personal-consumption loans, as it was in most backward agricultural societies. Foreign trade was financed abroad. In medieval times, Italian bankers did not establish branches in Russia as they did throughout Western Europe. Instead, German, Dutch, and English traders financed the Baltic trade in Antwerp. As time passed, however, foreigners came to Russia and engaged in trade and manufacture. In this way Western financial methods gradually infiltrated and were imitated in the big cities.

Early Russian banks were rudimentary. By 1754, the state had established two banks, a "State Loan Bank for the Nobility" and a "State Commercial Bank." (557) Loans, however, were based on favoritism and lacked good collateral; both banks were closed in 1786. Further attempts by the state to organize banks met with limited success.

In the 1860's, following the emancipation of the serfs, a serious effort was made to create a banking system in the Western manner. The "State Bank" was organized in 1860 "to promote trade and stabilize the currency." It accepted demand and time deposits; made loans secured by securities, land, or merchandise; discounted commercial paper; bought securities and precious metals; and issued bank notes. Monetary troubles, however, persisted until the 1890's, and the ruble sold at heavy discounts in world markets. The monetary reforms of 1895–1897 devalued the ruble by one-third, provided for specie payments, and established a gold standard. Thereafter, for fourteen years, foreign capital was attracted in large volume and played a very important part in the economic development of Russia. The State Bank followed a very conservative policy; with foreign aid, the currency weathered the Russo-Japanese war, 1904–1905, and the revolution of 1905–1906.

After 1860, joint-stock commercial banks were also organized. By 1914,

Russia had 47 such banks, with 743 branches. (558) Like German banks, these banks conducted both commercial and investment banking and helped to finance a very rapid growth in Russian industry and commerce. A large part of their stock was foreign owned. By 1913 there were also some 300 private banking enterprises; largely unregulated, they represented the growth of an indigenous business class before World War I. (559)

In the nineteenth century, small municipal banks and mutual credit societies were organized. Joint-stock land banks sprang up, which issued their own ten- to sixty-six-year bonds and loaned the money on farm mortgages. Some of these banks helped the newly liberated peasants to buy their farms, and others helped the aristocracy to retain their estates. State savings banks were also organized, and by 1912 more than 8000 were in existence. Securities markets were organized to trade in state bonds, railway bonds, and shares. During these few decades of rapid Westernization after 1860, Russian credit forms and interest rates bore a rough resemblance to those of Western Europe.

World War I and the Revolution of 1917 brought this capitalistic development to an abrupt end. Russia's new dependence on foreign capital and on foreign commodity markets made her financial system highly vulnerable to war. Russia's total war expenditures of 67 billion rubles were covered 25% by taxation, 29% by long-term loans, 23% by Treasury bills, and 23% by note circulation. Between 1914 and 1917, currency circulation increased fifteenfold, and retail prices rose fifteenfold. (560)

The period of "War Communism," 1918–1921, and the period of the "New Economic Policy," 1922–1925, together witnessed the hyperinflation described earlier. In 1917–1918 the private ownership of land was abolished; workers took control of all branches of the national economy; all public debts were annulled; and banks were nationalized. The joint-stock banks and the mortgage banks were liquidated. A catastrophic decline in economic activity followed, which, in 1921–1922, led to the New Economic Policy. This program of expediency recognized that three-fourths of the nation's production and trade was still in private hands and required a medium of exchange and some access to credit and capital. The next few years witnessed a revival of commercial activity, continued inflation, and the highest recorded Russian interest rates.

The current Communist banking system is built around the state bank (Gosbank), which was organized in 1921. Its declared purpose was to aid by credit and by other banking operations the development of industry, agriculture, and trade and to secure a sound monetary circulation. It paid interest on time and demand deposits owned by government enterprises and by others, and loaned at interest on collateral or overdraft. It bought and sold securities, commodities, foreign exchange, and precious metals. It did not, however, control the issue of notes, which remained in the hands of the state, and hence it could hardly provide a sound monetary circulation. The first few years of its existence saw the great inflation proceed and accelerate. In 1922, the Gosbank began to receive deposits repayable in gold rubles and to protect itself against inflation by requiring that loans be similarly repaid. It also developed a more stable unit of account, the *chervonetz*, to permit orderly credit operations.

Financial settlements in money, bank loans, bank deposits, and the payment of interest on both loans and deposits continued in Russia, even though economic activity became increasingly socialistic, and private trade dwindled. Interest rates served a different function from that in a capitalistic economy. Legal interest rates were established by official decision. Depositors in savings banks were paid high or low interest depending on how urgently the government wished to encourage savings in this form and how effective a means interest payments were to this end. State enterprises were charged interest on their overdrafts as an encouragement to use resources efficiently and as a penalty for excessive working capital requirements. Interest rates under communism are not comparable in any important sense with interest rates in free market countries. Soviet Russia, however, does provide a unique interest-rate history. Official and unofficial interest rates were very high in the 1920's; later, official rates became low. Unofficial rates of interest in modern Russia are not reported, but may exist in informal situations.

In 1923, the Soviet government reestablished the system of savings banks. As inflation was still rampant, these banks sometimes protected small depositors from depreciation by calculating deposits in terms of a fixed currency from day of deposit to day of withdrawal (561), when they were paid off in paper money at its new value. By 1924, there were 2506 savings banks, and by 1928, there were 16,924 such banks. These financial agencies of the government were located at post offices, railroad stations, drugstores, factories, and other places where people came together. The banks invested in government bonds, which sometimes paid them a special rate of interest as reimbursement for expenses and high interest payments. After the "currency stabilization" of 1924, they ceased to protect depositors against currency depreciation. They were the agents for the government in the sale of government bonds to the public, and they also offered an arrangement for paying depositors' recurrent bills and for making other remittances. In 1933 the savings banks had 24 million depositors (562); they became the only banks to receive individual deposits. In the 1930's, their interest payments, then high by Western standards (6–9% per annum), were exempt from the income tax.

After the currency reform of 1924, other credit institutions were organized by the state. A Central Agricultural Bank granted long-term and short-term credit to local agricultural cooperative banks and to credit societies. (563) Since real estate was no longer privately owned, there were no farm mortgages; long-term farm loans ran up to five years and were for the purpose of enlarging cultivated areas or making improvements. After 1924, provincial and municipal authorities were permitted to organize local banks, provided that they retained 51% of the stock. The first and largest of these was the Moscow City Bank. These municipal banks assisted municipal construction projects and financed local commercial activity. By 1928, fifty municipal banks had been organized to grant long-term credits for municipal purposes. A Bank for Foreign Trade was organized by the government in 1924 to finance imports and exports.

Mutual credit societies were also permitted, and by 1927, 285 were functioning. These attracted private capital, since members were required to contribute 10% of their maximum credit requirements. Borrowers were subject to double liability. The societies discounted acceptable two-name paper with maturity up to six months (564) and made other secured loans. They accepted deposits, arranged transfers, and themselves borrowed from other banks. They financed the private sector of the economy. Therefore, by 1930, when private trade had become a very small proportion of the total, the mutual credit societies had all but vanished. Mention should also be made of legally organized pawnshops; they continued to operate. In addition, there was an illegal private money market in the 1920's, which provided some very high interest rates.

In 1928, a period of rapid industrialization began. At the end of the first Five Year Plan, 1928–1932, socialized industry was said to account for 99% of total industrial production. Credit planning played an important part in the state's economic programming. The state bank and its branches closely controlled the remittances of all state enterprises. It held their excess funds on deposit and paid interest on them; it made loans at interest to them for working-capital purposes and charged higher penalty rates for overdue loans; it made loans at exceptionally low rates against goods in transit.

This early credit planning worked badly. Loans could be demanded by state enterprises and were automatically made on shipment of completed goods. It sometimes turned out that the goods were faulty or that the purchasing enterprise was not prepared to receive them or had exhausted its line of credit. In 1930 and 1931, credit procedures were thoroughly overhauled. The bank was given great powers: It could deny credit and even seize the funds of defaulting government enterprises; it could execute forced sales of the goods or other property of the defaulter; it was permitted to grant only seasonal credit. Enterprises were provided with, and required to maintain, a normal working capital.

Inflation continued from 1928 through 1933, although it did not appear in the official prices of rationed commodities. In 1933, however, the state finally succeeded in balancing its budget. In 1935, rationing was ended. In 1936, the foreign exchange value of the ruble was reduced, and the ruble was effectively stabilized.

These were years of rapid growth and financial stability. The long-term debt of industry to the government was canceled, since it no longer served a useful purpose. The enterprises ceased to pay interest on "charter funds."

Cooperatives, however, continued to pay interest on capital funds, and industry continued to pay interest on short-term loans. During the 1930's, official interest rates were reduced progressively and entered a range which resembled that of Western Europe in prosperous times.

This period of growth and financial stability was interrupted in 1939 by World War II. A gigantic mobilization was financed by foreign aid, by a return to rationing, by the forced sale of bonds to the public, and by another expansion of the currency.

Following World War II, and in spite of its disasters, the basic economic and financial system that had been established in the 1930's was not greatly modified. The war brought no new revolution, although it did bring further devaluations of the ruble. The state bank, the Gosbank, with more than 4000 branch offices, continued to dominate the flow of credit. It was supplemented by a bank for long-term industrial credits, a bank for foreign trade, and the chain of national savings banks. In 1957, the forced sale of State lottery bonds to the public was discontinued, and a twenty-year moratorium on redemption of the outstanding bonds was declared. By the late 1950's, only one issue of government bonds, which paid 3%, was outstanding and freely bought or sold (to or from the government). In 1958, consumer installment credit was introduced for the first time; down payments of 20–25% were required, with six to twelve months to pay the balance. Economic reforms in the 1960's sought to increase the role of the banking system in the long-term financing of socialist enterprises; earlier, banks had played only a marginal role. (565) By the 1970's, the state had redeemed its publicly held 3% bonds; these had been the only securities available to the Soviet population.

IMPERIAL RUSSIAN INTEREST RATES

In the eighteenth century, Russia's legal maximum rate of interest was 5%. It was not enforced, and the lowest ordinary rate on best securities was 8–10% (566) As late as 1911, a rate of 8–9% is mentioned for first mortgages in Russia. (567) Such quotations come to us from English reporters, who considered those rates newsworthy because, by English standards, they were high. By other standards, such as Chinese ones, they do not seem so high.

We have no true history of indigenous Russian interest rates until 1917. Imperial Russia was striving to imitate the finance of Western Europe and in some measure succeeded in the late nineteenth century. The interest rates quoted in the tables below reflect this effort at imitation based largely on foreign capital. As such, they are scarcely indigenous. They probably do not reflect the rates at which Russians customarily borrowed from Russians.

These rates were under the influence of Western European money markets. They came down in the 1890's and rose during the next decade. Thus, although they were higher than English and French rates, they followed

IMPERIAL RUSSIAN GOVERNMENT LOANS

Years	Kind of Loan	Short and Medium Term, %	Long Term, %	Source
1817	Nominal rate on 7-year loan	6.00		(568)
	Nominal rate on undated loan		4.50	(568)
1857–1867	Government-guaranteed bonds of railroads paid		5.00	(569)
1859	Government issued certificates, nominal rate	4.00		(569)
1850–1900	Mortgage banks issued bonds, which paid nominal rate of		4.50	
	and reloaned money at		6.00	(569)
1859	Government issued 37-year certificates, at nominal rate of		5.00	(570)
1863	Government issued 8-year bills at nominal rate of	4.32		(571)
1888–1894	Conversions of government debt from 6% or 5% nominal rate to		4.00	(572)
1894	Government floated a loan at nominal rate of		3.50	(572)
1895	Most government railroad debt paid nominal rate of		4.00–5.00	(572)
1875	Government 4% bonds sold to yield		4.64	(573)
1877	Government 4% bonds sold to yield		6.49	(573)
1883	Government 4% bonds sold to yield		5.48	(573)
1891	Government 4% bonds sold to yield		4.06	(573)
1893	Government 4% bonds sold to yield		4.28	(573)
1896	Government 4% bonds sold to yield		3.76	(573)
1903	Government 4% bonds sold to yield		3.99	(573)
1907	Government 4% bonds sold to yield		5.89	(573)
1908	Government 4% bonds sold to yield		4.71	(574)
1909	Government 4% bonds sold to yield		4.55	(574)
1910	Government 4% bonds sold to yield		4.26	(574)
1911	Government 4% bonds sold to yield		4.21	(574)
1912	Government 4% bonds sold to yield		4.30	(574)
1913	Government 4% bonds sold to yield		4.45	(574)
1914	Government issued 1-year Treasury bills at nominal rate of	5.00		(575)

similar trends. They seem to have been influenced as much by the commercial crisis of 1906–1907 as they were by the Russo-Japanese War and the revolution of 1905. The 3.75–6.50% range of government bond yields was high only by contemporary Western standards; it is probable that very few Russians bought bonds at those rates of interest.

IMPERIAL RUSSIAN BANK CREDIT

Years	Form of Credit	Rate, %	Source
Before 1857	Banks pay on deposits	5	(576)
Before 1860	Nobles' State Land Bank loans at	5	(577)
1882–1893	Peasant bank loans at	$5\frac{1}{2}$	(578)
1895	State bank charges: discounts	5–7	(579)
	collateral loans	4–$6\frac{1}{2}$	(579)
	grain loans	$4\frac{1}{2}$–$5\frac{1}{2}$	(579)
	agricultural machinery loans	$5\frac{1}{2}$	(579)
	loans to manufacturers	6–7	(579)
1888	Call loan rate in St. Petersburg	6–8	(580)
1889	Call loan rate in St. Petersburg	$4\frac{1}{2}$–8	(580)
1890	Call loan rate in St. Petersburg	$4\frac{1}{2}$–7	(580)
1891–1892	Call loan rate in St. Petersburg	4–8	(580)
1893	Call loan rate in St. Petersburg	4–7	(580)
1888–1893	State bank pays: current accounts	1.50–3.50	(580)
1897	Market discount rate in St. Petersburg	5.24	(581)
1898	Market discount rate in St. Petersburg	4.96	(581)
1899	Market discount rate in St. Petersburg	6.85	(581)
1900	Market discount rate in St. Petersburg	6.68	(581)
1901	Market discount rate in St. Petersburg	6.39	(581)
1902	Market discount rate in St. Petersburg	5.60	(581)
1903	Market discount rate in St. Petersburg	5.75	(581)
1904	Market discount rate in St. Petersburg	6.61	(581)
1905	Market discount rate in St. Petersburg	6.29	(581)
1906	Market discount rate in St. Petersburg	8.04	(581)
1907	Market discount rate in St. Petersburg	7.71	(581)
1908	Market discount rate in St. Petersburg	6.54	(581)

SOVIET INTEREST RATES

The history of Soviet interest rates begins in 1921–1923 in the midst of the hyperinflation. At this time, the state began to organize several specialized banks, some to finance the socialized economy and some to finance the temporary private economy.

The banking system of the Soviet Union was built around the Gosbank. To protect itself and government enterprises from the disastrous inflation, this central state bank created an independent unit of account, the *chervonetz*, which purported to equal 10 gold rubles, was secured by a metallic reserve, and shared only moderately in the continued wild depreciation of the ruble. The state bank made loans and received deposits in *chervonetz* units as well as in paper rubles. It also made loan and deposit contracts payable in foreign exchange or calculated in terms of gold.

The table below provides a brief summary of the rates of interest paid by the Gosbank on deposits of various types at widely separated dates. The high rates of the hyperinflation period of 1920–1924 are contrasted with lower rates paid during the period of moderate inflation, 1924–1934, and the still lower rates paid thereafter. Gradually all forms of market rates of interest vanished and were replaced by these arbitrary rates enforced by the state.

INTEREST RATES PAID BY THE GOSBANK ON DEPOSITS

Years	Type of Deposit*	Interest, %	Source
1921–1922	Ruble deposits	36–60	(582)
1922–1923	Ruble deposits	48–72	(582)
	Gold deposits	4	(582)
1927–1934	Demand deposits	6	(583)
	Time deposits	7–8	(583)
1934–1936	Demand deposits	3–6	(584)
	Time deposits	5–6	(585)
	Demand deposits to collective farms	8	(585)
	Time deposits to collective farms	12	(585)
1936	To state enterprises	$1\frac{1}{2}$	(586)
	To municipal banks	2	(586)
	To savings banks and collective farms	$3\frac{1}{2}$	(586)
	To the agricultural bank	$3\frac{3}{4}$	(586)
1950–1952	To state enterprises and others	$0–1\frac{1}{2}$	(587)
	To savings banks and collective farms	$3\frac{1}{2}$	(587)
1960	To state enterprises and others	$\frac{1}{2}$	(588)
1965	To state enterprises and others	$\frac{1}{2}$	(589)
	To collective farms	$\frac{3}{4}$	(589)
	To population, sight and time deposits	2–3	(589)

*Ruble deposits unless otherwise noted.

The Gosbank did, of course, charge more on loans than it paid on deposits. In the hyperinflationary years, its charges, quoted in the table below, were chiefly set to protect itself against inflation. Alternatively, in 1922–1923 the

INTEREST RATES CHARGED BY THE GOSBANK FOR LOANS

Years	Type of Loan	Interest, %	Source
1921	Ruble loans	96–144+	(590)
1922	Ruble loans	144–204+	(590)
1923	Ruble loans	216+	(591)
	Chervonetz loans to government enterprises	8–12	(591)
	Chervonetz loans to others	$10–15\frac{1}{2}$	(591)

INTEREST RATES CHARGED BY THE GOSBANK FOR LOANS
(*Continued*)

Years	Type of Loan	Interest, %	Source
1927	Loans to government enterprises	8–10	(591)
	Loans to others	15½	(591)
1931	Loans for goods in transit	8	(592)
	Loans for planned requirements	8	(592)
	Loans for unplanned requirements	10	(592)
	Loans for overdue payments	18	(592)
1934	Loans for goods in transit	4	(593)
	Loans for planned requirements	6	(593)
	Loans for overdue payments	8	(593)
	Loans to other banks	5	(594)
1936	Loans for goods in transit	2	(595)
	Loans for other purposes	4	(595)
	Loans for overdue payments	6	(595)
1950–1952	Loans for goods in transit	2	(596)
	Loans for other purposes	4	(596)
	Loans for overdue payments	6	(596)
	Loans to collective farms	1	(596)
1960	Loans to state enterprises, secured	1–2	(597)
1965	Loans to state enterprises, secured	1–2	(598)
1968	Loans for goods in transit	1	(598)
	Loans for carrying inventories	6	(598)
	Other loans	8	(598)

bank made a specific charge of 50–75% of the foreign exchange depreciation of the ruble during the life of a loan plus its discount rate. Sometimes it entered into agreements to receive payments in commodities or in gold or dollars. Its loans at that time were mostly against commercial transactions; two-thirds were to state enterprises, and the rest were to cooperatives, private banks, and the private sector, which at that time carried on two-thirds of the economic activity of the nation.

While these were dictated rates that were not directly responsive to supply and demand, it is probable that economic objectives were among the considerations that influenced the government in its interest-rate decisions. The course of the Gosbank's rates after 1922 are summarized in the table on page 603.

These rates were at their highest in the 1920's, declined in the 1930's, had changed very little by 1952, and declined again into the 1960's before the reforms of that decade raised some loan rates. The 8–12% rates of the early 1920's were only moderately above the short-term market rates of interest that prevailed during the last decades of czarist Russia: The market rate of discount ranged from 5.60 to 8.04% annual averages between 1900 and 1908. Russians were not unaccustomed to 8% or more. As the nation developed its

GOSBANK RATES CHARGED FOR GENERAL-PURPOSE LOANS TO GOVERNMENT ENTERPRISES

Years	Rate, %
1923	8–12
1927	8–10
1931	8
1934	6
1936	4
1950–1952	4
1960	1–2
1968	1–8

heavy industry, and after rationing had been abandoned in the 1930's, these rates were brought down. They reached levels that were above the Western European prime rates of the 1930's, but were below most earlier Russian rates. The great new inflation that followed World War II was apparently not allowed to bring back high official interest rates. The private economy that had been important in the 1920's was almost entirely liquidated.

In the days of the New Economic Policy (N.E.P.), 1922–1925, the private economy had several sources of credit. It could occasionally borrow from government banks, it could form mutual credit societies, or it could borrow from municipal banks. The revival of the private economy under the N.E.P. was brief. Some estimates of the interest rates charged and received have been reported, however, and are summarized in the table below.

INTEREST RATES OF MUTUAL CREDIT SOCIETIES (599)

Years		Pay on Deposits, %	Charge on Loans, %
1923–1925	Range	3–36	
	Usual Rate	18	36
1927	Range		18–48
	Average	10.1	33.2

Rates of Moscow City Bank (600)

Years		Pay on Deposits, %	Charge on Loans, %
1923–1925	Range		12–48
1927	Instructed not to charge over		10
1927–1928	Range	6–9	8–14

INTEREST RATES OF MUTUAL CREDIT SOCIETIES (599) (*Continued*)

Years		Pay on Deposits, %	Charge on Loans, %
	Rates in the Illegal Private Market Charged on Short-Term Loans (601, 602)		
1922	Never below 1% a day, reached 2% a day or higher (rubles)		360–720
	Private gold loans commanded		180
1925	After stabilization, ruble loans, in Moscow		72
	in Provinces		96–120
	up to		240

Pawnshops flourished in Soviet Russia during the 1920's. Before World War I, pawnshop rates had been limited by law to 18–24%. In the 1920's, they were permitted to charge 10–36% for small loans and 24–120% for loans over 10 rubles. In recent decades, pawnshops were still a recognized source of consumer credit.

Agricultural credit played an important role in Soviet planning. The Central Agricultural Bank, which received deposits from and made loans to local agricultural credit agencies, charged the rates of interest shown in the table below.

RATES CHARGED BY THE CENTRAL AGRICULTURAL BANK
TO LOCAL AGRICULTURAL AGENCIES

Years	Type of Loan	Rate, %	Source
1924	Short loans	10–12	(603)
	Long loans	6–8	(603)
1931–1936	Long loans to collective farms and tractor stations	4	(604)
	Long loans to others	6	(604)

In the early 1950's specialized credit agencies under certain circumstances granted loans up to 10,000 rubles to individuals to improve homes. They charged 2–3% per annum, repayable over a ten-year period. (605) Such loans are among the very few forms of consumer credit reported by the Soviet Union before 1958. A six- to twelve-month installment purchase program inaugurated in 1958 charged 2% per annum interest and grew rapidly in popularity. (606)

The consumer's ruble had attracted the attention of the government since the early days of the Revolution. The savings banks were the chief vehicles for permitting individuals to loan the fruits of their frugality to the government. Interest rates paid by savings banks at scattered dates were as follows:

RATES PAID BY SOVIET SAVINGS BANKS

Years	Type of Deposit	On Demand Deposits, %	On Time Deposits, %	Source
1923	With protection against inflation	6	6	(607)
1924	Protection withdrawn after "stabilization"			
1925	To individuals	8	9	(607)
	To legal entities	6	6	(607)
1934	To individuals	8	9	(608)
	To collective farms	6	6	(608)
	To legal entities	3	3	(608)
1936	To individuals and collective farms	3	3	(609)
	To legal entities	1	1	(609)
1950–1952	To individuals	3	5	(610)
1959	To individuals	2	3	(611)
1975	To individuals	2	3	(611)

Finally, a few rates are reported on government loans. Some of the loans were sold directly to government-owned banks, others to government-owned industrial enterprises, and some to the public.

When the government sold bonds to individuals, the loans were managed by the savings banks. The subscriptions were voluntary in name only. (612) Two weeks' wages were at times a standard for annual subscription. Resale was not often permitted without the sanction of the authorities. These loans have been considered a form of tax. One indication of the acceptability of the rate of interest is the fact that the public often showed a decided preference for the lottery tranche of these loans over the interest-bearing tranche. A few examples of rates of interest paid by the Soviet government on loans of various types are as follows:

RATES PAID ON GOVERNMENT LOANS

Years	Type of Loan	Rate, %	Source
1922–1923	Treasury issues 6-months–1-year notes at	6	(613)
1925	"Economic Reconstruction Loan" sold to state enterprise at	10	(614)
Up to 1935	Seven 10-year loans sold to public at	10	(615)

RATES PAID ON GOVERNMENT LOANS (*Continued*)

Years	Type of Loan	Rate, %	Source
1934–1935	10-year bonds sold to public at	8	(616)
After 1936	Government loans converted to one 20-year issue (or lottery), pays	4	(617)
1947	Bonds given to war workers for back wages, pay	3	(618)
1953	Interest on bond issues reduced to	3	(619)
1955	Average interest rate paid by government	2.4	
1957	Only one marketable issue remains, pays	3	
1971	National lottery bonds, pay	3	(620)

Interest rates in the Soviet Union obviously do not serve to regulate the volume of currency or of credit. Interest, however, does serve other purposes: It pays or helps pay the operating expenses of a very large and complex state-owned banking system. It penalizes state enterprises that are inefficient in regulating their cash flow or that hoard inventory or delay deliveries; these costs—losses of interest income—can be minimized by efficient management. Interest rates also can be used to encourage individuals to save or to place their savings at the disposal of the state. A large part of the interest payments in the Soviet Union is paid by the state, and a large part is received by the state by virtue of its ownership of enterprise and the banking system. Whatever may have been the government's motivation, the tables make it clear that all forms of official interest rates in the Soviet Union declined from the 1920's to the 1930's and were held down after World War II until the 1960's. Their downtrend in the 1930's and 1940's resembled the trend of interest rates in the West, but since the 1950's, Russian interest rates have not been permitted to rise when Western interest rates have risen. Rigid, administered interest rates were merely one of many forms of state control of the socialist economy.

Chapter XXVII

China

BACKGROUND

Throughout China's long history, its credit structure has remained under-developed. Credit in China has usually taken the form of personal-consumption loans from individuals or from pawnshops. Credit for productive purposes has been rare even in modern times. Commercial credit has usually been devoted to speculative purposes. The rate of interest ordinarily has been far above the normal earning power of agriculture or industry.

China has always been predominantly an agricultural country. The ownership of land was preferred to commerce even when the rate of return on capital invested in land was far below the rate of return on capital invested in trade and in money lending. Social opinion and government policy were unfavorable to the merchants and bankers, who in early times were considered malicious and were heavily taxed.

Barter has always been important in China; nevertheless, money in the form of coins and bullion was used as a medium of exchange as early as the fourth century B.C. (621) and probably much earlier. Copper or iron coins with a hole in the middle were the standard "cash" for small transactions for more than 2000 years. Large transactions were settled variously in gold or silver by weight, in bolts of silk, or in other valuable commodities, but until recently, payment of rents and of taxes was usually made in kind. After A.D. 1000 there were several experiments with paper money, which was called "flying money" because it originated in drafts used to transmit funds to distant places. Overissue often led to heavy depreciation. In the thirteenth century, China adopted a silver currency. Paper money did not reappear until the nineteenth century, when China fell under European influence.

Banking transactions in China can be traced back for well over 2000 years. A bureau of currency and produce exchange was established by the government during the first millennium B.C. to make advances of money and seed to farmers. Private credit was then subjected to legal regulation. Limits on the rate of interest were decreed, as in the earliest historical periods of the Babylonian and Roman cultures. Early Chinese banking, however, was not as advanced as that which developed independently in the Mediterranean world in classical times or in the Middle Ages. (622) The writings of Marco Polo do not indicate the existence in China of anything as complex as the financial institutions of medieval Italy.

The oldest credit institution in China was probably the monastery pawn-shop. (623) In A.D. 200–300, Buddhist monasteries, like Babylonian, Greek, and Roman temples, practiced pawnbroking. They extended credit to rich and poor against precious metals, farm produce, and a wide variety of articles, which they held in warehouses. Private pawnshops were reported as early as A.D. 800, and by 1500 they had supplanted the monasteries. By the eighteenth century, pawnshops were required to register with the government and pay a license fee. Pawnbroking became one of the most profitable businesses in China; it grew spectacularly in the eighteenth and early nineteenth centuries, when pawnshops were entrusted with public funds for investment. At that time, pawnshops functioned almost like commercial banks by making loans on commodities. Speculators used their facilities to accumulate inventories of raw materials, and farmers pawned grain in order to hold it for better prices. After 1850, pawnshops were supplanted in many of these functions by banks, which relied more on the personal credit of their customers.

Cooperative loan societies have been traced back to A.D. 800. These informal groups provided mutual help for funerals, weddings, travel, emergencies, and productive purposes. Often they maintained community granaries. Interest was usually charged for these loans. Access to the use of the club funds was sometimes determined by lot (a dice-shaking society), sometimes according to whichever member offered to pay the highest interest (an auction society), and sometimes by turn (a rotating society).

Modern banking was foreshadowed by (a) deposit shops, which from 800 on accepted cash and precious metals, charged a fee for storage, honored drafts, and issued deposit certificates, which eventually circulated; and (b) gold and silver shops, which dealt in precious metals and ornaments, cast and guaranteed ingots, and eventually issued secured notes, which circulated. In the eighteenth century a more advanced type of bank appeared: the Shansi banks, or draft banks, which originated in northern China from the need to protect remittances from robbery during transportation. Drafts were substituted for shipments of metal. The Shansi bankers set up branch offices throughout the country and arranged remittances for a fee. In time, they transported and stored government funds, received other deposits, and made loans. They backed promising candidates for government office and in return handled the successful candidates' official finances. They were the strongest indigenous financial institutions in China until they were ruined by the revolution of 1911.

In the nineteenth century, many other types of indigenous banks developed. These were called "money shops" and conducted a local business. They exchanged money, issued their own notes, made loans, and received deposits. The largest Chinese banks in the big cities belonged to clearing associations; these gathered together daily and set the rate charged that day for interbank credits, called "chop loans." Modern banks developed late in the nineteenth century after the model of the branch offices of foreign banks, which were then well established.

After 1840, it became impossible for the government to maintain the traditional policy of meeting public expenditures on a cash basis. The government then began to rely on internal loans and loans from foreign banks. After 1911, four official banks were established to handle the government's finances and to carry out some of the functions of Western central banks. These banking institutions of the nineteenth and twentieth centuries were adaptations of European institutions.

The practice of lending money at interest in China has been traced back at least to 400 B.C. (624) Government regulations concerning maximum rates of interest and terms of loans were proclaimed from dynasty to dynasty but were often ignored. Loans were typically for short terms, at a high rate of interest, and for consumer expenditure; commercial sales on credit were very rare. Loans were often repayable on demand, but were usually for periods of three to six months. In case of default, the property of the debtor could be seized and sold. Compound interest was usually illegal. (625)

The ultimate creditor was often the government. After A.D. 700 the government entrusted its funds to "money-catching clerks," who loaned them out to the people. The interest received by the government was assigned to specific public purposes. Often the rates were very high. In 1069, however, a reform program was inaugurated; money was loaned from the funds of the government to farmers in the spring for repayment at 10–20% interest in the fall. Loans at this benevolent rate were called "green sprout money." In the thirteenth century, government funds were loaned to friendly merchants at a nominal rate of 9.6% per annum, and these merchants sometimes reloaned the funds to the public at 100% per annum, so that in ten years the principal and compound interest amounted to 1024 times the original principal. This was known as "young lamb interest." (626) The legal ceilings on interest were rarely enforced. A common method of evasion in the eighteenth century was known as "seal print money," whereby the principal of a loan was repaid in daily or monthly installments while the legal interest was charged on the original principal. Alternatively, less was loaned than appeared on the face of the loan.

During the late nineteenth and early twentieth centuries, the ancient Chinese credit institutions existed side by side with modern institutions organized in the European manner. The latter, however, never became dominant factors in the life of the majority of the population. No large popular investment market ever developed for either bonds or stocks. The dealings in the securities markets were confined largely to banks and a restricted group of speculators. New issues of government bonds were usually sold not to the public but to the banks.

In China credit has rarely served the purposes of economic development that it has served so well in Europe and America. The regular flow of funds from savers to investors through the medium of securities or of institutions apparently never began. Chinese credit continued over the centuries to consist almost entirely of consumption loans made by individuals to individuals.

In modern China, approximately 70% of the households are still rural. A survey in 1933 showed that more than half of the rural population was burdened by cash debts arising from consumption needs. The sources of this farm credit were as follows: (627)

Sources of Credit	Percent of Credit
Private moneylenders	74
Mortgages	17
Loan clubs	4
Pawnshops	2
Stores	2
Other	1
	100

Half of this credit was unsecured. The purposes for this credit, mostly nonproductive, were as follows:

Purpose of Loan	Percent of Credit
Family expenses	32
Weddings, funerals, illness	20
Lawsuits, bandits, etc.	13
Commercial	11
Investment and other productive purposes	17
Other	8
	100

The term of this credit was usually short:

Term of Credit	Percent of Credit
Under 6 months	13
6–12 months	65
12–24 months	4
24–36 months	5
Over 36 months	2
Indefinite	11
	100

The annual rate of interest charged in 1933 on this rural credit was broken down in the survey as follows:

Interest, % per Annum	Percent of Loans
10–20	9
20–30	36
30–40	30
Over 40	24
	100

The individual moneylenders who provided most of this credit belonged to the class of landlords, merchants, and retired officials. They advanced seed and cash. Loans secured by land usually ran for two or more years and were in the form of conditional sale of the land or of a mortgage up to 50 to 60% of the value of the land. As mortgage interest at 20% or more usually exceeded the productivity of the land, such loans could rarely be used for productive purposes.

This survey of Chinese agricultural credit has been reported in detail because it gives a picture of the nature of many of the loans on which Chinese interest rates will be reported in the next section. Although the survey is relatively modern, the character of rural indebtedness has not changed greatly. These loans resemble the ancient personal loans of Babylonia, Greece, and Rome. They are far removed from the commercial and government loans of modern Europe and America that have been surveyed in earlier chapters.

During the nineteenth century, foreign investment brought an influx of silver to China, which reinforced the traditional silver standard. Bank notes were also issued by the new modern banks and by the older indigenous banks. After 1911, four government banks attempted to control the currency. The silver standard lasted until 1935, when it was replaced by a foreign exchange standard.

The war with Japan, 1937–1945, was marked by a classical paper-money inflation, which fell into three parts: (a) 1937–1939, when prices rose an average of 50% per year; (b) 1939–1941, when prices rose 160% per year; and (c) 1941–1945, when prices rose 300% per year. (628) After the war ended in 1945, prices dropped for a few months; but in 1946 a hyperinflation began, and prices doubled every two or three months. Many attempts at currency reform were then made and were unsuccessful. By October of 1948, prices were more than doubling every day. Thus, China provides us with one more example of interest rates in a period of hyperinflation.

INTEREST RATES

Our earliest information on Chinese interest rates comes from the Han dynasties of 200 B.C. to A.D. 220. This information consists largely of government regulations and scholars' opinions on equitable rates of interest. An early Han historian wrote that in the second century B.C., the returns on moneylending ranged between 33⅓% and 20% per annum (629); he considered the former rate too greedy. These are lower rates than are mentioned for later centuries. Toward the end of the first century B.C., credit conditions led to a reform movement. The government provided free loans for funerals and provided other loans to the needy poor at 36% per year. As this rate was considered philanthropic, prevailing rates must have been higher.

The third, fourth, fifth, and sixth centuries were marked by internal conflict and many dynasties. We have no information on interest rates for these centuries. Beginning with the Tang dynasty, 618–907, information is more abundant: Interest rates began high and seemed to decline. Legal limits on loans and actual rates charged by the government, which was then an important creditor, were as follows:

Years	Legal Limits		Rates Charged by the Government, %
	Private Loans, %	Government Loans, %	
600–650	72	84	96
650–728	72	84	84
728 and after	48	60	60
960 and after	48	60	?

The decline in official rates of interest during the Tang dynasty is noticeable, although the rates did not return to the 20–33⅓% level mentioned for the early Han period. In 765, seed loans from the government warehouses were made at rates as low as 45% per annum, but in the same century and the ninth century, seed loans by the government were also reported at 50% for four months, or an annual rate of 150% (630).

Private loan contracts during the seventh to tenth centuries indicate that legal limits were not enforced. One specific loan contract from 782 states that Ma Ling-Chih, a soldier in need, borrowed cash from a monk of the Hu-Kuo monastery at interest of 10% per month, payable on demand; the loan was secured by the right to seize his property without adjustment for overage, and endorsed by his mother and younger sister. This was an uncompounded interest rate of 120% per annum. Most of the contracts of the Tang period that have been examined specify repayment in three to six months and interest at 6–10% a month, or 72–120% a year.

During the Sung period, 960-1279, and the Yuan period, 1280–1368, there seems to have been a decline in official and conventional interest rates. Legal limits on loans of all types were reported as follows: (631)

Year	Legal Limits, % per Annum
960	48–60
1260	36
1368	36

Although these limits were still not enforced, private loan contracts also indicate a decline in rates. These have been estimated as follows: (632)

Century	Private Loan Contracts, % per Annum
Seventh–tenth century	72–120
Twelfth century	50–70 (sometimes 100%)
Thirteenth century	36–60 (sometimes 120%)
Fourteenth century	36–60 (sometimes 100%, "young lamb interest")

Government loans of seed to farmers were a usual part of China's ever-normal-granary plan. The interest rates were higher than those mentioned for loans of money. They were often at levels as high as 50% for the months from planting to harvest, which equals about 100–150% annual rate. Reform programs occasionally brought these rates down. For example, in 1069, the "green sprout money" was loaned to farmers in the spring and collected in the autumn at 10–20% interest, which equals annual rates of 20–50% (633).

During the Ming period, 1368–1644, no further decline in interest rates is evident, but during the succeeding Ching dynasty, 1644–1912, there seems to have been a further decline. This has been reported as follows: (634)

Time	Legal Limits, % per Annum
1368	36
1644	36
Late seventeenth century	18–36
Eighteenth century	10–36
Nineteenth century	24
Twentieth century	20

That the decline of interest rates was not confined to legal limits is suggested by the following quotations:

Century	Private Loan Contracts, % per Annum	Source
Fourteenth century "normal rates"	36–60	(635)
Fifteenth century "normal rate on silver"	60	(635)
Seventeenth century	36–60	(636)
Eighteenth century loans by government to merchants	24	(637)
Nineteenth century loans by government to merchants	12	(637)
Nineteenth century Shansi banks charge	9.6–10.8	(638)

There is no evidence that these lower rates quoted for the eighteenth and nineteenth centuries applied to consumer credit or other loans away from the big cities. Modern forms of commercial credit were developing in eastern China, and it is these that were quoted at lower interest rates.

The mainstream of Western interest-rate history touched briefly on China's shores in the nineteenth and early twentieth centuries. It brought with it a few decades of commercial activity financed at rates of interest that were low by Chinese standards but usually high by European standards. In the late nineteenth century, European banks at the treaty ports and especially at Shanghai were instrumental in bringing rates down in these areas. (639) Large sums were attracted from the pocketbooks of European investors, who considered 6–10% a high rate of interest.

In contrast to low treaty-port rates, rates in the interior remained high. As late as 1920, installment loans in Chinese villages were quoted at 60%. In 1933 it was estimated that Chinese farmers were paying an average of 85.2% for seed loans and an average of 34% for loans of money. (640) The highest rates must have been well above these averages. In 1927–1937, pawnshops in fact charged from the legal maximum of 20% up to 72%; loan clubs charged up to 30%; and farm mortgages cost 20% or more. (641) As recently as 1959, the government of Taiwan organized an agency to make production loans at 18% because the prevailing private rate was over 30% (642)

China thus remained a country of very high interest rates in the nineteenth and twentieth centuries. Some of the early twentieth-century rates from Shanghai quoted in the table below were part of a brief episode when Western economic customs were for a time imitated in China. The following tables attempt to sample late nineteenth- and early twentieth-century rates paid by, and charged by, Chinese and foreign banks in Shanghai and other large cities; the first of these tables contrasts the Shanghai rates with those charged in the interior.

RATES AMONG BANKERS FOR CALL ("CHOP") OR OTHER SHORT LOANS

Years			Rate, %	Source
1844	Peking		4.8–6	(643)
	Soochow		7.2	(643)
1870–1920	Shansi banks		7.2–10.8	(643)
		Interior	Shanghai	
1930			2.52	(644)
1931			4.68	(644)
1932		54.0	3.60	(644)
1933		32.0	1.80	(644)
1934		23.0	3.24	(644)
1935		48.0	5.44	(644)
1936		24.0	2.88	(644)

RATES CHARGED BY BANKS AT LARGE CITIES FOR STANDARD LOANS

Years	Banks	Rate, %	Source
1870–1920	Indigenous banks lend to industry at	8.4–14.4	(635)
1926	Foreign banks lend to foreign industries at	6½–10	(646)
1926	Indigenous and foreign banks lend to industry at	12–24	(646)

RATES CHARGED BY BANKS AT LARGE CITIES FOR STANDARD LOANS (*Continued*)

Years	Banks	Rate, %	Source
1927–1937	Indigenous banks' charge on long-term loans	8–17	(647)
	Indigenous banks' overdrafts minimum	8.4	(647)
	Government banks lend to commerce at minimum of	6	(648)
	Provincial banks make small loans at	12	(648)
	Commercial banks loan to cooperatives at	8–10	(649)
	(which relend to members at 13.2–16.8%)		

RATES PAID BY BANKS AT LARGE CITIES ON DEPOSITS

Years	Banks	Rate, %	Source
1870–1920	Indigenous banks pay	4.8–9.6	(650)
1926	Foreign banks pay on 3–5 year deposits	9–11	(651)
1927–1937	Indigenous banks pay on fixed deposits	4.8–9.6	(652)
	Government banks pay on current deposits	2	(653)
	Government banks pay on savings deposits	8–9.5	(653)
	Commercial banks pay on fixed deposits	4–8	(654)
	Commercial banks pay on savings deposits		
	(to 10 yrs.)	5–10	(654)
1939	Government banks issue thrift certificates at	6–9	(655)
1940	Government banks issue thrift certificates at	8–12	(655)

These tables suggest that in the areas not under Western influence, China remained a country of high interest rates, while in the treaty ports, lower rates often prevailed.

The Japanese war, which began in 1937, led to an inflation that turned, after the war ended in 1945, into a classical hyperinflation. Rates of interest on commercial credits during this period may be summarized as follows:

RATES AMONG BANKERS FOR CALL ("CHOP") LOANS DURING AND AFTER THE JAPANESE WAR

Average Market Rate	Kweichow, % (656)	Chunking, % (657)	Shanghai, % (658)
1937	18	12	4.82
1938	18	14.4	3.96
1939	22.8	15.6	5.04
1940	30	18.0	5.40
1941	36	22.8	2.16

RATES AMONG BANKERS FOR CALL ("CHOP") LOANS DURING AND AFTER
THE JAPANESE WAR (*Continued*)

Average Market Rate	Kweichow, % (656)	Chunking, % (657)	Shanghai, % (658)
1942	40.8	33.6	
1943	45.6	72	
1944	72	111.6	
1945	180	121.2	
Black Market Rate			
1946 January			132 (659)
1947 January			216
December			276
1948 June			360
October			1440
1949 April			3000

The government during these years often attempted to curb the inflation
by limiting speculative credit and the rate of interest. In early 1946, the central bank's rediscount rate stood at 21%, and private banks were not permitted to pay more than 8.4% on deposits or to charge more than 84% on call
loans, while at the time the black market rate was 132%. This was called an
"easy-money policy." In 1948, to check the inflation the central bank
changed its policy: Price ceilings were abandoned, the bank offered to pay
180% on deposits, and it sold one-month Treasury bills at 234–291% interest. (660) Later in 1948, the policy was again changed: 6% was set as the
maximum legal rate of interest, and all central-bank credit was banned.

In the twentieth century, the Chinese government, under Western influence, ceased to be a hoarder-creditor and became a borrower abroad and at
home. A few quotations on the modern domestic loans of the Chinese government are as follows:

INTERNAL GOVERNMENT LOANS

Years	Type of Loan	Rate, %	Source
1912–1920	Secured by customs, nominal rate	6	(661)
	Unsecured nominal rate	8	(661)
1919–1922	Short loans	6–22	(661)
1920–1925	Secured by customs, nominal rate	6–8	(661)
1913–1926	Twenty-seven issues with nominal rate of	8	(662)

INTERNAL GOVERNMENT LOANS (*Continued*)

Years	Type of Loan	Rate, %	Source
1923	8% bonds sold as low as 20	40	(662)
1923	Short-term loans at	8.4–21.6	(662)
1926	Loans secured by customs at nominal rates of	6–8	(663)
1927–1933	Market yield on bonds with 7–8% nominal rates	10–20	(664)
1927	New issues at 9.6% nominal rate at 80	20.6	(665)
1932	Proposed moratorium, market yield	27.7	(665)
1936	With credit high, debt refunded at	6–7.6	(666)
1937	6% bonds sell at 89	6.75	(667)
1938	6% bonds sell at 40	15+	(667)
1941	6% bonds sell at 68–78	8+	(667)

During the Japanese war, efforts to sell bonds to the public were generally unsuccessful. Bonds were sold to banks, which used them as a base for banknote expansion. Quotations, therefore, had little significance as an index of the prevailing rate of interest.

Few interest rates with any market significance have been available during recent decades. In China, as in Soviet Russia, the Communist government set interest rates by administrative fiat. Several deposit and loan rates for years from the 1950's through the early 1980's are given in the table below; in all cases the quoted monthly rate from the source (668) has been annualized by multiplying by 12.

CHINESE DEPOSIT AND LOAN RATES: 1953–1982

Year	Deposit Rates, %		Loan Rates, %				
	Demand	Time (1 Year)	State Industrial Enterprises	State Commercial Enterprises	Agricultural Collectives and State Farms	Rural Credit Companies	Individual Peasants
1953	5.40	14.40	5.40–5.76	8.28	9.00	14.40	9.00
1955				7.20	7.20	10.80	9.00
1958	2.88	9.72	7.20	7.20	5.76	6.12	8.64
1959	2.16	4.80–6.12	7.20		7.20		7.20
1961			7.20	7.20	5.76		5.76
1965	2.16	3.96					
1971	2.16	3.24					
1972			5.40–5.76	7.20	4.32–5.76		
1979	2.16	3.96					
1980	2.88	5.40					
1982	2.88	5.76	5.04–7.20	5.04–7.20	4.23–5.76	2.16	4.32–8.64

Chapter XXVIII

Latin America

Latin American interest rates have usually been well above European and North American rates. Scattered quotations for the nineteenth and early twentieth centuries were comparatively high, and more abundant quotations after 1930 suggest that rates had become even higher. Rates generally stayed up during the 1930's, when interest rates were declining in most other parts of the world. Many Latin American rates declined in the 1940's, but the inflation of the 1950's often was accompanied by very high rates.

The much more virulent inflations from the 1960's and through the 1980's in many Latin American countries brought fantastically high rates, reminiscent of rates in the German inflation of the early 1920's. If the United States could not avoid double-digit inflation, it could hardly be expected that underdeveloped Latin American countries could avoid worse—sometimes triple-digit inflation and triple-digit interest rates. The 1980's even witnessed quadruple-digit interest rates in Latin America.

In preceding chapters, a few small or underdeveloped countries that maintained low interest rates in the 1950's have been reviewed. In a few instances they reported lower rates than those that prevailed in the largest trading nations of the world. In Portugal, India, and Pakistan, the policy of low interest rates was maintained for Westernized market credit instruments long after the policy had been abandoned in England and elsewhere. This was not the case during this period in Latin America. Although the money markets in Latin America were small and political dictatorships were not uncommon, the money markets were usually either free to reflect the scarcity of capital or controlled at traditionally high rates. In more recent decades, however, inflation rates at times have gotten so out of control that functioning money and capital markets have contracted and even disappeared.

CHILE

Table 81 presents some Chilean interest rates from 1870 through 1988. The series of prevailing rates on short-term bank loans, 1870–1919 and 1937–1988, is based on three- to six-month loans. These were usually secured by stocks and bonds, sometimes they were secured by mortgages, and sometimes they were unsecured. This credit was often extended to farmers who did not have adequate liquid capital; therefore, at expiration the loans were usually renewed upon payment of interest, commission, and a certain amortization. Since 1937, the bank loan series has been based on a weighted average of rates charged by all banks in Chile or on the bank lending rate reported by the IMF.

The table also presents the discount rate of the central bank, 1930–1960 and 1969–1975. However, the central bank charged higher rates when any deposit-money bank borrowed over 50% of its capital funds, and this was usually the case. Therefore, the effective discount rate was well above the official figures presented in the table.

Finally, the table presents a series of long-term bond yields is presented for 1872–1917 and 1930–1953. The early yields are current yields derived from the average quotation of an issue of 5% mortgage bonds of the Caja de Credito Hipotecario. These bonds were usually quoted at heavy discounts, and their yields were less than the simultaneous yields of higher-priced bonds of the same obligator, which carried higher nominal rates. From 1930 on, the bond yields are based on the current yield of 7% government bonds. These were pegged at 8.33% from 1947 on, and quotations were discontinued after 1953. The trends of these yields are summarized by decennial averages.

Chilean yields tended to decline from 1878 to 1905. They rose thereafter to a high point in 1915, shortly before the end of the first series. Thus, before World War I, they followed very roughly the general international pattern. When the new series began in 1930, yields were very high at 7.79% and promptly rose to 11.82% annual average in the crisis of 1931, which was the highest quotation in this series. Their average for the 1930's was also the highest average, although the 1930's were a period when outside of Latin America most bond yields were declining to very low levels. During World War II, these Chilean bond yields were stabilized at around 8.33–8.50%. Thus, Chilean yields ranged higher in the twentieth century than they did in the nineteenth century. Only in the late nineteenth and early twentieth centuries did the Chilean yields average below 6%.

Short rates in Chile also tended to range much higher in recent decades than in the nineteenth century. Their low decennial average (see Table 81) occurred in the 1880's. A rate as low as 7% was not reported after 1905. During the late 1950's, the high average rate of 16.32% reported in the official statistics was often exceeded on good credits. One prominent U.S. corpora-

TABLE 81

CHILEAN AND BRAZILIAN INTEREST RATES: ANNUAL AVERAGES, 1870–1989

Year	Chile			Brazil	
	Short-Term Bank Loans, %	Central Bank Discount Rate, %	Long-Term Bond Yields, %	Central Bank Discount Rate, %	Government Bond Yields, %
1870	8.00–10.00				
1871	8.00				
1872	8.00–9.00		6.19		
1873	8.00–10.00		6.66		
1874	8.00		7.03		
1875	10.00–12.00		6.95		
1876	10.00–12.00		7.03		
1877	10.00		7.23		
1878	10.00–12.00		7.81		
1879	9.00–11.00		7.23		
10-yr. av.	9.10		7.02 (8-yr. av.)		
1880	7.00–9.00		5.80		
1881	7.00		5.58		
1882	7.00		5.58		
1883	8.00–9.00		5.75		
1884	7.00		5.67		
1885	7.00–8.00		5.67		
1886	7.00–8.00		5.80		
1887	7.00		5.62		
1888	7.00		5.42		
1898	7.00		5.58		
10-yr. av.	7.10		5.65		
1890	7.00		5.67		
1891	7.00		(Civil War)		
1892	8.00–9.00		5.58		
1893	9.00		5.88		
1894	9.00		6.10		
1895	10.00		6.33		
1896	10.00		6.70		
1897	8.00		6.40		
1898	8.00–10.00		6.66		
1899	7.00		6.20		
10-yr. av.	8.30		6.17 (9-yr. av.)		

TABLE 81 (*Continued*)

Year	Chile			Brazil	
	Short-Term Bank Loans, %	Central Bank Discount Rate, %	Long-Term Bond Yields, %	Central Bank Discount Rate, %	Government Bond Yields, %
1900	7.00		5.80		6.32
1901	8.00		5.80		6.02
1902	8.00		5.67		5.56
1903	8.00		5.74		5.21
1904	8.00		5.51		5.18
1905	7.00		5.39		4.61
1906	8.00		5.58		4.55
1907	9.00		5.67		4.89
1908	9.00		7.14		4.85
1909	9.00		6.51		4.77
10-yr. av.	8.10		5.88		5.20
1910	9.00		6.40		4.46
1911	9.00		6.31		4.52
1912	9.00		6.75		4.62
1913	9.00		7.15		4.97
1914	9.00		7.40		
1915	9.00		7.90		
1916	9.00		7.05		
1917	9.00		6.90		
1918	8.00				
1919	8.00				
10-yr. av.	8.80		6.98 (8-yr. av.)		4.64 (4-yr. av.)
1929					6.52
1930		6.41	7.79		6.79
1931		7.36	11.82		6.50
1932		5.23	11.42		6.35
1933		4.50	7.85		5.88
1934		4.50	7.53		5.92
1935		4.31	7.48		6.25
1936		4.50	8.26		6.49
1937	7.84	4.50	8.58		6.30
1938	8.20	4.50	8.43		6.21
1939	8.34	4.50	9.03		6.26
10-yr. av.	8.13 (3-yr. av.)	5.03	8.82		6.30

TABLE 81 (*Continued*)

Year	Chile			Brazil	
	Short-Term Bank Loans, %	Central Bank Discount Rate, %	Long-Term Bond Yields, %	Central Bank Discount Rate, %	Government Bond Yields, %
1940	8.37	4.50	9.28		6.23
1941	8.41	4.50	8.94		6.23
1942	8.85	4.50	8.41		6.10
1943	8.90	4.50	8.37		5.23
1944	9.03	4.50	8.33		5.11
1945	9.21	4.50	8.31		5.43
1946	9.22	4.50	8.20		5.54
1947	9.40	4.50	8.33		6.37
1948	10.00	4.50	8.33	6.00	7.17
1949	10.20	4.50	8.33	6.00	7.06
10-yr. av.	9.16	4.50	8.48		6.05
1950	10.68	4.50	8.33	6.00	6.86
1951	11.72	4.50	8.33	6.00	7.08
1952	12.14	4.50	8.33	6.00	7.02
1953	12.30	4.50	8.33	6.00	7.22
1954	13.16	4.50		6.00	7.09
1955	13.67	4.50		6.00	7.30
1956	13.89	4.50		6.00	7.60
1957	14.36	6.00		6.00	7.60
1958	15.69	6.00		8.00	7.50
1959	16.32	6.00		8.00	8.40
10-yr. av.	13.39	4.95	8.33 (4-yr. av.)	6.40	7.37
1960	16.64	6.00		8.00	
1961	15.58			8.00	
1962	14.95			8.00	
1963	14.41			8.00	
1964	14.63			8.00	
1965	15.30			12.00	
1966	15.58			12.00	
1967	15.84			22.00	
1968	16.61			22.00	
1969	19.59	13.50		21.50	
10-yr. av.	15.91			12.95	

TABLE 81 (*Continued*)

Year	Chile			Brazil	
	Short-Term Bank Loans, %	Central Bank Discount Rate, %	Long-Term Bond Yields, %	Central Bank Discount Rate, %	Government Bond Yields, %
1970	20.00	14.00		20.00	
1971	15.00	11.00		20.00	
1972	17.50	7.00		20.00	
1973	40.00	7.00		18.00	
1974	62.00	7.00		18.00	
1975	185.34	7.00		18.00	
1976	n.a.			28.00	
1977	163.15			30.00	
1978	86.14			33.00	
1979	62.11			35.00	
10-yr. av.	65.12 (9-yr. av.)			24.00	
1980	47.14			38.00	
1981	52.02			49.00	
1982	63.87			49.00	
1983	47.82			156.60	
1984	38.33			215.30	
1985	41.33			219.40	
1986	29.72			50.70	
1987	38.28			391.50	
1988	22.24			816.10	
1989	n.a.			2,485.30	
10-yr. av.	38.08 (9-yr. av.)			447.09	

SOURCES
Guillermo Subercaseaux, *Monetary and Banking Policy of Chile* (Oxford: Clarendon Press, 1922), pp. 191–92, 208.
League of Nations, *Statistical Year Book, 1939–40*, p. 223.
Canada, Report of Official Board of Enquiry, *Cost of Living* (1915).
IMF, *International Financial Statistics.*

tion reported that its subsidiaries paid interest on local bank loans in Chile at 22% in 1958 and up to 24% in 1959, both of which were higher than the official average. This is a common occurrence when inflation is high.

After World War II, Chile suffered from an inflation even more severe than that experienced by most Latin American countries. The monetary unit lost 95% of its dollar value between 1945 and 1960, and during these years, the cost-of-living index rose fiftyfold. Chilean interest rates since the 1960's provide one more example of interest rates during a severe inflation. By these standards the rates reported were not very high; they did not approach the rates reported in the more severe German, Russian, and Chinese inflations. In the 1960's, however, the bank loan rate in Chile edged up to 20%. Early in the 1970's, there was a brief period of declining interest rates. The central bank discount rate came down from 14 to 7%, and the bank loan rate came down from 20 to 15%. However, this attempt at lower interest rates and a stable economy failed. In 1974 the inflation grew worse, and the bank loan rate rose to 62% (in the face of a 7% central bank rate). The bank loan rate rose to 185% in 1975 and to 163% in 1977. From 1980 to 1987, annual average bank lending rates in Chile ranged from 30 to 64%.

BRAZIL

Table 81 presents Brazilian interest rates in two series: government bond yields from 1900 through 1913 and from 1929 through 1959; and the official discount rate from 1948 through 1989. The government bond yields are based on the current yield of a 4% issue through 1913; yields from 1929 to 1959 are based on the current yield of an issue of unified 5% bonds. The official discount rate applied to eligible commercial paper rediscounted by banks.

In 1900, these Brazilian government bond yields were above the Chilean bond yields: 6.32% versus 5.80%. During the first decade of the twentieth century, however, Brazilian yields declined and became much lower than Chilean yields; by 1913, they were 4.97% versus 7.15%. This decline in Brazilian yields ran counter to the international upward trend of bond yields during the first two decades of the century.

When the record of Brazilian government bond yields was resumed in 1929, the yield of 6.52% was far above the 1913 level. No spectacular yields, such as were reported in Chile, however, were recorded for the next few years; yields remained close to 6% through the 1930's. In the 1940's, the Brazilian yields declined briefly to 5.11% in 1944, their low point of the period surveyed. By 1949, they were up above 7%. Brazilian bond yields rose further in the 1950's, but not spectacularly. In 1959, they were up to 8.40%, which was the high point of the century for these quotations. Thereafter, quotations for long-term Brazilian government bond yields were discontinued. The inflation grew worse, and a military government tried to achieve stability by indexing wages, prices, and bond yields to a cost-of-living index. The inflation nevertheless continued. It is impossible to quote yields for such index bonds on a basis comparable with other yields in this history. The earlier long-term trend is indicated by the decennial averages in Table 81. These averages indicate that there was no easy-money period in Brazil in the 1930's. While yields declined in the 1940's, the high yields for the century to 1959 were those of the late 1950's, when the series stops.

The reported official discount rate was always relatively high compared to discount rates in other countries. It stood at 6% from 1948 to 1958, and then was raised to 8%. Between 1964 and 1979, it rose from 8 to 35%. The Brazilian discount rate then reached triple-digit levels in 1983 and quadruple-digit levels at times in 1989.

ARGENTINA

Argentine interest rates are represented in Table 82 by four series: long-term government bond yields from 1900 through 1913 and 1929 through 1953; the official discount rate from 1935 through 1960; Treasury bill rates from 1936 through 1953; and occasional commercial loan rates from 1930 through 1958 and 1984 through 1989. The government bond yields through 1913 are based on the current yields of an issue of 5% bonds. From 1960 to 1976, no Argentine interest rates were officially reported by the IMF; the loan rate in Table 82 is available only after 1983.

The Argentine bond yields reported for the early years of the century were below those quoted for Chile and Brazil, but were above most European yields. They tended to decline in the first decade, when bond yields in the great financial centers were rising. When a new series began in 1929, yields were higher at 6.34%, but not as high as the Brazilian yields quoted and not nearly as high as the Chilean yields. After rising further, to 7.15% in 1932, the Argentine bond yields declined steeply in the 1930's and even more in the 1940's; they came down to 4.97% in 1939 and to 4.18% in 1945. From 1946, a different series reported yields as low as 3.11–3.26% until the IMF discontinued quotations in 1953. This episode is the only example of really low Latin American yields reported in this history.

In the 1940's, other Argentine interest rates also became low. The rate on Treasury bills declined from 2.40% in 1936 to 0.56% in 1944 and had risen only to 1.50% by 1953, when reports cease. This was below the 1953 short rates reported in a number of great financial centers. The official discount rate was held at 3.50% from 1935 to 1957, when it was raised to 6%, where it was held through 1960.

In the 1950's Argentina also suffered from the ubiquitous inflation. The dollar value of her currency declined 94%, and the cost-of-living index rose elevenfold; this was not as high an inflation as in Chile, but it was still very severe. The economic situation worsened in the 1960's, and by the 1970's, the Argentine inflation had become a hyperinflation at rates over 400% per annum. It can be surmised that unofficial interest rates were correspond-

TABLE 82
Argentine and Uruguayan Interest Rates: Annual Averages, Twentieth Century

Year	Argentina				Uruguay		
	Commercial Loans, %	Treasury Bills, %	Official Discount Rate, %	Long-Term Government Bonds, %	Government Bond Yields, %	Discount Rate, %	Lending Rate, %
1900				5.14			
1901				5.24			
1902				5.29			
1903				5.01			
1904				4.86			
1905				4.87			
1906				4.87			
1907				4.90			
1908				4.86			
1909				4.81			
10-yr. av.				4.99			
1910				4.82			
1911				4.83			
1912				4.84			
1913				4.88			
4-yr. av.				4.84			
1929				6.34			
1930	7.04			6.26			
1931	7.64			6.52			
1932	7.66			7.15			
1933	6.51			7.00			
1934	5.50			5.39			
1935	6.07		3.50	5.24			
1936	5.62	2.40	3.50	5.09	4.43		
1937	5.28	2.25	3.50	4.99	4.24		
1938	5.30	2.39	3.50	4.99	4.83		
1939	5.75	2.50	3.50	4.97	4.61		
10-yr. av.	6.24	2.39 (4-yr. av.)	3.50 (5-yr. av.)	5.76	4.53 (4-yr. av.)		
1940	5.75	2.43	3.50	4.99	5.02		
1941		1.79	3.50	4.96	5.08		
1942		0.95	3.50	4.15	5.06		
1943		0.93	3.50	4.15	4.94		
1944		0.56	3.50	4.13	4.74		

TABLE 82 (*Continued*)

Year	Argentina					Uruguay	
	Commercial Loans, %	Treasury Bills, %	Official Discount Rate, %	Long-Term Government Bonds, %	Government Bond Yields, %	Discount Rate, %	Lending Rate, %
1945		0.64	3.50	4.18	4.46		
1946	6.00–7.00	1.08	3.50	3.11	4.30		
1947		1.42	3.50	3.20	4.59		
1948		1.48	3.50	3.26	4.92		
1949		1.50	3.50	3.26	5.67		
10-yr. av.		1.28	3.50	3.94	4.88		
1950		1.53	3.50	3.26	5.64		
1951		1.50	3.50	3.26	5.52		
1952		1.49	3.50	3.26	6.05		
1953		1.50	3.50	3.24	6.00		
1954			3.50		6.55		
1955			3.50		6.23		
1956			3.50		6.41		
1957	8.00–9.50		6.00		6.05		
1958	9.50–10.00		6.00		6.18		
1959			6.00		7.06		
10-yr. av.		1.51 (4-yr. av.)	4.25	3.26 (4-yr. av.)	6.17		
1960			6.00		8.50		
1961					7.24		
1962					6.88		
1963					6.43		
1964					6.34		
1965					6.98		
1966					6.74		
1967					7.04		
1968					6.13		
1969					7.57		
10-yr. av.					6.99		
1970							
1971							
1972							
1973							
1974							
1975							
1976							62.00
1977							76.60

TABLE 82 (*Continued*)

Year	Argentina					Uruguay	
	Commercial Loans, %	Treasury Bills, %	Official Discount Rate, %	Long-Term Government Bonds, %	Government Bond Yields, %	Discount Rate, %	Lending Rate, %
1978							71.20
1979							68.10
10-yr. av.							
1980							66.60
1981							72.10	60.40
1982							83.70	58.50
1983							112.70	93.60
1984	869						83.20
1985	1160						94.60
1986	108						94.70
1987	243						95.80
1988	430						102.00
1989	622						113.50
10-yr. av.	572						86.29

SOURCES

Canada, Report of Official Board of Enquiry, *Cost of Living* (1915).

League of Nations, *Statistical Year Book, 1939–40*, pp. 220, 221, 224.

Wendell C. Gordon, *The Economy of Latin America* (New York: Columbia University Press, 1950), p. 242.

IMF, *International Financial Statistics.*

ingly high, in the six-figure range, but they are not officially reported. The hyperinflation continued in the 1980's. The reported lending rate reached over 1000% in 1985. In 1989, rates at times reached astronomical levels: An annualized rate of 14,177% was reported in April, for example.

URUGUAY

Interest rates in Uruguay are represented in Table 82 by a series of government bond yields, 1936–1969, and by a bank lending rate, 1976–1989. The bond yields are based on the yields to maturity of an issue of 5% bonds due in 1974. Uruguayan bond yields from the 1930's through the 1960's followed trends more similar to those in England than to those in other Latin American countries. Starting at 4.43% in 1936, the Uruguayan yields rose after 1937 and reached 5.08% in 1941. Thereafter, they declined to 4.30% in

1946, the year of lowest yields for the period in England and the United States. They rose steeply to 5.67% in 1949 and to 8.50% in 1960. This sharp rise resembled the concurrent rise of English yields from 3 to 6% or higher. Throughout the years following World War II, Uruguayan yields were usually the lowest of the Latin American yields reported in these tables. During the 1960's, Uruguayan government bond yields were stable between 6% and 8% and did not rise like most other yields around the world. However, official reports of yields ceased in 1970.

The short-term bank loan rate in Uruguay, reported for recent years, was high by world standards but more moderate in the Latin American context. It ranged from roughly 60 to 110% per annum from 1976 to 1989. The trend was upward during these years.

MEXICO

Interest rates in Mexico are represented in Table 83 by three series: the official discount rate, 1936–1978, commercial loan rates, 1942–1963 and 1978–1989, and mortgage loan rates, 1947–1959. Until recent years, the data do not suggest strong trends, although the official discount rate rose from 3% in the 1930's to 4.50% in 1943 and remained there until 1975. The discounting privilege was very valuable because bank loan rates were usually above 10%. Hence, the volume of rediscounts was very large.

Bank loan rates crept up in the 1940's from 8.46% annual average to 10.22%, but rose only a little further in the 1950's and early 1960's. The series resumed in 1978, and the rates climbed steadily to reach 92% in 1987. In 1988 and 1989, short-term Mexican loan rates dropped back to the levels of the early years of the decade.

The reported rates on mortgage loans remained slightly above 10% most of the time from 1947 through 1959. While these were high rates by U.S. standards, they were below the corresponding rates in many other Latin American countries, and they were remarkably stable.

PERU

Peruvian interest rates are represented in Table 83 by two series: the official discount rate from 1932 through 1985, and government bond yields from 1936 through 1965. The latter are based on average current yields of an issue of 7% bonds that in 1943 were converted to 6% bonds.

These Peruvian interest rates were high. The discount rate fluctuated between 5% and 6% from 1932 through 1958, and then rose to 9.50% in 1960. This was at the time the highest discount rate reported by any Latin American country. The discount rate remained unchanged at 9½% from 1960 through 1975. In the following decade, it climbed steadily to 72% in 1985, when reports cease.

TABLE 83
Mexican, Peruvian, and Colombian Interest Rates: Annual Averages, 1930–1989

Year	Mexico			Peru		Colombia	
	Commercial Loans, %	Mortgage Loans, %	Official Discount Rate, %	Official Discount Rate, %	Government Bond Yields, %	Official Discount Rate, %	Government Bond Yields, %
1930						8.00	11.67
1931						7.00	13.95
1932				6.00		6.00	13.92
1933				6.00		4.50	9.40
1934				6.00		4.00	8.66
1935				6.00		4.00	9.31
1936			3.00	6.00	8.10	4.00	9.68
1937			3.00	6.00	7.99	4.00	8.73
1938			3.00	6.00	8.24	4.00	8.92
1939			3.00	6.00	9.09	4.00	8.17
10-yr. av.			3.00 (4-yr. av.)	6.00 (8-yr. av.)	8.36 (4-yr. av.)	4.95	10.24
1940			3.00	5.50	8.00	4.00	8.46
1941			4.00	5.00	7.25	4.00	6.98
1942	8.46		4.33	5.00	6.93	4.00	6.36
1943	8.30		4.50	5.00		4.00	6.28
1944	8.84		4.50	5.00	6.42	4.00	6.51
1945	9.28		4.50	5.00	7.07	4.00	6.62
1946	10.44		4.50	5.00	7.04	4.00	6.64
1947	9.94	10.62	4.50	5.25	6.66	4.00	7.12
1948	9.71	10.72	4.50	6.00	6.94	4.00	7.13
1949	10.22	10.89	4.50	6.00	7.11	4.00	6.61
10-yr. av.	9.40 (8-yr. av.)	10.74 (3-yr. av.)	4.28	5.28	7.05 (9-yr. av.)	4.00	6.87
1950	10.88	10.34	4.50	6.00	7.37	4.00	6.49
1951	9.88	10.61	4.50	6.00	7.43	4.00	6.58
1952	10.30	10.43	4.50	6.00	7.42	4.00	6.34
1953	10.41	10.27	4.50	6.00	8.12	4.00	6.33
1954	10.41	10.44	4.50	6.00	8.06	4.00	6.25
1955	10.21	10.18	4.50	6.00	7.82	4.00	6.74
1956	10.21	9.50	4.50	6.00	7.70	4.00	
1957	10.32	9.59	4.50	6.00	7.71	4.00	
1958	10.62	9.61	4.50	6.00	9.36	4.00	
1959	11.35	10.90	4.50	6.87	11.50	4.50	
10-yr. av.	10.46	10.19	4.50	6.09	8.25	4.05	6.46 (6-yr. av.)

TABLE 83 (*Continued*)

Year	Mexico			Peru		Colombia	
	Commercial Loans, %	Mortgage Loans, %	Official Discount Rate, %	Official Discount Rate, %	Government Bond Yields, %	Official Discount Rate, %	Government Bond Yields, %
1960	11.48		4.50	9.50	9.79	5.00	
1961	11.63		4.50	9.50	8.24	5.00	
1962	11.64		4.50	9.50	7.69	5.00	
1963	11.32		4.50	9.50	7.14	6.75	
1964			4.50	9.50	7.23	8.00	
1965			4.50	9.50	6.74	8.00	
1966			4.50	9.50		8.00	
1967			4.50	9.50		8.00	
1968			4.50	9.50		8.00	
1969			4.50	9.50		8.00	
10-yr. av.			4.50	9.50		6.98	
1970			4.50	9.50		14.00	
1971			4.50	9.50		14.00	
1972			4.50	9.50		14.00	
1973			4.50	9.50		14.00	
1974			4.50	9.50		16.00	
1975			4.50	9.50		16.00	
1976			4.50	12.50		20.00	
1977			4.50	14.50		20.00	
1978	18.20		4.50	28.50		22.00	
1979	19.90			29.50		30.00	
10-yr. av.			4.50 (9-yr. av.)	14.20		18.00	
1980	28.10			29.50		30.00	
1981	36.60			44.50		30.00	
1982	45.83			44.50		27.00	
1983	62.37			60.00		27.00	
1984	54.37			60.00		27.00	
1985	55.23			72.00		27.00	
1986	75.91			n.a.		n.a.	
1987	92.44			n.a.		30.00	
1988	52.70			n.a.		30.00	
1989	31.05			n.a.		30.00	
10-yr. av.	53.46			31.05 (6-yr. av.)		25.80 (9-yr. av.)	

Sources

League of Nations, *Statistical Year Book, 1939–40*, p. 221.

Bank of Mexico statistics.

IMF, *International Financial Statistics.*

Peruvian bond yields of 11.50% in 1959 were also the highest reported in this chapter for the 1950's. These bond yields were first reported at 8.10% in 1936. They declined in the 1940's to a decennial average of 7.05% and advanced in the 1950's to a decennial average of 8.27% and a high of 11.5% annual average in 1959. Thus, during these twenty-five years, they followed the general pattern by declining through World War II and rising in the postwar period. They reached their high of 11.5% in 1959, and thereafter declined to 6.75% in 1965, when the official reports were discontinued.

COLOMBIA

Colombian interest rates are represented in Table 83 by two series: the official discount rate from 1930 through 1989 and a series of government bond yields from 1930 through 1955. The latter were based on the current yield of an issue of bonds due in 1971 that had a coupon of 7% prior to 1941 and 6% thereafter.

The interest rates reported by Colombia in the 1950's were not as high as those reported by many other countries. In the early 1930's, however, Colombian interest rates had been very high. The discount rate began in 1930 at 8%, declined to 4% by 1934, and stayed there until 1959, when it was raised to 5%. Commercial loan rates were reported at 6% in 1946 and 6–9% in 1958. Both rates were moderate for Latin America. After 1962, the Colombian discount rate rose steadily to reach 30% in 1979, a level that was more or less maintained through the 1980's.

Colombian government bond yields were very high in 1931–1932, rising almost to 14%. They declined thereafter, but did not go below 8.17% in the 1930's, and averaged 10.25%. In the 1940's, the new series of 6% bonds sold at lower yields: 6.28–7.13%. In the early 1950's, yields fluctuated in a similar range, which was well below the Peruvian, Chilean, and Brazilian bond yields. They were the highest reported here for Latin America in the early 1930's and the lowest, except for Uruguay, in the early 1950's, when reports cease.

Notes

Chapter I

1. Einzig, Paul. *Primitive Money*. London: Eyre & Spottiswoode, 1948. P. 372.
2. Heichelheim, Fritz M. *An Ancient Economic History*. Leiden: A. W. Sijthoffs Uitgeversmaatschappij N. V., 1958. Vol. I, pp. 21ff.
3. *Ibid.*, p. 54.
4. *Ibid.*, p. 55.
5. *Ibid.*, p. 104.
6. *Ibid.*, p. 219.
7. Einzig, *op. cit.*, p. 507.
8. *Ibid.*, p. 114.
9. *Ibid.*, p. 102.
10. Herskovitz, Melville J. *Economic Anthropology*. New York: Alfred A. Knopf, 1952. P. 228.
11. Einzig, *op. cit.*, pp. 64ff.
12. Herskovitz, *op. cit.*, p. 226.
13. Einzig, *op. cit.*, p. 176.
14. *Ibid.*, p. 169.
15. *Ibid.*, p. 145.
16. *Ibid.*, p. 117.

Chapter II

17. Delaporte, L. *Mesopotamia*, tr. V. G. Childe. New York: Alfred A. Knopf, 1925. Pp. 126, 231.
18. *Ibid.*, p. 101.
19. *Ibid.*, p. 115.
20. *Ibid.*, p. 126.
21. *Ibid.*, p. 134.
22. Heichelheim, *op. cit.*, pp. 133, 135.
23. Delaporte, *op. cit.*, p. 121.
24. *Ibid.*, p. 306.
25. *University of California Publications in Semitic Literature*, X (1940), 9.
26. Delaporte, *op. cit.*, p. 127.
27. Niefeld, M. R. *The Personal Finance Business*. New York and London: Harper & Bros., 1933. P. 21.

28. Delaporte, *op. cit.*, p. 305.

29. *Ibid.*, p. 127.

30. *Ibid.*, p. 129.

31. Moldenke, A. B. (ed. and trans.). *Cuneiform Texts in the Metropolitan Museum of Art.* New York: The Museum.

32. Knight, F. H. *Encyclopedia of the Social Sciences.* New York: The Macmillan Company, 1932. Vol. VIII, p. 139.

CHAPTER III

33. Glotz, Gustave. *The Aegean Civilization.* New York: Alfred A. Knopf, 1925. P. 194.

34. Andreades, A. M. *A History of Greek Public Finance,* tr. C. N. Brown. Cambridge: Harvard University Press, 1933. Vol. I, pp. 6–21.

35. Einzig, *op. cit.*, pp. 228–234.

36. Heichelheim, *op. cit.*, p. 254.

37. Einzig, *op. cit.*, pp. 225–227.

38. Glotz, Gustave. *Ancient Greece at Work.* New York: Alfred A. Knopf, 1926. P. 68.

39. *Ibid.*, p. 61.

40. *Ibid.*, p. 69.

41. *Ibid.*, p. 230ff.

42. Michell, H. *The Economics of Ancient Greece.* New York: Barnes & Noble, 1957. P. 320.

43. Glotz, *Ancient Greece at Work, op. cit.*, pp. 238ff.

44. *Ibid.*, p. 343.

45. Finley, Moses I. *Studies in Land and Credit in Ancient Athens.* New Brunswick, N.J.: Rutgers University Press, 1951. Pp. 9ff.

46. *Ibid.*, p. 32.

47. *Ibid.*, p. 84.

48. Andreades, *op. cit.*, pp. 168–172.

49. *Ibid.*, p. 126.

50. *Ibid.*, p. 168.

51. *Ibid.*, pp. 137–141.

52. Glotz, *Ancient Greece at Work, op. cit.*, p. 305.

53. Casson, Lionel. *The Ancient Mariners.* New York: The Macmillan Company, 1959. P. 108.

54. Glotz, *op. cit.*, p. 365.

55. Day, John. *An Economic History of Athens Under Roman Domination.* New York: Columbia University Press, 1942. P. 4.

56. Glotz, *Ancient Greece at Work, op. cit.*, p. 325.

57. Day, *op. cit.*, pp. 14, 27.

58. Boeckh, Augustus. *The Public Economy of the Athenians.* Tr. Anthony Lamb. Boston: Little, Brown & Co., 1857. P. 179.

59. Andreades, *op. cit.*, p. 360.

60. Inglis Palgrave, R. H. (ed.). *Dictionary of Political Economy.* London and New York: The Macmillan Company, 1894–99. Vol. II, p. 429.

61. Day, *op. cit.*, p. 48.

62. Glotz, *Ancient Greece at Work, op. cit.*, p. 243.

63. Boeckh, *op. cit.*, p. 156.

64. Oxford Classical Dictionary, The. Oxford: Clarendon Press, 1950. P. 455.

65. Glotz, *Ancient Greece at Work, op. cit.*, p. 365.

66. Larsen, J. A. O. In *An Economic Survey of Ancient Rome,* ed. Tenney Frank. Baltimore: Johns Hopkins University Press, 1933. Vol. IV, pp. 368ff.

67. Heichelheim, Fritz M. *Wirtschaftliche Schwankungen der Zeit von Alexander bis Augustus.* Jena: G. Fisher, 1930. Pp. 126–127 (table).

68. Day, *op. cit.,* p. 251.

69. Larsen, *op. cit.,* p. 373.

70. Boeckh, *op. cit.,* p. 182.

71. Larsen, *op. cit.,* p. 491, quoting Gustav Billeter, *Geschichte des Zinsfusses* (Leipsig: B. T. Teubner, 1898), pp. 103, 109.

72. Finley, *op. cit.,* p. 32ff.

73. *Ibid.,* p. 86.

74. *Ibid.,* p. 64.

75. *Ibid.,* p. 78.

76. Larsen, *op. cit.,* pp. 363, 364.

77. Andreades, *op. cit.,* p. 175, quoting Billeter and F. R. Poland.

78. Larsen, *op. cit.,* p. 373, quoting Billeter.

79. Andreades, *op. cit.,* p. 177.

80. Boeckh, *op. cit.,* p. 174, quoting Cassaubon.

81. *Ibid.,* pp. 177ff.

82. *Ibid.,* p. 181.

83. *Ibid.,* p. 159.

84. Glotz, *Ancient Greece at Work, op. cit.,* p. 264.

85. Larsen, *op. cit.,* pp. 368ff.

CHAPTER IV

86. Einzig, *op. cit.,* pp. 234, 239.

87. Frank, Tenney. *An Economic Survey of Ancient Rome.* Baltimore: Johns Hopkins University Press, 1933. Vol. I, pp. 5, 13ff.

88. *Ibid.,* pp. 26, 31.

89. *Ibid.,* p. 23.

90. *Ibid.,* p. 209.

91. *Ibid.,* p. 52.

92. *Ibid.,* p. 387.

93. *Ibid.,* pp. 206, 350.

94. Rostovtseff, M. *A History of the Ancient World,* tr. J. D. Duff. Oxford: Clarendon Press, 1928. Vol. II, p. 159.

95. Frank, *op. cit.,* vol. I, p. 352.

96. Frank, *op. cit.,* vol. V, pp. 18ff.

97. Suetonius, *Lives of the Caesars,* Augustus 41–1. D 10.

98. Frank, *op. cit.,* vol. V, pp. 32ff.

99. *Ibid.,* p. 58.

100. *Ibid.,* p. 300.

101. Neifeld, *op. cit.,* p. 21.

102. Bentham, Jeremy. *Defense of Usury.*

103. Oxford Classical Dictionary, *op. cit.,* p. 456.

104. Angell, Norman. *The Story of Money.* New York: Garden City Publishing Co., 1929. P. 183.

105. Gardiner, Alan H. (ed). *The Wilbour Papyrus.* London: Published for the Brooklyn Museum at Oxford University Press, 1941–52. Vol. II, p. 206.

106. Moller, G. *Sitzungs Berichte der Preuss.* Akademie der Wissenschaften, 1921. Pp. 298, 304 (The Berlin Papyrus).

107. *Ibid.,* p. 302.

108. Malinine, M. *Choix de Textes Juridiques en Hiératique Anormal et en Demotique: Première Partie.* Paris: H. Champion, 1953. Pp. 15, 20, 25ff.

109. Johnson, A. C. In *An Economic Survey of Ancient Rome, op. cit.,* vol. II, p. 445.

110. *Ibid.,* p. 148.

111. *Ibid.,* p. 353.

112. Haywood, R. M. In *An Economic Survey of Ancient Rome, op. cit.,* vol. IV, pp. 6ff.

113. *Ibid.,* p. 79.

114. Heichelheim, F. M. In *An Economic Survey of Ancient Rome, op. cit.,* vol. IV, pp. 123ff, 224ff.

115. Broughton, T. R. S. In *An Economic Survey of Ancient Rome, op. cit.,* vol IV, pp. 505ff.

116. *Ibid.,* pp. 888ff.

117. *Ibid.,* p. 898.

118. Billeter, Gustav, *Geschichte des Zinsfusses.* Leipsig: B. T. Teubner, 1898. Pp. 103ff.

119. Frank, *op. cit.,* vol. I, pp. 28ff.

120. *Ibid.,* p. 269.

121. Frank, Tenney. *An Economic History of Rome,* 2d ed. Baltimore: Johns Hopkins University Press, 1927. P. 294.

122. Frank, *An Economic Survey of Ancient Rome, op. cit.,* vol. I, p. 171 (quoting Cato's *De Agricultura*).

123. *Ibid.,* p. 262.

124. *Ibid.,* p. 322.

125. Frank, *An Economic History of Rome, op. cit.,* p. 425.

126. Billeter, *op. cit.,* p. 181, quoted by Larsen, *op. cit.,* p. 491.

127. Broughton, *op. cit.,* p. 560.

128. *Ibid.,* p. 545.

129. *Ibid.,* pp. 898ff.

130. Johnson, *op. cit.,* p. 148.

131. *Ibid.,* pp. 450ff.

132. Haywood, *op. cit.,* p. 79.

133. Heichelheim. *op. cit.,* p. 227.

134. Knight, *op. cit.,* vol. VIII, p. 139; Nelson & Stair, *The Legend of the Divine Surety and the Jewish Money Lender* (1944), p. 59; Oxford Classical Dictionary, *op. cit.,* p. 456.

135. *Cambridge Economic History of Europe.* Cambridge: Cambridge University Press, 1952. Vol. II, pp. 97, 109.

136. Cassimatis, Grégoire. *Les Intérêts dans la Législation de Justinien.* Paris: Librairie du Recueil Sirey, 1931.

137. Andreades, *op. cit.,* p. 177.

CHAPTER VI

138. Noonan, John T., Jr. *The Scholastic Analysis of Usury.* Cambridge: Harvard University Press, 1957. P. 15.

139. Nelson, Benjamin N. *The Idea of Usury.* Princeton: Princeton University Press, 1949. Pp. 3–4.

140. Noonan, *op. cit.,* p. 17.

141. *Ibid.*, p. 18.

142. *Ibid.*, p. 33.

143. Nelson, *op. cit.*, p. 13.

144. *Ibid.*, p. 14.

145. Noonan, *op. cit.*, p. 34.

146. *Ibid.*, p. 35.

147. *Ibid.*, p. 100.

148. *Ibid.*, p. 105.

149. *Ibid.*, p. 108. Also, Thorndike, Lynn. *The History of Mediaeval Europe.* Boston: Houghton Mifflin Co., 1917. P. 355.

150. Noonan, *op. cit.*, p. 110.

151. *Ibid.*, p. 120.

152. *Ibid.*, p. 121.

153. *Ibid.*, p. 133.

154. *Ibid.*, p. 203.

155. *Ibid.*, p. 213.

156. *Ibid.*, p. 154.

157. *Ibid.*, p. 155.

158. *Ibid.*, p. 171.

159. deRoover, Raymond. *Money, Banking and Credit in Mediaeval Bruges.* Cambridge: Mediaeval Academy of America, 1948. P. 318.

160. Lane, F. C. "Venetian Bankers, 1496–1533," *Journal of Political Economy,* XLV (April, 1937), p. 190.

161. Noonan, *op. cit.*, p. 192.

162. *Ibid.*, p. 176.

163. *Ibid.*, p. 176.

164. deRoover, *op. cit.*, p. 53.

165. *Ibid.*, p. 55.

166. *Ibid.*, p. 62.

167. Noonan, *op. cit.*, p. 179.

168. *Ibid.*, p. 179.

169. *Ibid.*, p. 295.

170. Bentham, *op. cit.*

171. Noonan, *op. cit.*, p. 305.

172. Nelson, *op. cit.*, p. 18.

173. *Ibid.*, p. 78.

174. *Ibid.*, p. 29.

175. *Ibid.*, p. 45.

176. *Ibid.*, p. 65.

177. *Ibid.*, p. 74.

178. Noonan, *op. cit.*, p. 377.

179. *Ibid.*, p. 392.

180. *Works of John Locke.* Vol. V, pp. 4–18.

CHAPTER VII

181. *Cambridge Economic History of Europe,* vol. II, pp. 159, 269.

182. Pirenne, Henri. *Economic and Social History of Mediaeval Europe,* tr. I. E. Clegg. London: Routledge & Kegan Paul, Ltd., 1936. Pp. 1, 37.

183. *Ibid.*, p. 5.

184. *Cambridge Economic History of Europe, op. cit.*, vol. II, pp. 156, 158.

185. Pirenne, *op. cit.*, p. 3.

186. *Cambridge Economic History of Europe, op. cit.,* vol. II, p. 271.
187. Pirenne, *op. cit.,* p. 108.
188. *Ibid.,* p. 12.
189. *Cambridge Economic History of Europe, op. cit.,* vol. II, p. 262.
190. Pirenne, *op. cit.,* p. 18.
191. *Cambridge Economic History of Europe, op. cit.,* vol. II, p. 159.
192. Pirenne, *op. cit.,* p. 4.
193. *Cambridge Economic History of Europe, op. cit.,* vol. II, p. 161.
194. Pirenne, *op. cit.,* p. 37.
195. *Cambridge Economic History of Europe, op. cit.,* vol. II, p. 183.
196. *Ibid.,* p. 293.
197. Pirenne, *op. cit.,* p. 67.
198. *Cambridge Economic History of Europe, op. cit.,* Vol. II, p. 273.
199. Pirenne, *op. cit.,* p. 33; *Cambridge Economic History of Europe, op. cit.,* vol. II, p. 157.
200. Pirenne, *op. cit.,* p. 25.
201. *Ibid.,* p. 53.
202. *Ibid.,* p. 53; *Cambridge Economic History of Europe, op. cit.,* vol. II, p. 172.
203. Pirenne, *op. cit.,* p. 181.
204. *Ibid.,* p. 19.
205. deRoover, *op. cit.,* p. 9.
206. Pirenne, *op. cit.,* p. 121.

CHAPTER VIII

207. *Ibid.,* p. 31.
208. *Ibid.,* p. 37; *Cambridge Economic History of Europe, op. cit.,* vol. II, p. 184.
209. *Ibid.,* p. 68; *Cambridge Economic History of Europe, op. cit.,* vol. II, p. 160.
210. Pirenne, *op. cit.,* p. 148.
211. *Ibid.,* p. 98; *Cambridge Economic History of Europe, op. cit.,* vol. II, p. 181.
212. Pirenne, *op. cit.,* p. 102.
213. *Cambridge Economic History of Europe, op. cit.,* vol. II, p. 236.
214. Munro, D. C. *The Middle Ages.* New York: The Century Co., 1921. P. 309.
215. Noonan, *op. cit.,* p. 34.
216. Parkes, J. W. *The Jew in the Mediaeval Community.* London: The Soncino Press, 1938. P. 34.
217. deRoover, *op. cit.,* p. 312.
218. *Cambridge Economic History of Europe, op. cit.,* vol. II, p. 306.
219. Pirenne, *op. cit.,* p. 137.
220. Thorndike, *op. cit.,* p. 343.
221. *Cambridge Economic History of Europe, op. cit.,* Vol. II, p. 135.
222. *Ibid.,* p. 160.
223. *Ibid.,* p. 165.
224. Pirenne, *op. cit.,* pp. 68–83.
225. *Cambridge Economic History of Europe, op. cit.,* vol. II, p. 301.
226. *Ibid.,* p. 126.
227. deRoover, *op. cit.,* p. 51.
228. *Cambridge Economic History of Europe, op. cit.,* vol. II, p. 141.
229. Pirenne, *op. cit.,* p. 127.
230. Cipolla, C. M. *Money, Prices and Civilization in the Mediterranean World.* Princeton: Princeton University Press, for the University of Cincinnati, 1956. Pp. 64–66.

231. Hazlitt, W. C. *The Venetian Republic.* London: Adam and Charles Black, 1900. Vol. I, p. 349.

232. Pirenne, *op. cit.,* p. 131.

233. Knight, M. M. *Economic History of Europe at the End of the Middle Ages.* Boston and New York: Houghton Mifflin Co., 1926. P. 116.

234. *Cambridge Economic History of Europe, op. cit.,* vol. II, p. 334.

235. Ehrenberg, Richard. *Capital and Finance in the Age of the Renaissance.* Tr. H. M. Lucas. London: Jonathan Cape, 1928. P. 57.

236. Noonan, *op. cit.,* pp. 122, 172.

237. deRoover, *op. cit.,* p. 11.

238. Noonan, *op. cit.,* p. 122.

239. Information on thirteenth- and fourteenth-century Venice is principally derived from Gino Luzzatto, *I Prestiti della Repubblica di Venezia Nei Secc. XIII–XV* in *Documenti finanziari della Repubblica di Venezia* (Padova, 1929), Series III, Vol. I; and from unpublished notes of Professor F. C. Lane, of Johns Hopkins University.

240. *Cambridge Economic History of Europe, op. cit.,* vol. II, pp. 191, 338; also Pirenne, *op. cit.,* p. 173.

241. *Cambridge Economic History of Europe, op. cit.,* vol. II, pp. 215–216.

242. *Ibid.,* p. 339.

243. Ehrenberg, *op. cit.,* p. 50.

244. Pirenne, *op. cit.,* p. 194.

245. *Ibid.,* p. 219.

246. Ehrenberg, *op. cit.,* p. 43.

247. Shumpeter, Joseph A. *Business Cycles.* New York: McGraw-Hill Book Company, Inc., 1939. P. 617.

248. deRoover, *op. cit.,* p. 119.

249. *Ibid.,* pp. 104, 126.

250. Parkes, *op. cit.,* p. 355.

251. Cipolla, *op. cit.,* p. 64.

252. *Cambridge Economic History of Europe,* vol. II, p. 349.

253. Cipolla, *op. cit.,* p. 64.

254. Parkes, *op. cit.,* p. 317.

255. deRoover, *op. cit.,* p. 118.

256. Noonan, *op. cit.,* p. 172.

257. *Cambridge Economic History of Europe, op. cit.,* vol. II, p. 334.

258. Cipolla, *op. cit.,* p. 63; also Noonan, *op. cit.,* p. 122.

259. Luzzato and Lane, *op. cit.* See note 239.

CHAPTER IX

260. *Cambridge Economic History of Europe, op. cit.,* vol. II, pp. 194, 197.

261. Pirenne, *op. cit.,* p. 173.

262. *Ibid.,* p. 88; also *Cambridge Economic History of Europe, op. cit.,* vol. II, p. 215.

263. *Cambridge Economic History of Europe, op. cit.,* vol. II, p. 201.

264. *Ibid.,* p. 245.

265. *Ibid.,* p. 252.

266. Pirenne, *op. cit.,* p. 189.

267. deRoover, *op. cit.,* p. 349.

268. *Cambridge Economic History of Europe, op. cit.,* vol. II, p. 349.

269. *Ibid.,* p. 351.

270. Pirenne, *op. cit.,* p. 215.

271. Ehrenberg, *op. cit.,* p. 23.

272. *Ibid.,* p. 36.

273. *Ibid.,* p. 62.

274. *Ibid.,* p. 204.

275. Young, G. F. *The Medici.* New York: E. P. Dutton, 1909. Vol. I, p. 315.

276. Roscoe, William. *Leo X.* London: George Bell & Sons, 1888. Vol. 1, p. 85.

277. deRoover, *op. cit.,* p. 130.

278. Noonan, *op. cit.,* p. 295.

279. *Cambridge Economic History of Europe, op. cit.,* vol. II, p. 344.

280. Pirenne, *op. cit.,* p. 215.

281. Cipolla, *op. cit.,* p. 64.

282. Lane, *op. cit.* See note 239.

283. Ehrenberg, *op. cit. passim.*

284. *Cambridge Economic History of Europe, op. cit.,* vol. II, p. 217.

285. Noonan, *op. cit.,* p. 172.

286. deRoover, Raymond. *The Medici Bank.* New York: New York University Press, 1948. Pp. 54–65.

287. *Ibid.,* pp. 1–2.

288. Cipolla, *op. cit.,* pp. 64–65.

289. Noonan, *op. cit.,* p. 240.

290. *Ibid.,* p. 161.

291. Ehrenberg, *op. cit.,* p. 63; also Cipolla, *op. cit.,* p. 64.

292. Houtzager, D. *Life Annuities and Sinking Funds in the Netherlands Before 1672.* Schiedam: Hav-Bank, 1950. P. 11.

293. Luzzatto, *op. cit.,* Series III, vol. 1.

294. Hazlitt, *op. cit.,* vol. 1, p. 807.

295. Lane, "Venetian Bankers," *op. cit.,* pp. 198–199.

296. Pirenne, *op. cit.,* p. 173.

297. *Cambridge Economic History of Europe, op. cit.,* vol. II, p. 191.

298. Information on Genoa in the sixteenth and seventeenth centuries is derived largely from Professor Carlo M. Cipolla, of the University of Venice, who, in his paper, *Note Sulla Storia del Saggio d'Interesse; Corso, Dividendi e Sconto Dei Dividendi del Banco di S. Giorgio,* presents series from 1509 to 1625 of the annual dividends declared by the bank, the market price of the *luoghi,* the rate of discount on the dividends, and the ratio of discounted dividends to the price of the *luoghi.*

299. *Cambridge Economic History of Europe, op. cit.,* vol. II, p. 232.

300. *Ibid.,* p. 353.

301. Ehrenberg, *op. cit.,* p. 27.

302. *Ibid.,* p. 31.

303. *Ibid.,* p. 40.

304. *Ibid.,* pp. 101, 104.

305. Motley, J. L. *Rise of the Dutch Republic.* New York: Harper & Brothers, 1901. Vol. I, p. 85ff.

306. Del Mar, Alexander. "The Future of the Rate of Interest," *Bankers Magazine,* December, 1905 (New York: Bankers Publishing Co.).

307. Ehrenberg, *op. cit.,* pp. 69, 72, 93, 95, 106, 113, 116, 125.

308. *Ibid.,* p. 180.

309. *Ibid.,* pp. 256, 258ff.

310. Knight, Frank H. *Encyclopedia of the Social Sciences, op. cit.,* vol. 8, p. 139.

311. Noonan, *op. cit.,* p. 303.

312. Ehrenberg, *op. cit.,* p. 120.

313. Noonan, *op. cit.*, pp. 209–223.

314. *Ibid.*, p. 303.

315. Angell, *op. cit.*, p. 224.

316. Ehrenberg, *op. cit.*, pp. 89–94.

317. *Ibid.*, p. 165.

318. Noonan, *op. cit.*, p. 240.

319. *Ibid.*, p. 209.

320. Ehrenberg, *op. cit.*, p. 109.

321. *Ibid.*, p. 170.

322. Houtzager, *op. cit.*, pp. 43–45.

323. Information on Genoa in the sixteenth and seventeenth centuries is derived largely from Professor Carlo M. Cipolla, of the University of Venice, who, in his paper, *Note Sulla Storia del Saggio d'Interesse; Corso, Dividendi e Sconto Dei Dividendi del Banco di S. Giorgio,* presents series from 1509 to 1625 of the annual dividends declared by the bank, the market price of the *luoghi*, the rate of discount on the dividends, and the ratio of discounted dividends to the price of the *luoghi*.

324. Ehrenberg, *op. cit.*, pp. 334–336.

325. *Ibid.*, p. 339.

326. *Ibid.*, p. 343.

327. *Ibid.*, p. 347

328. *Ibid.*, pp. 357ff.

329. *Ibid.*, p. 349.

330. *Ibid.*, p. 357.

331. Hirst, F. W., *The Stock Exchange.* London: William & Norgate, 1911. Pp. 27, 29.

332. MacLeod, H. D. *History of Banking in Great Britain,* 1896. Pp. 2–3.

333. Ehrenberg, *op. cit.*, p. 347.

334. Macaulay, T. B. *History of England.* Boston: Houghton Mifflin & Co., 1901. Vol. I, p. 284.

335. Turner, B. B. *Chronicles of the Bank of England.* London: Swan, Sonnenschein & Co., 1897. Pp. 15ff.

336. Macaulay, *op. cit.*, vol. IV, pp. 433ff.

337. Clapham, J. *The Bank of England.* Cambridge: Cambridge University Press, 1944. Vol. I, p. 299.

338. Ehrenberg, *op. cit.*, pp. 347, 353.

339. Habakkuk, H. J. *Economic History Review,* 2d Series, V (1952), 1.

340. Macaulay, *op. cit.*, vol. V, p. 152.

341. Barbour, Violet. *Capitalism in Amsterdam in the 17th Century.* Baltimore: Johns Hopkins Press, 1950. Pp. 82–83.

342. Ehrenberg, *op. cit.*, p. 360.

343. *New York Times,* Sept. 21, 1957.

344. Ehrenberg, *op. cit.*, p. 362.

345. *Ibid.*, p. 341.

346. *Ibid.*, p. 336.

347. Hazlitt, *op. cit.*, vol. II, pp. 276, 643.

CHAPTER XI

348. *Bankers Magazine,* October, 1927.

349. Macaulay, *op. cit.*, vol. IV, p. 432.

350. *Ibid.*, p. 429.

351. *Ibid.*, p. 433.

352. *Ibid.*, p. 594.

353. *Ibid.*, p. 603.

354. Turner, *op. cit.*, pp. 18ff.

355. Clapham, *op. cit.*, vol. I, p. 18.

356. Hirst, *op. cit.*, p. 30.

357. Clapham, *op. cit.*, vol. I, p. 37.

358. *Ibid.*, p. 59.

359. Ashton, T. S., *An Economic History of England: The 18th Century*. London: Methuen & Co. Ltd., 1955. P. 105.

360. *Ibid.*, p. 2.

361. *Ibid.*, p. 177.

362. *Ibid.*, pp. 27, 38, 45, 84.

363. *Ibid.*, p. 27

364. *Ibid.*, p. 58.

365. Hirst, *op. cit.*, p. 39.

366. Clapham, *op. cit.*, vol. I, p. 92.

367. Ashton, *op. cit.*, p. 251.

368. Clapham, *op. cit.*, vol. I, p. 93.

369. *Ibid.*, p. 94.

370. Clapham, *op. cit.*, vol. I, p. 103.

371. John, A. H. "Insurance Investment and the London Money Market of the 18th Century," *Economica*, May, 1953, p. 137.

372. Pressnell, L. S. *Studies in the Industrial Revolution*. London: University of London, Athlone Press, 1960. Pp. 186–193

373. Niefeld, *op. cit.*, p. 21.

374. Clapham, *op. cit.*, vol. I, p. 299, for all Bank of England rates.

375. Fenn, Charles. *Compendium of the English and Foreign Funds*, rewritten and brought up to date by Robert Lucas Nash. London: Effingham Wilson, Royal Exchange, 14th ed., 1889. P. 30.

376. Turner, *op. cit.*, p. 25.

377. Ibid., p. 28.

378. Clapham, *op. cit.*, vol. I, p. 224.

379. *Ibid.*, p. 119.

380. *Ibid.*, pp. 78, 130.

381. *Ibid.*, p. 81.

382. *Ibid.*, p. 124.

383. *Ibid.*, p. 121.

384. *Ibid.*, p. 92.

385. *Ibid.*, p. 176.

386. Turner, *op. cit.*, p. 61.

387. Clapham, *op. cit.*, vol. I, p. 191.

388. Fenn, *op. cit.*, p. 67.

389. Turner, *op. cit.*, p. 82.

CHAPTER XII

390. Bogart, Ernest L. *Economic History of Europe, 1760–1939*. London: Longmans, Green & Co., 1942. P. 72.

391. Ehrenberg, *op. cit.*, p. 369.

392. *Ibid.*, p. 370.

393. Clough, S. B., and C. W. Cole. *Economic History of Europe*. Boston: D. C. Heath & Co., 1947. Pp. 283ff.

394. *Ibid.*, p. 284.
395. Fachan, J. M. *Historique de la Rente Francaise.* Paris: Berger-Levrault et Cie., 1904. P. 139.
396. Bogart, *op. cit.*, p. 180ff.
397. *Ibid.*, p. 185.
398. McCulloch, John R. *Essay on Interest.* Philadelphia: A. Hart, 1851. P. 18.
399. Ehrenberg, *op. cit.*, p. 345.
400. Saugrain, M. Gaston. *The Decline of the Interest Rate.* Paris: 1896.
401. Fachan, *op. cit.*, p. 34.
402. Clough, *op. cit.*, p. 286.
403. Loutchitch, L. J. *Des Variations du Taux de l'Intérêst en France de 1800 à Nos Jours.* Paris: Libraire Félix Alcan, 1930. P. 45.
404. Defoe, Daniel. *A Plan of the English Commerce.*
405. Langer, W. L. *Encyclopedia of World History,* Boston: Houghton Mifflin Company, 1940. P. 439.
406. Clough, *op. cit.*, p. 275.
407. Ashton, *op. cit.*, p. 193.
408. Wilson, C. H. "The Economic Decline of the Netherlands," *Economic History Review,* IX (London) (1938–1939), 111.
409. Ehrenberg, *op. cit.*, p. 350.
410. *Ibid.*, p. 352.
411. *Ibid.*, pp. 357ff.
412. Clough, *op. cit.*, p. 294.
413. Ehrenberg, *op. cit.*, p. 362.
414. McCulloch, *op. cit.*, p. 3.
415. Wilson, *op. cit.*, p. 122.
416. Clapham, *op. cit.*, vol. I, p. 93.
417. *Encyclopedia of Social Sciences, op. cit.*, vol. 8, p. 139.
418. Weeveringh, J. J. *Handleiding Tot de Geschiedenis der Staatsschulden, eerste deel.* Haarlem: 1852.
419. Noonan, *op. cit.*, pp. 226, 247.
420. Bentham, *op. cit.*, p. 80.
421. Saugrain, *op. cit.*
422. Noonan, *op. cit.*, p. 306.
423. *Sveriges Riksbank, 1668–1924 Statistiska Tabeller,* 1931. Pp. 129ff.

CHAPTER XIII

424. Clough, *op. cit.*, p. 586.
425. *Ibid.*, pp. 503, 662.
426. *Ibid.*, p. 464.
427. *Ibid.*, p. 486.
428. Clapham, *op. cit.*, vol. II, p. 226.
429. Clough, *op. cit.*, pp. 508, 662.
430. Clapham, *op. cit.*, vol. II, p. 298.
431. Clough, *op. cit.*, p. 385.
432. Clapham, *op. cit.*, vol. II, p. 4.
433. *Ibid.*, pp. 9, 57, 78.
434. *Ibid.*, pp. 36ff.
435. *Ibid.*, pp. 50ff.
436. *Ibid.*, p. 100.
437. *Ibid.*, p. 183.

438. Hawtrey, R. G. *A Century of Bank Rate.* London: Longmans, Green & Co., 1938. P. 37.

439. *Ibid.,* p. 69.

440. *Ibid.,* p. 46.

441. Fenn, *op. cit.,* p. 10.

442. Macaulay, *op. cit.,* vol. IV, pp. 432ff.

443. Fenn, *op. cit.,* pp. 8, 9, 16, 33.

444. Clapham, *op. cit.,* vol. II, p. 32.

445. Hirst, *op. cit.,* p. 70.

446. Böhm von Bawerk, Eugen (1851–1914), quoted by J. A. Schumpeter in *Ten Great Economists* (New York: Oxford University Press, 1951), p. 182.

447. Bloomfield, Arthur I. *Monetary Policy Under the International Gold Standard.* New York: Federal Reserve Bank of New York, 1959. P. 24.

448. Fenn, *op. cit.,* pp. 146ff.

449. *Ibid.,* pp. 180ff.

450. Hirst, *op. cit.,* pp. 53ff.

451. Clough, *op. cit.,* p. 656.

452. Roth, Cecil. *Benjamin Disraeli.* New York: Philosophical Library, 1952. P. 44.

453. Clough, *op. cit.,* p. 582.

454. Clapham, *op. cit.,* vol. II, p. 15.

455. National (U.S.) Monetary Commission, vol. XXI, *Great Britain,* p. 143 (The Aldrich Report).

456. Hawtry, *op. cit.,* pp. 84ff.

457. Clapham, *op. cit.,* vol. II, pp. 263ff.

CHAPTER XIV

458. Fachan, *op. cit.,* p. 139.

459. Clough, *op. cit.,* p. 637.

460. Dunham, Arthur Louis. *The Industrial Revolution in France, 1815–1848.* New York: Exposition Press, 1955. P. 19.

461. *Ibid.,* p. 55.

462. Clough, *op. cit.,* p. 586.

463. Fachan, *op. cit.,* p. 122.

464. Fenn, *op. cit.,* pp. 436ff.

465. Fachan, *op. cit.,* p. 204.

466. Dunham, *op. cit.,* p. 240.

467. Loutchitch, *op. cit.,* p. 50.

468. Dunham, *op. cit.,* p. 236.

469. *Ibid.,* p. 238.

CHAPTER XV

470. Clough, *op. cit.,* pp. 653ff., 662.

471. *Ibid.,* p. 623.

472. *Ibid.,* p. 624.

CHAPTER XVI

473. Wright, Chester W. *Economic History of the United States.* New York: McGraw-Hill Book Company, Inc., 1941. P. 163.

474. Dewey, Davis Rich. *Financial History of the United States.* New York: Longmans, Green & Company, 1931. P. 8.

475. Wright, *op. cit.,* p. 129.

476. Dewey, *op. cit.,* p. 19.

477. Wright, *op. cit.,* p. 167.

478. Childs, C. F. *Concerning U.S. Government Securities.* Chicago: C. F. Childs & Co., 1947. P. 4.

479. Dewey, *op. cit.,* pp. 24–26.

480. *Ibid.,* pp. 37–39.

481. *Ibid.,* p. 46.

482. *Ibid.,* pp. 56ff.

483. Wright, *op. cit.,* p. 472.

484. *Ibid.,* p. 476.

485. *Ibid.,* p. 509.

486. *Ibid., frontis.*

487. *Ibid.,* p. 541.

488. *Ibid.,* p. 872.

489. Dewey, *op. cit.,* p. 322.

490. Macaulay, Frederick R. *The Movements of Interest Rates, Bond Yields and Stock Prices.* New York: National Bureau of Economic Research, 1938. P. A215.

491. F. R. Macaulay, *op. cit.,* pp. A142, A174.

492. Bayley, Rafael A. *National Loans of the United States.* Washington: U.S. Government Printing Office, 2d ed., 1882. P. 109.

493. Dewey, *op. cit.,* p. 95.

494. *Ibid.,* p. 113.

495. Bond prices from: Martin, Joseph G. *Martin's Boston Stock Market.* Boston: 1886. P. 127.

496. Dewey, *op. cit.,* p. 137.

497. Bayley, *op. cit.,* p. 59.

498. Dewey, *op. cit.,* p. 272.

499. *Ibid.,* p. 316.

500. Lerner, E. M. "Monetary and Fiscal Programs of the Confederate Government," *Journal of Political Economy,* LXII (August, 1954).

501. Cleland, Robert G. *The Cattle on a Thousand Hills.* San Marino, Calif.: The Huntington Library, 1951. Pp. 102ff.

502. *Los Angeles; the Transition Decade.* San Marino, Calif.: The Huntington Library.

503. Plehn, C. C. *Yale Review,* VIII (May, 1899), p. 52.

504. Cochran, Thomas C. *The Pabst Brewing Co.* New York: New York University Press, 1948. Pp. 23, 46, 85.

505. Sumner, William Graham. *History of Banking in the United States.* New York: 1896. P. 83.

506. Burns, Robert H., Andrew S. Gillespie, and Willing G. Richardson. *Wyoming's Pioneer Ranches.* Laramie, Wyo.: Top-of-the-World Press, 1955. Pp. 177, 633.

507. *Business History Review,* XXIX (1950), p. 325.

508. *Ibid.,* XXXII (1958), pp. 293–310.

509. *Ibid.,* XIX (1945), p. 71.

510. *Ibid.,* XXXIII (1959), p. 136.

CHAPTER XVII

511. Wright, *op. cit.,* p. 876.

512. Childs, *op. cit.,* p. 112.

513. *Ibid.,* p. 120.

514. Wright, *op. cit.,* p. 882.

515. Childs, *op. cit.,* p. 138.

CHAPTER XVIII

516. Durand, David. *Basic Yields of Corporate Bonds, 1900–1942* (and supplements). New York: National Bureau of Economic Research, 1942.

517. Hickman, W. Braddock. *The Term Structure of Interest Rates*. New York: National Bureau of Economic Research, 1942.

P. 7, ch. 4. (Unpublished)

518. Kaufman, Henry. *Interest Rates, the Markets, and the New Financial World*. New York: Times Books, 1986. Chs. 3, 14.

519. Niefeld, M. R. *The Personal Finance Business*. New York: Harper & Brothers, 1933; and *Trends in Consumer Finance*. Easton: Mack Publishing Co., 1954. P. 59.

520. Niefeld, *op. cit.*, p. 292.

521. Niefeld, *op. cit.*, p. 209.

522. *Encyclopedia of the Social Sciences, op. cit.*, vol. 8, p. 139.

523. *New York Times*, Feb. 19, 1959, p. 1.

524. An exact formula for the one-year real rate is $(1 + i)/(1 + p) - 1$, where i is the nominal, or market, rate of interest per annum and p is the expected one-year inflation rate. The formula is equivalent mathematically to a real rate of $(i - p)/(1 + p)$. It is often stated that the real rate of interest is the nominal, or market, rate less the inflation rate. Clearly, this is an approximation that is only roughly correct for low rates of inflation.

525. An excellent book-length study of real rates—the first of its kind—appeared in 1989, the last full year of this HISTORY. See Peter S. Spiro, *Real Interest Rates and Investment and Borrowing Strategy*. New York, Westport, CT, and London: Quorum Books, 1989.

526. This is discussed by Henry Kaufman, *op. cit.*, p. 19.

527. See Spiro, *op. cit.*, ch. 7.

528. Macaulay, *op. cit.*, Pp. 85ff.

529. Durand, *op. cit.* See Table 53 for additional sources.

CHAPTER XIX

530. Bogart, *op. cit.*, p. 421.

531. Clough, *op. cit.*, pp. 662, 664.

532. *Ibid.*, p. 740.

533. *Ibid.*, p. 824.

534. *Ibid.*, p. 846.

535. Spiro, *op. cit.*, ch. 7.

CHAPTER XX

536. Material on the German inflation from: Constantino Bresciani-Turroni. *The Economics of Inflation*. New York: Barnes and Noble, 1937. Pp. 76–78, 317; and C.-L. Holtfrerich. *The German Inflation, 1914–1923*. Berlin and New York: Walter deGruyter, 1986. Part One.

537. Holtfrerich, *op. cit.*, p. 73.

CHAPTER XXII

538. *Canada Year Book, 1950*, p. 1089.

539. Fenn, *op. cit.*, p. 193.

CHAPTER XXIV

540. For an excellent account of the old and new Japanese financial markets, see Yoshio Suzuki, ed., *The Japanese Financial System*. Oxford: Clarendon Press, 1987.

541. Phra Sarasas. *Money and Banking in Japan*. London: Heath Cranton, 1940. Pp. 106ff.

542. Suzuki, *op. cit.*, p. 26.

CHAPTER XXV

543. Butlin, S. J. *Foundation of the Australian Monetary System 1788–1851*. Melbourne: Melbourne University Press, 1953. P. 31.

544. *Ibid.*, pp. 61–62.

545. *Ibid.*, p. 123.

546. *Ibid.*, pp. 237–238.

547. *Ibid.*, pp. 309–310.

548. *Ibid.*, p. 410.

549. *Ibid.*, p. 246.

550. *Ibid.*, p. 634.

551. Butlin, S. J. *The Australian Monetary System 1851–1914*, Sydney: Ambassador Press, 1986. Ch. 1.

552. *Ibid.*, appendix.

553. *Ibid.*

CHAPTER XXVI

554. Arnold, Arthur Z. *Banks, Credit, and Money in Soviet Russia*. New York: Columbia University Press, 1937. Pp. 3ff.

555. *Ibid.*, p. 91.

556. *Ibid.*, p. 198.

557. *Ibid.*, p. 6.

558. *Ibid.*, p. 20.

559. Anan'ich, Boris V. "The Russian Private Banking Houses, 1870–1914," *Journal of Economic History*, 48 (June 1988), pp. 401–407.

560. *Ibid.*, p. 49.

561. *Ibid.*, p. 195.

562. *Ibid.*, pp. 500, 501, 504.

563. *Ibid.*, p. 302.

564. *Ibid.*, p. 319.

565. Garvey, George. *Money, Financial Flows, and Credit in the Soviet Union*. Cambridge, MA: Ballinger Publishing Co. for National Bureau of Economic Research, 1977. P. 69.

566. Bentham, Jeremy, *Defense of Usury*.

567. Hirst, *op. cit.*, p. 95.

568. Horn, Antoine E., "Banking in the Russian Empire," in *A History of Banking in All the Leading Nations*, vol. II. New York: Journal of Commerce and Commercial Bulletin, 1896. Pp. 347ff.

569. Arnold, *op. cit.*

570. Horn, *op. cit.*, pp. 347ff.

571. *Ibid.*, pp. 393ff.

572. *Ibid.*, pp. 430–435.

573. Raymond, W. L. *American and Foreign Investment Bonds*. Boston: Houghton Mifflin Company, 1916. P. 77.

574. Canada, Report by a Board of Enquiry, *Cost of Living*, 1915, p. 711.

575. Arnold, *op. cit.*, p. 39.

576. Horn, *op. cit.*, p. 353.

577. Arnold, *op. cit.*, p. 24.

578. Horn, *op. cit.*, p. 404.

579. *Ibid.*, pp. 393ff.

580. *Ibid.*, p. 414.

581. Albert, Hermann. *Geschichtliche Entwickelung des Zinsfusses in Deutschland, 1895–1908*. Leipzig, 1910, p. 170.

582. *Ibid.*, pp. 133ff.

583. *Ibid.*, pp. 245, 254.

584. Hubbard, L. E. *Soviet Money and Finance.* London: Macmillan & Co., 1936. P. 85.

585. Arnold, *op. cit.*, pp. 245, 254.

586. *Ibid.*, pp. 385–386.

587. Grossman, Gregory. "Soviet Banking," in B. H. Beckhart, ed., *Banking Systems.* New York: Columbia University Press, 1954. Pp. 739–766.

588. Korovushkin, Alexander. *The Financial Times* (London), June 26, 1961, supplement, p. 25.

589. Garvey, *op. cit.*, pp. 58–59.

590. Arnold, *op. cit.*, pp. 133ff.

591. *Ibid.*, pp. 245, 254.

592. *Ibid.*, pp. 385–386.

593. *Ibid.*; and Hubbard, *op. cit.*, p. 59.

594. Hubbard, *op. cit.*, pp. 85ff.

595. Arnold, *op. cit.*, pp. 385–386.

596. Grossman, *op. cit.*

597. Korovushkin, *op. cit.*

598. Garvey, *op. cit.*, pp. 131–132.

599. Arnold, *op. cit.*, p. 170.

600. Horn, *op. cit.*, pp. 347ff.

601. Arnold, *op. cit.*, pp. 245, 254.

602. *Ibid.*, p. 319.

603. *Ibid.*, p. 302.

604. *Ibid.*, pp. 480ff.

605. Grossman, *op. cit.*

606. Boris Gogol. *The Financial Times* (London), June 26, 1961, supplement, p. 25.

607. Arnold, *op. cit.*, p. 325.

608. Hubbard, *op. cit.*, pp. 85ff, 500, 501, 504.

609. *Ibid.*, pp. 500, 501, 504.

610. Grossman, *op. cit.*

611. Garvey, *op. cit.*

612. Arnold, *op. cit.*, p. 192.

613. *Ibid.*, p. 192.

614. *Ibid.*, p. 290.

615. *Ibid.*, pp. 500, 501, 504.

616. Hubbard, *op. cit.*, pp. 181–202.

617. Arnold, *op. cit.*, pp. 500, 501, 504.

618. Grossman, *op. cit.*

619. Schwartz, Harry. *Russia's Soviet Economy.* Englewood Cliffs, N.J.: Prentice-Hall, 1954.

620. Garvey, *op. cit.*, p. 68.

CHAPTER XXVII

621. Lien-Sheng Yang. *Money and Credit in China.* Cambridge: Harvard University Press, 1952. Pp. 1ff.

622. Tamagna, Frank M. *Banking and Finance in China.* New York: Institute of Pacific Relations, 1942. P. 13.

623. Lien-Shang Yang, *op. cit.*, p. 71.

624. *Ibid.*, pp. 5, 92.

625. *Ibid.*, p. 95.

626. *Ibid.*, p. 97.

627. Tamagna, *op. cit.*, pp. 203ff.

628. Chang Kia-Ngau. *The Inflationary Spiral.* New York: John Wiley & Sons, 1958. P. 12.

629. Lien-Shang Yang, *op. cit.*, p. 95.

630. *Ibid.*, p. 96.

631. *Ibid.*, p. 95.

632. *Ibid.*, p. 98.

633. *Ibid.*, p. 96.

634. *Ibid.*, p. 98.

635. *Ibid.*

636. Noonan, *op. cit.*, p. 289.

637. *Ibid.*, p. 99.

638. *Ibid.*, p. 100.

639. For an account of the activities of one of these banks, see Frank H. H. King, *Eastern Banking: Essays in the History of the Hong Kong and Shanghai Banking Corporation.* London: Athlone Press, 1983.

640. Lien-Shang Yang, *op. cit.*, p. 96.

641. Tamagna, *op. cit.*, pp. 86, 87.

642. *International Financial News,* June 19, 1959.

643. Lien-Shang Yang, *op cit.*, p. 100.

644. Tamagna, *op. cit.*, p. 66.

645. Lien-Shang Yang, *op. cit.*, p. 100.

646. Lee, Frederic E. *Currency, Banking and Finance in China.* Washington: U.S. Department of Commerce, 1926.

647. Tamagna, *op. cit.*, p. 70.

648. *Ibid.*, p. 150.

649. *Ibid.*, p. 195.

650. Lien-Shang Yang, *op. cit.*, p. 100.

651. Lee, *op. cit.*

652. Tamagna, *op. cit.*, p. 63.

653. *Ibid.*, p. 133.

654. *Ibid.*, p. 162.

655. *Ibid.*, p. 266.

656. Chang Kia-Ngau, *op. cit.*, pp. 254, 265, 268, 274.

657. *Ibid.*

658. Tamagna, *op. cit.*, pp. 229, 234, 292.

659. Chang Kia-Ngau, *op. cit.*, pp. 254, 265, 268, 274.

660. *Ibid.*

661. Lee, *op. cit.*

662. Tamagna, *op. cit.*, pp. 44, 45.

663. Padoux, George. *The Consolidation of China's Unsecured Indebtedness.* Peking: La Libraire Franchise, 1925. P. 11.

664. Tamagna, *op. cit.*, p. 217.

665. Chang Kia-Ngau, *op. cit.*, pp. 118–120.

666. Tamagna, *op. cit.*, p. 217.

667. *Ibid.*, pp. 229, 234, 292.

668. Byrd, William. *China's Financial System—The Changing Role of Banks.* Boulder, CO: Westview Press, 1983. Pp. 154–156, tables 10 and 11.

Index

A

Accord of 1951, Treasury-Federal Reserve, 369, 393
Actium, battle of, 48
Aldrich-Vreeland Act, 344
Alexander (the Great), 38–39
Alexander III, Pope, 70
Ambrose, Saint, 70
Amsterdam *Wisselbank, see* Bank of Amsterdam
ancient interest rates, 57–65
Anne, Queen, 157
annuities and mortgages, 75–76, 91, 97, 100–101, 103, 107, 117, 121, 131, 135
Aquinas, Saint Thomas, 71, 74, 92
Arbela, Temple of, 7, 30
Argentina, interest rates in, 6, 626–629
Aristotle, 71
Asia Minor, ancient finance in, 51–52
assignats, 169, 218
Assyria, 7, 27–32
Athena, Temple of, 37
Athens, 35–39, 58
Augustine, Saint, 70
Augustus, 48, 49, 51, 53
Australia, interest rates in, 581–587
   annual averages, 584–585
   decennial averages of government bond yields and discount rates, 586–587
Austria, interest rates in, 527, 534–535
Austro-Hungarian empire, 527

B

Babylonia, 5, 27–32
Baldwin, King, 7

Baldwin, Emperor, 7, 94
Bank Charter Act, 185, 187, 211
banking, medieval, 76–78, 136
   in England, 154, 186–188
Bank of Amsterdam, 136, 174
Bank of Canada, 542
Bank of England, origin of, 126–127, 136, 147–152, 164–165
Bank of France, 168, 171, 217, 218, 228–233, 461, 477
Bank of Italy, 514
Bank of Japan, 572–573, 578–579
Bank of New South Wales, 582
Bank of Sweden, 136, 179–180, 271–273, 533
Banks of the United States, 283, 296, 302
Baring crisis, 184, 282
basic corporate and government bond yields, history of yield spreads of, 399–409
basic yields of corporate bonds, by maturity, 394–399
bear bond market, first, 20th century United States (1899–1920), 339–346
   average prices and yield changes in, 340–341
   U.S. government securities, 1900–1920, prices and yields of, 343
   yields of corporate and municipal long-term bonds, 341–342
second, 20th century United States (1946–1981), 366–387
   average prices and yield changes in, 368–369
   prices and yields of long-term U.S. government securities, 375–376
   yields of corporate and municipal long-term bonds, 370–374